NEW PERSPECTIVES IN
GERMAN LITERARY CRITICISM

NEW PERSPECTIVES IN
GERMAN LITERARY CRITICISM

A Collection of Essays

Edited by
Richard E. Amacher and Victor Lange
Translated by
David Henry Wilson and Others

PRINCETON UNIVERSITY PRESS
PRINCETON, NEW JERSEY

Contents

CONTENTS

Acknowledgments

THE editors wish to express a very special debt of gratitude to the Wilhelm Fink Verlag of Munich for permission to reproduce in English translation these papers which were first published in Fink's distinguished and extensive multi-volume contribution to international esthetic discourse—its *Poetik und Hermeneutik* series. The essays we have selected from the Fink volumes originally appeared there in German—with the exception of those by René Wellek and M. H. Abrams (which were printed in English).

For permission to reprint Wolfgang Iser's two essays "Fiction—The Filter of History: A Study of Sir Walter Scott's *Waverley*" and "Patterns of Communication in Joyce's *Ulysses*," which appeared in Iser's *The Implied Reader* (as well as in the original Fink edition), we also thank the Johns Hopkins Press.

Cornell University Press kindly permitted us to use Herbert Dieckmann's "The Transformation of the Concept of Imitation in Eighteenth-Century French Esthetics," which is to be included in its forthcoming edition of his collected papers.

The translation of these papers is largely the work of David H. Wilson, who holds a joint appointment at the University of Konstanz and the University of Bristol. Almost singlehandedly he accomplished the very difficult task of translating most of the essays. Credit must also be given to Mrs. Mary Mennicken for her assistance to Mr. Wilson on Manfred Fuhrman's "Myth as Recurrent Theme in Greek Tragedy and Twentieth-Century Drama" and to Mrs. Angela Schirpf for her work on Herbert Dieckmann's "The Transformation of the Concept of Imitation in Eighteenth-Century Esthetics." Richard E. Palmer translated the first half of Dieter Henrich's "Art and Philosophy of Art Today," while J. S. Morgan did the second half. Gird Birkner and Juergen Schlaeger, erstwhile colleagues of Mr. Wilson, also assisted in the checking and proofreading of the manuscript.

The selection of the essays was made by a committee whose members at the time represented various departments at the University of Konstanz: Wolfgang Iser (English), Wolfgang Preisendanz (German), Jurij Striedter (Slavic), and Wolf-Dieter Stempel (Linguistics).

This American edition of the German Poetics and Hermeneutics papers has been the work of many hands—writers, translators, typists. At least two major foundations have played roles in the dissemination of these essays of the Poetics and Hermeneutics series. In Germany the Volkswagen Foundation has liberally supported not only the costs of the various symposia of the *Forschungsgruppe* but also the publications of the individual volumes emanating from each conference. In the United States the American Council of Learned Societies has generously provided a grant to defray the cost of translating the present selection of these papers into English. A grant-in-aid from the Auburn University Research Council assisted with typing costs.

Mrs. Esther Breisacher of the Princeton Department of Germanic Languages and Literatures typed the final complete version of the manuscript.

Frances Lange helped prepare the manuscript and Anne Ward Amacher assisted with proofreading and indexing.

Finally, the editors of this volume acknowledge with thanks the aid of R. Miriam Brokaw, Associate Director and Editor of the Princeton University Press.

NEW PERSPECTIVES IN
GERMAN LITERARY CRITICISM

VICTOR LANGE

Introduction

I

THE essays contained in this volume are contributions to that intense and self-conscious assessment of the perspectives, resources, and terms by which contemporary literary criticism has sought to justify its validity, its function, and its historical legitimacy. If literature itself seems in our time to have lost its innocence, if neither its subjective nor its objective character is self-evident but demands of its readers a sharp awareness of its modality, it has by this challenge called forth a breathtaking variety of systems of critical discourse; indeed, it has created a pre-eminence of theoretical consciousness that may tend, at times, to dissolve rather than illuminate the textual substance which occasioned it. The literary text has been subjected to a closer formal rhetorical or poetological scrutiny than ever before; it has been subordinated to stringent social or political judgments. But whether it is regarded as the configuration of psychological or mythological archetypes, whether the mobility and creativity of its author or its dependence upon the disposition and receptivity of the reader has offered the more appropriate form of access to its substance, whether its linguistic materials have been taken to enhance or to delimit its communicative scope—none of these alternatives has failed to convey the seriousness with which modern criticism has explored the implications of its object and specified the articles of its theory and practice. Inevitably, and to a striking, even alarming, extent, literary theory has become preoccupied with terminological issues; that is to say, it has been concerned more with a meticulous description of its tools and their sophisticated, at times pointedly abstract, capacity than with the character and the authority of its recalcitrant object.

It is symptomatic of much important contemporary criticism that it has tended to define the text that is before the reader or critic essentially as an interdependent system of functions. Yet, what has given it an unmistakable cast of radicalism is not the novelty or the scope of its techniques of access to the literary text, or its manner of interpreting it; it has, on the contrary, with compelling logic, insisted that the linguistic material as well as its social and poetological conditions require (or make feasible) a form of understanding and systematized "reading" that differs in essential respects from the traditional exercise of "interpretation." Interpretation, it is argued, can proceed effectively only as long as it regards a given text as an autonomous and essentially incomparable vehicle that contains and conveys a substance of immanent meanings to be elicited in an act of objectifying analysis. That this assertion is open to various and irrefutable forms of disagreement is the tenor of the history of recent European and American criticism: the insistence of Marxist critics on the ideological character of literature as well as the overwhelming effect of contemporary structuralism have strengthened the notion that a literary text offers a potential of more or less unlimited challenges that must be identified and met in the critical act. The burden of criticism is thus no longer primarily that of determining the adequacy and manner in which a set of philosophical or spiritual convictions is rendered in a given text; its function is rather to relate the implications of a work that is constituted by its language and its appropriate rhetorical devices to certain general modes and structures of experience.

Whatever we may think of this categorical turn in modern literary theory, whether we accept or deplore its conclusion that literature is not so much a superior form of insight and representation as one of several means of describing and understanding the complex interplay of culture, it is impossible to deny its energy and the range of its consequences.

But the object of literary criticism is not merely the text in its present susceptibility to classification; the most compelling, perhaps, indeed, the constitutive, element in the critical procedure is the recognition of the historical matrix in which the special nature of the document must be determined and in which alone the conditions of its production and reception can be sufficiently understood. If structuralism in its early and classical phases tended to declare its skepticism towards the traditional principles of historical understanding, its fundamental legitimacy has been confirmed and enriched by the insistence of literary critics upon a recognition of the dimension of history, without which, ultimately, works of literature can neither be adequately identified nor judged. To the issue of understanding the literary text in its broadest definition, yet as an object of historical determinacy, the essays contained in this volume offer a variety of reflections.

II

The impression of miscellaneity which this collection may at first sight suggest will be confirmed only if it is read as a body of work directed at a coherent topic or field, or at a series of interconnected figures and texts. The essays are, in fact, contributions by German,

French, American, and East European scholars of various methodological cal dispositions and of different philosophical assumptions who met between 1963 and 1972 for a series of symposia at the University of Konstanz and elsewhere in Germany. It was their intention to bring the resources of particular disciplines to bear upon topics which were, in each case, formulated in such a manner as to provide not merely a purview of contiguous interest but a sense of common concern. That concern was, on the one hand, with the literary document as an object of the widest possible resonance, requiring both the most specific and the most general critical attention; and the conviction, on the other hand, that the literary work can be satisfactorily described and defined only if it is recognized (together with the critical assessment) as an element in the historical process. In the tradition of German literary scholarship these essays insist on an assumption which is at present not altogether common: a sense of life as culture. While the authors do not explicitly attack or reject the modish assertion of criticism as technique, as grammar, or as topological system, they are of one mind in regarding literature as a discriminating mode of life, as a concurrence of language and history in which a given society incomparably constitutes its convictions. Literature in this sense is neither a privileged nor a casual institution, but its linguistic character and its cultural function need to be specified. It is for this reason that the unifying issue of these essays is the interlocking relationship between poetics and hermeneutics. This conjunction of the two central facets of criticism on the ground of history has for long been an unmistakable impulse in German literary theory. It has emerged as a crucial configuration in the work of several recent "philosophical" critics whose hypotheses and conclusions it may be useful to outline in some detail.

Whether in its beginnings in classical textual studies or in the more modern context for which Friedrich Schlegel provided the decisive impulse and vocabulary, German criticism has proceeded from "philological" premises and has almost invariably regarded the reading and understanding of a literary document as an exercise in comprehending its historical dependency. This nearly absolute faith in a genetic method, in history as an eminently telling signature of the text, is, of course, itself the result of an historical, an ideological, decision. Its most rigorous and dynamic defender and practitioner was W. Dilthey, whose theory of literature (*Die Einbildungskraft des Dichters*, 1887; *Das Erlebnis und die Dichtung*, 1905) gave systematic coherence to the "romantic" heritage of philosophical, theological, and historical idealism and at the same time regarded literary criticism as one, perhaps the most congenial, mode of understanding "non-scientific" cultural documents. Neither the

idealistic cast of Dilthey's theory of criticism nor his distinction between
an esthetic and a scientific strand of judgment is today considered
adequate: the concept of *Geistesgeschichte*, the notion that the history
of esthetic documents can be written as a history of "ideas" embedded
equally clearly in systems of thought and works of art, has long since
been shown to discriminate insufficiently between specific intellectual,
social, and formal conditions. Sociologists such as E. Troeltsch, M.
Weber, and K. Mannheim, the resurgence of interest in Marx and in the
tradition of Marxism, the impact of modern psychological investigations, the several currents of formalist theory, Russian as well as Czech
or American, have decisively modified and enlarged the horizon of German criticism.

The topography of that critical endeavor is rich and varied; a mere
summary of its characteristic features cannot do justice to its complexity. Although it is, at the moment, a mirror of the two distinctly motivated societies, issues central to the modern critical debate emerge
equally clearly, though within different social and political systems,
from East and West. The line, for instance, for long stubbornly drawn in
Germany, between academic and "casual" criticism, between literary
theory as an aspect of esthetics and literary history, on the one hand,
and the practice of literary judgment without recourse to sustained historical or esthetic reflection, on the other, has almost disappeared. Long
before the Second World War, men of letters of various intellectual dispositions, such as Karl Kraus, Alfred Kerr, and H. Jhering, had attacked
from a conservative, contemporary, or "revolutionary" point of view
the time-honored notion of literature—and criticism—as an elevated
and academically sanctioned exercise, all of them intensely preoccupied
with the rhetorical devices that determine the social function of literature.

Equally effective in broadening the scope of criticism were the reflections on literary matters by poets such as H. von Hofmannsthal,
Gottfried Benn, or Hermann Broch; indeed, non-academic criticism received in post-war Germany decisive impulses from a series of Frankfurt
lectures on poetics in which younger writers of different persuasions acknowledged the importance for their creative work of European and
American forms of criticism that had not been available to German
readers during the National Socialist decade. H. Holthusen drew attention to the later criticism of T. S. Eliot, H. Heissenbüttel to the uses of
the new linguistics for a modern theory of composition, I. Bachmann to
Wittgenstein, R. Baumgart to the contemporary French view of fiction.
All these writers, however different in their particular premises, were
agreed that the literary text, whether or not it offers explicit access to

meaning, can no longer be judged either in terms of Platonic metaphysics or—excepting Brechtian or neo-Marxist views—by any esthetics
of mimesis. They all—and this obviously is a dominant issue in all contemporary criticism—reflected an overriding interest in the problematical nature of language; and the functioning of speech has remained one of the chief topics of academic investigation as well as poetic
experimentation. The range of offered points of view has extended from
a re-examination of the special character of poetic language in the terms
of Mallarmé or Valéry—in Germany most uncompromisingly asserted
in Gottfried Benn's theory of the lyric—to an examination of the deceptions of language and the German contributions to the current debate
(seldom without recourse to Saussure or Jakobson) on the relationship
between linguistic theory and poetics, stylistics, or rhetoric.

These poets and critics have appeared surprisingly unwilling to en-
quire into the nature of the poetic experience, that is, the character of
the imagination, or into the effect of a text upon the individual—as
against the collective—sensibility. In striking contrast to important English or American critics, they and their successors were relatively un-
interested in psychological or psychoanalytical approaches, either in
Freudian terms or in Jungian mythological patterns of the archetypal
imagination. What has engaged nearly all German criticism of the past
thirty years—clearly in reaction to the mass of speculative, spiritualist,
and mythographic criticism produced before 1945—is the problem of the
public effectiveness of literary works, either within a given social and
philosophical context or in deliberate isolation from it, the interlocking
relationship between text and reader, and, altogether, the historical (and
ideological) conditions of literature.

It is safe to say that without the hostility of many of these critics to
traditional assumptions as to the nature of literature, the character of the
literary work, and the determinants in its creation and reception, the
turning from academic historicism and esthetic speculation towards
modern theories of literature would have occurred far more reluctantly.
The varieties of *Geistesgeschichte* and other neo-idealistic methods that
developed between the wars had, it is true, proved to be increasingly removed from the contemporary philosophical and scientific climate.
Dilthey, from a vitalist position, equated poetic production with an intense projection of a "presence of life" and elaborated large and elusive
topologies of style, attitude, movement, and of ingenious synthesis. He
and his successors were inclined to be altogether skeptical of empirical
procedures and—with the notable exception of R. Petsch—indifferent to
the problem of recognizing and formulating distinct poetological
categories. In their hands the specificity of the work of art tended to dis-

solve or to be consumed in the pursuit of a perennial human essence that maintained itself throughout the ages of literature with only incidental historical adjustments.

It is not surprising that in reaction to these critical and historical (as well as implicitly political) preconceptions, German literary scholarship should gradually have been willing to pay attention to the text itself and to the forms of access to it. Two handbooks of criticism, in retrospect significant primarily as indications of an historical shift in the critical climate, determined much of German post-war literary scholarship. One was Emil Staiger's *Grundbegriffe der Poetik* (1946), which reassessed certain tenets of classical esthetics, especially a theory of genres, that were indebted to Goethe's notion of "natural" typological forms. Indebted to Heidegger's ontological view of the three states of temporality, Staiger evolved a set of persuasive definitions of "lyrical," "epic," and "dramatic" attitudes and projected corresponding stylistic principles. An admirable sensibility enabled him as well to offer subtle exegeses of individual works (*Die Kunst der Interpretation*, 1955); but the fundamentally traditionalist character of his position emerged ever more rigid, and eventually involved him in a passionate polemic against all forms of "modernist" writing and criticism.

The other and more fundamental attempt at a comprehensive theory of literature was Wolfgang Kayser's *Das Sprachliche Kunstwerk* (1948), a work, like Staiger's, written outside Germany during the war and with a close awareness of the formal and formalist theories that had developed in Russia and later in the United States. Kayser sharply focused upon the linguistic and constructivist characteristics of the text; he adopted some of the critical principles that German historians of art such as Alois Riegl and Max Dessoir had formulated earlier, and insisted on the specifically esthetic nature of the literary work.

Although Kayser's "intrinsic criticism" was bound eventually to come under attack from those who rejected his formalism, there can be little doubt of its immediate effect. It produced a series of studies, by Kayser himself and others, in which the classical genres—ballad, satire, elegy, comedy, etc.—were subjected to rhetorical and poetological scrutiny; it created a fresh interest in the formal features of modern European poetry and justified the intellectual framework and the methodology of Hugo Friedrich's *Die Struktur der Modernen Lyrik* (1956); it turned the attention of younger critics to allegory, metaphor, and symbol; and it was instrumental in drawing a number of scholars towards recognizing the interdependence of linguistics and poetics. Broadly speaking, Kayser stimulated and confirmed a tendency—especially appealing as an antidote to the German propensities for spiritual generalization—towards empirical criticism, an interest at once strengthened and sensibly tempered by René Wellek and Austin Warren's *Theory of Literature*, which appeared in German translation in 1959.

The German counter-arguments to this "intrinsic" or "immanent" approach echoed or reiterated the patterns of challenge, modification, or rejection that have emerged to similar formal theories in France or America. The debate has concerned itself with several large issues: the first focused upon the need for an historical framework within which the literary text in its recognized esthetic mode could be illuminated more adequately than in any formal criticism. The second and more radical challenge to immanent criticism came, in Germany as elsewhere, from those who found that procedure altogether inadequate for a definition of criticism and the function of literature, since intrinsic criticism can only indirectly pay attention to the sociological and ideological premises of literature and of literary judgment. And to perform a critique precisely of those implications or limitations of a text that are likely to remain unreflected in a strictly esthetic assessment should be one of the legitimate intentions of any theory of literature.

III

Throughout the 1960's this anti-ideological kind of criticism has in Germany exercised an extraordinary appeal. With all its consequences for the theory of poetics and hermeneutics, its implied view of history, of language, and of the function of art, it is one of the pervasive impulses which must be kept in mind in reading the essays in this volume. Its unmistakable idiom was developed in the dialectical manner of Th. Adorno and the "critical" theory of the "Frankfurt school." As an Hegelian and Marxist, anti-phenomenologist, anti-ontologist, and anti-existentialist, Adorno defended, in occasional essays on the contemporary condition of fiction and poetry, on Valéry, Proust, or Balzac, his thesis that the great documents of modern literature reveal the paralyzing character of a fundamentally disfigured and dehumanized world which can be made transparent, intelligible, and tolerable only in a "poetic" rendering of its inherent contradictions.

Indebted to Hegel's hypothesis that art can at times be the most adequate and the most exalted medium in which the historical self-consciousness of a society articulates itself, Adorno, like G. Lukács in his early work, defined the present state of society as profoundly and demonstrably disjointed and disoriented. Art, in confronting this deficient condition, must exercise its potentially creative function by demonstrating, obliquely, the devalued and alienated character of that society. The reflecting mind, made impotent within the collective compulsions of late capitalism, has developed a differentiated critical sensibility that can become productive only by its resolute detachment and by its confidence in the rare manifestations of authenticity. It is the power of art, Adorno has argued, to make the present state of negativity palpable and thus to create a "mirror image of its very opposite." Precisely through its negative energy, the work of art thus offers a telling statement of the anguish in which the writer of poetry (or music) can and must face the present social reality. Only in this severely "critical" sense can art today be said to have redemptive value—by its rendering of insufficiency, by its denial of any form of immanence or of history as a continuum of meaning, by its insistence that being can claim our attention in its sublimest representation as form.

Adorno's intellectual procedure is aphoristic yet fascinating. At the same time his historical horizon is limited and the chosen topics of his critical attention are miscellaneous and accidental. Nevertheless, he encircles and displays his objects with extraordinary perception and intelligence. His style, wilful and circumstantial to the point of preciousness, suggests in every gesture a relentless groping for a language equivalent to the movement of his thought. It conveys precisely the discrete rather than systematic form of his discourse, which seldom discursively describes but rather demonstrates the tension between the "damaged" historical substance and its utopian foil by the very intermingling within a given metamorphic statement of the concrete and the abstract, of denial and affirmation, the objective and the subjective, the familiar and the surprising. It was this style of argument, the "negative dialectic" of Adorno's procedure, the compelling allegories of his nihilistic fervor, that gave, for more than a decade, extraordinary currency to his "Critical Theory."

Adorno's work is one of several German philosophical undertakings that aim at deriving a somewhat eccentric form of esthetic Marxism from Marxist esthetics, a paradoxical but consistently argued position that is the premise of another dithyrambic rather than systematic treatise of considerable power, Ernst Bloch's *Prinzip Hoffnung*. Written during nearly twenty years in exile, and published in part in East Germany, and in 1959 in its totality in the West, it is the projection of a utopian vision (or principle) in language reminiscent of the German expressionist idiom and, in fact, sketched as early as 1918 in Bloch's first major work, *Der Geist der Utopie*. This vision of a process of history suggests a movement toward the fulfillment, the total realization, of the principle of hope in a state of integrity and identity in which modern man may achieve his immanent promise. The work is an encyclopedic survey, organized in five sections profuse with metaphysical and poetic imagery, of the forms and concepts that have throughout the historical experience shaped the emerging consciousness of hope. Not as an elusive "meaning of life" but as a dynamic agent, the principle of hope sustains the monument of Bloch's philosophical enterprise. Myths and dreams, cyphers, emblems and symbols, forever materialized and renewed in the language of the imagination, are the means of holding together the mass of disparate human experience within that single perspective of hope.

To understand the operation of this principle within a universal culture is the purpose of Bloch's Marxist hermeneutics. This is to say that, insofar as Bloch's frame of reference rests on Marxist principles, it does so by virtue of his faith in the ultimate capacity of historical materialism to bring about the compelling progression from a utopian vision to the reality of a truly humane life. If Bloch is equally attached to the German tradition of speculative spiritualism, his eschatological projection is directed at the efficacy of the historical process itself rather than towards any religious or idealistic transcendental abstraction. Hope, he argues, is not a chimerical illusion; it can, reassessed, restated, reiterated at every moment of history and with an ever-alert awareness of its function at a given time, find its fulfillment in that state of freedom in which the present condition of alienation and division must be superseded.

IV

What Adorno and Bloch have in common is the conviction, not shared by the German tradition of *Kulturphilosophie*, that culture and art, however negative in their particular content, have, by their formal reality, by the continuing energy of their "signs," an ultimately redemptive function. It is this issue, the question of the "expressive" character of the indices of culture, of the accretions of historical consciousness in the artifacts of language, and, altogether, in the documents of social and historical experience, of their "truth" and of the accessibility of that truth, that is at the center of Walter Benjamin's work. Despite its impressive range, its extraordinary variety of topics, and its intensity of reflection, this work is pointedly esoteric, profoundly contradictory, and difficult to grasp in its intellectual preconditions. Benjamin was in one sense a romantic, with a deep attachment to German idealistic thought: his first work is a study of the esthetics of German romanticism. But he was, in another context, a Marxist thinker. His tenets were theological and Talmudic as well as materialist and dialectical. Within this paradoxical framework of belief, Benjamin produced a fragmentary but altogether compelling body of writing which is, even in its ephemeral pieces, richly allusive, serious, and carefully reasoned. His first work, *Ursprung des deutschen Trauerspiels (The Origin of German*

Tragic Drama, 1977), written in 1925 and published in 1928, attempts to develop not a literary history in the conventional sense but, by examining certain aspects of German baroque tragedies, a theory of knowledge derived from historical and linguistic premises: cognition and truth share in the critical act in that truth is in the objective phenomenon and not in the subjective consciousness. However obscured by history, truth is therefore an immanent factor. To rediscover its lost identity in the appearance of "name" and "object," to be aware of it, gathered and represented symbolically in the word, is the task of criticism. The truth that resides in every "form" must in the critical act be given utterance. The special truth of the baroque tragedy is embodied in its forms of allegory, by which that genre represents the *Leidensgeschichte*, the passion of the world as a process of fallibility and as the permanent flux of negativity that is only momentarily arrested in formalized acts of resistance such as the splendid theatrical spectacles of the baroque court. In these formal accretions, a vision of "paradisical timelessness" seeks to transcend the destructive thrust of history.

Even in this early work, Benjamin asserts his faith in the dialectic between destruction and redemption, a conviction equally present in his notion of the intrinsic and melancholy inadequacy of the act of understanding which in its subjective self-assertiveness may fail to recognize the truth that is the concrete presence of the object. Benjamin's theological belief in the reconciliation of the opposites of subject and object, of truth as the identity of the phenomenal present and its infinite challenge, is in his later work made concrete by an increasing attachment to Marxism or, at least, to certain congenial features of it.

A collection of incisive sketches, aphorisms, and brief descriptive passages entitled *Einbahnstrasse* (1928) (One Way Street) illuminates, by means of carefully established echo-effects and cross-references, a landscape of objects and places, "configurations" in which "allegorically," the flux and restlessness of life is arrested and phenomenologically understood. Another project, "Charles Baudelaire, Ein Lyriker im Zeitalter des Hochkapitalismus" (1927-1940), only partially completed, was intended to "interpret" the Parisian "passages," those shopping arcades between the major boulevards, their blend of commercial and artistic intentions and their fetishism of merchandise as indicators of the physiognomy of an era and a society. Against this background it was to examine the character of lyric poetry at the high noon of capitalism. These texts are Benjamin's most characteristic attempt to describe, from the point of view of a modern Marxist, the "creative" forms of the bourgeoisie, those striking indications of an ideological blindness towards the authentic energies of the artistic tradition.

Benjamin's commitment to a Marxist theory of art, originally stimulated by Bloch's *Geist der Utopie* and Lukács' *Geschichte und Klassen-
bewusstsein* (1923), gives to one of his later essays "Das Kunstwerk im
Zeitalter seiner technischen Reproduzierbarkeit" (The Work of Art in
the Era of Mechanical Reproduction), first published in French in 1936,
its particular force and eloquence. The function of the work of art, he
maintains, has been radically changed by modern technology; the ease
of reproducing, transporting, and distributing it, and the immense expansion of its public have deprived the work of art of its sometime aura,
that peculiar power and authority derived from its uniqueness. He describes the process of the disintegration of the "aura" and of the autonomous sphere within which, in bourgeois esthetics, that character of art
could be maintained. If the "aura" of a work, its "presence," gives authenticity to it, if it contains an almost infinitely rich accretion of tradition, these qualities of a significant work of art will henceforth no longer
be felt, because art is now effective primarily as an object of display and
of marketing. As it has emancipated itself from a ritualistic, introspective purpose, it has turned into a vehicle of dissipation and diversion.
Individual reception and critical contemplation have been replaced by a
collective enterprise that is increasingly susceptible to manipulation. At
the moment, Benjamin warned, when fascism offers the devalued and
sterilized categories of "creativity," "originality," and "eternal values"
as the terms of its artistic creed, art and its interpreters must be ready to
face the compelling logic of the historical circumstances and, avoiding
large commonplaces, must, in a specific, rational, and critical sense, become aware of the political consequences of the changed character of the
work of art.

The double impulse in Benjamin's thinking is indicated by a meticulous and immensely rewarding capacity for the closest and most searching attention to the phenomena and texts of culture, to the concrete existence of the object, and by his fundamental attachment to a philosophy
of history which is ambiguously drawn from two intellectual sources,
one by inference pessimistic, derived from the Jewish faith in an ultimate reckoning and the messianic redemption of the human insufficiency, and the other, a basically optimistic Marxist belief in the
dynamic, dialectical logic of the historical process.

Nowhere is Benjamin's central preoccupation with the compulsion of
temporality more evident than in a series of convoluted "Theses on the
Theory of History," presumably his last work posthumously published
in 1942 but conceived ten, or even twenty, years earlier. In these eighteen propositions, Benjamin mounts his attack upon the fatally false assumption of an "empty continuum" of history. To articulate the past,

he insists, is not merely to record what in fact happened; it is rather to seize a memory that flashes up (vorüberhuscht) at a moment of danger—danger to the tradition as well as to its recipients.

Alluding to Klee's picture "Angelus Novus," Benjamin sees (in the ninth thesis) the angel of history facing the past. "Where we perceive a chain of events, he sees only one single catastrophe which keeps piling wreckage upon wreckage and hurls it in front of his feet. The angel would like to stay, awaken the dead and make whole what has been smashed. But a storm is blowing from paradise; it has got caught in his wings with such violence that the angel can no longer close them. This storm irresistibly propels him into the future to which his back is turned, while the pile of debris before him grows skyward. This storm is what we call progress." The historian who "blasts a piece of history" from the presumed continuum and applies it to the present, rescues a singular image of the past. In this sense, to grasp the significance of a moment in time is to "redeem" that time from meaninglessness; it is to illuminate the messianic concept of a past fulfilled in the present. This is the necessary premise of every act of "criticism"; it can proceed only from an adequate understanding of the relationship of the past to the present, a comprehension of the past not as objective meaning but as the result of an awareness of the coincidence of past and present at a moment of Jetztzeit.

Benjamin's tentative theory of history, developed in statements and images of powerful seriousness, is an attack upon non-committed historicism; instead of continuity and progression, he recognizes the disturbing power of agonizing "splinters" of history to appear in the body of the present at once as a challenge to self-satisfaction and as a plea for their recognition and preservation as witnesses to tradition.

If "interpretation," as Benjamin understood it, must concern itself with texts that are formal accretions of historical instants and are therefore shot through with opinion and error, this was "in keeping with the Talmudic teaching of the forty-nine levels of meaning in every passage in the Torah." Indeed, much of his writing, Adorno observed, seems to deal with profane texts as though they were sacred. With the surrealists he shares a categorical distaste for seeking an "intention" on the part of the artist, and instead insists on the "accidental" origin of the work as a necessary assumption of criticism. It is precisely in such accidental products that the critic should seek to identify the signature of the age. Benjamin was determined to destroy the reassuring notion that the historical phenomenon or the work of art could be assumed to offer an immanent, objective meaning accessible to any of the practiced forms of more or less intuitive "interpretation."

The truth of a poem, he was inclined to say—and it is hardly necessary to point out the proximity of much contemporary criticism to this
conviction—can be recognized only if we are aware of the evocative
power of the spoken word. In a celebrated essay on "The Task of the
Translator" (1923), he reminds us of the astonishing capacity of human
speech to testify to the ever-renewed resource of a primal, unified language: speech, neither as "imitation," as a device by which we point to
the data of the objective world, nor as a mirror of subjectivity, but, supremely, as a system interlocking and enhancing the two in a symbolizing grasp. Adam, not Plato, is for him the father of philosophy. The
truth to be heard is—in terms formulated in Mallarmé's esthetic as well
as in Heidegger's assertion that it is language that speaks—the constituent element of existence. Criticism, then, was for Benjamin not so
much a manner of discourse that elaborates the causal nexus between
fixed textual entities, nor was he interested merely in the pragmatic
relationship between social forces and a given work or in explaining the
surface signs of a work of art. Criticism meant for him the act of jux-
taposing the most telling aspects of a moment, of establishing its "constellation," of "quoting" those forms in which a substance buried in the
debris of historical accident has become tangible and "sayable."

The concern with particularity, not generality, is thus the mode of
Benjamin's criticism; if he sought insistently to identify "ideas," it was
with the (Kantian) proviso that an idea cannot be abstracted but becomes
palpable only as sensed appearance. "Appearances" of this sort he subjected to the double scrutiny of Jewish mysticism and Marxist materialism, and altogether to a theory of interpretation in which the problem of the temporality of all knowledge is the haunting center. The
importance of time and of language as constituent functions for our
awareness of truth are the issues to which he returned from beginning to
end. They have remained the cardinal themes of much German and
European criticism, not least through their systematic exploration in the
work of M. Heidegger.

V

The evident impact of Heidegger's thought on modern critical
theories has resulted from three aspects of his system: he replaces, first,
in *Sein und Zeit* and in his later lectures, particularly in his re-
examination of Nietzsche, the classical concept of thought by a modern
notion of thinking, idea by process, *Gedanke* by *Denken*. Thinking is for
Heidegger the act of giving "presence" to an object, to remain within the
resonance of the object which offers itself to thinking in order to be
"realized." The phenomenal world is for him not a fixed given to be re-

produced in the act of reflection, but the result of a production, a "practice," in which the world is integrated into our consciousness of being. The origin of this view in Marx as well as in Nietzsche has often been demonstrated. Subject and object are not opposites, but constitute one another. In the critical systems that have taken cognizance of Heidegger, the search for ontological meaning has given way to attempts at developing functional theories of appropriate structures.

The second context of Heidegger's philosophy which, despite basic differences in other regards, is related to Benjamin's thinking, is the preeminence of the historical experience as the condition of all reflection. Heidegger shares Nietzsche's belief that truth is not timeless or general; history alone gives shape to the absolute. However pervasive the energy and direction of this notion in Heidegger's philosophy, in his analysis of our present state of alienation as an elemental experience, it transcends but is not incompatible with Marx's theory of history: "The Marxist view of history," he wrote to Jean Beaufret in 1946, "is superior to any other." To limit the scope of subjective reflection, to derive his epistemological categories from the "ground of Being" rather than from a traditional distinction between the authority of the object and the discriminatory power of the subject has from the beginning of his work been a fundamental premise.

This refusal to think in anthropocentric terms has qualified his conception of temporality (or historicity) as in no sense teleological or pragmatic. It is, finally, his notion of language that Heidegger offers as one of the instrumental categories by which object and subject are drawn into the common experience of Being. It is an axiom of Heidegger's philosophy that it is not man who speaks but "the word in man." Language is not an expression of man but an appearance of Being. Speech reveals at every moment of our awareness its character as process or procedure, not as a vehicle for the distinguishing or conveying of universal meanings. It is the word, therefore, that gives its Being to the phenomenal world; everything owes its "is" to the word which is not related to the object but is itself that relationship.

It is clear that these contentions are of the greatest importance for a modern theory of poetry. The essence of language, of which "reflection" (*Denken*) and "composing" or "intensifying" (*Dichten*) are the two modes, lies for Heidegger in the "saying" (*Sage*); "saying" is tantamount to bringing Being into its own, to be heard and seen. But the essence of language is ultimately in the stillness which the act of differentiation accrues, at once to the object as a thing in the world, giving it its specific character, and to the world as a constituent of Being. Language, Heidegger formulates in an often quoted phrase, is the "sound-

ing" or "chiming" of stillness (*Geläut der Stille*); man speaks only insofar as he hears or listens to what language itself speaks: not the spoken
word, itself an objectification, but the saying, that "chime of stillness"
establishes the sense of Being or, as Heidegger puts it, that which we
name by the word "is." In another metaphoric phrase, language is described as the "house of Being," because all Being is in its guardianship.

Without claiming to offer a contribution to literary history or to
esthetics, Heidegger has attempted to extrapolate an application and
confirmation of his theory of Being and Language from the work of a
number of German poets, notably Hölderlin. Each poet, he suggests, in
Mallarmé's image, speaks out of a single, over-arching "poem" that is
never pronounced: "only out of the place of the (unspoken) poem does
the individual poem shine and sound." In a similar fashion Heidegger
defines the function of the great work of art as "speaking," and in speaking, "bringing the world to stand." By making the truth into an historical
event, the "performance" of the poem at once reveals and conceals the
truth. To interpret a work of art is, for Heidegger, the attempt "to move
into" the open space which the work has "brought to stand." Heidegger
has admitted the affinity of his own theory of time to Nietzsche's "Eternal Recurrence." Time is for him—as it is for Benjamin—not a mere
flow of duration, but the "arrival" of what has been: transitoriness, or
merging into the past, is the essence of time. Theories of criticism or of
literary history such as Derrida's have drawn the consequences of
Heidegger's statement that history is "not so much the past, for that is
just what does not happen any longer; much less is it a passing event
which comes and goes by. History, as happening, is the acting and being
acted upon in and right through the *present*, determined from out of the
future and taking over what has been." Heidegger's preoccupation with
the problem of Being and Historicity dates back to his inaugural lecture
on "The Concept of Time in Historiography" (1916); but if he there
speaks of the need for a conception of time more adequate than that of
mere chronology, he moves, after his encounter with Dilthey's *Lebens-
philosophie* and Husserl's *Phänomenologie*, beyond this elementary
frame towards an "hermeneutics of facticity."

From Dilthey, Heidegger derived the conviction that the historical
concretizations of life require an understanding from within the phenomena rather than a mere causal explanation, a comprehension of the
manner in which "life" has constituted itself in history. The theory of
hermeneutics as Schleiermacher had formulated it, beyond its original
application to Scripture, for all projections of human endeavor, and A.
Boeckh applied it to the philological enquiry into secular literary texts,
provided methodological access to this "understanding from within" by

recognizing the historical context of the individual creative act that mirrors the supra-personal presence of life. Heidegger rejects the subjectivist implications of Dilthey's "Erlebnis"-complex and, in *Sein und Zeit*, gives to the hermeneutical principle and practice a radical efficacy: it is the fundamental procedure by which man comprehends and articulates his existence. In this sense, *Sein und Zeit* has been called a hermeneutical phenomenology. "Understanding" is no longer, as it was for Dilthey, merely a manner of investigation but a constituent element of being-in-the-world. All understanding is temporal, intentional, historical; it is not a subjective confrontation of an object, but the way of being of man himself.

Heidegger's influence upon German criticism has been sporadic and indirect; its ontological bias has been met by resolute refutations on the part of analytical and "critical" thinkers such as Adorno. But its impact has been most striking in France, where, despite its *germanicité* and its anti-cartesian ontology, it has profoundly affected not only poets such as René Char but, to an altogether astonishing extent, critics such as Lacan and Derrida.

The implications of Heidegger's hermeneutical theory have in Germany been systematically unfolded in H. Gadamer's *Wahrheit und Methode* (1960; *Truth and Method*, 1975), a work that has, in its own right, aroused the liveliest debate. Gadamer, like most contemporary critics, rejects the concept of an "esthetic consciousness" and insists on the epistemological character of art which reveals "Being" and is a world with its own dynamics totally mediated into image and form. In becoming experience, it transforms the experiencer: "the work of art works." The act of reading (or interpretation) is appropriately directed at the text, not the author; its efficacy is dependent upon an analytical awareness of the present and a sense of participation in the stream of tradition realized in every moment that fuses past and present. If Gadamer's notion of understanding is predicated upon a cognizance of historicity, it is determined by his view of language. As in Heidegger's system, the word is here no mere sign; language is not an instrument of communication. Like understanding itself, it is a mode of disclosing our world, it is the means of having world. Yet language is not the tool of subjectivity; it is finite and historically determined, a repository and vehicle of the measure of Being which has accrued to it in the past. The purpose of understanding—and thus the task of hermeneutics—is to recognize and show the "linguisticality" of experience. "Everything that is, is reflected in the mirror of language." Thinking, understanding, and perception are altogether linguistic; it is only through language that we can have the world of understanding by which the phenomena take their place in our consciousness.

Gadamer's theory of hermeneutics, anti-subjectivist, processive, dialectical, and eminently concerned with the historicity of judgment, is not intended to offer directions for an objectively valid understanding. It conceives of understanding as an event, as a dynamic progression towards the recognition of an ontological structure and offers a coherent system of scrutiny within which the several disciplines of contemporary reflection are examined as to their premises, the logic of their terminologies, and their usefulness for literary and historical criticism. Gadamer regards the literary text not as a closed object with an accessible meaning but as an occasion for a process of reflection that concerns itself with the substantive and formal efficacy of language as well as with the proximity in purpose between its own intentions and those of the text. He enquires, ultimately, into the consequences for the critical performance, of the unceasing challenge to criticism by a given text.

VI

Like the other theories upon which I have touched, Gadamer's work has contributed importantly to the definition of the field—and at times the style—of discourse within which the essays gathered in this volume must be considered. Indeed, what has prompted these papers is precisely the recognition of the fact that the procedures of literary criticism must be accompanied by a steady recourse to hermeneutical reflection. They are preoccupied in a variety of ways with the insights, directions, and concepts which modern theories of poetics, analytical philosophical discourse, and the findings of the contemporary social sciences have made available; they address themselves directly or indirectly to the tension between structuralist formalism and its philosophical and history-oriented alternatives.

Ever since the publication of H. R. Jauss's "Literary History as a Challenge to Literary Criticism" (1969), the need for redefining the relationship between literary criticism and its presumed "grounding" in literary history, as well, of course, as the definition of sufficient principles for the writing of literary history, has been widely and contentiously discussed. Jauss based his defense of literary historiography on a categorical proposition: what Marxist and formalist criticism have in common, he argued, is the rejection of positivism as well as of the metaphysical implications of *Geistesgeschichte*. Each deals with the problem of the sequentiality of literary works in its own unsatisfactory way: a Marxist interpretation of literature derives its historical scheme and judgments from an overriding faith in social evolution and, at best, extracts from the literary constellation of the past preliminary—or exemplary—modes of social insight. Marxist literary historiography and criticism are committed to operating within the evidence of national and economic experiences which can grasp only a small measure of the total esthetic complex.

The theories of formalism, on the other hand, deliberately aim at removing the literary object from its historical determinants and define its efficacy functionally, as the sum of all its artistic devices. The distinction made by formalist criticism between poetic and non-poetic features of a text requires of the critical act a focusing upon specific formal characteristics of a given work and an awareness of its relative place in a series of comparable products. It is true that in admitting a synchronic relationship between poetic and non-poetic modes of literature, and in admitting a diachronic relationship of works and genres (and thus an evolutionary succession of esthetic systems), later formalist critics have moved closer to providing a possible scheme of historical judgment. But to understand a literary text within the limits of the history of its particular formal systems, Jauss argues, is not the same as understanding it within the more comprehensive categories of its production, its social function, or its historical consequences. Like language itself, the text must be comprehended as a specific structure as well as an historical phenomenon, but, beyond the diachronic or synchronic succession of its forms, within the larger context of general history.

Jauss concludes that both Marxism and formalism remain enclosed in self-imposed historical insufficiency and that their methods can achieve an understanding of the literary work only within an "esthetic of production and representation." In neither theory is the factor of reception and impact, of reader, listener, or spectator, sufficiently taken into account. Marxist criticism regards the reader, if at all, as virtually identical with the author, and is, at best, concerned merely with identifying his place in a given society. Formalism, on the other hand, requires the reader only as a perceiving subject who follows the directions of the text and differentiates formal characteristics and features. In both systems of criticism the reader operates with a quasi-scientific sort of attention. But literary works are not, as a rule, written to be read and judged by philologists or social scientists; they transmit information to a suitably perceptive recipient and are designed to produce a constant interaction of question and answer. This relationship between the work and its readers is of considerable consequence for an understanding of literature. It has esthetic as well as historical implications: even the earliest reception of a work of art demands of the reader evaluative judgments that are derived from a familiarity with comparable works or procedures; each receptive act, necessarily more elaborate than the previous one, contributes to an understanding of the accumulated historical complexity as well as to the esthetic potential of a given text.

From the general premise of an esthetic concerned with the reception of a literary text, Jauss has here, and subsequently, argued the case for a new conception of general literary history, and altogether for a *Rezeptionsaesthetik* which assumes that a literary text can be said to reveal its character—or meaning—only by the evidence of its successive historical effects. A poem, Jauss insists, has no necessary consequences: it continues resonant only so long as it is received and judged by its readers. It is one of Jauss's important, though not unquestioned, convictions that the mode of reception can be objectively defined by an analysis of the manner in which a work meets the expectations of its readers—expectations emerging from available forms, genres, themes, or linguistic structures—that is to say, of the response to explicit or implicit signals contained in the work itself. Novels such as *Don Quixote, Tristram Shandy, Werther,* or *L'Education Sentimentale* mobilize the reader deliberately within an intended "horizon" of critical opinion. How a work is received at the time of its first appearance as well as subsequently, whether it surpasses, disappoints, or refutes, whether it irritates or merely confirms contemporaneous expectations—all these amount to a history of its critical effect which is an indispensable premise of our own critical judgment. What is important in such an esthetic of reception is the mutual exercise of challenge and response: the challenge of a work which, without claiming any fixed meaning, yet contains a variety of objectively describable esthetic stimuli; and the responses of a succession of readers who bring their particular perception (and philological or rhetorical assumptions) to bear upon the work and the accumulated critical experience of previous readers, and thereby in turn "define" the work as well as their own historical condition.

Jauss's theses are, of course, related to premises which we suggested earlier: to Heidegger's notion of temporality, to Husserl (who first used the term "horizon of expectation"), and to Gadamer's *Wahrheit und Methode,* which itself maintained that the historical character of all interpretation can be adequately demonstrated only through an understanding of the history of successive aspects of the experienced text. The hermeneutical procedure must not isolate the text as an object but show the unfolding of a potential of meaning that is virtually given in the work, historically actualized in its reception and made concrete in the history of its relevance.

Jauss's concept of an esthetic of reception, or of literary history as a history of certain major texts embedded in the continuous tradition of their critical assessment, has been a recurring motif not only of the Konstanz symposia; it has been widely discussed in Germany and America and has offered W. Iser the vantage point for several studies devoted to a systematic enquiry into the intertextual role of the reader. Iser transfers Jauss's conclusions from an historical scheme to a theory of the esthetic functioning of the text. In two comprehensive investigations, *Der implizite Leser* (1972) (*The Implied Reader*, 1974) and *Der Akt des Lesens* (1976) (*The Act of Reading*) he submits that, in reading, no fixed categories of access or significance can be presumed; it is in the act of reading itself that criteria and codes are established by which, in turn, prevailing intellectual or social norms are insistently put in question. The reader is called upon in this negative performance to achieve a state of esthetic consciousness in which meanings may be construed.

To overemphasize the centrality of Jauss's theory would neglect the readiness of German literary scholarship to explore and adopt a plethora of critical procedures that have come from abroad. It has at any rate decisively detached itself from the traditional forms of interpretation, whether impressionistic or "immanent," and has, like the various alternatives of structuralism, denied the feasibility of any procedure that is directed at discovering unequivocal contents of meaning. Instead, it has concerned itself vigorously with the social conditions of literary life and its consequences, historical, political, and poetological, for an adequate assessment of the functions of the text. Much German criticism has seized upon, even at times radicalized, the emancipatory potential of literature, and has sought to define its efficacy as a vehicle of ideological critique; it has, in consequence, sought to remove the customary distinction between esthetically elevated literature and texts of a non-literary sort, and has attempted by its attention to contemporary linguistic theories, such as socio-linguistics or textual linguistics, to give validity to empirical applications of descriptive methods. German scholarship has, especially, shown itself interested in the results of Russian formalism and its structuralist elaborations, particularly in their Czech form and the methodology of the Copenhagen linguists. Finally, it has developed poetic theories based on formalized grammatical models and has shown considerable energy in employing quantitative criteria and the results of new information theory to stylistic analysis.

VII

While the essays that follow should not be read with an expectation of discovering the consensus of a "school" of criticism or even a common strategy of discourse, they demonstrate the importance of interdisciplinary perspectives for the discussion and interpretation of any facet of modern cultural studies. If scholars concerned with the history and theory of literature and the arts, linguistics, philosophy, and theology here address themselves to the hermeneutical issue, they share an interest in certain problems and methodological alternatives. It is not surprising that the modalities of language should be a recurring theme; it could also be expected that the contributors to this volume should argue within the determinants of a "philological" faith. They are not attached to obsolete theories of historicism or to the classical chimera of a teleology of the spirit, but are firm in their belief in the word as the focus of critical enquiry, indeed, as the inexhaustible means of access to an understanding of the nature and the value of literature. At the same time, the essays confirm that literary criticism must, in our time, redefine the scope of its traditional resources and draw upon the whole range of method and insight that have emerged in the social sciences. Analytical philosophy, linguistics, psychology, anthropology, and modern theories of communication are therefore the self-evident ingredients in the procedures and conclusions of these papers.

The philosophical, poetological, and rhetorical concerns that gave urgency and wide interest to the six symposia to which these papers were conspicuous contributions are indicated by the general topics to which the participants addressed themselves. The first (1963) dealt with the historical shift in sensibility and practice from the classical principle of *imitatio naturae* to the theories of illusion which have in modern literature affected not merely the function of the several categories of genre but the basic view of creativity and the balance between subjective and objective criteria. Hans Blumenberg's essay on the impact of that shift, of the historical transmutation of the category of truth upon modern forms of fiction, explores with remarkable ingenuity the topos that poets are liars. H. Dieckmann enquires into the modifications of the principles of imitation in eighteenth-century French esthetics; W. Iser analyzes W. Scott's *Waverley* novels as model instances of the use of illusion as a device in enlarging the scope of historical narrative.

The theme to which, in 1964, the second Konstanz gathering turned its attention was the effect of contemporary esthetic reflection upon the arguable assumptions of "immanent" esthetics. Its ostensible material was lyric poetry, since it is in terms of that mode that the decisive theorists of modernism have argued their claims. Why is it, the participants asked, that modern literature is described pre-eminently in negative terms such as estrangement, reification, provocation, obscurity, discontinuity, or irony? Dieter Henrich's paper on "Art and the Philosophy of Art" is a superb survey of that central issue to which two other contributions give concrete application: W.-D. Stempel's "Syntax and Obscurity in Poetry" and the interpretation directed by H. Robert Jauss of Apollinaire's poem "Arbre."

The third symposium (1966) was devoted to the various modern deviations from the norms traditionally implied in the category of the "esthetic." The conventional connotations of that term must necessarily be transcended if criticism is to deal appropriately with artistic phenomena that cannot be accommodated and evaluated within the established canon, but require judgments for which "beauty" is no longer an adequate criterion. Several of the contributions demonstrated the historical alternation from prescriptive norms to their deliberate violation or refutation and a new configuration of shared assumptions and conventions. At two periods in the European history of consciousness can this phenomenon be clearly observed: when the anti-esthetic mainspring of Christian art disavows its classical antecedents and in due course itself establishes canonical esthetic norms; and at the more recent turn in which Hegel saw the end of art as the paramount vehicle of cognition: the experience which effectively broke the confining conceptual bracket of the "fine arts" and made the "ugly" a creative dimension of indubitable esthetic legitimacy. Four of the papers included in this collection speak directly or indirectly to this topic of the "no longer 'fine arts.' " R. Koselleck investigates, as a social historian, the play of accidence and coincidence as a residual motif in historiography; O. Marquard examines (as a philosopher) the bearing of theories of the unconscious upon a modern theory of art; the art historian M. Imdahl deals with the relationship between esthetic and non-esthetic features in the modern pictorial art; and W. Preisendanz explores the transition from poetry to certain journalistic forms of artistic effectiveness in the paradigmatic instance of Heine's work.

What gave to the fourth symposium (1968) its coherence is indicated metaphorically in the title: "Terror und Spiel" (Terror and Play). Its topic was the reception (or creation) of secularized myths in modern literature and their appearance as ingredients in utopian or ideological writing. The unreflected character of myths can no longer be taken for granted. What are the conditions and contexts in which myths operate in an age that has ostensibly emancipated itself? To what extent, the participants asked, can history be said to shape myths; in what manner can myths be said to have an effect on history? Myth, it was argued in another programmatic paper by Hans Blumenberg, continues to fascinate our time as "terror and poetry," as a political and an esthetic impulse; if the classical substance of myth was transformed during the Middle Ages into religious allegory, the original multi-valent range of the meaning of myths turns into singleminded dogma and thus becomes a tool, ultimately, of political purpose. The German romantic philosophers attempted to reclaim the capacity of myth-making for utopian ends: F. Schlegel and Schelling assigned to poetry and art the task of articulating the myth for political ends. When this proved illusory, when the political reality made such a "poetic mission" irrelevant, Novalis and Hölderlin created a self-referential mythology of poetry itself: mythology is from now on subjective and its public authority becomes increasingly arbitrary.

The essays by Jurij Striedter and M. Fuhrmann investigate the transformation of certain historical myths with distinct philosophical as well as esthetic implications, into modern variable alternatives that lose their self-evident "public" credibility and, justified as subjective constructs only, take on an ideological character. Mayakowsky's interpretation of the Christ-myth in revolutionary terms ceases to have general significance as soon as the vagaries of the Russian Revolution reduced that myth to a merely private statement. The contention of M. Fuhrmann's paper that Giraudoux and Anouilh have successfully reasserted the meaning of classical myths must remain debatable: precisely these playwrights remind us of the incompatability of the traditional substance of myth with the abstract realities of present-day living. Indeed, as myth functions in our time more and more as a subjective experience, it may come to serve in modern fiction as a contrasting foil against which, as in Joyce's *Ulysses*, the substance of contemporary life is shown as dissolved into countless incidents and shades of meaning. Myth offers, as Wolfgang Iser has argued, an infinite potential of the imagination which must in turn be organized by the reader; reader and novelist together establish the coherence of meaning which was originally contained and palpable in the myth itself.

The fifth symposium (1970) had as its topic the relationship between history and its rendering in narrative forms, between pragmatic events and their ordering within appropriate schemes of "storytelling." What could at one time be related as a succession of biographies of those who made history has, since the Enlightenment, been seen and ordered as the unfolding of a meaning which in turn (argued Dieter Henrich) has tended to be described and narrated in episodic form. This is to say that historiography is itself subject to esthetic categories which inevitably affect the truth-character of what is related. If history is seen altogether as a secularized form of mythological thinking, what are the terms of an understanding of such a structure? K. Stierle, for instance, analyzes the dimensions of subjectivity by which Montaigne gives to the "exempla" of history, those corollaries of admirable actions that are for long transmitted as features of a fixed system, their modern relativistic significance. The writing of history—like all modern literature—must convey not merely the presumed facts of its material but the theoretical implications of its particular point of view. To what extent and in what manner a history of literature depends upon an understanding of the successive esthetic judgments and prejudices of its readers was the question which led H. R. Jauss to his reiteration of an esthetic of reception. R. Wellek, in his magisterial paper on "The Fall of Literary History," arrives at the melancholy conclusion that a satisfactory theory of literary historiography does not appear to be feasible.

A sense of challenge, of resistance to all assumptions of objectivity, immanence, or normative idealism determined the cast of all Konstanz symposia as well as the presuppositions of aim and methodology in the essays that are here published. The force of negativity in modern thinking, as the condition of any contemporary theory of literary criticism or historiography, was the theme of the sixth conference (1972), whose summary topic was "Negation und Negativität." How has that disquieting principle affected and clarified the various disciplines that converge in the hermeneutical enterprise? How has it determined the means of discovering, describing, and discriminating structures of experience in the formal accretions of culture, in the configurations and conventions of the imagination, in the deceptive gestures of speech?

The essays that follow offer a partial and tentative answer to these questions. Together they represent patterns of thought common to the most important among contemporary theories of knowledge; yet, they are judicious and in no sense dogmatic. Not unlike systems such as structuralism, for instance, they distrust the subjective resources of intentionality and judgment. But these essays are nearly unanimous in deriving their assessment of the character and place of the text or the document from the notion of temporality that is contained in Benjamin's metaphor of the angel of history: history, that is to say, not as linear progression which each successive event propels towards a more lucid future. History is here understood rather as a process in which the dialectic of experience and failure, of creation and destruction, of confidence and frustration, offers an unending rhythm of challenge. This "provocation" constitutes the resonant character of the text which draws the reader into its sphere and by its presence alerts the reader's *Betroffenheit*, in the double sense of that term, his being affected as well as concerned. The text and its readers, critics and historians, are joined as participants in the hermeneutical process of discovering not a set of meanings but the forms and signs of the continuing tradition of historical reflection.

Literary history, for long abused as a speculative construction or devalued as an unrewarding chronological linkage, has once again become a crucial component of the critical pursuit: it is a syntagma, a concatenation of moments of insight and speech in which each is given its place and value by virtue of the junctures at which it is created, received, recreated, and made part of the constellation of past and present, of the specific and the general, of cognition in complicity and dissent.

I

Imitation and Illusion. From *Poetik und Hermeneutik I*

HANS BLUMENBERG

The Concept of Reality and the Possibility of the Novel

THE history of Western literary theory can be summed up as a continuous debate on the classical dictum that poets are liars.[1] Even Nietzsche was still under the influence of this assertion, when, claiming a metaphysical dignity for art, he had to invert it, contrasting the *truthfulness of art* to the *falseness of Nature*.[2] Halfway between the classical

[1] For the history of its influence, the origin of this dictum is scarcely relevant; but for a proper understanding of the matter, it is worth noting that at first there was no general devaluation, but a critical reminder that the epic is obliged to be truthful—it should not bring up the unprofitable writings of earlier times, but ought to reveal noble deeds through the power of memory (ἐσϑλὰ ἀναφαίνει) (Xenophanes, fr. B I, 19-23, Diels). The reproach of untruthfulness is therefore based on the premise that the epic should communicate truth. As B. Snell has shown in *Die Entdeckung des Geistes* (Hamburg, 1946), p. 87 et seq., the reproach takes on a general significance only through problems connected with dramatic illusion in the theatre; here the technique of actualization, arising from the mythical significance of the lyric and tragic chorus, no longer coincides with the consciousness of reality underlying the epic. The transition from ecstatic identification in the cult of Dionysos to technical accomplishments of *representation* tears open the differences between reality and art, a split which, typically, is thought out to its ultimate theoretical consequences by the Greeks: even for Aeschylus, Agatharchos not only painted a decor in perspective, but also left behind a treatise on it (Diels, 59 A, 39; vol. 1, 14 et seq.). There has also survived a piece by Gorgias (fr. B 23, Diels), with a moralizing justification of illusion in tragedy which is apparently excused by its effect upon the spectator. And so in classical times, as in the eighteenth century with Diderot, the starting-point for these reflections on poetic illusion was provided by the drama. In both eras this starting-point was soon abandoned. For the tradition of this saying—that poets are liars—two points became significant: Plato's critique of the truth content of art in general, and the Stoic-Christian habit of allegorizing, which depended on defending a *relic of truth* in literature in order to be able to *rescue* it from dispersal or concealment.

[2] *Der Philosoph. Betrachtungen über den Kampf von Kunst und Erkenntnis* (Entwürfe von 1872) (WW, Musarion-Ausg., VI, 31). Now the concept of *Nature* is completely oriented towards scientific objectification and its command over the concept of truth, which fulfills itself in the destruction of anthropomorphic immanence. But the *taming of science* offers a questionable justification for *the need for illusion* (WW, VI, 12); ultimately, this kind of truth cannot escape from the tradition of *imitation*, but is committed only to a world interpreted as an *appearance* that liberates the desire for cognition: *Art therefore treats appearance as appearance, and so does not seek to deceive at all, but is true* (WW, VI, 98). This interpretation of *art as a true appearance* remains bound to the metaphysical tradition of art theory, for it pins art down to the character of given reality, even if this is

topos and the modern antithesis stands the scholastic concession to literature of a "minimum veritatis."

If we are to consider the pros and cons of the classical dictum, we must first decide what is meant by its antithesis—i.e., that poets "tell the truth." There are, I believe, two sorts of truth involved: first, when it is claimed that literature refers to a given outside reality—whatever that reality may be; second, when literature is said to create a reality of its own. We must also bear in mind the purely logical possibility that both thesis and antithesis may be ignored, and art may be regarded as totally divorced from such considerations as truth and falseness or any criterion connected with "reality." However, this logical scheme does not necessarily coincide with the historical possibilities.

At no time in the history of Western esthetic theory has there been any serious departure from the tendency to legitimize the work of art in terms of its relation to reality, and so any critical assessment of the foundation of traditional esthetics must begin with a clarification of what is meant by "reality." This is difficult, for generally in our dealings with what we regard as real, we never get down to the predicative stage of defining exactly what it is that constitutes the reality. And yet the moment a doubt is cast on the reality of an action or a proposition, our attention is drawn to the specific conditions which have led us to regard it as real. The very fact that the "truth" of literature has always been contested has made literary theory a focus for the critical assessment of concepts of reality and for the unmasking of implicit preconceptions. Ultimately we shall have to recognize what at a given time has been taken for granted as most obvious and trivial, i.e., not even worth stating— and hence never specifically formulated. Our immediate task, then, must be to define the various historical concepts of reality.

The first historical concept that I should like to discuss here is what we might call the "reality of *instantaneous evidence.*" This concept is not explicitly propounded but is presupposed when, for instance, Plato unhesitatingly proceeds from the assumption that at the first sight of ideas the human mind immediately and with total confidence realizes that it is confronted with the ultimate and unsurpassable reality and, at the same time, is aware that the sphere of the empirical and the sensual is not and could never be such a reality. However, it is by no means taken for granted that anyone could view the duality of the empirical world and the ideal world without risking a corresponding split in his own consciousness of reality—a risk we should certainly apprehend the moment

---

called *incognizability*. As regards the function intended for art in this reversal of history, it cannot be anything different: such efforts always assume the premises of that which they set out to *repeat*.

we tried to imagine our minds transferred from the world around us to one that was completely different. The classical concept of reality that gave rise to Plato's doctrine of ideas—though not identical to it—presumes that reality presented itself as such and of its own accord, and that at the moment of its presence it was there and totally incontrovertible.[3] For these formal characteristics, the metaphor of light is particularly apt. This concept of reality also gave sustenance to a way of thinking that saw nothing problematic in biblical and other accounts of the appearance of God or of a god, who could present himself as such in a moment of direct revelation, leaving absolutely no room for the suspicion or the fear that he was illusory.[4] "Instantaneous evidence" is a concept that involves the instant recognition of ultimate reality and can be identified precisely through this implication.

A second concept of reality, basic to the Middle Ages and after, may be called *guaranteed reality*. The length of time philosophy took to grasp and express the implications behind man's understanding of an at-

[3] Although I should not maintain that the Platonic world of ideas is representative of the classical concept of reality, I do believe that it would be virtually unthinkable without the implication of that concept. It has been said often enough that the Greeks' access to their world was not just through their eyes but also through their thoughts. This may need elaborating: the Greeks preferred *seeing in repose* and the seeing of *given realities in repose*—ὁρᾶν is leaving the eyes at rest on the outside appearance of something, on a shape or a picture, as I have learned from Snell's lectures "Homerische Bedeutungslehre." Aristotle referred to the momentariness of sight as an analogy to pleasure (*Eth. Nic.*, x, 3; 1174 a, 13 et seq.): ὅρασις is at all moments complete and has no need of additional integration in time, like ἡδονή. Reality for sight does not constitute itself within time; although of course objects accumulate, the course of experience does not endow them with anything that could increase their given character. In the here and now, seeing, without any reference to γένεσις, is a whole (1174 b, 9-13). The direct consequence of this is the concept of any αἴσθησις (x, 4; 1174 b, 14-17). The fact that sight takes place in a series of aspects, that it is a process which essentially takes in *events*, relations, and representations, causes no difficulties and has no bearing on the formation of concepts.

[4] A late, ironic reflection of such instantaneous evidence is to be found in a novel whose theme is the interweaving of fiction and reality, their equivalence as far as human destiny is concerned, and the consequent irrelevance of their identity. This novel is André Gide's *Caves du Vatican*. After the funeral of the poor crusader Amadeus, who had failed in his attempt to prove the alleged exchange of popes, there is a conversation in the coach between Count Julius Baraglioul and Anthimos, who is told by the count that the present pope in fact is not the real one. Anthimos, the one-time atheist, who has been as totally converted as he has been totally cured of lameness, thinks over this revelation and returns instantly to his atheism; who can reassure him now that Amadeus Fleurissoire, as he enters Paradise, will not have to recognize that his God is also not "the real one"? The count's answer implies an unclouded faith, for in such a case there can be nothing but momentary evidence: for him it is a bizarre idea that there could be a false presentation of God, a mix-up *as if one could imagine another God being there*. But, typically, this argument makes not the slightest impression on Anthimos. Undoubtedly, he no longer shares this concept of reality, stops the coach, gets out, and—limps again.

titude to the world may be gauged from the fact that the history of modern philosophy had its starting point in the systematic formulation of this particular concept. For Descartes there is no instantaneous evidence of the ultimate reality, either for the self comprehending itself in a quasi-syllogism (*cogito, ergo sum*), or for God, whose existence is deduced from the concept of God. The given reality becomes certain only by virtue of a guarantee which has to be secured by thought in a complex metaphysical process, because only by means of this process can the suspicion of a world as gigantic hoax be eliminated. The idea of God as the guarantor of the reliability of human knowledge—the schema of the third instance—of the absolute witness, had been emerging throughout the history of the medieval concept of the human mind ever since Augustine. This schema precludes the possibility of any one characteristic that might pinpoint the total reality of a given object. The characteristic of clarity and distinctness which Descartes attributes to evidence can only be explained in terms of the metaphysical assumptions arising from his philosophical doubts; otherwise, as has rightly been observed, there would be no difference between this sort of clarity and that found in a state of paranoia. The schema of guaranteed reality, with a third instance mediating in the relationship between subject and object, has had a considerable impact on modern theory of art. It is still to be seen in the attempt to guarantee the truth of the artistic product by referring to the underlying experiences of the artist and the psychological integrity with which he has transformed these experiences.

A third concept of reality may be defined as the *actualization of a context in itself*.[5] This concept differs from the others through its time component: reality as "evidence" makes itself felt in the present moment; guaranteed reality refers back to the instance that creates and mediates between the world and human reason—in other words, to what scholasticism called *"ceritas ontologica"* that has its place in the past. The third

[5] It has rightly been pointed out that this is the reality concept of Husserl's phenomenology. Perhaps I should have insisted on being more precise—it is the reality concept presented by phenomenology. But I doubt whether this description of the constitution of reality could have been possible at any time; this is why it was important for me to determine what such a phenomenological thematization presupposes, and since when it could have been written and understood. Precisely in this context it becomes clear that concepts of reality do not simply take over from one another, but that the exhaustion of their implications and the excessive strain on their capacity to answer questions inspire a search for a new basis. The fact that *here* I am confining myself to an enumeration of concept-types is due to the thematic interest in the *vertical* foundation structure. More recent discussion on the connection of the reality concepts is contained in my "Vorbemerkungen zum Wirklichkeitsbegriffe" in *Abhandlungen der Akademie der Wissenschaften und der Literatur*, No. 4 (Mainz, 1973), 3-10.

concept takes reality as the result of an actualization, a progressive certainty which can never reach a total, final consistency, as it always looks forward to a future that might contain elements which could shatter previous consistency and so render previous "realities" unreal. Even when a person's life-space is complete, we can only say that *his* reality has been continuous, and that such and such constituted *his* illusions, delusions, and imaginings—in other words, "his" reality. It is typical of this particular concept that the possessive adjective is linked with the word *reality*. The transcendency of time either invalidates the self's concept of "its" reality, or, at best, allows it the quasi-justification that it is nothing but a single perspectivistic topographical view. Reality as a self-constituting context is a *borderline concept* of the *ideal totality* of all selves—it is a confirmative value for the experience and interpretation of the world that take place in *intersubjectivity*. Obviously this concept of reality has a sort of "epic" structure, relating to the totality of a world that can never be completed or grasped in its entirety—a world that can be only partially experienced and so can never exclude different contexts of experience which in themselves constitute different *worlds*.[6]

The last concept of reality that we shall discuss here is based on the

[6] The reality concept of the "open" context legitimizes the esthetic quality of the *novitas*, the element of surprise and unfamiliarity, whereas "guaranteed" reality does not allow anything new or unfamiliar to become *real*, ascribes to tradition and authority a world that is already mastered and rounded off as the sum total of all that is knowable, and so leads inevitably to the postulate of "nihil novum dicere" (e.g., Petrarch, *Epist. fam.*, VI, 2; cf. X, 1). The change in the concept of reality removes the dubiousness from what is new, and so *terra incognita*, or the *mundus novus*, becomes possible and effective as a *stimulus* to human activity; if one might phrase the process as a paradox, surprise is something to be expected. This is also relevant to the history of the "falseness" of poetry: esthetic pleasure in *falseness* becomes legitimate so long as it can be regarded as *newness* as well (i.e., as something possible, as a reality lying just beyond the horizon). Julius Caesar Scaliger, author of an oft-quoted poetics (1561), discusses in his even more interesting work *De subtilitate ad Hieronymum Cardanum* (1557; I use the edition of 1582), Cardanum's dictum: "Falsa delectant quia admirabilia" (*Exerc.* 307, 11; p. 936 et seq.). Scaliger protests against his commentary that it is only children and fools that could have such pleasure in the untrue, because they assume that there is *plus veritatis* in it, so that ultimately it would actually *be* a (supposed) form of truth, which gives rise to pleasure. However, art can give far more satisfaction than Nature to a naturally infinite, reasoning mind; those falsehoods in which even *sapientes* find pleasure (e.g. the *Homerica phasmata*) are revealed as the rich overflow by which art exceeds the (still) constant quantity of Nature. "At quare delectant admirabilia? Quia movent. Cur movent? Quoniam nova. Nova sane sunt, quae nunquam fuere neque dum existunt. . . . Mentem nostram esse natura sua infinitam. Quamobram et quod ad potentiam attinet aliena appetere, et quod spectat ad intellectionem, etiam e falsis ac monstrorum picturis capere voluptatem. Propterea quod exsuperant vulgares limites veritatis. . . . Mavultque pulchram imaginem, quam naturali similem designatae. Naturam enim in eo superat ars."

experience of *resistance*. Here illusion is understood as the desires enter-
tained by the self: unreality as the threat to and seduction of the self
through the projection of its own wishes; the consequent antithesis is
reality as that which cannot be mastered by the self, i.e., which resists it
not merely as an experience of contact with an inert mass, but also—
most radically—in the logical form of the *paradox*. This would explain
why paradox has become the favorite form of testimony in theology,
which in the very frustrations and vexations of its logically inconsistent
contents sees the proof of an ultimate reality that overwhelms the self
and demands that it subjugate itself. Reality here is that which is totally
unavailable, which cannot be relegated simply to the level of material for
manipulation, but can only occasionally appear to be processed by one
technique or another, then to reveal itself in the full potency of its overwhelming autonomy as a *"factum brutum,"* of which it may afterwards
be said, though not conceived, that it might have emanated from a free
and constructive process of creative thinking. The significant feature of
this concept is that which cannot be further analyzed—the basic constant, the "atomic fact"; it is typified by such claims as Heisenberg's,
that playing off two mutually exclusive images against each other can
ultimately convey the correct impression of a particular reality—or
George Thomson's, that a "complicated section of mathematics is just as
representative of reality as 'mass,' 'energy' etc." The beginnings of this
concept are perhaps to be found where awareness of reality is supposed
to involve an *instinct*, the practical workings of which need not necessarily exclude or remove theoretical doubts, but make them irrelevant to
our assertions concerning our existence or that of the self in general.
D'Alembert suggests this in the introduction to the *Encyclopédie*. One
might perhaps also cite Lessing's letter to Mendelssohn—written more
or less at the same time—in which he states that *"with every violent
desire or detestation we are aware to a larger extent of our reality"*[7]—
an idea that separates awareness of reality from thought and removes
this awareness of reality to the sphere of experiences unavailable to the
mind with itself. Clearly, then, we must face the possibility that the
modern era is one in which there is no longer any one homogeneous
concept of reality, or that if one particular form of awareness predominates, it does so through confrontation with another fully developed or
developing experience of reality.

This historical sequence of concepts of reality and the different ways
of understanding works of art, are dependent on each other. Without
doubt, the theory of imitation[8]—the concept that is dominant in our

---

[7] Lessing, *Gesammelte Werke* (Berlin, 1957), ix, 105 (letter of Feb. 2, 1757).

[8] The following description of the origin and historical role of the mimesis theory
not only refers to but also partly corrects the corresponding section of my study

esthetic tradition—is based on the notion of *instantaneous evidence*. The theory of imitation depends upon two ontological premises:

1. A realm of actual, self-evident *exemplary* reality that is given or may be assumed;

2. The *completeness* of this realm as regards all possible contents and forms of reality.

It follows from these premises that an artist can only *repeat* Nature, because there is no scope for him to transcend it. Furthermore, it is a fundamental feature of this exemplary given reality that not only *can* it be repeated, but indeed it *should* be repeated: it demands imitation of itself because if, in its exemplariness, it failed to instigate such images of itself, it would remain totally sterile. Thus Platonic idealism demonstrates why there are such things as works of artifice and art, but also why nothing essential can be "achieved" by them. Herein lies the peculiar *ambivalence of Platonism* in the history of esthetics: it has always been at one and the same time a justification and a devaluation of artistic activity. Plato himself verifies this in the tenth book of his *Republic*, where he attacks literature and the pictorial arts in general, arguing that in depicting given objects the artist is already creating something second-hand, insofar as whatever he is basing his work on is not itself the true and ultimate reality, but merely an imitation of it by Nature or by a craftsman. The work of art, then, is an imitation of an imitation. The fact that the image of an image demands a completely different evaluation from that of the image of the original is also based on the concept of instantaneous evidence: in the unsurpassable evidence of the "original," reality can be experienced as something reliable, and the image of this original is legitimized by the *fact* that it has to be, and not by *what* it has to be (a definition applicable only to the original). This is confirmed by Plato's example of artistic representation of elementary household objects through the art of painting. There is no such thing in Nature as a table or a bed; also, for Plato there can be no question of the craftsman's having *invented* such objects for a particular practical purpose, for this would mean that the craftsman was the originator of the idea. According to Plato, for every meaningful human design there must already be "originals" in the world of ideas, and it is upon these that the craftsman bases his work. And so the copy of the original is ac-

"Nachahmung der Natur" in *Studium Generale* (1957), x, 266-83; esp. 270 ff. Above all I am no longer satisfied with establishing the ambivalence of the Platonic schema, but would like to show that positive and negative evaluation, and emphasis on participation or deficiency, belong to different levels of reference, which might be labelled real and merely relational imitation. This will clarify what takes place in the Aristotelian theory of art, which cannot make this difference and is open only to the positive evaluation of mimesis, and also what Neoplatonism and Platonic Gnosis have "left out."

complished by the man who manufactures the table or bed. The painter, however, who in turn reproduces such objects, bases his work on something that has already been produced—in other words, he creates a copy of what is already a copy.

But why does Plato not concede that the painter—just like the craftsman—may himself see the idea, when depicting such objects, thus fulfilling the requirements for producing a copy of the original? The tenth book of the *Republic* offers no answer to this question. But the problem is not unimportant if one wishes to understand the ambivalence of Platonism in esthetic theory. It also plays a significant role in justifying the thesis that the Platonic residue within our esthetic tradition is what denies the *novel* a legitimate place in the traditional system of esthetics, making it a *genre of the bad esthetic conscience* that has constantly had to be transcended or assimilated into other legitimate genres.

Platonic ideas fix a canon of what is both demanded of and permitted to the copier. They were, first of all, the basis of our abstract concepts, not yet themselves the primal images of forms, but norms for the accomplishments of reason, say, for establishing relations between objects, for comprehending geometrical proportions, and, finally, for evaluating actions. In all these spheres, ideas had the prescriptive character of rules; they were representative not of reality as it ought to be, but of the actual obligation. The fact that the original, preexistent experience of the ideas had to be visualized in the imagination led to their eidetic character's becoming more and more clearly defined, so that they formed primal images of all the vague copies we see in the visible world around us. But these ideas were not only images of pure essences—they were primal images with the true exemplary character that demands and compels imitation. The terms "primal image" and "copy" are not just relational concepts arising out of the completed imitation, but they themselves have an ideal quality, corresponding to the origin of the doctrine of ideas: i.e., the primal image is independent of the actual imitation, and preceded it as a norm that could be substantiated only through the actuality and the faithfulness of the copy. This consequence of the doctrine of ideas, which had already come to the fore in the *Republic* through the singling out of goodness as an idea of ideas, is revealed in its full significance in the dialogue *Timaeus*: here the fact of the creation of the world is shown to need no further motivation than that of a mere glimpse of the ideas by a craftsman who is considered capable of performing this task, and who only requires affirmation of the truthfulness of his work, but not of any particular disposition of his will to take on and execute such a work. The visible world is, accordingly, a fulfillment of the compulsive implications of the primal images, which demand imitation as the correlative that completes their meaning. However, it is clear that in this system only the first, direct copy can be the legitimate fulfillment of the demands of the original, and this first copy therefore represents the end of the process of imitation; its imitative nature, though accepted itself as real predication, precludes the possibility of its becoming a binding model in its own right. The artist therefore only copies something which itself is *already* a copy and can be nothing but a copy, and he thereby raises it to the level of an original—a level which intrinsically it is not qualified to occupy. It is not every copy, or copies as such, that Plato derogates, but only those that did not directly imitate the original—i.e., the "unreal" copies, the indirect secondhand imitations that are based on what is already an imitation. One of the misunderstandings of Neoplatonism is that it gives a totally negative evaluation to all imitations, so that even the creating of the world itself, and not just that of the copies worked by the artist, becomes a dubious event. However, this Neoplatonic misconception of Plato's criticism of imitation at the same time clarifies the curious fact that Platonic elements had a part in a development which led eventually to the liquidation of imitation as a basis for the artistic creativity.

We must not forget that the esthetic theory of imitation is part of the *Aristotelian* tradition.[9] With Aristotle, ideas became formal principles of Nature itself, so that actuality and necessity merged in the world to such an extent that the artist's function was to extract from the external world what ought to be and the way it ought to be. Artistic representation therefore became a direct copy, and was not, so to speak, a copy once removed. The dignity of imitation as the essence of artistic activity was thus established, not by revaluing mimesis itself, but simply by reducing the number of levels of reference: art now took over the position which in Plato had been occupied by Nature itself or by the demiurge that created it, a position in which artistic activity had been essentially superfluous and even inconsistent with the system.

It is true that this is but a residue of Platonism in Aristotelism, explaining why a work of art may be possible, but endowing it with neither justification nor necessity. This is why the Aristotelian tradition in esthetics, even though it sets out to define artistic activity as an imitation of nature, accounts for it and evaluates it almost exclusively in terms of man's emotional needs and its effect on these needs. In Aristotelian

---

[9] We must also bear in mind the fact that in this tradition the general metaphysical interpretation of *art* ($\tau \acute{\epsilon} \chi \nu \eta$) in the broadest sense was predominant, before what we would call Aristotelian *esthetics* could take effect with the rediscovery of his *Poetics*. Medieval criticism resulted in Aristotelianism minus the *Poetics* (which only follows Arabic lines of tradition); the consequences of this are something that urgently require closer study.

esthetics, the basic concept of *man* is more important than that of reality; it is a system conceived from the standpoint of the viewer or listener. Against such a background, the original, angry dictum that artists, and particularly poets, are liars is deprived of its negatively critical
substance, insofar as the Aristotelian definition of art as imitation does
not concern what *ought* to be done, but only what *can* be done.

The revival of Platonism during the Renaissance[10] did not signify a
reversal of the original derivation—Aristotelian concept arising from
Platonian; the critique of the ideal of imitation was now based on a shift
in metaphysical interest. In the late Middle Ages, man's interest in himself and in his position in the world became the overriding consideration,
and the answer to his questions lay first and foremost in man's own
works and achievements. Together with the dignity of man's works, the
dignity of art itself became the central theme of the Renaissance. An
esthetic system concerned principally with the observer's reactions
scarcely fitted in with such an approach. The comparability of man's creations with those of God was implicit or even explicit in this newly
developing concept of the artist; this meant returning directly to the
question of art's relationship to reality, and the extent to which this relationship was inevitable or contingent, necessary or dispensable. If this
reinterpretation of the early symptoms of the modern view of art is correct, then the result of such an approach is not only a new definition of
the difference between physical and esthetic objects but also an inherent
rivalry between the artist and the outside world as a whole—in other
words, the artist offers not only a transformation, idealization, or variation of the world, but works that are, so to speak, of *equal rank* to it.
Both in terms of the classical concept of instantaneous evidence and the

[10] It is difficult to define in detail what is really "Platonic" about this revival. In study-
ing the history of concepts, we must not forget that the "Platonism" of the Renaissance
after Petrarch originated from Cicero criticism and its capacity for comprehension was determined by this. As a result, a guideline such as the *idea* is unsuited to the discovery of
Platonisms, as can be seen from Erwin Panofsky's "Idea" (*Studien der Bibl. Warburg,*
1924; 2nd ed., 1960): by choosing *species* as the Latin equivalent, Cicero had removed all
precision from the term (even though he also left it in Greek), out of which humanism
made an all-round word. When Panofsky refers, for instance, to Melanchthon's express
equation of *idea* with *notitia* for the "pulcherrima imago humani corporis" included in the
in animo of Apelles, in order to demonstrate the immanence of Platonism, he is contradicted by Melanchthon's own embarrassment, who, when compelled, at one stage, to
reproduce an authentic Platonic idea, uses, for instance, *imitatio*, which is scarcely compat-
ible with *notitia*, and so the *statuarius* has in himself a *certa notitia* of his work, which
guides his hand: "donec efficiatur similitudo eius archetypi quem imitatur (*Corp. Ref.*,
xiii, 305). If *idea* were really taken here "almost as a specifically esthetic" concept, *ar-
chetypus* would not need to be smuggled in in this way; but *idea* is, of course, the nice
academic term which in fact can be used for anything except something Platonic.

medieval concept of reality guaranteed by God, this idea of the artist's competing with given reality would have been senseless and groundless. Only a new concept, bestowing upon the inter-subjective consistency of the given in space and time the sole right to recognition through a mind conscious of reality, could give substance, and even intelligibility, to the artist's claim to totality as against the claim of the factual world.

The same concept of creation, now involving the possibility of totality in a single work—without this possibility's being systematically made explicit—removed the very foundations of the Aristotelian concept of the artificial and the artistic. While Nature appeared as the expression of an omnipotent, divine will, idealization as the task of the artist had become something not only dubious but daemonic by the implication that Nature was perhaps not what it ought to be; the artist had, as it were, to "catch up" with its possibilities and make up for its deficiencies in relation to what it ought to be. What according to the Aristotelian definition could it mean that art and technology completed what Nature could not finish? For the medieval view of the world, Nature had lost its specific, authentic evidence as reality. The fact, now constituted and guaranteed by an absolute will, was a great new element of ambiguity: it allowed the reassurance of not having to ask questions, and at the same time gave rise to the annoyance that anything factual is bound to arouse in man's reason. The fact that no esthetics came forth from the premises and postulates of Cartesian philosophy was clearly due to this philosophy's being—in respect of its concept of reality—"medieval," clinging to the guaranteed schema of reality. Cartesian esthetics could not have been anything but, at best, a theory of medieval art. We should not be surprised or misled by this historical phenomenon; it is quite natural that the most deeply hidden implication of an era—namely, its concept of reality—should become explicit only when the awareness of that reality has already been broken.

If the question of the *possibility* of the novel is put as an ontological one, searching out the foundations of the concept of reality, this means that one is also inquiring into the origin of a new claim of art—its claim, not merely to represent *objects* of the world, or even to imitate *the* world, but to actualize *a* world. A world—nothing less—is the theme and postulate of the novel.[11] It is odd that the premise underlying this

[11] There is a certain affinity between Georg Lukács' comment that the novel is the "épopée of the God-forsaken world"—*Die Theorie des Romans* (Berlin, 1920), p. 84—that is to say, the epic under the conditions of the modern view of the world—and the arguments developed here. The longed-for revival of the Greek epic, and the claim that it set the absolute standard, foundered against a view of reality that took the world for *a* world, the *cosmos* for a *universe*. The ultimate failure of Leibniz and Wolff to ensure the *ratio*

approach was created by the renewal of Platonism, for, in this context, Platonism took on a historical function that was quite extraneous to it. Its inherent negative evaluation of imitation was, at the beginning of the modern age, more or less the "desired" effect, whose genuine *premises* certainly were not to be renewed: the difference between what is and what ought to be, as the scope of art, was a possibility that had in the meantime been excluded. Art was rather to concern itself with that sphere which had not been actualized by God or by Nature, and so there was no longer any duality of existent reality and formative art. Instead, every work, measured against the new concept of reality, was the *reality of the possible*, whose unreality had to be the premise for the relevance of its actualization.

If our original thesis is correct—namely, that the history of esthetics is one long debate on the classical dictum that poets are liars—this history must always be intimately related to concepts of the human capacity to "tell the truth." It is *the change in the concept of truth* which opens up new possibilities for art to be "true." The classical concept of truth, valid throughout most of the Middle Ages, maintained that in cognition, ontologically, there were present and effective the same constituent factors that made objects themselves what they were—in Aristotelian terms, their essential form. Between the object and the act of perception there exists a causal link of clearly *imitative* representation. Connected with the medieval concept of a *transcendentally guaranteed reality*, there arose a new possibility of abandoning this direct causal link and, instead, viewing the sphere of cognition as a heterogeneous, individual world of mere *signs for objects*—a world whose internal order needed only to correspond precisely to the internal order of the elements of things for truth to be attained. The concept of *non-imitative cognition*, in which words and figures and their correlations can stand for objects and their correlations, has its metaphysical foundation in the premise of a *third instance*, which guarantees the strict coherence even of that which is totally heterogeneous. The Aristotelian claim that the soul is everything of the possible—a view that gave the most abstract definition

---

sufficiens of the factual world opened the gates for a critique of the factual from the standpoint of the rational and the possible—a critique which was bound to work on the imagination and stimulate it into testing out the meaning of its own "worlds." The uniqueness of the cosmos and the Greeks' commitment to the epic as an interpretation of the world were just two aspects of the reality given by *instantaneous evidence*. The novel could not be a "secularization" of the epic after the world's loss of religion; on the contrary, the contingency, the factualness of the indefinite article, the inrush of *possibilia* all go back to the theologizing of the world. The "worlds" which the esthetically minded self is willing to belong to only provisionally, in the accessible finiteness of a context, are the quintessence of the novel's thematization of reality and the irony essential to it.

to the age-old principle of cognition through similarity and affinity—
takes on a new meaning: the cognitive mind, with its capacity for putting symbols in place of things and their correlations, is capable of *every*
formulation of objective facts. The late Middle Ages had to abandon the
concept of cognition through similarity and imitation mainly because it
seemed to set the human spirit up too close to the divine. The new *concept of cognition*, however, radically separates the divine spirit, which
sees all things directly and in their essence, from the human spirit,
which can only represent them symbolically; the human spirit thus loses
its receptive openness to things, and becomes instead a creative principle
employing its own symbolic tools.[12] The enhanced *transcendency* of the
divine rule over things forcibly gives rise to the *immanence* of the new
concept of human mastery over these things. The correspondence between cognition and its objects is no longer *material* but *functional*. The
immanent consistency of the symbolic system of concepts remains the
only—though adequate—approximation to the given reality. The *concept of the image* is released from its hitherto inescapable confinement
between the original and the copy.[13] Truth, in the strict sense of
adaequatio, remains possible only for what man himself has created and
of which he can therefore be completely aware without any symbolic
mediation: this includes the structural laws governing his symbolic tools
of cognition—laws that are formulated by logic—mathematics, history,
language, and, last but not least, art. No longer is absolute truth to be
seen somewhere in the relation between the representational work of art
and Nature; it now lies between the subjective mind perceiving the work
and the product which is viewed as a possible piece of reality created by
the artist. It is no longer through his relationship to Nature, as a form of
creation from which he is alienated, but through his cultural works, that
man can match God's direct contact with his own works both as creator
and as observer. This hitherto unknown metaphysical dignity of the
work of art has its foundation in what is, at one and the same time, a
limiting and an intensifying transformation and dissolution of the concept of truth.

The consequences of this new view of man's spiritual achievements

[12] For the *similitudo divini intellectus in creando*, see my book *Die Legitimität der
Neuzeit* (Frankfurt, 1966), pp. 503-513.

[13] Already in the (disputed) Platonic vii letter, εἴδωλον and ὄνομα are put on a level as
regards their distance from truth (342 et seq.), but in a derogatory sense, as provisional
measures for what is then an unsurpassable immediacy. The modern levelling-out of the
difference between *image* and *concepts* as suppositions which are free of any similarity-
relation to reality knows no greater approximation or immediate access to reality *as such*.
It is in fact one of the features of the modern concept of reality that it excludes the "ontological comparative" (W. Bröcker).

are far-reaching. Reality can no longer be considered an inherent quality of an object, but is the embodiment of a consistently applied *syntax of elements*. Reality presents itself now as ever before as a sort of text which takes on its particular form by obeying certain rules of internal consistency. Reality is for modern times a context; even such an important phenomenon in the history of ideas as criticism of the theological interpretation of miracles as testifying to the divine, is totally compelled to maintain this concept of reality. Now, if esthetic objects can have such a thing as a specific reality, they, too, are not only bound by the criterion of context as proof of their reality but are also constrained, as regards their scope and the wealth of elements they incorporate, to compete with the context of *Nature*, i.e., to become *secondary worlds*: they no longer extract, by imitation, realities from the one reality, but imitate the fact of being real.

Ultimately, art claims as its subject matter the formal proof of reality and not the material content that presents itself with this proof. Without doubt, the *non-possible* would represent the fulfillment of this claim—namely, the infinite context, which alone could be counted as the normal equivalent to the open-endedness of physical experience. This is the starting point from which modern literature—and the esthetics appropriate to it—proceeded towards the novel as the most comprehensively "realistic" genre, representing a context which, though finite in itself, presumes and indicates infinity. The *potential infinity* of the novel represents its *ideality*, arising out of the concept of reality, as well as the esthetic *irritation* inevitable in view of the fact that its task of representing an infinite context can be fulfilled only by esthetically binding principles of form. Perhaps the clearest embodiment of the problems of the genre is to be seen in the humorous novel: already in Sterne's *Tristram Shandy* the subject is the possibility as well as the impossibility of the novel. The increasing incongruity between the real and the represented existence brings out the novel's implication of infinity, and shows the dilemma created when a finite text tries to evoke an infinite context. As a finite and discontinuous work, the novel thwarts the reader's expectations of the "et cetera," and so focuses his attention on its true theme: that it is ultimately not concerned with proving its own validity as a work of art through a sequence of edited events, but with the conflict between the imaginary reality of a context and the reality of the existing world. Another such humorous novel that is not only in fact incomplete but also incompletable, and that has reality itself as its subject matter, is Jean Paul's *Der Komet*.[14] Here the theme is the "experimental" presen-

---

[14] Jean Paul himself, in his introductory *investiture* of the reader with the story, points out this thematization by so projecting history and novel onto one another that to convey

tation of the illusory world of the supposed crown prince Nikolaus Marggraf, interwoven with the real, or supposedly real, world of the German petty principality; as the two worlds act upon each other, the predicates of illusion and reality appear to be interchangeable. This very fact shows that what we tend to call "representation" in a novel is in fact "asemantic"—i.e., it represents nothing but itself; it removes the boundaries between being and meaning, matter and symbol, object and sign, destroying the correspondences that had been integral to our whole tradition of truth concepts. This destruction, nevertheless, involves continuing dependence on the tradition it negates, indirectly creating the uncreatable by removing the hitherto unchallenged function: the sign no longer purports to represent a "thing," and so itself takes on the substantiality of a thing. This, of course, is an approach that ranges beyond the novel and its basic concept of reality, to an awareness of reality that is determined by resistance, and to a corresponding and confirmatory art form that is made up of means of expression that annihilate themselves, and use their own inconsistencies to demonstrate their own lack of meaning.[15] Once more the novel takes itself as its own subject matter; by demonstrating the impossibility of the novel, a novel becomes possible.

I should like to go into rather more detail concerning this problem of

----

this given *historical* subject he wishes for himself the capacity of the novelist, so that with *one mighty stroke* he could complete the creation of his hero: "and I shall reach *my goal if I can set out the historical truths* of this story in such a way that they seem to the reader like successful fictions, with the result that, raised above the juridical law of *fictio sequitur naturam* (fiction, or appearance, follows Nature), here conversely Nature or history follows fiction—or, to put it in Latin, natura fictionem sequatur."

[15] Such a substantialization through annihilating the function of "means of meaning" has not been discovered in the immanent history of the novel; the reality that occurs in *resistance* is, from the viewpoint of the esthetics of genre, basic to *lyric poetry*. Late nineteenth-century esthetic experiences gained from poetry in its strictest and narrowest sense, have become prototypical—among other things, for the changing of novel esthetics into the thematization of the "impossibility" of the novel. Perhaps I can best define this prototypical discovery of lyric poetry through the passage in Paul Valéry's letter to J.-M. Carré, 23rd February 1943 (*Lettres à quelques-uns*, Paris, 1952), p. 240, in which he tries to systematize the experience of shock caused 50 years back by Rimbaud's *Illuminations*: ". . . le système, conscient ou non, que supposent les passages les plus virulents de ces poèmes. Il me souvient d'avoir résumé ces observations—et, en somme, mes défenses— par ces termes: R. a inventé ou découvert la puissance de l'incohérence harmonique. Arrivé à ce point extrême, paroxystique de l'irritation volontaire de la fonction du langage, il ne pouvait que faire ce qu'il a fait—fuir." The anticlimax of the "actualization," the exhaustibility of the ontological basis of this reality concept, are preconditions for the transposition of the principle to other genres and arts (e.g., the abandonment of tonality); but the novel (in a different way from the drama) has shown itself to be particularly resistant to the "paroxysmal" consequence of the principle, and so, as extremely flexible and productive as far as experiments are concerned.

form. The idea of reality as context imposes on the novel the form of
linear consistency within a given system of space and time. But, as I
have pointed out, this concept of reality becomes valid only through an
agreement among subjects that are capable of understanding one
another—i.e., through *intersubjectivity* and its various possible perspectives. So far as I am aware, the novel first took on a *perspective pattern*
with Balzac, whose cycle of novels creates the illusory reality of a whole
human society through the recurrence of identical characters viewed
from changing perspectives. As far as the question of reality is concerned, there is a big difference between the epic-linear and the perspective recurrence of characters—the spatial consciousness is different, and
the world created is far subtler. Balzac's perspective system enables a
linear series of episodes to be translated into simultaneous events. But it
demands more than mere consistency with elements already dealt with,
for perspective consistency allows a transformation of those elements as
the emphasis shifts, for instance, from one character to another, or from
one aspect of character to another. The result is a highly complex process
of reconciling individual aspects to one another and to the overall identity of the object to which they belong. This is basically quite different
from the traditional introduction of individual characters drawn in preparation for their ultimate meeting at the climax of the plot. It is no
longer merely the characters in the novel that move through the various
events contained in the plot; the reader now moves around the body of
imaginary reality, passing through all the different aspects from which it
can be viewed. Balzac himself believed, and expressly indicated as one of
his most daring intentions, that the recurrence of individual characters
in his *Comédie Humaine* would endow this fictitious cosmos with more
life and movement;[16] but in fact it is not the world of the novel that is
set in motion so much as the reader himself as he experiences the various
changes of perspective. The world of the novel itself takes on a greater
degree of stability and substance, which seems both to the author and
the reader more and more to defy total mastery, compelling them to
ever greater efforts, by which the imaginative reality itself remains quite
unaffected. The more the novel's reality depends on the *standpoint* of
the mediating self, the less it seems to depend on that *self* and his imagination, and in fact the more he seems to depend on it.

[16] "This is something which one might call a 'fiction-mobile,' a totality that consists of a
certain number of parts, which we can observe in virtually any sequence we like. . . . It is
clear that the recurrence of characters or their continuation from one novel to another has
a far greater significance in Balzac than in the so-called *roman-fleuve* . . ." (Michel Butor,
Balzac et la réalité, 1959). ". . . The final triumph of Balzac over his great predecessor
(Walter Scott), and his liberation from him, is to be seen in an extraordinary innovation,
which completely changes the structure of his work . . . the recurrence of characters" (p.
64).

Clearly, then, the idea of reality as an intersubjective context can lead to an idea of it as the experience of the resistance of any given object. In the novel, this transition is marked as a breaking up of connections between aspects resulting from different perspectives. The beginnings of this process are to be seen in Jean Paul's humorous novel *Der Komet* ;[17] and it came beyond all humorous implications to full fruition, for instance, in Robert Musil's novel *Der Mann ohne Eigenschaften*. In this immense fragment even the (existing) conclusion does not begin to bring together the different threads of the plot or to lead them towards any common end; epic perspectivism is here virtually exploded, wrecked on the consequences of its own precision. In 1932 Musil wrote of his *Mann ohne Eigenschaften*: "This book has a passion for something which nowadays is to a certain extent out of place in the field of literature: namely, correctness and precision. What the story of this novel amounts to is the fact that the story which is to be told is not told." The increasing specificity of the narrative leads to a demonstration of the impossibility of narrative itself. But this impossibility in turn is felt to indicate the unbreakable resistance of the imaginary reality to being described, and in this sense the esthetic principle inherent in the reality concept of immanent consistency leads at a certain point of transition to a different reality concept altogether. Herein lies the reason why the constantly anticipated "liquidation" of the novel has never been achieved. It also explains why irony seems to have become the authentic mode of reflection as far as the esthetic claims of the modern novel are concerned: the novel becomes ironic through the connections with reality that it is unable to dispense with and yet incapable of forming. Thomas Mann once spoke of the *seeming accuracy* of scientific discourse used as a stylistic means of irony: in his 1942 lecture on *Josef und seine Brüder* he calls this the application of the scientific to the totally unscientific—and this precisely is for him the purest expression of irony.

I should like to deal with just one more facet of the basic connection between the reality concept and the feasibility of the novel. I have tried

---

[17] It is worth noting how the dialogues in Jean Paul's *Der Komet* always "function" only through misunderstandings and never allow the fictional context to be exploded. But as the structure of intersubjective communication is shown to be strong enough to reify even unreality into quasi-reality, the concept of reality is not only thematized, but also used as an esthetic element—one might almost say it is instrumentalized. Inevitably the esthetic instrumentalization creates, indeed even presupposes, critical awareness: suspicion as regards the malleability of reality for specific purposes is here implied, this suspicion is also contained in the unexpected, socially critical virulence of the novel, in the ceaseless *probing*, for instance, of the deformability of elements of reality, up to the discovery of the breaking-point as in the solipsistic dialogues of Kafka or Beckett. The triumph (as yet not properly understood) of finally having hit upon something stable, is what marks the phrasing of this development: the functional collapse of intersubjectivity releases a new concept of reality.

to show that the concept of reality as a phenomenal and immanent consistency lies at the root of the autonomous reality of the work of art.
What I have not mentioned, but what actually brings together man's
created works in competition with the existing reality of Nature, is the
strange fact that, on the one hand, man asserts himself in the actualization of his creative potential, while, on the other, he must seek to conceal the dependence of his art on his own abilities and will; he must do
this, because only then can his works take on the unquestionable autonomy and individuality that will make them indistinguishable from
the products of Nature. It may therefore be taken as a characteristic feature of modern art and literature that they have undergone a sort of de-
reification; the more familiar *alienation* is only a partial phenomenon
within this trend. Human art presents itself neither as an imitation of
Nature nor as a "piece of Nature," but it is to have the same rank and
dignity as natural objects; it is to be the work of Man, but it is not to be
characterized by the contingency of the individual will, or the actuality
of the mere idea. In other words, it must be, at one and the same time,
both novelty and fossil. We want to be able to disregard ourselves as the
condition of the possibility of these works, because we do not want them
to be a part of our conditional or our historical nature, of which we are
proud despite the afflictions they cause us; we do not want our works to
be *objects* dependent on subjects, but to be *things* in themselves. And
these works for their part should not *represent* aspects but should *offer*
us aspects of themselves. From the perspective structure systematically
prepared and laid out in the novel, there can emerge a perspective potential that is stimulated by the work and yet at the same time is not
fulfilled by it; we recognize this potential when we realize the essential
openness of modern art to commentary and varied interpretation which
is apparent from Romanticism onwards. This *hermeneutic ambiguity* is
integral to the "reality" of the work of art, insofar as it is this which
proves its independence of our own subjectivity. This is why we tend
artificially to *historicize* the work of art, in order to strip it of its dependence on ourselves and to "reify" it. Just as archaic sculpture exists in the
landscape, such as the *things* tossed on to the green grass of Otterloo,
there is also the novel distanced by language or by the artifice of a narrative framework—the type of novel of which we "know too much" for it
to have its desired effect of alienation on us. In the same way that we can
artificially historicize, we can also artificially *naturalize*, but no longer
can we do this by representing or imitating Nature; we must instead
claim "naturalness" for our works, erecting things which resemble the
products of eruptions or erosions, like the *objet ambigu* in Paul Valéry's
Eupalinos. Corresponding to these in the novel is the artificially artless

transcript of streams of consciousness and interior monologues—the "writing-the-minutes" type of novel (*Protokollroman*), which claims to create and at the same time renounces the creation of a whole world.

The reality concept of the context of phenomena presents a reality that can never be assured, is constantly in the process of being actualized, and continually requires some new kind of confirmation. This idea of reality, even when transformed into the reality of an esthetic object, remains a sort of consistency which is, so to speak, open at both ends and dependent on continuous proofs and accomplishments, without ever achieving the finality of evidence that characterized the classical concept of reality. This is one reason for the uneasiness and dissatisfaction that have been a constant critical undercurrent throughout the history of the novel. One way out of this dissatisfaction is to resist the need for an endless actualization by deliberately breaking through set patterns of formal consistency—a breaking-through which shows by the way it is handled that it does not spring from any failure or exhaustion of creative powers but, on the contrary, represents a conscious effort which can afford to disregard the quasi-objective principle of formal consistency. The idea that poets are liars can be completely invalidated only if they no longer set out to prove its antithesis—namely, that poets tell the truth—but concentrate on deliberately breaking the bonds of this antithesis and indeed all the rules of the reality-game itself. Commitment to reality is rejected as an unwanted limitation on form, an esthetic heteronomy wearing the mask of authenticity. Herein lie the roots of an esthetic concept that can now present as "true" what all previous concepts of reality would have designated as unreal: paradox, the inconsistency of dreams, deliberate nonsense, centaurian hybrids, objects placed in the most unlikely positions, the reversal of natural entropy, refuse used to make *objets d'art*, newspaper cuttings to make novels, the noises of technology to make a musical composition.

Modern art, however, has not freed itself from the compulsion to refute its dependence on the given realities of Nature; its anti-physicism is not even directed against a constant *Nature* whose dimensions are known or defined. The liberation of the imagination always being proclaimed, for instance by Breton, goes so far as to dissolve even the (now merely formal) connection between the reality concept of immanent consistency and its commitment to the reality value of *Nature*, and so it is again and again compelled to make desperate efforts to actualize itself despite its extreme improbability, in what remains, when all is said and done, a type of *instantaneous evidence*. The fact that the novel still adheres to the reality concept of immanent consistency can be gauged from the problems that accrue to it from any heterogeneous concept of reality. It cannot actualize itself simply by contradicting whatever has hitherto been regarded as significant evidence of reality. The ideal of the *perfetta deformitá* cannot be fulfilled by the novel. But it is characteristic of the novel that at this point it takes its own possibility as its subject matter, thus demonstrating its dependence on the concept of reality. I need only point to the technique of uncommunicative dialogue to explain what I mean: the failure of conversation, its hypertrophy in meaningless chatter, misunderstanding as a constituent product of language —all this remains essential to the novel, embedded in a world that is still presumed and produced with too much imagination for it ever to be said that pure absurdity can really become the subject matter. The novel has its own "realism," which has evolved from its own particular laws, and this has nothing to do with the ideal of imitation, but is linked precisely to the esthetic illusion which is essential to the genre. Fixing (or causing) a world (*Welthaftigkeit*) as a formal, overriding structure is what constitutes the novel. When the absurd was proclaimed the program of art, its function was defined as "transcending the foundations," and ultimately even architecture showed itself suited to this function of the absurd. But the novel had advanced much earlier and much more spontaneously to this transcending of the foundations—i.e., to the resolution of the conflict between reality and fiction—and, as I have shown, it had taken as its theme its own possibility, not as a fiction of reality, but as a *fiction of the reality of realities*. The novel's preeminence in the actualization of basic modern ideas of esthetics is comprehensible only if one realizes that it has not adopted absurdity, that new criterion of absolute poetry, because it has no need of such a stigma. The novel fulfills the esthetic norm which, according to Boswell's diary, was first formulated by Samuel Johnson during the famous conversation in the Literary Club about the excessive price of an antique marble dog: "Everything that enlarges the sphere of human powers" (3rd April 1778), whereas even the broadest interpretation of the Aristotelian ideal of imitation—perhaps Breitinger's—is concerned with the sphere of the *naturally* possible.[18]

[18] The notes added subsequently to this paper have been written, with grateful acknowledgments, as a result of suggestions, doubts, and objections raised during the discussion.

HERBERT DIECKMANN

The Transformation of the Concept of Imitation in Eighteenth-Century French Esthetics

THE topic suggested to me was: "The concept of fidelity-to-nature in French esthetics and its development by Diderot." I changed this to: "The transformation of the concept of imitation in eighteenth-century French esthetics." I have done this not in order to broaden the scope of the subject, but because a change in formulating the title is appropriate. *La Vérité de la nature* is, of course, a common term in the esthetics of eighteenth-century France, but it is neither productive nor central. Moreover, the meaning of the term seems to me to have been unduly influenced by the contrasting terms—fidelity-to-nature (vs) fidelity-to-art, natural beauty (vs) artistic beauty—which were used in German esthetics at the end of the eighteenth and the beginning of the nineteenth century. It is therefore advisable not to use these terms when referring to the *ars poetica* and the esthetics of eighteenth-century France, as they apply to a later period. In a discussion of these problems, it is, after all, important to see them in their proper context. The subject which I am to deal with here must doubtless be seen in the context of the principle of *imitatio naturae* and the formula of *ut pictura poesis*. This means that the imitation of nature is not only a question of *ars poetica* but of esthetics in general. It also means that the point of view from which it is discussed undergoes a change: the eighteenth-century discussion of *imitatio naturae* was not concerned solely with the object imitated, but also—and in increasing measure—with the means of imitating. In the eighteenth century, literature was no longer supreme, either as a form of art or as a theory. Painting, sculpture, and music held an equal place with literature, and all became united in the comprehensive genre of opera. It is not surprising that the two most important theoretical essays in the first half of the eighteenth century, the Abbé Du Bos's *Réflexions critiques sur la poésie et sur la peinture* (1719) and *Les beaux arts réduits à un même principe* (1746), were based on a comparative study of art, and that Diderot should connect the theory of literature with the theory of painting and of music. This development broadened the concept of *imitatio naturae* to cover several forms of art as well as the way in which they are presented.[1] However, the fact that this concept was broadened may lead to a certain confusion. Statements concerning imitation of nature that are applicable in one art form should not automatically be applied to all art forms. For example, the same author may offer a very broad definition of the concept of imitation, when dealing with architecture or music, but a much narrower one when he speaks of painting or sculpture. From this, one can see that the classical tradition still had a very strong influence over esthetics in the eighteenth century, and that the concept of genres proved far more durable in theory than in practice. In theoretical writings a systematic critique of the genre concept and its acceptance as a fact often go hand in hand. But problems and imprecisions notwithstanding, discussions concerning *imitatio naturae* were in France very extensive at the end of the seventeenth and during the first two-thirds of the eighteenth century. In Germany, on the other hand, Winckelmann and Lessing reduced the range of descriptive art, which, in turn, led to a narrowing of the concept of *imitatio naturae*.

Before we turn to the various points of view from which the imitation of nature has been discussed, certain more general questions must be clarified. Although it is obvious that the principle of *imitatio naturae* has been claimed for widely varying notions of art—e.g., primitive, literal naturalism as well as abstract forms of idealizing—there is a tendency to claim this principle for a particular school and to limit its validity to that school, i.e., to assert that a critic or theoretician who advocates the principle belongs to a certain school. It has often been maintained that Diderot's esthetics are not in the least "modern," and, for instance, do not go much beyond the principles of French classicism; such a judgment is based on his close adherence to the rules of *imitatio naturae*. This tendency has only increased the difficulties of understanding eighteenth-century esthetics. The meaning both of *imitatio* and of *natura* changes according to different trends and genres. In my opinion it is wrong to say that the esthetics of sentiment, or the gradual recognition of creative ge-

---

[1] Here it is important to mention that the end of this rivalry between different arts meant that the discussions concerning *imitatio naturae* and *ut pictura poesis* were freed from the pseudo-arguments so typical of Renaissance esthetic theories, i.e., from arguments which were said to refer to the theory of art, but which in fact merely served to prove that one art was supreme, or at least entitled to equal recognition. For example: in his works the painter should convey passion (like the poet); his paintings should have a persuasive, moving effect on the observer (like the orator); it is the story, which lends value to the landscape, and it (the landscape) should therefore be presented as the development of an action (Lomazzo); the painter should convey *eruditio* (like the classical poet), and so on. Leonardo's *Paragone* is a comprehensive attempt to show that the painter is superior to the poet.

nius, have invalidated the principle of the imitation of nature. Instead they have merely modified its meaning. I also feel it is misleading to assume that the principle of *imitatio naturae* gradually disintegrated in the eighteenth century. Such an assumption may lead us to search for signs of this process in the works of individual authors, and thus one forces these authors into a pattern of development which distorts their individuality. Of course, the objection can be raised that I myself am dealing with the transformation of the concept of imitation, and that I therefore assume a fixed point against which this transformation can be measured; also, that there was undeniably a critical discussion of the concept of imitation in eighteenth-century France. I certainly assume that there is a fixed point, but I do not regard transformation as development; as far as the critical discussion is concerned, there are obvious signs of it and of an examination of the conditions imposed by the concept of imitation, but criticism does not necessarily lead to crisis.

Before I give the fixed point to which the transformation refers, I would like to define my point of view. In his article "Nachahmung der Natur" Professor Blumenberg has shown the philosophical causes and the foundations of the concept of *imitatio naturae*, and above all the meaning of imitation, imitative creation, and creation, as well as of nature and reality. My examination, however, will be based solely on the esthetic conception of the principle. Although in eighteenth-century discussions the connection with the foundations is sometimes clear, since the seventeenth century and the Renaissance there has developed a somewhat indeterminate world of esthetic and rhetorical conceptions and perceptions. I feel that we must understand these conceptions before we can determine the philosophical elements. It is surprising to note that esthetic speculations in France in the eighteenth century were not based on the works of Plato and Aristotle, as was the case in, for example, the works of Lessing; instead, terms were used which had been changed by a long and often inconsistent tradition, and an explanation of the basic terms was often avoided. When one considers how drastically Descartes changed Aristotle's conception of nature, it seems almost unbelievable that there is no sign of a change in the use of the term *nature* in the *ars poetica*, *ars graphica*, or in esthetic theories. This is also true of Newton's conception of nature; only the term *rapports* has been adopted, but it is used in a purely formalistic way, or as a kind of magic key to open up the meaning of definitions.[2]

My point of reference as regards the transformation of the concept of

---

[2] I have gone into details in my *Cinq Leçons sur Diderot*; see pp. 101, 102. Professor Blumenberg's article appears in *Nachahmung und Illusion* (Munich, 1964).

imitatio naturae is seventeenth-century French classicism. I shall deal
with both theory and literary works. This point is not chosen arbitrarily;
it is determined by history. One could say that all discussions on the
imitation of nature in eighteenth-century France have one thing in
common: they all link up with the *doctrine classique* or the French classics. In this respect they differ from similar discussions in England and
Germany, where the problem *imitatio naturae* was not considered to be
so important. In these two countries the main concern was with problems of art and nature, imitation and original work, nature in general or
in detail, and the different degrees of reality. Moreover, although the
theory of English neo-classicism was influenced by the *doctrine classique*, England lacks such great dramatic works as the tragedies of Corneille and Racine, or the comedies of Molière, which one could quote as
examples of the *doctrine classique*. England also had no *siècle de Louis
XIV*, during which classicism developed, and which lived on into the
eighteenth century—not only in ways of life but also in art and language. In English neo-classicism we find theories which are independent
of masterpieces and even, to a certain extent, of culture generally. However, this is only one aspect of the situation. The esthetics of English
neo-classicism could not only be applied to the French classics, but,
under the sway of Shakespeare's works, it had to explain and reconcile
their greatness and originality. Only a few strict critics or authors on
esthetics are prepared to sacrifice Shakespeare for the French classics.
One of the few who were, Thomas Rymer, influenced Voltaire's rejection of Shakespeare.[3] One must keep this basic difference in mind, and
not compare single separate theories without observing the relations in
which they stand to one another.

In another of my essays[4] I have attempted to explain the powerful and
lasting effects of the French classics on the eighteenth century as being
due partly to admired masterpieces and partly to clear, rational, systematic, and convincing theory and doctrine. Here I must add that this effect
on eighteenth-century French authors is a hindrance to closer examination of the principles underlying the *doctrine classique*. We may find
analysis of individual concepts, but this leads neither to their basis nor to
any coherent new theory.

The prestige of the great works and of the *doctrine classique*, which
seemed to be justified by their "perfection," probably played a big part
in preventing insight into the difference between historical and normative interpretations. However, it was in the tradition of the Renaissance
that descriptive theories (Aristotle, Horace), linked to specific historical
forms, were not only regarded as generally valid, but also that the in-

[3] Voltaire, *Lettre à l'Academie française*, in *Œuvres*, ed. Moland, xxx, p. 363.
[4] See *Cinq Leçons*, pp. 104-107.

terpretation of these theories which itself was again historically conditioned was presented as timeless and rational and appeared as the norm. It seems to me that the main difficulty in rethinking the classical concept of the imitation of nature so that it would fit the eighteenth century, was the fact that the *doctrine classique* placed nature on equal terms with reason and also identified it with *bon sens*. This is what the writers did, too. In the preface to *Iphigénie*, a work which was admired in the eighteenth century as much as *Phèdre* was in the nineteenth and twentieth, Racine writes: "le bon sens et la raison étaient les mêmes dans tous les siècles. Le goût de Paris s'est trouvé conforme à celui d'Athènes. . . . "In other fields as well (science, law, politics), reason and nature were regarded as principles of criticism and reform; they dissolved the rigid prevailing forms which had hindered free development. In works of art and esthetic theories, the element of historical conditioning was rarely seen or attacked, and the basic error of transforming historical forms into universally valid rules was not perceived.

A further difficulty in rethinking the concept of *imitatio naturae* lay in the fact that the *doctrine classique* contained a mixture of naturalism and idealism. Idealism led to the exclusion of everything which was base, ugly, humdrum, coincidental, limited in time or place, even concrete and direct; it led also to the demand for decorum, i.e., for those characteristics which corresponded to the norms of society. Naturalism is found in the unities of time and place.[5] Without a doubt Corneille often violated these principles—usually in the name of history (what had actually happened), and of necessity (which he conceived of as objective)—and Racine sometimes interpreted the unities symbolically (in *Athalie*); however, these naturalistic ("true") tendencies were usually regarded as rules. Voltaire often makes use of this fact when defending the unities (*Préface à Œdipe*).

These various factors explain the confusion which arose when the attempt was made to rethink the concept of imitation, as it was understood in the classical era, in the name of reason or nature. In the classical era both principles already existed as norms. Only a far-reaching dissociation of the historical from the rational elements would have led to a solution—but this required a historical way of thinking.

The complex process that brought about the eighteenth-century transformation of the *imitatio naturae* can be understood only against the background of these difficulties. Both the concept of imitation and the concept of nature change, and the attempt is made to give them a new philosophical basis. Perhaps even more important is the change of per-

[5] Cf. D'Aubignac, *Pratique du Théâtre*, chaps. 3, 6, 7, Castelvetro's commentary on Aristotle. It would be more correct to classify these arguments under Verism, but they were considered to have their foundations in nature.

spective in which the esthetic problems are viewed—but at the same time the basic categories remain the same and retain their earlier meanings, in defiance of the changes. For all the modifications of tenets in the *doctrine classique*, the overall system was adhered to, for otherwise there would have been no foundation at all to build on. Many of the innovations were due not so much to conscious reform as to factual changes in the taste and structure of society; they were, so to speak, grafted onto the esthetic thinking without really fitting in. Therefore, when one is dealing with the esthetics of eighteenth-century France, one must not demand, or try to construct, thoroughgoing consistency or an unbroken line of thought.

An example will clarify the conflict between the permanent basic concepts and the wish for change. In his article "Encyclopédie" Diderot writes of the swift progress of knowledge and philosophy in the eighteenth century.[6] If the *Encyclopedia* had been compiled in the seventeenth century, it not only would now be out of date but would also show the power of authority and precept. Now, however, man follows the laws of reason and the truth of nature, instead of the models created by mankind. Then, unexpectedly changing his line of thought, Diderot applies these ideas to esthetics: "certains genres de littérature qui, faute d'une vie réelle et de mœurs subsistantes qui leur servent de modèles, ne peuvent avoir de poétique invariable et sensée, seront négligés; et d'autres qui resteront, et que leur valeur intrinsèque soutiendra, prendront une forme toute nouvelle. Tel est l'effet du progrès de la raison; progrès qui renversera tant de statues, et qui en relèvera quelques-unes qui sont renversées. Ce sont celles des hommes rares qui ont devancé leur siècle. Nous avons eu, s'il est permis de s'exprimer ainsi, des contemporains sous le siècle de Louis XIV." (XIV, p. 425.)

After a few remarks which refer to the then outdated *Dictionnaire de Bayle* Diderot continues: "Mais, si tel a été le sort de Bayle, qu'on juge de ce qui serait arrivé à l'*Encyclopédie* de son temps. Si l'on en excepte ce Perrault, et quelques autres, dont le versificateur Boileau n'était pas en état d'apprécier le mérite, La Mothe, Terrasson, Boindin, Fontenelle, sous lesquels la raison et l'esprit philosophique ou de doute a fait de si grand progrès, il n'y avait peut-être pas un homme qui en eût écrit une page qu'on daignât lire aujourd'hui. Car, qu'on ne s'y trompe pas, il y a bien de la différence entre enfanter à force de génie un ouvrage qui enlève

---

[6] Diderot is often used as an example, because in research on this period he is considered to be the most original and most imaginative author writing on esthetics in eighteenth-century France. The quotations I have used are, unless otherwise stated, taken from the Assézat & Tourneux edition of his works (20 volumes).

les suffrages d'une nation qui a son moment, son goût, ses idées, et ses préjugés, et tracer la *poétique du genre*, selon la connaissance réelle et réfléchie du cœur de l'homme, de la nature des choses et de la droite raison, qui sont les mêmes dans tous les temps. Le génie ne connaît point les règles; cependant il ne s'en écarte jamais dans ses succès. La philosophie ne connaît que les règles, fondées dans la nature des êtres, qui est immuable et éternelle. C'est au siècle passé à fournir des exemples; c'est à notre siècle à prescrire les règles." (*ibid.*)[7]

The surprising thing about this, in my opinion, is not the assumption that, with the exception of a few predecessors, compilers of poetics and theorists had been basing their works on something changeable, but had now chosen something lasting as a basis (in other words, that history was now at an end); nor is it the indeterminacy and abstractness of the concepts or the choice of authors. The surprising thing is that the new scale of values which Diderot announced corresponds exactly in its conception to the *doctrine classique*. Boileau, whom Diderot dismisses as a verse-maker, also criticized genres that were not based on reality and existing tradition. His poetics also claimed to be built upon the ever valid nature of things and on healthy reasoning (*droite raison*); the works which Boileau cited as models also show a "connaissance réelle et réfléchie du cœur de l'homme." Even the idea of genius which, although it does not abide by any fixed rules, does not diverge from them either, reiterates Boileau's idea. Later in the article we can see how "new" ideas on art theory again refer back to the standards set up by Boileau:

"Il faut fouler aux pieds toutes ces vieilles puérilités, renverser les barrières que la raison n'aura point posées, rendre aux sciences et aux arts une liberté qui leur est si précieuse, et dire aux admirateurs de l'antiquité: Appelez *le Marchand de Londres* comme il vous plaira, pourvu que vous conveniez que cette pièce étincelle de beautés sublimes. Il fallait un temps raisonneur, où l'on ne cherchât plus les règles dans les auteurs, mais dans la nature, et où l'on sentît le faux et le vrai de tant de poétiques arbitraires: je prends le terme de *poétique* dans son acception la plus générale, pour un systeme de règles données, selon lesquelles, en quelque genre que ce soit, on prétend qu'il faut travailler pour réussir." (xiv, pp. 474-475.)

The admiration for the middle-class tragedy *The London Merchant*, and the rejection of the ancient authors as the model, are modern, and, in fact, change the classical conception of *imitatio naturae*; Boileau,

---

[7] See a similar passage in *Lettre sur les sourds et muets*: "Aujourd'hui qu'on est à l'abri des hémistiches du redoutable Despréaux, et que l'esprit philosophique nous a appris à ne voir dans les choses que ce qui n'y est, et à ne louer que ce qui est véritablement beau . . ." (I, p. 380).

however, advocates the same freedom of reason in the face of barriers which have not been set up by reason itself, and he respects the classical authors only because their rules were based on nature. Diderot identifies certain historical forms with abstract nature and timeless reason, just as the classical theorists did. As regards antiquity, Diderot makes as many appeals to it as Boileau did, even if his starting point is dramatic forms and not the hypostasis of reason and nature; and he justifies their use as models for the same reasons as Boileau. This observation also applies to other concepts of classical esthetics. In the *Entretiens sur le Fils naturel*, Dorval (Diderot) cries out: "Ah! bienséances cruelles!"[8] They were indeed cruel, for only with great difficulty could Diderot free himself from them. In *le Fils naturel* and *le Père de famille* he follows them. Not until *Est-il bon? est-il méchant?* which was conceived as a game and not as an example of reform, did he manage to throw off these chains. And yet Diderot's poetics and his concept of *imitatio naturae* differ essentially from those of the classical era; but one cannot capture this individuality with the terms *Nature* or *Reason* or other terms derived from these, insofar as they are used in the theoretical argument. This argument is far more important for Diderot than for other French estheticians. As I have written elsewhere[9] of the innovations in Diderot's esthetics, I will not discuss them again here.

The transformation of the concept *imitatio naturae* was due to a number of causes, the most general of which was the disintegration of the culture and society of the *siècle de Louis XIV*. The historical character of the tastes and values of this period was concealed by the abstractness and the timelessness of the terms Nature, Reason, Truth, and Decorum, so that one is not always conscious of the transformation. Voltaire was one of the few who recognized that reason with the rationalistic *modernes* (modern authors)[10] had become "geometric," and that it had therefore lost the meaning given to it during the French classical era.[11] The differences in the concept of nature were clearer; they concerned mainly the idea of a beautiful, general, universal, or typical nature. In contrast to this, anything limited to one time or place, anything individual and concrete, anything non-representative, even anything ignoble and unbeautiful, was recognized as being worthy of imitation. To put it another way: the term *Nature* was gradually cleared of all those elements which had been introduced into it by the principles of ideal beauty and of the universally valid, of decorum ("biénseances internes et externes"), and of probability (from which results the "aver-

---

[8] *Œuvres esth.*, ed. Vernière, p. 117.   [9] *Cinq Leçons*, chap. IV.
[10] Diderot names them all; see above quotation at n. 7.
[11] R. Naves, *Le goût de Voltaire*, chap. I.

age reality," inasmuch as it serves to exclude the miraculous and the supernatural).[12] The presentation of everyday reality, of the world in which we live, was discussed in connection with art and sculpture and with the theatre and the novel. In art this was linked with the change in the order of precedence of the portrait, the still-life, and the genre-picture—the valuation of Teniers and Ostade is a good example of the development from the seventeenth to the eighteenth century.[13] In sculpture the presentation was of a purely theoretical nature, as this form of art retained idealization. In the theatre a good deal of idealization was also retained, though realism was to be found in the setting and in the total illusion of reality. The most advanced presentation of every-day reality, both in practice and in theory, was to be found in the novel, the genre freest of restrictions. In mid-eighteenth-century France, the most illuminating document was Diderot's *Éloge de Richardson*—and it is a pity that Diderot never wrote an "Éloge de Fielding," as Fielding was much closer to him as regards his ideas on realism.[14]

In the eighteenth century, the reality deemed worthy of imitation expanded; indeed, the principle of *imitatio naturae* seemed occasionally to be defined in a new way and thus to be rediscovered: in its name, the demand was made for the recognition and artistic portrayal of areas of nature which, until then, had either been excluded or had gained a

[12] The following quotation from La Mesnardière's *Poétique* (Paris, 1639) is a good example of the limits set by classical poetics. Exceptions are: "la bassesse d'une avarice, l'infâmie d'une lâcheté, la noirceur d'une perfidie, l'horreur d'une cruauté, l'ordure d'une pauvreté" (p. 314, see also p. 125).

[13] Cf., e.g., Du Bos, I, p. 70, and Diderot, XI, p. 302; *Œuvres esth.*, pp. 749, 784, 790, 826.

[14] At this point I would like to refer to a possible difference of opinion between H. R. Jauss ("Diderots Paradox über das Schauspiel," *GRM* 11, October, 1961) and myself, concerning a passage in the *Éloge de Richardson*: I interpret the phrase "Il me montre le cours général des choses qui m'environnent" as referring only to close and familiar surroundings; I do not consider that there is any reference to a law of nature. Prof. Jauss seems to read: "le cours général / des choses qui m'environment," and to consider "cours général" to be analogous with "système de la nature"; he then leaves out the words "qui m'environnent" and quotes "le cours général des choses." I believe that in this passage the laws of nature are not connected with the theory of imitation; the former belong to another region of thought. Moreover, Diderot expresses great misgivings about their applicability, because in order to apply them one would have to know them all—which is impossible (e.g., *Essai sur la peinture, Œuvres esth.*, p. 666). I would translate this passage as follows: the general course of surroundings; in this context "cours général" is contrasted to "biais chimériques," "contrées lointaines," and "régions de la féerie," as well as impossible or exceptional situations. Here Diderot again complies with the *doctrine classique*, i.e., the concept of the universal as opposed to the improbable and the subjective. In the *doctrine classique* the universal does not always possess, as is often maintained, an ideal quality—especially when it is used polemically. The *doctrine classique* and Diderot are both opposed to the chimeric novel.

critical significance as a result of changes in the social structure. This principle often expressed a reaction against ideal beauty which led away from nature. The reaction was so strong that it resulted in a demand for naturalism and verisimilitude.[15] It is a mistake to regard this as a retrograde step towards primitive forms of imitation. On the contrary, it can be the expression of a new sense of reality, especially when it is connected with the sensualism of taste. I shall return to this matter later.

One of the most important consequences of the transformation of the "nature" concept was the upheaval or new relationships it brought about in the traditional hierarchy of the genres. This hierarchy had been based on the primacy of ideal beauty or of universal and purified reality. Now the minor genres gained more importance, while the epic and the ode, in fact even if not always in theory, lost ground. The novel and the short story, which until then had been treated as poor relations, unworthy of the *art poétique*, now received a poetics. This development was, however, very gradual, and was attended by great difficulties in terminology. It led to significant changes in the conception of *imitatio naturae*.[16]

Another important factor concerning the imitation of nature was the criticism, even the destruction, of the exemplary status of classical works. This was not a consequence of the changes I have dealt with so far, although it is connected with them. It developed out of the critical and rationalistic or scientific movements which united in the *Querelle des Anciens et des Modernes*. The separation of the concept of classical exemplarity from the concept of nature[17] was a complicated process which must be examined in detail. The reasons for its being so complicated are, as far as France is concerned, to be found partly in the *doctrine classique*, which laid down that nature (which must be imitated as it is the quintessence of all rules) is identical with antiquity. One should

---

[15] The use of unarticulated sounds on stage (instead of the melodramatic, rhythmical, disciplined diction of classical tragedies), the direct expression of the "cri du coeur" and of the passions, the portrayal of feelings in music, the—as I feel—absurd idea of scars and warts given to the classically beautiful face in order to make it more real (*Entretiens sur le Fils naturel, Œuvres esth.*, pp. 101-102; *Neveu de Rameau*, ed. Fabre, pp. 77 et seq.; "Les Deux Amis de Bourbonne," in *Contes*, ed. Dieckmann, London, 1963, pp. 81-82; and *Cinq Leçons*, p. 108) are all examples of Verism arising from the reaction against ideal beauty.

[16] Cf. *Cinq Leçons*, pp. 123 et seq.; "The Presentation of Reality in Diderot's Tales," in *Diderot Studies*, III, pp. 101 et seq.; Diderot, *Contes*, edited with an Introduction by H. Dieckmann.

[17] The origin of the connection between the concept of imitation and the model character of the classics probably lies in Horace's *Ars Poetica*. Here he recommends that the playwright should follow the Greek models, and not search for new ideas. (*Ars Poetica*, 128-131, 268-269.) In the sixteenth century the theory of imitation and the classics were closely connected.

not, however, imitate the ancient models because they are ancient, but because they correspond to reason. In this way, at least in theory, reason became the guiding principle. The categories of those critics who rebelled against the supremacy of classical works, basing their arguments on reason and nature, are somewhat confused owing to the association of antiquity and nature in the *doctrine classique*. Moreover, the term *classical* does not represent a simple or constant idea. Thus it happened that, in the name of nature and of reason, a critic might attack some classical poets and refer to others as being examples of true nature. And yet as a result of the *Querelle des Anciens et des Modernes* a critical consciousness of the problematic relationship between nature and antiquity developed, which led to the liberation from academicism to a new and broader concept of nature, and to independence from certain traditional forms of art. The principle of *imitatio naturae* became connected with the desire for change and the courage to break with tradition. We shall return to this question when dealing with the principle of *ut pictura poesis*.

The rationalistic criticism of antiquity and of tradition is, as regards its judgments on art and the principle of imitation, less radical than one might suppose. Above all, it is not directed basically against poetry and not always against the *doctrine classique*. There could hardly be a greater admirer of the *siècle de Louis XIV* and of Boileau than Perrault. A few examples taken from Fontenelle, Houdard de La Motte, and Perrault will make the opinions of the rationalists clearer.

Fontenelle is especially important because he freed the controversy over "Ancients" and "Moderns" from the endless comparison of old and new works, and from philological and critical differences of opinion. He led the way back to philosophic and scientific principles; human beings, like objects, are created by nature, which always remains the same; just as, in ancient times, trees were no bigger than they are now, so were the Greeks no bigger than we are *per essentiam* as well as *per naturam*. On the other hand, ways of life, culture, and reason grow and develop through progress of knowledge, refinement of customs, and perfection of powers of reasoning. Descartes' way of thinking is superior to everything which has gone before (*Digression sur les Anciens et les Modernes, De l'origine des fables*). Fontenelle recommended that this method be applied to all areas of human activity:

"L'esprit géométrique n'est pas si attaché à la géométrie, qu'il n'en puisse être tiré, et transporté à d'autres connoissances. Un ouvrage de morale, de politique, de critique, peut-être même d'éloquence, en sera plus beau, toutes choses d'ailleurs égales, s'il est fait de main de géomètre. L'ordre, la netteté, la précision, l'exactitude qui règnent dans les bons livres depuis un certain temps, pourroient bien avoir leur première source dans cet esprit géométrique, qui se répand plus que jamais, et qui en quelque façon se communique de proche en proche à ceux mêmes qui ne connoissent pas la géométrie. Quelquefois un grand homme donne le ton a tout son siècle; celui à qui on pourrait le plus légitimement accorder la gloire d'avoir établi un nouvel art de raisonner, étoit un excellent géomètre."[18] (Préface: *Sur l'utilité des mathématiques et de la physique, et sur les travaux de l'Académie des sciences.*)

Descartes himself excluded poetry from his observations on this method.[19] In the case of Fontenelle, this basic belief was united with a weariness of the eternal repetition of the same material, fables, pictures, and comparisons—mythology especially bored him to death (a frequent exclamation of his was: "tout cela est usé, extrêment usé!"). The contempt which the *bel esprit* and the cultured human being felt for whatever was crude, sensual, primitive, and undisciplined[20]—a *scepticisme désabusé* in the renewing capacity of heart and mind—was opposed by admiration for thought and for the ability to invent and to reach perfection.[21]

Although the classical principle of *imitatio naturae* was not specifically discussed by Fontenelle, he did indirectly bring its basic tenets into question. The validity of ancient poetry and art as models was based, as a result of classical esthetics, upon the fact that they imitated nature in an exemplary way. But as nature is the primitive in Fontenelle's view, the equation of nature with antiquity loses its esthetic meaning. Of course, Fontenelle did not exclude a certain amount of nature from a work of art, but it had to be supplemented by the intellectual capacity of the human being. Art was for him the expression of intellectual activity (the activity and movement of thought are for Fontenelle all important), and everything sensual must first pass through the filter of the intellect.

Moreover, Fontenelle destroyed the elementary principle of classical esthetics: the equation of the Ancients with reason; according to Fontenelle the latter developed during the course of the centuries and did not reach its perfection until Descartes:

"Sur quelque matière que ce soit, les anciens sont assez subjets à ne

---

[18] Fontenelle, *Œuvres*, ed. Bastien, 1790, VI, p. 67.

[19] *Discours de la méthode*, Classiques Larousse, p. 13.

[20] "Je crois qu'Eschyle était une manière de fou, qui avait l'imagination très vive et pas trop réglée"; (*Œuvres*, ed. Bastien, III, p. 108).

[21] "Le cœur ne change point et tout l'homme est le cœur" (*Dialogue des morts: Socrate-Montaigne*). "Le champ de la pensée est sans comparaison plus vaste que celui de la vue. On a tout vu depuis longtemps; il s'en faut bien que l'on ait encore tout pensé" (III, p. 185). However, in connection with the scientific methods, the senses do lead to new observations.

pas raisonner dans la dernière perfection. Souvent de faibles conve-
nances, de petites similitudes, des jeux d'esprit peu solides, des discours
vagues et confus, passent chez eux pour des preuves; aussi rien ne leur
coûte à prouver: mais ce qu'un ancien démonstrait en se jouant, don-
nerait à l'heure qu'il est bien de la peine à un pauvre moderne; car de
quelle rigueur n'est-on pas sur les raisonnements? On veut qu'ils soient
intelligibles, on veut qu'ils soient justes, on veut qu'ils conclurent."
(*Digression sur les Anciens et les Modernes.*)

We should add that Fontenelle excluded the usual metaphysical and
ethical arguments from his observations on beauty, and viewed the problem from a purely psychological and genetical point of view.[22] The most
fruitful application of his ideas is to be found in his theory of poetic images, a theory which he developed in connection with his defense of the
poète-philosophe Houdard de La Motte.

La Motte's polemic against the classics is not only in principle the
same as that of Fontenelle, but it is also directed at certain works which
are each subjected to criticism. Above all he attacked the veneration of
antiquity and the authoritarian beliefs which resulted from it. When he
insisted on imitation of nature, he often simply meant that one should
not imitate authors and models from the past. In other words, the poet
should create and invent. Because of the great emphasis he placed on *inventio* La Motte became dissociated from the classical theory of imitation. He was, as it were, rationally preparing the way for the idea of the
"genius."

His conception of nature also shows new characteristics: he does not
regard nature as static and timeless. He opposes the old concept of nature with a newer, more progressive one. The world becomes more
beautiful through art, more perfect through morality; thus the imitative
poets also improve.[23]

The emphasis La Motte placed on invention is also illustrated by the
importance he attaches to the poet's intention and desire to express himself. When La Motte speaks of a selective imitation, he means this intention and not *belle nature* or idealized nature (III, pp. 189-191).

In his reflections on beauty and pleasure the intellectual elements
serve mainly to arouse ideas (III, p. 252-255, 264). "C'est donc de la dig-
nité, ou de l'agrément des idées que les mots tirent leur force ou leur
grace, et par une suite nécessaire, c'est de la beauté du sens que les vers
tirent leur plus grand mérite" (III, p. 262). He makes excellent observa-

[22] On the basis of Locke's sensualism, this became the fundamental feature of
eighteenth-century esthetics in England. In Fontenelle's works we find an independent
French rational form.

[23] *Œuvres de Monsieur Houdard de La Motte* (Paris, 1757), III, p. 189.

tions on the "beauté du sens" in Racine's works. At times he approaches
Valéry's conception of *poésie pure*.

Of the three participants in the *Querelle* that we have mentioned, the
best known is Charles Perrault; but as regards the originality and modernity of his basic position in the *Parallèles*, he seems to me the least
interesting. In principle he belonged to the *modernes* and with pedantic
exactitude refuted the idea that the classics were supreme. His way of
thinking was influenced to such an extent by this theory that his ideas on
art and his conception of *imitatio naturae* can be really understood only
in the light of it. As the cult of the classics was based on the argument
that they faithfully imitated nature and as the doctrine of imitating nature came from antiquity, Perrault proceeds to attack doctrine and practice. In my opinion nothing could be more mistaken than to take literally
his idea that in sculpture the human body is directly imitated and that in
architecture one follows natural proportions,[24] or to regard Perrault as a
representative of naturalism in the imitation theory, or even a precursor
of eighteenth-century naturalism. Since Perrault could not completely
deny the greatness and exemplarity of classical sculpture, he maintained
that although this art was indeed beautiful, it was also simple and restricted: "particulièrement lorsqu'il ne s'agit que de figures de ronde
bosse. Il n'y a qu'à choisir un beau modèle, le poser dans une attitude
agréable et le copier ensuite agréablement" (i, p. 129). If one considers a
higher form of art (e.g., relief), one notices immediately how primitive
ancient art is. As for columns and overhanging roofs—these are also to
be found among the savages: the model is simply a tree, and the proportions are common to all people, and not peculiar to antiquity. When
Perrault praises perspectives, "clair-obscur," as well as the harmony of
the nuances in painting, it is in order to denigrate the classics, in which
these higher forms were unknown. As far as he is concerned, the anecdotes concerning Zeuxis and Parrhasios merely go to prove how primitive ancient art was. His long criticism of the "trompe-l'œil" proves this
point *ad nauseam* (i, pp. 136-160). He applies the same principles and
methods to literature: in an attempt at least to reduce the incontestable
reputation and effect of Horace's satires, he classifies this genre as a secondary one (pp. 150-151). He has a low opinion of classical comedies
because they merely imitated nature:

". . . ce n'est pas un grand mérite à Terence d'avoir imité la nature
comme il a fait, d'avoir fait parler un vieillard comme un vieillard, un
jeune homme comme un jeune homme, un valet comme un valet; cela
n'est pas bien difficile, car il ne suffit pas que les caractères soient assez

---

[24] *Parallèles* (Amsterdam, 1693), i, pp. 89 et seq.

marquez (sic) pour être reconnus, il faut les porter en quelque sorte à la perfection de leur idée, qui est comme je l'ai déjà dit, non seulement au-dessus de la pure nature, mais de la belle nature même, ce que Terence n'a fait." (I, pp. 149-150.)

Molière is far superior to Terence.[25] Of course, his polemic against "pure nature" (II, pp. 144-145) cannot be explained away by zeal against the admiration and veneration of the classics, although it was certainly nourished and determined by it. His prejudices probably blinded him to the fact that he had actually borrowed his theory of imitation from the Renaissance interpretation of antiquity, and that it shows a typical Renaissance eclecticism of Aristotelian and Platonic elements. The only difference is that in his three-stage theory, rationalism is given more emphasis.[26] He follows the *doctrine classique* in his principles of selection—from nature, *belle nature*, *bienséances*, the unities, and (to some extent) from morality. However, he emphasizes more strongly the ideal moment in a work of art, and the rational, in the composition as well as in the observer or the reader. His rationalism separates him from seventeenth-century French classicism in other respects as well. Although Boileau and other theorists said that one should not imitate the classics because they were classics but because their work corresponded to reason, it was not this justification that concerned the imitative artist, and his observer, reader, or listener schooled in the understanding of art, so much as actual study of classic works. This study reconciled the artist and the observer much more than any theories could. As long as the classics served as models, work and theory supplemented each other. Now, however, only the theory remained, and it became more and more rational and formal, so that feeling in all its forms and sense for the intrinsic in art finally revolted. It was precisely through arousing this reaction that the rationalism of geometrical reasoning had such a great influence on the development of the theory of imitation.

In the changes thus far described, *imitatio naturae* has been viewed from the traditional point of view: it is essentially a question of the object imitated. In the eighteenth century two more points of view devel-

[25] This confrontation is one of the many examples showing that Perrault is by no means a direct forerunner of the eighteenth century. Terence was a model for reforms in the theatre in the eighteenth century: cf., e.g., Diderot's *Sur Térence*, critical text in *Studia philologica et litteraria in honorem L. Spitzer* (Bern, 1958). "Modernism" alone is not the same as progress.

[26] A work of art should unite three characteristics and should appeal to three different faculties; see, e.g., I, pp. 142-146; he summarizes the principle in the following way: "Car il faut remarquer que comme la peinture a trois parties qui la composent, il y a aussi trois parties dans l'homme par où il en est touché, les sens, le coeur, et la raison" (I, p. 145).

oped: that of the reader, observer, or listener, and that of the means of presentation.[27] If the *imitatio naturae* is discussed from the standpoint not of the model or of the object but of the effect, then one's concern is with the pleasure which the act of imitating or the thing imitated gives. This pleasure can be sensuous or intellectual, depending on the arousal through content or form.[28]

The growing interest in the effect of a work is without a doubt influenced by currents of sensibility, sentimentality, or, more generally, emotionality. A work of art, and hence an imitation, should above all appeal to feelings, and this appeal is investigated empirically, often by means of the genetic method of sensualism.

To illustrate these ideas, I have chosen as an example the part played by appearance in imitation, because illusion in a work of art is one of our main subjects. I think we must distinguish between the views held by French esthetes of the eighteenth century (until the 1760's) and those of Goethe and Schiller; we should try especially not to be unduly influenced by Schiller's idea of the "beautiful appearance."

Abbé Du Bos, whose views were dominated by his interest in the effect of a work of art, is the most important author in the reorientation of French esthetics. The question of *imitatio naturae*, appears at the very beginning of his *Réflexions critiques sur la poésie et sur la peinture* (1719). The titles which he gives his chapters show clearly the idea of pleasure in imitation or the thing imitated; the subject dealt with in chapters 3 and 4 is: "Que le mérite principal des Poèmes et des Tableaux consiste à imiter les objets qui auroient excité en nous des passions réelles. Les passions que ces imitations font naître en nous, ne sont que superficielles" (3); "Du pouvoir que les imitations ont sur nous, et de la facilité avec laquelle le cœur humain est ému" (4). The title of chapter 43, in which this question is mainly dealt with, is "Que le plaisir que nous avons au théâtre n'est point l'effet de l'illusion." Before we turn to the contents of this chapter, we must distinguish between various meanings in the concept of Illusion or Appearance, insofar as this is conceived as an effect upon observer, reader, or hearer. In *imitatio naturae*, appearance can be taken as something naturalistic or literal. In connection with this idea, which can be linked with painting, the anecdotes about Zeuxis' grapes and Parrhasios' curtain are often quoted. This same idea is applied to poetry by means of *ut pictura poesis* (Horace). This phrase is, however, not taken in the way the author meant it to be, but is given

[27] The various points of view are in reality not as clearly defined as they are here, for the sake of clarity.

[28] I am not setting up any antitheses, but merely mean a predominance of interest. Of course, there is sensual enjoyment of form, but intellect plays a greater part in this enjoyment than in material pleasure.

the meaning Plutarch ascribed to Simonides: painting is mute poetry and poetry is painting in words. Charles du Fresnoy succeeded in uniting Horace and Simonides in an oft-quoted part of his poem *"De arte graphica"* (1667):

> Ut pictura poesis erit; similisque Poesi
> Sit Pictura; refert par æmula quæque sororem,
> Alternantque vices et nomina; muta Poesis
> Dicitur hæc, Pictura loquens solet illa vocari.
> Quod fuit auditu gratum cecinere Poetae;
> Quod pulchrum aspectu Pictores pingere curant:
> Quæque Poetarum Numeris indigna fuere,
> Non eadem Pictorum Operam Studiumque merentur.

In this way descriptive poetry and *imitatio naturae* are linked together.[29] The naturalism of imitation is also applied to music by means of description. A good example of this is Fontenelle's "Sonate, que me veux-tu?" The sonata is not a description, it has no realizable meaning. As regards music, some authors were also of the opinion that the composer reproduced in his medium the outcry of the heart, the sound of emotions. Several instances of this view can be found in the works of Batteux: they serve his pseudo-Cartesian reduction of all forms of art to one principle. We can call this concept of appearance or illusion *duplication*, for this word enables us to avoid the confusing terminology of sightsense. As regards this theory of duplication, we must ask whether it was used bona fide or to express some other postulate: for example, it could be used to criticize rational poetry and its theory (poetry as a process of thought or a thinking game), overemphasis of elements of form in art, or as an antidote against allegory and mythology in art. The demand was made for an exact copy, in order to reestablish spontaneous feelings and direct impressions of reality, uninfluenced and unaltered by reflection. This idea is to be found in eighteenth-century esthetics of sentiment, which arose in protest against rationalist ("geometrical") and neo-classical currents of thought. Together with the concept of *imitatio naturae* that we have already examined, it demanded a widening of artistic reality. Descriptive poetry also underwent a change: the stylized classical descriptions of nature with their set clichés were replaced by something similar to Rousseau's rediscovery of nature. This new descriptive poetry at times competed with painting, which till then had monopolized matters of description.

---

[29] This criticism of the *descriptio* in literature (poetry and the novel) in the eighteenth century, a criticism which often does not stem from *imitatio naturae*, has nevertheless influenced this concept.

We also find various forms of criticism of the imitation[30] we have called duplication. This criticism often continued the tendency of the *doctrine classique* to idealize and generalize. We see here, as so often before, that the terms *imitation* and *nature* signify little in themselves; one must ask what they express and what they stand for.

In the *Réflexions critiques* (Abbé Du Bos) the demand for imitation is linked with the esthetics of sentiment, and is seen from the point of view of the observer or the reader. This line of thought is explained in two different ways: the feeling aroused by a work of art is identical to the feelings aroused by the original object or event which has been imitated.[31] The actor who moves us is one who is himself moved.[32] He may lack the gift "d'exprimer les passions avec la noblesse [ou] la justesse convenable (sic)" (I, p. 41); but the nature which he gives voice to will make up for what is missing.[33] However, Du Bos criticizes the opinion that the esthetic pleasure given by art and the theatre (typically his concern is with the visual) is based on the illusion of reality which they give us. In chapter 43 of the first volume, "Que le plaisir que nous avons au Théâtre n'est point produit par l'illusion," he writes:

"Des personnes d'esprit ont cru que l'illusion étoit la première cause du plaisir que nous donnent les spectacles et les tableaux. Suivant leur sentiment, la représentation du Cid ne nous donne tant de plaisir que par l'illusion qu'elle nous fait. Les vers du grand Corneille, l'appareil de la Scène et la déclamation des Acteurs nous en imposent assez pour nous faire croire, qu'au lieu d'assister à la représentation de l'événement, nous assistons à l'événement même, et que nous voyons réellement l'action, et non pas une imitation. Cette opinion me paroît insoutenable." (I, pp. 453-454.)

According to him it is unthinkable that a normal human being could imagine that, when watching something on the stage, he is watching reality; he is conscious of his surroundings even when he is moved by what is happening on the stage. A young and sensitive person could, for a moment be taken in by the illusion, but Du Bos says: "il n'est pas vrai qu'elle ait cru, durant son ravissement, voir Rodrigue et Chimène. Elle a

---

[30] See passages above, concerning Fontenelle, La Motte, and Perrault.

[31] See 1754 Paris edition, Book II, chap. 22.

[32] Horace is often quoted as an authority for this concept, which arose again and again in the seventeenth and eighteenth centuries: *Ars Poetica*, 102-103 ("*Si vis me flere, dolendum est primum ipsi tibi*"). This concept is also linked with the demand that art should above all be the expression of emotions, and in many respects anticipates the later theory of empathy. (See, e.g., Giampaolo Lomazzo, *Trattato dell'arte della pittura*, Milano, 1584, vol. II, i, p. 105.)

[33] This corresponds to Diderot's conception of the sensitive actor in the *Entretiens sur le Fils naturel*, *Œuvres esth.*, p. 104, for example.

seulement été touchée presqu'aussi vivement qu'elle l'auroit été, si réellement elle avoit vu Rodrigue aux pieds de sa maîtresse dont il vient de tuer le père." (I, p. 455.) This is very interesting, for the idea of an illusion is here, as it were, doubled. Du Bos denies an outright illusion, but without realizing it he assumes an "as-if" illusion. As a further example he chooses a painting of Raphael's and says that we cannot really see the people, but the imitation is so true to life that it impresses the observer almost as much as the scene itself would (I, p. 456). Again, this effect could be ascribed to an "as-if" illusion. The adjective *vraisemblable*, which plays such an important part in classical esthetics, takes on a new meaning here: it applies neither to reason nor to the criteria of educated society, but instead it refers to an inner concordance and to the so-called truth to life of the picture. Du Bos quotes more examples of *trompe-l'œil*, and then he arrives at what concerns him most of all: examples of complete illusions are numerous and, factually, correct, but this illusion is not the source of esthetic pleasure. To prove this he writes that works of art also please us even when we know that they are works of art and not actual reality (I, pp. 457-458). In my opinion this line of thought becomes completely clear when we turn back to those chapters whose titles I have quoted above. In chapter 4 Du Bos speaks of the power imitations exercise on us, especially on a sensitive heart. In chapter 3, however, he admits that they imitate things which have themselves aroused our real passions. But feelings aroused by imitations differ from real passions in that they have no disturbing or upsetting consequences, and are less strong:

"Comme l'impression que les imitations font sur nous est du même genre que l'impression que l'objet imité par le Peintre ou par le Poëte feroit sur nous; comme l'impression que l'imitation fait n'est differente de l'impression que l'objet imité feroit, qu'en ce qu'elle est moins forte, elle doit exciter dans notre âme une passion qui ressemble à celle que l'objet imité y auroit pû exciter. La copie de l'objet doit, pour ainsi dire, exciter en nous une copie de la passion que l'objet y auroit excitée. Mais comme l'impression que l'imitation fait n'est pas aussi profonde que l'impression que l'objet même auroit faite; comme l'impression faite par l'imitation n'est pas sérieuse, d'autant qu'elle ne va point jusqu'à la raison pour laquelle il n'y a point d'illusion dans ces sensations, ainsi que nous l'expliquerons tantôt plus au long, enfin comme l'impression faite par l'imitation n'affecte vivement que l'âme sensitive, elle s'efface bientôt. Cette impression superficielle faite par une imitation, disparoît sans avoir des suites durables, comme en auroit une impression faite par l'objet même que le Peintre ou la Poëte a imité.

"On conçoit facilement la raison de la différence qui se trouve entre l'impression faite par l'objet même, et l'impression faite par l'imitation. L'imitation la plus parfaite n'a qu'un être artificiel, elle n'a qu'une vie empruntée, au lieu que la force et l'activité de la nature se trouvent dans l'objet imité. C'est en vertu du pouvoir qu'il tient de la nature même que l'objet réel agit sur nous.'' (ɪ, pp. 27-28.)

Later in the chapter he says: "Le plaisir qu'on sent à voir les imitations que les Peintres et les Poëtes sçavent faire des objets qui auroient excité en nous des passions dont la réalité nous auroit été à charge, est un plaisir pur. Il n'est pas suivi des inconvéniens dont les émotions serieuses qui auroient été causées par l'objet même, seroient accompagnées.'' (ɪ, p. 29.) Du Bos sets up an equation: the greater the force and power of nature, the more powerful and lasting and completely compelling the impression on us; imitation produces the weaker, more transient impression, which affects only our sensitivity. Here we again find the hierarchy of the powers (or perceptive faculties) which had been dismissed by empiricism and sensualism: *imitatio* moves the *anima sensitiva*, not the *ratio*. The kind of impression is unimportant, it is only the degree of intensity and proximity which separate impressions. We can now understand why Du Bos was so strongly opposed to the idea that esthetic pleasure was based on the illusion of reality. Esthetics based on emotional impressions stand or fall according to whether Art and Nature are divided or joined. It is probable, too, that Du Bos's line of thought, which was completely dominated by the idea of the effect of art, prevented his seeing that the question of appearance or illusion in art can be profitably considered only if one takes up factors beyond mere illusion. In other words, illusion in art only becomes problematic when it is dealt with from the point of view of the relationship between the imitation and its object. In Du Bos's case it is not a matter of this relationship, nor is it natural beauty and artistic beauty, or reality in nature and reality in art, but the effect of nature and the effect of art; the problem of illusion is linked with that of esthetic pleasure.

Similar questions are to be found in Diderot's writings on esthetics. I will deal with only certain aspects of this subject as revealed in his earlier works, which show his basic position most clearly.

In my opinion it is important, when judging Diderot's ideas on esthetics, to bear in mind their origin, direction, and context. Diderot's ideas did not originate from seventeenth-century classical esthetics (*doctrine classique*), or from the concept of *imitatio naturae*; poetics play only a small part, rhetoric none at all. His first reflections on esthetical questions arose from his reading and translation of Shaftesbury (*Essay on Virtue and Merit*) and from his own work on mathematics and physics. He was preoccupied with the origin and the nature of beauty, as well as with esthetic pleasure and taste. The laws and purposes of nature provided the foundation for his concept of beauty. He based pleasure, in connection with music and architecture, on *rapports*, a term which he defined according to the laws of acoustics or mathematics, but which also refers to a more general concept of relationships in the natural sciences.[34] Diderot pursues these ideas further in his article "Beau" in the *Encyclopédie* and connects them with epistemological questions in the *Lettre sur les sourds et muets*.

Apart from these reflections, which base beauty and pleasure on objective laws (Diderot repeatedly attacks the subjective, the arbitrary, and the imaginary), there is, in his works, another starting point for esthetical questions. Here the terms *rapports* and natural law play no part; it is not until the later development that these two points of view occasionally link up.

In the same year as the *Mémoires sur différents sujets de mathématiques*, Diderot's pornographic novel *Les Bijoux indiscrets* also appeared, in which one can find observations on music and the theatre. Diderot later returned to these observations, and therefore we can take them seriously, but one must not forget the irony and the arbitrariness which predominate in this novel.[35] The point of view which he chooses when discussing the theatre is completely different from that of the first *Mémoire*: he bases his discussion on a comparison between the classical and seventeenth-century theatre (e.g., on a subject of the "Anciens et Modernes") and chooses one representative of each side. When the debate on the equality of the "Modernes" reaches the question of the imitation of nature, the Sultan's favorite steps in and settles the debate with common sense, and not with learning or with rules. This intervention is significant: the favorite gives preference to the "Anciens"—in their works the action and the dialogue seem natural. In Sophocles' *Philoctetes*, for example, nothing destroys the illusion. What we are to understand by this is shown us a few lines later after the praise of *Philoctetes*. The favorite speaks: ". . . je sais qu'il n'y a que le vrai qui plaise et qui touche. Je sais encore que la perfection d'un spectacle consiste dans l'imitation si exacte d'une action, que le spectateur, trompé sans interruption, s'imagine assister à l'action même. Or, y a-t-il quelque chose qui ressemble à cela dans ces tragédies que vous nous vantez?" (IV, pp. 284-285.)

These latter tragedies are the French classics: their action is over-

---

[34] See the first *Mémoire* on the general principles of acoustics, in the *Mémoires sur differents sujets de mathématiques*, 1748, IX, p. 104.

[35] Here I am dealing with a subject which has been dealt with in detail by H. R. Jauss; see *op.cit.* (footnote 14). I shall, however, be examining it in a different context.

loaded, complicated, forced, and therefore improbable; the illusion is thus destroyed. The artificial dialogue, the stylized or exaggerated gestures, have the same effect. Furthermore, the author speaks through his characters. But classical tragedies are full of "pure nature" (IV, p. 286). In order to make her argument more persuasive, the favorite thinks up a hypothesis: a stranger who is acquainted with the court and all its intrigues, but who knows nothing of the theatre, comes to the capital. The favorite tells him of a scandal in the court and invites him to be a hidden witness; she places him in a box in the theatre and there, without knowing it, he watches a modern tragedy. Until now the illusion has been successful. However, the performance soon destroys it: the action and presentation are so improbable that the appearance of reality is lost. The advocate of the "Modernes" objects: "mais ne pourrait-on pas vous observer qu'on se rend au spectacle avec la persuasion que c'est l'imitation d'un événement et non l'événement même qu'on y verra?" (IV, p. 287.) The favorite replies: "Et cette persuasion . . . doit-elle empêcher qu'on n'y représente l'événement de la manière la plus naturelle?" (ibid.)

The subject, terms, and perspective of this passage are different from those in the Mémoires and the article Beau. In the Bijoux Diderot links up with a literary debate and thinks in the accepted categories of theatre poetics. It is true that he changes the meaning of natural and real, but he bases the new meaning, as does the doctrine classique, on antiquity. Like Boileau he finds nature and truth in Greek tragedy. And yet he uses these terms to attack classical French works. Here we have an example of the confusion of terms in eighteenth-century poetics which I have already mentioned earlier.

For us the subject of illusion is especially important. As in the works of Du Bos, it is discussed from the point of view of the observer and the effect of the work, and is also linked with the confusion between theatre and reality. But this confusion, which Du Bos considers to be impossible and which Diderot uses merely as a hypothesis in his discussion and then casts aside again, is only one form of illusion. Diderot discusses an esthetically significant illusion which Du Bos mentions only implicitly: the spectator does not witness the real action, but he imagines that he is witnessing it (". . . le Spectateur, trompé sans interruption s'imagine assister à l'action même" [IV, p. 285]). He is not listening to a real conversation, but a dialogue "fort voisin du naturel" (IV, p. 284). Diderot bases this illusion above all on the trueness of the style and presentation (here he is thinking in particular of the true-to-life screams of Philoctetes), but he is also referring to the action in a broader sense. In the chapter from Bijoux, Diderot does not generally discuss the confusion of theatre with reality, but the stirring of the emotions and the pleasure given by an exact illusion. The spectator does not compare the original and the imitation and judge the similarities; he is not aware of the art, but is simply tricked: in the appearance he sees the natural which is the true.[36]

The point of view of the observer, the listener, the hearer, etc., and the high valuation Diderot places on appearances seem to be the most significant features of his reflections on imitation. A passage from the postscript to the *Lettre sur les sourds et muets* will, I hope, make this idea clearer.

The esthetic sections of *Letter on the Deaf and Dumb*, which was probably written shortly before the article *Beau*, are, like the chapter quoted from the *Bijoux*, related to the problem of the imitation of nature. The theory of perception, which is the fundamental element of this letter, influences all the other problems. We shall return later to the pivotal question of this letter (imitation in various forms of art), but for the moment we shall concentrate on illusion. In the postscript to the *Letter on the Deaf and Dumb*, which answers questions and critical observations made by Mlle. de la Chaux, Diderot replies to the objection that music can be pleasing even when it does not arouse direct or symbolic pictures:

". . . je vous prie de considérer que ces morceaux de musique qui vous affectent agréablement sans réveiller en vous ni peinture ni perception distincte de rapports, ne flattent votre oreille que comme l'arc-en-ciel plaît à vos yeux, d'un plaisir de sensation pure et simple; et qu'il s'en faut beaucoup qu'ils aient toute la perfection que vous en pourriez exiger, et qu'ils auraient, si la vérité de l'imitation s'y trouvait jointe aux charmes de l'harmonie. Convenez, mademoiselle, que si les astres ne perdaient rien de leur éclat sur la toile, vous les y trouveriez plus beaux qu'au firmament; le plaisir réfléchi qui naît de l'imitation s'unissant au plaisir direct et naturel de la sensation de l'objet. Je suis sûr que jamais

---

[36] Here we see a constant feature of Diderot's works, which is not restricted to the theatre—the place where the greatest illusions are possible. The *Salons* provide many examples, as does Diderot's first encounter with the works of Richardson. "O Richardson! on prend, malgré qu'on en ait, un rôle dans tes ouvrages, on se mêle à la conversation, on approuve, on blâme, on admire, on s'irrite, on s'indigne. Combien de fois ne me suis-je pas surpris, comme il est arrivé à des enfants qu'on avait menés au spectacle pour la première fois, criant: *'Ne le croyez pas, il vous trompe. . . . Si vous allez là, vous êtes perdu.'* Mon âme était tenue dans une agitation perpetuelle." (*Œuvres esth.*, p. 30.)

Du Bos, however, as we have seen, separates imitation from reality. Rousseau distinguishes between nature and appearance, especially with regard to the theatre, which as the social art "par excellence" is also the illusion "par excellence." Society (as it is, and not as it ought to be) conceals true nature and displays a false appearance; the actor and the theatre epitomize this lie.

clair de lune ne vous a autant affectée dans la nature que dans une des Nuits de Vernet." (ɪ, pp. 407-408)[37]

In a letter to the Père Castel, who doubted whether Diderot's observations were correct, he again deals with the subject of moonlight, as depicted by Vernet: "Quant à la nuit de Vernet, je conviens que, tout admirable qu'elle soit dans son tableau, elle n'avait pas la majesté ni le pathétique de la nature, ce qui signifie tout au plus que mon exemple est mal choisi, mais ce qui n'empêche pas mon principe d'être vrai. Il est certain, je crois, que toutes les fois que le plaisir réfléchi se joindra au plaisir de la sensation, je dois être plus vivement affecté que si je n'éprouvais que l'un ou l'autre." (xɪx, p. 426.) In this passage Diderot combines two ideas: pleasure given by imitation is greater, because it is added to the pleasure given by the original, and moonlight in Vernet's picture moves one more than natural moonlight. The latter seems to me Diderot's spontaneous feeling; the former, a reflection on this feeling and an explanation.

The pleasure Diderot gained from art was pleasure gained from an appearance, and this appearance gave him an illusion of reality (Diderot calls it nature or truth), i.e., pleasure in the original object arose through the imitation aimed at. But at the same time (at first anyway), Diderot often regarded the imitation as a kind of mediator, showing the way to nature and reality. It has surprised many Diderot scholars that his stories and novels do not contain many descriptions of people, action, and scenery, but that in his *Salons* he describes everything down to the last detail, and with deliberate variations of style. He needed the transposition (from nature) to art in order to capture the concrete reality; but he then described the illusion as reality. A convincing example of this characteristic is the description of a series of Vernet's pictures, in the 1767 *Salon* (xɪ, p. 98 et seq.).[38] Diderot tells a story: he writes that he wanted to discuss Vernet's pictures when his friends invited him into the country, near the coast; there he went for walks with his friend's children and their tutor; he describes what he saw during these walks. In the end it turns out that he has, in fact, been describing the pictures hanging in the Louvre. This extraordinary ambivalence is not limited to the pic-

[37] In later years, too, Diderot was concerned with this question. See e.g., the following passage taken from the *Salon de 1767*: "Il y a des sensations composées; et c'est la raison pour laquelle il n'y a de beaux que les objets de la vue et l'ouïe. Ecartez du son toute idée accessoire et morale, et vous lui ôterez la beauté. Arrêtez à la surface de l'oeil une image que l'impression n'en passe ni à l'esprit ni au coeur; et elle n'aura plus rien de beau" (xɪ, p. 116).

[38] The problem of the relationship between reality and appearance, nature and the impression given by a work of art, remains connected to Vernet's pictures; see, e.g., xɪ, pp. 113, 140, 416. It also occurs, of course, in other contexts.

torial arts. Diderot's exposition on the esthetics of realistic dramas and the composition of plays, which is said to exemplify his theories, is constructed around a similar story. He claims to have learned of the events of the *Fils naturel* during a visit to the country; in fact he had taken them from Goldoni's *Vero Amico*, and in the *Entretiens sur le Fils naturel*, which was supposed to explain his theory, he gets involved in an inextricable *qui pro quo*. His theory of narrative, which was also supposed to be exemplary (cf. *Les Deux Amis de Bourbonne*), is based on a mixture of fiction and reality which remains to this day quite inseparable.[39] The intention behind the *qui pro quo* is obvious, and the theories on which Diderot based his idea of realism have been analyzed many times. But it is just as important to consider his conception of imitation and illusion from the same point of view as he discussed them himself, i.e., from the standpoint of "plaisir esthétique," and to connect this conception to his taste and his ideas on reality. In the theory the demand is for more exact imitation of nature and truth to nature; esthetic pleasure, however, is directed towards appearance, which, inasmuch as it is a perfect imitation (i.e., "exacte"), is regarded as nature itself. When reading the *Salons* and thinking about the stories of the *Fils naturel* and the *Deux Amis de Bourbonne*, I am always convinced that Diderot arrived at "plaisir directe" by way of "plaisir réfléchi," i.e., he arrives at nature by way of art. What is natural is taken to be the source and the model, but Diderot sees it through the medium of art. The pleasure gained from the imitation transmits an impression of the original. Of a still-life by Chardin he writes:

"c'est qu'il n'y a qu'à prendre ces biscuits et les manger, cette bigarade l'ouvrir et la presser, ce verre de vin et le boire, ces fruits et les peler, ce pâté et y mettre le couteau.

"C'est celui-ci qui entend l'harmonie des couleurs et des reflets. O Chardin! ce n'est pas du blanc, du rouge, du noir que tu broies sur ta palette: c'est la substance même des objets, c'est l'air et la lumière que tu prends à la pointe de ton pinceau et que tu attaches sur la toile." (*Œuvres esth.*, p. 484.)

He is not dealing here with a new version of the "sparrows in front of the picture of Zeuxis"; Diderot is not taking the "biscuit," nor is he cutting into the pâté. He is not dealing with an identification of art and reality, but with the joy gained from a *perfect* illusion. One can speak

[39] As H. R. Jauss has dealt with the *Entretiens sur le Fils naturel*, in the above-mentioned article (see footnote 14), and I have discussed the relationship between Diderot and Goldoni, as well as the creation of the *Deux Amis de Bourbonne* elsewhere, I shall not go into details here. See *Diderot and Goldoni* (Köln, 1961) and Diderot, *Contes*, Introduction, and pp. 64-69.

equally of Diderot's naturalism, and of his art-cult. The same applies to his attitude towards the French classical period: in accord with his realistic theories on the theatre he attacks the artificiality—the elevated, idealized, universal, refined, select, and stylized "nature"—of French classicism. But, in spite of his protests, his taste still remains attached to this form of art. I do not believe that he ever overcame this ambivalence of feeling and taste between art and reality; there is evidence of this in all his works, even his later writings.

The ambivalence of the impressions given by nature and by art—in other words, the difficulty of separating feelings aroused by art and feelings aroused by the natural object, even occasionally the confusion of the two—is connected with those factors (feeling, sensibility, sentimentality) which oppose rationalism, the *esprit géométrique*, and the intellectual elements of taste; it is also concerned with the recognition of the "baser" senses (taste and touch) in esthetic pleasure and judgment.[40] Traditionally the sense of sight plays the most important part in the theory of *imitatio naturae*, occasionally hearing is also mentioned; the former is the most "spiritual," the latter approaches it in the perception of harmony. Examples of *imitatio naturae* are taken almost exclusively from painting and from descriptive poetry. When we discuss the means of presentation, we shall return to this subject. What matters for the moment is the fact that the sense of sight, thanks to its traditional spiritual connotations, corresponded to and enhanced the idealizing, universalizing trends underlying the *imitatio naturae* principle. On the other hand, there is also a connection between the trend towards the concrete object, the close environment, the everyday reality, and the recognition of the "baser" senses of touch, taste, and, to a certain extent, smell. The reasons for the fact that taste played a commanding part in the esthetic discussions of the eighteenth century probably lie in social upheaval as well as in the philosophical question of the construction of the world of the senses. A remark made by the Marquis d'Argens on the *Réflexions critiques* is a convincing example of the point of view of the *honnête homme*, who steadfastly maintains the tradition of the *grand siècle*:

"Le système général de M. l'Abbé du Bos souffre quelque [sic] difficultés. Il prétend qu'on juge mieux des ouvrages d'esprit par le sentiment, que par la raison, et par les connoissances qu'on peut avoir acquises par l'étude. Cette opinion me paroît sujette à de grands incon-

[40] In the *Lettre sur les sourds et muets*, Diderot characterizes the senses in the following way: ". . . je trouvais que, de tous les sens, l'oeil était le plus superficiel; l'oreille, le plus orgueilleux, l'odorat, le plus voluptueux; le goût, le plus superstitieux et le plus inconstant; le toucher, le plus profond et le plus philosophe" (I, pp. 352-353).

véniens; et c'est soumettre les tragédies de Racine, et les pièces de Molière à la décision de tous les bourgeois les plus ignorans: c'est rendre le peuple maître du sort des meilleures pièces. L'expérience nous a cependant montré que la Phèdre de Racine, que le Misanthrope de Molière ne plurent point par le sentiment à la multitude; et que ce furent les véritables connoisseurs, qui jugent des choses par la connoissance des règles, qui soutinrent ces chefs-d'oeuvres contre le mauvais goût de ceux qui ne jugent que par le sentiment." (*Mémoires secrets de la Republique des Lettres*, 1744, vii, p. 156.)

The image used by the Abbé to prove that it is feeling alone that decides what is good and what is bad in art, must have disgusted d'Argens and the society he represented. The image is that of *ragoût*! It is not reason or rules that decide whether *ragoût* is good or bad, but taste (ii, p. 341). Taste is used here both esthetically and sensually, and after this comparison comes the following sentence: "Il est en nous un sens destiné pour juger du mérite de ces ouvrages, qui consiste en l'imitation des objets touchans dans la nature. Ce sens est le sens même qui auroit jugé de l'objet que le Peintre, le Poëte, ou le Musicien ont imité." (ii, pp. 341-342.) The *imitatio*, the appearance, affects the senses, and these pass judgment as they are acquainted with the original object. The examples Du Bos gives are taken from the sphere of sight and hearing, and later he calls the esthetic sense the sixth sense, but again identifies it with feeling. Therefore his protest against reason, rules, formalism, and privilege in esthetics is far more radical in theory than in practice.[41] Diderot, however, who was far more cold-blooded, went much further in the materialization of taste and esthetic judgment. The passage quoted above, concerning one of Chardin's paintings, shows that in fact every sense plays a part in judging to what extent the illusion is true. In the *Salons* the sense of touch plays a particularly important part;[42] the same applies to Diderot's theory of perceptions—the sense of touch is basic to the world of perception.

Diderot drew another conclusion from the primary importance of feeling in esthetics: he assumes a direct effect of the artist's sensibility on the audience. Thanks to his sensibility the actor can find the sound, the rhythm, and, more important, the suspense (or tension) which the author wishes to communicate; and he conveys this by means of sound and metaphoric gestures to the audience. The composer makes our nerves vibrate like the strings of an instrument. Our own sensibility makes us

[41] This feature can be found everywhere in the *Réflexions*. In my opinion, the sixth sense has only been introduced as an explanation for what is direct and spontaneous, and independent of the judgments passed by taste.

[42] With reference to these questions, see the last of the *Cinq Leçons*.

resound as we listen. This direct effect conveys for Diderot not art, but nature itself by means of illusion through imitation. But, apart from this peculiarity, it is undeniable that the significance of imitation and appearance changes when, in analyzing the effect of the work of art and the essence of taste, one incorporates the appeal (and the directness of the appeal) to the "baser" senses. To a certain extent, the appearance seems subtler, even if the "baser" senses are "cruder." Less "raffinement" is required to visualize the illusion of an apple than to imagine the illusion of its taste.

Earlier we mentioned two points of view which are important for the transformation of the *imitatio naturae* principle in eighteenth-century France: one, which we have been dealing with up to now, is that of the effect of a work of art; the other is the means used by the artist, and the media in which he works. A few reflections and examples will illustrate the problems of *imitatio naturae* as they appear when they are seen from this standpoint. First, we shall deal with the part played by illusion.

From the point of view of the artist, and the means with which he imitates nature, the illusion is not seen in connection with the original or with the effect of the imitation, but with regard to the ways and means by which it is created. Diderot examined this question in his works on the theatre, in the *Salons*, and in his reflections on the novel and the *conte*. Here we will deal only with the latter aspect of the question, since Diderot treated it more clearly and more thoroughly. (The illusion of reality in narrative was not primarily a theoretical problem but a matter of personal experience, even an experience which repeated itself in different forms. This idea is very important, and so we must look at it a little more closely.)

It is a known fact that Diderot's novel *La Religieuse* and the accompanying *Préface-Annexe* (1760) were not planned originally as a literary work but as a conscious deception. However, while working on it, Diderot and his friends came to regard the fictitious letters, the nun's life-story (of which only a few details were really true),[43] and her fate, as being completely real. The events of the *Fils naturel* and *Entretiens sur le Fils naturel* were partly borrowed and partly invented, so that Diderot was always aware of their fictional character, but as the *author* of *La Religieuse* he came face to face with the ambivalence of art and reality, appearance and actuality.[44]

Diderot was probably confronted by this same ambivalence in the

---

[43] See Georges May, *Diderot et "La Religieuse"* (Yale University Press, 1954).
[44] See my critical edition of the *Préface Annexe* in *Diderot Studies* II.

same year (1760) when reading the works of Samuel Richardson. He was carried away by the novels and could not free himself from the belief that they were true. He noted the same reaction in his friends. When, in 1762, he wrote the "Éloge de Richardson" his enthusiasm was still as fresh and keen as when he had first read the novels. In the *Éloge* he asks himself how Richardson achieved such convincing reality. He does not set out to ask this question, but keeps coming to it, as it were, by chance. His answers, in brief, are as follows: Richardson writes about events which take place in the world we live in, but which we ourselves often do not see; we perceive the world in general, but not all the fleeting moments, the changes and the rapid developments from one event to another. The illusion arises out of all these small details: ". . . c'est à cette multitude de petites choses que tient l'illusion: il y a bien de la difficulté à les imaginer; il y en a bien encore à les rendre."[45] Diderot makes the same observations with regard to the fullness of events and characters: the details are the overwhelming feature; each character speaks with his very own voice, or with a voice which corresponds to the circumstances. "Dans ce livre immortel, comme dans la nature au printemps, on ne trouve point deux feuilles qui soient d'un même vert. Quelle immense variété de nuances! S'il est difficile à celui qui lit de les saisir, combien n'a-t-il pas été difficile à l'auteur de les trouver et de les peindre!" (*Ibid.*, p. 39.) The remarks concerning the different shades of green are not supposed to remind us of Leibniz but of nature (reality). There are other explanations which are, however, not as important, as Diderot always uses them when comparing the objective and permanent to the subjective and fleeting. "Le coeur humain, qui a été, est, et sera toujours le même, est le modèle d'après lequel tu copies" (*ibid.*, p. 40). The French classical theorists also used these arguments, even though they were opposed to emphasizing the transitory, individual, complex, self-changing, fleeting elements of situations, and of daily life, and indeed gained part of their realistic effect through this opposition.[46]

The question of the form of the illusion is also posed in the *Préface-Annexe* of the *Religieuse*. This was added later (probably 1781), but we mention it here as it is relevant to the composition of the novel. In the *Question aux Gens de Lettres*, an afterthought added to the *Préface-Annexe*, Diderot says that the fictitious letters were at first very artistic, well-thought-out, touching and novel-like, but that he then purposely spoiled them (on the advice of his friends and his wife, he adds): "en

---

[45] *Œuvres esth.*, p. 35.
[46] Diderot's argument that the realistic novel is more "real" than history inverts the traditional difference made between the novel and history, and is due to the skeptical view of history, which was common in the eighteenth century.

supprimant tout ce qu'elles avaient de saillant, d'exagéré, de contraire à l'extrême simplicité et à la dernière vraisemblance; en sorte que si l'on eût ramassé dans la rue les premières, on eût dit: 'Cela est beau, fort beau . . .' et que si l'on eut ramassé les dernières, on eût dit: 'Cela est bien vrai. . . .' Quelles sont les bonnes? Sont-ce celles qui auraient peut-être obtenu l'admiration? ou celles qui devaient certainement produire l'illusion?'' (*Œuvres rom.*, p. 868.)

Maximum probability creates the illusion of reality, but the author has to sacrifice art and poetry in order to achieve it. What should he pay most attention to? Beauty or exactitude? Here the question remains open; but while revising the *Religieuse* Diderot preferred to *faire beau* (as study of the different versions shows). Elsewhere in a different context he again posed the question and tried to answer it.

At the end of his story *Les Deux Amis de Bourbonne* Diderot outlines a poetic of the *conte*; to a certain extent the *conte* is actually a poetics itself. (I have tried to demonstrate this in my critical edition of Diderot's short stories.) Diderot's attempt is especially interesting as at that time there was no such thing as a poetics of the novel or the short story. He distinguishes three kinds of short story: the *conte merveilleux*, the *conte plaisant*, and the *conte historique*. The last, the "true story," interests us most. The *conteur historique* tries to deceive the reader; his aim is "strict truth," i.e., exactitude. Here Diderot seems to contradict himself. His terminology is indeed very confusing, but his meaning is clear: he means, as he did in the *Bijoux*, the illusion (deception) of reality. In the following quotation "illusion" also means the appearance of reality. The aim of the *conteur historique* is twofold:

"... Il veut être cru: il veut intéresser, toucher, entraîner, émouvoir, faire frissonner la peau et couler les larmes; effets qu'on n'obtient point sans éloquence et sans poésie; l'une et l'autre exagèrent, surfont, amplifient, inspirent la méfiance. Comment s'y prendra donc ce conteur-ci pour vous tromper? Le voici: il parsèmera son récit de petites circonstances si liées à la chose, de traits si simples, si naturels, et toutefois si difficiles à imaginer, que vous serez forcé de vous dire en vous-même: Ma foi, cela est vrai; on n'invente pas ces choses-là. C'est ainsi qu'il sauvera l'exagération de l'éloquence et de la poésie; que la vérité de la nature couvrira le prestige de l'art, et qu'il satisfera à deux conditions qui semblent contradictoires, d'être en même temps historien et poète, véridique et menteur." (*Contes*, p. 81.)

To make this clearer, Diderot gives an example from graphic art:

"Un peintre exécute sur la toile une tête; toutes les formes en sont fortes, grandes et régulières; c'est l'ensemble le plus parfait et le plus rare. J'éprouve, en le considérant, du respect, de l'admiration, de l'effroi: j'en cherche le modèle dans la nature et ne l'y trouve pas; en comparaison tout y est faible, petit et mesquin. C'est une tête idéale, je le sens; je me le dis. . . . Mais que l'artiste me fasse apercevoir au front de cette tête une cicatrice légère, une verrue à l'une de ses tempes, une coupure imperceptible à la lèvre inférieure, et, d'idéale qu'elle était, a l'instant la tête devient un portrait; une marque de petite vérole au coin de l'œil ou à côté du nez, et ce visage de femme n'est plus celui de Vénus; c'est le portrait de quelqu'une de mes voisines. Je dirai donc à nos conteurs historiques: Vos figures sont belles, si vous voulez; mais il y manque la verrue à la tempe, la coupure à la lèvre, la marque de petite vérole à côté du nez qui les rendraient vraies . . . .

> Atque ita mentitur, sic veris falsa remiscet,
> Primo ne medium, medio ne discrepet imum.''
> Hor., *Art. poet.* (*Ibid.*, pp. 81-82.)[47]

This example is, I feel, a bad one, as it destroys the original train of thought.[48] I have only mentioned it for the sake of completeness and for the Horace quotation. In this case we are dealing with the means with which the artist achieves the illusion of reality, and with the difference between *faire beau* and *faire vrai*. The answer to this problem is to be found in the original reception of Richardson's novels—the so-called "Richardson experience." But here the author's own experiences are still noticeable; Diderot knows that our creative activity guides us and changes what we experience; the attention given to minute details not only simulates reality, but also binds our inventive power to reality. Elsewhere Diderot also suggested various other methods of fighting against the tendency to pull oneself away from truth and reality.

Although Diderot quotes a passage from the *Ars Poetica* and uses the same terminology (i.e., the lie and the mixture of true and false), he does not actually deal with the problem in a traditional way. Not only does he set the Horace quotation in a new context, but he also alters its meaning.[49] Horace speaks of the liberties Homer took for the sake of artistic form: Homer introduces us into the middle of the story, and omits everything which could spoil the beauty of what he is portraying; for the sake of *nitescere* he makes up certain things, mixes true and

[47] Here I am quoting the original text; in the latest version, a short anecdote consisting of three lines separates the "rendraient vraies" from the Horace quotation.

[48] See *Cinq Leçons*, p. 125.

[49] Here we have one of the many examples of "wrong" quotation in the eighteenth century. In many cases the classical quotation was used merely as an ornament or reference, and the person quoting often did not refer to the original sense of the quotation. This common feature is often intentionally ignored by those who wish to connect the eighteenth century with the tradition of the classics.

false, as long as this does not spoil the structure. The story (*fama*), which is true and probable, is supplemented by fiction and invention (*fictum*), for the pleasure of the reader. Here Horace is in agreement with Aristotle, who allows the epic writer this freedom for the sake of esthetic pleasure. Invention consists of details which are added to the main line of the true action; the structure of the work is the criterion of justification for such a mixture. For Diderot, it is the added details which constitute the truth; it is they that constitute the appearance of reality. He does not say a word about the structure of the overall work.[50] Diderot emphasizes the artist's powers of invention, and examines the problem of realism from the point of view of the creative faculties. Although this invention is not supposed to deviate from reality but to lead to it, one can see that there is a change here from the traditional view of *inventio*. According to classical tradition, the artist should confine himself to accepted material and subjects; his *inventio* is limited to the manner of the presentation. But, according to Diderot, the artist chooses his material from the everyday world (in his theories—as opposed to his stories—Diderot did not yet recognize that this reality changes and that it is social as well as political). The psychology of the creation of an illusion of reality is the central esthetic and critical point of interest.[51] The importance of the *inventio* is also to be seen in the fact that for the creative artist there was no longer any ambivalence between the real and the invented, no longer any deceptive mixture of purported reality and actual happenings such as characterizes the *representative* concept of nature-imitation and is to be found in reflections on esthetic effect.

Our last example of the transformation of the principle of *imitatio naturae* is the discussion of *ut pictura poesis*, from the standpoint of the means and the media of presentation.[52] Horace's formula, seldom taken on his own terms, has been given several different interpretations since the Renaissance: it is used to justify the equivalence of art and poetry, and states that these two forms of art are related. The relationship can be explained as follows: the arts are sisters, both imitate nature, and both have the same purpose—to describe the outside world. The means of expression are different (drawings, color—words, sound), but they have

[50] It is worth noting that in the original version the Horace quotation follows on immediately after the idea that the wart, the pock-mark, and the scratch make an ideal face "real"—an idea completely opposed to classical tradition. Here Diderot abandons the ideal and the criterion of *perfectio*. Taken this way, the passage on warts, pock-marks, and scratches is not contradictory.

[51] Perhaps there is a connection here with the bourgeoisie seizing power over *de facto* reality and becoming conscious of the means by which this power is to be gained. Work itself becomes problematic.

[52] On the history of *ut pictura poesis*, see especially R. Lee's essay: "*Ut pictura poesis*: The Humanistic Theory of Painting," *Art Bulletin*, xxii, no. 4 (Dec. 1940).

both the same representative character, i.e., they both present the external world. To this we must add that poets and theorists understood Horace's maxim to mean that poetry was like painting, whereas the representatives of graphic art understood it to mean that painting was like poetry.

It was very important for eighteenth-century esthetics to link up with *ut pictura poesis* and its traditions when comparing the various forms of art, and for music to be included in these comparisons. Du Bos used this idea as a motto and Batteux used it to back up his Cartesian claim that all forms of art were based on one principle. Batteux is the starting point for Diderot's critical reflections.

For our purposes, it is unnecessary to consider the question of the equality of the arts, their reduction to one principle, the analysis of their similarities and their differences as well as the formalistic separation of the arts according to means employed and senses appealed to in presentation. As Batteux and others showed, it is not just this separation of the arts that leads to an understanding of their essential differences. These latter are appreciated only by those authors who recognize that the means of presentation differ according to the various forms of art, since they employ different media of expression and since the perceptive faculty differentiates according to the different senses at which they are aimed. This realization developed from a comparison of the arts in connection with the *ut pictura poesis* and led to a separation which is quite contrary to the identification in Horace's maxim.[53] Abbé Du Bos's *Réflexions* show this development; the subject is *ut pictura poesis*, and in fact the analysis frequently proceeds along the lines of comparative observation. Music remains completely given over to description.[54] In the case of poetry and painting, Du Bos indicates their limits and establishes the difference between the object imitated in poetry and in art, according to the criteria of simultaneity and sequence—the single visual moment and the succession of moments in time (categories later developed in full by Lessing's *Laokoön*). Above all he is opposed to the idea that poetry is descriptive, and claims that this feature is peculiar to painting, while poetry presents the world of thoughts and feelings, its nuances, its diversity, its complexity, as well as its accompanying circumstances. (See I, chap. 13.) A. Lombard[55] feels that these categories contradict the

[53] The return to the empiric foundations of imitation as one of the forms of perception, and the principle of the genesis of our ideas, play an important part in this process.

[54] See I, chap. 45. To this excuse of Du Bos's one can add that he is thinking above all of opera, as is often the case in his *Réflexions*, which proceed mainly from the art form of the theatre.

[55] A. Lombard, *L'Abbé Du Bos: un initiateur de la pensée moderne* (Paris, 1913), part 2, chap. II, sections 2 and 3.

principle of *ut pictura poesis*, and interprets the engraving which decorates the 1755 quarto edition as a misunderstanding of the *Réflexions* (the title page shows art with a bandaged mouth). If one takes *ut pictura poesis* literally, then he is right, but Du Bos probably took it to mean a general comparison, and, as we have seen, the maxim had a different meaning for poets and for painters. The engraving means simply that painting is silent poetry, and this meaning fits in with chapter 13 and other sections of the *Réflexions* where the subject of painting is given a very literary definition. Du Bos's concern with descriptive painting corresponds to his sensualism, for, as he so often says, a picture can move us more deeply than any written account.

Du Bos's critique of descriptive poetry is aimed at one of the elementary claims of *imitatio naturae*, and is all the more effective because it is based on an analysis of the means and media of art. Its counterpart in the esthetics of the *Réflexions* is the emphasis given to form as opposed to instruction and to content (see I, chap. 34, and II, chap. 35). For Du Bos the most essential thing in poetry is style, the beauty of which constitutes the reader's pleasure. The magic of a beautiful style, like beautiful colors in a painting, makes us overlook mistakes and improbabilities. "Si l'on veut rappeller les choses à leur véritable principe, c'est donc par la poësie du style qu'il faut juger d'un poëme, plutôt que par sa régularité et par la décence des mœurs (I, p. 309). . . . S'il est permis de parler ainsi, dans la poësie, le mérite des choses est presque toujours identifié avec le mérite de l'expression" (II, p. 554). This expression consists of the harmony of the verses, the sound, the rhythm, and the choice and positioning of the words (chap. 35 in Books I and II).

From these observations and distinctions we can see that the traditional form of the *imitatio naturae* gave way to a subtler, more refined, concept, offering the poet more self-reliance and independence. Diderot carried out a more thorough analysis of the differences between imitations in various arts than did the Abbé Du Bos, whose writings appear to have been unknown to him when he first tackled the problem. In the *Lettre sur les sourds et muets*, which was addressed to the Abbé Batteux, he argued against the idea that all forms of art could be reduced to one principle, i.e., the idea already adopted and systematized by the French classics. Batteux simply followed this more closely and with more emphasis on form. In the course of this letter Diderot noted the arbitrariness and the simplifications of the Abbé.

He maintained that every form of imitative art has its own *hiéroglyphe*. This term, which plays a significant role in the letter and in any study of Diderot, can be understood in several different ways: here it means metaphoric or pictorial expression. Diderot invites Batteux to compare the imitation of *belle nature* in the different forms of art. He

says that literary works have often been compared—the famous
parallèles—but no one has examined how the painter, the composer,
and the poet express the same beauty. Why is it that we admire a poem,
but laugh at a picture which presents exactly the same thing?[56] The
beauty of nature is not the same for all arts! Here Diderot has come up
against the differences in imitation which result from the different ways
and means of presentation; at the same time he points out the limitations of *ut pictura poesis*.[57] After a brief effort to imitate the same thing
in three different arts, he arrives at the conclusion that the painter is
limited to one particular moment, and that he cannot imitate the sequence of poetry; but he can show the original as it really is, and so
achieves a more powerful impression: "les expressions du musicien et du
poète n'en sont que des hiéroglyphes" (I, p. 388), i.e., they are only
metaphorical expressions.

All these ideas, which we find in the letter, are in theory meaningful,
but if one pursues them, they become restricted. We might look at a
later passage concerning the same lines of Virgil, where the ideas implicit in the *Letter on the Deaf and Dumb* are brought to full fruition. In
order to avoid the boredom of having to discuss a bad picture, Diderot di-
gresses a little *(Salon,* 1767). The picture had been sketched by the person who commissioned it, and Diderot takes this opportunity for a short
diatribe against those who demand that the artist merely fulfill their own
wishes. Not even *gens de lettres* should do such a thing; they justify
their wishes by means of the Horace quotation and do not realize that it
would be better to say: ". . . *ut poesis pictura non erit. Ce qui fait bien
en peinture fait toujours bien en poésie; mais cela n'est pas réciproque.
J'en reviens toujours au Neptune de Virgile, . . . Summa placidum caput
extulit unda."* (Virgil. *Ænid. lib.* I, v. 131; XI, pp. 72-73.)

One must not take the first part of this sentence literally; Diderot is
attacking the presentation of a literary subject in a painting. In the *Letter
on the Deaf and Dumb* he maintained that the image Virgil uses of the
head rising up out of the water would be disturbing, as it would look as if
the head had been chopped off. In the 1767 *Salon* he is not talking about
one particular detail, but about the most important differences in the
possibilities of presentation in the arts; his copious knowledge of painting and sculpture had helped him to develop these ideas:

"Il n'y sur le papier (i.e., the medium of the epic poet) ni unité de

---

[56] See I, p. 386; cf. there, too, the example from Virgil.

[57] Here he is fighting against a belief which had a great deal of influence in the eighteenth century, both in theory as well as in poetry and in painting. Descriptive poetry was
triumphant in England, France, and Germany. Count Caylus sanctioned *ut pictura poesis*
by means of his *Tableaux tirés de l'Iliade* (1757). It is well known that these problems were
at the center of Lessing's esthetical reflections.

temps, ni unité de lieu, ni unité d'action. Il n'y a ni groupes déterminés, ni repos marqué, ni clair-obscur, ni magie de lumière, ni intelligence d'ombres, ni teintes, ni demi-teintes, ni perspective, ni plans. L'imagination passe rapidement d'image en image; son œil embrasse tout à la fois. Si elle discerne des plans, elle ne les gradue ni ne les établit; elle s'enfoncera tout à coup à des distances immenses; tout à coup elle reviendra sur elle-même avec la même rapidité, et pressera sur vous les objets. Elle ne sait ce que c'est qu'harmonie, cadence, balance; elle entasse, elle confond, elle meut, elle approche, elle éloigne, elle mêle, elle colore comme il lui plaît. Il n'y a dans ces compositions ni monotonie, ni cacophonie, ni vides, du moins à la manière dont la peinture l'entend. Il n'en est pas ainsi d'un art ou le moindre intervalle mal ménagé fait un trou; où une figure trop éloignée ou trop rapprochée de deux autres alourdit ou rompt une masse; où un bout de ligne chiffonné papillote; où un faux pli casse un bras ou une jambe; où un bout de draperie mal colorié désaccorde; où il ne s'agit pas de dire: 'Sa bouche était ouverte, ses cheveux se dressaient sur son front, les yeux lui sortaient de la tête, ses muscles se gonflaient sur ses joues, c'était la fureur'; mais où il faut rendre toutes ces choses; où il ne s'agit pas de dire, mais où il faut faire ce que le poëte dit; où tout doit être pressenti, préparé, sauvé, montré, annoncé, et cela dans la composition la plus nombreuse et la plus compliquée, la scène la plus variée et la plus tumultueuse, au milieu du plus grand désordre. Dans une tempête, dans le tumulte d'un incendie, dans les horreurs d'une bataille, l'étendue et la teinte de la nue, l'étendu et la teinte de la poussière ou de la fumée, sont déterminées.'' (xi, pp. 73-74.)

A few pages later he comes back to the same subject while referring to the first lines of *De rerum natura* (the greatest poetic image):

''Il faudrait un mur, un édifice de cent pieds de haut, pour conserver à ce tableau toute son immensité, toute sa grandeur, que j'ose me flatter d'avoir sentie le premier. Croyez-vous que l'artiste puisse rendre ce dais, cette courronne de globes enflammés qui roulent autour de la tête de la déesse? Ces globes deviendront des points lumineux, comme ils sont autour de la tête d'une vierge dans une assomption; et quelle comparaison entre ces globes du poëte et ces petites étoiles du peintre? Comment rendra-t-il la majesté de la déesse? Que fera-t-il de ces mers immenses qui portent les navires, et de ces contrées fécondes qui donnent les moissons? Et comment la déesse versera-t-elle sur cet éspace infini la fécondité et la vie?

''Chaque art a ses avantages. Lorsque la peinture attaquera la poésie sur son palier, il faudra qu'elle cède; mais elle sera sûrement la plus forte, si la poésie s'avise de l'attaquer sur le sien.'' (xi, p. 78.)

In these two passages Diderot not only recognizes that the poet and the artist think and create with different concepts of time and place, but that the poet uses a power of imagination *sui generis*. According to Diderot, this power consists not only of perception or of memories of images, but of a creative faculty that extends beyond the simple presentation of an object. This faculty is discontinuous—it does not carry out or execute, it sees distances, connections, and an intensity of light which it is impossible to convey in a picture. Without abandoning Nature as the embodiment of objective existence, Diderot managed to free the concept of imitation from being an exact copy, a duplicate, a mere description, and linked it with *inventio*, which is not restricted to the "modus." The insight, first apparent in the *Letter on the Deaf and Dumb*, into the metaphoric and symbolic character of art and the creative power of the artist, took on clearer form as more attention was paid to the works themselves. The reader of the *Salons* and of Diderot's literary criticism will find plenty of evidence; we have selected just one such piece.

If one were to examine more closely the principle of *ut pictura poesis* in eighteenth-century French thought, one would see that the criticism of this principle has greatly changed the concept of *imitatio naturae*. This criticism is aimed at the rational systematization of the arts on the basis of the imitation principle; it emphasizes the importance of media and means in artistic expression. This change of perspective leads from the prevalence of objectivity, from the adaption of the artistic form to the object (*adequatio rei*), which is the foundation of the theory of imitation, to the recognition of the subjective, of the creative in artistic production, as well as to the valuation of the suggestive in form.

WOLFGANG ISER

Fiction—The Filter of History:

A Study of Sir Walter Scott's *Waverley*

I

IN the "General Preface" to the *Waverley Novels*, Scott reflects on his own situation as narrator. He tries to clarify his intentions, which—unlike those of earlier novelists—are no longer concerned with expounding moral norms. Instead, he takes as his guide his own personal development, as he seeks to explain the curious innovation of history as the subject of fiction. His starting point, he says, is as follows: "I had nourished the ambitious desire of composing a tale of chivalry, which was to be in the style of the *Castle of Otranto*, with plenty of Border characters and supernatural incident."[1]

This "ambition" links Scott to a form of novel that had arisen specifically out of reactions against the morally oriented novels of the eighteenth century. The Gothic novel restored to the genre the element of the mysterious and the uncanny which the moral novels of the eighteenth century had tried hard to eliminate. Fielding had taken care to make his own position clear as regards the principles underlying his novels: ". . . I would by no means be thought to comprehend those persons of surprising genius, the authors of immense romances, or the modern novel and Atalantis writers; who, without any assistance from nature or history, record persons who never were, or will be, and facts which never did, nor possibly can, happen; whose heroes are of their own creation, and their brains the chaos whence all their materials are selected."[2] Here he was clearly excluding all elements of the "unnatural" from his presentation of human nature. But the Gothic novel of the eighteenth century was built up round the fantastic and the supernatural, the purpose of which Horace Walpole outlined himself in the preface to the second edition of the *Castle of Otranto*:

"Desirous of leaving the powers of fancy at liberty to expatiate through the boundless realms of invention, and thence of creating more interesting situations, he (i.e., the author) wished to conduct the moral

---

[1] Sir Walter Scott, *Waverley* (*The Nelson Classics*) (Edinburgh, n.d.), p. xiii.
[2] Henry Fielding, *Joseph Andrews* (*Everyman's Library*) (London, 1948), p. 143.

agents in his drama according to the rules of probability; in short, to make them think, speak, and act, as it might be supposed mere men and women would do in extraordinary positions. He had observed, that, in all inspired writings, the personages under the dispensation of miracles, and witnesses to the most stupendous phenomena, never lose sight of their human character."[3]

Walpole is at pains to show that he introduces the supernatural in order to create situations that will call forth new and unexpected reactions from his characters. This increase in interesting situations and the resultant diversification of human conduct arose out of the desire to reconcile the old form of the novel with the new.[4] Walpole points out that in the old novel *imagination* was predominant, but the action or plot proved to be improbable. In the new novel, on the other hand, though there is no lack of *invention*, the primary claims of nature mean a restriction of *imagination*. Now Walpole wishes to break this *strict adherence to common life*, and to introduce the *extraordinary* in order to extend what he regards as the hitherto limited sphere of action in the novel. This, he feels, is the only way to disclose forms of human conduct that had been excluded by the moral novels of the eighteenth century. His declared aim is to make the *extraordinary* seem probable.[5]

It was this intention that made the Gothic novel interesting for Scott; the link between his "Border characters" and "supernatural incident" corresponds to the technique with which Walpole strove after a diversification and extension of human reactions. The many "supernatural incidents" were also meant by Scott to derestrict the natural, and he intended to show the consequences of this derestriction in a world of historically verifiable characters. However, Scott confesses that this intention soon took a turn in a different direction,[6] for in his increasing

---

[3] Horace Walpole, *The Castle of Otranto and the Mysterious Mother (Constable's Edition)*, ed. Montague Summers (London, 1924), p. 14.

[4] See *ibid.*, pp. 13 f. Concerning the difference, see also Clara Reeve, *The Progress of Romance*, ed. Esther M. McGill (New York, 1930), p. 111: "The Romance is an heroic fable, which treats of fabulous persons and things.—The Novel is a picture of real life and manners, and of the times in which it is written. The Romance in lofty and elevated language, describes what never happened nor is likely to happen.—The Novel gives a familiar relation of such things as pass every day before our eyes, such as may happen to our friend, or to ourselves; and the perfection of it, is to represent every scene, in so easy and natural a manner, and to make them appear so probable, as to deceive us into a persuasion (at least while we are reading) that all is real, until we are affected by the joys or distresses, of the persons in the story, as if they were our own." See also John Colin Dunlop, *History of Prose Fiction*, ed. Henry Wilson (London, 1898), I, 1.

[5] See Walpole, *The Castle of Otranto*, p. 14.

[6] See Scott, *Waverley*, p. xiii; see also Sir Herbert Grierson, *History and the Novel: Sir Walter Scott Lectures 1940-1948* (Edinburgh, 1950), p. 37.

preoccupation with the folklore and history of Scotland, he found the historical supplanting the supernatural, and this immediately ensured a greater degree of probability for the variety of human reactions than Walpole had been able to achieve. History stood as guarantor for all the quirks and peculiarities of human conduct; and history also opened the way to an even greater variety of situations than the supernatural could create. And so Scott's original attachment to the Gothic novel prepared the way for his new subject matter: the representation of historical reality.

Walpole's Gothic novel had broken with the principle of *imitatio naturae*[7] and through the introduction of the fantastic had brought about an artificial extension of the possibilities for presenting human conduct. As Scott's starting point was this same Gothic novel, we can hardly expect him to adhere to classical poetics in presenting history. Nevertheless he was faced with the massive problem of how he could actually mould historical reality in the form of diverse modes of individual human conduct. To start with, he considered his own personal experience of the publication of a historical novel. He had himself arranged publication of Joseph Strutt's posthumous novel *Queen-Hoo-Hall*, but this had proved a failure.[8] Scott attributed the failure to the fact that the wealth of historical detail in *Queen-Hoo-Hall* could appeal only to the antiquarian. He concluded that historical information and situations could only be taken as subject matter for a novel if it was possible for them to be translated into terms that were relevant for the reader. In the preface to *Ivanhoe*, Scott again refers to *Queen-Hoo-Hall*; he describes the quality which that work lacked and which he considered to be a basic principle for his own novel:

"It is necessary, for exciting interest of any kind, that the subject assumed should be, as it were, translated into the manners, as well as the language, of the age we live in. . . . The late ingenious Mr. Strutt, in his romance of *Queen-Hoo-Hall*, acted upon another principle; and in distinguishing between what was ancient and modern, forgot, as it appears to me, that extensive neutral ground, the large proportion, that is, of manners and sentiments which are common to us and our ancestors. . . ."[9]

It is on this "neutral ground" that the links must be forged between the reader and historical reality. The technique of communication is thus of fundamental importance in this type of novel, and we shall now try to analyze how the technique is made to operate in *Waverley*.

[7] See Walpole, *The Castle of Otranto*, pp. 13 f.
[8] See Scott, *Waverley*, pp. xvi f.
[9] Sir Walter Scott, *Ivanhoe*, ed. by Andrew Lang (London, 1901), pp. xlvii f.

The direction of Scott's style, as outlined in the "General Preface" to the *Waverley Novels*, is given a revealing, concrete form right at the beginning of *Waverley, Or, 'Tis Sixty Years Since*. Scott deliberately chose this title because it points to the intended process of animating history and making it real in the reader's mind. The title outlines the interrelationship between the main character and historical reality, and in order to make his intentions quite clear, Scott runs through a few more variants of the title. "Had I, for example, announced in my frontispiece, *Waverley, a Tale of Other Days*, must not every novel-reader have anticipated a castle scarce less than that of Udolpho?"[10] Such a title would have blurred the historical outline, for the indeterminacy of the period would have made the past seem like a fantasy without any connection with the present. *Waverley* would then have been a Gothic novel, leaving unlimited scope for the invention of fantastic situations. Clearly, then, for Scott the past can take on historical reality only if it is linked with the present, for the world portrayed in the Gothic novel remains unhistorical precisely because it lacks this link. The title that he did choose brings together the character and the period, and this tells us a good deal about the function of Waverley himself.

He is to mediate between the historical events of 1745 and the present day, and so embodies the "neutral ground" on which historical reality is to be "translated" into terms conceivable for the contemporary reader. This function of transforming a given reality makes him very different from, for instance, the Fielding hero. The latter's exemplary course of life was the focal point of interest, and the reader was oriented to this interest by the realization of moral principles. Waverley, however, does not dictate the course of events—he is dependent on the given reality that he is to bring to life.

This fact is confirmed by another title variant:

"Or if I had rather chosen to call my work a 'Sentimental Tale,' would it not have been a sufficient presage of a heroine with a profusion of auburn hair, and a harp, the soft solace of her solitary hours, which she fortunately finds always the means of transporting from castle to cottage, although she herself be sometimes obliged to jump out of a two-pair-of-stairs window, and is more than once bewildered on her journey, alone and on foot, without any guide but a blowzy peasant girl, whose jargon she can hardly understand?"[11]

With this allusion, Scott separates his own intentions from those of the sentimental novel, which, in the second half of the eighteenth century, had as its subject the passions and sufferings of the "enlightened"

---

[10] Scott, *Waverley*, p. 10.   [11] *Ibid.*, pp. 10 f.

hero. In a sentimental novel, reality would have been reduced to the trials and tribulations of a wounded heart. Reality would have been determined by the sufferings of tearful characters, and would have taken on an abstract connotation to the extent that it could be presented only as a round of knavery alternating with beautiful dreams. Such an overvaluation of the sentiments would make the reality presented most improbable, and Scott would be transplanting the implicit heroine of his title into a kind of fairy-tale atmosphere. Furthermore, if the main character were to be given too much importance in relation to the events, he would disturb the balance so vital to Scott's intentions, and so satisfactorily established by the actual title of the novel.

Finally, Scott asks what expectations the reader would have formed if the title had promised an account of contemporary conditions: "Or again, if my Waverley had been entitled *A Tale of the Times*, wouldst thou not, gentle reader, have demanded from me a dashing sketch of the fashionable world?"[12]

The presentation of contemporary reality would raise two problems for Scott. First, he would have to work out a principle of selection in order to pinpoint the representative elements of contemporary events. But he sees himself in no position to establish such a principle, as he cannot choose between foreground interests and the desire for sensations. Second, he would be obliged to act merely as a reporter of current events, so that the figure of the hero would become an increasing embarrassment as far as the structure of the novel was concerned. For a reporter is expected to give many details about many people, and since he himself thus acts as the mediator, Waverley's function would become superfluous. And so, for Scott, the present day was no subject matter for a novel, and in this respect he was quite different from his great successors in France, who tended more and more to set their novels in the present.

These reflections on possible titles are a clear indication that Scott was not aiming exclusively at a description of the past, or an illustration of the present, or the life-story of a hero. So long as these three elements remain separate, they are irrelevant for Scott, for it is only through their interaction that the novel attains its subject matter. The historical past must be brought to life, to avoid the label of the Gothic novel; interest in the fate of the hero must be kept down, so that the historical novel will not be taken for a sentimental novel; and, finally, the present can be only a point of reference and not a subject of portrayal, or else the novel would "sink to the level of mere reporting." Bringing the past to life

---

[12] *Ibid.*, p. 11.

requires the presence of the main character, for he—the passive hero[13]—represents the thoughts and feelings of the contemporary reader; in this way, historical reality is transformed for the reader to experience for himself.

II

What does Scott mean by historical reality?

"I beg pardon, once and for all, of those readers who take up novels merely for amusement, for plaguing them so long with old-fashioned politics, and Whig and Tory, and Hanoverians and Jacobites. The truth is, I cannot promise them that this story shall be intelligible, not to say probable, without it. My plan requires that I should explain the motives on which its action proceeded; and these motives necessarily arose from the feelings, prejudices and parties of the times. I do not invite my fair readers . . . into a flying chariot drawn by hippogriffs, or moved by enchantment. Mine is a humble English post-chaise, drawn upon four wheels, and keeping his Majesty's highway. Such as dislike the vehicle may leave it at the next halt, and wait for the conveyance of Prince Hussein's tapestry, or Malek the Weaver's flying sentry-box."[14]

Scott feels that what may seem like a lot of tedious historical details are in fact essential if one is to discern the human motives underlying and formulating historical reality. The individual impulses that drive men to act are, in their turn, answers to existing historical situations. Historical reality, then, for Scott, is a network of interactions arising out of situation and response. Such situations are concrete manifestations of human motives, and each motive is conditioned by and, in turn, conditions the particular circumstances surrounding a sequence of events. In this feature of historical reality, Scott comes closest to the intention which had germinated out of his original "model," Walpole's *Castle of Otranto*. However, there now arise so many individual possibilities of reaction that an account of them all might become tedious. And yet Scott considers such a display to be the basic driving-force behind his novel,[15] for it is only in this way that he can attain the necessary degree of verisimilitude.

Thus the presentation of individual human conduct and of the events arising out of that conduct is endowed with verisimilitude by history, and no longer depends on a set of pre-established norms, as was the case in the eighteenth-century novel. Verisimilitude is not guaranteed by

---

[13] See Georg Lukács, *Der historische Roman* (Berlin, 1955), p. 31. A closer analysis of Lukács's ideas is not possible here if the subject under discussion is to be adhered to.

[14] Scott, *Waverley*, pp. 43 f.

[15] *Ibid.*, p. 44, in a footnote Scott again lays emphasis on this fact.

personal experience, as with Defoe and Richardson; nor does it arise out of the norms of human conduct that Fielding deduced from the tempo- rary aberrations of his heroes and the complicated machinations of the "reality" around them; nor is it linked with what Fielding called "ex- perience"[16]—the trying and testing of potentially existing virtues. If the verisimilitude of events and reactions is vouched for by history alone, then it cannot be interpreted either as an adumbration of truth,[17] or as an esthetic effect.

This built-in verisimilitude testifies to the originality of Scott's con- ception of reality, for this no longer serves to illustrate moral norms but, instead, is taken as an end in itself. It can be successfully disclosed only through the "wandering viewpoint" of the reader, which Scott depicts with the metaphor of the post-chaise.[18] This indicates the problems at- tending comprehension and perception of historical reality—a continual change of viewpoint is necessary, because it is no longer possible to find a single, ideal position that will command a total panorama. Thus Scott warns his readers that they will have to be patient, or else wait for an Oriental magic carpet to enable them to get a total view of reality. If reality is to be uncovered only by means of a long and difficult journey, then obviously it is no longer going to be the clear-cut setting for some underlying, philosophical system. Scott's images of the post- chaise and the magic carpet show the basic difference between a reality that is a subject in itself, and a reality that is only the testing-ground for a philosophical idea.

While Scott disguises his methods of presentation in metaphors, our task is to find out precisely how the new subject matter of reality is translated and transplanted into the mind of the reader. Our starting point is that interrelationship between human motivation and historical situation from which Scott derives the network of interactions that con- stitute his "reality." For this network to be communicated to the reader, he needs a hero whose individuality will be played down rather than em- phasized, for the character must never take precedence over the events. Thus even the name Waverley hints at the hero's function, since he is to take no decisive part himself, but is, rather, to reflect historical situa- tions and the conduct of genuine historical figures.[19]

---

[16] See Henry Fielding, *Tom Jones* (*Everyman's Library*), ii (London, 1909), xiii, 1:158.

[17] For a thorough discussion regarding this question, see H. Blumenberg, *Paradigmen zu einer Metaphorologie* (Bonn, 1960), pp. 88 ff.

[18] The metaphor of the post-chaise can also be found, incidentally, in a similar context, in Fielding's *Tom Jones*, which Stendhal greatly admired (see *Tom Jones*, xi, 9, vol. ii, pp. 91 ff.).

[19] See also Stewart Gordon, "*Waverley* and the 'Unified Design' " *ELH*, 18 (1951), p. 111.

III

Both in the introduction and the epilogue to *Waverley*, Scott emphasizes the fact that the troubles of the civil war, as described in his novel, are gathered mainly "from the narrative of intelligent eye-witnesses."[20] While Scott the narrator uses eye-witnesses to link the events of 1745 to the present, the same process is repeated in the action of the novel. Waverley is made aware, by the accounts of people he meets, of the impending decline of Scotland.[21] The first time he realizes the difference between past and present is in the meeting with the Baron of Bradwardine. This Lowland nobleman still recalls the days when traditional customs governed life in the Scottish villages. He himself tries to adhere to these old traditions, but this only makes him seem odd;[22] his narrative, however, authenticates the reality of the past world he describes. The political present has so distorted the relics of Scottish village life, that now only eye-witnesses can describe how things used to be, and details of old folklore can be brought to life for Waverley only by the words of the Baron.

This fanning out of history into sections of the past depending on the age and standpoint of the eye-witness is the dominant principle of presentation in *Waverley*. It is repeated when Waverley himself comes into contact with the archaic-seeming Highland clans. Here, though, the technique undergoes a subtle refinement, which might be described as the telescoping of different sections of reality, as offered by the eye-witnesses. The more peculiar and archaic past reality becomes, the more complicated is the process of its resuscitation. Waverley first learns from Rose Bradwardine all about the age-old relations between the Highland clans and the people of the Lowlands.[23] The impression arising from this is then elaborated on through the account given by the bodyguard of the Highland chief whom Waverley meets after leaving the Baron's estate.[24] The conversation with Fergus Mac-Ivor reveals another aspect of clan life,[25] and this, in turn, is extended by Flora Mac-Ivor's descriptions in an unforeseeable direction.[26] Thus from several points of view, comprising several different social levels, we are presented with historical rituals and rhythms of life within a single clan. This eradicates the one-sidedness of the single eye-witness account, and the picture of this clan's history thus becomes fuller and fuller, though at the same time we realize that

[20] Scott, *Waverley*, pp. 554 f.; see also pp. lxxiv, 123 f., footnote, 570; also references to a similar guarantee of events in *Heart of Midlothian*, made by Dorothy Van Ghent, *The English Novel. Form and Function* (New York, 1961), p. 115.

[21] See Scott, *Waverley*, pp. 96, 98 ff., 117, 121, 128 f., 146 ff., 149, and 172.

[22] See esp. *ibid.*, pp. 109 ff.   [23] *Ibid.*, pp. 118 ff.   [24] *Ibid.*, pp. 146 ff., and 149.

[25] *Ibid.*, pp. 160 ff.   [26] *Ibid.*, pp. 172 ff.

these sections do not constitute the whole picture, which will in fact be extended and diversified with every new viewpoint. This additional potential adds more fuel to the reader's imagination, where the various sections of reality merge into a vivid mosaic. And so historical reality is shown as a checkered variegation of the past according to the standpoints in time and space of the different eye-witnesses. The sections are presented in no special order of importance, and indeed this lack of specific orientation and of any overriding conception of reality is what endows the eye-witness presentation with its own special quality. Scott himself says that his intention is simply to preserve the past from oblivion,[27] and it is precisely this multiplicity of viewpoints that enables him to fulfill his intention. The minor characters in the novel ensure that historical ways of life are continually communicated to the present, and thus a reality is saved that would otherwise have perished with the passing of time. This process depends on the presence of Waverley, who acts as the link between the reader and the past. As for the story, it is no longer concerned with a single event enclosed within a particular period of time; instead, the novel shows how situations of the Civil War begin to reach out into an ever-expanding past, revealing more and more aspects and more and more surprises.

Historical reality, then, is a cohesively patterned phenomenon that has to be communicated; its relative homogeneity is brought about by the fact that the authenticity is guaranteed each time by an eye-witness, who does not allow the past to disintegrate into a pile of amorphous facts, but instead reports on his own world, which seems to him to be a complete and unquestionable one. Thus, although each section of reality is permeated by the reactions of the particular character, it is these reactions that make the past credible, that give the events narrated a sort of spontaneous order, and that provide the reader with personal access to an otherwise alien reality. Similarly, when he is describing the events of the war itself and the period leading up to it, Scott again takes care to authenticate his account with eye-witness reports.[28] This care shows that Scott's view of history coincides neither with the Hegelian idea of a continual process nor with the mere accumulation of facts. Scott had learned his lesson from the failure of *Queen-Hoo-Hall*. He did not impose any idealistic construction on history. His eye-witnesses bring to life only their own particular section of the fading past, so that each account clearly presents only one aspect of reality and never the whole. If

[27] *Ibid.*, p. 554; see also David Daiches, "Scott's *Redgauntlet*" in *From Jane Austen to Joseph Conrad. Essays collected in memory of James T. Hillhouse*, ed. R. C. Rathburn and M. Steinman, Jr. (Minneapolis, 1958), p. 46.

[28] See Scott, *Waverley*, pp. 554 f., 570 and lxxiv.

the individual sections do sometimes overlap, this simply serves to make one aware that reality can be presented only through a continual expansion of what we know.

The eye-witness accounts ensure that only those aspects of reality are captured that have actually been in existence. But by revealing Scotland's past through a variety of different characters, Scott also draws attention to the inevitable individualization of reality, for each aspect carries with it the limitations of its reporter, and is clearly only a part of a far greater whole. Reality is something that is constantly individualized and diversified. And so each particular section of the narrative restricts the reality presented, and at the same time points to the open-endedness of its own presentation. And thus we perceive, at one and the same time, the self-containment of historical events, and the unceasing movement and changeability of historical processes.

Scott defined historical reality as an interaction of human motivation and historical situations.[29] In order to understand this idea more fully, we shall look at two specific examples. At the beginning of the novel, the close relationship between character and reality is outlined in the person of Richard Waverley, the father of the "hero." As the second son of a noble family, Richard Waverley feels that he is underprivileged, for he believes that the title is really due to him and not to his elder brother.[30] It is therefore quite natural for him to join the new party of the House of Hanover and to abandon his family's traditional loyalty to the Stuarts.[31] The Tory, then, becomes a Whig and begins to take an active part in political affairs at the start of the Civil War. The interweaving of motivation and historical reality—the structural principle behind Scott's characters—is strikingly reflected in Richard Waverley. His firm political views, in fact, arise out of the personal disadvantage of his birth, which Richard hopes to counteract through a political career. He involves himself in matters which, as regards their political goals, are of no concern to him. Hence Scott's talk of the *mixed motives*[32] underlying Richard's decisions and the political opportunism which in various ways endangers his own family.[33] He takes an active part in the troubles of the Civil War, and yet has no genuine political conviction, since his attitude stems from a personal problem connected with the historical reality of primogeniture. If Richard Waverley had been out to do away with primogeniture, then his political fight would at least have had a political motive, but his motive is merely to cover up the damage done to his self-esteem, by actively contributing to the political formation of the present. However, the personal motives are in fact diverted until they are almost un-

[29] *Ibid*., p. 44.   [30] *Ibid*., pp. 14 f.   [31] *Ibid*., pp. 15 f.
[32] *Ibid*., p. 14.   [33] *Ibid*., p. 469.

recognizable, and finally he himself can no longer tell what gave rise to his actions, the consequences of which become his sole preoccupation.[34] The reality which is shaped by people arises from origins that can no longer be kept check on. Again, though, it must be stressed that the network of motives that give rise to historical reality is not to be interpreted as a platform for a priori ideas. If reality arises out of subjective reactions to historical conditions, then clearly there must be as many sides to reality as there are subjective reactions. Since these subjective impulses can lead to any number of possible consequences, reality takes on an element of opacity very far from the clear-cut orientation of the traditional novel. And, indeed, the reality shaped by the characters in this novel is often radically different from that connected with their original motives, which represented their original reaction to the given reality confronting them.

The Baron of Bradwardine is another case in point. He sides with the Stuarts, fights in the army of the Pretender, loses all his possessions, exposes his daughter to the greatest danger, and is finally forced himself to live as an outlaw.[35] He is committed perhaps to a greater extent than any other character in the book, and one is bound to suppose that all his actions are governed by his loyalty and his conviction of the divine right of the Stuarts. And yet we learn that this total devotion arises out of his desire to be allowed to take off the King's shoes after the battle—"which was the feudal service by which he held the barony of Bradwardine."[36] This eccentricity, revealing the impenetrability of human motivation, shapes political reality, and this contributes to the imponderability of history.

All the most important minor characters are based on this principle. There is always a strange contrast between the factual reality of political events and the motives of the people involved in them. The imaginations of the characters are inspired by historical facts: Richard Waverley by primogeniture, the Baron of Bradwardine by a ceremony. And so it is a concrete historical circumstance that sets off the subjective impulses of these people, but the consequences of their reactions show in what unexpected directions a historical situation can lead once it has sown its seed in the human mind. It is this mirroring of events through their surprising consequences that first enables Scott to produce an illusion of historical reality. For the reality conceived in the novel is fictitious—it is not a chronicle of the Civil War. The fiction is based on the reflections and reactions of the individual characters, whose subjective transformation of historical situations gives rise to the reality of the novel. This

[34] *Ibid.*, pp. 201 ff.   [35] *Ibid.*, pp. 488 ff.
[36] *Ibid.*, p. 110; see also pp. 374 f. and 377 f.

reality, being historical, inevitably precludes any superimposed symbolic dénouement. This is why the reactions of the characters to given situations are so erratic, and would, in different times and under different circumstances, themselves be quite different—as Scott states explicitly of the most important of the minor characters, Fergus Mac-Ivor.[37] The vast potential scope of reaction bears witness to the constant individualization and consequent dynamic diversification of history. The facts are true, but they are made probable by means of fiction, and it is only this fiction that enables Scott to produce the illusion of historical reality. In the epilogue to *Waverley*, he himself comments on this form of illusion: ". . . for the purpose of preserving some idea of the ancient manners of which I have witnessed the almost total extinction, I have embodied in imaginary scenes, and ascribed to fictitious characters, a part of the incidents which I then received from those who were actors in them. Indeed, the most romantic parts of this narrative are precisely those which have a foundation in fact."[38] In transforming eye-witness accounts of historical facts into a fiction, Scott ensures that the highly romantic-seeming situations retain their basis of fact, for they would seem incredible were it not for the fictitious characters that authenticate them.

This apparent paradox is what underlies the special illusion of historical reality. If the past is to be made tangible in all its individualized ramifications, it must seem to be consistent. But historical consistency can only be a fiction, as otherwise the past would be artificially structured by non-historical categories. A fictitious consistency enables the singularities of history to be related to one another, and this is why Scott transplanted his authenticated reality into fictitious figures and imaginary situations. On the other hand, if an individual historical fact is given in isolation, its effect will be romantic, because stripped of any fictitious connections it will seem as if it can only have been invented. Truth, as they say, is stranger than fiction—and, in this case, fiction prevents the truth from seeming too strange. But if this fictitious consistency ensures that the past will be comprehensible, it is only natural that the contingent elements of the past should begin to take on a fantastic character—and this Scott attempts to play down by constant reference to real historical events. He had learned from the *Queen-Hoo-Hall* affair that the mass of historical facts needed consistency if it was to be brought to life, and so the fictitious consistency is what guarantees the truth-to-life of the historical reality presented. This would seem to imply, in fact, that if history is to be linked to the present, its presentation is bound to fall back on esthetic means.

[37] *Ibid.*, pp. 154 f.   [38] *Ibid.*, p. 554.

IV

We must now take a closer look at the function of the hero, Waverley himself. Our discussion of the various possible titles has already drawn attention to the functional connection between the past, the "passive hero," and the present. Waverley has the task of bringing a differentiated past into the present. At the beginning of the novel, Scott ponders on the name of his hero. He wants to free him from all associations with traditional heroes: "I have, therefore, like a maiden knight with his white shield, assumed for my hero, WAVERLEY, an uncontaminated name, bearing with its sound little of good or evil, excepting what the reader shall hereafter be pleased to affix to it."[39] With this neutrality, Waverley, being uncommitted, is clearly to represent the world of the reader; he is in fact the viewing-glass through which the reader may observe the events that are to form his experience of historical reality. Like the reader, Waverley has no immediate connection with the ancient Scotland that he is to discover. His initial feeling of unfamiliarity with and secret embarrassment at Scottish customs—which is only to be conquered through his gradual understanding of them[40]—automatically establishes a link between his own and the reader's reactions. Scott observed that distance allowed only an unclear perception, but this in its turn began to act as something magic and attractive.[41] Waverley's comprehension is inextricably bound up with his imagination. Scott gives repeated descriptions of the process which leads from the imagination to an understanding of the world. In his youth, for instance, Waverley heard many tales of the past: "From such legends our hero would steal away to indulge the fancies they excited. In the corner of the large and sombre library . . . he would exercise for hours that internal sorcery by which past or imaginary events are presented in action, as it were, to the eye of the muser."[42] Through "internal sorcery" Waverley brings past events to life by transforming them into actions. Here we have one important function of the imagination: by investing and reenacting traditional or legendary facts with imaginary human actions and reactions, it can resuscitate the past. Here Scott is simply indicating the way in which the process can take place.

He gives further indications when, for the first time, Waverley makes contact with an unfamiliar world through his meeting with the Baron of Bradwardine: "But although Edward and he differed *toto coelo*, as the Baron would have said, upon this subject, yet they met upon history as

---

[39] *Ibid.*, pp. 9 f.

[40] See also Alexander Welsh, *The Hero of the Waverley Novels*, in *Yale Studies in English*, 154 (New Haven, 1963), p. 51.

[41] Scott, *Waverley*, p. 235.   [42] *Ibid.*, p. 32.

on a neutral ground, in which each claimed an interest. The Baron, indeed, only cumbered his memory with matters of fact; the cold, dry, hard outlines which history delineates. Edward, on the contrary, loved to fill up and round the sketch with the colouring of a warm and vivid imagination, which gives light and life to the actors and speakers in the drama of past ages."[43]

According to the definition given by Scott in the preface to *Ivanhoe*, history as "neutral ground" comprises both the factual uniqueness of an event and the feelings and reactions of people toward this event. Historical facts do not disclose the motives of the "actors and speakers," and this is why Waverley tries to reenact in his imagination the conditions that gave rise to, or arose out of, a particular event. Thus the context of historical situations becomes vivid again, after being, as it were, squeezed out by the passage of time. The imagination fills the framework of historical fact with the picture of dramatic human confrontations, and it is this which makes historical reality genuinely interesting. Events are freed from their fixed abode in the past, and are brought back to life with the attendant diversification that characterizes all real events.

Scott speaks of the "drama of past ages," and it is Waverley's imagination that animates the "actors and speakers." Scott began his *Essay on the Drama* with the following definition: "A DRAMA (we adopt Dr. Johnson's definition, with some little extension) is a poem of fictitious composition in dialogue, in which the action is not related but represented. A disposition to this fascinating amusement, considered in its rudest state, seems to be inherent in human nature."[44] The active imagination, then, is an integral part of human nature, which does not relate but reenacts what happened in the "drama of past ages." In this way, the time gap between past and present is bridged, and history loses the apparently clear-cut dimensions it had assumed through the passage of time. The imagination releases all the circumstances that cannot be perceived in the mere historical fact, and it brings to life all the conditions that led to the formation of historical reality. Imagination and reality interact upon one another, so that, in the reality of the novel, neither history nor imagination can assume a completely dominant role. The imagination establishes what Collingwood called the "emotional charge"—the response to the "sensum" of a given situation.[45]

There are moments when Waverley experiences an exciting convergence of reality and imagination:

"Waverley could not help starting at a story which bore so much re-

---

[43] *Ibid.*, p. 98.
[44] Sir Walter Scott, *The Miscellaneous Prose Works* (Edinburgh, 1878), II, 575.
[45] See R. G. Collingwood, *The Principles of Art* (Oxford, 1938), pp. 162 f.

semblance to one of his own day-dreams. Here was a girl scarce seven-teen, the gentlest of her sex, both in temper and appearance, who had witnessed with her own eyes such a scene as he had used to conjure up in his imagination, as only occurring in ancient times, and spoke of it coolly, as one very likely to recur. . . . It seemed like a dream to Waver-ley that these deeds of violence should be familiar to men's minds, and currently talked of, as falling within the common order of things and happening daily in the immediate vicinity, without his having crossed the seas, and while he was yet in the otherwise well-ordered island of Great Britain."[46]

At this moment, imagination and reality, past and present, seem to have become interchangeable for Waverley, for a scene conjured up by his imagination does not, in fact, belong to some distant age but is hap-pening here and now. This surprising coincidence of imagination and re-ality is confirmed by the eye-witness, and so historical reality is restored to the present by the imagination, while the imagination fulfills itself by the bringing to life of history. Waverley is so excited by this interaction because his imagination has always been fired by those elements of the past that seem to have vanished into obscurity.[47] The imagination must create a path to the apparently inaccessible, and historical reality is ideal material for it, insofar as past human conflicts are not totally wrapped in mystery. The imagination can achieve comprehension of them through animation, and this represents a perfectly valid category of historical comprehension.[48] The imagination endows the individual events of the past with a consistency that is quite different from any philosophical pat-tern-forming. It is disciplined by the concreteness of events, while the unconfinable fluidity of events attains consistency without being re-stricted to any single, ultimate purpose. Thus reality and imagination become virtually inseparable, and this in turn implies that history can best be captured by esthetic means. In *Waverley*, Scott has set history free from its chains of fact; he uses the imagination of his hero to com-municate the live reality behind the facts. Scott took care to particularize this function of the imagination by contrasting his own hero with that of Cervantes: "My intention is not to follow the steps of that inimitable author, in describing such total perversion of intellect as misconstrues the objects actually presented to the senses, but that more common aber-ration from sound judgment which apprehends occurrences indeed in

---

[46] Scott, *Waverley*, pp. 121 and 123.

[47] See, for instance, *ibid.*, pp. 133 and 112.

[48] See Heinrich Rickert, *Kulturwissenschaft und Naturwissenschaft* (Tübingen, [3]1915), pp. 79 f.

their reality, but communicates to them a tincture of its own romantic tone and colouring."[49]

Scott's hero is aware of the gap between his imagination and reality. He cannot produce a purely imaginary world, if only because his imagination depends on reality for its importance. At the same time, though, whatever is communicated by the hero is bound to be colored by his own personality. However, Waverley is a "passive hero," representing the sentiments of the reader himself, and so the coloring he gives to the reality he communicates will in fact be a vital aid in establishing contact with the reader. It is the very imperfection of the hero that guarantees his esthetic effectiveness.

Though Waverley differs from Don Quixote in that, despite his imaginativeness, he does not construct an imaginary world, nevertheless he is exposed to the danger of getting lost in his imagination: ". . . a thousand circumstances of fatal self-indulgence have made me the creature rather of imagination than reason."[50] The imagination tends to be perilous when it develops into a vehicle for the hero's wish-fulfillments. At such moments it becomes obvious that the imagination can perform its proper function only when it is directly related to a given reality. This observation is confirmed by the blotting out of "romantic spirit" and "exalted imagination" when the hero is temporarily involved in war emergencies and is thus totally preoccupied with saving his own skin.[51] Once he is forced to concentrate completely on getting out of such situations, imagination fades right away, for it is not an instrument to dictate forms of action. Only when the hero is free from the immediate pressures of distressing situations will his imagination fulfill the purpose of reenacting historical reality.

As we have seen already, this process involves a change in the hitherto conventional conception of the novel-hero. He can no longer be the focal point of interest. The ideal intentions which still permeate even Waverley's life[52] are gradually squeezed out by his new function. His imagina-

---

[49] Scott, *Waverley*, p. 35.   [50] *Ibid.*, p. 214.   [51] *Ibid.*, p. 296.
[52] The recent monograph by Welsh is concerned with this form of presentation: "The argument of the book is a simple one. The passive hero has always seemed to me the most extraordinary and significant feature of the *Waverley Novels*. I set out to account for this hero's inactivity from a study of the text of the novels. The result of the inquiry is a thematic study centering on the relations of property, anxiety, and honor, and supported by excursions into the history of ideas" (pp. vii f.). For a different conception of the passive hero, see Walter Bagehot, *The Works*, ed. Mrs. Russel Barrington (London, 1915), III, 67; Gerhard Buck, *In Fortsetzung Bagehots. Die Waverley Romane Sir Walter Scotts* (*Britannica*, 13), p. 3; David Daiches, *Literary Essays* (Edinburgh, 1956), p. 89; and Donald Davie, *The Heyday of Sir Walter Scott* (London, 1961), p. 30.

tion is not allowed to dwell upon any one single event, for such a preference would imply an evaluation of reality. Indeed, the communication of historical reality through the imagination leads almost to a loss of identity in Waverley, for he must be open to all situations but must identify with none. Only in this way can his imagination create a trustworthy experience out of the contingencies of historical reality.

The potential limitlessness of this whole process makes it a problem how to end the novel. While the hero's function is to bring past reality to life, history itself does not come to any end—as Scott's subtitle indicates—and so the novel can come to a stop only if the main figure once more steps into the foreground. But this would mean a total change of emphasis as regards the subject matter of the novel, with Waverley taking precedence over events, and history supplying only the trappings for the hero's development. Scott deals with this problem by adopting an ironic style in depicting his hero at the end. The reader is bound to be interested in Waverley's personal situation after the Civil War, but Scott dampens down this interest by constantly interrupting his description of Waverley whenever he is on the verge of tying up the various ends of the action.[53] He merely indicates how things reached this particular point, and then adds apologetically that he does not want to overtax the reader's patience. Thus he tends more and more to gloss over the personal details of Waverley's life, and when finally he comes to the obligatory marriage—in the tradition of the eighteenth-century novel—he makes the following ironic observation:

"But before entering upon a subject of proverbial delay, I must remind my reader of the progress of a stone rolled down hill by an idle truant boy . . . it moves at first slowly, avoiding by inflection every obstacle of the least importance . . . but when the story draws near its close, we hurry over the circumstances, however important, which your imagination must have forestalled, and leave you to suppose those things, which it would be abusing your patience to relate at length."[54]

Scott simply leaves it to the reader to imagine and paint in the details of the conventional ending, for to describe the obvious and expected would be again to overtax the reader's patience. This ironic treatment of convention shows that Scott certainly did not want the end of his novel to be interpreted as the visible self-fulfillment of the hero. And so he uses irony and omission to preserve the integrity of his intentions, to push his hero discreetly into the background, and to leave historical reality—as conjured up with the aid of that hero—properly situated in the foreground.

[53] See Scott, *Waverley*, pp. 497 and 517.   [54] *Ibid.*, p. 539.

V

There remains, finally, the question of how Scott manages technically to communicate the picture of an individualized historical past. A full discussion of this technique would require a separate essay, and we must restrict ourselves here to only a few basic observations. When, as narrator, Scott wishes to produce a vivid.idea of specific persons or events, he splits them up into a variety of aspects, and, as we view the characters and the situations from different perspectives, so the pictures gradually become fuller, and the potential expands. This process emerges, for instance, in the portrayal of Gilfillan when he meets Waverley in Major Melville's house. First the narrator offers a detailed description of Gilfillan; then Waverley supplements this with another, quite unexpected, view, which vividly intensifies the impressions given by the narrator: ". . . Waverley was irresistibly impressed with the idea that he beheld a leader of the Roundheads of yore, in conference with one of Marlborough's captains."[55]

This is typical of Scott's technique of presentation. By fanning out the character into a series of perspectives, Scott creates a heightened awareness of the *potential* character. The way is laid open for the imagination to penetrate the diversification and to bind the various aspects together in a unified picture, as we can see from Waverley's reaction when he meets Gilfillan. It is the imagination that gives consistency to the narrator's apparently disordered presentation, and it is this consistency that raises the description to the level of vivid perception. There are many instances of this technique in *Waverley*, and it is used to describe situations as well as characters. The exodus of the Highland clans from Edinburgh is one example.[56] The narrator sets out his series of observations, and these are then drawn together through Waverley's reactions, which bring the whole event to life in the reader's imagination.

This very technique is what gave rise to Stendhal's objections to the historical novel. The danger attendant on such detailed historical descriptions is that they may become boring, because Scott's historical "tableau" and the communicative reactions of the hero do not leave the reader enough free play to involve himself personally: the reactions and the historical facts are presented by the author or his minor characters in such a clear-cut manner that the reader is bound to become too passive. Scott's French successors kept reality and reaction apart, so that the world to be deduced from the behavior of their characters took on a

[55] *Ibid.*, p. 281.
[56] *Ibid.*, pp. 348 ff.

suggestive note very different from Scott's technique of intermediary communication.[57]

Furthermore, we cannot equate Scott's "perspectivism" with that of the modern novel since Flaubert and Henry James. Scott's splitting of his subject matter into perspectives always serves the specific aim of communicating historical events. While the modern novel seeks to create its subject through a profusion of perspectives, Scott's subject is already present and is divided up purely for the sake of achieving an enhanced vividness. At the same time, Scott's aims separate him from his predecessors, such as Fielding, in that he is no longer committed to the principle of *imitatio naturae*. The principle of *imitatio historiae* demands only that history be made vivid in the present; this involves translating factual reality into "fictitious characters" and "imaginary scenes," because only in this way can historical diffuseness be overcome and presented coherently for subjective comprehension and experience. Fiction, however, is a phenomenon of form; traditionally it had always served art in completing what in nature appeared to be incomplete. With history for its subject matter, the novel now had to cope with the problem of presenting a fixed reality *without* making it seem complete, since historical reality is continuous and indeterminable. It might be said that Scott's greatness lies in his ability to create the illusion of historical reality without confining that reality to the illusion he created.

[57] Concerning Scott's reception in England, see John Henry Raleigh, "What Scott meant to the Victorians," *Victorian Studies*, 7 (1963), 7 ff.

II

Immanent Esthetics and Esthetic Reflection, The Lyric as Paradigm of the Modern. From *Poetik und Hermeneutik II*

DIETER HENRICH

Art and Philosophy of Art Today:

Reflections with Reference to Hegel*

I. On the Situation in Philosophy of Art

At the present time there is only a loose connection between the philosophical discipline of esthetics and efforts to diagnose the condition of the arts today. The assumption would hardly be disputed that art and philosophical theory move forward in such a way as to permit their situation of the moment to be reciprocally illustrated and interpreted; nevertheless, scarcely any effort has been made to test the circumference and limits of this presupposition.

A project of this sort must exert itself to do two things: It must designate the basic conditions pertaining in philosophical theory today. Secondly, it must try to show that contemporary art can be made intelligible in relation to these conditions. It should do this in such a way that, except by means of the concept as worked out by theory, the endeavor would fail. And such a theory should, if not guide the interpretation of works and texts, at least be able to corroborate their interpretation and bring it into a broader context.

In such an endeavor, a possible orientation for philosophical theory is also generated. Indeed, there are good grounds for the hypothesis that philosophical theory can trace its train of thought back to legitimate sources only if these are ultimately the very sources upon which the persuasive functions of the arts are based. So the question of the interpretive power of philosophical theory in relation to contemporary art is here to be posed from the standpoint of an interest in maintaining philosophy's own contemporaneity. If this important question is ignored or denied in contemporary philosophy, then this gives weight to the claim of

---

* This paper (1964) was not written as a treatise directed to professional philosophers but for a more general audience with a main interest in criticism. The philosophical arguments which lie in its background may be found more fully elaborated in my *Fichtes ursprüngliche Einsicht* (Frankfurt, 1967); "Selbstbewusstsein," in *Hermeneutik und Dialektik*, ed. R. Bubner, K. Cramer, and R. Wiehl (Tübingen, 1970), I, 257-84; and "Selbsterhaltung und Geschichtlichkeit," in *Poetik und Hermeneutik*, ed. R. Koselleck and W. D. Stempel, v (Munich, 1972).

those who diagnose philosophy as a thing of the past, based on the symptom of the disappearance of philosophy's own diagnostic power. To them, what philosophy formerly claimed to do is now done or can be done by sociological analysis of art. But sociological analysis of art, even more than psychological, is just the beginning of a possible development which, on its side, does not claim to define historical epochs of art from their basic tendencies.

In view of this situation, it is meaningful to try to determine the situation in which philosophy finds itself today by considering its relationship to modern art. It should be mentioned here that in what follows we presuppose that contemporary art has found its valid manifestations in works which because of their opposition to customary connotations have come to be known as non-objective.

If one now inquires into the prevailing philosophical theories of today as to what implicit or explicit meaning can be gotten from them for such non-objective works and texts, one arrives at a result that is as surprising as it is instructive. The general compass of today's philosophical interpretations is far narrower than the multiplicity of theories would lead one to expect; this would suggest that such a horizon is not adequate for grasping the consciousness and dynamics of the modernity of the arts.

First, all the possibilities for interpretation seem to fall within one of two alternatives which correspond to the two main traditions of philosophical esthetics. Contemporary art can be understood as presentation of reality and mediation of insight, or as a way of arousing emotions or inducing forms of behavior. The first possibility, rooted in Platonic motifs, found its most significant formulation in the classical esthetics articulated by idealism. The other possibility stands in historical continuity with Aristotelianism and takes over essential themes from the psychological esthetics of the late eighteenth century. It is the only possible position for a theory of art in the context of logical positivism. This explains its predominance in English-speaking countries, and its large number of variants. It has certainly not been to the benefit of real progress in this area of study that in continental philosophy this second position has still been given little attention.

Positivist esthetics has only in limited measure given interpretations of what is modern, and these have been of little weight. Such interpretations could, however, have been accomplished within the basic thinking of their theory, which holds that the arts are various ways, within a self-transforming reality, to discover or to become familiar with new modes of experience. Contemporary art would then appear to be the effort to make a world of machines bearable, familiar, and the foundation of an ever-broadening feeling of life. This world of machines, of technologically prepared materials, and of a universal information which gradually dominates and deforms all language, is one to which the customary ways of living have not matured. Or, in place of this more obvious interpretation, a "crisis" theory could be advanced, according to which modern art has simply reached its limits, since it no longer succeeds in projecting generally binding and fulfillable patterns of behavior. For this reason, it is falling into a whirlpool of self-surpassing conceptions and of programs whose persuasive power is quickly left behind as obsolescent, and it stands in isolation over against society. Yet only as an established style could art be what it is in essence: immediately persuasive, and showing a sure path into the open through a reshaping of the primarily unformed emotional life. Positivist theory of art, however, as opposed to all "crisis" theories, has a natural tendency to see modern society in terms of progress, and its arts as at the forefront of this development.

For presentational esthetics in the idealist tradition, the very reverse applies: presentational esthetics seems inevitably to have to arrive at a crisis theory of the historical situation. To a philosophy of art that understands art as a presentation of the powers and forms of a world, modernity seems able to appear only as the reflection of a way of life that has become abstract and impoverished, ultimately of a disintegrating reality. So presentational esthetics, in the form of a theory of the crisis of the arts and contemporary society, has remained the only meaningful alternative to positivistic emotionalism.

The presentationalist view today is by no means restricted to the Marxist variant; rather it also extends to the opposite extreme of a neothomist conservatism. Its most significant achievements, however, are indebted to reformed Marxism, which builds on Georg Lukács and Walter Benjamin, and the Heideggerian conception of the historical situation. What is common to both the latter diagnoses, which have been carried out without contact with each other, is the conviction that contemporary art is truest when it brings forward undisguised the emptying of reality, or the self-empowering of man in conformance with the nature of his technology. They differ in that, for the Marxist the reproduction of a reality from which the inner tendencies to sham must be wrested away is already, as critique, itself a part of the power to overcome such reality, while for Heidegger, alongside the art which has declined into technological triviality, there remains possible an "essential" poetry which preserves the primordial nature of language and prepares for the advent of a new time. Both, however, do hold fast to the utopia of a coming, richer art which, like the Homeric epic, transfigures the present fallen reality and opens up a sound and healthy world in image and song.

Alongside the strictly philosophical interpretations of art, numerous philosophies formulated by artists themselves have emerged. Because most of these are tied to popular and at the same time lay-theological premises which have not attained the level of conceptuality and development of insight found in recent philosophy, they in themselves cannot be taken as an adequate explanation of the situation of art. Nevertheless, it is not good that there is scarcely a productive relationship between them and the philosophical theory of art. For, although the consciousness that expresses itself in these artist philosophies may use formulations which cannot be carried over into philosophy of art, it is still significant that this consciousness can in no way be subsumed under either of the two major positions in philosophy of art. Artist philosophies today hold fast, as a rule, to the presentational function of art, and they agree to a notable extent with the view that art today tries to bring into image and word an invisible world lying behind appearing things. For the most part, however, they are not ready to accept the theory of an ever-sharpening crisis, or to understand their task as the unmasking of the crisis through artistic dismantling of its illusions.

The artists' esthetic, then, constitutes an index of the narrowness of philosophical theory, even if it is not in a position to contribute to broadening it. Thus, the endeavor must be made to overcome a limitation to the two stark alternatives in present philosophy of art. Such an endeavor must approach more nearly the contemporary self-consciousness of the arts, and provide a possibility of seeing the most recent developments in art in a way that goes beyond the questionable schemata of either progressive degeneration or anticipation of progress. At the same time, it must let us know the reasons why philosophical theory could fall into its narrowness without at least calling into question the evidence on which the two alternative positions were based. The following considerations will make a beginning, at least, in the direction of such an endeavor.

II. On Hegel's Prognosis of Art in the Future

Hegel's theory may serve as a paradigm of a philosophy of art which seeks to make the historical present intelligible. It may serve as a model, too, in that it designates basic tendencies of recent art which have been largely left unnoticed in some of the predominant recent theories. In these tendencies, one finds elements of modernity which were already claimed in romantic theory of art, along with those which are the result of Hegel's distance from all variations of romantic theory of art. In fact, when we look at his project for itself alone, even though we are separated from it by three half-centuries, it seems to belong to the immediate present.

(1) The first of these elements is *the renunciation of a utopia* of the imagined art of the future, not simply because the utopia cannot be thought out, but, more importantly, because a utopia is in itself intrinsically incompatible with what can be thought out beforehand. Such renunciation signifies taking leave of programs of the "universal artwork" which, in an infinite progression of self-renewing reflection and mirroring, manifests itself throughout all the forms of art, as well as from Schelling's dream of the epic of the new world, in which the idealist gods of the modern age would be newly implanted into nature in some kind of last and highest synthesis. (This latter was a dream which Lukács also was to dream in his *Theorie des Romans*.) Rather, every art of the future will have to proceed from the level and stance of the contemporary consciousness, and in all future art the artist will have achieved a free relationship to his object. On this free relationship all future art will be based which does not belong to an epoch of regression in the history of man.

(2) The freedom of the artist in his *métier* arises from *reflectedness*. This reflectedness is the foundational conditioning factor in our present consciousness and life. Neither the artist nor the general consciousness prevailing in an age are confined within a certain *Weltanschauung* whose genesis and limits he cannot know. It really amounts to an act of violence to wish to be free of reflection, either through extravagant ingenuity or a firm "fixing of the mind" on some resolve that turns back to a past religiosity; and this violence punishes itself through the triviality of the works produced by it. The artist of today must proceed on the basis that reflection and criticism have become basic elements of his own practice, and he acknowledges this state of affairs in the nature of the work itself.

This concept of an art which is self-reflective, and the warning against breaking out of consciousness in fearful response to the distress at freedom (*Not der Offenheit*)—these are Hegelian concepts which are still of undiminished significance today. They enable us to see in a proper light the many efforts to ideologize art which have come forward since Hegel, and to see through the illusions of immediacy in which arts have in the past few decades sought to disclose a life world prior to all consciousness, yet with techniques which in reality are highly reflected.

(3) The level of consciousness in which art can still be contemporary brings with it the fact that the artist today has also become a *tabula rasa*

in his relation to historical forms of style. Since the artist is no longer immediately identical with any content or any form, today he relates to both, like the dramatist who represents persons alien to him. He can freely draw on the immense store of past art forms and their ways of shaping their materials, and he can make them serviceable for his own purposes. The whole history of the arts can be retrieved by him and modified to have present significance. The burden of the "imaginary museum" (Malraux) appears as the modern stigma of the freedom of the artist.

Obviously Hegel himself would rather have anticipated the Victorian rail stations in this conception than the archaism and Japanizing practiced by modern architects. This does not prevent us, however, from relating this concept also to this latter, or from supposing that a coming time will see both cases in a closer relation than ours does, which still finds itself in a transition from disdain of the nineteenth century to genuine reception.

(4) The fundamental conception found in Hegel in which the modernity of the three points above culminates is that of the *partial character* of the most recent art. It is well known that Hegel held that the end of art had arrived, and that art could no longer be regarded as the place of the unique and peculiar appearance of truth. In other words, no art work is still, as Schelling would wish to have it, the medium in which spirit comes to itself and in which, submerged in intuition, it has knowledge of its own essence. No art work, according to Hegel, is any longer adequate to the deeper requirement of self-mediation in faith and philosophy; by virtue of the higher certainty of these latter, art is relegated to a more incidental and ancillary function. Only in Greece, said Hegel, was the essential form of the art work able to stand in agreement with the essential content of consciousness, a harmony which brought art into its own as the highest form of the presence of the absolute and developed its uttermost potentialities. Since then art has made progress and may also make further progress, but the Greek epoch of its fulfillment belongs to the past.

In this familiar thought of Hegel's there lies another, hidden and inexplicit, which is well suited to help us comprehend recent art. If it remains unmentioned, it would appear that for Hegel in an epoch of deeper and more mediated self-reference of spirit, art is only surpassed, without, however, ceasing to make present in the intuition that which consciousness comprehends about itself. Art is then only qualitatively surpassed, without being restricted in its circumference. But Hegel's thinking about the end of art is not adequately presented in this way, for the form of mediation of truth in the art work also in-

volves limits within which alone art, as such, is able to bring its contents
to intuitive appearance. Greece was able to concentrate the essential content of its life in art images. But already the Christian world that followed could relate to art only within its more encompassing faith. And
the life relationships of modernity finally have become abstract and thus
are in no position to ground an appropriate integral consciousness in the
work of art. Art has not only stepped back behind other ways of awareness with which it must now attune itself; it has also in its very content
become "partial"—a part rather than the whole.

In Hegel's own prognosis of the future of the art of his time, this consequence of his thought is only in a covert way validated. Hegel foresaw
a period that would be characterized by historicism in architecture, by
the humoristic novel, and by lyric poetry in the style of late Goethe and
Rückert. These would all have in common that they are produced in full
awareness of the fulfillment and omnipotence of the spirit; they would
be works for which the whole history of art forms was freely available to
the artist, and in which the mind plays lovingly and understandingly
through everything finite without losing itself in it. Such art accomplishes the unification of the subjectivizing art, as proclaimed by the
romantics, with naturalism, whose theory Diderot had developed.

Hegel was one of the first to trace and express the potently effective
impulses within the art of his time and of his people. But his prediction
held true only for a short period of time after his death. This circumstance makes it necessary to analyze the formulae with which he wished
to decipher the inner context of these movements. These formulae easily
betray the fact that Hegel had understood art no longer as the making
present of a truth for consciousness, but more as merely the consequence of truth: Its works presuppose a knowing deepened by reflection,
a knowing of the fulfilled and fulfilling union of consciousness and actuality, and they move only within this union. They corroborate this in
application to random segments of actuality, and they mediate to us a
feeling of the all-livingness and omnipresence of a spirit that has become
aware of itself. But they presuppose an insight into the fulfillment of
this mediation whose foundation and content they themselves are in no
way able to reproduce. The external sign of this is the fact that, as over
against Christian art, these art works have been excluded from the
fulfillment of the reconciliation. In the prose of philosophical knowledge
today and of modern political life, art finds no place, not even an ancillary one.

This helps us determine more exactly the sense in which modern art is
of a partial character. For Hegel himself, this meaning does not arise
from a restriction of art to certain objects. This sense lies in its incapacity

to bring to presentation the context of actuality as something rational in itself. Art offers this meaning, in any event, through the manner in which it proceeds with a special finitude warmed and made alive by a self-certain subjectivity. But the mood of ease and sovereign peace into which art transports us takes place based on an already worked-out knowledge. On the basis of this knowledge, art wins its justification and the possibility of making itself understood; art is incapable, from within itself, of yielding place to such knowledge.

This is a matter that Hegel did not expressly carry through in its consequences. Had he done so, he would have found himself on the other side of the limits of his own theory of art. For, according to this, the intuitive presentation of truth is the defining characteristic of art as such. But if art is understood only as the consequence of truth and as a playful preservation of knowing, then the very conditions of its definition are no longer fulfilled.[1]

For this reason, it is obvious that for the sake of the consistency of Hegel's project, we must while holding to the "partial" character of modern art do so in such a way as to leave intact the function of *presentation* in the full sense of Hegel's theory. This means, of course, we are obliged to rethink Hegel's project, in which art is conceived as an activity that is following truth instead of initially bringing it to appearance.

The essential reason for trying to accomplish such a revision is that only through it do we have the prospect of disengaging Hegel's theory of art from his own short-term predictions for the art of the mid-nineteenth century. His prognosis as to the future shape of the arts simply cannot be extended into the present without becoming untenable. To the person who today traces modern art back to its roots, the range of what to Hegel appeared "the future" is now seen as just a portion of a development rising up and subsiding in longer measures of time. And so, in this respect, other premises must come into play than those found in Hegel.

With regard to these premises, it would be necessary to show, above all, whether such new premises can make Hegel's analyses intelligible without becoming dependent on other Hegelian assumptions, and whether they permit a modernistic presentational theory to be maintained while getting rid of what is captive to the past. A few steps in the direction of demonstrating this will be presented in what follows.

---

[1] Since I originally wrote this essay, I have found in unpublished manuscripts that his diagnosis of the art of the future is a late amendment to Hegel's philosophy of art. It was presented for the first time in his lectures of 1828. This fact helps to explain the inconsistency of that diagnosis with the main principles of his esthetics.

Our cursory recurrence to Hegel's theory has already allowed us to push the limits of a possible philosophical theory of modern art beyond what appeared to be possible. The philosophy of art in recent times that is probably the most significant, and certainly the most widely received, substantiates the fact that a presentational esthetics does not have to be a "mirror" theory of representation. Thus, a diagnosis of modern art which wishes to employ philosophical means is made free from ruinous alternatives: it is not obliged, in order to establish the seriousness and weight of contemporary art, either to see the basic tendency of contemporary actuality as deformation and disintegration, or, in the interest of a more appropriate understanding of contemporary actuality, to pass off the most significant contemporary art as ephemeral, destructive, and trivial. And, at the same time, the way out of this dilemma does not necessarily have to be sought through renouncing the principle of presentation in esthetics.

Presentation can, after all, be of a partial character, and just for this reason be combined with the openness, reflectedness, and historical constitution of the modern artist. In other words, the actuality which art brings to appearance does not have to be interpreted as a larger, universal actuality.

Admittedly, this result of a critical revision of Hegel does compel us to face the question of how the moment of truth peculiar to the work of art is to be more exhaustively determined. On the one hand, if it were isolated from every actuality but experienced in the mind, then one would come back to Hegel's predictions, which fall short and do not think forward fully into modernity. If, on the other hand, it were merely a random actuality, the question would remain undetermined as to what has the prerogative to be rendered present by art, and on what grounds. Cutting our ties with Hegel's concept but not with presentational esthetics will mean that we interpret contemporary art as manifestation of a *particular and significant* actuality.

Of what kind would such an "actuality" be? It appears that, unhoped and unintentionally, the revision of Hegel recommends turning back to a Platonizing esthetic. In accordance with this, the composition and inner law of any random, finite essent among others is simply made visible in art as order, agreement, and harmony. This thought can be joined with Hegel's theory in two ways: it would be possible to say that an abstract context can be presented only *in abstracto*, or, that a reconciliation that has not yet occurred can be anticipated only *in abstracto*. Both of these lines of thought yield a way of explaining the non-objectivity of recent art. Both, however, leave essential tendencies in the consciousness of modern art out of view—indeed, they omit precisely those tendencies which subsequently prove to be more important. And the thought that the nature of art itself may have experienced a striking and peculiar transformation is juggled away in favor of a harmless traditionalism.

It will be impossible to cut away the aspect of Hegel's forecast about the future of art from the general modernity of his diagnosis of recent art without reformulating his theory of art as a whole. Only one who knows the conditions under which its defects arose can begin this task of reformulation; one can make use of its foundations only when one understands the grounds on which the foundations were laid.

III. Basic Elements of the Modern in Philosophy

Wilhelm Dilthey has shown in his brilliant treatise on the anthropology of the sixteenth and seventeenth centuries that the systems of metaphysics in the seventeenth century can be understood as a rationalizing of a new view of man, a new anthropology whose most important texts had already appeared in the early sixteenth century. This anthropology was both the articulation of a new experience of the nature of life for man and a reaction against the Aristotelian tradition. Its basic principle was the Stoic conception of the self-preservation of all that exists. Out of this principle the new anthropology proposes to understand the system of the faculties of the soul, and to trace the gradual organization of human society into the state. It is probable that both the concept of the Principle of Inertia (*vis inertiae*) in the emerging new physics and the concept of the causa-sui nature of God in theology were related to or motivated by the new anthropology.

This central principle of self-preservation, although originally a teaching of the Stoics, has been of incomparably greater impact and dynamism in the modern era. The reasons for this are not to be discussed here. But they stand in close connection with implications of the Stoic notions (which for the first time received support and which concern the fact that self-preservation had reference to self-relatedness as a presupposition): because the principle of self-preservation was supposed to serve as a counteraction against the established Aristotelianism, in place of the Aristotelian concept of the relation of all things to their essential inner goals and natural position, it had to install their relation only to themselves—in other words, *reflection*.

When one takes this circumstance into consideration, it seems very improbable that the transition from renaissance anthropology to the systems of the seventeenth century was more than simply the first phase of a development which extends much further in time and which, indeed, still determines the presuppositions we hold today. In Hobbes and

Spinoza, self-preservation is the basis of a system, but without the help of its reflective essence. The elaboration of this is accomplished only in idealist speculative philosophy, which can be derived from Hobbes and Spinoza through a series of intervening stages, the most important of which are the philosophies of Leibniz and Rousseau. And even in idealism only a beginning is made at thinking out and fulfilling the consequences implicit in modern consciousness.

Just this short sketch of the development of modern philosophy is enough to make clear how wrong and misleading is the opinion advanced by Heidegger, that the self-power of subjectivity and its violent mastery of the existent as such is radicalized to an ever-increasing degree in modern consciousness. The fact is that modern consciousness from its very beginnings is far removed from mere self-empowerment; for, the experience of maintaining and enhancing oneself only in one's own being is, even in the early stages of the new anthropology, bound up with an awareness of not holding sway over this being. The self-relation of self-preservation, along with reflection on it, is what it is not through itself alone; and this fact raises the question, for reflection, of its deeper foundation. Such a foundation, however, could no longer be thought of as extrinsic, as a ground which generates the being of the self in the interest of a higher purpose. For all ontology must justify itself to self-reflection, and it is implicit in the concept of a goal that this goal can be defined only on the basis of the self-relationship of life. Thus, the experience that on account of inner principles the being of the self is related to itself and only to itself has as its complement not only the certainty of being based on a foundation not within its arena of control but also the knowledge that this foundation will remain inaccessible to it. The more the thought of man's self-relatedness and self-determining power was developed in later philosophy, the more the complementary side of this same consciousness also had to become its theme.

The double nature of the reflective being of the self demands a clarification of the interaction between the two sides and an integration of both into that unity which experience as such already presents. The developmental course of modern philosophy can be described as the succession of stages in the effort at such a clarification. Its most important problem had to be thinking the self-relation of subjective life in such a way that the rendering present of its as yet unthought ground came to stand, not as a second something alongside it, but could be comprehended within the self-relation and as a moment of its own essence.

Hegel's thought had an important place in the sequence of such efforts. He wanted to bring about the integration of both moments of subjectivity by thinking the fulfilled self-relationship as a task of the self, a task on a foundation which in its own right included both moments in itself. Thus, for Hegel the abandonment of self-reflexivity is entailed in the way in which the self finally actualizes itself.

The progress of philosophical insight following Hegel has brought the downfall of this concept. In fact, it could reasonably be said that only after that point were man's experience and a number of basic ideas of recent times grasped in distinctness and raised with full clarity as problems. For the period which began as the persuasiveness of Hegel's solution to the problem had vanished only intensified the problem in such a way that the task of mediation must now be accomplished, even though the transition from the one moment of self-experience to its other pole cannot ever seamlessly take place.

This premise, overt or covert, is a presupposition for all modern thinkers: for Kierkegaard as well as Marx, for Darwin and Nietzsche as well as Cohen and Freud. In what follows, they will serve to free Hegel's project of a theory of art in modern times from its defects, and to outline a philosophical diagnosis of the present situation of the arts.

This diagnosis cannot orient itself simply to one or the other thinker during the time since Hegel. Rather, it must specify structures of the greatest possible universality, which nevertheless are well-defined enough to allow us to understand from one context the multiple techniques, aspects, and changes of modern art. These structures should, where possible, also be designed to incorporate modern forms of thinking into the same context. In cognizance of its own history, philosophy is obliged not only to lay its own foundation, but on this basis to understand its tradition and present.

This does not mean that one should strive to unfold the contemporary philosophy of art in deductive fashion. Leaving aside the fact that the considerations which would serve as a foundation could not bear such weight, they also could not be convincing without a verification of their powers of interpretation on art itself. For to interpret the situation of the arts from the vantage point of philosophy means in equal measure that philosophy comes to an understanding of its own situation.

IV. On the Character of Art in Modern Times

The critical revision of Hegel's theory had led to the question of how the partial character of modern art could be comprehended in a different and more suitable way than that of which Hegel himself was capable. The guiding thread of the contemporary philosophy of art leads one to suspect that its proper object is the unpremeditated mediation of self and being. For Hegel this mediation was total. This distinction will seem overly formal at first, for it seems to posit a merely quantitative difference. In place of Hegelianism carried to its conclusion, it tries to substitute a Hegelianism which has been weakened in its consequences without having been expanded in its presuppositions. It should become apparent, however, that what appears to be a weakening allows us to draw conclusions which are further reaching than those which Hegel was able to draw. This state of affairs must arise when the conditions under which Hegel's thought itself was unfolded are described from Hegel's point of view. That is here the case. The most significant attempt to force the opposing experiences of modernity together serves but as a means of conceiving how they are present in its art. Taken by itself, this attempt cannot be considered decisively valid.

If mediation is called unpremeditated, this means that it must be completed without our being able to be assured of it. Mediation already corresponds thereby to previous understandings of modern consciousness. Modern consciousness, namely, is merged with itself and lives from the power of such presence, which, however, is effected for reasons which are inaccessible to and thus beyond consciousness. This structure is fundamentally different from the one in which Hegel thought to sublate all finite reflection, as well as from his concept of finitude. All moments, therefore, which belong to an unpremeditated mediation never became moments of his thought. It is precisely for this reason that his esthetics cannot make concrete patterns of modern art intelligible. It is useless to try to drive this structure beyond the limits of its capacities, as one only limits or supplements it.

The manner of mediation in relation to the mediated and the mode in which we are certain that there is a mediation both belong to the moments of unpremeditated mediation. Hegel was unable to grasp these moments with his means. These moments are developed, not for themselves, but as fundamental characteristics of modern art, in the following chapters (v and vi). We can tentatively interpret them as follows:

(On Chapter v) As soon as the problem of mediation is seen under the condition that the being of the self cannot be unfolded in its presence to itself, it becomes possible and necessary to distinguish the things mediated as such from their mediation. This means, first of all, that they are themes of mediation in one respect only, although not in a random, but in a significant, respect. In mediation, a fundamental characteristic of the self relation in the Self is brought to the fore, a characteristic which the latter covertly or overtly dominates without being identical with it. Self-motion is also more than the unfolding of this basic characteristic. This has in self-motion only the presence of an origin, which is the basis of what makes it possible as well as of its limitation. Thus, it is also possible to indicate the mediation in various ways which are of equal value. As the things mediated do not dissolve in the mediation, each can then be the verification of the mediation in a different way. Works of such mediation are, therefore, partial by virtue of what they achieve as well as how they fulfill their function. The difference between the mediated and the mediation can finally have the further consequence that the mediated forfeit their clear-cut meaning (unequivocality) in the mediation. Indeed, the mediation is immanent within them. Their phenomenal fullness is brought into suspension when mediation occurs. In the tension between their concretion and their mediation into the unpremeditated, a medial dimension opens up. It may be that the actuality of the concrete first comes to light in this tension. It can also appear, however, that the independence of the mediated is melted asunder in it.

(On Chapter VI) If mediation takes place in the unpremeditated, then it cannot attain the certainty of one who sees the completion in the *speculari* of Hegelian reconciliation. The retrogression into the presuppositions of the self which never become manifest is, to be sure, as a mediation, an affirmation of the self. It takes place, however, under the twofold condition that that which mediates remains undetermined, and that moments of uncertainty thus enter into the mediation. Only in the fulfillment of the retrogression, which may possibly have to recur constantly, and in the results which it brings into maturity for the self can it be verified. Everything affirmative in the mediation of the retrogression is accompanied, therefore, by a counterpart which holds in suspension the certainty reached. This ambivalence of the retrogression in regard to its confirmation must ultimately lead to transformations in the essence of art itself. Historically, art could generally be understood as a glorification of the visible which unfolds the play of forms in the pathos of reconciliation. More recent art, however, places the "beautiful semblance" on the boundary beyond which gloom and monotony extend. Modern art wrests from them something which indicates that the being of the self rests on an eluctable basis. It can be art most convincingly where it has become a problem to itself and has this problem as its theme.

These conclusions concerning the character of modern art are in correspondence with similar conclusions that concern the possibility of philosophical esthetics after Hegel. Presentational esthetics and the esthetics of action alone are not in a position to grasp contemporary structures of art. For any art which brings the underlying essence of the being of the self to the fore possesses to that extent the character of presentation. But it is distinguished from forms of art which correspond to the traditional presentational esthetic in two ways:

(1) It can bring neither a comprehensive relationship of actuality (Hegel) nor even the structure of the actual itself (Platonism) into pre-

sentation and intuition. It is possible only within an integral consciousness which enables such art to be. Such a consciousness needs art, but it
does not find itself encompassingly (i.e., comprehensively) made present
in it. It seems peculiar to a contemporary consciousness to know itself as
simultaneously being abroad on unbounded ways and yet constrained.
Each of these two forms of knowledge can assume a threatening character for the other. This occurs when self-motion and self-augmentation
are experienced as a meaningless restlessness which is cut off from the
origins. It occurs as well when the uncertainty of its antecedents and the
inaccessibility of the constituents of this motion appear to be a limitation
of power or the danger of its senseless rupture. Such experiences encourage escaping by a fixation of the mind which has rendered possible
the acts of violence of our century in diverse disguises such as
mythologies about the origins or utopias *par force*. But neither of these
threats can be avoided by fleeing into the arms of the other. Rather, the
real threat is the flight before that which threatens as such. Only a consciousness which settles down in the midst of the tension and which can
hold out until it succeeds in integrating the opposing elements of the
threat can turn the threat away.

Contemporary art has within such a consciousness and the task which
it takes upon itself the possibility and the function of indicating the unpremeditated mediation of its moments. It holds fast to a twofold truth
in the face of the temptation toward fixation. It maintains that subjectivity can be understood only in the mediation of its being with its motion
and that this mediation cannot be accomplished *in concreto* and in the
present. One cannot, therefore, attain the point of mediation which
makes subjectivity possible by idealizing the order of the actual. Such
idealization exhibits something, to be sure, but as a presentation of the
unpremeditated, it is interested less in the glorification of that which
concretely comes into appearance, but rather attempts to overcome and
transcend it. In bringing the basic element which dominates the life motions of subjectivity to the fore, it assumes at the same time the aspect of
a retrogression behind its everyday presence. Although it is a presentation, its efforts are nonetheless opposed to those acknowledged by traditional theories of art. Instead of transposing the actual into the essentiality of its appearance, it compels the actual to emerge from its previous
manner of appearance. The fact that art nevertheless shows thereby
what it really signifies is due to the dependence of this actuality on a
ground which precedes its appearance without the possibility of becoming manifest.

(2) If modern art is contrary to traditional presentational esthetics in
yet another way, this is a consequence of its partial character and of its

ability to bring the unpremeditated point of indifference to the fore only
as a retrogression out of appearance. By virtue of this, contemporary art
possesses certain peculiarities which are associated with the positivist
esthetics of emotion and action. It does not cease thereby to be a presentation. It cannot, therefore, be conceived as an image in the familiar
sense, nor as copying or mirroring. For modern art is just as much a
fulfillment which is opposed to the imageable and which refuses the
enjoyment in the presence of pure appearance. It indeed creates
images. But the purport of such images is to remould or even distort
the familiar and already understood, whereas, according to Aristotle's
theory, modern art would have to perfect these into their essentiality.
Worlds of images thus arise which are distinctive solely through their
mediation of a consciousness which is emancipated from imageability.
They arise from a process which runs along underneath visible objectivity. They are only fittingly perceived when they occasion a similar activity. It is necessary to attribute an *emotive meaning* to them in this
sense. Nevertheless, they present something. For the activity, from
which they proceed and which they trigger, serves only to clarify the
being of the Self.

Modern presentation approaches positivist esthetics in one further
sense. The retrogression into the unity of self and being does not leave
the integral consciousness in which it takes place unchanged. The truth
brought forth by the retrogression is indeed not the truth of all its actuality. But the experience which it effects is simultaneously an impetus
and an appeal to appropriate it anew and more adequately. The modalities by virtue of which such an impetus occurs and in which it can become effective cannot be defined for the time being. But it is clear that
they cannot be interpreted from the imageability of the image alone. Although they belong to an art which is directed toward presentation, they
nevertheless lack none of the marks which a positivist theory places
under the category of *appraisive signs* of a language related to action.

It turns out, therefore, that the attempt to take Hegel's thesis on the
state of the arts in modern times more seriously than he does also brings
with it valuable conclusions for philosophical esthetics. If the thought of
the partial character of art in an integral consciousness is more closely
determined by the retrogression into the unpremeditated unity of self
and being, then both of the positions which are meaningful in contemporary esthetics are brought together without constraint. This thought
unites them by simultaneously making possible an interpretation of recent art which lies beyond the alternative according to which the art
must be either a symptom of crisis or a medium of progress. The pre-

suppositions of such an interpretation are thereby sufficiently recommended. We must now proceed to it.

V. The Basic Structures of Modern Art

Contemporary art is a retrogression into a mediation of self and being which can come to pass neither in the self-motion of the self nor in a phenomenologically establishable actuality. For this reason it is called unpremeditated. It follows from this that such a retrogression can take place in two ways: (1) as a transposition of phenomenal givenness back to a basis which is no longer explicable and (2) as a presentation of the constrained motions of subjectivity. This distinction produces the first division of a theory of art in modern times. It is elementary and must be presupposed in all of its other essential characteristics without these having to be deduced from it.

The problem which subjectivity presents to itself is the one which lies at the basis of both forms of art. That could not be said as well if Hegel's original scheme remained valid. He wanted to present the mediation of being and self as a desideratum which arises from both in a like manner. No essent is itself until it has been liberated to subjectivity, just as an unactual subjectivity remains without essence. One can indeed consider if and how this formula can be transposed into the contemporary scene. If, however, it comprises nothing but a stage in the movement of modern thought, then Hegel's formulation must be abandoned in favor of one in which the problem of subjectivity alone produces the impetus to a more comprehensive problematic. For an attempt which remains within the range prescribed by Hegel, a retrogression into the mediating ground would be just as much a consequence of the ontological constitution of things as of the concept of subjectivity. On the contrary, a scheme which is oriented toward the origin of modern consciousness must concede a hegemony to the ontological problematic of the being of the self. It would not be difficult to exhibit this problematic in Hegel's philosophical development and in the movement of thought in his system.

This does not, however, prevent introducing both basic forms of modern art as elementary. For the twofold essence of subjectivity offers primarily a twofold outcome for the presentation of its unpresentable unity. Even if the being of the self is an inaccessible motion in itself, its unity must be rendered possible in the essent in the same way that it is in fact carried out in the self. Art will, therefore, present every essent in such a way that it points above and beyond itself to a ground which, lying beyond manifestation, is equivalent to the moment of facticity in the motion of the being of the self. By this means art will no less initiate the self-mediation of consciousness than by bringing self-consciousness to the fore in its dependence upon inaccessible facticities.

Both elementary forms of modern art correspond to the duality of two principles of style which Fritz Baumgart has pointed out in contemporary painting. His distinction of an abstract form of art from an art of expression which likewise tends toward abstraction deserves preference to distinctions such as Sedlmayr's, which opposes, as the theme of modernity, the abstract thing to an abstract form. Sedlmayr's thesis presupposes a special sort of philosophical crisis theory. According to him the modern era bears on its forehead a mark of guilt for having dissolved the *analogia entis* of spirit in the material world and for having thereby sacrificed the unity of matter and form. Baumgart's distinction not only appears to be more suitable for describing the relationships within contemporary painting, but also presupposes a freer relation to modernity and allows its accomplishments to be perceived as something other than symptoms of the agony of humanity. It commends itself to philosophers through remaining in secret agreement with the consciousness which keeps modern philosophy in motion.

The art of "abstract form" and of "pure expression" are but the most general of titles for a manifold of structures which accomplish the retrogression into the mediating ground of being and self in particular ways. Their relevance must prove itself in their power to make such structures intelligible. Some of them are to be specified in the following. Because the modern epoch does not lie before us as a finished epoch, we cannot hope for completeness. No epoch can, to be sure, be described in its fundamental characteristics without elements of prognosis arising. But not all variations of these can be anticipated, however.

(1) The art of modernity makes intuitable the ambivalence of the inaccessible autonomy in the being of the self.

(a) That can occur by the self confirming itself as a power over the natural order of things. The given is broken down into its elements. New orders are produced from them, which possess a peculiar attraction precisely because they stand in immediate contrast with the actual. They provoke a conception of a second actuality which, because it lies in the background, cannot be made concrete. It cannot be said that such works are creations of a free fancy and that they can be perceived as such. It is true that the law which presents itself in them can be made visible only through construction. The law turns out, however, to manifest an unimaginable world unity in itself in which the subjective origin of the work is latent. This order beyond the usual condition of things and meanings is no longer the order of thing-hood itself. This new order cannot be imposed upon or mastered any further by efforts of the self. It traces the opposition of both back to the peaceful unity of a common, but inaccessible, ground. All construction finds therein its justification as well as its limits. This reference to the material from which the work arises is seen in the reduction of that material to its metaphorical minimum. This, however, becomes an insurmountable obstacle to further reduction. In a pure construction, pure materiality and pure qualities of word, tone, and color stand out foremost.

(b) The same truth appears in those works which represent the inner connection of all motions of subjectivity, but without taking the way of the second actuality of things. They originate in an act of production which is spontaneous and at the same time inaccessible. It belongs to the meaning of the work itself and thus to a suitable reception of it to let them develop on their own. Unconscious mechanisms and preintentional moments of language are consciously set into motion and guardedly brought to the fore. This can, once again, take place in various ways. Expressionism thus negated the world of objects with an ecstatic retrogression into origins. This bears a distant relation to the romantic intention of liberating the creating subject through its pure deed. The surrealism, which followed expressionism, had already attained a deeper concept of the subject, whose immanent dependency caused surges of emotion to appear trivial. It was followed by more thoroughgoing attempts at unpremeditated mediation.

(c) The first two modes of an art of subjectivity are presentations of its presenceless essence which are brought into motion by the work through its activities and accomplishments. It succeeds above all in works which strive toward an order without objects. What it presents is revealed in the act of a productive subjectivity alone. But the being of the self can also become the *object* of presentation. It is revealed in its inaccessible unity when passive geneses of its motion are made visible. The temporal structure and the linguisticality of consciousness are suitable media for such works. Art does not set consciousness into the motions of its activities, but only confronts it with its own unfreedom. It is very easy, therefore, to misinterpret it as an art of impotency. It is such, however, only when the renunciation of an extravagant lust for power of the being of the self, a lust which holds its right to being to be self evident, already mounts to impotency. Partial art of the retrogressive mediation of self can itself be understood as both: it can be interpreted as a demise into the threatening ground of dark origins, or as the joy of the authorization of action from an inaccessible freedom. What it actually is and what it effects in the integral consciousness of its time remains, however, unaffected by this distinction.

Beside music, poetry appears to be the most suitable medium for the first basic form of modern art. One can find examples of its three modes in Eliot's lyrics, along with the above-named features of Dada and the Theater of the Absurd, as well as in the novel since Proust, but especially in Samuel Beckett. In painting, cubism and constructionism must be conceived as falling within the first mode.

(2) The second basic mode seems to have had an influence chiefly on the development of the modern fine arts. The works which belong to it retrace given actuality to a ground which can also be present in the self as its being. At least three possible modifications of it can be distinguished. Here we shall merely note them.

(a) Each thing as such can, when placed before an unfamiliar background, attain a second, "higher," actuality, and thereby attest to it. This is true above all for things which have been removed from a purposive or a utilitarian context. They are thus transformed from apparatuses which lie at our disposal into images which, for an obscure reason, have a peculiar meaning all their own. Subjectivity experiences a resistance to its mastery of the world in this meaning, and thereby an impetus to retrogress within itself. ("The Magic of Things")

(b) Upon release from their worldly relations, things can be combined into new associations and configurations. If this be an arranged order, then it corresponds to the first mode of subjective art. But it can also very well be an order which has grown of itself. The work can show how fragments of actuality combine of themselves into new relations. They can indicate another actuality in which the essence of things does not resist the being of the self. (Technique of Collages)

(c) Things can reveal a secret, self-like essence in other ways than through contrasts and combination into new functions. Preliminary forms of their objective actuality may be traced in them which have their own esthetic environment of colors and images. When things are so depicted, they entice us into an unimaginable and ineffable sphere of the potentiality of all that which is.

(d) One can also surpass objectivity in the direction of pure materiality. A peculiar order becomes manifest in pure materiality, in that materials, which may also be colors, are consigned to their own lawfulness. It turns out, therefore, that the material of the world of things and that of technological images come from a source which does not succeed in appearing within the system of relation of objectivity. (Posttachistic Painting)

It would hardly be possible to associate structures of works of art which differ from each other as extensively as the above-named in one train of thought if each of them could, in itself, raise the claim of making present an actuality in its entirety. Being partial is, however, common to all forms of modern art. None of them is to be understood as a presentation of the whole even if each, in its own particular way, accomplishes and evokes the retrogression into one and the same ground. That which forms the basis of the particular unity of modernity makes possible at the same time its openness for the multiplicity of forms of art, an openness which the unity of style of the historical epochs of art would not have permitted. Thus, it is not only the subjective training of the artist, but the function of his art, which makes him flexible toward experimenting with various structures without, however, breaking out of the problematic position of his work and of his time.

If being partial bestows the character of modernity on the arts, it must certainly be admitted that other sorts of works than those which possess this character completely are possible. These other forms occupy the space which, in historical epochs, belonged to the arts, in that they bring the worldly mediation of self and actuality into presentation. They are not partial in the same sense as the retrogressive art forms. For it is their intention to present an integral consciousness. They thereby forego, however, making the essential, fundamental character of consciousness into a theme. They must intimate it in silence. The contemporaneity of their presentation is thus not deduced from an unfolded consciousness. For this reason they are constantly in danger of ineffectually conjuring up a richer actuality which is already past and of accordingly gliding out of the dimension of art over into the dimension of *belles lettres* and applied art. This danger can be mastered only through a developed reflection and extensive historical training. These, however, introduce once again the other danger of destroying the unity of the pattern of the form or of pressing the work beyond the limit which separates art from science into a work which attempts to present phenomenal actuality in its own context. Two attempts at such art at its limits which have succeeded in contemporary literature are those of Thomas Mann and T. S. Eliot. If they are misunderstood, they encourage undertaking an art which understands the conditions of modern art only as signs of its weakness. Such art gives in to the temptation of seeing in the open and unpremeditated a demand for fixedness. Insofar as this fixation is only willed, it can obtain its persuasive power only through violence. A will of this sort is at work where art is reduced to the realm of the application of supposed scientific knowledge or to the position of turning back to the salutary blessings of myth. The worst happens when, in order to escape the doubts of each at once, one falls for both deceptions.

VI. Reflection in the Contemporary Work of Art

Once again it is necessary to return to Hegel. The defects of his theory are corrected by taking his thesis of the partial significance of art in contemporary consciousness in a way which, however, deviates considerably from his own. His modernism should be maintained. His modernism manifests itself above all in his renunciation of a utopia of the arts, which once again presupposes the recognition that the reflectedness of modern art is a consequence of its partial character. The reflection peculiar to art itself attains another meaning in the conception which has been developed in the meantime.

Modern art is reflective for Hegel because it belongs to an epoch of the cultivation of reflection. In contrast to Hegel's opinion, this cultivation must be looked upon as the result of the ambivalent experience of self which modern consciousness has had. That art, however, does not leave this reflection behind in order to bring unreflectedly a world produced by reflection into intuition lies rather in its being something other than a making present of a total situation. Art must above all occupy a place in a larger context, and it must do this explicitly. This occurs when art puts into effect a reduction which refuses to enter into other tendencies of contemporary actuality. Art is thereby only one element in the more general movement of reflection which is kept in motion by the problem of the mediation of being and the power of self.

If these are the reasons for demanding a cultivation of reflection from art, it can easily be seen that the space which Hegel concedes to reflection is still too narrowly circumscribed. Hegel did not allow for the reflectedness *of the work of art itself*. He could at best describe reflection as the education of the *poeta doctus* who is an artist without art's meaning for him the fulfilling of knowledge. Hegel's own theory confirms, in spite of his own intentions, that the work of art must possess the character of being reflected and of implying itself as a work of art. It is well known that his theory places art alongside faith and philosophy as means of the complete self-mediation of spirit. In this triad, art, however, lacks the essential characteristic which makes the faith of religion and the knowledge of philosophy into final forms of knowledge, beyond which it is impossible to go. In contrast to art, faith and philosophy imply themselves. Faith is simultaneously faith in salvation through faith itself and in the sanctification of the congregation. Philosophy is the concept of its method and of its system.

In Hegel's theory there is no reason for denying to art the same characteristics. Hegel's all too short-winded prognosis for the art of the future may have stood in the way of this. For, in truth, a modern work of art is reflected into itself to the same extent if not also in the same sense that Hegel only wanted to acknowledge for faith and knowledge. A modern work of art is even suited to the tendency of bringing forth works which stand in a double reflection: through their reflection on the character of being art works, and through reflection on the consequences which are necessarily bound up with the formal structures of a successful work.

(1) The reflection of art in the work is not brought about by art's refusing to build Daedalian statues which try to compete with products of nature in naturalness. That fine art should look like nature is a demand which very few epochs have heeded. And it can be convincing only when it relates to the attunement and to the self-sufficiency of the work. For the surprise at the capacity to deceive through imitation is wholly different from the experience of the work of art. Wherever art does not deny being a work, it has not yet made itself known in the work itself as art.

The modern work, however, takes itself for a theme. It wishes to show in what manner it has arisen and to bring its genesis to the fore through itself. At the same time this becomes a program. It does not mediate any ideality without simultaneously declaring that the presentation of the ideality is more essential. Its meaning is not revealed in the order of things, but rather in the manner in which order comes to stand forth and hold together. For art is a retrogression within the medium of presentation and representation which makes that which is presented visible by wresting the unpremeditated from the semblance of things.

Such art must simultaneously alter the relation of the work to the manner of its intuition. As regards its illusion, it appears at first to assure the autonomy of its reception. For it explains itself and lays claim to the reflection of the viewer, which must already come into play when the work is perceived, and not first when that which is perceived is later interpreted. The claim to reflection is, however, a call to freedom.

The same state of affairs also leads, however, to a lessening of freedom in reception. Since, namely, the work explains itself, the reflection which it demands and induces is determined by it. The freedom of observation can be restored only in a second stage which reduces the reflection itself to an element in the intuition. The work indeed pushes toward a completion of this transition. For a reflection, once set into motion, inclines toward liberating itself from every determination and toward bringing itself into its own proper distance to the thing reflected. Nevertheless, all knowledge which finally breaks away from the reflectedness of the modern work remains related and bound up with it in other ways than art of earlier times.

Cubist *peinture-peinture* (painting of the painting) was the first to conceive and realize a program of such works. Related structures also set in a little later in other branches of art.

(2) The reflection of the work as a work forms the presupposition for the possibility of a second reflection. That it must occur is a consequence of the inability of modern art to unfold itself as art without question.

As a work of art, each successful work is subject to a series of conditions which formal esthetics is quite capable of delimiting. Interpreters of art, critics, and juries have used them tacitly as criteria of quality, regardless of the epoch. A good or even a significant work must be harmonious and consistent; it must create a unity from manifold or opposing elements.

This basic form of art cannot, however, be realized without a further meaning rising above and beyond that which the work as such presents. One of the riddles which art poses is understanding how any content of art is bound to mediation through form and consequently to its connotations. Such connotations are those of rest, order, the compatibility of things to the unity of life and meaning, harmony, and reconciliation. The legitimate skepticism toward such terminology does not prevent them from being indispensable for every analysis of the esthetic structures.

The link with such connotations of form, however, has itself become a problem for modern art. For it cannot tacitly allow to come to pass the increase in meaning which results from its becoming form. Modern art is an art of reduction, and it mediates self and being beyond all manifestation. The peculiarity of this mediation is that any affirmation which lies in it can never become present as such. Any interpretation of form as presentative affirmation must be openly suppressed by the modern work.

Contemporary art is affirmative only in an integral consciousness, as it provides an orientation without representing it and its context. Thus, its mediation, as unpremeditated, is not the reconciliation of consciousness with its opposite in the intuition of an absolute. So different is this mediation that not even a missing presence can be made present abstractly or symbolically without the meaning of recent art being transformed into its opposite. The mediation, which factually does result, occurs with the consciousness that the indifference of self and being can just as easily mean the selflessness of the self as the self-like character of being. The self has in this ambivalence the essence which it has first come to experience in modern times. This essence is made present to it in the movement of retrogression of modern art and, to be sure, such that it can accomplish the mediation of its essential moments into a unity without compelling their reduction to one or the other.

Contemporary art, therefore, can only maintain its truth by retracting its claim to be art and nevertheless not ceasing to be art. It must deny the connotations of form within itself. If contemporary art became formless and accordingly thoroughly rejected mediation, it would throw away its entire truth just as much as if it were to conjure the self-like mediation in unbroken form. Contemporary art must be form and the breach of form at once and through this unity allow both of its elements of significance to oscillate against each other. Each opposite denies the other, but does this nevertheless within the other.

Thus, the endeavor of contemporary art becomes the apparently paradoxical striving of form against itself. Form structures are supposed to arise which destroy the associations of meaning of form but are nonetheless completed forms. Breach of form thereby becomes a principle of composition. Something quite other than the titanic striving beyond the limits of finite forms or the wreck of greatness at the boundary of traditional forms is brought to completion in such art. For the first time such failure is not a testimony for art transcending itself or being a state on its way to an Absolute. The intention of modern art is fulfilled in the broken form. It establishes therein a principle of form all its own, whose potentialities cannot be surveyed at present.

It had already resulted from the reflectedness of the work as such that the relation of the work to the observer had to be a different one than that which holds in traditional art. Reflection was also implicated in the observation. The same thing occurs once again, but in a more significant manner, in the exertion of art against the form. The first reflection still allowed the possibility of the freedom of the observer, even if the first reflection gave this freedom a character other than that which the traditional division of interpretation and intuition implies. Reflection on the meaning of form, however, leads to the genesis and the technique of the work's no longer being the sole object of the work. It now includes the question as to its meaning and to the possibility of being suitably perceived. It does not thereby integrate reflections into a pleasing form in which reflections could be played off against or suffused with other reflections. It forces a process on consciousness which can no longer be brought into esthetic distance. For all reflections by means of which that could occur have been woven into the work and therewith eliminated as means of distancing. The modern work gains thereby an intensity which, even if with an entirely altered meaning, appeared to be reserved to the mythical epochs of the arts and which the art of modern times, emancipated from the religious sphere, could not have previously.

The reflectedness of modern art also works out a special way of developing its basic structures. Every form in which a state of consciousness takes shape is capable of explication. And it requires explication, partially for unfolding the possibilities which lie within it, but, even more, in order not to lose its evocative force in habituation. The original evidence and meaningfulness of the form can be maintained only when it can be successfully modified and made visible in a new originality. This dynamism is hermeneutically conditioned and is just as valid today as ever. The reflectedness of the modern form suggests, however, experiments with form which cannot be understood by means of such a dynamism. For where the emergence of a work becomes its theme, a modification of form means bringing about a new manner of emergence. Moreover, the reflection of the observer is implicit in such works. The unrest of reflection accelerates the process of form variation on this account. It is conjointly responsible for the hectic motion of surpassing oneself, from which motion the critics of modernity can most easily derive their arguments. It does not, however, prevent the success of the intensifications of modern form, nor does it hinder them from occurring neither more seldom nor more frequently than in past epochs of art. They certainly oppose everything which has gone before with a radicality previously unknown. They remain, notwithstanding, modifications of a situation whose peculiarity demands reflected works, which are theme and program for themselves.

The lines of the development of art in modern times have certainly become more diverse and intertwined. Its partial character conditions its capacity to be entirely itself in diverse forms. And its fundamental problem is overlaid with that of the doubled reflection which results from it as its consequence. Even these reflections in the work have their own history of development. On this account, it becomes increasingly difficult to exhibit a unified continuity of modern art in linear developments.

We have no reason for holding the possibilities of modern art to be exhausted or thinking their exhaustion near. One succumbs to an illusion such as the theory of a radical crisis if one believes that modernity is racing toward its end and stands before the alternative of either emptying out life or of an art from a new source. The consequences of the second reflection have hardly been comprehended in their beginning, even though it cannot be expected that its greatest achievements will be immediately followed by others of equal magnitude.

The hope for a world art of free originality which has gotten away from the blemish of reflection must be counted among the self-delusions of the philosophy of art of our time. It is predominant wherever this theory of art has gone the farthest and also wherever it is paired with the greatest sensibility toward contemporary art. One of the goals of this essay has been to search out the reasons for it and to enable us to dispense with them.

There is no reason for suspecting that the art of the future could free itself from partiality and reflection. Actually, there is no motive for longing for such a liberation from the essential. If having to produce himself and to bring himself into his essence is peculiar to man, it is nevertheless only so in that he becomes simultaneously a problem for himself. Even art, as self-mediation, arises from such a foundation and has, in modern reflectedness, comprehended and realized itself more than before. The way of modern art can, to be sure, lead it to stagnation and crises which allow it to dream the dream of the past even though the actualization of this dream would only mean collapse. If, however, the way leads farther, then it leads through and beyond contemporary art without leading back behind it. The goddess in the olive tree can appear to be the lost truth only until the statue of Athena is successfully completed.

Modern art is certainly threatened from many sides. It fits into an integral consciousness in a different way than ever before. Modern art can form and intensify itself only if the meaning of art is changed at the same time. It requires, therefore, a public which executes such a change. This public must overcome the temptations of fixity of mind, as well as of habituation in the art of the past, which is already mediated with reality and only therefore enjoyed. Modern art contains an evocative moment which can only be carried out in a consciousness which has, at its disposal, another orientation than that which it receives from art. On this account, modern art can very easily be misunderstood. Such misunderstanding is present above all when art conceives itself to be a sphere of freedom which arranges for itself a world beyond the actual and its constraints, and makes possible the existence of an enjoyable connoisseurship. This connoisseurship thus reflects itself out of the reflection of actuality. As such, it is the correlate of a society which remains largely indifferent to the evocations of art, a society which cannot yet grasp and fulfill the potentialities and demands of modernity.

WOLF-DIETER STEMPEL

Syntax and Obscurity in Poetry:

On Mallarmé's *A la nue accablante*

"Guerre à la rhétorique et paix à la syntaxe!" With this war-cry Victor Hugo declared, in his oft-quoted *Réponse à un acte d'accusation* (1854), donning the mantle of a romantic Malherbe ("Alors . . . je vins . . ."), that he had brought about a "quatre-vingt-treize" in French literature. Concerning the nature of his campaign against rhetoric, Hugo tells us two things: at his very appearance, he says, all metaphors fled in terror to hide beneath the robes of the "Académie, aïeule et douairière"; but at the same time he lets us know, as so often in his lyrical language, that in this war he was fighting, so to speak, on both sides. In the light of this, one can only guess what fate he had devised for syntax. Immediately before the war-cry, he had laid his curse on "les Bouhours, les Batteux, les Brossettes," who "à la pensée humaine . . . ont mis des poucettes," and from this one can assume that it was to be a syntax untroubled by purists and pedants, allowing the poet a free hand in exploiting all its stylistic possibilities.[1] And so Victor Hugo also regards it as an achievement to have made "un jacobin du pronom personnel, Du participe, esclave à la tête blanchie, Une hyène, et du verbe une hydre d'anarchie." We need not go into the precise significance of this statement here. French poets of the next generation did not strive after "revolutionary" attainments of this nature, but they, too, had a new attitude towards syntax which helped form the foundations of modern "obscure" poetry, and found its ultimate fruition in the work of Mallarmé.

In order to understand the importance of syntax in the development of modern poetry, we must first look closely at two fundamental questions. The first concerns poetic forms of syntax in relation to poetic *obscuritas* (a); the second, the dividing line between these forms and non-syntactic methods of poetizing (b).

(a) The most important group under this heading—and the only one we shall be concerned with here—deals with the way in which individual parts of a statement are brought together. Classical *ornatus* figures, which outside literary and poetic texts are put in a standardized order,

---

[1] Cf. G. Antoine, *La Coordination en français*, I (Paris, 1959), p. 65.

can be shifted to create a totally new relationship. The purpose of this technique is to restrict the directness with which information is conveyed, and to guide the reader's attention, to a greater or lesser degree, towards the artistic *modus dicendi;* the separation of elements that normally belong together, or the inversion of normal thought processes, leads to the creation and subsequent relaxation of tension. A simple example of this is *anastrophe,* such as inversion of the genitive attribute:

> Pour moi, qui ne pourrais y mêler que des pleurs,
> D'un inutile amour trop constante victime . . .
>
> Racine, Bérénice, 1, 4

> Oh! de pôles, d'axes, de feux,
> De la matière et du fluide
> Balancement prodigieux!
>
> V. Hugo, Magnitudo parvi

> Sale, inutile et laid comme une chose usée,
> Il faisait des enfants la joie et la risée.
>
> Baudelaire, Châtim. de l'orgueil

> De vos forêts et de vos prés
> O très paisibles photographes!
>
> Rimbaud, Ce qu'on dit au poète

An even wider range of complications is offered by *hyperbaton:*

> De ce juste devoir sa piété contente
> A fait place, seigneur, aux soins de son amante.
>
> Racine, Bérénice, 1, 4

> Enfant, comme deux hirondelles,
> Oh! si tous deux, âmes fidèles,
> Nous pouvions fuir . . .
>
> V. Hugo, Magnitudo parvi

> Que j'aime voir, chère indolente,
> De ton corps si beau,
> Comme une étoffe vacillante,
> Miroiter la peau!
>
> Baudelaire, Le serpent qui danse

A second category is made up of forms of contraction, through which certain parts of the statement—generally of a functional nature—are left out, and the reader himself has to supply the missing links in order to complete the implied message (unless the poet is actually aiming at ambiguity or incompleteness). Apart from certain exceptions such as syntactic zeugma, we are not concerned here with ornamental figures of speech, but with intensive forms of verbal expression which, depending on the degree of evocativeness, can give rise to a poetic effect. Common constructions such as participial clauses, in which the implicit and the explicit often amount to the same thing, are not so relevant here as, for instance, contractions for the sake of emphasis, giving force and expression to the dynamic impulses of the mind. Cf. Victor Hugo, in *Magnitudo parvi*:

> Monde rêve! idéal réel!
> Lueurs! tonnerres! jets de soufre!
> Mystère qui chante et qui souffre!
> Formule nouvelle du gouffre!
> Mot nouveau du noir livre ciel!

There are also unemphatic types of contraction which can sometimes be used to create a special effect.

Between the two categories we have dealt with so far, there is an important difference. Forms of contraction may be quite arbitrary, whereas the effectiveness of, for instance, hyperbaton depends on the extent to which it diverges from the norm, and is therefore inseparably linked to normative syntax. The mere fact that such figures of speech have *official* names is an indication that in certain contexts, or in a particular literary *genre*, they can themselves have a kind of normative character. However, we must bear in mind that the term *hyperbaton* refers only to a linguistic technique, and the question naturally arises as to where and when one can put a limit on divergence from the syntactic norm. In other words, what restrictions are there on individual poetic freedom, either from the point of view of intelligibility, or from that of recognizable usage of language? The scope of this question is too large for it to be dealt with in detail here, but one thing that does seem certain is that the answer will not depend merely on the conveyance of information; this is obvious from the fact that many types of freedom are attributed to particular epochs, after which they have lost their esthetic validity but not their intelligibility. Thus Dámaso Alonso observed, of a particular form of hyperbaton used by a nineteenth-century Spanish poet, that it would be "esthetically impossible" for a modern poet to use the same construction.[2] The same applies to constructions like "j'ai la chanson chantée," to be found in seventeenth-century poetry, but no longer used by the lyrical poets of the Romantic era. Furthermore, the possibilities of hyperbaton were never so extensively exploited by French poets of the

---

[2] *La lengua poética de Góngora* (Madrid, 1935), p. 178.

sixteenth and seventeenth centuries as by their contemporaries in Spain; as far as one can judge, those types used in French poetry remain well within the limits imposed by intelligibility. If, then, from a historical point of view, we are dealing with changing esthetic norms, nevertheless we can say that these norms can, in retrospect, be transcribed, but the extent of new creative freedom cannot be determined *in advance*.

The situation is different with the constructions of our second category. These are not in opposition to normative syntax; but, in varying degrees, they dispense with its support in order to convey impulses more powerfully through unfettered language. Unlike set figures of speech, they are not so dependent on historical changes in the linguistic norm, but in many cases can even transcend time. Far more complicated is the question of their poetic character. While to a certain extent the figures are automatically endowed with a degree of poetic effect—as becomes obvious the moment they are used in ordinary prose, for instance— forms of contraction are quite lacking in any specifically poetic features; they are as much a part of everyday language as of poetic language, and depend entirely on their context for any poetic effect they may have. In the right context, of course, they may then be far more effective than the set figures. If, for instance, we remove the exclamation marks from the Hugo quotation, and replace them with commas and full stops, then the motivating force of emphasis will be lost; as a result, there will arise a huge area of indeterminacy, in which all kinds of connections will be formed and then dissolved, perhaps without ever arriving at any single consistent pattern. This state of oscillation is richer in meaning and in mystery than a simple, emphatic contraction, and this is why the relevant syntactical technique is so apposite to modern poetry (we shall come across a good example of this in our analysis of the Mallarmé poem).

(b) In considering poetic effects based on syntax, one must naturally draw a dividing line between them and expressions that have no real connection with syntax. Apart from such obvious cases as archaism, cultism, etc., there are those figures that are concerned exclusively with content or with meaning. The fact that connections also come into play in this context as well has sometimes led to the assumption that syntax is involved here, too. But if one considers carefully the nature of *hysteron proteron* (inversion of the chronological order of events), of parenthesis, or of semantic zeugma (these correspond more or less to the set figures of speech mentioned above), one is bound to come to the conclusion that syntax remains quite unaffected by them, in just the same way as a metaphor makes its point independently of syntactic connections. Syntactically speaking, it does not matter in the least whether Achilles was a "lion" or a "hero" in the battle. Even the *hypallage* or *enallage* of an adjective must ultimately be categorized as a figure of speech; the observation that in Goethe's phrase "des Knaben lockige Unschuld" the adjective *lockig* really belongs to *Knaben* and not to *Unschuld*, cannot be based on any functional, syntactical evidence, but is purely and simply a matter of content or of logic.[3] Indeed, it can be regarded as at least debatable whether, from an esthetic point of view, such an observation can be justified at all;[4] one need only think of the phrases, quoted by Hugo Friedrich, "rotgefärbten Wiesen" and "blaugefärbten Bäume," such as were demanded by Baudelaire and accomplished by Rimbaud.[5] Here there is no context (the function of the *Knaben* that precedes *lockige Unschuld* is quite unmistakable), and so it is a waste of time to try and work out what imaginary attribute has given rise to these puzzling adjectives, and it is utterly irrelevant to talk of a displacement of adjectives. Syntax remains quite untouched by all this; it is not even put under any strain—indeed, it is only "correct," normal syntax that can make these figures of content effective.

At this point, before we turn our attention to Mallarmé, we must look briefly at earlier forms of poetic *obscurities*. It will suffice if we just take one poet who in fact is often linked with Mallarmé—Góngora. Of great help in this context are the studies by Dámaso Alonso, who was the first to shed light on the obscurity of Góngora.[6] The most common form of syntactic alienation in Góngora is hyperbaton, and this is the prime factor in the obscurity of, especially, his second period.[7] The transpositions are far more complicated than those of the French examples we have quoted, and, even if one allows for the fact that the comparatively fluid word order of Spanish sentences favors this technique, nevertheless the extent to which he split up his nouns and adjectives, his verbs and negative particles, etc., led to the accusation that this Andalusian poet had offended the spirit of the Spanish language. It is also worth mentioning that the figures of our second category, the contracted forms such as par-

[3] This example is taken from H. Lausberg, *Elemente der literarischen Rhetorik* (München, ²1963), 103 (§315).

[4] Cf. the discussion between Vossler and Croce on the sentence "The round table is square," which Croce said was meaningless. Vossler was probably right to say that what he called the *mathematical absurdity* was meaningless in the sphere of esthetics, where *nothing can be excluded a priori*. Above all, he is right to claim that a grammarian could accept the sentence completely. Cf. *Carteggio Croce—Vossler 1899-1949* (Bari, 1951), pp. 84 et seq. Croce's attitude explains why Mallarmé remained inaccessible to him. Cf. L. de Nardis, *Mallarmé in Italia* (Milan, 1957), pp. 69 ff. See also note 14.

[5] H. Friedrich, "Die Struktur der modernen Lyrik," *Rowohlts Deutsche Enzyklopädie*, xxv (Hamburg, 1956), pp. 42, 62.

[6] Particularly in the work already quoted, *La lengua poética de Góngora*.

[7] D. Alonso, pp. 177, 201.

ticipial clauses and certain noun phrases, gain in significance as well.[8] But this is the full extent of Góngora's syntactic individuality. We need not take into account the complicated sentence construction, which often contributes to the obscurity of the text; if this is regular, which is always the case here,[9] then the complication is only gradual; if it is irregular, the cause will not be found in the construction as such, but in the relevant figures of speech or contractions, which take on an even greater effect of alienation when incorporated into a larger sentence. In brief, we can say that the difficulty of Góngora's poetic language is purely quantitative in character: it arises out of his exploitation of the rich qualitative possibilities of, in particular, hyperbaton, and out of the frequency with which he employs this figure.[10] But an obscurity that arises out of addition can be reduced by a simple process of subtraction, and so a clear understanding of the syntax of a Gongorian text, even though it is bound to take time, is nonetheless always attainable.

It is worth noting that in those poets who paved the way for modern "obscurity," we do not find any such alterations of syntax. It has often been pointed out that in Baudelaire and Rimbaud the sentence construction is "normal" and the syntactic framework solid and firm.[11] There are also plenty of exhortations, particularly by Baudelaire, that true poetry must have a "flot régulier: tout ce qui est brusque ou cassé lui déplaît."[12] That this precept was put into practice can easily be seen from the poems themselves. And here one is struck by the fact that only familiar syntactic means of alienation such as hyperbaton are used, and these are reduced to very few forms, and are employed only rarely (the examples quoted from Baudelaire and Rimbaud are exceptional). This may well be due to an aversion to that kind of poetizing, regarded as "parasitical," which depended on a number of set figures, such as anastrophe, that belonged to the inventory of poetic language right up to the Romantic period (Rimbaud's "De vos forêts et de vos prés O très paisibles photographes" was certainly meant as a parody). But in this very aversion, in the levelling out of poetic language and its liberation from complicated figures, we can see the first stage of a new development in the function of syntax: it is to give formal clarity to an obscure content. The idea that an obscure style is enhanced by a syntactic clarity finds confirmation in the works of Nerval, Baudelaire, and particularly Rimbaud. To a certain extent this is an inversion of Góngora's poetic

---

[8] D. Alonso, pp. 162 ff.

[9] *Ibid.*, p. 131, and *Estudios y ensayos gongorinos* (Madrid, 1955), pp. 88-90.

[10] Cf. *id.*, *La lengua poética de Góngora*, pp. 210 et seq., 218, 219.

[11] Cf. R. Vivier, *L'originalité de Baudelaire* (Brussels, 1952), reprint, pp. 45 et seq.; H. Friedrich, pp. 45, 56, 63, 67, et al.

[12] *Œuvres complètes* (Pléiade, 1961), p. 698.

technique: there, the simplicity of content is a pre-condition for the obscurity of form, the complexity of the syntax; but for Baudelaire and, in particular, Rimbaud the new type of poetic communication is linked to a simple and "correct" arrangement of language. Góngora is, as Dámaso Alonso states, difficult but clear; the forerunners of modern poetry prior to Mallarmé are clear, but—in content—difficult; the vital difference is that in the first case the quantitative difficulty can be broken down, whereas in the second the difficulty is qualitative, and hence irreducible. This will explain why, apart from all historical considerations, modern poetry did not immediately follow the course of combining difficult language with difficult content: there is no path leading from quantitative to qualitative difficulties; Góngora's road was a cul-de-sac. However, once the initial step has been taken towards qualitative obscurity and ambiguity—in other words, taking content as the starting-point—then it is possible also to take the second step of incorporating syntax in the overall mystification. Mallarmé made use of this possibility.

The poem that is the basis of our syntactical interpretation is one of Mallarmé's later works. It was first published in May 1895 by the magazine *Pan*, founded in the same year by O. J. Bierbaum in Berlin. It reads:[13]

> A la nue accablante tu
> 2 Basse de basalte et de laves
> A même les échos esclaves
> 4 Par une trompe sans vertu
>
> Quel sépulcral naufrage (tu
> 6 Le sais, écume, mais y baves)
> Suprême une entre les épaves
> 8 Abolit le mât dévêtu
>
> Ou cela que furibond faute
> 10 De quelque perdition haute
> Tout l'abîme vain éployé
>
> 12 Dans le si blanc cheveu qui traîne
> Avarement aura noyé
> 14 Le flanc enfant d'une sirène.

This sonnet is regarded as one of the most difficult of all his works.[14] It is immediately obvious that the difficulty is not only a matter of our not

---

[13] Quoted from the Pléiade edition of the *Œuvres complètes* (Paris, 1951), p. 76.

[14] H. Charpentier in: *Nouvelle Revue Française*, 27 (1926), p. 544. Croce, in a discussion of the ten interpretations of E. Noulet (cf. the following note), chose this particular

understanding the meaning of the poem; it is also due to the fact that the basis of understanding, the use of language as a means of communication, is made so questionable. Let us begin by having a look at those elements of the poem that seem to offer some sort of starting-point for an interpretation.

The first thing that strikes one is the fact that, apart from the parenthesis in the second quatrain, and the full stop at the end, the poem is completely devoid of any punctuation. And so, on the positive side, we can say that the sonnet may be regarded as a single sentence; on the negative, we cannot pinpoint any clear divisions within the sentence. The importance that punctuation can assume becomes obvious when we examine the form of the parenthesis: (tu le sais, écume) as opposed to (tu le sais écume); here the absence of the comma would also be relevant, and would ensure the clarity of the statement, assuming that the isolation through punctuation of "mais y baves" were proof that punctuation was used in principle within a parenthesis. As there is no punctuation of this sort in the rest of the text, there is no such determinant factor, and so, theoretically, one could for instance understand line 14 as "le flanc, enfant d'une sirène."[15]

However, our understanding of the syntax is not totally blocked by this lack of punctuation, for the division between units of meaning can also be established through certain words. For example, a certain orientation is given by *Quel* at the beginning of the second quatrain and *Ou* at the start of the following tercet. Then there are several syntactic groups of different sizes that can easily be divided off from the rest: the construction of lines 2 and 4 seems as clear as that of the second quatrain as a whole, or the section "faute . . . haute" (lines 9 and 10). Of course,

---

poem as a basis for his ironic comments on Noulet's interpretation, and also as an illustration of the meaninglessness of Mallarmé's verse (. . . *il complesso di parole e di rime che il Mallarmé ci ha messo innanzi . . . , manca della profonda chiarezza ed univocità che è della poesia*, in: *Quaderni della critica*, v [1949], p. 97).

[15] In a later edition of the sonnet (1902), the two commas of the original text have been left out; cf. E. Noulet, *Dix poèmes de Stéphane Mallarmé. Exégèses* (Lille-Genève, 1948), pp. 132 et seq.; in this case, the overall syntactic ambivalence also applies to the parenthesis. It is worth noting in this context that the absence of punctuation in Mallarmé's poetry, at least in his later poems, is in contrast to his prose, which, as has often been remarked, is "hacked to pieces" by commas, or "atomized" by punctuation marks. Cf. W. Naumann, *Der Sprachgebrauch Mallarmé's* (Marburg, 1936, p. 185, and L. Spitzer, in *Stilstudien*, II, unchanged reprint (Darmstadt, 1961), p. 349, note 2. This difference, which we cannot go into fully here, may be attributed to the general freedom of prose language, which Mallarmé counters by frequent interruptions of the flow; his prose writing is mainly conditioned by a content that is more closely geared to communication, though of course the excessive chopping up into smaller and smaller units of communication gives this content an element almost of deformity.

after we have recognized the few syntactically coherent passages, our troubles really begin. If, for instance, we return to the line already mentioned, "le flanc enfant d'une sirène," is *enfant* in apposition to the metonymic *flanc*,[16] standing for *homme*, or is it attributive?[17] Is this syntagma to be understood as the subject[18] (in which case *cela que* in line 9 should be related to *noyer*) or as the object?[19]

Doubts of this kind are perhaps not unduly disturbing; with arguments that are largely independent of the possible meaning of the poem, one can make out a case for preferring one particular solution, even if one cannot call it the authoritative solution. The translation of *flanc* as *sideswipe* incongruously transfers the *flanc* of the presumed agent to the recipient; the linking of *flanc* with the definite article makes it unlikely that in this context it can be interpreted simply as "pars pro toto" ("Man"). But all too often one seeks in vain for convincing arguments. "Basse (de basalte . . .)" can be a noun and so a metaphor ("Abyss"), or an attributive adjective qualifying *nue*.[20] "A même (les échos)" can be explained as "même aux . . . ," but can also be regarded as a prepositional phrase[21] (cf. "taillé à même le roc"); the idea of inversion, assuming a parallelism to "A la nue," is questionable, and in any case this, too, cries out for interpretation. "Dans le si blanc cheveu" (line 12) fits equally well as an adverbial qualification to "aura noyé" and to "abîme . . . éployé (*Dans* . . .). *Cela* (line 9) is quite vague, and could be regarded as a demonstrative or as a verb;[22] and even if one excludes the latter possibility, one still does not get very far. Small wonder that, with such vagueness, one editor finally imposed his own reading and printed "Tu/ . . . / As même."[23]

---

[16] Cf. K. Wais, *Mallarmé* (Munich, 1952), pp. 751 et seq. ("der Leib, welcher der Sohn einer Sirene war"), and Lit. Also p. 582.

[17] See most recently J. P. Richard, *L'univers imaginaire de Mallarmé* (Paris, 1961), p. 125, and most other interpreters.

[18] Wais's paraphrase, p. 582: "was hier ertränkt worden sein mag durch den wutentbrannten Flankenhieb einer mädchenhaften Sirene" (What may have been drowned here through the enraged sideswipe of a child-like siren).

[19] The most common view, also considered by Wais, pp. 751 et seq.

[20] The first explanation of S. Johansen, *Le symbolisme* (Copenhagen, 1945), p. 326—though he also speaks of a "périphrase pour les nuages," as does de Nardis, pp. 72, 73.

[21] The interpretation given by de Nardis, pp. 72, 73 ("fuor di dubbio . . .").

[22] Later interpretation by de Nardis, pp. 72, 73.

[23] Cf. Noulet, p. 132. The version of the sonnet printed in Croce's ironic discussion of Noulet's exposition, *Quaderni della critica*, 5 (1949), pp. 94 et seq., is also distorted (*trombe*, l. 4, *blanc enfant*, l. 14, a colon after *dévêtu*, l. 8, a comma after *éployé*, l. 11). But since in other cases there is no apparent interpretative intention (cf. *basalthe*, *sépulchral*, *dévêtu*, *éployé*), and also Croce bases all his comments on the original version (cf. p. 96 on "fianco"), this may well be due entirely to incompetent printing.

More disconcerting is the problem of trying to make out the overall construction of the poem. Here it is of little use to us that we were initially able to discern a few syntactic groups, unless we can find out their connections to one another or to the general composition. E. Noulet (*op. cit.*, p. 134 et seq.) follows H. Charpentier[24] in reversing the order of the two quatrains ("Quel . . . naufrage . . . abolit le mât . . . , naufrage tu à la nue accablante"), which makes it difficult to connect up the alternative "Ou cela que. . . ." Naumann's interpretation is more satisfactory, making "Quel naufrage" a nominative clause dependent on *tu*, thus also coordinating the tercet (*cela* in this case heralding the second nominative clause introduced by *que*).[25] But then how is one to understand *tu*? Certainly not, as de Nardis thinks, in conjunction with *A* as a predicate to an inverted *la nue*,[26] but as a contracted form, dispensing with the usual substantiation of an exclamation mark. When are the two possibilities kept secret (*tu*)—in the past, in the timeless present, in the future? Is something being kept secret, or is something to be kept secret? The uncertainty, which cannot be reasoned away, is symptomatic of the new syntactic situation to be found in Mallarmé's later works. We come across structures which we think we recognize as hyperbaton, only to find that we are no longer in a position to measure the degree of dislocation, as there is no clear point of reference. In this confusion we can only seek refuge in our discernment of the fact that this new system of "connectabilities" offers no such thing as a hyperbaton with a recognizable, calculable divergence from the norm, that the familiar *déterminé-déterminant* relation generally no longer applies, and that as a result normal relations must also be newly assessed. The obvious and inevitable consequence of this continual uncertainty is that, to a far greater extent than ever before, non-syntactic factors increase in value, produce their own connections, and thus either confirm or contradict connections suggested by the syntax. First among these factors is the attraction of neighboring words with similar sounds—a principle through which the poem takes on "richness" or an "undercurrent of meaning" (Poe).[27] Even on a first reading of the sonnet, one is aware of a number of echoes, and these become even more apparent on closer inspection: line 2 is very closely akin to *accablante*, whose two oral *a* sounds are echoed in duplicate, while the most important consonants, enclosing the accented syllable (*bl—t*), undergo a kind of double semantic epexegesis ("Basse de

---

[24] In *Nouvelle Revue Française*, XXVII (1926), p. 544.   [25] Pp. 67-69.
[26] "*L'opprimente nube—ha taciuto direttamente agli echi schiave . . . ,*" p. 73.
[27] Cf. R. Jakobson, "Linguistics and Poetics," in *Style in Language*, ed. by Th. A. Sebeok (New York/London, 1960), pp. 371 ff. Concerning sound textures that establish their own meaning, see also Friedrich, p. 37.

basalte et de laves": b—b—lt—$[d]$ l), and are themselves arranged like a reflection (b—alt / d—lav). In line 3 there is an almost telescopic arrangement of consonants: "les échos esclaves" (l—z—k / z—skl); in line 4, "par une trompe sans vertu," the system is actually in three parts (p—r / tr—p / v—rt); in line 5, "Quell sépulcral naufrage" links up k—l / —$lkra$— (f)ra; and in fact practically every line contains examples of these connecting "undercurrents," and indeed towards the end these extend over several lines (11, 12, 14): "l'abîme—éployé" (lab / $plwa$), "dans le—blanc" ($dãl$ / $blã$), "le flanc enfant" (l—$flã$—$fã$). In addition there are internal rhymes such as nue / tu (line 1), $sais$ / $mais$ (line 6) etc. Obviously these sound-echoes produce no more in the way of communication than the parallelism, equivalence, or contrast of the activated semantic units, but in the circumstances the technique seems to take on a greater significance, evincing a new form of poetic communication which at the same time presupposes a new form of comprehension.[28]

The fact that the individual connections do not converge into a single clear function certainly does not mean that all is chaos or that it is impossible to establish any syntactic coherence at all—as we have already seen in this poem. The syntactic freedom that characterizes the new system is not a freedom *from* the rules of syntax, nor is poetic freedom in the manipulation of language a mere license which the individual can find offensive or can magnanimously forgive, according to his temperament; this is a freedom leading *to* a new esthetic convergency. Inevitably, this freedom can be valid only within the work itself, and is "poetic" through the very fact that it becomes comprehensible by means of the convergency, for clearly the "meaning" of the poem is not contained in any concrete, factual information ("the transmission of information is secondary to the manner of presentation," as E. Stankiewicz recently said, echoing the old principle of Russian formalism).[29] If our main impression is of an interdependence of incomplete discernments, this is the result of an analytic grasp of elements of effect, which crystallize on a suprainformative level into a new poetic substance; in this, the "mot total, neuf, étranger à la langue et comme incantatoire,"[30] lies the individual esthetic quality of the poem.

[28] Sound attraction also has a semantic counterpart: ambiguous words bring about associations with particular spheres that are illustrated by dominant word-groups. Thus *Basse* (l. 2) could belong to the acoustic sphere of "bass instrument" evoked by tu—$échos$—$trompe$, or to the *naufrage* image ("abyss," "reef")—though because of the context the first possibility does not merit consideration; Johansen and de Nardis have settled for the second, cf. note 20.

[29] Cf. his contribution "Linguistics and the Study of Poetic Language" to the collective volume *Style in Language* (see above, note 27), p. 73.

[30] Mallarmé, *Variations sur un sujet*, Pléiade edition of *Œuvres complètes*, p. 368.

In order to elucidate the syntactic structure of this sonnet in the sense indicated, we should, of course, have to give a complete interpretation, taking into consideration every single element of effect. Here we must be content just to observe a few salient points.[31] However vague and mysterious may be the connections between the different sections of the poem, the effect achieved by the individual elements that make up the overall picture is clear and concrete. Cloud, rock, sea—shipwreck, sea-bed—death of a siren: these form a poetic and coherent landscape, which is animated in a rich variety of ways through a polarity of attributes or actions. Contrasted with things of a blurred or changing outline (*nue, écume, abîme*) are the sharp contours of *trompe, mât dévêtu, flanc*; there are spatial oppositions such as "high—low" (*suprême, mât, [perdition] haute—sépulcral, abîme*), intensified in such combinations as *nue / basse*, perhaps *perdition haute*, or, if one accepts Richard's interpretation,[32] *basalte = basse + alte* "high"[33]; "narrow—broad" (*cheveu, mât—abîme éployé*) is another of these oppositions; soft things contrast with hard (*nue, écume, cheveu—trompe, basalte, laves, mât*), dark with light (*basalte, laves—écume, blanc cheveu*), solid or heavy with animated (*nue accablante, basalte, laves—écume, cheveu qui traîne*). Destroyer and destroyed belong partly to the inanimate, partly to the living world (*naufrage—mât* or *abîme* with subjective attributes *furibond, avarement—sirène*), etc. This principle finds a certain parallel in the sounds as well: there is an alternation between lines with a single dominant vowel sound (I), lines with two contrasting types (II), and those that are thrown into relief through maximal variation (III); cf. I[34]: a (l. 2), a (l. 13); II: a/ü (l. 1), e̦/o̦ (l. 10); III: a ü õ ã e̦ ü (l. 4), ü e̦ ü ã e̦ e̦ a (l. 7), a o̦ i a e̦ e̦ ü (l. 8), u a ü i õ o̦ (l. 9) etc. Furthermore, the composition of the sonnet is also based on a contrast: the fact that the first quatrain presents an (impeded) act of speech, while the remaining stanzas are events, points to two time levels; the speech is thrown into relief by the thematic silence—a contrast that is underlined by the parallelism of

---

[31] As we are concerned here with an individual problem of esthetic effect there is no place for references to parallel cases of language and content in Mallarmé's poems, however rewarding this may be in other contexts. The close affinity of this sonnet to *Un coup de dés* has often been pointed out and used in interpretation, cf. Naumann, pp. 67 et seq.; Johansen, pp. 128, 325 et seq., Ch. Mauron, *Introduction à la psychoanalyse de Mallarmé* (Neuchâtel, 1950), pp. 158 ff.; Wais, p. 582; de Nardis, p. 74; Richard, pp. 216, 390. Wais and Johansen, who are mainly concerned with interpreting the meaning, are of the opinion that *"A la nue . . ."* can be properly understood only when taken in conjunction with "Un coup de dés."

[32] P. 276.

[33] *Alt* is, of course, to be thought of here in the sense of *altitude, altimètre*, etc.

[34] The neutral vowel is not counted.

the two rhyming *tu*'s, each placed at the beginning of a quatrain (the striking element of this contrast is the fact that the second *tu*, as the second person subject pronoun, is an immediate indication of direct speech). And, finally, there are similar effects in the thought content as well, following the typical Mallarmé type of paradox: silence, in order not to break itself, can only take on existence in speech;[35] the elimination of uncertainty through precise information can only be brought about by a dumb, speechless object—*écume*.

These few observations should suffice to give us a somewhat clearer insight into the syntax of this poem. Our analysis has shown that the individual parts, whatever overall system they may belong to, create a varied and lasting esthetic effect (one word, for instance, being the starting point for several polarities).[36] It is now quite clear to what situation the manifold sensual and intellectual stimuli can be ascribed, or rather to what situation they owe their whole effect: namely, the fact that syntactic connections remain, as it were, in suspense, and in their place come potential connections through which the esthetic content can take its full effect. By the obscuring of syntactic divisions, new possibilities are revealed for poetic experience, and, provided they have been perceived, they make virtually irrelevant the question of correctness or clarity of syntax. Thus it makes no difference to our understanding of the sonnet if, to take one last example, we try to transform the *tu* of line 1 into a complete verbal expression; *tu* stands as a kind of contracted form for the spiritual potential of silence; when we come to direct speech, the poet has chosen a clear and punctuated form of communication.

We can understand this new poetic situation better if we have a look at the syntactic make-up of a "genre" diametrically opposed to poetry—a species of writing that demands the utmost precision and concreteness of information, and so dispenses with all poetic and indeed literary pretensions—the *telegram*. As we are all aware, the syntax of telegrams departs from normal grammar: *passed exam arriving tomorrow midday meet me station* scarcely corresponds to the rules. But this irregularity only strikes us as odd outside the "genre"; in a telegram we actually expect it and regard it as normal—so normal, in fact, that we find an explicitly, grammatically worded telegram—such as a telegram from a head-of-state which does not need to be abbreviated—quite abnormal. Of course, there are no rules specific to telegram syntax; there is simply the characteristic tendency towards brevity, which is naturally restricted by the need for clear information. Now, just as a telegram is reduced to

[35] Cf. Friedrich's discussion of the banishment through language of the absent or the destroyed, in connection with his interpretation of *Sainte* and *Surgi de la croupe et du bond*, pp. 75, 81.

[36] Cf. also Richard's comments, pp. 550 ff.

the substance of its information, a poem can be reduced to the substance of its esthetic effect; we can contrast the external necessity for the telegram of a particular form of language, with the internal necessity for the poem of not being prose and of creating values *sui generis* which can be applied outside the realm of intellectual comprehension. Up to and including the Romantic era, the freedom of poetic language was restricted by the fact that it had to convey a complete and clear message to the reader; poetic techniques, disregarding rhyme and rhythm, etc., were confined to ornamentation through various formal and abstract figures. But from the moment when the poet took the plunge and dispensed with completeness and clarity of message, poetic syntax was opened up to new possibilities, and the process of individualizing poetry could advance through syntactic constructions that ran contrary to the norm. The linguistic outcome was, in principle, the same as with the telegram: *outside* the "genre," the peculiarities of the syntax were bound to seem abnormal, and even, in some critics' eyes, antisocial and offensive to the spirit of the language, which was only rarely so with the syntactic figures of traditional poetry (such as Góngora's hyperbaton); the correlative was missing, that compensating element without which the process of contraction is inconceivable. As the extent of the reader's requirements from the poet remains the same, the reader must, to put it simply, be compensated for the loss of information by new esthetic qualities,[37] even if he must pay for them by making an extra effort himself in order to gain access to this new form of poetry.

If we apply to Mallarmé's syntax what B. Eichenbaum said in 1919 about literature in general—namely, that it is "always something made . . . not only artful, but artificial in the good sense of the word,"[38] then we need scarcely bother to go into the many speculations concerning foreign influences on Mallarmé's language. It has been suggested that Mallarmé, who was a teacher of English, either in a kind of *déformation professionnelle* or even deliberately, adopted English syntagmata—an idea which Scherer took seriously enough to set about refuting, though with the somewhat surprising argument that, as evinced by the reports of various school inspectors and acquaintances of the poet, his knowledge of English was only moderate, and in any case he never mentioned any such influence.[39] Others have observed the influence of Latin

---

[37] These are probably what made the young Valéry feel "qu'il y avait dans l'œuvre de Mallarmé, quelque chose *de plus* (et non pas quelque chose *d'autre*) que dans le reste des ouvrages poétiques; quelque chose de plus important . . ." (*Variété* [lecture of 1933] in: *Œuvres*, Pléiade edition, I, 668; italicized in the text).

[38] Quoted by V. Erlich, *Russian Formalism* (The Hague, 1955), p. 163.

[39] J. Scherer, *L'expression littéraire dans l'œuvre de Mallarmé* (Paris, 1947), pp. 20 ff. (esp. pp. 29 ff.).

syntax,[40] of German syntax,[41] or of tendencies towards the occult—a view advocated by Scherer.[42] But even if one did take such influences into consideration, the question of the meaning and effect of these syntagmata within the poem would remain unanswered. Nowadays the view is gaining ground that Mallarmé's syntax is in fact consistent with the spirit of the French language; there is little mention now of the *petit-nègre* character of a syntagma, or of *solécisme*,[43] and not very many scholars share the view of Marouzeau ("les libertés qu'on prend avec la syntaxe conduisent vite à l'incorrection," with reference to the "almost unpardonable offenses" of Mallarmé).[44] But even the champions of the "correctness" of Mallarmé's syntax can be convincing only if they make their judgment intelligible through the work itself; if what is generally regarded as normal French syntax is taken as the criterion, then many peculiarities of construction, such as the occasional end position of the verbal predicate (which Giraudoux parodied in *Elpénor* as a typical feature of German syntax), or the syntactic arrangement of the first quatrain of this sonnet, can well be regarded as lapses. Scherer has for the most part neglected to explain the esthetic functions of his Mallarmé grammar; the result is that, in spite of its undeniable merits, the book is rather like a kind of old curiosity shop.[45] His claim that Mallarmé's use of language anticipates the development of modern French (e.g., the nominal style)[46] is equally open to question. In a similar way, Spitzer thought that the symbolist Henri de Régnier, with his syntactic "accomplishments," "so recht den Weg weist, den die Sprache in Zukunft nehmen wird" (thus shows the way language will take in the future).[47] Mallarmé's syntax stands or falls with his work, for it functions in accordance with "immanent laws" which, in the phrase used by

[40] Cf. Scherer, pp. 33 ff.

[41] "Nous sommes (. . .) à l'opposé même de la syntaxe française, et presque dirait-on un Allemand s'efforçant à tirer de la logique de sa langue un Ueberdeutsch," says A. Thibaudet at one point in *Divagations, La poésie de Stéphane Mallarmé* (Paris, [5]1926), p. 326. Cf. also L. Spitzer, in *Stilstudien* II, 348, note 2: "Wirklich Deutsch mit französischen Worten redet (dagegen) Mallarmé, wenn er . . . das Verb unnatürlich gegen den Satzschluss hinauszögert."

[42] Pp. 155 ff.

[43] Thibaudet, pp. 321, 322.

[44] *Précis de stylistique française* (Paris, [5]1963), p. 166.

[45] Occasionally he makes surprise effects or emphasis responsible; see pp. 136 et seq., 144. Naumann's book (*Der Sprachgebrauch Mallarmé's*) is far more illuminating in this respect.

[46] Cf. the section "Mallarmé et l'évolution du français moderne," pp. 240-43.

[47] *Aufsätze zur romanischen Syntax und Stilistik* (Halle, 1918), p. 228. Cf. Vossler's critique in the *Literaturblatt für germ. und rom. Phil.*, XL (1919), p. 246, and Spitzer's agreement in *Stilstudien*, II, 505.

Jakobson somewhat exaggeratedly in the early days of Russian Formalism (1921) but most appositely when applied to Mallarmé, make of poetry "an utterance oriented towards the mode of expression."[48] The syntactic achievement of Mallarmé does not lie in the fact that he gave particular syntactic innovations to later generations of poets, but in the fact that he paved the way for new expectations from poetic language, which were to have a decisive influence on the form of modern poetry for decades to follow, and which Remy de Gourmont, a contemporary of Mallarmé and author of an *Esthétique de la langue française* (1899), expressed in the following words: "Une poésie pleine de doutes, de nuances changeantes et de parfums ambigus, c'est peut-être la seule où nous puissions désormais nous plaire."[49]

[48] Quoted by Erlich, p. 155.
[49] Quoted by Ch. Mauron, *Mallarmé l'obscur* (Paris, 1941), p. 26.

M. H. ABRAMS

Coleridge, Baudelaire, and Modernist Poetics

I HAVE been asked to say something about Coleridge, both as a representative Romantic critic of poetry and in relation to Symbolist and Modernist theories of poetry. An intimidating assignment! Yet clearly pertinent to the topic of this conference,* and timely as well. Although on the continent Coleridge as a critic has been important mainly to scholars, in England and America he has played not only a prominent, but a double, role, as both villain and hero of the major literary movements of the last half-century. By participating in post-Kantian intellectual currents Coleridge, more than any English writer of his time, represented the central tendencies of Romantic criticism in Europe. As a consequence he has been a key target in the general assault mounted against "Romanticism" more than a generation ago: F. R. Leavis, with characteristic briskness, declared in 1940 that the continued currency of Coleridge "as an academic classic is something of a scandal."[1] Yet excerpted elements in Coleridge's criticism—his exaltation of the imagination over the "understanding" of unenlightened scientism, his concept of "the balance or reconciliation of opposite or discordant qualities," his opposition of organic to mechanical form, his discussions of the "symbol"—have been praised and assimilated to their own doctrines by such central personages in the modern movement as T. E. Hulme, I. A. Richards, and T. S. Eliot, as well as by the American New Critics; to an extent which stimulated Stanley Edgar Hyman, in a survey of recent English and American criticism, to the startling claim that Coleridge, next to Aristotle, was the "most important progenitor" and his *Biographia Literaria* "almost the bible of modern criticism."[2] However one may wish to qualify this pronouncement, it is at any rate evident that the major Romantic critic in England provided concepts with which modern critics have attacked English Romantic poetry, including some of Coleridge's own. On the other hand, Coleridge's poems of magic and mystery, especially *The Ancient Mariner*—as distinct from the great bulk of his lyrics, which are concerned with what he called "things of

* Conference on the "Lyric as Paradigm of the Modern," held at Cologne in 1964.
[1] F. R. Leavis, "Coleridge in Criticism," *Scrutiny*, IX (1940), p. 69.
[2] S. E. Hyman, *The Armed Vision: A Study in the Methods of Modern Literary Criticism* (New York, 1948), p. 11.

every day"—are often excepted from the modern indictment against
Romantic vagueness and emotional indulgence, because they exhibit
narrative impersonality and a clarity of image, as well as a seeming
structural inconsequence which makes them readily eligible for analysis
as symbolist poems *avant la lettre*.

Coleridge's traditional posture in literary history, with a foot both in
the Romantic and Modernist camps, makes him especially relevant to
our consideration of the origins of modern poetics. But more than this,
my assigned topic is a timely one, because it provides an opportunity to
examine a recent tendency to revise the standard view of this development by controverting the claims of Hulme, Pound, Eliot, and other
founding fathers of the Modernist Anglo-American movements that
they were counter-Romantic writers, and by proposing instead that the
new poetry and new criticism which developed after the First World
War, whether imagist or post-symbolist, was essentially a continuation,
in some ways even a culmination, of early nineteenth-century Romantic
innovations. Edmund Wilson, whose *Axel's Castle* (1936) marked an
epoch in the historical perspective on modern English and American literature, was equivocal on this point. The main movement of our day, he
said, is "a counterpart" to Romanticism, "a second flood of the same
tide." But he added that "even the metaphor of a tide is misleading:
what we have today is an entirely distinct movement" which "must be
dealt with in different terms."[3] The revisionist history of recent years
can be represented by two books. In 1957 Frank Kermode wrote *Romantic Image* to demonstrate that two basic assumptions bind most of the
major twentieth-century poets and critics writing in English with the
French symbolists and English estheticists of the latter nineteenth century: that the poem is an autonomous image, insulated from social and
human concerns, and that this poem is engendered by a poet who is
necessarily and agonizingly estranged from his age. But the image of the
moderns, Kermode maintains, together with "the Symbol of the
French," is simply "the Romantic Image writ large"; and the entire
esthetic of the sufficient image and the poet-apart originated in Romantic
poets and theorists, including in England Blake, Wordsworth, and
Keats, as well as Coleridge.[4] And Richard Foster's *The New Romantics*
(1962) proposes the thesis that the New Criticism, from Richards and
Eliot through the reigning American group, whatever the overt claims to
be anti-Romantic in the "principles of art and life," has in fact harbored
a version of Romantic "aesthetics, epistemology, and metaphysics," and

[3] Edmund Wilson, *Axel's Castle: A Study in the Imaginative Literature of 1870-1930*
(New York, 1936), pp. 1-2.
[4] Frank Kermode, *Romantic Image* (London, 1957), Preface, and pp. 5 ff.

that "it is this romanticism of viewpoint or sensibility which most truly constitutes . . . the 'real' identity of the New Criticism as a literary movement."[5]

There are certainly some assumptions, ideas, and poetic practices which are shared by Romantic writers in England and innovative poets and critics of the last half-century. Nevertheless, attempts to assimilate symbolist and modernist literary tendencies to Romantic theory and practice in essentials rather than details are, I believe, mistaken; and I am the more concerned to put forward some important distinctions between these movements because in a book that I wrote more than a decade ago, I undertook to show that Romantic innovations included "many of the points of view and procedures which make the characteristic differences between traditional criticism and the criticism of our own time, including some criticism which professes to be anti-romantic."[6] Such an assertion, while not invalid, seems to me to need qualification if it is not to be misleading, and I should like in this paper to outline the kind of qualification I have in mind.

"What gives Romantic poetry as a whole its strong, deep and steady movement," Graham Hough has remarked, was that it participated in "a more inclusive movement in thought, politics, and society," and that "the most living questions of the age were actually worked out in poetry."[7] In order to understand not only certain characteristic ideas in early Romantic writers in Germany and England, but also one important cause of later reactions against these writers, as well as some characteristic ideas which these reactions manifested, we must remember that Romantic poetics and poetry were not an isolated development. They were an integral part of radical changes in metaphysics, theology, morals, politics. And in their origins and early development, they were revolutionary, in the literal sense that these radical changes in inherited schemes of thought and values accompanied, and were in important ways, stimulated and shaped by the profound expectations and feelings aroused by the great and obsessive event of the age, the French Revolution, in its promise, its event, and its aftermath.

Their involvement with the liberal concepts and revolutionary events of their day was plainly evident to many participants in the movements of thought and literature in the 1790's and later. Fichte declared that the

[5] Richard Foster, *The New Romantics: A Reappraisal of the New Criticism* (Bloomington, Indiana, 1962), pp. 21, 29.

[6] M. H. Abrams, *The Mirror and the Lamp: Romantic Theory and the Critical Tradition* (New York, 1953), p. vii.

[7] Graham Hough, *Reflections on a Literary Revolution* (Washington, D.C., 1960), p. 112.

first presentiments of his *Wissenschaftslehre*, written in 1794-1795, "surged up in me" while "I was writing a work on the Revolution," and that his system was the metaphysical equivalent of the French deliverance of humanity "from its material chains."[8] At the seminary in Tübingen, Schelling and Hegel, together with the poet Hölderlin, developed their early ideas under the same revolutionary impetus and enthusiasm. In England, Shelley, Hazlitt, Francis Jeffrey, and other commentators, radical and conservative alike, attributed the new literature to what they called "the Spirit of the Age," and explained that spirit as the consequence and literary counterpart to the ideas and events of the French Revolution—that "great moral tempest," as the Tory De Quincey wrote in retrospect (1839), which had an effect so nearly "miraculous" that "in Germany or England alike, the poetry was . . . entirely regenerated, thrown into moulds of thought and feeling" that were completely "new."[9] That this estimate, if exaggerated, is grounded on the historical facts is demonstrated by the life and early poetry of Hölderlin, Blake, Wordsworth, Coleridge, Southey, and Shelley; the belated Romantic movement in France was also related to liberal and revolutionary ideas and events, after-waves of the first French Revolution. And when these poets lost their faith in the Utopian possibilities of radical social change, though a few recoiled into reaction, most of them did not simply turn against their earlier values and aims, but instead attempted so to reconstitute their views as to substitute a spiritual and imaginative base for hopes earlier grounded on radical political action.[10]

To a striking degree the various forms of modernist poetics were formulated with persistent reference to Romantic precedents, so that these movements are patently post-Romantic. But when we judge them not by the retention of isolated elements and ideas, but by the premises and general directions of their thinking, we see that the various founders of Modernism who thought of themselves as anti-Romantic were not mistaken. Against Romantic views of poetry which, in their provenience, had been part of an inclusive political and intellectual radicalism, later critics opposed theories in which the esthetic elements typically involved a philosophical world-view, and in many cases a political and theological stance as well; and these, in their totality, were antithetic to the basic

[8] Letter to Baggesen, April, 1795 [?], in Xavier Leon, *Fichte et son temps* (Paris, 1927), II, Part 2, p. 288.

[9] "William Wordsworth," *The Collected Writings of Thomas DeQuincey*, ed. David Masson (14 vols., Edinburgh, 1889-1890), II, 273-74.

[10] On the relations of the French Revolution to the Romantic imagination, cf. M. H. Abrams, "English Romanticism: The Spirit of the Age," in *Romanticism Reconsidered*, ed. Northrop Frye (New York, 1963).

prepossessions of the major Romantic writers about man, his world, his primary values, his hopes, and his aims in all lines of endeavor, including literature.

In this paper I have no intention of defining a Modernist poetic, but shall merely put forward a number of basic concepts which turn up repeatedly and prominently in many of the most influential theorists and poets of the last hundred years. To provide a focus for the discussion, I shall set beside Coleridge a French critic and poet, Charles Baudelaire. For the main development of these persistent modern ideas did not occur in England; it began in the ante-bellum American South, with Edgar Allan Poe, and was elaborated in France, in the mid-nineteenth century and later, by Baudelaire and his symbolist and post-symbolist successors. (T. S. Eliot spoke for many writers of his generation when he remarked that "the kind of poetry that I needed, to teach me the use of my own voice, did not exist in English at all; it was only to be found in French.")[11] There is no evidence that Baudelaire knew Coleridge's criticism except at second hand, through Poe, in whom Coleridge's ideas had already been drastically transformed. But as Coleridge, in his philosophical grasp and range, best represents central tendencies in Romantic thought and criticism, so Baudelaire—of whom T. S. Eliot said that, despite "a good deal of romantic detritus," he was "the first counter-romantic in poetry," "far in advance of the point of view of his own time"[12]—has to an astonishing degree been the fountain-head of the most prominent ideas and viewpoints in post-Romantic criticism. To Rimbaud, Verlaine, Mallarmé, and Valéry, Baudelaire was an acknowledged master; members of the Decadent and esthetic groups developed elements from his writings into their own specialized programs; and he continues to be both hero and exemplar, no less outside of France than within it, to major writers in the modernist modes, from 1910 to the recent past.[13]

1. The analogical universe and the poetic image

Beginning with his writings of the 1850's, when he had assimilated Poe's doctrines to his reading in Swedenborg and various Illuminist writers, Baudelaire posits two worlds, one *"naturel," "terrestre,"* and

---

[11] T. S. Eliot, "Yeats," in *On Poetry and Poets* (London, 1957), p. 252. Cf. also René Taupin, *L'Influence du symbolisme français sur la poésie américaine* (Paris, 1929).

[12] T. S. Eliot, "Baudelaire," in *Selected Essays 1917-1932* (London, 1932), pp. 367, 371-72.

[13] Cf. e.g. Marcel Raymond, *From Baudelaire to Surrealism* (New York, 1950), and Hugo Friedrich, *Die Struktur der modernen Lyrik von Baudelaire bis zur Gegenwart* (Hamburg, 1956), especially pp. 25 ff., 107 ff.

the other *"surnaturel,"* *"extraterrestre."* The two are sharply differentiated, yet related by a "correspondence," or "universal symbolism," "une analogie réciproque, depuis le jour où Dieu a proféré le monde comme une complexe et indivisible totalité."[14] The artist operates in three modalities of analogy. There is an intercorrespondence among the senses in which "Les parfums, les couleurs et les sons se répondent," and there is also an analogy between mind and the outer world, in which you can "contemplate yourself, to speak as the mystics do, in your own correspondence." Baudelaire most emphasizes, however, the third plane of analogy, that between the sensible and spiritual world, where "tout, forme, mouvement, nombre, couleur, parfum, dans le *spirituel* comme dans le *naturel*, est significatif, réciproque, converse, *correspondant.*"[15] Hence poetry, in rendering the hieroglyphs of this world, is that "qui n'est complètement vrai que dans un autre monde."[16] The artist accordingly, does not "copy nature," as the "realist"—or rather, Baudelaire adds, "better to characterize his error, the 'positivist' "—would have it, but rather, by the power of his imagination, "queen of the faculties," he repeats the act which produced the original world of correspondences, by decomposing the world in order to create it anew: "[L'imagination] a créé, au commencement du monde, l'analogie et la métaphore. Elle décompose toute la création, et, avec les matériaux amassés et disposés suivant des règles dont on ne peut trouver l'origine que dans le plus profond de l'âme, elle crée un monde nouveau, elle produit la sensation du neuf."[17] The poet is for us "un traducteur, un déchiffreur," because by his native clairvoyance he is able to detect the symbols and to render them in his images—"ces comparaisons, ces métaphores et ces épithètes [qui] sont puisées dans l'inépuisable fonds de *l'universelle analogie*, et . . . ne peuvent être puisées ailleurs."[18]

These and similar passages in Baudelaire were a frequent point of departure for the later theorists of symbolism; and one cannot read them without being reminded of Coleridge's exposition of the role of the creative imagination. Indeed Baudelaire's description of the creative power of imagination is based on Coleridge, by way of a distant echo of Coleridge's distinction between fancy and imagination, together with his parallel between the divine and the poetic creativity, which Baudelaire himself quotes from Mrs. Catherine Crowe's *mélange* of spiritualist phenomena called *The Night Side of Nature, or Ghosts and Ghost Seers*

---

[14] *Correspondance*, in *Œuvres complètes de Charles Baudelaire*, ed. F.-F. Gautier and Y.-G. Le Dantec (Paris, 1933), VII, 130; and *Œuvres complètes de Baudelaire*, ed. Y.-G. Le Dantec (Bibliothèque de la Pléiade, 1961), pp. 689, 1213.

[15] *Ibid.*, pp. 11, 254-55, 705.   [16] *Ibid.*, p. 637.

[17] *Ibid.*, pp. 1036-38, 1044.   [18] *Ibid.*, p. 705.

(1848).[19] Moreover Coleridge, like Baudelaire, was fascinated by hermetic literature, and much concerned to define the nature of the symbol (though primarily in order to define the symbolic character, not of secular poetry, but of Scriptural narrative). Indeed the metaphysics underlying Coleridge's theory of the poetic imagination, based in large part on Schelling and other post-Kantian philosophers, is itself an elaborate doctrine of correspondences between levels of being. These similarities, however, overlie differences which sharply set off the poetic theory of Coleridge from that of Baudelaire and the symbolists who succeeded him.

We can begin with Coleridge's essay "On Poesy or Art," in which he undertakes, like Baudelaire, to distinguish between the behest to copy nature and the procedure of the true artist:

"If the artist copies the mere nature, the *natura naturata*, what idle rivalry! . . . Believe me, you must master the essence, the *natura naturans*, which presupposes a bond between nature in the higher sense and the soul of man. . . .

"The artist must imitate that which is within the thing, that which is active through form and figure, and discourses to us by symbols—the *Natur-geist*, or spirit of nature. . . . The idea which puts the form together cannot itself be the form."[20]

Coleridge is not claiming here that the artist reproduces spiritual forms which he discerns behind the symbolic surface of nature. In context these passages turn out, instead, to be a way of saying that a genuine work of art does not reproduce fixed objects or forms, whether in nature or beyond it, but is the result of an evolving *process* of imagination which accords with the generative process going on within vital nature itself.[21] "Painful copying" produces "masks only, not forms breathing life"; the difference is "between form as proceeding, and shape as superinduced." Since the artist's "own spirit . . . has the same ground with nature," he can refer to that spirit to acquire, not "cold notions—lifeless technical rules—but living and life-producing ideas," which "contain their own evidence, the certainty that they are essentially one with the germinal causes in nature." "For of all we see, hear,

---

[19] *Ibid.*, pp. 1040-1041; and see Margaret Gilman, *Baudelaire the Critic* (New York, 1943), pp. 128-133.

[20] S. T. Coleridge, "On Poesy or Art," in *Biographia Literaria*, ed. John Shawcross (2 vols.; Oxford, 1907), II, 257, 259.

[21] Cf., e.g., *Coleridge's Miscellaneous Criticism*, ed. T. M. Raysor (Cambridge, Mass., 1936), p. 43: As nature "works from within by evolution and assimilation according to a law," so Shakespeare "too worked in the spirit of nature, by evolving the germ within by the imaginative power according to an idea."

feel and touch" we can be sure "that the life which is in us is in them likewise."[22]

We find in this essay the cardinal principle of all Coleridge's mature writings, one which he shares with most of the Romantic philosophers and critics in Germany after J. G. Herder. His great premise and paradigm, the invariable point of departure in his reasonings about both truth and value, is Life. From the attributes of living things he derives the categories for what is valid and excellent in all areas of human intellection and productivity, whether metaphysical, moral, political, or esthetic. And for this way of thinking the prime character of a living thing is that it grows, by a self-starting process which assimilates diverse materials and organizes them by an inherent lawfulness into an organic whole: "It shapes," as Coleridge says, "as it develops itself from within, and the fullness of its development is one and the same with the perfection of its outward form. Such is the life, such the form."[23] The mode of this growth Coleridge translates, in philosophical terms, into the polar dialectic of successive and progressive antithesis and synthesis, opposition and reconciliation; as he says, "To the idea of life victory or strife is necessary. . . . So it is in beauty."[24]

In Coleridge's theory of poetry, accordingly, as he expounds it in his *Biographia Literaria*, the correspondence between planes of being is not, as it is in Baudelaire, a correspondence between component parts, whether sensations, objects, or forms, but a correspondent process of living, evolving growth and creativity, exhibited in an ascending order in nature, in man, and in Divinity. Thus "the primary Imagination" of man, "the living Power and prime Agent of all human Perception," parallels the living, creative principle in nature; the "secondary Imagination," which effects poetry, is "an echo" of the primary Imagination, since "it dissolves, diffuses, dissipates, in order to recreate"; and both of these in turn can be said to correspond to the continuous generation of the universe in God—"a repetition in the finite mind of the external act of creation in the infinite I AM."[25] And in evolving the organic unity of a poem, that "synthetic and magical power," the secondary Imagination, operates by the dialectic process which governs all growth; namely, "the balance or reconciliation of opposite or discordant qualities: of sameness, with difference; of the general, with the concrete; the idea, with the image. . . ."[26]

I have dwelt on this matter because it is a key to a prime difference

[22] "On Poesy or Art," ii, 258-59, 262.
[23] *Coleridge's Shakespearean Criticism*, ed. T. M. Raysor (2 vols.; Cambridge, Mass., 1930), i, 224.
[24] "On Poesy or Art," ii, 262-63.   [25] *Biographia Literaria*, i, 202.   [26] *Ibid.*, ii, 12.

between Coleridge's view and a widely prevalent post-Romantic view of the elements and structure of a poem. What the symbolists and post-symbolists (however diverse among themselves) had in common with Anglo-American imagists (who were themselves strongly indebted to symbolist theories)[27] was the concept that the primary component of a poem is the image, which is "distinguished," as A. G. Lehmann has said, "by some special efficacy" from the elements of ordinary discourse.[28] For symbolists this efficacy derives from the revelation by the image of an Idea or Essence; and whether this Idea subsists in its own superterrestrial realm, or in the mind and affects of the poet, or glows at the heart of the image itself, or is simply evoked by the incantation of a word, or (in Yeats's version) floats up from the racial memory, it is fixed, discrete, and (it is usually claimed) eternal. To imagists, as Pound said, "the proper and perfect symbol is the natural object,"[29] so that the poetic image is not translucent, but opaque, owing its efficacy to a concreteness beyond abstract discursive language that enables it, as T. E. Hulme said, to "hand over sensations bodily," "to convey a physical thing";[30] but, like the Symbol, the image is a static, isolated poetic entity.

"Glorifier le culte des images (ma grande, mon unique, ma primitive passion)," Baudelaire wrote in *Mon coeur mis à nu*.[31] The cult of the unitary image or symbol has been a prime legacy of modernist poetics. In *The Poetic Image* (1948) C. Day Lewis, in stating his own views, neatly epitomizes the pervasive assumption: "The image is the constant in all poetry, and every poem is itself an image"; it is "an image composed from a multiplicity of images."[32] Such a premise has opened the way to a total revision in inherited concepts of the order and structure of poetry. Traditionally, the structure of a poem had been grounded on such matters as the representation of men whose interactions, in their complication and dénouement, constitute a plot; or on the marshalling of ideas to form a coherent and persuasive argument; or on the presentation of a meditation moving toward resolution. According to the new poetic, the poem is constructed of elemental images or symbols, or of the words evoking these elements. In the line of esthetics inaugurated by Rimbaud, these images derive from a distortion of nature by means of "a systematic derangement of all the senses," and are put together by

---

[27] Cf. Taupin, *L'Influence du symbolisme français*, Deuxieme partie.
[28] A. G. Lehmann, *The Symbolist Aesthetic in France* (Oxford, 1950), p. 271.
[29] *The Literary Essays of Erza Pound*, ed. T. S. Eliot (London, 1954), p. 9.
[30] T. E. Hulme, *Speculations*, ed. Herbert Read (London, 1936), pp. 134-35.
[31] *Œuvres complètes*, p. 1295.
[32] C. Day Lewis, *The Poetic Image* (New York, 1948), pp. 17-18.

an irrational process of free phantasy. In the alternate and more influential view propounded by Mallarmé, the aim is to allow the structure to
be entirely determined by inherent forces in the component elements
themselves: the poet "cède l'initiative aux mots, par le heurt de leur in-
égalité mobilisés. . . . Une ordonnance du livre de vers point innée ou
partout, élimine le hasard. . . . ni le sublime incohérent de la mise en
page romantique ni cette unité artificielle, jadis, mesurée en bloc au
livre. Tout devient suspens, disposition fragmentaire avec alternance et
vis-à-vis. . . ."[33]

It has become a commonplace of modern criticism that the poem is a
structure of dynamic images, ordered by such inherent principles as dissonance and harmony, disparity and conciliation, or irony, tension,
paradox, or else by thematic and counter-thematic relevance. The sharp
departure from traditional forms, in poems written in consonance with
such theories, is patent, from the lyrics of Rimbaud and Mallarmé to
The Waste Land of Eliot, *The Bridge* of Hart Crane, and the *Cantos* of
Ezra Pound. By a number of New Critics, this modern principle of structure has been extended back to account for all good poetry, no matter
when it was written. Shakespeare, for example, is made out to be essentially a symbolist poet; so that in many modern explications of his plays,
we find Macbeth, Lear, and Othello elbowed off the stage by images and
symbols, protagonists in a drama which is a "symbolic action," or else
(in an amalgam of symbolist and Coleridgean theory) an "inherent
dialectic," in which the initial oppositions between the component elements compel them toward an ultimate reconciliation.

For Coleridge, as we saw, the imaginative Idea was not a component
image but a seed, or seminal principle—"living and life-producing
ideas," he called them, "essentially one with the germinal causes in
nature"—which controls the process of poetic development, and reveals
itself only in the achieved fullness of that development. What Coleridge
and like-minded contemporaries contributed to traditional poetics was
the view of poetic structure as essentially process: an evolving organization, of which the key attributes are genesis and growth, and all parts
lose their separate identities in an organic whole; as Coleridge said of
Shakespeare's plays, "All is growth, evolution, *genesis*—each line, each
word almost, begets the following."[34] To Coleridge a structure achieved
by a combination of distinguishable images or symbols, in whatever relations of opposition and conciliation, would have been an instance, not
of the imagination, but of the fancy, which he defined as having "no

[33] "Crise de vers," *Œuvres complètes de Stéphane Mallarmé*, ed. Henri Mondor and
G. Jean-Aubrey (Bibliothèque de la Pléiade, 1945), pp. 366-67.
[34] *Miscellaneous Criticism*, p. 89.

other counters to play with, but fixities and definities." And the difference between collocation and growth was to Coleridge—in the basic
terms to which his philosophy invariably recurs—ultimately a matter of
life and death. The imagination "is essentially *vital*, even as all objects
(*as* objects) are essentially fixed and dead."[35] The mechanic system
"demanding for every mode and act of existence real or possible visibil-
ity . . . knows only of distance and nearness, composition . . . and de-
composition, in short, the relations of unproductive particles to each
other. . . . This is the philosophy of Death, and only of a dead nature
can it hold good. In Life, and in the view of a vital philosophy, the two
component counter-powers actually interpenetrate each other; and generate a higher third."[36]

2. *Original sin and fallen nature*

"De Maistre et Edgar Poe," Baudelaire confided to his
notebook, "m'ont appris à raisonner."[37] We can say, with an equivalent
simplification, that Poe clarified for Baudelaire his incipient scheme of
art in its relation to life, and that Joseph de Maistre provided that scheme
with its principle and sanction—a theological sanction. In the middle and
later 1840's, at the very time of his own brief overture at an artistic *rap-
prochement* with the *bourgeoisie* and short-lived attempt to combine
Romanticism, progressivism, and revolutionary enthusiasm, Baudelaire
found in Poe, with an extraordinary sense that he was reading in him his
own secret heart and mind, a distinctive conjunction of ideas entirely
opposed to these. For Poe posited the existence of two worlds, terrestrial
and supernal, and attributed to poetry the struggle "to grasp *now*,
wholly, here on earth . . . those divine and rapturous joys" which ap-
pertain only to the realm of "supernal Loveliness" and "eternity";[38] he
expressed contempt for the theory and products of the American
revolution—democracy, equality, social reform, progress—and proposed in their place a social order and aristocratic hierarchy in accordance
with "the laws of *gradation* so visibly pervading all things in Earth and
Heaven";[39] and he emphasized the night side of human nature with its
"radical, primitive, irreducible sentiment" which he called "perverse-
ness," the "unfathomable longing of the soul to *vex itself*," "the overwhelming tendency to do wrong for the wrong's sake."[40] Baudelaire

[35] *Biographia Literaria*, ii, p. 202.
[36] *Hints Towards the Formation of a More Comprehensive Theory of Life*, ed. Seth B.
Watson (London, 1848), p. 63.
[37] *Œuvres complètes*, p. 1266.
[38] "The Poetic Principle," in *The Complete Works of Edgar Allan Poe* (Virginia edition;
New York, 1902), xiv, 274.
[39] "The Colloquy of Monos and Una," *ibid.*, iv, 203.
[40] *The Black Cat* and *The Imp of the Perverse, ibid.*, v, 146; vi, 145-147.

found in de Maistre ("le grand génie de notre temps,—*un voyant!*" he called him)[41] a simple principle to reconcile and justify all these views: "le péché originel," as de Maistre said, "qui explique tout et sans lequel on n'explique rien."[42] In his *Notes nouvelles sur Edgar Poe* (1857), Baudelaire brought together all these elements. "More important than anything else" in "a century infatuated with itself," Poe in his idea of perversity has affirmed "the natural wickedness of man" against all the humbugs who say "all of us are born good," when we are in fact "all born marked for evil!" Poe as a true poet "uttered the ardent sighs of *the fallen angel who remembers heaven;* he lamented the golden age and the lost Eden." And the admirable pages of Poe's anti-rational, anti-scientific, and anti-democratic phantasy, "The Colloquy of Monos and Una," "eussent charmé et troublé l'impeccable de Maistre."[43]

After this period Baudelaire's treatment both of man and his universe assumed the simplicity of an all-comprehensive dualism. His basic critical opposition between the "natural" and "supernatural" worlds is also a theological opposition between a fallen and an unfallen realm of being, for by primal inheritance not only man, but external nature as well, is radically corrupt: "La *nature* entière participe du péché originel."[44] The consequences Baudelaire draws from this premise are no less esthetic than moral; in itself "la nature est laide," trivial, terrifying, shocking, "marécages de sang . . . abîmes de boue," producing only monsters and crime.[45] In it remain no more than vestiges and distorted reflections of the uncorrupted world, and it is only because he possesses the imaginative faculty that the artist is able "de saisir les parcelles du beau égarées sur la terre, de suivre le beau à la piste partout où il a pu se glisser à travers les trivialités de la nature déchue."[46]

If in these views, as it has become the fashion to say, Baudelaire is eminently a Christian moralist, his is an extraordinarily truncated Christianity. The kinds of things it leaves out is indicated by the full range of the doctrines of St. Paul who, if he founded the doctrine of original sin—"Wherefore, as by one man sin entered into the world, and death by sin; and so death passed upon all men, for that all have sinned" (Rom. 5:12)—did so to emphasize the fact and magnitude of salvation—"much more the grace of God, and the gift of grace, which is by one man" (Rom. 5:15)—and also proclaimed that "now abideth faith,

[41] *Correspondance*, VII, 130-31.

[42] Joseph de Maistre, *Les Soirées de Saint-Pétersbourg* (Paris, 1960), p. 53.

[43] "Notes nouvelles sur Edgar Poe," in *Nouvelles histoires extraordinaires, Œuvres complètes*, ed. Gautier and Dantec, x, 15-17.

[44] *Correspondance*, I, 131.

[45] *Œuvres complètes*, pp. 1037, 739-40; and "Notes nouvelles sur Edgar Poe," *Œuvres complètes*, x, 19.

[46] *Œuvres complètes*, p. 1067.

162   M. H. ABRAMS

hope, love, these three, but the greatest of these is love" (I Cor. 13:13).

Christian millennialism and the cardinal virtues of faith, hope, and above all love, translated into non-theological equivalents, were the ultimate roots of the secular optimism and the belief in the fraternity of equal men which were at the heart both of the political theory of the French Revolution and of the humanism of revolutionary Romanticism. No doubt the extraordinary appeal to Baudelaire of the stark doctrine of inherited corruption, unqualified by the idea of love or redemption, inhered in part in his own inner division ("Il y a dans tout homme, à toute heure, deux postulations simultanées, l'une vers Dieu, l'autre vers Satan"), and in his love-hate ambivalence toward life ("Tout enfant, j'ai senti dans mon coeur deux sentiments contradictoires, l'horreur de la vie et l'extase de la vie").[47] But its appeal lay also in the fact that de Maistre had demonstrated the sweeping utility of the dogma of original sin as a political instrument, enabling him to attack the optimistic assumptions about the potentialities of political man of Rousseau and the theorists of the French Revolution, and to claim instead the indispensability of hereditary monarchy, Papal supremacy, a strictly hierarchical social order, and an authoritarian government.

On the theological premise of fallen man and a fallen nature, Baudelaire, combining the views of Poe and de Maistre, based the principles both of his counter-Revolutionary and anti-democratic politics and his innovative poetics. And ever since Baudelaire there has been in Anglo-American, as well as French and German letters, the sporadic but persistent recurrence of a combination of dogmatic theological orthodoxy, political and social conservatism, and (through the continuing association of Romanticism with libertarian and egalitarian ideas) an anti-Romantic poetic, usually called "classical," but often used to justify an avant-garde art—all presented as mutually implicative positions. Thus in the 1890's, Charles Maurras, citing among his predecessors Joseph de Maistre and Poe,[48] conjoined the advocacy of absolutism in government and of an orthodox religious establishment to supply and enforce order, together with a total opposition to Rousseauism in thought, to the results of the French Revolution in society and politics, and to the associated movement of Romanticism—to which he also added symbolism—in poetry. T. E. Hulme, identifying as his models "Maurras, Lassere and . . . L'Action Française," charged that "it was romanticism that made

[47] *Ibid.*, pp. 1277, 1296.

[48] In the early statement of his position in *Trois idées politiques*, e.g., Maurras used as epigraph Poe's attack against democracy in "The Colloquy of Monos and Una," on the grounds of the universal laws of gradation on earth and in heaven; see Maurras, *Œuvres capitales* (Paris, 1954), II, 69.

the revolution" of 1789, that "romanticism both in England and France" continues to be "associated with certain political views," and that "the root of all romanticism" was the teaching of Rousseau "that man was by nature good." Hulme proposed instead "the sane classical dogma of original sin" as the sole possible base for order, tradition, limitation, impersonality, and control—the common elements in an authoritarian politics, a dogmatic religion, and a "classical" (which was in his case, an Imagist) poetic.[49] The ideas of Ezra Pound paralleled those of his friend T. E. Hulme in politics and poetics, though not in religion. T. S. Eliot admired Poe and Baudelaire, praised and defended the views of Maurras, and joined some of those views with a number of poetic concepts derived from French writers in the symbolist tradition. Eliot also supported the doctrines of Hulme—of whose ideas about original sin and discipline, ethical and political, he remarked, "Baudelaire would have approved";[50] propagated the opposition of tradition and a dogmatic theology against heterodoxy as a "more fundamental" equivalent for the standard opposition of classicism against Romanticism;[51] attributed much of the blame for the weakness of modern society, "worm-eaten with Liberalism," and of modern literature as well, to the "disappearance of the idea of *Original Sin*";[52] and in the famous phrase which is an echo of Maurras, identified his triple position as "classicist in literature, royalist in politics, and Anglo-Catholic in religion." With Allen Tate, a Southern Agrarian and one of the earliest exemplars of the American New Criticism, who drew upon both Hulme and Eliot, the line of development from Edgar Allan Poe returns to the place of its origin. In Tate the correlated positions, though qualified, recognizably recur: the deprecation of liberalism, progressivism, and the Romantic literary example; the return, in a search for authority and hierarchy, to a traditional social order and a revived religious orthodoxy; and the support, in the name of tradition, of the experimental new poetry and the post-symbolist esthetic of the autonomous, "autotelic" poem.

A few words about Coleridge in this connection. T. E. Hulme defined Romantics "as all who do not believe in the Fall of Man,"[53] but this definition does not apply to Coleridge. As early as March 1798, he wrote a letter to his brother George in which, recanting his earlier advocacy of the French revolutionaries, he also affirmed by way of corollary that "I believe most steadfastly in original Sin . . . that our organization is de-

[49] T. E. Hulme, *Speculations*, pp. 114-17, 254-55.
[50] T. S. Eliot, "Baudelaire," *Selected Essays* (London, 1932), p. 378.
[51] *After Strange Gods* (New York, 1934), pp. 22, 33.
[52] *Ibid.*, pp. 12, 45, 61-62.
[53] *Speculations*, p. 256.

praved, and our volitions imperfect."[54] A later statement is sufficiently sweeping to have charmed even the impeccable de Maistre: "A fall of some sort or other . . . is the fundamental postulate of the moral history of man. Without this hypothesis, man is unintelligible; with it, every phenomenon is explicable."[55]

But Coleridge's differences from the de Maistre-Baudelaire-Maurras tradition are fundamental. He grounded his indictment of the course of the French Revolution not on man's innate corruption, nor on denial of the possibility and desirability of political and social progress, but on his basic philosophical antithesis between the mechanical attempt forcefully to impose a ready-made political scheme and the organic growth of living political institutions: valid meliorism in a state, Coleridge held, must work toward the better realization of its innate, evolving "Idea." And Coleridge repudiated the view that original sin is "Hereditary Sin—guilt inherited" as no other than a "monstrous fiction," proposing instead the interpretation that sin re-originates, inevitably, in the free will of each individual; this is not even, he says, an exclusively Christian tenet, but a "fact acknowledged in all ages, and recognized . . . in the Christian Scriptures."[56] And since the fall of man is thus a recurrent moral act, it cannot for Coleridge, as it does for Baudelaire, involve the primal fall of "la nature entière." Indeed Coleridge, like Schiller, Schelling, Hölderlin, and other German Romantic thinkers, tends to interpret the theological doctrine of the fall, in metaphysical terms, as a falling away, a fragmentation, of man from his primal unity with uncorrupted nature; and consonantly to think of "Redemption," as he wrote to Wordsworth, as a reintegration, a "Reconciliation from this Enmity with Nature."[57] When Coleridge looks upon the natural scene in a meditative mood, he finds in it, not ugly and monstrous reminders "du péché originel," but precisely the opposite: a surviving instance, in natural, living beauty, of man's simple and primal unity with himself and with nature before the fall, and a reminder of what man must strive deliberately to regain, but on the higher level of a complex and conscious reconciliation of the divided and conflicting elements:

"In the flowery meadow, on which my eye is now reposing . . . there is . . . no one character of guilt or anguish. For never can I look and meditate on the vegetable creation without a feeling similar to that with

---

[54] *Collected Letters of S. T. Coleridge*, ed. E. L. Griggs (I; London, 1956), pp. 395-96.

[55] *The Table Talk*, ed. H. N. Coleridge (London, 1917), p. 84 (May 1, 1830).

[56] *Aids to Reflection* (London, 1913), pp. 172-200.

[57] 30 May 1815, in *Collected Letters* (IV; 1959), p. 575. Cf. e.g., Hölderlin's Preface of 1795 to his novel, *Hyperion*, in *Sämtliche Werke*, ed. F. Beissner (Stuttgart, 1957), III, 194-95.

which we gaze at a beautiful infant. . . . It seems as if the soul said to herself: From this state hast thou fallen! Such shouldst thou still become. . . . But what the plant is by an act not its own and unconsciously—that must thou make thyself to become."[58]

Coleridge's theological view of nature as unfallen, and of man as fallen away from a nature with which he must strive to be reconciled, has esthetic consequences which are entirely opposed to those which follow from Baudelaire's view that nature is fallen hence, until modified by art, no less ugly than it is evil. Thus, in his essay "On Poesy or Art," Coleridge describes nature as "to a religious observer the art of God," and posits as both the identifying attribute and chief value of art that it is "the mediatress between, and reconciler of, nature and man," "the union and reconciliation of that which is nature with that which is exclusively human."[59]

3. Nature and art

It is already apparent that the conflict between Romantic and anti-Romantic theories of art was fought out in part on the traditional esthetic battleground of "nature" as against "art," in the root sense in which nature signifies that within man which is spontaneous, emotional, instinctual, plus whatever external to man exists without human intervention; while art signifies that within man which is studied, deliberate, the turning of known means to foreseen ends, and whatever in the external world has been introduced or changed by human contrivance. In his early critical writings Wordsworth, like the eighteenth-century primitivists, tended to elect entirely for nature and "the spontaneous overflow of powerful feelings," as against art. Coleridge, however, while confirming the superior status of "nature," employed his ruling organic principle of the reconciliation of opposites to propose as norm a synthesis in which the element of conscious art is incorporated into a higher-order parallel to simple natural process: the imagination, as he says, "while it blends and harmonizes the natural and the artificial, still subordinates art to nature."[60] To Coleridge, as to many German theorists, great poems were thus indeed natural, but only in a sense which involves the contrary attributes of craft and artistic cunning, in "a

---

[58] *The Statesman's Manual*, in *Lay Sermons*, ed. Derwent Coleridge (London, 1852), pp. 75-76. Cf. Schiller's description, in the opening paragraphs of *Über naive und sentimentalische Dichtung*, of the human response to the simple beauty and self-unity of the natural objects in a landscape: "Sie sind, was wir waren; sie sind, was wir wieder werden sollen."

[59] "On Poesy or Art," *Biographia Literaria*, II, 253-55.

[60] *Biographia Literaria*, II, 12.

union, an interpenetration . . . of *spontaneous* impulse and of *voluntary* purpose."[61] So Shakespeare "first studied patiently, meditated deeply, understood minutely, till knowledge [became] habitual and intuitive," and his process of composition became that of "a nature humanized, a genial understanding directing self-consciously a power and an implicit wisdom deeper than consciousness."[62]

In the theory of Baudelaire's maturity the term "nature," when used as esthetic norm in opposition to "art," no less than when it denominates this world in opposition to the supernatural world, usually connotes a theological, fallen nature. "La plupart des erreurs relatives au beau," he says, "naissent de la fausse conception du dix-huitième siècle relative à la morale. La nature fut prise dans ce temps-là comme base, source et type de tout bien et de tout beau possibles. La negation du péché originel ne fut pas pour peu de chose dans l'aveuglement général de cette époque. . . . La nature ne peut conseiller que le crime. . . . [Dans] toutes les actions et les désirs du pur homme naturel, vous ne trouverez rien que d'affreux."[63]

In the later writings of Baudelaire, therefore, the beautiful and the good tend to be identified with art and the artifical; while the artificial, as the antithesis of the corrupt "natural," tends to fall into synonymity with the uncorrupted "supernatural": "Tout ce qui est beau et noble est le résultat de la raison et du calcul. Le crime . . . est originellement naturel. La vertu, au contraire, est *artificelle*, surnaturelle. . . . Le mal se fait sans effort, *naturellement*, par fatalité; le bien est toujours le produit d'un art. Tout ce que je dis de la nature comme mauvaise conseillère en matière de morale, et de la raison comme véritable rédemptrice et réformatrice, peut être transporté dans l'ordre du beau."[64]

Baudelaire thus responded to the Romantic ideal of an art reconciled with, but subordinate to, nature, by the precisely opposite demand, on grounds that are at once religious, moral, and esthetic, and in all the inherited senses in which art is the non-natural. In describing the process of poetic composition, Baudelaire derides what he says is the Romantic laudation of spontaneity, inspiration, and the expression of personal feelings, and makes poetry almost exclusively a matter of impersonal

[61] *Ibid.*, II, 50.

[62] *Ibid.*, II,19, and *Coleridge's Shakespearean Criticism*, I, 224. A passage from Hölderlin demonstrates clearly how, in Romantic organicism, life provides the paradigm for art, so that the product of human artistry is viewed as a higher order natural organism. The poetic masterpiece is a systematic whole, "das aus lebendiger Seele des Dichters und der lebendigen Welt um ihn hervor und durch seine Kunst zu einer eigenen Organisation, zu einer Natur in der Natur sich bildete." (To Goethe, July 1799; Hölderlin, *Sämtliche Werke*, Stuttgart, 1946-1958, VI, Part I, p. 350.)

[63] *Œuvres complètes*, p. 1182-83.   [64] *Ibid.*, p. 1183.

calculation and craft. He expresses contempt for the modern school of realistic landscape painting: "dans ce culte niais de la nature, non épurée, non expliquée par l'imagination, je vois un signe d'abaissement général."[65] He recoiled from the abundance, fecundity, and exuberance of living, vegetative nature. "Je suis incapable," says his letter of 1855 to Desnoyers, "de m'attendrir sur les végétaux. . . . Je ne croirai jamais que *l'âme des Dieux habite dans les plantes* . . . légumes sanctifiés. J'ai même toujours pensé qu'il y avait dans *la nature* florissante et rajeunie quelque chose d'affligeant, de dur, de cruel."[66] His taste is for "la majesté superlative des formes artificielles," and his dream is not mankind's immemorial dream of a natural, flourishing Eden-garden, but of "un vrai pays de Cocagne . . . supérieur aux autres, comme l'Art l'est à la Nature, où celle-ci est réformée par le rêve, où elle est corrigée, embellie, refondue."[67] This *paradis artificiel* is sometimes envisioned as a tropical or Oriental setting, too exotic to seem "natural" to the European sensibility; more commonly, it is an urban dream—of a Lisbon of which "on dit qu'elle est bâtie en marbre, et que le peuple y a une telle haine du végétal, qu'il arrache tous les arbres . . . un paysage fait avec la lumière et le minéral, et le liquide pour les réfléchir";[68] or else of a Paris which has been denaturalized and devivified, "le végétal irrégulier" banished for the inorganic regularity of metal, stone, and imprisoned water: "L'enivrante monotonie / Du metal, du marbre, et de l'eau."[69] Baudelaire shares the delight he ascribes to his friend Constantin Guys in civilized ceremony and in ritual behavior according to a strict code, "*la pompe de la vie*, telle qu'elle s'offre dans les capitales du monde civilisé, la pompe de la vie militaire, de la vie élégante, de la vie galante,"[70] which reaches its apogee in the pure ritualism of the dandy. And in the brilliant paradoxes of *Le Peintre de la vie moderne*, Baudelaire carries his systematic preference of art over nature to a laudation of cosmetics, of rouge and kohl, over the natural features and the living hue, as "une déformation sublime de la nature" which instances man's noble struggles for a "réformation de la nature" and of "tout ce que la vie naturelle y accumule de grossier, de terrestre et d'immonde."[71]

Baudelaire's anti-naturalism, in all its diverse aspects, has remained a persistent strain in post-Romantic esthetics, which has tended—in fastidiousness, or luxuriousness, or horror, or perversity, or in a combination of these motives—to set both the artist and his art in opposition to

[65] *Ibid.*, p. 1077.
[66] *Correspondance*, I, p. 111.
[67] *Œuvres complètes*, pp. 1184, 254.
[68] *Ibid.*, pp. 303-04.
[69] *Ibid.*, p. 97.
[70] *Ibid.*, p. 1175.
[71] *Ibid.*, p. 1184.

instinctual and organic nature and the conditions of ordinary life. In the extreme form it took in the Decadent movement the esthete, epitomized in Huysman's Des Esseintes, isolated himself from life in order to live *à rebours*, systematically deranging his senses and flouting nature by every available device of artifice and perversity. Most symbolists and post-symbolists have, in various more moderate ways, proposed an art of anti-nature, in which the poet deliberately employs his craft to shape a superior alternative to this natural existence. Baudelaire's visions of the city of Lisbon or of Paris, in which all organic life is replaced by metal, marble, and geometric artifice, are echoed in the modern preoccupation with the city of Byzantium, persisting through Hulme, Pound, and Yeats. This city is viewed as the point in cultural history in which intellect and artifice triumphed over nature and organic life, and it is held to have fostered an art, as T. E. Hulme said, in which "there is nothing vital," which arises from "disgust with the trivial and accidental characteristics of living shapes" and seeks "a *perfection* and rigidity which vital things can never have," in anti-humanistic, life-alien, abstract and "geometric" forms.[72] So, in order to escape "out of nature" and its "sensual music" of generation, birth, and decay, Yeats represents himself as an old man sailing (though very reluctantly) to Byzantium in order to assume the "artifice of eternity"; it is a city of gold and marble in which an artifical bird scorns aloud

> All that man is . . .
> The fury and the mire of human veins.[73]

Yeat's description in *Byzantium* of the flames burning away the fleshly life,

> Dying into a dance,
> An agony of trance,

introduces an equally current modern emblem, the dance, a subject on which Frank Kermode has written illuminatingly in *Romantic Image*. Its unanalyzable fusion of dancer and dance and its fluid fixity of ever-altering but always perfect self-containment, made it a favored instance of life translated into artifice, in which vital process is simulated, but perfected, by turning control over to abstract, non-vital laws of rhythm and form. The favorite dancer is Salome—a preoccupation of Mallarmé, Flaubert, Yeats, no less than of the Decadents, Moreau, Huysmans, and Wilde—the dancer who, feminine but sterile, erotic yet passionless, with a beauty of feature utterly mask-like, weaves her remote and self-absorbed arabesque in a ritual dance of death.

[72] *Speculations*, pp. 9, 53 ff., 92.
[73] W. B. Yeats, *Sailing to Byzantium* and *Byzantium*.

The passage in which Coleridge represents a very similar fusion of matter and form and ceaseless motion in total rest, is a description, not of an artificial simulacrum of life, but of a natural thing exhibiting the essential processes of life itself. Coleridge's instance is a growing plant, which is self-evolving and self-contained, yet only by virtue of a ceaseless reciprocation with an environment from which it takes in order to give:

"Lo!—with the rising sun it commences its outward life and enters into open communion with all the elements, at once assimilating them to itself and to each other. At the same moment it strikes its roots and unfolds its leaves, absorbs and respires . . . and breathes a repairing spirit . . . into the atmosphere that feeds it. . . . Lo! . . . how it . . . effectuates its own secret growth . . . Lo!—how upholding the ceaseless plastic motion of the parts in the profoundest rest of the whole it becomes the visible *organismus* of the entire silent or elementary life of nature."[74]

4. "La poésie pure" and the "absolute poem"

When Arthur Symons, in his influential exposition for English readers of *The Symbolist Movement in Literature* (1899), said of the new literature that "in speaking to us so intimately, so solemnly, as only religion had hitherto spoken to us, it becomes itself a kind of religion, with all the duties and responsibilities of the sacred ritual," he pointed to an obvious aspect of symbolism, and one which has profoundly affected later esthetic theory. The Romantic writers of the 1790's and later had already begun the process of translating theological into esthetic ideas. Hölderlin, Blake, Wordsworth, Shelley, Hugo, for example, reviving the ancient notion of the poet as *vates*, seriously represented themselves as inspired priests, in the great line of succession from the Biblical poet-prophets through Dante and (for the English poets) Milton. So Wordsworth opened *The Prelude* by describing how, inspired by "the sweet breath of Heaven," he assumed the prophet's sacred mission:

> To the open fields I told
> A prophecy: poetic numbers came
> Spontaneously, and cloth'd in priestly robe
> My spirit, thus singled out, as it might seem
> For holy services. . . .

In the writings of various French symbolists, the infiltration of esthetics by theology (though often a theology seen through Hermetic or

---

[74] *The Statesman's Manual*, pp. 77-78.

Illuminist concepts) was carried to the point of constituting a full-formed religion of art. The resulting theories differed radically, however, from those of their Romantic predecessors, not only in the degree to which they assimilated religious ideas, but in their essential esthetic perspective—the view they took of the nature of the work of art and its relation to the artist, the audience, and the world without.

The major Romantic poets had thought of themselves as poet-prophets because they felt they had been granted an illumination which desperately needed to be conveyed to mankind in a time of revolution and reaction, social disintegration, and a civilization in crisis. As Wordsworth had begun *The Prelude* by acknowledging his election to "holy service," so he closed it by calling on his fellow-poet, Coleridge, in an age threatening to "fall back to old idolatry," "servitude," "to ignominy and shame," to carry on with him as

> joint-labourers in a work . . .
> Of [men's] redemption, surely yet to come.
> Prophets of Nature, we to them will speak
> A lasting inspiration . . . teach them . . .
> Instruct them. . . .[75]

We can indicate the altered perspective of the post-Romantic religion of art by saying that the focus shifted from the poet, regarded in one of his functions as expressing a revelation to his fellow-men, to the poem, regarded as existing in total self-sufficiency as an end in itself. In the full development of this theological esthetic, the poem, "l'oeuvre pure," was envisioned as a sacred object, the embodied Idea, or Essence, or Absolute, existing in and for itself in a closed circle of perfection. To this work the poet was subordinated as the agent and ministrant who, in a painful renunciation of this world, has lost his life to find his art. And the work, veiled from the profane and vulgar, "la foule," by its sacred mystery, is accessible—insofar as it is accessible at all—only to an audience of the elect, initiates and communicants in the rites of art.

As Paul Valéry has noted, the "remarkable will to isolate Poetry once for all from every other essence than itself," "in its pure state," had been predicted by Poe; and "it is therefore not surprising to see in Baudelaire the beginnings of this striving toward a perfection that is concerned only with itself."[76] Baudelaire's theory, as we saw, rests on a distinction between fallen nature and the supernature which is evoked or reflected in the poem; the anomaly is that from this theological ground

---

[75] *The Prelude* (edition of 1805), XIII, 431 ff.

[76] Paul Valéry, *The Art of Poetry*, translated by Denise Folliot (New York, 1958), "A Foreword," p. 40.

he does not develop the claim that poetry has a religious or moral purpose, but the opposite claim that a poem has no purpose beyond its own existence. In objecting, for example, to the fact that in Hugo's *Les Miserables* "la morale entre directement à *titre de but*," Baudelaire raises the question "si l'oeuvre d'art doit n'avoir d'autre but que *l'art*, si l'art ne doit exprimer d'adoration que pour *lui-même*."[77] His own answer to this question he had often expressed: "teaching," "truth," and "morality" in poetry are "heresies." For "la poésie . . . n'a pas d'autre but qu'elle-même; elle ne peut pas en avoir d'autre, et aucun poème ne sera si grand, si noble, si véritablement digne du nom de poème, que celui qui aura été écrit uniquement pour le plaisir d'écrire un poème."[78] Baudelaire echoes Poe, who had said that "there neither exists nor *can* exist any work more thoroughly dignified—more supremely noble than . . . this poem *per se*—this poem which is a poem and nothing more—this poem written solely for the poem's sake."[79]

Statements of this type have become a staple of our critical discourse, and they carry for the modern reader a heavy weight of esthetic pathos. But if we break out of the standard categories of modern poetics, the assertion seems by no means self-evident that a poem achieves not only its identity, but also its value, and indeed its supremacy over all other works of man, by the very fact that it is self-sufficient and self-bounded, free from any relation or aim outside the perfection of its own existence—as Baudelaire put it, without the need "to express adoration except for itself." Kant, following Baumgarten, had earlier made the limited claim that the work of art, as contemplated by the spectator, is an object whose value is intrinsic, without reference to its truth or utility. The unqualified assertion that the poem is a self-enclosed and utterly sufficient entity, however, moved against the full current of the European critical tradition; for even when an earlier critic had proposed that the *dulce* rather than the *utile* is the defining characteristic of poetry, he had asserted no more than that the poet alters and orders the materials he takes from this world with the aim of providing the maximum pleasure to his audience.

It seems clear that modern claims about the nature and superlative value of the autonomous work of art owe both their form and their persuasive force not to an esthetic, but to a theological prototype. For in traditional Western thought, only one Being had possessed the attributes of absolute self-sufficiency; and post-Romantic theorists, following the direction indicated by Poe and Baudelaire, imported into esthet-

---

[77] *Œuvres complètes*, pp. 787-88.
[78] "Notes nouvelles sur Edgar Poe," in *Œuvres complètes*, x, 29-30.
[79] "The Poetic Principle," in *The Complete Works*, xiv, 272.

ics the concept of God's unique nature—and *ipso facto* the apex both of
reality and value—and applied it to the work of art. This concept made
its appearance in Plato's description of the Idea of Ideas; this is the Idea
of the Good, and the Good, Plato said, "differs from all other things . . .
in that the being who possesses good always everywhere and in all
things has the most perfect sufficiency, and is never in need of anything
else."[80] Aristotle's God was an unmoved mover who, in his total sufficiency, is the criterion of goodness: "One who is self-sufficient can have
no need of the service of others, nor of their affection, nor of social life,
since he is capable of living alone. This is especially evident in the case of
God. Clearly, since he is in need of nothing, God cannot have need of
friends, nor will he have any."[81] In the Absolute of Plotinus, too, perfection was equivalent to self-sufficiency: "The One is perfect because it
seeks for nothing, and possesses nothing, and has need of nothing. . . ."[82]

These thinkers were the most powerful classical influences on Christian theology, and they helped generate the strain of otherworldliness
which, though among other and conflicting currents of ideas, became a
durable element in the philosophy of Christendom. This is the view that
the *ens perfectissimum*, the highest mode of existence and the supreme
form of value, is alien to the categories of this world, and characterized
by a timeless self-sufficiency; and that the resultant ideal for mankind is
to approximate such a severance from ordinary reality and experience,
by a *contemptus mundi* and *contemptus vitae* whose aim is a pure contemplation (or else as nearly as possible, an imitation) of the perfect
Being who exists outside of this world. It is this persistent set of ideas
and attitudes which provided the paradigm for the otherworldly strain
we have noted in much post-Romantic esthetics.

The movement of *l'art pour l'art* had begun as a rebellion against the
triviality and ugliness of the present-day world and the standards of its
bourgeois and utilitarian society, in the defiant declaration that the aim
of a work of art is not to be useful, but only to be beautiful. But the
esthetic ideas I am describing, in their radical form, are more complex
and far-reaching than a defiance against an indifferent or hostile contemporary milieu. The aim, in the English title of one of Baudelaire's
prose-poems, is nothing less than to seek a way "Anywhere Out of the
World"—"N'importe où! N'importe où! pourvu que ce soit hors de ce
monde!"[83] The tendency is to undertake to disengage the poem from the

---

[80] *Philebus*, 60.   [81] *Eudemean Ethics*, VII, 1244b.   [82] Enneads, V, 2, 1.

[83] *Œuvres complètes*, pp. 303-04. Or, as Flaubert said, "Tout ce qui est de la vie me
répugne; tout ce qui m'y entraîne et m'y plonge m'épouvante." "La vie est une chose tel-
lement hideuse que le seul moyen de la supporter, c'est de l'éviter. Et on l'évite en vivant

ineradicable conditions of human life in the natural world—regarded as fallen, sordid, hideous, contemptible, or absurd—by defining the poem in categories alien to ordinary human experience and attributing to it a detached and self-enclosed perfection of being. And as Baudelaire's pure work of art takes on some of the attributes of a self-sufficient Deity, so Baudelaire's "dandy" assimilates to the figure of the social aristocrat the qualities of the Christian saint who emulates God by substituting the detachment from life of the *vita contemplativa* for the engagement with life of the *vita activa*. Dandyism, says Baudelaire, is "a cult of oneself" which "borders on spirituality" and, with its disciplines "to fortify the will and to discipline the soul," constitutes "a kind of religion"; and the dandy, by his "unshakable resolution never to be moved," cuts himself deliberately off from common humanity and—detached, remote, imperturbable—devotes himself to the utterly self-centered, and for that reason supreme, existence of "cultivating the idea of beauty in his own person."[84] In a parallel fashion Baudelaire's ideal poet undertakes to sever himself from worldly and human relations in a self-sufficing existence, though in order to devote himself (in Yeats's later antithesis) to the perfection not of the life, but of the work: "Goût invincible de la prostitution dans le cœur de l'homme, d'où naît son horreur de la solitude. —Il veut être *deux*. L'homme de génie veut être *un*, donc solitaire. . . . Foutre, c'est aspirer à entrer dans un autre, et l'artiste ne sort jamais de lui-même."[85]

That the modern concepts of the sufficient and impersonal image and the dedicated and estranged artist are related, and by the fact that they derive from related religious prototypes, comes very clear in James Joyce, who beyond most of his predecessors was systematic in constructing his esthetics out of a secularized theology. "The esthetic image," explains Stephen Dedalus, "is first luminously apprehended as self-bounded and self-contained. . . ." In drama, highest in the hierarchy of literary forms, "the esthetic image . . . is life purified in and reprojected from the human imagination," accomplishing "the mystery of esthetic like that of material creation," with "the artist, like the God of the creation," become "invisible, refined out of existence, indifferent, paring his fingernails." And when Stephen himself, at the end of *A Portrait of the Artist*, determines to embrace his artistic destiny in "silence, exile, and

---

dans l'Art. . . ." (20 Dec. 1846 and 18 May 1857; Flaubert, *Correspondance*, Paris, 1926 ff., I, 429; IV, 182).

[84] *Œuvres complètes*, pp. 1177-80.

[85] *Œuvres complètes*, pp. 1294, 1296. Baudelaire also images the poet as "L'enfant déshérité," exiled and condemned, who recapitulates, like the saintly martyrs, the sufferings and passion of Christ; see "Bénédiction," *ibid.*, pp. 7-9.

cunning," the poet-apart bears a patent likeness to Aristotle's self-sufficient deity who has "no need of friends": "Cranly, now grave again, slowed his pace and said: —Alone, quite alone. You have no fear of that. And you know what that word means? Not only to be separate from all others but to have not even one friend. —I will take the risk, said Stephen."[86]

More than a generation before, however, Stéphane Mallarmé had explored the possibilities of esthetic otherworldliness to their farthest consequences. Very early in life Mallarmé, expressing contempt for the world, had turned his back on life and the sordid impurities of reality in order to find in his art a purer self and world:

> Ainsi, pris du dégoût de l'homme à l'âme dure . . .
> Je fuis et je m'accroche à toutes les croisées
> D'où l'on tourne l'épaule à la vie et, béni,
> Dans leur verre, lavé d'éternelles rosées . . .
> Je me mire et me vois ange! et je meurs, et j'aime
> —Que la vitre soit l'art, soit la mysticité—
> A renaître, portant mon rêve en diadème,
> Au ciel antérieur où fleurit la Beauté![87]

By "la poésie pure" Baudelaire had signified a poetry unalloyed either by adaptation to a purpose beyond its own existence, or by exhibiting rhetorical awareness of an audience, or by expressing the personal passion of the poet—"car la passion est *naturelle*, trop naturelle pour ne pas introduire un ton blessant, discordant, dans le domaine de la beauté pure" in "les régions surnaturelles de la poésie."[88] Mallarmé's prose, when put to the question, is no less elusive than his verse; but it seems clear that he aimed at the ultimate purgation which would free the poem from all earthly or human relations whatever: not content with making it embody the Idea or reflect the Absolute beyond reality, he undertook, with unremitting single-mindedness, to transform the poem itself into the Absolute. He aspired to ascend "la montagne sainte," on which Wagner's dramas are but a half-way house, to "cette cime menaçante d'absolu" which haunts us too lucidly, "fulgurante, nue, seule: au-delà et que personne ne semble devoir atteindre. Personne!"[89] And though Mallarmé's talk of the Absolute was probably derived by hearsay from

---

[86] "A Portrait of the Artist," in *The Portable James Joyce*, ed. Harry Levin (New York, 1947), pp. 478, 481-82, 518-19.

[87] *Les Fenêtres, Œuvres complètes de Stéphane Mallarmé*, ed. Henri Mondor and G. Jean-Aubry (Bibliothèque de la Pléiade, 1960), p. 33.

[88] "Notes nouvelles sur Edgar Poe," in *Œuvres complètes*, x, 25, 31, 35.

[89] "Richard Wagner," in *Œuvres complètes*, p. 546.

Hegel, he means by it very much what Plotinus had meant: the One that "is perfect because it seeks for nothing, and possesses nothing, and has need of nothing." Mallarmé's aim was to achieve the sufficient poem, absolute in its purity in the sense that it is totally inhuman and unworldly, because independent not only of poet and audience, but even of reference to anyone or anything outside of itself.

In discussing the coming-into-being of a poem, Mallarmé likes to replace the inherited terms of imitation, representation, or expression (which imply a relation to the world or to the poet) by metaphors taken from necromancy or the occult, implying the conjuring up of a poem out of nothing and nowhere. There is "une parité secrète" between poetry and magic, and "évoquer . . . l'objet tu, comporte tentative proche de créer: vraisemblable dans la limite de l'idée uniquement mise en jeu par l'enchanteur de lettres. . . ."[90] The poet like a mage utters the word and there rises up, not the concrete object, but "la notion pure," a flower which is an "idée même et suave, l'absente de tous bouquets."[91] As to the author: "L'oeuvre pure implique la disparition élocutoire du poëte, qui cède l'initiative aux mots. . . . Encore la faut-il, pour omettre l'auteur"; so that a work of art is "anonyme et parfait."[92] Nor does the pure poem require a reader: "Impersonnifié, le volume, autant qu'on s'en sépare comme auteur, ne réclame approche de lecteur. Tel, sache . . . il a lieu tout seul: fait, étant."[93] And only, "reportage," not literature, aims to "narrate, instruct, even to describe"; the words of poetry do not denote, but function beyond reference, like elements in a dream, or an incantation, or (in a favorite analogue of advocates of pure poetry) like the notes in the non-representational art of music. "Au contraire d'une fonction de numéraire facile et représentatif," the speech of the poet, "avant tout, rêve et chant," which "de plusieurs vocables refait un mot total, neuf, étranger à la langue et comme incantatoire, achève cet isolement de la parole."[94] Poetry achieves its purity by devouring and wearing away the reality it has no recourse except to employ as its initial material. "Tout le mystère est là: établir les identités secrètes par un deux à deux qui ronge et use les objets, au nom d'une centrale purité."[95]

---

[90] "Magie," ibid., p. 400.   [91] "Crise de vers," ibid., p. 368.

[92] Ibid., pp. 366-67. Mallarmé wrote to Verhaeren, Jan. 22, 1888, that "the poet disappears (this is absolutely the discovery of our time)." In Propos sur la poésie, ed. Henri Mondor (Monaco, 1953), p. 158.

[93] "Quant au livre," in Œuvres complètes, p. 372.   [94] "Crise de vers," ibid., p. 368.

[95] To Viélé-Griffin, 8 August 1891, in Mallarmé, Propos sur la poésie, p. 174. Mallarmé had earlier said: "Je n'ai créé mon œuvre que par élimination, et toute vérité acquise ne naissait que de la perte d'une impression qui, ayant étincelé, s'était consumée et me permettait . . . d'avancer plus profondément dans la sensation des Ténèbres Absolues. La Destruction fut ma Béatrice." (To Eugène Lefébure, 17 May 1867, ibid., p. 91.)

For although "la Nature a lieu, on n'y ajoutera pas: as the source of poetry, yet to create poetically is to unrealize or abolish it—"a l'égal de créer: la notion d'un objet, échappant, qui fait défaut."[96]

Freed from the last bonds of worldly contingency and of relationship to anything outside itself, the poem becomes an isolated, introverted object constituted solely by the internal relations of its words. "Le hasard n'entraîne pas un vers, c'est la grande chose. . . . Ce à quoi nous devons viser surtout est que, dans le poème, les mots—qui déjà sont assez eux pour ne plus recevoir d'impression du dehors—se reflètent les uns sur les autres jusqu'à . . . n'être que les transitions d'une gamme."[97] The absolute poem, then, in the perfection of its beauty, is self-contained, self-signifying, self-adoring; in describing it Mallarmé, like Joyce later, recalls Aristotle's claim that the self-sufficient deity needs no friends, and has none: "Il n'y a que la Beauté,—et elle n'a qu'une expression parfaite: la Poésie. Tout le reste est mensonge—excepté pour ceux qui vivent du corps, l'amour, et cet amour de l'esprit, l'amitié. . . . Pour moi, la Poésie me tient lieu de l'amour, parce qu'elle est éprise d'elle-même et que sa volupté d'elle retombe délicieusement en mon âme."[98]

Now, a self-bounded perfection of existence which neither expresses, communicates, nor describes, however it may suit the Deity, offers difficulties as the ideal for an art whose medium is language, the human instrument of expression, communication, and description. A. O. Lovejoy has raised the question with respect even to God whether, by positing an otherworldly Being who is defined exclusively by antithesis to the mode of existence of anything in this world, "many of the great philosophers and theologians have been occupied with teaching the worship of—nonentity."[99] This, at any rate, is what, seeking the absolute poem, Mallarmé seems very early in his career to have discovered:

"Malheureusement, en creusant le vers à ce point, j'ai rencontré deux abîmes, qui me désespèrent. L'un est le Néant . . . et je suis encore trop désolé pour pouvoir croire même à ma poésie."[100]

"Je te dirai que je suis depuis un mois dans les plus purs glaciers de l'Esthétique—qu'après avoir trouvé le Néant, j'ai trouvé le Beau,—et que tu ne peux t'imaginer dans quelles altitudes lucides je m'aventure."[101]

"Pour garder une notion ineffaçable du néant pur, j'ai dû imposer à

---

[96] "La Musique et les lettres," in Œuvres complètes, p. 647.

[97] To François Coppée, 5 December 1866, Propos sur la poésie, p. 85.

[98] To Henri Cazalis, 14 May 1867, ibid., p. 89.

[99] A. O. Lovejoy, The Great Chain of Being (Cambridge, Mass., 1936), p. 30.

[100] To Henri Cazalis, March 1866, Propos sur la poésie, pp. 65-66.

[101] To Henri Cazalis, July 1866, ibid., p. 77.

mon cerveau la sensation du vide absolu. . . . Il me reste la délimitation parfaite et le rêve intérieur de deux livres, à la fois nouveaux et éternels, l'un tout absolu *Beauté*, l'autre personnel, les *Allégories somptueuses du Néant*. . . . Vraiment, j'ai bien peur de *commencer* . . . par où notre pauvre et sacré Baudelaire a fini."[102]

"Pour moi, voici deux ans que j'ai commis le péché de voir le Rêve dans sa nudité idéale. . . . Et maintenant arrivé à la vision horrible d'une œuvre pure, j'ai presque perdu la raison et ce sens des paroles les plus familières."[103]

In his pursuit of absolute purity Mallarmé exploited his ingenious tactics of negating, eliminating, absenting, disembodying, refining to the verge of non-entity the objects of this world; and though he produced a slim body of extraordinary verse, he was haunted by the apprehension that even his best achievements, "d'une pureté que l'homme n'a pas atteinte," may in truth be of a purity that man "n'atteindra peut-être jamais, car il se pourrait que je ne fusse le jouet que d'une illusion, et que la machine humaine ne soit pas assez parfaite pour arriver à de tels résultats."[104] "Mon art," Mallarmé once said, "est une impasse." Of an art of language which aspires to the condition of pure notation without denotation, the inevitable result is—in that mode of *coincidentia oppositorium* to which otherworldly theologians have always been reduced in defining their Absolute—an eloquent silence. Mallarmé was fascinated by the idea of the tacit poem—"l'écrit, envol tacite d'abstraction," and "le poëme tu, aux blancs."[105]

From this extremity poetics had nowhere to go except back. Mallarmé's successors, in the generation of symbolists after 1890, typically felt the attraction of the ideal of a pure poetry disengaged from the impurity of ordinary life, yet found it necessary to bring poetry into some kind of relationship with the world and mankind. "L'univers," Valéry wrote in *L'Ebauche d'un serpent*, "n'est qu'un défaut / Dans la pureté du Non-Etre"; but his *Cimetière Marin* ends in the recognition that "Il faut tenter de vivre." And as Valéry acknowledged in his retrospect of the symbolist movement, the concept of the absolute poem, as it developed after Poe and Baudelaire, turned out to be beyond existential possibility: "A l'horizon, toujours, la poésie pure. . . . Là le péril; a précisément, notre perte; et là même, le but. . . . Rien de si pur ne peut coexister avec les conditions de la vie. . . . La poésie absolue . . . comme le vide parfait

---

[102] To Villiers de l'Isle-Adam, 24 September 1866, *ibid.*, pp. 82-83.
[103] To François Coppée, 20 April 1868, *ibid.*, p. 97.
[104] To Henri Cazalis, 14 May 1867, *ibid.*, p. 88.
[105] "Le Mystère dans les lettres," in *Œuvres complètes*, p. 385; "Crise de vers," *ibid.*, p. 367.

... ne se [laisse] même approcher qu'au prix d'une progression épuisante d'efforts ... [et ne laisse] enfin que l'orgueil de n'être jamais satisfait.''[106]

By and large, prominent modern theories of art, from the Formalists through many of the New Critics, have inherited from the symbolist doctrine of an absolute work their view of the nature of a poem and, in consequence, their central esthetic problem. In maintaining the central insight of modern esthetics since Baumgarten and Kant—that a work of art has intrinsic values, to be contemplated independently of the state of mind in which it originated, or the truths it states, or the moral and other ends it effects—the modern theorist has usually, although need-lessly, committed himself to the ontological claim that the work of art is "self-sufficient," "autonomous," "autotelic," "autarchic," "absolute," existing "for its own sake," "*per se*," as "an object in itself," in entire independence of any intent of its author, any reference to the outer world, any effects on an observer, and, indeed, of any extra-poetic human concerns or values whatever. Such a view, since it appropriates to a poem the attributes originally assigned to an otherworldly deity, readily verges on poem-worship, and is often associated with the opinion that poetry has assumed the function which is no longer fulfilled by reli-gion, or else that art is itself a kind of religion, or intimately related to religious experience. This criticism continues to deploy other concepts preempted from theology; a phenomenon visible, for example, in the claim that poetry provides a supreme and privileged knowledge immune from ordinary criteria or logic, and in the designation of competing views of poetry, not as products of error in esthetic observation or rea-soning, but as violations of a creed—that is (in the term introduced into esthetics by Poe and Baudelaire) as "heresies." Consonantly, the central problem for modernist theory has been to maintain the position that the work of art is a self-contained object, yet to relate the work once again to the world outside itself, and to reengage it with the emotional, intellec-tual, and moral concerns of common humanity.

An esthetic of an otherworldly, self-sufficient poem is entirely remote from the views of the early and most influential Romantic philosophers and poets. They were all in some sense Idealists, but their critical theories were, in the final analysis, of this world, and their basic criteria humanistic. "Poetry," Coleridge wrote in "On Poesy of Art," "is purely human; for all its materials are from the mind, and all its prod-ucts are for the mind"; it binds man with the objects of the external world, and these share his humanity, in that "the life which is in us is in

---

[106] Paul Valéry, "Avant-propos," *Variété* (Paris, 1924), pp. 103-05.

them likewise.''[107] On this issue the greatest statement was uttered by Wordsworth, in the Preface to *Lyrical Ballads* which, Coleridge declared, whatever his exceptions to Wordsworth's theory of poetic diction, had been "half a child of my own Brain."[108] When Wordsworth says that "Poetry is the first and last of all knowledge,"[109] he does not mean that it is an equivalent for the Deity, the *Alpha* and *Omega*. For "however exalted a notion we would wish to cherish of (his) character," what, Wordsworth asks, is a poet? "He is a man speaking to men," and his "poetry is the image of man and nature. . . . The Poet writes under one restriction only, namely, the necessity of giving immediate pleasure to a human Being possessed of that information which may be expected from him . . . as a Man"; and this condition is not demeaning, but "a homage paid to the native and naked dignity of man, to the grand elementary principle of pleasure, by which he knows, and feels, and lives, and moves." At the farthest extreme from the modernist's alienated and sufficient poet, needing no friends, Wordsworth's poet expresses that which by "habitual and direct sympathy" connects "us with our fellow beings," and is eminently "an upholder and preserver, carrying everywhere with him relationship and love," and uttering "the general passions and thoughts and feelings of men."[110]

Wordsworth's poet, then, deals with this world and the universal human concerns, expresses those ideas and feelings which bind him to man and men to each other, and undertakes to appeal to the moral interests and springs of pleasure he shares with his audience. From other men he differs, not in kind, but only in the degree of his powers; and, above all, he differs in his ready and joyous responsiveness to the very thing from which advocates of "l'oeuvre pure" later sought, with ascetic zeal, to disengage both poet and poem entirely—namely, life itself. The poet, says Wordsworth, is a man "who rejoices more than other men in the spirit of life that is in him, delighting to contemplate similar volitions and passions as manifested in the goings-on of the Universe, and habitually impelled to create them where he does not find them."[111]

These differences between such views and these characteristic symbolist and post-symbolist views of art derive from a radical cleavage in basic schemes of value. The early Romantics committed themselves on

---

[107] "On Poesy or Art," in *Biographia Literaria*, ii, 254, 259.

[108] To Robert Southey, 29 July 1802, *Collected Letters of S. T. Coleridge*, ed. E. L. Griggs, ii (Oxford, 1956), p. 830. In the same letter Coleridge describes Wordsworth's section (added in 1802) on "the Dignity and nature of the office and character of a Poet" as "very grand, and of a sort of Verulamian Power and Majesty."

[109] Preface to "Lyrical Ballads," in *Wordsworth's Literary Criticism*, ed. N. C. Smith (London, 1905), p. 28.

[110] *Ibid.*, pp. 23-29.   [111] *Ibid.*, p. 23.

the side of life—life in this world. In their writings Life played a role equivalent to that of the Absolute in the otherworldly thinkers, functioning as the premise of their thinking and the residence and reference of their major values, including esthetic values. This fact is epitomized by a passage in which Coleridge identifies as Absolute, not the state in which we disengage ourselves from this world, but on the contrary, that in which we reunite severed man and nature, subject and object, in an intuition which combines the central Romantic values of life, joy, and that total relationship for which Coleridge, like many of his contemporaries, used the term "love":

"The ground-work, therefore, of all true philosophy is the full apprehension of the difference between . . . that intuition of things, which arises when we possess ourselves, as one with the whole, which is substantial knowledge, and that which presents itself when . . . we think of ourselves as separated beings, and place nature in antithesis to the mind, as object to subject, thing to thought, death to life. . . . [The former] is an eternal and infinite self-rejoicing, self-loving, with a joy unfathomable, with a love all-comprehensive. It is absolute. . . ."[112]

For Coleridge, as for Wordsworth, such a full intuition of "the one Life within us and abroad," whose sign is the unison of all the faculties which he calls "joy,"[113] is the essential condition of the highest poetry. Shelley was not indulging in rhetoric, but putting forth a considered view he shared with his contemporaries, when he spoke of "the joy of the perception and still more of the creation of poetry," and described poetry as "the record of the best and happiest moments of the happiest and best minds."[114] In *Romantic Image* Frank Kermode has read back into Coleridge's *Dejection: An Ode* the Modernist concept of the poet-apart, whose estrangement and anguish are the inescapable price he pays for his ambiguous joy in accomplishing the self-sufficing image which is the poem.[115] The claim of Coleridge's poem, however, is precisely the opposite: that the severance of his responsive mind and feelings from the outer world is an unmitigated disaster which leaves him isolated in a nature that has been rendered dead and alien; that this state of "dejection," far from being necessary to creativity, has suspended his "shaping spirit of Imagination"; that the contrary state of "joy," attending full community with what is external to him, is the necessary condition for the imaginative recreation of the world in poetry; and that this new world is

---

[112] *The Friend* (3 vols.; London, 1818), III, 261-62.

[113] Cf. Coleridge's *The Eolian Harp*, ll. 26-29.

[114] Shelley, *A Defence of Poetry, Shelley's Prose*, ed. D. L. Clark (Albuquerque, New Mexico, 1954), pp. 292, 294.

[115] *Romantic Image*, pp. 6-10, 89-91.

not a remote and purified otherworld or supernature, but merely the present and imperfect world, experientially transformed by the joyous power emanating from the poet's abundant sense of life. "Joy," he says, which is "Life, and Life's effluence,"

> Joy, Lady! is the spirit and the power,
> Which, wedding Nature to us, gives in dower
> A new Earth and new Heaven.

HANS ROBERT JAUSS

Group Interpretation of Apollinaire's *Arbre* (From *Calligrammes*)

JAUSS (*in the chair*): This group interpretation* is to be a kind of specimen test—that is to say, we shall try and clarify certain still unsettled questions concerning relations between clarity and ambiguity, indeterminacy and form *in praxi*. We shall discuss what functions ambiguity can have in poetic language, how in its various possible stages it is to be understood as a positive esthetic category, whether observation of poetic ambiguity (or a subsequent removal of it) can count as part of the esthetic pleasure, and how one is to conceive the "new clarity" of the poem that will arise from a process of understanding that must not be just a mere decoding.

My suggestion for a *modus procedendi*—we should not begin by offering up clear-cut interpretations; first we should describe the surprising, strange, and bizarre aspects we see, and then show the different possibilities of organization ("positive determinants").

ARBRE

A Frédéric Boutet[1]

(I)   1   Tu chantes avec les autres tandis que les phonographes
galopent
Où sont les aveugles où s'en sont-ils allés
La seule feuille que j'aie cueillie s'est changée en plusieurs
mirages
Ne m'abandonnez pas parmi cette foule de femmes au
marché
Ispahan s'est fait un ciel de carreaux émaillés de bleu
      6   Et je remonte avec vous une route aux environs de Lyon

(II)   Je n'ai pas oublié le son de la clochette d'un marchand de coco
d'autrefois

---

* The chairman was Hans Robert Jauss. Also participating in this discussion were students and graduates of the French Department at Giessen University.

[1] In *Calligrammes*, Ed. de la Pléiade (Paris, 1956), pp. 178 et seq.; the poem is dedicated to Frédéric Boutet (b. 1874, French novelist and short-story writer).

J'entends déjà le son aigre de cette voix à venir
Du camarade qui se promènera avec toi en Europe
Tout en restant en Amérique

(III) 11 Un enfant
Un veau dépouillé pendu à l'étal
Un enfant
Et cette banlieue de sable autour d'une pauvre ville au fond
de l'est
Un douanier se tenait là comme un ange
16 A la porte d'un misérable paradis
Et ce voyageur épileptique écumait dans la salle d'attente des
premières

(IV) Engoulevant Blaireau
Et la Taupe-Ariane
Nous avions loué deux coupés dans le transsibérien
21 Tour à tour nous dormions le voyageur en bijouterie et moi
Mais celui qui veillait ne cachait point un revolver armé

(V) Tu t'es promené à Leipzig avec une femme mince déguisée
en homme
Intelligence car voilà ce que c'est qu'une femme intelligente
Et il ne faudrait pas oublier les légendes
26 Dame-Abonde dans un tramway la nuit au fond d'un
quartier désert
Je voyais une chasse tandis que je montais
Et l'ascenseur s'arrêtait à chaque étage

(VI) Entre les pierres
Entre les vêtements multicolores de la vitrine
31 Entre les charbons ardents du marchand de marrons
Entre deux vaisseaux norvégiens amarrés à Rouen
Il y a ton image

(VII) Elle pousse entre les bouleaux de la Finlande

(VIII) Ce beau nègre en acier

(IX) 36 La plus grande tristesse
C'est quand tu reçus une carte postale de La Corogne

(X) Le vent vient du couchant
Le métal des caroubiers
Tout est plus triste qu'autrefois
41 Tous les dieux terrestres vieillissent

L'univers se plaint par ta voix
Et des êtres nouveaux surgissent
Trois par trois.

TREE

For Frédéric Boutet

(I) 1 You sing with the others while the phonographs gallop
Where are the blind where have they gone
The single leaf that I picked has changed into several mirages
Do not desert me amongst this crowd of women in the
market
Ispahan has made itself a heaven of blue enamel tiles
6 And I reascend with you a road near Lyon

(II) I have not forgotten the sound of the bell of a coconut vendor
in former times
I hear already the shrill sound of that voice to come
Of the comrade who will wander with you in Europe
While staying in America

(III) 11 A child
A skinned calf hanging in the slaughterhouse
A child
And that suburb of sand round a poor town down in the East
A customs officer stood there like an angel
16 At the door of a miserable paradise
And that epileptic traveller foamed in the first-class waiting
room

(IV) Goatsucker Badger
And Mole-Ariadne
We had reserved two compartments in the trans-Siberian
21 In turns we slept the traveller in jewels and I
But the man on guard did not hide at all an armed revolver

(V) You went walking in Leipzig with a slender woman disguised
as a man
Intelligence for that's what an intelligent woman is
And the legends should not be forgotten
26 Dame-Abonde in a streetcar at night in the depths of a
deserted quarter
I saw a chase as I went up
And the elevator stopped at every floor

(VI) Between the stones
Between the multicolored clothes in the shop-window
31 Between the glowing coals of the chestnut seller

> Between two Norwegian vessels anchored in Rouen
> There is your image

(VII)   It grows between the birch trees of Finland

(VIII)   That beautiful Negro in steel

(IX)   36 The greatest sadness
           Was when you received a post card from La Coruña

(X)   The wind comes from sunset
           The metal of the currant trees
           Everything is sadder than in former times
       41 All the earthly gods grow old
           The universe laments through your voice
           And new beings surge up
           Three by three.

KRACAUER: We could start asking what sort of reality is represented. The *phonographes* in the very first verse refer to the reality of modern civilization, that disorderly, unbeautiful world that is principally reproduced by photography and the cinema. The following evocation of the confusion of a lively city street—a basic motif of modern times—is a typical opening scene for a film. All this is an indication of Apollinaire's historical situation, of our modern photographic experience of reality, of attempts to carry the reality of the camera over to art (somewhat as in Dos Passos' novel [*U.S.A.*]). Chance becomes a sort of necessary phenomenon. In the associative course of the poem, the omnipresence of chaotic reality becomes obvious (names of towns, stations, people in the street). "Tout est plus triste qu'autrefois" (l. 40) shows the way in which Apollinaire experiences this reality. But it does not stick at this *tristesse*, at the elegiac mood arising from vague impressions of a godless, technocratic world. Apollinaire tries to extract a new beauty out of this very reality. The sadness changes into an Orphic vision and almost drunken representation, in which reality itself experiences an implicit recognition.

DIECKMANN: The film analogy does not apply just to the representation of the world. The whole movement of the poem, the sequence of visual impressions—this is obviously influenced by the cinema.

ISER: Cinema techniques have often been used deliberately in modern literature. They enable impressions to be freed from the one-sided perspectives they are usually caught up in. The pictures are cut and joined abruptly together, so they seem like fragments that need to be completed, though they never could be. Gertrude Stein actually worked out her prose style in accordance with this film technique, using a series of superimposed images in order to convey the various facets of the thing she wanted to depict.[2] In her book on Picasso she wrote that in this century air travel has uncovered completely new and undreamt-of perspectives through which the earth and countryside can be observed.[3] This enrichment of perspective vision also means a change in what is looked at. If one is aware that one has a large number of possible perspectives at one's disposal, one's technique of composition is bound to be influenced, in order that the impression of a potential multiplicity can be evoked in the depiction of the object.

WARNING: Are there real associations in this poem? If so, what is the principle connecting them? In the first lines it is difficult to link things up (what links the title *Arbre* to "tu chantes, les phonographes" to "les aveugles," and this to "la seule feuille," the "femmes au marché," "Ispahan," and "Lyon")? If you are going to have associations, you must have some kind of connection (at least a recognizable *état d'âme*, which you have not got here).

JAUSS: On a first impression, the poem is obviously not based on recognizable links of association, but rather on observations of a disparate "chaotic reality" (Kracauer). So-called associations and the principle behind their arrangement are given only as it were a posteriori: they emerge only when one links up impressions and tries to define them.

HARTFELDER: Are not associations established syntactically through *et*? The linking together of disparate things at the end of the first verse, of "Ispahan" with "Lyon," (of perfect with present), of impersonal forms with the very personal "je" and "vous"—this all *creates* connections. In the same way, the return to the personal sphere of the first line, which starts with "tu," establishes formal connections and so a unification of the verse. Although these connections cannot be followed through as regards the content, they are confirmed by the personal elements. The reader must be prepared right from the beginning to accept visually established associations that are strange to him.

KRACAUER: Is the character of the association a kind of inner monologue (J. Joyce)?

TSCHIŽEWSKIJ: We should avoid the term "association." There are no associations in the sense of a link-up of individual isolated elements; rather, each idea belongs to a larger whole, to a complex of ideas and

---

[2] Cf. G. Stein, *Lectures in America* (Boston, 1957), pp. 177 ff.
[3] Cf. G. Stein, *Picasso* (London, New York, Toronto, 1948), p. 49.

other, mainly emotional, experiences; one single idea arouses in the conscious mind the whole of this complex, or at least its essential, important part. As far as the interpretation of a poem is concerned, this means that right from the start we should consider the poem as a whole, even if it is only an indistinct whole—in other words, we have to have an overall impression of it. It is only against the background of this overall conception that the individual parts become apparent to us (and in some cases can be understood by us). The suggestion that in interpreting a poem we should proceed from the individual elements of that poem reminds me of a saying attributed to Talleyrand: *one must never act according to the first impulse of one's heart, for it is always right.* Perhaps one should not insist that the "first impression" of a poem is always right, but it is certainly more right than the impression arising from the individual elements of the poem.

BUDDEMEIER: The poem can be divided into three sections, according to the different stages of time that it contains. The first section is predominantly in the present, and embraces the first stanza. The two perfect tenses in lines 2 and 3 bring us directly up to the present.

The second stanza forms the transition to the central part of the poem, which is in the imperfect. That second stanza contains in just a few lines the largest variety of tenses (perfect, present, future). This striking change of tenses can be interpreted as a minute description of a memory process, which is set off by acoustic elements. Line 7 (perfect) begins with the memory—still at the stage of reflection—of the sound of a vendor's bell. In line 8 (present) the sound, now the voice of the friend, is actually heard in the imagination. The future (l. 8) anticipates memory images that are to come. The friend is going to wander through Europe with the *je* (which is presumably concealed behind the *toi*), though in reality at the time of remembering he is actually in America ("Tout en restant en Amérique").

The second section of the poem (stanzas III-v), if this interpretation is right, contains memories of events connected with the *je* and the *camarade*. This seems to be borne out by the fact that in this part of the poem there are the three personal pronouns *je* (l. 27), *tu* (l. 23), *nous* (ll. 20, 21), whereas the introductory stanza II contains only *je*. *Nous* does not occur again throughout the rest of the poem.

Stanza VI like stanza II forms the transition to the next section; in a subtle way it leads out of memory and back into the present. On a first reading, one thinks that line 29 is an adverbial qualification dependent on the preceding sentence. But from line 30 on, this syntactical link-up becomes more and more improbable, until line 33 finally shows that line

29 was the beginning of a new sentence. But the original effect of linking stanzas v and vi cannot be cancelled by this awareness, and in fact the impression of homogeneity is added to by this impression of a transition.

The third section of the poem is in the present again, which significantly starts only in the last line of stanza vi. The present tense in this line refers directly back to the preceding memories: for the *je*, the image of the friend is still between the stones, clothes etc.

PREISENDANZ: I think it is even possible, to a certain degree, to organize what looks like complete disparity in relation to a thematic vanishing point. Of course one would have to substantiate this claim from line to line. One could start with the contrasting relations of lines 1-3: "tu chantes" stands against "les phonographes galopent," and this acoustic contrast is again opposed to the deficient optical reality of "les aveugles" while the third line, with the contrast of "seule feuille . . . plusieurs mirages"—a clear reference to the title (*Arbre-feuille*)—seems to connect these oppositions to the situation of poetic composition. There are other vanishing lines that are immediately obvious, arising out of all sorts of correspondences: the reference to the past, to which "les légendes" also belong (e.g., ll. 5, 7, 25-26, 41), connects up with the shrill sound of the "voix à venir" or the emergence of "des êtres nouveaux" (ll. 8, 43); the first four lines of the second section quite clearly stand halfway between what is remembered and what is to come. It is also worth noting the taut relationship between East and West, in which the line "Le vent vient du couchant" is particularly weighty as it sets the scene for the increase in sadness, the aging of the earthly gods, and the universe complaining through someone's (whose?) voice. And does not everything flow into this focal line of the last section "L'univers se plaint par ta voix?" Is not everything directed towards this line, which describes the tragic, or rather elegiac, function of what is presumably a human voice?

JAUSS: Now we should ask if and how the possibilities of connection or of clarification that have been suggested so far, affect, modify, or cancel one another out. Kracauer's idea of an "Orphic transformation of the civilized world," Preisendanz's emphasis on a dualism in the poem's composition, and Buddemeier's time perspectives of a lyrical, reminiscing *I*, do not refute one another—or at least only in certain dispensable details. As "positive determinants," insofar as they can be verified against the text, they all have a partial interpretive validity; but individually they cannot embrace all the impulses of poetic perception or their meaning.

SCHRAMM: As with pictures, it is a matter of standing the right distance away from the poem; this is controlled by the overall impression. It does not push you into searching for individual "associations," because there are clearly wider contexts: in the first four lines, thematically and rhythmically, the movement of the loss of self, fading away; in contrast to this is the intensive compression of line 5, beginning with the name that is strange both in sound and meaning ("Ispahan . . . carreaux émaillés de bleu"): the dwindling away comes up against an obstacle; then with a very gentle rhythm and conception ("avec vous" in contrast to the loss of the self in the crowd), line 6 starts a return movement, a "homecoming." The first verse gives the overall movement of the poem; in stanzas II-VI, the immediacy is gradually dissolved (though in a homecoming movement that reflects the fading away), stanzas VII and VIII have an external compression that corresponds to line 5; stanzas IX and X correspond to line 6: the whole poem is an absorption of the strange diversity into the context of the subject's own experience, as an internalization.

NEUMEISTER: One's impression on a first reading is irregularity of image sequence, openness of form, and obscurity of title and dedication. The direct reference in the first line to the dedication ("tu chantes") immediately draws attention to the importance of the personal pronouns in the poem. If you follow up where they occur, you will uncover a contrast: opposite the community of "tu" ("toi," "ton," "ta") with "les autres," "vous," "camarade," "femme," right through the poem stands the "je," in weak isolation. Only in line 6 are the individual and the community brought together: "je remonte avec vous."[4]

[4] The community of the "tu" (lls. 1, 9, 23, 33, 37, 42) with "les autres," etc. (lls. 1, 4, 6, 9, 23) is emphasized by the fact that the connecting "avec" occurs only in this context (lls. 1, 6, 9, 23). Cf. the cry of the "je": Ne m'abandonnez pas" (l. 4) in fear of being excluded; but also the word "camarade" (l. 9). The forsaken state of the "je" emerges from the situations he is involved in: the leaf falls apart in his fingers (l. 3); he is in danger of being lost in the crowd (l. 4); he recalls past security (l. 7); he hears the voice of whoever was a comrade of the "toi" (lls. 8-9). And even the sleeping compartment shows itself to be a treacherous shelter, with the "revolver armé" (l. 22). The only instance of community between "je" and "vous" (l. 6) forms a positive upward movement in the "remonte" (cf. the "ascenseur," l. 28, in which the "je" finds time to observe). This shows the importance of the vertical (upward movement) and the horizontal (movement into the distance) for the message of the poem. The horizontal contains the various onward movements (lls. 2, 9, 17, 20, 23, 26, 27). Also the bad news (l. 37) and the west wind (l. 38), the immensity of the market (l. 4), and the extensiveness of the suburb (l. 14). Against these images of desolation, distance, homelessness—most powerful in lls. 17-22—is the vertical, as a "positive" force: twice with direct climbing (lls. 6, 27), twice with growing (lls. 34, 43). In particular, the "surgissent" of the final verse (l. 43) shows the positive value of the vertical, as well as referring back to the title (*Arbre* as the quintessence of upward growth).

JAUSS: Could not "tu" also refer to *Arbre*?

GERHARDT: It obviously is left open whether "tu" refers to *Arbre* or to *Frédéric Boutet*. (Anyway, who was Frédéric Boutet? This question naturally ought to be settled before any interpretation.) It is possible that *Arbre* is also to be seen as part of the series "feuille" (l. 3), "coco" (l. 7), "bouleaux" (l. 34), "caroubiers" (l. 39). The *tu* has two functions—another person, as in line 9, or an indefinite agent (on a par with "je").

JAUSS: Does that mean the persons are deliberately introduced in such a way that they cannot be brought to a common or differentiating denominator?

BEYER: The *raison de la série* for this poem remains indiscernible. Overall it reveals no unity of place, first person, other persons, poetic subject matter etc. Even the modus of an evocation of memories, offered by the twofold "ne pas oublier" (ll. 7 and 25) and the final verse, cannot embrace all the elements of the poem. Apollinaire's predilection for using heavily disguised autobiographical material, which are comprehensible only to the author or some poetic *you* (*toi*? *Frédéric Boutet*?), connected to him through shared experience, can also be excluded as a unifying perspective, although the five demonstrative adjectives (ll. 4, 8, 14, 17, 35) which consistently dispense with the grammatically necessary cross-references, can be justified only by the modus of reminiscence. But this very consideration of minor (grammatical) structures seems to offer one possible starting point for a solution. The personal pronouns ("je"—"tu," "vous"—"les autres") can no longer be connected to any recognizable reference; the unconnected demonstratives point into a void; and the conjunction "mais" lacks any logical counterbalance. The linguistic determinants used in this way make the obvious juxtaposition of the disparate statements of the poem even more obvious. The paratactic construction with the conjunction "et," strengthened by the two demonstrative adjectives "ce," "cette" (ll. 14, 17), typifies this technique of disjointed alignment. The juxtaposition of disparates, which can be observed right through the poem (see, for instance, "Taupe-Ariane," l. 19), may well be the actual *raison de la série* of this poem. It is Apollinaire's answer to cubist techniques, which he got to know through Picasso and others, in the medium of language.

ABRAMS: The question is, what, if anything, holds this poem together, and makes it more than a congeries of fragments? Can we propose a principle of organization which binds the parts into a single whole?

I should like to propose, as an hypothesis to be tested by application to the text, that at the center of the poem there is a single "persona," a lyric "I." What we read in the poem is the sequence of his memories, thoughts, and observations. The seeming randomness of the details derives from the fact that the author does not connect these together for us; but the apparently free associations, and the seemingly intrusive observations, are in fact subdued into a kind of unity by a prevailing mood: a mood of nostalgia for a missing friend. This friend is the one whose remembered voice mingles with the sounds heard in line 1 ("Tu chantes avec les autres . . ."); whose remembered face intrudes in lines 31 ff. ("Entre les charbons . . . Entre deux vaisseaux . . . Il y a ton image"); and whose absence gives the elegiac coloring to the conclusion of the poem ("Tout est plus triste qu'autrefois . . . L'univers se plaint par ta voix").

JAUSS: Abrams coordinates the poem through a lyric I, as a lament in an interior monologue. But many lines could also be disconnected fragments of conversation (e.g., ll. 2, 4, 6, 9, 10). How much of this is memories suddenly recalled, and how much observation? Could this question be answered by the syntactic structure?

STEMPEL: What elements of form contribute towards transforming the text into a poem? There is practically no rhyme, apparently no consistent metrical scheme; and yet one can see general semantic correspondences which have a similar functional effect to that of recurrent sounds or rhythms. This applies for instance to the geographical names, which appear in nearly every verse, mostly in a transitional position at the end of a line. Cf. in stanza I / "Ispahan—Lyon" /; these are drawn parallel through the *et*, in a similar relation (though with a different nexus) to / "Europe—Amérique" / (stanza II), "une pauvre ville au fond de l'est" / (stanza III), "transsibérien" / (stanza IV), "Leipzig" (stanza V), "Rouen" / (stanza VI), "Finlande" / (stanza VII), "La Corogne" (stanza IX), all summed up or at least echoed in "univers," in the last stanza.

DIECKMANN: "Et" is accumulative, additive: so is it an addition of disparates?

NEUMEISTER: H. Dieckmann's suggestion can be demonstrated. Stanzas I, III, V, X are rounded off with clauses that are joined on with an *et*. So these closing lines take on the character of a summary, a "result," and they give a semantic justification to the group division.[5]

[5] The self-containment of the verses, accomplished here through "et," also comes about quite naturally in the other groups: in stanza IV through "mais," in stanzas II and VI through anaphoric preparation for the last line (twice "je" leading to "tout en restant," and four times "entre" leading to "il y a ton image"). The brevity of stanzas VII, VIII, IX prepares the way for the last stanza X.

STRIEDTER: If there is no obvious coherence in a poem, then a starting point for structural analysis would be easily recognizable, traditionally familiar, principles of division. Here, these are the division into lines and sections, which for all their divergence from tradition, can still be regarded as genuine lines and stanzas. The influence of the stanza division on an interpretation of this poem can be demonstrated by changing the division—if you make lines 23-33 into *one* stanza. Then on a first reading lines 29-32 would most likely appear to be "étages" for the "ascenseur" in line 28. With the four "entre's," this would give a syntactically perfectly correct sentence, in which the semantic connection would be established through association with the "climbing" of individual memory images (see, too "montais" in l. 27). Only the last line, 33, would invalidate this at first apparently clear syntactic-semantic connection, since now lines 29-32 have to be linked with "Il y a ton image." Or rather can be linked, because with the general independence of the individual lines and the frequency of elliptical constructions in the poem, line 33 could also remain on its own, so that neither the initial link with line 28 nor the later one with line 33 could be regarded as obviously the correct one. So is this a deliberate syntactic "switch," to jerk the reader out of his belief in the possibility of "clear" solutions, and so draw his attention to "ambiguity" as a structural element of this poem?

In fact between lines 28 and 29 there is a stanzaic division. The impact is strong enough, even on a first reading, for us to take line 28 as a kind of conclusion, and line 29 as a syntactic-semantic beginning, which builds up through a "crescendo" of anaphora, in the four *entre* lines, to line 33, which gives rise to a self-contained, and clearly divided verse. This, of course, does not mean that the possibilities of association I have mentioned, or the ambiguity of the poem, are generally removed. But one's second interpretation of the section differs considerably from one's first and is no longer evidence of constant ambivalence; in fact, on the contrary, it shows, rather, how dangerous it is to rush into an attempt to prove that ambiguity or obscurity is an underlying principle.

HENRICH: One must try to get a vision of the poem as a whole. Schramm was right that the impression of an overall movement in the text is of prime importance. It can be explained by the sequence of associations: they follow the course of an agitated unhappiness through to a new, calm, and collected sadness. The release from disquiet and menace seems to come about by means of memory. This movement arches through the image sequence of the text: images of ecstatic excitement—the presence of the friend that holds promise of reassurance—images of modern everyday life. You can deduce one theme of the poem from its movement: a new age, which destroys the home and so at first is felt as a threat, may come and may hold out expectations of a future—in a calm that will not need any "residence."

JAUSS: Henrich's interpretation amounts to giving semantic precedence to one theme ("The image of the friend is in everything"), so that the linguistic form is explained as a suitable means of expression for this "new clarity." This is an interpretation as if we were dealing with a classical form of art. It seems to me to be an approach that has to leap over the disparate sequence of visual impressions in this modern poem, that rushes headlong into a complete solution, which demands a total reorganization of all the impulses, thus removing the incongruence between perceptible linguistic form and possible content, and so missing out the effect intended by Apollinaire, which it has been our so far laborious, but enjoyable, common task to describe. Also, with Henrich's solution, the identity of the lyric "I" and of the pronominal persons remains undiscovered, and it sheds no light on the individual unmotivated contrasts and obscure interspersions in the overall movement of the poem.

NEUMEISTER: The following might be regarded as evidence in favor of Henrich's "classical" interpretation:

1. The juxtaposition mentioned, of "je" and "tu," "vous" etc.
2. Possibly deliberate rhymes (of the 44 lines, 28 rhyme, i.e., more than half, though apart from stanza x the rhymes are very far apart). The last five lines have alternating rhymes.[6]
3. The use of time stages, which in the midst of the chaotic present build a bridge from lost childhood across to an as yet indeterminate future security.[7]

STRIEDTER: The "reassurance" at the end of the poem, which Henrich spoke of, is clear at all events in the rhyming technique. Whereas at first regular rhymes only occur very rarely, the last stanza is the only one with a constant, strict rhyme scheme (*a b a b a*), in which the "*a*" rhyme

---

[6] E.g., "*-ois*," "*-oix*," in lls. 7, 21, 40, 42, 44; "*-é*" in lls. 2, 4, 22, 35, 39; there are other possible group links through such lines as 31 (=6), 32 (=11, 13, 38), 33 (=3, 28), 34 (=25).

[7] (a) The predominantly "positive" value of the "passé composé" (lls. 3, 7, 23; not 2) combined with concrete statements ("autrefois," lls. 7, 40; "légendes," l. 25; childhood joys, from stones to [sailing?] ships, lls. 29-32) draws a picture of a lost, happy childhood.

(b) Set against this, and spread out over all stages of time, is isolation in the chaos of the present world (*passim*).

(c) Out of this, and emphasized by the fourfold anaphora and the rhyming scheme, emerge the two present-tense utterances of lls. 33-34 and 43-44, which are both activities of growth, pointing towards a future. Cf. the presence of this threefold development beneath the surface of four present tenses in stanza x.

is reinforced by the repetition in "trois par trois," and the "rocking" of the rhyme is balanced out in the symmetry of the last line.

ISER: It is questionable whether the search for "positive determinants" in the poem can result in the elucidation of the "obscurity" that we want. Each of the individual interpretations suggested has an indisputable foundation, but at the same time each of them leads to a progressive clarification of the poem. The very variety of interpretations shows that different impressions arise according to the different distances at which the observer chooses to stand. This distance relationship, which Schramm emphasized, has so far undergone several variations. It is obvious from this that every attempt to make the contingent details of the poem even approximately coherent is bound to ignore opposing possibilities of interpretation. The unity we are striving after can be obtained only if we shut out all that cannot be integrated. So all the interpretations developed so far are right, even if their intentions are very different. Whatever form of coherence is to be attributed to the poem, the principle of selectivity has to be applied. And in this there is an element of illusion—insofar as it pretends to be able to comprehend the whole, without actually being able to do so. Even if all-embracing explanations seem to generate their own validity, the shape that they give to the whole soon proves to be nothing but one among many possibilities. In this way the discrepancies excluded from any overall interpretation come out into the open again, and so it is clear that the poem contains a number of possibilities for comprehension. The attraction of it lies in the fact that the different possibilities cannot be realized all at the same time. And this in fact seems to be what the poem aims at. The intention of the poem can never be completely fulfilled. But as each individual interpretation experiences its own inadequacy, it succeeds in evoking the other possibilities. The indications contained in the *broken images* of the poem, that we should form a conception of the intention of the whole, all have to be tested, because this is the only way in which the reflecting mind can uncover the many possibilities wrapped up in the poem. But if the text harbors different possibilities of comprehension, which form the intention of the poem only in company with one another, then this intention consists in the interaction of the realized with the possible, for each explanation releases other possibilities of explanation. The poem seems like a frame that can be filled with different pictures, and as the explanations given do not exclude one another, they collectively reveal the potential of the text, though the size of this cannot be accurately estimated.

TAUBES: In spite of the unmotivated contrasts and obscure interspersions in the overall movement of the poem, it does not seem to me to be a definite example of the obscure style. It is clearly bipartite. Stanzas I-IX are in contrast to the last stanza. The last stanza forms a lyrical, rhyming poem in itself, and offers a contrasting commentary on the rest of the poem.

PREISENDANZ: The poem seems to me to be only *prima vista* completely obscure or hermetic. Actually I feel tempted to relate it to themes of Rilke in the *Duino Elegies* and *Sonnets to Orpheus*. In the broad sweep from the opening "Tu chantes . . ." right through to the quite unequivocal final section, with its focal line speaking of a universal lament uttered in a human voice—in this broad sweep a theme is unfolded which, if one were more familiar with the poem, would enable one to reveal the coherence of what at first certainly seem to be incoherent images and evocations, as far as the sense, the tone, the "key" (elegiac) are concerned. Unless there is some a priori objection, one may be confident in approaching the immediate aspects of the surprising, strange and bizarre, under the premise "unity in diversity."

Someone has spoken of the completely obscure "interspersions," giving as an example *La Taupe-Ariane*. But are not the three creatures— the goatsucker, badger, and mole—named in a unified and easily discernible context? Allow me to give you a little lecture on zoology: the mole has eyes that are almost atrophied, so that he is popularly believed to be blind; also, like the badger, he lives in a ramified, underground system of tunnels, which people often like to call labyrinthine: hence the pairing off with Ariadne. The badger is an emphatically nocturnal creature, as is the goatsucker. The latter is a *nightjar* (a European bird, related to the American whippoorwill and nighthawk). It flies only at night, and so is popularly believed, like the bat, to be blind, although in fact, like the bat, it has an uncanny sense of direction during its zig-zag flights on the hunt for insects. Finally, the nightjar, unlike the swift to which it is akin, nests on the ground, and as it does not actually build a nest, everyone thinks it makes its home in nooks and crannies. So here in lines 18-19 we have three creatures that have in common the fact that they are nocturnal, chthonian, and can find their way in the dark and in labyrinths. I must say that, on the grounds of what I have gleaned from regular study of my *Brehm* and my *Brockhaus*, these animal names do not arouse in me any impression of obscurity. Can one not look back from them at line 2 "Où sont les aveugles?" And does not the apostrophizing of these particular animal names, with their epideixis of labyrinth, darkness, and underground existence, give us a key with which we can reveal the confusing, cryptic, remembered features that are contained in the images and data of the poem? And, finally, could not the evocation of Ariadne again be a reference to the situation of the speaker, to his relations with what he speaks of, and to the structure of this speech, this linguistic representation?

STRIEDTER: But as we have seen on our first reading, the animals are at the beginning of the *transsibérien* stanza—as if they were stations.

KRACAUER: As regards the character of our discussion so far, it seems to be suffering from the completely formal way in which we have approached the poem. We have not yet been able to determine the reason for the poet's sadness (l. 40), or the meaning of the title. The situation from which the poem proceeds is experience of the modern, mechanized world. The "I" is overwhelmed by this reality: a fragmented "I" expresses itself in arbitrary associations. And so the interpreter must reach the conclusion that there is no point in searching for a unified meaning in the sequence of associations. The title *Arbre* is to be related to the atomized world. The tree as an organic image indicates consolation and ultimate hope.

PREISENDANZ: In Rilke (he translated Valéry's *Palme*) the tree is often a metaphor for the poet, his glorification and especially his lamentation. The *Sonnets to Orpheus* begin with the lines: "There rose a tree. O pure transcension! O Orpheus sings! O lofty tree in the ear." In the late poem *Klage* the poet calls his early lamenting an unripe fallen berry of exultation, but now in the storm his whole tree of exultation is falling. There are corresponding images in the tenth *Duino Elegy*, with the trees of tears in "the landscape of lamentation,"the significance of the fig-tree for the elegiac "I" in the sixth elegy, because it almost omits to flower and thrusts its "pure secret" straight "into the early-resolute fruit," because it lets the sap leap "from its sleep, scarce waking, into the joy of its sweetest achievement." Perhaps I am seeing only what I want to see, but I at once linked up the title—disregarding the other trees named in the text—with "Tu chantes," with the single leaf which the "I" had plucked, and with the voice through which the universe laments at the end.

DIECKMANN: I see the title quite differently—as a contrast. From *Arbre* as a title, everything that follows goes off in the opposite direction: in the poem itself there is nothing else that is organic.

JAUSS: Even well-grounded interpretations of our poem do not just leave behind a residue of unexplained details, but are also conditioned by the

omission of another, equally tenable perspective. Kracauer's idea, showing the cinematic reality of a mechanized world but disregarding the possible perspective of a reminiscing "I," is not "refuted" by the
Schramm-Henrich view of a "counter-movement to memory" or to a
calmly accepted *tristesse* showing up the fragmented world as nothing
but "disquiet." The disparity of the image sequence need not necessarily
(even from stanza II onwards) be explained as incoherent memory. It can
also relate to a particular mode of perception, or to the special situation
of a perceiving "I" sitting on the boulevard recording snatches of other
people's conversation. Some poems in *Calligrammes* were in fact conceived by Apollinaire as "poèmes-conversations, qui prétendent repro-
duire, non sans humour, les bruits ambiants, les bouts de phrases en-
registrés par le poète dans un lieu public."[8] An example in our text: the
obscurity, the mysterious paradox of lines 10 and 11: "Du camarade qui
se promènera avec toi en Europe / Tout en restant en Amérique" disappears quite harmlessly if you think of it as two separate fragments,
which join up in a grotesque unit for someone listening (this would invalidate all previous conjectures about the identity of the *tu* and the
other persons; cf. a similar technique in stanza v).

Now you could also see an "organizing principle" in the *poème-
conversation*, and, using that as a basis, undertake a new interpretation
of the whole. This principle would present yet another view of the image
sequence, though without quite excluding the contrast we found earlier
between the world observed and the world remembered.[9] For the ambiguity of the image sequence still allows it to be applied to the
boulevard situation, the situation of the poet (l. 3), the remembered
image of the friend (l. 33), or the elegiac lament in line 42. And so the
process of expected clarification would lead here to the juxtaposition of
possible themes, which would also reveal themselves in the contrasts
we have observed in the contingent image sequence. We can draw a conclusion from this, which makes another interpretation possible: as our
poem cannot be completely subsumed under *one* theme, could not the
contrasts through which the possible themes present themselves actually
be thematic?

This is the premise of my attempt at an "unclassical interpretation."
Unclassical, because it is not to be orientated by the primacy of statement or the search for congruence of form and content. This approach is
necessary when observation of formal connections no longer coincides

---

[8] G. Apollinaire, *Œuvres Poétiques*, Edition de la Pléiade (Paris, 1956), p. 1074.

[9] If one looks closely at the possible snatches of conversation, regardless of context, it is
clear that Apollinaire enjoyed choosing fragments which in detachment could themselves
seem uncommon and poetic (cf. lls. 2, 4, 5, 23, 26, 27, 37).

with the emergence of a clear meaning or representation, or when—as in
the particular case of this poem—the disparate image sequence no longer
merges into the motivated order of a theme, but by itself poetizes the
unforeseeable, the contingent. The so-called time-stages (better, verbal
aspects and types of action) do not illustrate any kind of set course, but
they rather transfer certain phases of the image sequence into a different
atmosphere. Each of the twelve stanzas, which are all divided up differently, has its own tone, which contrasts with the stanza before and the
stanza that follows. For instance:

1. Speed and nearness of impressions, snatches of conversation, at the
tempo of "les phonographes galopent."

2. What is observed is suddenly jerked away into the distance, both
in time and space ("marchand de coco d'autrefois, en Europe, en
Amérique").

3. Now pictorial elements within the stanza seem to be contrasted
("veau" with "enfant," "douanier-ange" with "pauvre ville"), and only
with the "voyageur épileptique" in the waiting-room can one begin to
see "loneliness" as a possible common denominator.

4. Sentimental image sequence of lonesomeness now ousted by sudden onset of movement ("trans-Sibérien" variants, animal names as stations, see Striedter) and motif of grotesque twosomeness.

The analysis can easily be continued (particularly striking is line 35:
"Ce beau nègre en acier"—an absurd detail forming a stanza that over-
balances rather than counterbalances, to be understood as a contrasting
"patch" of color or something stuck on, like a collage). The alternating
optical and acoustic impressions continually give rise to new groupings
and refractions, the new verse puts the previous one in a different light,
so that a succession can also be seen as a juxtaposition. The analogy with
the art of that period is obvious, and is illustrated by M. Imdahl's Delaunay interpretation.[10] Even the last verse does not mark the end of an
irreversible order, but again splits up the foreseeable *tristesse* conclusion
through the counter-image of the "êtres nouveaux" ("trois par trois"
reminds one, among other things, of a marching unit), so that once
again the unexpected and inconclusive contingency is thematized.

IMDAHL: In this poem synchronism itself is intended as a theme. *Simultanéité* is a determinant factor in the whole Apollinaire, Delaunay circle.

---

[10] Cf. M. Imdahl, *Poetik und Hermeneutik II*, pp. 219 et seq., on the dissolution of the
tangible, material world by the pictorial means of colors, which themselves turn into a
reification of these pictorial means; Apollinaire's judgment on Delaunay's achievements
(p. 220) can also pass for a description of the effect of our poem: " . . . la nature n'est plus
un sujet de description, mais un prétexte, une évocation poétique d'expression par des
plans colorés qui s'ordonnent par des contrastes simultanés. Leur orchestration colorée
crée des architectures qui se déroulent comme des phrases en couleurs. . . ."

The contrasts of the poem are meant to give the effect of simultaneity: "Le simultanisme littéraire peut être donné par l'emploi des contrastes des mots."[11] And in this sense, what might seem chaotic in Apollinaire's poem is not the theme of chaos, but a condition of simultaneity. For in a poem this can be achieved only through the heterogeneous, through fragments, through *broken images*, through the destruction of associations.

HESELHAUS: The Apollinaire idea of the *poème-conversation* is part of the larger sphere of simultaneity in poetry, which the German Expressionists discussed a great deal. (Georg Heym: "I think my greatness lies in the fact that I have realized that there is little progression [Nacheinander]. Things lie mostly on one level. It is all a simultaneity [Nebeneinander]."[12] The structural principle of simultaneity is that the "Nacheinander" appears as a "Nebeneinander." This means that the lyric author no longer reports or narrates, nor does he describe his own "experiences" as a succession of events; he experiences the simultaneity of what enters into him. The category of the line as an organizing force of sequence falls by the wayside, and only the category of space as exposure to world and environment is left. This simultaneity of multiple experiences and observations can be given different genetic explanations: perhaps the modern experience of accelerated movement (which has led to the film as a new medium of representation), or the psychological instability of authors, perhaps even the ontological disorientation of modern socialized man. But what remains determinant is the fact that simultaneity represents a new structural principle within which the relation of parts to whole and whole to parts can be newly formulated. An example of this new formulation in the simultaneity poem is the contrast in Apollinaire's *Arbre* between distraction and attention (concentration). The alternation between distracted observations and concentration on memories is a rhythmic structure running right through the poem.

STIERLE: Can you talk of synchronism when the course of the poem changes perspectives with the different time stages? When differences in space and time merge into the ideational activity of the lyric subject?

HESELHAUS: The lyric *I* (Benn) as the *I* of the simultaneity poem keeps the heterogeneous associations together. It is not enough to say the contrasts are thematic: they are a way to a new concentration.

STIERLE: Through a more precise definition of the lyric subject, one can get a more precise definition of the connection between the fragmentary

[11] Delaunay, *Du Cubisme à l'art abstrait* (Paris, 1957), p. 112.
[12] G. Heym, *Tagebücher, Träume, Briefe*, 21st June 1910, III, *Dichtungen und Schriften* (Darmstadt, 1960).

images—if not semantically, at least functionally. The subject emerges in his jerky reminiscences as a *voyageur*. This motif seems particularly important to me, both for the poem and in the wider context of the whole history of this "genre." Not long before, V. Larbaud published his *Poésies de Barnaboth*, poems of a traveller devoted to the intoxication of distances; Blaise Cendrars had written his *Prose du Transsibérien*, which made an enormous impression on Apollinaire, and a part of which he quoted almost word for word in our poem. Apollinaire himself wrote a poem called *Le Voyageur*, in which he tried out the same theme, even before *Arbre*, and used a quite similar technique of presentation.

In the poetry of this period there is a new pathos of distance and the conquest of vast spaces, which is given a lyrical form in our poem. The fragment seems to me here to indicate not so much a fragmented world as the experience of the *voyageur*, which itself can only be fragmentary and broken—a fleeting glimpse. In the memory of a *voyageur* who by chance has come to rest for a moment in one corner of the earth; fragmented, disconnected images come crowding from all parts in the form of a snapshot of the conscious mind.

IMDAHL: According to Jauss, the discontinuous time stages of the poem are not illustrative of any progression, but create different atmospheres. This shows, like the interspersion of snatches of conversation, that the time continuum of a lyric "I"-experience is no longer there. It is the hindering, or even prevention, of empathy in this poem that enables one to experience simultaneity as a consequence of the discontinuity. In the time-bound arts, it does not seem possible to represent simultaneity in any other way.

HARTFELDER: But in the poem there are also common elements that mediate between the contrasts, as we have seen: time, place, sounds, as units that overlap. In these thematic structures there is a form of mediation.

HENRICH: A question on the principle binding the overall structure of the poem. Even if the contrasts are thematic, again the poem still constitutes only a sequence of impulses connected with content. So the only interpretation possible *is* according to content. What is the principle behind the individual sequences? Is it enough to say the simultaneous, the contrasting, as such—as Jauss and Imdahl think? One must be able to see the overall sequence of the contrasts if the poem is to be regarded as successful. It is a question of finding the right terms.

TAUBES: Jauss's claim that modern poetry needs modern analysis is a hermeneutic trap. Analysis of modern poetry does not need itself to be hermetic. There is no reason at all why one should not interpret in accordance with classical rules. The ultimate question is still that of what the poem says. In this case, elegiac lament for a lost "organic" or "natural" world, the *Arbre*.

HESELHAUS: The entering into simultaneity and the exit from it (coming to an end) is the formal problem here. The classical method is not so far off target. The classical questions can still be asked of this poem: the beginning of the poem and the end are "classical."

JAUSS: The methods of modern theories of style were developed from classical forms of art. They follow the principle of this form of art—coincidence of being and appearance, of image and meaning—in interpretation both of ancient and modern literature (with continual search for evidence that form corresponds perfectly to content), although according to Hegel the principle of these non-classical forms of art is to be defined as the non-coincidence of *gestalt* and meaning. The question is how this form of interpretation can be methodically correct with a modern art form which no longer aims at a form perfect in itself and at "new clarity" of statement, but at incongruence of presentation and thing presented, together with the resultant incomplete and hence ambiguous perception of the poetic whole.

Certainly one can also approach this poem with "classical expectations," and ask, as Taubes does, "what the poem says," and looking at it from lines 40-42 interpret Apollinaire's *Arbre* as an "elegiac lament" for a lost, more beautiful, or even "wholesome," world. But then, as we have seen, behind Apollinaire comes the unmistakable figure of Hölderlin—and by no means to the advantage of our poem. I think that differentiating here is more rewarding than identifying: if one regards *Arbre* as a Hölderlin-type elegy, then one automatically loses the originality of Apollinaire—namely, the coming and going of all themes in the simultaneity of the perceptive activities. The interpreter cannot brush aside the sequence of perception intended by the poet without doing some damage. The need for any interpretation constantly to refer back to the *sens vécu*, to the intentional effect of the first reading, is an inevitable and basic principle for the philological interpretation of poetic texts (also of classical texts). [13] The line showing the poetic situations (l. 3), and also

---

[13] In support of this argument I refer not only to Leo Spitzer's interpretative method and his dictum: "Défense absolue de renverser l'ordre littéral d'une poésie" (*Romanische Literaturstudien*, 1936-1956, Tübingen, 1959, p. 376), but also to the very noteworthy essay by Arthur Nisin: "La littérature et le lecteur" (Paris, 1959). Cf. my critique, *Archiv für das Studium der neueren Sprachen und Literaturen*, 197 (1961), pp. 223 ff. Here Nisin, in conjunction with Valéry's challenge to philology, develops the hermeneutic rela-

the elegiac lines 40-42 (especially since they are not the conclusion), are just one possible "positive determinant" out of several; their subject matter must again be referred back to the *sens vécu*, to their "Thus," "Here," "Now" and "Nevermore," if one's overall impression of the poem is not to lose its effect through a reified "skeleton key" at the end.

HENRICH: For a concrete interpretation and for a judgment on the quality of the poem, it is not enough just to outline its structural principle and describe Apollinaire's poetic technique. A series of ambiguities is still not a cogent whole. If this whole, thanks to the technique in which it is set out, invites a constantly new interpretation, this is neither arbitrary in detail nor devoid of a basic orientation running convincingly right through the composition of the text. The first reading conveys this cogency through the suggestion of the rhythm. The interpretation must be in compliance with this medium, in which the whole poem moves. Otherwise the interpretation could be used in the same way for any poem of this type, and so it would reveal too little. It does not seem right to me to call an explanation of the rhythmic structure "content" interpretation. It sets out to grasp the particular form of *this* poem. Naturally every rhythm contains ideas of content and has affinities to a world of images. That is especially clear in this poem, which incidentally seems to me to be comparatively traditional. Its technique of composition may be modern. So in this case it has just given rise to a poem that lies in the "anteroom" of modernity.

ABRAMS: What we have all, in fact, been doing at this session, is to propose diverse "interpretations" of this poem which are in the nature of hypotheses. These hypotheses emerge from a reading of the poem, and must in turn be tested (somewhat in the mode of scientific hypotheses) by the degree to which they account for all the elements of the poem; the preferable hypothesis is the one which is simplest in itself, yet best fits all the details of the text. Since such a hypothesis sets out from, and also terminates in, an appeal to our response to the poem, the first impression that the poem makes on the reader is important, but not in itself determinative. A later impression, which emerges from a correction of our initial hypothesis by the details of the text, may prove to be preferable to the first one.

---

tionship between "sens vécu" and "sens vérifiable." In interpreting poetic texts it must always be possible for the latter to be referred back to the former, i.e., the critically evaluating "sense" to be referred back to the direct experience and sequence of perception of the text when first read; an interpreter who only considers the "sens vérifiable"—i.e., interprets directly from the altered standpoint of his second reading—runs the risk of masking the "lecture poétique" with his "lecture prosaique"; in other words, clinging to "what the verses say" at the expense of "what the verses are."

JAUSS: According to Henrich it is not enough to reveal the technique—but one must reveal the perfection of the technique. What I was concerned with, though, was to emphasize the preeminence of the formal, and so the openness of interpretation. Perfection of form seems to me to be a specifically classical expectation. In our poem, such an expectation proves to be illusory, because the constantly renewed perception of possible connections and contrasts within the simultaneity prevents any ultimate conformity with the classical harmony of form and content. With this modern poem, the process of understanding turns into an inconclusive movement between representation and thing represented, form and content, the incongruence of which constantly swings the reader's perception from one pole to the other, from image to meaning and vice versa.

STRIEDTER: Is not the thesis of an "incongruence" of "form and content" even more problematic than that of a "perfection"? In this poem, what is supposed to be "form" and what "content"? Are not particular experiences here—such as lack of unity, lack of clarity, obscurity, simultaneity etc.—both structural and "thematic"? And cannot such a "thematization" of the form, or "formalization" of the theme, from an esthetic point of view, very possibly become "perfect," though without this perfection having to be a "classical" one?

BLUMENBERG: I would like to take up Taubes' statement that "The claim that modern poetry needs modern analysis is a hermeneutic trap. Analysis of modern poetry does not need itself to be hermetic." I agree with this statement, which rather upsets the beautiful unanimity of our exegetic demonstration, though my conclusions may look rather different from those that Taubes intended. Heselhaus said that there is no reason why one cannot ask the classical questions of Apollinaire's poem, and I would like to go even further and say that one *must* ask them, because those questions are preconditions of the poetic effect. This does not apply just to this poem: the possible response to a modern work of art depends precisely on the ineradicable "classicality" of the expectations towards it, the fulfilling, shattering, or frustration of which is one of the elementary effects. "Modernity," whatever definite meaning you give it, can only be the *ultima ratio* of a process of interpretation in which the "burden of proof" for the unanswerableness of the classical questions has been undertaken and found wanting.

And so the outcome of a "classical" hermeneutic inquiry will depend not only on *which* questions are asked, but also in what *order* they are asked. With Apollinaire's poem, it seems basic to me that the question of "what it says," which Taubes wanted to ensure was asked, cannot be

answered before one has asked about the addressee of the statement—
not, of course, in the sense suggested by Gerhardt, that one must know
more about the actual character of Frédéric Boutet, though I will not dispute that this would also be extremely desirable. The question of who is
being spoken to is, in accordance with Stempel's suggested list, one of
the possible ambiguities. The classical work of art offers the percipient the
chance to identify himself with the standpoint and presuppositions of the
addressee, insofar as the work contains them; even occasional lines presuppose that one takes part in the "occasion" and that they are not inac-
cessibly intimate. With the poem we are discussing, it is this classical
expectation in particular that is deprived of its self-evidence, if not actually destroyed—and this is what gives the poem its fascination: the
reader is excluded from identifying himself with the addressee—and so,
indirectly, also with the lyric "I." The speaking "I" does not shut himself off by withdrawing into the labyrinth of his interior monologue, but
on the contrary by addressing another I and talking with him about an
intimate and singular possession that the two "I" 's have in common.
The poem as a whole does not have an addressee in the sense that a coherent gift is presented to a particular partner for all eyes, as it were, to
admire; nor does it consist of a series of messages conveyed to a third
party, with the reader as an accidental, fictively unwanted, witness. The
apostrophe addressed, as it were, past the reader is the evocation of a
potential that is unknown and inaccessible for him. He does not learn
that or how the speaking and the listening subjects integrate the community of their possession. The ambiguity of the poem lies in the fact
that it compels the reader to think in the place of the undefined addressee, whose existence in the reader's imagination has the function of
preserving his trust in the meaningfulness of the obscure, mysterious
composition, without ever having to confirm or satisfy it. And so the
poem is not a context of information, the elements of which can be integrated into a tableau of "represented reality." Its basic process is that of
anamnesis or, perhaps to be more precise, proceeding towards anamnesis, as the one still possible common factor with a partner whose answers and confirmations the reader could not imagine, and with whom
he has no hypothetical common history that could be verified. Everything is "allusion" in discreet pigeon-holes for which there must be a
system of reference in the continuum of time and space, without this
becoming thematic. In this way the diagram of past evocations changes
into a structure of "advances" pushing off into ever new directions, and
coming more or less close to the time vector, after starting at a point
outside this line. The figure involved in this anamnetic activity, groping
towards its end but never reaching or restoring what is lost, might be the

tree evoked in the title, which of course is not viewed as a self-contained gestalt, but as a developing, sprouting texture indicating the uselessness of the attempt to reach the past. It is a "third instance," for which every line of the poem has correlatives and fulfills the intention that has broken down for the reader. The "eccentric" adjustment of the disparity of the poem lies neither in the associations nor in the formally facilitated representation of a "chaotic reality," but in the anamnetic substructure which bears the material elements. Buddemeier rightly drew our attention to the change of time stages in the poem and to the resultant possibility of an organizing connection principally with the chaotic. But if this thesis of the constitution of an anamnesis is correct, then one must draw a careful distinction between time stages and types of action. The present tense with which the poem begins is a remembered present, alluding to a past situation of the addressee; it then returns into the present of the speaker, who asks where the blind people are now, whom he once met with his friend. Ambiguity remains, because we can never decide whether one molecule of the poem authentically forms part of the speaker's present or is a "quotation" from a common memory, whether we are confronted by a descriptive memory of a shared spectacle, or a recalling of words that had already been spoken at the time. Jauss is right in saying that many lines could be snatches of conversation, evocative repetitions of things once spoken, in which it is a matter only of attesting to the accuracy of detail, the effect of which is an induction of someone else, perhaps shaming his forgetfulness, his infidelity, or lamenting the incomprehensibility of his fatal silence—the function also remains in the ambiguity. Unsuccessful, off-target anamnesis may also slip in, perhaps allegorical interjection as well, like badger and mole who live in the underground of the present just as memory itself. Allegory as an interjection, and not as a clarification of the overall gestalt—one must be prepared for this in modern poetry.

Now I would like to go into the question that has arisen several times during the discussion, concerning the procedural connection between esthetic response and interpretation. Schramm made it clear that it rests with the percipient to adopt the distance prefigured by the poem, and he felt that the first impression fixed this distance and so invalidated the search for "associations." Neumeister also suggested that one should proceed from the first impression—but has he really followed this procedure in defining, as one of his first tasks, where *je, tu, vous* come in the poem? If it is right to designate the obscurity of modern poetry as ambiguity, then the first impression cannot be given hermeneutic primacy. The distance at which the reader has to stand is not determined by the first impression, but proves to be a variable adjustment during which histories or aspects—it does not matter which one chooses—can be tested and joined together, so that the meanings within the overall ambiguity can be, if not exhausted, then at least tapped. Whereas, if one gives oneself up wholly to the first impression, which is started off by the *Tu chantes* . . . of the first line, one is at once led astray by the false, imperfect present-tense and the false second person mode of address of a personal poem, which loses its grip on the "I," that comes into being along with the anamnesia, and its need for its own identity, in the time which the poem itself cannot, as it were, maintain. The fine, molecular structure of the poem has the effect of frustrating every "settled" first impression and every incipient stabilization of expectations in a single aggregate, and continually tearing them away from the concrete "intentions" they have formed. And so it is not the impression that decides the distance, but the choice of distances that leads to particular impressions. The "overall movement" that Henrich spoke of, is not the teleology prevailing in the poem itself, but the dynamic "entropy" arising from the succession of constant adjustments that have to be made by the reader. Only the imaginary picture of an addressee, evoked in the breaks and omissions, whose function is the potentiality of the integrated memory and the release of the sadness and torment of an always unfulfilled search for a lost reality that is not to be found again in isolation—only the projected occupation and imaginative elaboration of this "third position" leads to the "reassurance" that Henrich mentioned as the point at which the supposed overall movement of the poem converges. But this overall movement does not go through the poem as a unit—it goes through the many discontinuous stages of our responses. The teleology is in the eating, not in the pudding. Extracting the immanent poetry here, then, would mean recognizing that it is suspended during the first impression and the demand for esthetic pleasure inherent in the first impression, and so deducing the need for an analysis whose leading questions concern formal, indeed grammatical observations. A formal revelation and perception of the immanent indications in this way will turn into provisional approaches, guides to possible adjustments. The obstacle to a "progressive elucidation" of the Apollinaire poem is not so much the formal structure as the element of lost dialogue that characterizes it and makes clear the formal character of the broken-off intentions. The hermetic side of the poem is not the alienation and mystification of a reality accessible for the author but arbitrarily withheld from the reader; it is the indication of a situation, common both to author and reader, of being referred to an unavailable "third instance," whose unavailability constitutes the impossibility of a convergence into clarity and also the resultant peculiar sadness that lies over the poem and affects the reader. Although this "third instance," unlike the instance of the medieval conception of reality with its built-in guarantees,[14] does not have possession of the hidden plan or the assured meaning of the whole, nevertheless it has taken with it the "other half" of the time-shattered images to where they can never be brought back again. Ambiguity here is the linguistically manifest contradiction of the possibility of *temps retrouvé*.

[14] See Blumenberg, "The Conception of Reality and the Possibility of the Novel," pp. 30 ff., in the present volume.

III

The No Longer Fine Arts: Border Phenomena of Esthetics. From *Poetik und Hermeneutik III*

REINHART KOSELLECK

Chance as Motivation for the Unexplained in Historical Writing:

Notes on Archenholtz's *History of the Seven Years' War*

I

THE main difficulty in discussing chance in historiography is the fact that this subject has its own history, which as yet is unwritten. It is certainly impossible to discuss the role of chance in any given situation without first taking into account the whole terminology of the historian concerned. One needs to ask what is the opposite term that will exclude chance, or what is the overall term that makes it relative. Raymond Aron, for instance, begins his introduction to the philosophy of history with the antithesis, based on Cournot, between *"ordre"* and *"hasard"*; he concludes: "Le fait historique est, par essence, irréductible à l'ordre: le hasard est le fondement de l'histoire."[1] In comparison with scientific order, history may well seem to have a basis of chance, but this is to ignore the time factor that influences all historical definitions. In the course of his treatise, Aron breaks up this rigid antithesis, and thus alters the significance of chance in his historical epistemology. An event can seem coincidental or not, depending on the standpoint of the observer. In the light of one set of circumstances it may seem accidental; in the light of another, it may seem inevitable. Carr also adopts the attitude that chance is a matter of perspective.[2] This at least brings us to a stage at which the term "chance" has been methodically restricted—a stage that has not always been in existence.

Temporally speaking, chance is purely a category of the present. It is independent of all future expectations—unless it be the shattering of them—and it cannot be deduced from past experience—otherwise it would no longer be chance. Therefore, insofar as history aims at elucidating historical events in their temporal context, chance must be regarded as "ahistorical." It is not "unhistorical." On the contrary, it is a term ideally suited to circumscribing the surprising, the new, the unforeseen, etc., in history. Thus a particular set of circumstances may originate with a coincidence, or an inconsistent course of events may re-

[1] R. Aron, *Introduction à la philosophie de l'historie* (Paris, 1948), p. 20.
[2] E. H. Carr: *Was ist Geschichte?* (Stuttgart, 1963), pp. 96 ff.

quire chance to fill in its gaps. Whenever the historian calls on chance, it is primarily to smoothe over such inconsistencies, and this is what gives chance its historical status.

Nowadays the historian will certainly try to avoid chance, if possible, but up to and including the eighteenth century it was customary to give chance or luck, in the guise of Fortuna, its due importance. This custom has a long and checkered history, of which we shall mention only a few basic features here.[3] Fortuna was one of the few heathen deities to be transposed into the Christian view of history. Augustine, with that sharp logic typical of the Christian "Enlightenment," ridiculed the contradiction inherent in the recognition of a goddess of luck: "Ubi est definitio illa Fortunae? Ubi est quod a fortuitis etiam nomen accepit? Nihil enim prodest eam colere, si fortuna est."[4] He attributed all accidents exclusively to the hand of God, and so Fortuna was to disappear from any truly Christian history. When Otto von Freising refers to coincidences, as he often does, it is only in order to explain that they are acts of God.[5] It is precisely their incomprehensible nature that reveals the hidden hand of God. Fortuna was placed in a theological context, and so lost her identity.

If nevertheless Fortuna was adopted by an increasingly Christian world—either through popular belief or following Boethius—it was certainly because her position in everyday life or in history could not simply be left unoccupied. With a range from good or bad luck right up to "Salvation," she offered a structural basis for individual histories,[6] representing the constancy of change and those impersonal events that are beyond the control of men. Whatever attitude virtue and faith might have towards her—regardless of whether she was answerable to or, later, replaceable by God—Fortuna always stood for the changing times and circumstances that prevail over the "best laid schemes."[7]

---

[3] Cf. Papers (Hugo Friedrich school) by K. Heitmann, *Fortuna und Virtus, Eine Studie zu Petrarcas Lebensweisheit*, Köln/Graz, 1958 (*Studi Italiani*, ed. by E. Schalk and M. Marianelli, Vol. 1), and H. Jansen (*Kölner Romanist. Arb. N.F. Heft 9*), and ancient literature quoted. Also F. P. Pickering, *Literatur und darstellende Kunst im Mittelalter*, Berlin, 1966 (*Grundlagen der Germanistik*, ed. by H. Moser, 4), pp. 112 ff.

[4] Augustinus, *De Civitate Dei*, IV, 18.

[5] Otto von Freising, *Chronica sive Historia de duabus Civitatibus*, ed. by W. Lammers (Darmstadt, 1960), pp. 10, 92 (a rare occasion on which he speaks of "worldly" Fortuna and not of "fortuitis casibus"), pp. 130, 210, 290, 446.

[6] Cf. H. Löwe, "Regino von Prüm und das historische Weltbild der Karolingerzeit," and H. Beumann, "Widukind von Korvei als Geschichtsschreiber und seine politische Gedankenwelt"—both essays in *Geschichtsdenken und Geschichtsbild im Mittelalter*, ed. W. Lammers (Darmstadt, 1961), pp. 123, 133, 154.

[7] Zincgref, *Emblematum Ethico-Politicorum Centuria* (Heidelberg, 1666), XCIV, and the résumé of Tradition in *Zedlers Universallexikon* (Halle and Leipzig, 1735), IX, 1545 ff.

To this extent, Christians and humanists were all agreed about the "Daughter of Providence" and the "Mother of Chance."[8] The metaphor of the turning wheel,[9] applied by Boethius to the Christian interpretation of history, referred to the repetition of all events and the fact that, with all the ups and downs, nothing new could come into the world until the Last Judgment. At the same time, Fortuna—in Boethius too—was regarded as a symbol of the incommensurable, a vindication of God. From both points of view it was possible to regard the good or bad luck that interfered with a human situation as the explanation of that situation, since good or bad luck did not appear to be immanent in it. With her two faces, Fortuna was versatile enough to embody all possible histories; at her table there was room for "all centuries."[10] It was her changeableness that guaranteed equal conditions for all earthly events and their depiction. Fortuna's place was in the theory and science, not in the events of history. Thanks to her, history could be raised to the status of something exemplary. Previously, Fortuna could be rationalized only theologically or ethically, not historically: she became a creature of pure chance the moment she was viewed empirically or pragmatically.

The problem of chance in history first became of significance when Providence was replaced by reasons which did not suffice to explain accidents, coincidences, and miracles. Furthermore, there was a need for some kind of historically immanent cause, psychological or pragmatic, which went beyond the scope of the old Fortuna. The famous nose of Cleopatra, which according to Pascal changed the face of the world,[11] shows the transition from one epoch to the next: chance has become an immanent cause to which massive consequences may be attributed. Through its very triviality and externality, chance takes on the character of *cause*. Thus Frederick II, in his *Antimachiavell*, attributes the Treaty of Utrecht to a pair of gloves ordered prematurely by the Duchess of Marlborough.[12]

In the eighteenth century, a whole historic movement arose from these causes: Richer wrote an *Essay sur les grands évenemens par les petites causes* (1758); affairs of state were traced back to the intrigues of mistresses; Voltaire attributes the devastation of Europe in the Seven Years' War to the *amour-propre* of two or three individuals.[13] Here

[8] Gracián, quoted by Jansen, pp. 191 f.

[9] Boethius, *De Consolatione Philosophiae*, lib. 2; ed. Gothein (Zürich, 1949), p. 80.

[10] Baltasar Gracián, *Criticón*.

[11] Pascal, *Pensées*, ed. Ch. M. Des Granges (Paris, 1948), p. 162; cf. p. 744 (Brunschvicg edition).

[12] Frédéric le Grand, *Œuvres* (Berlin, 1848), VIII, 151.

[13] See J. H. Brumfitt, *Voltaire Historian* (Oxford, 1958), pp. 105 ff.

chance stands in the service of causes which the historian sets forth with a moral intention. Thus Duclos wrote, concerning the policies of Louis XIV: "As regards our misfortunes, one can see that they are entirely our own fault, whereas our deliverance is due completely to chance."[14] Chance here signifies the absence of those moral and rational modes of conduct that should be a part of good politics, and any stroke of luck that may occur is merely a stopgap for rational politics.

"La fortune et le hasard sont des mots vides de sens," wrote Frederick;[15] they have sprung from the heads of poets and owe their origin to the profound ignorance of the world, which has given vague names to the effects arising from unknown causes. The misfortune of a Cato, for instance, is said to have arisen solely from the unforeseeableness of conflicting causes and effects, which brought about the contretemps, and which it was impossible for him to forestall. Frederick tried to develop a political system that could bring all the circumstances of his time into the service of his plans. He dismissed Machiavelli's old Fortuna, without quite being able to dispense with what she stood for. Terms connected with time (*temps* and *contre-temps*) took her place, but the scope of these was rationally restricted by questions of cause and intent. And so coincidence revealed itself, in fact, to be a whole collection of causes, and the word itself became a name without a reality. And this explains, adds Frederick somewhat mysteriously, why "Fortune" and "Chance" are the only heathen gods to have survived—a passage which Voltaire deleted from the proofs.[16]

The extent to which chance disappeared under the scrutiny of an enlightened historian—and also obtruded either through circumstances or from reasons of presentation—will become apparent from our study of Archenholtz.

II

Von Archenholtz, formerly a captain in the royal Prussian army, was one of the most widely read historians of the late eighteenth century, and was also one of the authors of the *Moral Pictures* that are regarded as a precursor of modern sociology. In his popular study of the Seven Years' War, Archenholtz frequently resorts to chance. In the context of our discussion, then, he is open to the suspicion of having wandered off into non-historical terminology, impermissible for a consistent presentation of historical matter, in order to conceal a lack of motivation in his account. Let us look closely at three of Archenholtz's "coincidences."

[14] Carl Duclos' *Geheime Memoiren*, German trans. (Berlin, 1792), I, 15.
[15] *Frédéric le Grand*, p. 149; the rest in Chap. 25 of *Antimachiavell*.
[16] P. 285.

At the very beginning, he describes the infamous coalition of the two Catholic courts of Vienna and Versailles, which seemed to turn the whole political system of Europe upside down—a shock, incidentally, not dissimilar to that of the Hitler-Stalin pact of 1939: "Diese Vereinigung Österreichs und Frankreichs, welche die Welt in Erstaunen setzte und als das grösste Meisterstück der Politik betrachtet wurde, war ein blosser Zufall."[17] (This union between Austria and France, which amazed the world and was regarded as the greatest masterpiece of politics, was a mere coincidence.) For France—so runs Archenholtz's explanation of the coincidence—never had any intention of destroying the King of Prussia, however angry she may have been at his treaty with England, and however much resentment Kaunitz may have stirred up in Paris against him. The real reason for France was that she wanted to conquer the Electorate of Hannover, in order to gain higher objectives (höhere Absichten) in America. This is a motive which Frederick in his memoirs also quoted as decisive, and which subsequent historians as well have regarded as central, since it indicates the global context that marks the Seven Years' War as the first genuinely world war in our history.

What, then, was the coincidence Archenholtz was referring to? He was perfectly aware of the worldwide context within which the coalition achieved its political aims. But what had been the main purpose in the eyes of the court at Versailles was, for the Prussian reader, a "blosser Zufall"—a mere coincidence. For the coalition turned its attention first, on behalf of the French Ministry (not of Pompadour), to England, against whom France was fighting for trans-Atlantic dominance. What seems absurd, or coincidental, against the background of the centuries-old struggle in Europe for the balance of power, immediately becomes meaningful when seen in its global context.

Chance for Archenholtz here was not just a stylistic means of making his tale more dramatic—though this was certainly one motive; it also served to delineate a particular perspective: that of the contemporary. As a contemporary who had fought in the great war himself, he had also helped to create this history. For the Central European reader, the introduction of chance, with its emphasis on the lack of motivation, was perfectly justified, before the historian, with his wider field of vision, ultimately produced the motives. For these motives lay in a different sequence of cause and effect, and in quite different causes from those which the Central European reader could have experienced. And so Archenholtz's "Zufall" is indeed a coincidence from one point of view, but

[17] J. W. v. Archenholtz, Geschichte des Siebenjährigen Krieges (1791), Halle/Saale, ed., no date, pp. 2 f.

fully motivated from another. A scientific historian of the nineteenth century, such as Ranke, would not countenance such a change of perspective; but the historians of the late Enlightenment were trained, as few others have been, to present history not just as knowledge, but also—in order to transmit this knowledge—as a convincing experience. The gaps in the experience of the German reader are clearly revealed— hence the "blosser Zufall" of the coalition—and also filled in, for even in 1790 historians were already seeking for causes wherever possible.

What is the significance of another coincidence which Archenholtz refers to in his analysis of the first decisive battle of the Seven Years' War? "A very common chance (*ein sehr gewöhnlicher Zufall*)" he writes, "a clever monk going for a walk during the first days of the siege, saved Prague and the [Austrian] monarchy. This man, who is not unknown in the history of literature, by name Setzling, observed a column of dust approaching the northern parts of the town."[18] There follows detailed description of how the monk suspected that this was the Prussians, hastened to the observatory, found his suspicions confirmed by what he saw through the telescope, and was able to inform the commanding officer in time, so that a tactically vital hill was taken over before the enemy could take it.

Archenholtz had learned from historians' discussions on Pyrrhonism to weigh historical certainty against historical probability in order not to wander off into the realm of romance, and so he hastens to qualify his tale of coincidence. As a fact he takes it seriously, but at once sets it against the military situation: "The surprise attack on a town that was occupied by an army of 50,000 seasoned warriors, and this in broad daylight, is unheard-of in the annals of war and incomprehensible for any soldier, and would have strained the credence of the present generation and have been regarded as pure invention by generations to come."

Thus Archenholtz transposes this apparently vital chance occurrence—an unmilitary event casting its influence on the course of a war—into the realm of military possibilities. In this context, the coincidence takes on a different complexion: it becomes an anecdote. It does, of course, throw a somewhat ironic light on the Protestant-Catholic confrontation in the struggle for Bohemia; but here the coincidence has been caught up in the whole complex of rational military techniques and strategies. The coincidence, inexplicable when interpreted as the cause of the relief of Prague—unless Archenholtz were to adopt the Prague legend and attribute it to the hand of God, which he could scarcely have done, being an enlightened Prussian—now takes its place, through its effect, in a credible context. Viewed from the standpoint of its effect, our

[18] Pp. 40 ff.

monk's decisive little stroll loses its coincidental character. Set in the context of rational causes and consequences of contemporary warfare, this extraordinary event is recorded by Archenholtz, but indirectly devalued, because it was exchangeable. The author gives us to understand that if this event had not saved Prague, then certainly another one would have done so. That it happened to be the monk going for a walk is in itself a singular occurrence—but strategically, this was quite irrelevant. *Someone* would have spotted the Prussians anyway.

In order to delocalize and in effect eliminate the coincidence in this way, Archenholtz follows two lines of thought: one, military feasibility, the other, the comparison between history and fiction. He quotes the old Ciceronian opposition of *res factæ* and *res fictæ*, handed down since Isidor from one generation of historians to the next,[19] to show military probability—not fact—against military improbability, or "fiction."[20] The non-occurrence of the coincidence would have led into the realm of the possible and conceivable but, at the same time, unlikely. If Prague had fallen, it would have been in an absurd manner, and only then would the chance element have been complete (i.e., had noone spotted the Prussians) and the unlikely have materialized.

That such experiences were not unfamiliar to the people of that time is shown by the commemorative coin struck by the city of Kolberg in 1760, after it had been freed at the last moment from the 23,000 Russian troops besieging it. The inscription, based on Ovid, runs: "res similis fictæ," translated by Archenholtz as "eine Begebenheit, wie erdichtet" (an incident as imagined).[21] The Kolberg example helps us to see what Archenholtz felt about the Prague incident. The monk on his walk is, historically speaking, mediatized. Retrospectively, the coincidence is stripped of its coincidental trappings. Fortuna is not excluded, but as a cause she is now put back in second place, however strongly she may at first have claimed to be the prime and only cause.

Montesquieu, in his paper on the greatness and the decadence of the Romans, offered an explanation that was as simple as it was rational. All elements of chance remain secondary to general causes. "Et si le hasard

[19] Isidor of Seville, *Etymologiarum sive originum libri*, xx, ed. Lindsay (Oxford, 1957), in 2 vols., I, 40 ff.

[20] That inner probability is more convincing than reality is an argument which since Aristotle's time (although not uncontested) has elevated poetry over history. For poetry is more concerned with probability than fact. Archenholtz makes use of this train of thought, which had become known to him through Lessing, in order to raise (by means of the classical argument in the *Poetics*) history above poetry—one of the ways whereby the revaluation of history above poetry occurred. See H. Blumenberg, *Paradigmen zu einer Metaphorologie* (Bonn, 1960), pp. 96-105.

[21] Archenholtz, p. 254.

d'une bataille, c'est-à-dire une cause particulière, a ruiné un État, il y avait une cause générale qui faisait que cet État devait périr par une seule bataille. En un mot, l'allure principale entraîne avec elle tous les accidents particuliers."[22] Anyone who looks for a cause will never be at a loss for a cause. It would, of course, be frivolous to dismiss the business of the historian in this way. Archenholtz's art as an historian lay in his ability to let incommensurable factors stand together and at the same time to give a historically satisfying answer. Thus he later described the siege of Breslau in 1760. Outside the walls were 50,000 Austrians under their most competent general, Laudon. In the town were 9,000 Austrian prisoners of war, ready to rebel, like many pro-Austrian citizens; the number of defenders was a mere 3,000 men, of whom only a thousand were active soldiers. Archenholtz describes the successful defense as an event which at best would pose a problem for the philosopher, and which the shrewd historian would scarcely dare tackle in view of its improbability. Such a miracle, he continues, could be performed only by the power of Prussian military discipline.[23] One can question this explanation of the miracle, and suggest other causes to make the miracle seem even less miraculous, but the tendency here is quite clear: miracles, accidents, etc., are introduced only in order to disabuse the normal reader who would in fact have expected them.

Now we come to the last example, that we have selected at random, from the history of the Seven Years' War. How does our author go

[22] Montesquieu: *Considérations sur les causes de la grandeur des Romains et de leur décadence*, chap. xviii, ed. Faguet (Paris, 1951), p. 475. Montesquieu's dictum was well-known in the eighteenth century (see Brumfitt: *Voltaire Historian* [Oxford, 1958], p. 113). Archenholtz certainly knew it, for he modified Montesquieu's sentence to the effect that recent history offered no example, "dass mit der Behauptung oder dem Verlust einer einzigen Stadt das Schicksal einer ganzen Monarchie verknüpft gewesen wäre" (". . . that the fate of a whole monarchy had ever been bound up with the holding or the loss of one single town"), p. 342. And, as Frederick's strategy was based on continual movement, he could have afforded to leave his most important fortress, Magdeburg, relatively unfortified. The enemies could not have found one single decisive turning point in this war. Ranke said later, in his essay on the great powers (*Hist. Polit. Zeitschr.*, ii), that the Seven Years' War differed from all previous wars in that, at every moment throughout its long duration, the existence of Prussia was at stake. A single unlucky day could have brought about its downfall. And to his own complementary question as to what general causes prevented Prussia from falling, Ranke replied that Frederick was not captive to the French philosophy of pleasure. He was a rule unto himself and depended upon his own truth. The main cause was that he kept himself morally upright. Disregarding the question of whether this observation is true or not, one can say that in Ranke the antithesis between general causes and coincidences is removed through the idea of individuality. Concerning Marx's and Trotsky's development of Montesquieu's differentiation between general trends and chance occurrences, see Carr, p. 99.

[23] Archenholtz, p. 241.

about explaining the defeat at Kolin? "Nicht die Tapferkeit und Kriegs-kunst, sondern Zufälle entschieden den Ausgang dieses denkwürdigen Tages." ("It was not boldness or tactics, but chance events that decided the outcome of this memorable day.") But at Leuthen, in contrast to Ko-lin, we read later that boldness and tactics alone brought about the vic-tory.[24] Here Prussian pride seems to run away with the old soldier, and it is clear that, in the case of Kolin, chance is brought into the battlefield as a kind of apology. In his account of the battle, Archenholtz describes the individual coincidences. As everyone knows, the battle was tactically lost because Frederick's extended lines were broken and, compared with the superior Austrian forces, he had no reserves with which to plug the massive gaps. The vital question of why the Prussian lines actually broke is explained by Archenholtz with psychological causes. Against the King's orders troops attacked when they were supposed to be waiting; and so the soldiers were attacking all along the line, instead of following up to support the flank attacks.

And so the rashness and military ardor of the junior officers are made responsible for the "chance events." But now the writer has to ask whether, after all, these are not soldierly qualities, and whether, after all, it was not bad tactics and misplaced boldness that led to this defeat. "Der Alte Fritz" in his later accounts never fell back on chance to excuse his defeats. He always identified the individual mistakes that ruined his plans, although he sometimes glossed over his own mistakes. He attrib-uted the defeat at Kolin to the tactical blunders of his generals, who dis-obeyed orders. This third coincidence of Archenholtz's obviously holds even less water than the others when we look into its causes.

Let us now summarize our findings so far. In the first example, the coalition between France and Austria, chance was a matter of perspec-tive. What seemed absurd in a European context—the novelty and un-expectedness of a Franco-Austrian alliance—became clear in a worldwide context. The second coincidence of the wandering monk arose out of causal contexts different from those of the outcome of the battle. The timing was, of course, coincidental, but, from the strategical point of view, this chance event became part of a completely rational context, so that the element of fortune disappeared. The third example is different again. Here "chance" is simply a word timely inserted for patriotic rea-sons, to cover up or to minimize the superiority of the Austrians and the deciding onslaughts of the Saxons. The psychological arguments Ar-chenholtz used are, practically speaking, on the same level. In this re-spect, chance is used as a rather lame way of dispensing with more de-

[24] Pp. 44, 98.

tailed explanations and self-criticism. In the same way Gibbon noted that the Greeks, after their country had been reduced to a province, attributed Rome's triumph not to merit but the good fortune of the Republic.[25]

Nowadays we can judge for ourselves how well Archenholtz fitted in two of his coincidences, and how labored was the third, as he unconsciously sought to mitigate what he felt as a personal calamity; this judgment would not have been conceivable before the theoretic destruction of "chance" in the eighteenth century. Gibbon and Montesquieu have already been called as witnesses for the prosecution, and we can also add Frederick himself. In deep depression after the defeat at Kolin, which he thought might be his Pultawa, he wrote to his friend Marshal Keith that "Fortune" had deserted him. "This day Fortune has turned her back on me. I should have guessed that luck was a female, and I am not gallant. She declares herself on the side of the women who are waging war on me." And in 1760 he wrote to the Marquis of Argens that he could not direct Fortune, but must reckon more and more with chance, as he lacked the means to carry out his plans on his own. This last remark, also made in private, is not, however, a renunciation of his system of cause and effect as formulated in *Antimachiavell* and so ironically brushed aside in his letter to Keith.

In his war memoirs Frederick appears consistently to disregard Fortune, which, if one views things unhistorically, eventually was to smile on him after all. In the memoirs he rationally assesses the mistakes and successes of the different sides, measured against their plans. The point at which these assessments converge is the action and its outcome—the outcome, of course, hardly ever conforming with the original plan of one of the two sides. This rational approach led Frederick to the conclusion that history always brings to fruition more, or less, than was contained in the sum of all its given factors. In this Frederick goes beyond the purely causal view of history, and anticipates what in the nineteenth century could be called the understanding school of history.

III

The nineteenth-century school of history disposed even of the last vestige of chance. As we shall see later, this was done not so much by means of a logical extension of the principle of cause, as through the theological, philosophical, and esthetic implications inherent in the modern idea of history. As an illustration of this, we can turn again to Archenholtz.

[25] Quoted by Carr, p. 98.

We have seen how Archenholtz was able to rationalize "chance" as a stylistic term of perspective, in order to make room for the principle of causality, but there is one striking, and historically supreme, instance in which even he allows the old Fortuna to take over the battlefield: the death of Tsarina Elisabeth in 1762. In dramatic cadences, death is introduced as Fate. Frederick, in his history of the Seven Years' War, simply remarks that this death upset all the politicians' plans and arrangements; Ranke later wrote that death had only revealed that a slight *innere Notwendigkeit* (inner necessity) had been inherent in the existing "Kombination von Umständen" (combination of circumstances);[26] but Archenholtz presents death as the Lord of Destiny. He builds up to a climax, at which this event is described as "die grösste Wohltat Fortunas" (the greatest benefit of Fortuna), which saved Frederick and Prussia from ruin.[27] Here Archenholtz makes use of the old Fortuna idea, which was not immanent in events, but was above them. This is not a stylistic means of rationalization; it is a clear indication that natural forces interfered with the military plans of all parties concerned. Fortuna is not a substitute for causality, but is totally independent of all events. In this respect, Archenholtz reverts to an old idea which he shared with the humanists and also with Christian historians: namely, that history remained embedded in Nature, and that historical events were to be referred back through Fortuna to their non-historical conditions.

The death of a ruler was generally included in calculations of probability, but it was not something that could be influenced by rational planning (except, of course, through assassination); it was not one of the pragmatic *causae*, even if its possible consequences were plotted and assessed, as in the "Pragmatic Sanction" of 1713. Succession to the throne was the subject of wars and diplomatic bargainings, and the political horizon of the future stretched only as far as the possible life duration of the ruler concerned.[28] And so by evoking Fortuna within this natural framework of history, Archenholtz was not being inconsistent in his manner of presentation.

For all his modernity, Archenholtz was living in a continuum that embraced all previous forms of history; in his accounts, he is always referring back to deeds and events of ancient times, in order to compare

---

[26] Ranke, *Friedrich der Grosse* (A.d.B.)   [27] Archenholtz, p. 350.

[28] The extent to which the possibility of Nature's influencing history has been excluded in modern times is shown by the death of Roosevelt in 1945. Nazi propaganda sought to draw a parallel between this and the death of the Tsarina in 1762, in order to find a historical way out of the impasse. In fact, Roosevelt's death could have had no influence on the course of the war. The individual hero has given way to historical structures which have left Fortuna with less and less descriptive and factual scope.

them with those of the Seven Years' War. The parallels he draws do not
serve any historical interpretation of the events; they are based on the
implicit assumption that all historical conditions are identical: Fortuna is
a yardstick for comparison and judgment, enabling one to view Frederick, Hannibal, and Alexander as potential contemporaries, or Cannae
and Leuthen as homogeneous.[29]

This ambivalence in Archenholtz, with his rational breaking down of
chance and his retention of the figure of Fortuna, shows us how distant
he is from the historical school of the nineteenth century. Humboldt,
the theoretical pioneer of that school, did not disavow the eighteenth-
century idea that all world history, past and future, could be worked out
in causal terms, with the only boundaries being set by our limited
knowledge of the effective causes. To this extent, chance was eliminated,
but Humboldt's objection to this approach was that it left out the unique
quality of history. The thing that distinguished history was its constant
newness and lack of precedent, the creative individualities and inner
forces which, even if they formed a coherent external sequence, through
their unique course and character could never be deduced from the accompanying circumstances.[30] The inner unity of history and its singularity eluded causal deduction—hence the continual forward drive of
world history—and left no room for Fortuna—symbol of recurrence—or
for chance, as the uniqueness of a coincidence was already absorbed by
the uniqueness of history itself.

Humboldt was inspired by a new idea of history, which he brought to
the point that enabled following historians to take it for granted. The
origin of this new idea will be dealt with more fully in the discussion,[31]
and here we shall simply trace the course that led to the demolition of
chance through the uniqueness of history.

Leibniz defined two kinds of truth: that of reason, which counte-
nances no contradiction, and that of facts, for which there are adequate
causes but also quite conceivable variations; with these *vérités de fait*, he
was circumscribing the whole region of thought that was later to be
termed "history." The historical facts of past and future are possibilities
which have been or will be fulfilled, but which exclude any inevitable
compulsion. Whatever the motivation may be, the facts remain contingent and come into being in the context of human freedom. In this respect the future, and the future in the past, have always been subject to

---

[29] Archenholtz, pp. 47, 174, 328, 350, passim.

[30] Wilhelm von Humboldt, *Über die Aufgabe des Geschichtsschreibers* and *Über die
bewegenden Ursachen der Weltgeschichte*, both Meiner, Leipzig, no date, pp. 24, 18.

[31] See later discussion III, closing summary, in *Die Nicht Mehr Schönen Künste*, ed.
H. R. Jauss (Munich, 1968), pp. 578-81.

chance; but for Leibniz the chain of "coincidences" in the history of the world has its unique definition, each one forming an integral part of the divine plan for the best of all possible worlds. Theodicy shows the contingent—historical—events to be inevitable, not in the sense of a geometrical proof, but "nécessaire . . . ex hypothesi, pour ainsi dire par accident."[32]

Seen from a more lofty perspective—to use later terminology—chance proves to be historically inevitable. Unexplained motivation is no longer covered up by chance, but unexplained motivation is excluded, as it were, a priori from the new theory of history, as it was slowly developed in the eighteenth century. It is the theological idea of the uniqueness of all earthly things in relation to God, and the esthetic idea of the internal unity of history, that have been incorporated in the modern philosophy of history and have emancipated it. Thus Wieland in 1770 could speak of the "thousand inevitable coincidences" that force the human race along the irreversible course of boundless perfection.[33] Thus Kant could talk of the cunning of Nature, anticipating Hegel's "cunning of reason," by virtue of which all apparent coincidences are given their true meaning. "Philosophical observation has no other object than to dispose of the accidental. Chance is the same as external inevitability, i.e., an inevitability that goes back to causes which themselves are only external circumstances. In history we must seek out a general purpose, the ultimate purpose of the world." These words of Hegel show how far he had progressed beyond the rationalization of chance that had been accomplished in the preceding century, and how the teleological unity of world history excluded chance far more consistently than had been possible in the Enlightenment. "Den Glauben und Gedanken muss man zur Geschichte bringen, dass die Welt des Wollens nicht dem Zufall anheimgegeben ist."[34] ("One must bring to history the belief and the idea that the world of volition is not left to chance.")

It was not only the theological heritage that excluded chance from the historical ideal; it was also forced out by literary and esthetic considerations, which demanded that the presentation of history be endowed with probability and hence with a maximum of reality. Novalis, in 1799, summarized the discussion current at the time: the mass of facts and

---

[32] Leibniz, *Metaphysische Abhandlung*, section 13, *Kleine Schriften zur Metaphysik*, ed. H. H. Holz (Darmstadt, 1965), p. 86; cf. *Theodizee*, 36 ff. and *Monadologie*, 31 ff. For previous history of theodicy as regards the elimination of chance, see Book Five of Boethius, *De Consolatione Philosophiae*.

[33] Chr. M. Wieland, *Über die Behauptung, dass ungehemmte Ausbildung der menschlichen Gattung nachteilig sei* (S. W. Leipzig, 1857), pp. 29, 311.

[34] Hegel, *Die Vernunft in der Geschichte* (Hamburg, 1955), p. 29.

data that historians generally studied would cause them "to forget what was actually worth knowing—that which makes history into history, and connects up the many coincidences into a pleasant and instructive whole. When I consider all this, it seems to me that an historian would also perforce have to be a poet."[35]

From poetry as well as from idealistic philosophy, the historical school received the impetus that led to history's being understood and scientifically studied as a teleological unity. "Let them measure and weigh, our business is theodicy" (Droysen). If all events are unique, "every epoch . . . directly to God,"[36] then miracles are not eliminated, but the whole of history, rather, becomes one single miracle. "One learns to worship," Droysen continued.[37] Thus even accident is robbed of its freedom to be accidental.

It would be pointless to try and separate the theological, philosophical, and esthetic implications that merged together in the historical school. For our purpose it is sufficient to note the result—that they all combined to form an idea of history which gave no place whatsoever to the workings of chance.

The esthetic element of "Historismus" was an even more potent factor in the exclusion of chance than theological motivations had been. The question as to whether this is of benefit to historical knowledge, and more so than when Fortuna was playing her part, is one that we are bound to ask again today. We might find that this very removal of chance demands a greater level of consistency, simply because, in the context of historical uniqueness, the dismissal of everything coincidental leads to chance's becoming something absolute. What earlier conceptions of history attributed to Fortuna, in modern times has turned into ideology, which can be manipulated in proportion to the degree in which it is understood as binding.[38]

---

[35] Novalis, *Heinrich von Ofterdingen* (*Schriften*, ed. Kluckhohn-Samuel, 1960, 2nd ed.), I, 259.

[36] Ranke, *Über die Epochen der Neueren Geschichte* (1854), ed. Hoffmann, *Geschichte und Politik* (Stuttgart, 1942), p. 141.

[37] Droysen, *Briefwechsel*, ed. Hübner (Leipzig, 1929), II, 282.

[38] An essential supplement to this paper is to be found in my closing comments at the end of the third discussion, to which the reader is here referred. [*Poetik und Hermeneutik*, III, 578-81.]

WOLFGANG PREISENDANZ

Bridging the Gap Between Heine the Poet and Heine the Journalist

It is a long journey from lyric poetry to a placard beside a tram-line, but it is a journey in which there are no breaks. —E. M. FORSTER, *Anonymity*

I

ALL contemporaries of Heine valued his prose writings as a new beginning, even as a revolution. We might quote just three voices from the choir:

Arnold Ruge, 1838: "Heine—starting from the *Reisebilder*—is 'the poet of the modern age.' With him, there has arisen in poetry an emancipation from the old belief in authority, and a new genre. Thus he takes a decisive place in the modern evolution that we have shared in, and have felt and are feeling in the agitations of our own hearts."[1]

Georg Herwegh, 1840: "The new literature is a child of the July Revolution. It dates from *Börne's* journey to *France*, and from *Heinrich Heine's Reisebilder*. It dates from the *opposition to Goethe*."[2]

Johannes Scherr, 1844: "The Paris July Revolution brought the Restoration Period to an end, but the July Revolution of German literature dates from earlier still—it dates from the arrival of Heinrich Heine, who with his *Reisebilder*, the first volume of which appeared in 1826, chased the Polignacs and Peyronnettes away from the ministerial desk, and gave rise, if not to a new sun, at least to a new dawn over the forest of German poetry."[3]

What his contemporaries also emphasize continually is that the new, revolutionary feature of Heine's prose writing is, first and foremost, his *Schreibart* (way of writing),[4] i.e., the manner of literary presentation

[1] *Die deutsche Literatur. Texte und Zeugnisse*, VI, *19. Jahrhundert*, ed. B. Von Wiese (Munich, 1965), p. 335.

[2] *Ibid.*, p. 341.

[3] *Das junge Deutschland. Texte und Dokumente*, ed. J. Hermand (Stuttgart, 1966), p. 96.

[4] Around 1830, as if by arrangement, Heine, Wienbarg, Engels, etc. replace the word *Stil* (style) with *Schreibart* (way of writing).

and communication, and not—in particular—his subject matter. Thus Wienbarg, for instance, writes that Heine, more than other great prose-writers, deserves the distinction of "serving as a model of the new prose"; no other author has the gift of "depicting the spirit of the age and of the latest movements through the reflections of [his] prose works." But what characterizes this prose and hence the difference between it and the works of the "immediately preceding esthetic period," as represented by Goethe and Jean Paul, lies "not just in the nature of the views given—i.e., the greater political freedom—but also in the hidden workings of the spirit, in the élan, in the concentration of thought in a particular direction, in the choice of expression, in the structure of periods, even in apparent trifles like paragraphing, full-stops, and commas." Wienbarg goes on to say that a comparison between this way of writing and Börne's makes it impossible to overlook "the deliberateness of Heine's presentation as something peculiar to it [Heine's way of writing]."[5]

Another example of the tendency to reveal the revolutionary element of Heine's prose, primarily in his way of writing, can be seen in the continuation of the Ruge passage quoted above. Like Wienbarg and others, he sums up the novelty of this way of writing with the term "wit," which—particularly in *Reisebilder*—is the formal principle governing this new genre, and is now interpreted by Ruge, as by other Hegelians, in a manner relating to the history of thought and mind, being designated as a formal correlative of emancipation (Wienbarg) or revolution (Ruge):

"In principle the same thing is represented poetically in him, as the revolution, which has itself as its purpose, is political. Both of them, Heine and the revolution as such, recognize only subjective preference, and not objective substance or its justification. However, this maelstrom, which hollows out the freedom of the subject till it is merely a formal movement empty of content, is an essential standpoint of the spirit, and it is precisely here that Heine's significance lies, in that he represents it poetically. The liberation of genius from intellectual content, from the chains of love and marriage, from the confinements of faith, from the fixed laws of freedom, is brought about by the wit which the genius brings to bear against all these; for wit is the *free, self-confident, dominant personality*, hence the enjoyment of the genius's choice. . . . As consistent and as powerful as Fichte, his mighty ancestor, this spirit of the independent, disinterested genius has travelled forth into the opposed forms of life and literature. . . . In belles-lettres,

[5] *Ibid.*, pp. 114, 116.

the principle of arbitrary genius animates all the bold, outrageously independent phenomena which recognize in Heine their progenitor."[6]

Clearly these statements concerning the novelty of Heine's way of
writing are inspired by Heine himself (and the concurrence often extends even as far as the wording), principally by his repeated remarks
concerning the beginning of "the end of the period of art which began at
Goethe's cradle and will end at his coffin" (IV, 72). The term "end of the
period of art"[7] (which Wienbarg calls the "esthetic period") refers
mainly to the break-up of the idea of classical esthetics through an emphatically committed form of literature. Heine recalls other periods,
whose works of art had been "only the dreaming reflection of their
time," and whose artists had stood "in holy harmony with their surroundings": "They did not separate their art from the politics of their
day, they did not work with that scanty private enthusiasm that easily
lies its way into any material it likes" (IV, 72 ff.). In contrast, this "period of art" was characterized by the idea that art was an "independent
second world" and "aimless as the universe itself," existing only for its
own sake and unconnected to the claims of the "first, real world" (V, 251
ff.). In the all-important demand for objectivity in art, Heine sees the
correlative of this egotistically isolated art-life, which holds the politics
of the day as well as the social movements at arm's length from art, and
which leaves the "futilely poetizing soul hermetically sealed against the
great sorrows and joys of the age" (IV, 72).

Heine speaks prophetically of a new art, which will be in fervent harmony with the new age it brings forth, and which will not need to borrow its symbols from the faded past, but will have to produce a new,
completely different technique of its own. But as yet there can be no
concrete conception of this new art and its new technique. So what is
there for those who have renounced the obsolescent "period of art"?
"Until then let the colors and sounds of self-intoxicated subjectivity,
world-unbridled individuality, and God-free personality with all its *joie
de vivre*, assert themselves—which anyway are more productive than
the dead outer show of the old art." In other words, poetic communication of a new consciousness and a moving human world is not possible as
a worldly communication, through the representation of a reality (epic

---

[6] *Die deutsche Literatur*, l. c., p. 337.

[7] The most important observations concerning the end of the *"Kunstperiode"* are to be
found in the discussion on Wolfgang Menzel's *Die deutsche Literatur* (1828), in *Französische Maler* (1831), and in the first book of the *Romantische Schule* (1835-36). The
quotations from Heine are translated from *Heinrich Heines sämtliche Werke*, ed. Ernst
Ester (Leipzig and Wien, n.d.).

or dramatic) that is "born of the spirit," but remains enclosed within its own world. For Heine, it is only in the more or less distant future that images are conceivable which, on the basis of a new and unforeseeable technique, will be a worldly representation of reality containing a modern consciousness, while the subjective reflection of the objective will itself become a dimension of the objective. For the moment, according to Heine, only subjectivity itself, as the point of reference for all experience of reality, can truly be represented.

These few observations indicate the extent to which those elements of novelty that his contemporaries found in Heine's way of writing, were already put on show by himself. We have the reference to a *littérature engagée*, through which poetry is no longer oriented by an "idea of art" or by esthetic considerations, but takes on the journalistic function of influencing the public; even the artistic element of this way of writing appears to serve intentions that are basically non-esthetic. On the other hand, the nature of this new way of writing is derived from wit as the a priori principle of form and language underlying all contents and intentions, and insofar as the modern consciousness and the new reality are to be poetically communicated through this wit, the way of writing does appear once more to be a primarily artistic phenomenon; the politicizing of literature, and the journalistic intentions seem to function as manifestations of a new conception of poetry.

Perhaps even more than his contemporaries, modern readers have continued to find Heine's prose, his way of writing, a mixture of poetry and journalism. An extract from the epilogue that J. Hermand has recently added to his admirable collection *Das junge Deutschland* (see note 3), shows the relevance of Heine's prose, and in particular the *Reisebilder*, to the theme of "Border Phenomena of Esthetics":

"To search for 'poetry' here would be to miss the point right from the start. For most representatives of this movement were proud to regard themselves as publicly active journalists and not as unworldly men of letters . . . whatever literary means were employed were only of secondary importance. . . . Everything was allowed, except the *'genre ennuyeux.'* They . . . wrote essays, letters, feuilletons, or travelogues which could be digested on the spot. Thus it is also perfectly possible to divide up the works of these modern Germans into parts and particles. . . . For what all the authors in this genre adored was the rhetorically sharpened point, as a result of which there seldom developed a complete narrative continuity. There is scarcely a single finished, polished work in this sphere of literature. . . . They simply did not want to be poetic. . . . The new image of the writer was therefore that of the prose-poet, as typified by Börne and Heine, who in a witty and popular manner embraced the cause of progressive emancipation."[8]

We are not concerned here (hence the numerous omissions) with what is right, misguided, or wrong in these assertions. More important at the moment is what is symptomatic of them—namely, the argument that forms the basis of the ultimate judgment: "To search for 'poetry' here would be to miss the point right from the start." Why should that be to miss the point, and what is Hermand's criterion for poetry, since he puts the word in quotation marks? If one disregards the arguments that seek support in the self-interpretation of the relevant authors,[9] the remaining evidence is "seldom . . . a complete narrative continuity" and "scarcely a single finished, polished work." And this reveals precisely what is wrong with searching for "poetry" here: it is the irreconcilability of the texts under consideration with the "period of art's" conception of poetry; it is—for Hegel's lectures on esthetics can be regarded as a "Summa" of the "period of art" from 1750-1830, from Baumgarten to Hegel, or from Goethe's cradle to his grave—the irreconcilability of these texts with Hegel's idea of the "free, poetic work of art"; it is, even more generally, the irreconcilability of this prose with the "idea of art" expressed through esthetics.

Hegel's idea of the free, poetic work of art need not be gone into here. It is sufficient to point out in general that wherever the poetic element is missing from Heine's way of writing and textual structure, it is the Hegelian definition of the poetic, of the genre and of representation that acts as criterion. Hegel's distinction between the prosaic and the poetic view, between the prosaic and poetic work of art, his idea of representation as a reconciliation of truth and reality not in thought and reflection

---

[8] Pp. 373 et seq.

[9] "They simply did not want to be poetic": this is at least questionable if applied to Heine, even if one disregards his verse. Although he proclaims the end of the "period of art" and advocates a "littérature engagée," on Aug. 23, 1838, he writes to Gutzkow: "My motto is still: Art is the purpose of Art." In Chap. 31 of the *Reise von München nach Genua*, we read: "Poetry, however much I loved it, was always nothing but a sacred toy for me or a means dedicated to heavenly ends" (III, 281). And as he goes on to explain these ends by describing himself as "a brave soldier in mankind's war of liberation" and also seems only to apply the word poetry to his songs, one might conclude that he wanted to abandon all claim to poetry for his *Reisebilder*. However, Chap. 15 of *Stadt Lucca* ends with the remark: "So, for instance, you, dear reader, are involuntarily the Sancho Panza of the mad poet, whom you follow through the wanderings of this book, shaking your head but following all the same" (III, 422). "The mad poet"—although he calls this essay, as we shall see, "inflammatory." In the "mattress-tomb" he finally sums up his existence, repeating such sentences as "I was always a poet . . . I die as a poet. . . . Nothing has become of me, nothing but a poet."

but in the imagined form of a real appearance, his definition of the poetic work of art as a complete free whole creating a self-sufficient world for itself, his definition of the relationship between parts and whole as an organic totality—all this has remained a generally determinant factor in the attempt to confine the sphere of creative writing within the bounds of literature. Herman Meyer, for instance, in his famous essay "Zum Problem der epischen Integration" (On the Problem of Epic Integration)[10] resolutely maintains that research into literary gestalt could not manage without the idea of totality, because it represents the ultimate criterion by which one can decide whether or not there is a gestalt in the true esthetic sense. For him, therefore, knowledge of the specific nature of the esthetic whole is an indispensable precondition for recognizing the nature of the art. And so the question of the interrelationship between part and whole, together with that of the integral unity of the work of art, becomes the terminal question of all gestalt study. The question of integral unity, and the definition of the work of art as a total "world" that is actually or intentionally enclosed and self-sufficient, have a complementary relationship: only when the "final whole" of a "reality with the character of totality" is realized, or at least intended, is a specifically esthetic order at all possible, according to Meyer.

These basic reflections of Meyer's seem to formulate the premises which lead Hermand to believe that it is wrong to search for poetry in Heine's witty prose. For, to put it briefly, regardless of whether Karl Kraus rages over the lack of a borderline between poetry and information (singing when it should deliver its message, informative when it is time to sing), or Gundolf condemns Heine as the disastrous simplifier, diluter, and twister of the German language, or Croce distinguishes between poets and artists and ranks Heine as an artist only, or W. Muschg, taking up Baudelaire's terms, talks of Heine's putrefied literariness, or Herman Meyer reduces the structure and way of writing of the *Reisebilder* to the denominator of "subjectively orientated wit," or—finally—whether such judgments contain more negative or more positive elements, it will be seen that throughout there is an overall, even if only latent, concurrence with Hegel's idea of the *free, poetic work of art*, precisely as there was with Hegel's contemporaries. For these obviously stood for the most part within the circle of Hegel's influence, and even those who applauded the end of the "period of art" must have found it hard to equate Heine's prose writings with esthetic categories, as a "gestalt in the true esthetic sense": because the frame of reference supplied by Hegel's esthetics was valid for them, too.

[10] *Trivium* 8 (1950), pp. 299-318; reprinted in: *Zarte Empirie* (Stuttgart, 1963), pp. 12-32.

The suspicion of violent non-conformism may be discounted. If this essay deals with Heine's way of writing within the framework of the subject "Border Phenomena Esthetics," then it may be supposed *a limine* that such a "border phenomenon" is present here. The main question is simply what perspectives are opened up through this apparently obvious hypothesis. Is it a matter of listing (with approval or disapproval) those features of the "prose-poet's" texts that cannot be fitted into esthetic categories? Or should we test how far a way of writing, for which "feuilletonism" is in my opinion a doubtful label,[11] could broaden the scope of what the Anglo-Saxons call "imaginative writing"? This latter perspective carries with it three heuristic preconditions. First, the intention not simply to equate the border phenomenon with primarily informative, explanatory, polemic or propagandist texts that have been hotted up with literary spices. Second, the willingness to recognize an imaginative way of writing even where texts do not correspond to the idea of the free, poetic work of art. Third, the thought that in addition to "Grenzphänomene des Ästhetischen" (border phenomena of the esthetic) there can also be "das Grenzphänomen der Ästhetik" (the border phenomenon of esthetics) and its implicit "idea of art." For what makes esthetic complementary to the "period of art"? The fact that art and poetry are considered in the light of their claim to give expression to what can only be expressed through, and as, art and poetry. Indeed, it is this claim that separates poetry from rhetoric, written art from spoken art, and it is this claim which, around 1750, paved the way for esthetics, for without it art and literature could not have become an independent

[11] *Feuilleton* originally referred to the sub-positioning of texts—as in *Almanach* or, outside the literary sphere, with reference to various numbers, as in *Variété*. However, the word *feuilleton* has long been adapted to refer to individual texts, and writers have become known as authors of *feuilletons*. So long as one is merely thinking of the positioning of texts, there are no problems, but if the word is used to indicate a literary genre, one is liable to overlook the great variety of types of texts which the term has to cover. It is quite impossible to define what specific characteristics (of subject-matter, style, technique) go to make up a text exemplary of this genre. As with "reading-books," there is any number of types, forms and species that might be called *feuilletonistic*. The term tells us far less about the nature of the text than does, for instance, the term *diary*. And so the description *feuilletonistic*—even when it is not loaded with critical overtones—cannot express any reasonably definite form of presentation or communication; for it is far too difficult to pinpoint the common ground amid the varied and heterogeneous texts that are included under it. Despite the introduction to Hesse's *Glasperlenspiel*, there really is no precise agreement as to what the term means. The failure of the attempt to classify the *feuilleton* as a genre, and the *feuilletonistic* as a relatively homogeneous form of presentation and communication, can be gauged from the epilogue to H. Bender's anthology *Klassiker des Feuilletons* (Stuttgart, 1966); every attempted definition actually proves to be an evasion of a definition.

problem for the philosopher.[12] If one upholds this claim, then Heine's prose and his way of writing allow only two approaches. Either one renounces the search for poetry in them—and then that esthetic character[13] that had already forced itself on the attention of his contemporaries must be regarded as something purely vehicular; or one assumes that even the journalistic intention can become the medium for a desire to express and to represent things, complete with its own values and to be classified under purely esthetic categories.

II

Or is the claim invalid, together with the alternatives to which it gives rise? The answer, of course, lies in the texts themselves,[14] the structure of which we must sketch out roughly, dispensing with concrete references since we are here concerned with features that cannot be illustrated even by a whole chapter, let alone by shorter passages. It must be sufficient to make the following abstract generalization.

There is no development of an enclosed situation, and even less representation of a worldly, coherent reality which, in epic form, generated by speech, might have a beginning, a middle, and an end. What does come under discussion is an almost continuous confusion of facts, phenomena, episodes, forecasts, intellectual data, a pot-pourri of realities on a variety of levels and in a variety of dimensions, which make contact with one another only through the associations, reflections, and thoughts of a never-quite-fictitious author. Under discussion comes "a series of riddles, of mystifying innuendoes, a mere rhapsodic hodge-podge of

[12] For confirmation and explanation of this point, I am indebted to J. Ritter (Münster) and his philosophical colloquy.

[13] Thus Wienbarg, for instance, with regard to "Intention and Art," sees a fundamental difference between Heine's way of writing and Börne's, and although he was convinced that "an intelligent man with a knowledge of history" after a hundred years "will not hesitate to link Goethe with Jean Paul and Heine with Börne, and will ascribe to each pair its own peculiar period," nevertheless he preferred, with regard to the "idea of art . . . to compare Börne with Jean Paul, and Heine with Goethe" (Das junge Deutschland, pp. 115 ff.).

[14] It is difficult to classify and name the spectrum of different texts in which Heine's "new way of writing" manifests itself—either on the basis of themes and contents, or in acccordance with fixed categories such as narrative, essay, treatise, report, interpretation, article, sketch, pamphlet, etc., or in accordance with their predominant forms of execution, attitude and communication. The present essay, in view of its subject, is concerned primarily, if not exclusively, with those writings which are semi-narrative and so seem best placed under the headings of poetics and esthetics—i.e., the Reisebilder, Aus den Memoiren des Herren von Schnabelewopski, Florentinische Nächte, Memoiren, the second book of Ludwig Börne, and the letters from Heligoland. However, this is by no means meant to imply that the text of these writings is basically any different from that of his other works; there are passages everywhere that could be used just as easily as these.

whims, moods and reflections."[15] Heine's saying (again inspired by Hegel) that modern poetry was not objective, epic, and naive, but subjective, lyrical, and reflective, is confirmed to the extreme. Instead of a "represented reality" that can make its own way, a self-contained world of esthetic appearance, we are confronted by a whole network of obtrusive or intended references to reality. And this presentation of references is further faceted by a sequence of the most varied subjective modes, the most heterogeneous "intellectual preoccupations" (A. Jolles, *Einfache Formen*), through which each particular reference is made: observation, analysis, imagination, reminiscence, dream, mood, passion, meditation, reflection, dialogue, reading—these are just a few of the roads, tracks, and canals that carry the traffic between mind and reality. The image of tracks or, as in Lichtenberg, canals comes to mind because it conjures up the picture of a turntable or a canal system; for everything that is observed, imagined, remembered, felt, learned, or thought, gives rise to something else, to desultory acts of consciousness and speech, and provokes the principle of intervention. The interaction of progression and digression—this might be an apt description of the prevailing movement in these texts.[16]

This rough outline can be supplemented by a list of those qualities that are absent and, through their absence, constitute the case against Heine's prose-writings being called "poetic" in the esthetic sense:

1. These texts are not an "outward show produced by the mind," and so they do not fulfill the condition of ideality which, according to Hegel, constitutes the "genuinely poetic in art."

2. They do not reveal the "imaginative character" of poetry, which marks the latter as an "organ of the imagination"; even less do they conform to the postulate that the artistic imagination should manifest itself in esthetic, i.e., in "figurative, completely sensuous representation."

3. They lack the "integral unity of the work of art" and so make it impossible to perceive a "gestalt in the true esthetic sense."

4. They do not fulfill the demand concisely formulated by H. G. Gadamer and providing the quintessence of the other three arguments: "The poetic utterance is speculative, insofar as it does not illustrate a pre-existent reality, and does not reproduce the view of species within the order of existences, but represents the new view of a new world in the imaginary medium of poetic invention."[17]

---

[15] H. J. Weigand, "Heine's 'Buch Le Grand,' " in *The Journal of English and Germanic Philology*, xviii (1919), p. 102.

[16] The reference to Sterne's "progressive digression" as a possible connection with Heine is made by W. Höllerer, *Zwischen Klassik und Moderne* (Stuttgart, 1956), p. 77.

[17] *Wahrheit und Methode* (Tübingen, 1960), p. 446.

WOLFGANG PREISENDANZ

And yet the claim is made that the "new genre" can, paradoxically, be called a poetic genre in that it destroys the notion of the esthetic, and abandons the "idea of art." We shall outline, and at the same time disavow, two possibilities for considering the structure of these texts as purely poetic:

First, we can proceed from Heine's thesis that, at the end of the "period of art," only subjectivity remained representable for poetry as the point of reference for all experience of reality. "Poetry is now no longer objective, epic, and naive, but subjective, lyrical, and reflective," writes Heine in *Zur Geschichte der Religion und Philosophie in Deutschland* (1) (IV, 204). The subjectivity that "bestrides" (Hegel) the *Reisebilder*, etc., might be interpreted as the reflection of a world whose nature and essence can be instinctively perceived in the "wanderings of the mad poet." For in Chap. 3 of *Ideen. Das Buch Le Grand*, the world is called "the dream of a drunken God," who does not know that "he also creates everything he dreams" (III, 136); Chapter 11 takes this idea up again in the closely related idea, often recurring in Heine, of an "Aristophanes in Heaven." In Chapter 8 of *Bäder von Lucca* he talks of the irony of "the great world-dramatist" (III, 32), and in Chapter 16 of *Stadt Lucca* he speaks of "world irony," of "the irony that God has built into the world" (III, 423); in the second book of *Romantische Schule* Heine comments on Tieck's nomination as Hofrat with the words: "the Lord is, after all, an even greater ironist than Herr Tieck" (V, 288). And last but not least is the reflection on the dialectics of folly and reason, which doubtless forms a key to the understanding of *Ideen. Das Buch Le Grand*.[18] One might be tempted by statements of this kind to interpret the structure and way of writing in *Reisebilder, Schnabelewopski*, and *Florentinische Nächte* as a means of conveying an experience of the world that can only be represented in the reflections of the subject concerned. Through their subjective character, these texts would then reflect the impossibility of "depicting the coherence of a reality that is rational in itself."[19] G. Lukács' explanation of Heine's form-content dialectics[20] would be as valid as W. Kayser's definition of style as "the

---

[18] Cf. Weigand, pp. 102-36, with an interesting reference to points of contact with Tieck and E. T. A. Hoffmann.

[19] D. Henrich, *Poetik und Hermeneutik*, II, p. 16; also pp. 113-14 of present volume.

[20] G. Lukács, *Heinrich Heine als nationaler Dichter*, in *Werke*, VII (Berlin, Neuwied, 1964), pp. 317 ff.: "Balzac presents the self-activation of contradictions in reality itself. He gives a picture of the real course of real contradictions in society. Heine's form is that of extreme subjectivity, the reduction of the poetic shaping of reality to the live and contradictory interaction of the reflections of reality in the head of the poet. . . . If Heine wanted to write an imaginative critique of German conditions at the international climax of the epoch, i.e., if he wanted to do it in a contemporary and not a German-anachronistic

unified perception beneath which stands a poetic world"; at the same time, however, the problem of the border phenomenon would be ignored.

Secondly, one might refer back to Kant's differentiation in §16 of his *Kritik der Urteilskraft*: "There are two kinds of beauty: free beauty (*pulchritudo vaga*), and merely adherent beauty (*pulchritudo adhaerens*). The former does not presuppose any idea as to what the object is to be; the latter does presuppose such an idea and the perfection of the object in accordance with it." As an example of free beauty, Kant names "drawings *à la greque*, the foliage on mountings or paper-hangings etc."—i.e., things included under the heading of "arabesque." One could also include amongst "free beauties" that which "in music is called improvising (without a theme), and indeed all music without a text . . . for it presupposes nothing, no object under a specific heading." This distinction of free beauty is of extreme significance for early Romantic poetry, and indeed the orientation of poetry towards music and the arabesque is one of its most important and characteristic facets. Heine, too, may have had in mind the arabesque as a model of free beauty when, in Chapter 10 of *Bäder von Lucca*, he twice called the text taking shape beneath his pen a "paper-hanging," and prefaced this tag with the following:

"This story [Candide's astonishment at the worthlessness of gold in El Dorado, W.P.] always comes into my mind when I am in the act of writing down the most beautiful reflections on art and life, and then I laugh and choose rather to keep my thoughts in my pen, or instead scribble some picture or little figure on the paper and convince myself that in Germany, the spiritual El Dorado, such paper-hangings are far more useful than the most golden thoughts" (III, 337).

The conjecture that the idea of a free beauty might be relevant to the question of the poetic "pole" in *Reisebilder* etc., becomes more substantial when Heine, in Chap. 11 of the same text, says that he "is thoroughly enjoying wielding the Protestant battle-axe," and adds later: "even if I previously adorned my axe with laughing flowers" (III, 362). For almost inevitably one associates with this picture that of the thyrsus, with which Baudelaire[21] often illustrates the relation between poetry and prose, between "matière-support" and "poésie-langage" in one and

---

manner, he could not possibly find on German soil and in realistic form a story framework that could bring this critique to satisfactory, realistic life. And so it is neither a weakness nor an eccentricity of Heine's that, for his great poetic critique of Germany . . . he chose the extremely subjective form of the *Reisebilder*. He chose what at the time was the only possible *German form* of the highest poetic expression of social anomalies."

[21] Quoted from: Baudelaire, *Œuvres complètes*, ed. Pléiade (1961).

the same text. Indeed, he illustrates it in such a way that one can scarcely escape the idea of an inner link with Kant's idea of free beauty, the "pulchritudo vaga" whose model forms are arabesques and music without a text. Baudelaire takes over the time-honored picture of the thyrsus from De Quincey, of whom he says, in *Mangeur d'Opium* (i):

"Il compare . . . sa pensée à un thyrse, simple bâton qui tire toute sa physionomie et tout son charme du feuillage compliqué qui l'enveloppe . . . (p. 390). Le sujet n'a d'autre valeur que celle d'un bâton sec et nu ; mais les rubans, les pampres, et les fleurs peuvent être, par leurs entrelacements folâtres, une richesse précieuse pour les yeux . . ." (p. 461).

In the thirty-second of the *Petits Poèmes en Prose*, entitled "Le Thyrse" (dedicated to Franz Liszt), this image is taken up again and further developed:

"Et une gloire étonnante jaillit de cette complexité de lignes et de couleurs, tendres ou éclatantes. Ne dirait-on pas que la ligne courbe et la spirale font leur cour à la ligne droite et dansent autour, dans une muette adoration?. . . Et quel est, cependant, le mortel imprudent qui osera décider si les fleurs et les pampres ont été faits pour le bâton, ou si le bâton n'est que le prétexte pour montrer la beauté des pampres et des fleurs?. . . Le bâton, c'est votre volonté, droite, ferme et inébranlable ; les fleurs, c'est la promenade de votre fantaisie autour de votre volonté ; c'est l'élément féminin exécutant autour du mâle ses prestigieuses pirouettes. Ligne droite et ligne arabesque, intention et expression, roideur de la volonté, sinuosité du verbe, unité du but, variété des moyens, amalgame toutpuissant et indivisible du génie . . ." (p. 285).

What we read here about the "promenade de votre fantaisie autour de votre volonté" connects up, through its metaphors alone (*dansent autour, fandango, pirouettes, caprice, pampres, fleurs, sinuosité, arabesque*), with free beauty as described by Kant, with his examples of arabesques, musical improvisation (Franz Liszt, remember, is the dedicatee), dancing as a free play of forms. This is not the place to discuss what perspectives *Le Thyrse* opens up on Baudelaire's poetry.[22] We are concerned here with what we learn about the connection between "bâton nu et sec" and "complexité de lignes et de couleurs,"[23] between *inten-*

[22] In *De l'essence du rire*, Baudelaire distinguishes between "le comique ordinaire" as "une imitation," and "le grotesque" as "une création," and he separates the grotesque as "comique absolu" from the normally comic as "comique significatif" (p. 985), which gives rise to the question of how far his poetics and theory of art might conform to the tradition—transmitted I know not how—of the Kantian distinction between free "ungegenständliche" and adherent "gegenständliche" beauty.

[23] Cf. in *L'Œuvre et la vie, d'Eugène Delacroix* Baudelaire's *remarks on the relation between esthetic effect and subject: "La ligne et la couleur font penser et*

tion and *expression*, and with what we may perhaps deduce from it in relation to the connection in Heine's work between the prosaic, informative or polemic "ligne droite" (my axe) and the poetic "ligne arabesque," fulfilled through the medium of language (adorned with laughing flowers).

Through the medium of language: for one is bound to ask what in language can correspond to such a "complexité de lignes et de couleurs." Well, the common denominator for all these aspects of the thyrsus is that of movement. Kinds of movements, relations of movement, dimensions of movement—they appear as a sort of meta-metaphor. Five times the word "autour" is used to describe the connection between the "complexité" and the "prétexte" or "sujet"; it is also this aspect of movement through which Baudelaire equates the author De Quincey with the picture of the thyrsus: *De Quincey est essentiellement digressif* (p. 390).

The conjecture that this aspect of linguistic movement, transcending all informative content, guarantees poetry as a possibility of creating a non-semantic form—this conjecture is strengthened by other statements in Baudelaire. But even where there is no mention of this transcendence or this transformation into the free beauty of the non-semantic (*digression, fandango, pirouette, entrelacements folâtres, ligne arabesque, sinuosité du verbe*, etc.), this movement aspect appears to be emphasized as a non-semantic, poetic value. Thus we read in a passage from the dedication of the *Petits Poèmes en Prose* to Arsène Houssaye: "Quel est celui de nous qui n'a pas, dans ses jours d'ambition, rêvé le miracle d'une prose poétique, musicale sans rhythme et sans rime, assez souple et assez heurtée pour s'adapter aux mouvements lyriques de l'âme, aux ondulations de la rêverie, aux soubresauts de la conscience" (p. 229)?

In this definition of a *prose poétique*, the phrase "soubresauts de la conscience" is particularly reminiscent of Heine—i.e., the section of the preface to the French edition of *Reisebilder* that deals with the problems of translation: "Le style, l'enchaînement des pensées, les transitions, *les brusques saillies* [W.P.'s italics], les étrangetés d'expression, bref, tout le caractère de l'original allemand a été, autant que possible, reproduit mot à mot dans cette traduction française des *Reisebilder*. Le goût, l'élégance, l'agrément, la grâce, ont été impitoyablement sacrifiés partout à la fidélité littérale. . . . Enfin, je veux instruire, sinon amuser" (III, 507).

Heine, too, characterizes his way of writing by emphasizing the aspect of movement, which he considers essential in all its forms and relations.

---

rêver toutes les deux; les plaisirs qui en dérivent sont d'une nature différente, mais parfaitement égale et absolument indépendante du sujet du tableau. . . . Une figure bien dessinée vous pénètre d'un plaisir tout à fait étranger au sujet. Voluptueuse ou terrible, cette figure ne doit son charme qu'à l'arabesque qu'elle découpe dans l'espace" (p. 1125).

The progression contained in "l'enchaînement, les transitions, les brusques saillies" strikes one as being the equivalent to Baudelaire's description of a poetic prose, insofar as perception of a non-semantic, poetic
value is identical with perception of the different types and lineations of
movement that can be realized in linguistic progression. In 1886, René
Ghil put forward the much-quoted thesis that art must be primarily
"mouvement, passage, et traduction de mouvement."[24]

Let us now leave this theme. Our concern has been merely to outline a
possible way in which Heine's *Reisebilder* might be legitimately called
poetry, without proceeding from the question of the "meaning of the
structure" (R. P. Warren), and without identifying the poetic element of
his way of writing as the constant transition from form to content and
from content to form (Hegel, Lukács). Baudelaire's *Le Thyrse* and his
description of a poetic prose have led us to consider the extent to which
Heine's image of the battle-axe adorned with laughing flowers, and his
reference to the polarity (difficult to preserve in the translation of *Reisebilder*) of *instruire* and *amuser* might be relevant to the relation of prose
and poetry in *Reisebilder* etc., and also the extent to which we might be
confronted here with the poetry of linguistic movement and lineation. It
may be argued that this possibility cannot simply be dismissed, and that
Heine's prose[25] generally in no way excludes this perspective—even if it
does arise only through consideration of later phenomena in modern literature. However, we shall see that this cannot be the last word, since
this accentuation of the aspect of movement does in fact have a semantic
and communicative function.

III

Let us return once more to the attempt to show how virtually
irreconcilable are the structure and way of writing of *Reisebilder* etc.
with the "idea of art" characteristic of the "period of art." "Design, continuity, structure, a coherent view or vision—all this seems to be as re-

[24] Quoted from F. Nies, *Poesie in prosaischer Welt. Untersuchungen zum Prosagedicht
bei Aloysius Bertrand und Baudelaire* (Heidelberg, 1964), p. 235.

[25] I am thinking even of such apparently unpoetic works as the accounts from Paris collected under the title *Lutezia*. For in the dedicatory letter to Prince Pückler-Muskau, Heine
calls even this work "at once a product of nature and of art": a product of nature because
the accounts could pass for "a daguerrotype history book, with each day counterfeiting
itself": a product of art "through the putting together of such pictures," in which the "ordering spirit of the artist" shows itself. With regard to this putting together, the word
arabesque occurs once more, when Heine defends the way in which he interweaves reports
and descriptions of oddities and curiosities. It is true that he again explains this idea, pointing to the polarity of *instruire* and *amuser* ("in order to brighten up the dreary reports") as
an element of his instructional intent, as an unavoidable prerequisite for a "true daguerrotype: and if, among such arabesques, I have drawn a foolish virtuoso caricature, this

mote from Heine as from any author we can think of"—so says B. Fairley in one of the most illuminating books on Heine,[26] dealing with "the travel-books with their parade of illogicality." He observes, however, that if we read them properly, step by step we arrive "at a sort of loose order in his writings, unsuspected before, like a shifting pattern seen and lost in the bed of the stream." This loose order, made vivid by a matchless image, cannot be described in any other way than as "an order of imagination, and therefore a creative order, an artistic one." And this insight finally permits us to "forget or suspend for the time being the usual distinction between poet and publicist and think only of the creative personality seeking expression at every turn."[27]

All this is very much to the point. Our concern here is to see how this "consistent inconsistency" can be linked and reconciled with a fundamental "order of imagination." In this, we are helped by a statement of Heine's which, at first sight, might seem hard to connect up with his own writings. In the introduction to *Shakespeare's Mädchen und Frauen*, we read of the poet that:

"It is often said that he holds the mirror up to Nature. This expression is inaccurate, for it is misleading as far as the poet's relation to Nature is concerned. Nature is not reflected in the poet's mind, but an image of it, similar to the truest reflection, is innate in the poet's mind; it is as if he brought the world with him into the world, and when, awakening from dreaming childhood, he becomes conscious of himself, every part of the external world of appearances is immediately understandable to him in its total context: for he carries a parallel picture of the whole in his mind, he knows the ultimate causes of all phenomena which puzzle the normal mind, and in the course of normal study can only be understood with difficulty, if at all. . . . And just as the mathematician, given the tiniest fragment of a circle, can at once supply the whole circle and its centerpoint, so can the poet, when just the smallest fragment of the world of appearances is offered to his view from outside, at once visualize the total, universal context of this fragment; it is as if he knows the circumference and the center of all things; he understands things to their widest extent and their deepest center-point" (v, 379).

---

was not done in order to give heartache to some long forgotten Philistine of the pianoforte or the Jew's harp, but in order to provide a picture of the time, even in its smallest nuances" (vi, 135 f.). Nevertheless, even an apparently quite journalistic piece of writing is a product of nature and of art, and the specific art element is partially covered by the category which, at least since the late Romantic era, accompanies music as a non-semantic, non-mimetic, poetical art of expression.

[26] *Heinrich Heine, An Interpretation* (Oxford, 1954), pp. 160 et seq.

[27] *Ibid.*, p. 163.

At most these sentences are irrelevant to Heine's own prose only up to the ellipsis points—the mathematical image. For, in his own particular way, he completely fulfills the demand that, like the mathematician, he take the smallest fraction of the world of appearances as an indication of its universal context. In his own particular way he writes in a manner that is completely speculative, from a minimal point he develops an all-embracing horizon, and he relates things to a center-point that is not given as a direct premise, just as he expects and demands of the poet in the second half of the passage we have just quoted.

The difference—which is significant enough—is that in Heine himself the "order of imagination," the "creative order" is not conditioned or determined by any mysterious image of the world innate in the poet's mind; there is no strange, a priori parallel picture of the whole that guides the "creative personality seeking expression at every turn." Instead there is, to put it quite simply, an ideological[28] frame of reference. This shows that the "shifting pattern" of the *Reisebilder* can without doubt be linked up with the ability illustrated in Heine's example of the mathematician as applied to the poet. For what is it that actually forms this "shifting pattern"? Where do the recurrent motifs and themes come from that form it? Which are the universal contexts conjured up by the tiniest fragments of the external world, and which the center-points that come to light through the revelation or circum-ambulation of the circumference? Over and over again we are confronted by the theme of that ideological aspect which made Thomas Mann call Heine a "world psy-

---

[28] A definition of the term *ideology* has always been, and still is, uncommonly difficult and controversial; cf. K. Mannheim, *Ideologische und soziologische Interpretation der geistigen Gebilde*, in *Jahrbuch für Soziologie*, II (1928), pp. 424-40. It is therefore necessary to point out that here, and throughout this article, the term is meant without any of its pejorative connotations—i.e., without any idea of "distortion of thought by interest," *Weltanschauung* as a reflection of class situation and class passions, or a vindicatory conciliation of empiricism and doctrine. Mannheim, *Das Problem einer Soziologie des Wissens*, in *Archiv für Sozialwissenschaft und Sozialpolitik*, LIII (1925), pp. 577-652, used the term *ideology* in a less orthodox manner to designate a specific structure of thought and experience which occurred at a specific point in time, and for which there was scarcely any other suitable term (self-relativism of thought and knowledge, transcendence of thought and the thought system with regard to the historic and the social, functionalizing of the immanent interpretation of phenomena with regard to the reference level of a dynamic social existence). A more recent and more decisive instance is H. D. Aiken's, *The Age of Ideology* (New York, 1956), pp. 13-26: "Philosophy and Ideology in the Nineteenth Century," where the term is used neutrally and without overtones of evaluation to designate a specific link, historically descended from Kant, between the formation of theory and the sphere of phenomena—a link which is principally determined by the fact that, instead of a given dogmatic correspondence between "reason" and "reality," now every mode of observation presupposes its own, non-rational "ultimate commitments or 'posits.' " My own use of the word is in this strictly neutral sense.

chologist";[29] his reduction—almost monstrous and yet, as a perspective, both fascinating and heuristically rewarding—of the history of mind, society, and civilization to that typological antagonism between what he called *Hellenen und Nazarener*:[30] "A dispute which, as old as the world, manifests itself in all histories of mankind, and was most fiercely in evidence in the duel fought by Jewish spiritualism against Hellenic *joie de vivre*—a duel that is still not decided and perhaps will never come to an end . . ." (*Ludwig Börne*, 1) (vii, 23).

Another no less important and recurrent theme is the contrasting conceptions of the flow of history: is history merely a multiplication of the "history of man," a "comfortless rotation" analogous to the cycles of nature, a "comfortless eternal repetition"? Or is it the progressive "history of mankind" and so the "history of emancipation," a linear, oriented process? This is an aspect that clearly links up with the perspective of the "world psychologist," for the second conception has its foundations in a "pathos of path and process" an "eschatological conscience"

[29] *Notiz über Heine* (1908): "His psychology of the Nazarene type anticipates Nietzsche. His deep insight into the opposition between spirit and art (not, for instance, merely between morals and art), and his question as to whether perhaps the harmonious blending of both elements—Spiritualism and Graecism—were not the task of all European civilization, anticipates Ibsen and more than him." This one sentence alone is sufficient to show that Thomas Mann's interest in Heine is linked to the central theme of his own work, and to the main problem on which he meditates. It would be well worth devoting a special study to the question of how far the perspective of "world psychology" in Heine is taken up in Th. Mann's writings and aspirations. As an example one might compare these two passages:

"Judea always seemed to me like a piece of the Occident lost in the middle of the Orient. In fact, with its spiritual faith, its strict, chaste, even ascetic customs—in short, its abstract introspection—this land and its people always formed the strangest contrast to the neighboring lands and the neighboring peoples who, paying homage to the most lewd and lustful cults of Nature, dissipated their existence in bacchanalian sensuality. Israel sat piously beneath her figtree and sang the praise of the invisible God and practised virtue and justice, while in the temples of Babylon, Nineveh, Sidon and Tyre were celebrated those bloody and obscene orgies, the description of which can still make our hair stand on end" (Heine, *Geständnisse*).

"The true opposition is that of ethics and esthetics. Not morals, but beauty is bound to death, as many poets have said and sung—and was Nietzsche supposed not to know that? 'When Socrates and Plato began to speak of truth and justice,' he said once, 'they were no longer Greeks, but Jews—or I know not what.' Now the Jews have, thanks to their morality, shown themselves to be good and enduring children of life. With their religion and their faith in a just God, they have survived for thousands of years, whereas the dissipated little nation of Greek esthetics and artists very soon disappeared from the stage of history" (Th. Mann, *Nietzsches Philosophie im Lichte unserer Erfahrung*).

And, incidentally, who would not be reminded by the Heine passage of Th. Mann's story *Das Gesetz?*

[30] Th. Mann's admiration of the "world psychologist" relates to *Ludwig Börne*; the other writings in which Heine explicitly develops this perspective are: *Französische Maler*

that "came to the world by way of the Bible."[31] These are just two elements of what is constantly emerging as the "shifting pattern," of what
is shaped by outlook, imagination, reflection, and association, of what
for Heine makes human phenomena and objectivations into a *Signatur*
(signature, symbol, or key): "I, who otherwise can so easily grasp the
'Signatur' of all phenomena, I yet could not solve this danced riddle,"
we are told in *Florentinische Nächte* (II) (IV, 358). *Signatur* is in fact a
favorite Heine word; for he is constantly preoccupied with grasping
Signaturen or introducing concrete points of reference in such a way
that they take on the character of a *Signatur*. This, indeed, is the
speculative aspect of his way of writing.[32] But this apprehension and
shaping of *Signaturen* in even the tiniest fragments of reality cannot be
traced back to any world innate in the poet's mind; it harks back to an
ideological frame of reference which, first and foremost, allows everything to be referred, everything to be taken as a *Signatur*—and primarily as a *Signatur* of political, social, economic, or ideological movements
and processes.[33] The "creative personality seeking expression at every
turn" and the "order of imagination" are indisputable, but one must
realize that the scope given is in the form of an ideological frame of reference. "Whoever is speaking is acting speculatively, insofar as his
words do not illustrate something existing, but express and introduce a

(L. Robert), *Zur Geschichte der Religion und Philosophie in Deutschland* (I), *Elemen-
targeister*, *Shakespeares Mädchen und Frauen* (Constanze), *Der Doktor Faust. Ein
Tanzpoem* (comments), *Geständnisse*, and the last great poem *Für die Mouche*.

[31] E. Bloch, *Das Prinzip Hoffnung, Gesamtausgabe* Frankfurt . . .v, p. 254. Apart from
the short essay *Verschiedenartige Geschichtsauffassung* (the title given to it by the pub-
lisher), Heine also discusses this subject in *Französische Zustände* (Robert and Delaroche),
Shakespeares Mädchen und Frauen (Constanze), and *Ludwig Börne* (Briefe aus Helgo-
land).

[32] If one considers the role played in Romantic poetry by the "chiffre" and the "hiero-
glyph," and its connection with the principle of the Romantic as set forth by Heine following on from Hegel ("The treatment is Romantic, if the form does not reveal the idea
through identity, but allows one to guess at this idea parabolically"—see *Zur Geschichte
der Religion und Philosophie in Deutschland I*, IV, 202), then the almost obsessive *Signatur* element of Heine's own way of writing reveals a hitherto almost unconsidered aspect
of the "romantique défroqué."

[33] This is borne out, for instance, by the following passage in the fifty-ninth part of
Lutezia (II), referring to the 1843 exhibition of paintings: "In vain I torment myself trying
to bring order to this chaos of the spirit, and to discover therein the thought of the time or
even just the kindred feature through which these paintings proclaim themselves to be
products of our present age. For all works of one and the same period have such a feature,
the painter's sign of the 'Zeitgeist'. . . . But what will our successors, when one day they
look at the paintings of our present-day artists, have revealed to them as the 'Signatur' of
the age? Through what common peculiarities will these pictures show themselves at once
to be products of this present era? Has the spirit of the bourgeoisie, of industrialism, which

relationship to the whole of existence."[34] This statement applies completely to Heine's way of writing; only the selection of empirical material, the dialectical categories, and the relationship to the whole are based on an ideological connection of thoughts and experiences. The specifically ideological correlation of the structure of experience, modes of thought, and modes of phenomena is the determinant factor in mediating between consciousness and world. This—let it be emphatically pointed out—is avowedly so. To be an "immemorial mediation" is neither expected of, nor attributed to, his own writings.

However, it would be a gross oversimplification and distortion if one were to regard the link between the ideological "matrix" and the "order of imagination" as meaning that the latter's function was merely to endow certain elements of the theoretical conception with a *"feuilletonistic* liveliness and to convey [them] to the people."[35] Though this very common interpretation has the advantage of being simple and straightforward, it can scarcely explain why Thomas Mann should have called Heine's book on Börne "the most brilliant German prose until Nietzsche."[36] For our counter-evidence, we must narrow our field of vision to the example of a text; in view of its relative shortness, we shall take *Die Stadt Lucca, 1831,* published in the fourth part of the *Reisebilder.* However, there seems little hope of obtaining this counter-evidence through a bird's-eye-view recapitulation of the text, and so I shall try to give a brief indication of the main contents of each chapter—though, of course, this will convey nothing of the character of the text itself:

I. Reflections on Nature. II. Conversation with an old lizard about the philosophy of Hegel and Schelling. III. Something about Italy and the Italians. IV. Typology of the Italian and German, Catholic and Protestant clergy. V. Description of the nocturnal procession in Lucca, meditation on things observed. VI. Listening to the organ in an out-of-the-way church, *with an extemporizing soul supplying the strange music with even stranger texts,* above all, *some involuntary words* on the turning-point of the world beginning with Christ; then a report on the remarkably unfriendly behaviour of Francesca on and after the return from evening mass. VII. Going to church with Francesca and Lady Mathilde; on

---

is now permeating the whole social life of France, perhaps also made itself felt already in the plastic arts, in such a way that the coat of arms of this new aristocracy is emblazoned on all present-day paintings?" (VI, p. 392.)

[34] H. G. Gadamer, p. 445.

[35] W. Harich in the introduction to Heinrich Heine: *Zur Geschichte der Religion und Philosophie in Deutschland* (Frankfurt am Main, 1966), p. 24.

[36] (Stockholmer) *Gesamtausgabe der Werke—Reden und Aufsätze,* II, p. 680.

Del Sarto's Marriage of Cana. vIII. The "Old Egyptian" of the Catholic liturgy. IX. Discussion with Lady Mathilde about immortality. X. On military obedience and the art of monarchic rule. XI. Francesca's ardent piety and Mathilde's disdain for religion as an expression of Catholic unity and the modern emotional schism and feminine deportment. XII. Mathilde's despairing and ambiguous confession to belief in the Bible; why Berlin has a bear as its heraldic symbol. XIII. On positive religions, churches, dogmas, ceremonies as material manifestations of the supernatural. XIV. Attack on the Established Church. XV. Revolution as the death-blow to aristocracy and clergy. XVI. Memory of reading Don Quixote in childhood; Don Quixote as *Signatur* of one's own existence. Post-script: *Aux armes, citoyens!* as background music to the *great firework display of the age.*

This highly inadequate reduction of an essentially irreducible text might well evoke the idea of light "feuilletonistic" critiques and polemics, especially when one takes into account what Heine himself wrote in a letter about *Die Stadt Lucca*:

"The book is deliberately so one-sided. I know perfectly well that revolution embraces all social interests, and that the aristocracy and church are not its only enemies. But for the sake of intelligibility, I have represented these as the only allied enemies, so that the struggle may be consolidated. I myself hate the *aristocratic bourgeoisie* even more.—If in Germany, where people are religious to the core, my book helps to emancipate feelings in matters of religion, then I will rejoice (Nov. 19, 1830, to Varnhagen) (I, 464 f.). The book is stronger in expression than in what is expressed; it is solely propagandist" (April 1, 1831 to Varnhagen) (I, 471).[37]

Thus the author himself says that his way of writing is calculated to create a propagandist effect, and his text is purely tendentious. But, in this case, we should not stick too closely to Heine's claims. For to do so would involve a prejudgment that would in turn lead us to overlook what, on closer inspection, constitutes the very fabric and texture of this way of writing: namely, the fact that all the realities expressed—subjective and objective, ideal and phenomenal, factual, invented, remembered and imagined—are significant because in, with, and behind them there arises a field of "Vermittlungsrelationen" (mediating relations) that is functionally bound up with the subject's ideological system of reference. In other words, the realities are presented and reflected not for their own sake, and not primarily *as* realities—not even with regard to "la realidad como función genérica"[38]—but as *Signaturen* or representatives of asso-

---

[37] Quoted from: Heinrich Heine, *Briefe*, ed. Friedrich Hirth (Mainz, 1949-1950).
[38] J. Ortega y Gasset, *Meditaciones del Quijote* (Madrid, 1914), p. 168.

ciations and dialectical connections, which they establish by referring to
an ideologically fixed and committed structure of experience and outlook. And this is why there is no thematic consistency, either through
the presentation—direct or symbolic, allegoric, or parabolic—of a coherent reality, or through the presentation of interacting subjective refractions, which Hegel describes as the principle of "subjective humor."
What is presented is neither the formation of a model corresponding to
the image of reality, nor the subjective adaptation of the world, but the
mediating relation of everything real for an imagination that is stimulated by an ideological interest, but is also an essential voice for this interest. This is very different from the claim that Heine's way of writing
is merely a vehicle for publicity, or a camouflaged or belletristic arrangement of information, propaganda, social criticism, or political discussion. For now we see how the "creative personality seeking expression at every turn," the creative, artistic "order of imagination," and
the ideological frame of reference not only square with one another, but
actually need one another, as elements that would be excluded by the
esthetics of the "period of art," and its explicit "idea of art," enter into a
functional relationship: the ideological element can become the hermeneutic key to poetic imagination, poetic imagination can become the
heuristic key to the ideological structure of experience.

Naturally this thesis demands verification through a text—as concise
an extract as possible. As indicated, we shall attempt to do this with the
aid of the first half of Chapter 6 in *Die Stadt Lucca*. However [as
we study this passage from Heine] let us constantly bear in mind
S. Kracauer's melancholy dictum that the detail can never come un-
damaged to the surface:

> And now he poured for the rest of the assembled gods,
> To the right, sweet nectar, busily draining the mixer.
> But enormous laughter rang out from the blessed gods,
> As they saw how nimbly Hephaestos went round the hall
> And so all day, till late when the sun was sinking,
> They feasted; and their hearts did not lack the communal meal,
> Or the stringed sounds of the sweet lyre of Apollo,
> Or the songs of the muses with graceful answering voices.
>
> (Vulgate)

"Then suddenly there came panting a pale, blood-dripping Jew, with a
crown of thorns on his head and a great wooden cross on his shoulder;
and he threw the cross onto the gods' high table, so that the golden
chalices shook and the gods were dumb and grew pale and ever paler, till
at last they faded utterly into mist.

"And now there was a sad time, and the world became grey and dark.

There were no more happy gods, and Olympus became an infirmary, where gods flayed and scorched and run-through slunk around in boredom, and bound their wounds, and sang sad songs. Religion gave no more joy, but only consolation; it was a woeful, bloody religion of offenders.

"Was it perhaps necessary for a diseased and crushed mankind? He who sees his god suffering bears his own pain easier. The cheerful gods of the past, who themselves felt no pain, did not know, either, how poor tormented people felt, and a poor tormented man could not truly confide in them in his need. They were feast-day gods, around whom one danced in joy, and whom one could only thank. And so they were never wholly loved with all the heart. To be wholly loved with all the heart, one must be suffering. Pity is the last consecration of love, perhaps it is love itself. Of all the gods that have ever lived, therefore, Christ is the god that has been most loved. Especially by women—.

"Fleeing from the human hurly-burly, I lost myself in a lonely church, and what you, dear reader, have just read is not so much my own thoughts as, rather, some involuntary words that were uttered in me as I stretched out on one of the old pews and let the sounds of an organ flow through my breast. There I lie, with extemporizing soul providing the strange music with even stranger texts; now and then my eyes wander through the dusky arcades and seek the dark acoustic figures that belong to those organ melodies. Who is that veiled one kneeling there before the picture of a madonna? The lamp, hanging in front, lights with hideous sweetness the beautiful Lady of Sorrows of a crucified love, the Venus dolorosa; but mysterious, go-between lights fall intermittently, furtively, on the beautiful shapes of the veiled woman in prayer. She lies motionless on the stone steps of the altar, and yet in the changing lights her shadow moves, runs over to me sometimes, then hastens back again like a dumb Moor, the fearful love-messenger from a harem—and I understand him. He announces to me the presence of his lady, the Sultana of my heart.

"But gradually it grows darker and darker in the empty building; here and there an indeterminate form scurries along the pillars; now and then a soft murmuring rises out of a side-chapel; and the organ drones its long, drawn-out tones like the sighing heart of a giant—.

"But it was as if those organ tones could never cease, as if those death-sounds, that living death would last for ever; I felt an unutterable oppression, a nameless fear, as if, seeming dead, I had been buried, or as if I had long been dead, and had risen from the grave and gone, with ghastly companions of the night, into the church of ghosts to hear the prayers of the dead and to confess the sins of corpses. Sometimes I felt as if I could really see them sitting next to me, in a ghostly twilight, the community of the departed, in ancient Florentine garb, with long pale faces, gold-mounted prayer-books in thin hands, furtively whispering, sadly nodding to one another. The whining sound of a distant funeral bell reminded me of the sick priest whom I had seen in the procession, and I said to myself: 'He has died, too, and is coming here to read the first nocturn, and only then does the sad ghost reality begin.' But suddenly, from the steps of the altar, rose the graceful figure of the veiled woman in prayer—.

"Yes, it was she, and her living shadow already frightened away the white ghosts; now I could see only her, and swiftly I followed her out of the church . . . " (III, 394 ff.).

The preceding Chapter 5 describes the nocturnal procession and the way in which it becomes for the spectator a *Signatur* of that which followed on from Christ's attitude towards the classical world evoked in the *Iliad*: "Life is a disease, the whole world an infirmary" (III, 393). The imaginary scenic memory of this world-turning-point at the beginning of Chapter 6 then leads into reflections on the philosophical, social, and historical necessity for a "turn" in perception of life and the world. Only after this do we learn that what has just been imagined and reflected on is no longer a reaction to the impression made by the procession, but an inner echo of the organ music in the dark and lonely church, and these thoughts are provoked by the music and projected onto it: "with extemporizing soul providing the strange music with even stranger texts." This is an example of how, in the realm of mood and atmosphere, there can arise that same poetic "filling out of the world," as was illustrated by the comparison with the mathematician, which we quoted earlier. According to the text, the organ music, church and setting are the starting point for involuntary reflections, but the reverse could be equally true—that the reflections are what give rise to the mood and manner of observation: the "order of imagination" bases itself on a reality that has already been conveyed ideologically. This becomes even clearer in what follows. His eyes search for "the dark acoustic figures that belong to those organ melodies." What are these synesthetic phenomena that correspond to the moans and sighs of the organ? Evidently they are everything real or imaginary that comes to mind before he leaves the church. But in order for all this to be properly captured in all its complexity, we must realize why it is that these real and imaginary phenomena belong to the death sounds of the organ, as dark acoustic figures. At the beginning, the author calls the *Iliad* the "Vulgate"—the bible of Hellenism, translated into German by Voss, like a second St. Jerome. And then he calls the Lady of Sorrows in the church, the "Venus dolorosa"—the

love-goddess of Nazarenism. By way of the cross, the two antagonistic
worlds are related to each other and contrastively linked by a part of each
world being designated with a name taken from the other world.[39] Indeed, this perspective of contrast and relation underlies everything that
at first appears to be pure impression and pure mood. Even that which
strikes the wandering eye or rises up in the imagination is pointedly related to the lines of the *Iliad*: the organ music droning like the sighing
heart of a giant runs parallel to the stringed sounds of the sweet lyre of
Apollo; the soft murmuring from the side-chapel, probably to be interpreted as the responses, is parallel to the songs of the muses with graceful answering voices; the furtive whispering and sad nodding of the
ghastly companions of the night, to the enormous laughter of the
blessed gods; the indeterminate form scurrying along the pillars, to the
nimble Hephaestos; the community of the departed in the church of
ghosts, to the assembly of the gods on Olympus; the nocturn, which
includes the Sacrament of the Last Supper, to the communal meal of the
gods. Feature by feature, the picture of the Olympian feast is reflected
by that of the religion of offenders.

However transitory, atmospheric, and even lyrical the description
may seem, the fact remains that whatever is described, whether it be real
or imaginary, is functionally orientated towards the "world-psycholog-
ical" level of reference. And this applies just as strongly to the veiled
woman kneeling before the picture of the madonna. Who would say that
this illustrated a theory on the link between Christianity and the
feminine mentality, between Catholicism and the libido, or that it was a
feuilletonistic presentation of the psychology of Nazarenism, so admired
by Thomas Mann? And yet what is described is so arranged that the at-
tuned, esoteric Heine reader[40] becomes aware of the interweaving of
sensualism and spiritualism, of "meek abstinence and brazen pleasure-
seeking" (vi, 500) (*Der Doktor Faust*, comments), as a recurrent pattern
moulded by an ideological structure of experience. The very name
"Venus dolorosa" becomes a formula for the ambiguous, the veiled,
which then makes itself felt in visual phenomena which indicate that
elemental sexuality operates as a hidden or suppressed force in the pious
man, that Nazarenism and Hellenism, as it were, change hands, and that

[39] Cf. in Chap. 3 of *Rabbi von Bacherach*, Isaac's confession: "Yes, I am a heathen, and
just as repugnant to me as the arid, joyless Hebrews are the gloomy, masochistic
Nazarenes. May our dear Frau von Sidon, the sacred Ashtaroth, forgive me, that I kneel
and pray before the afflicted mother of the Crucified One. . . . Only my knee and my
tongue pay homage to death, my heart remains true to life" (iv, p. 486).

[40] The fact that the Heine reader should be an esoteric reader may be deduced from the
presentation of the texts to him as the result of an esoteric (i.e., transcending the imma-

religious piety is basically an alienated or sublimated erotic devotion.[41]
An ideological pattern is here projected onto the inherent cohesion of
what is described, so that one might say ideological hermeneutics and
poetic heuristics are complementary. The reflections inspired by the
organ music condition the description of the physical setting: the veiled
woman, the madonna, the interplay of light and shadow, the movements and noises, and everything conjured up by the imagination; and
on the basis of this conditioning, every fragment of the world of outer

---

nent interpretation) exegesis of history and spiritual formation. Just as Heine enjoys talking about his ability to comprehend *Signaturen*, so, too, he likes to refer to his esoteric
way of reading human phenomena and objectivations: "Yes, for eighteen hundred years
already there has continued the grudge between Jerusalem and Athens, between the Holy
Sepulchre and the cradle of art, between life in the spirit and the spirit in life; and the
friction, the public and private attacks, that have resulted from it, reveal themselves to the
esoteric reader in the history of mankind. When we read in today's newspaper that the
Archbishop of Paris has refused some poor dead actor the customary funeral rites, this
procedure is not caused by any strange priestly whim, and only a myope will perceive
therein any narrow-minded malevolence. The dominant factor here is, rather, the zeal of
an old conflict, a fight to the death against art, which was often used by the Hellenic spirit
as a platform from which to preach life against the maceration of Judaism: the Church was
persecuting in actors the organs of Graecism, and not infrequently this persecution also
struck at poets, who derived their energies only from Apollo and assured the proscribed
heathen gods of refuge in the land of poetry" (*Shakespeares Mädchen und Frauen*, v, pp.
373 ff.). Here, as elsewhere, Heine wishes to be an esoteric reader, in that he interprets
history, social phenomena, and cultural objectivations from the viewpoint of a system of
factors transcending the immanent spheres of meaning, so that the immanent structures,
situations and references always take on an indicative or functional value. *Französische
Maler*, *Die Romantische Schule*, *Zur Geschichte der Religion und Philosophie in Deutschland*, and *Über die französische Bühne* are particularly striking examples.
[41] Cf. in Chap. 15 of the *Reise von München nach Genua*, the description of the
Cathedral in Trent. This is a fine example of the extent to which the ideological frame of
reference can give scope to an uncommon sensitivity to the atmospheric and the psychic,
and also what subtle esthetic and psychological aspects of a situation can come to light
when set against an ideological context. Even in this short chapter, a naive reader will overlook those dimensions which the—in Heine's sense—esoteric reader will notice in every
line of the description: for instance, in the comparison drawn between the soothing, magical light in the old Catholic cathedral, and the Protestant churches of Northern Germany,
"where the light shoots so impudently through the unpainted panes of reason"; in the
remarkable floridity of the praying women; in the praise of Catholicism as "a good sum-
mer religion," and of devotion of "a siesta of the soul"; in the description of the beautiful
lady's hand hanging out of the confessional, unlike those merely thoughtless, animal-
vegetable hands of young girls, "something so spiritual, something so historically charming," awakening the impression "as if it did not need to take part in the confession," etc.
In this chapter, too, one will only be aware of impressions and witty remarks, if one does
not understand the relation between sensory perception, imagination and background
ideology, and so misses the correlation of the imaginative, creative, artistic and ideological
pattern.

appearances is accompanied by a circumference, a center point, and a universal context. But the direction in which the reflections are steered is determined by an ideological context, for it is only through reference to this that the organ music functions as voice and expression of a living death. The subject of meditation—the substitution of a religion of offenders for a religion of *joie de vivre*—becomes the *Signatur* of the phenomena inside the church, but these phenomena in turn show themselves to be the *Signatur* of the subject of meditation—the *Signatur* of a way of thinking which has its religious projection in the "myth" imaginatively visualized at the beginning of the chapter. And in the light of this "myth," the account of the journey home with the veiled woman proves to be a realization of the mediating relations apparent throughout the episode:

"The streets had become empty, the houses slept with closed window-eyes, with just here and there a little light winking through the wooden eyelashes. But up in the sky, a wide, bright green expanse emerged from the clouds, and in this swam the crescent moon, like a silver gondola in the sea of Smaragden. In vain I asked Francesca to look up just once at our dear old friend; but she kept her little head dreamily lowered. Her gait, normally so gay and floating, now had a churchly restraint, her step was somberly Catholic, she moved as if in time to a solemn organ, and as in earlier nights it was sin, so now it was religion that had gone into her legs. On the way she crossed her head and bosom at every icon; in vain I tried to help her do it. But when in the market-place we came past the church of San Michele, where the marble Lady of Sorrows, with the gilded swords in her heart and the Chinese lantern crown on her head, shone forth from her dark niche, there Francesca flung her arm round my neck, kissed me, and whispered: 'Cecco, Cecco, caro Cecco!' " (III, 396 f.).

The kisses are meant, in fact, for an earlier love, who is now an abbot. Thus Francesca's connection with the "Lady of Sorrows of a crucified love" in the church, and the "Lady of Sorrows with the gilded swords in her heart" in the market-place, is highly ambiguous, in that Francesca finds her own love pains reflected, and Cecco himself is a crucified love, in the sense that he is a sacrifice to the religion of offenders.[42] Here, and

---

[42] Cf. in *Nachwort zu Weills Novellen* (1847): "Oh! I am still just a child of the past, I am not yet healed of that slavish humility, that grinding self-disdain, which for one and a half thousand years sickened the human race, and which we sucked in with our mothers' superstitious milk . . . but our healthier successors will, in most joyful peace, look at, confess, and insist on their divinity. They will scarcely be able to comprehend the disease of their fathers. It will sound to them like a fairy-tale, when they hear that once men renounced all pleasures of this earth, chastized their bodies and deadened their spirits,

in the preceding description in Chapter 5 of Lucca dreary in the daylight, we are confronted with the effects of renunciation and suppression so essential to Heine's view of the psychology of Nazarenism. This is particularly striking at the point where "a fine, ironic little bell" (III, 390) has all the stories of Boccaccio chuckling inside the author—i.e., where the scene with the monk and the picture of the naked, busty woman becomes the *Signatur* of the liberal, emancipating tendencies of the Renaissance; of course, this is without any amelioration of the horror that shudders through the soul at the sight of the grave-like, corpse-like town—a town that only comes to life with the nocturnal procession, under the spell of the cross, asceticism, and martyrdom, to celebrate its "marriage-feast with death . . . to which it has invited beauty and youth" (III, 390).

So much for our efforts to shed light on the interaction of an ideological structure of experience with an imaginative way of writing. The extent to which the "shifting pattern seen and lost in the bed of the stream" forms itself in accordance with this same principle, may be gauged from a look at the *Reise von München nach Genua*. Prospects and episodes, among other things, tend here to recur and to form patterns, in which the contrast between present-day Italy, tutored and depraved by Austria and the church, and the historical might of Ancient Rome and the Italian Renaissance, is brought to light. From this standpoint the author, as an esoteric reader, finds at every moment in history the opportunity to relate fragments of the world of outer appearances to the whole of the epoch and the political, social, and intellectual processes that shaped it. In Chapter 14, he writes of Trent: "This town lies old and broken in a broad circle of blossoming green mountains which, like eternally youthful gods, look down on the decayed works of man" (III, 241). This, together with the further description of "blossoming ruins" (sweet vines wind round tottering pillars, and even sweeter girls' faces peep out of gloomy arched windows), brings to mind a thoroughly luxuriant motif, halfway between Hainbund and Late Romantic, between Hölty and Eichendorff, proverbialized by Schiller's immortal line "And new life blossoms out of the ruins." But what falls outside this frame is the remark that in the likewise broken and decayed castle "live only owls and Austrian invalids." For through this remark, crumbling monuments, Nature's powers of restoration, and human vitality all come together in a real and specific relationship. Chapter 9 deals with the importance of comic opera, which allows a poor, enslaved,

---

slaughtered girl blossoms and youth pride, constantly lied and whined, endured the most flavorless misery . . . I need scarcely say for *whose* sake!" (VII, 376.)

muzzled Italy to "make known the feelings of her heart" (III, 251). All indignation at slavery and helplessness, all memories of past greatness, all ardor for freedom, all hope for change, have masked themselves in music:[43]

"That is the esoteric meaning of comic opera. The exoteric sentinel, in whose presence it is sung and acted, has absolutely no idea of the meaning of these merry love-stories, love-problems, love-teasings, beneath which the Italian conceals his most deadly thoughts of liberation, as Harmodius and Aristogiton hid their daggers in a myrtle wreath. This is just a load of nonsense, says the exoteric sentinel, and it is good that he doesn't notice anything" (III, 251).

In Chap. 24, the walls of the amphitheatre at Verona are speaking in their fragmentary, "lapidary style" to the evening visitor, describing the history of Ancient Rome, when "suddenly there came the dull ringing of a prayer-bell and the fatal drumming of the retreat. The proud Roman spirits disappeared, and I was once more right back in the Christian, Austrian present" (III, 263). Then in Chap. 25 his nocturnal stroll through Verona leads to further meetings with witnesses to the greatness of Italian history, but "When I came to the Roman triumphal arch, a black monk was just scurrying through, and from afar there came the muttered sound of a German 'Who's there?' 'Good friend!' whined a cheerful soprano" (III, 264). In Chap. 28 an icon, which has climbed down from the facade at midnight, raises the question of what might happen to Milan Cathedral, "once Christianity is past": "Once Christianity is past—I was thoroughly shocked to hear that there are saints in Italy that talk in such a way, and in a place where Austrian sentinels, with bearskin and knapsacks, are walking up and down" (III, 272 f.).

The "Constantine tradition" of the church, the link between throne and altar, between church and the privileged classes, the alliance of the Italian clergy with foreign rulers, the interested parties and the representatives of the Restoration—all this cannot be too often brought to mind. But for the esoteric exegesis of history, even this situation, pointed out by way of tiny splinters of the external world, is again only a *Signatur*. In Chap. 29, he looks at the future prospects of the Napoleonic Era. On the battlefield of Marengo, it seems to him "as if it were now intellectual interests that were being defended rather than material, and as if world history were no longer a tale of robbers but a tale of minds" (III, 274). He foretells that henceforth political quarrels will be determined by ideological confrontations; "intellectual party politics" will accompany and eventually orient "material state politics," for even

---

[43] Cf. in Chap. 27 the pale Italian's reply to the Briton's reproach that Italians are politically indifferent.

now "not even the smallest struggle [can] take place in the world without these party politics at once making clear the general intellectual implications, and the most distant, heterogeneous parties being compelled to take sides for or against" (III, 275). Even now, through the interlocking of "intellectual politics" and "state politics," there are arising "two great multitudes that stand in hostile confrontation and fight with speeches and with looks."

And with regard to these ideologically separate blocs, he asks the leading question:

"But what is this great task of our time?—It is emancipation. Not just that of the Irish, Greeks, Frankfurt Jews, West Indian blacks and other such oppressed peoples, but the emancipation of the whole world, especially Europe, which has come of age and is now tearing itself free from the iron leading-strings of the privileged classes, the aristocracy" (III, 275).

This is a direct expression of that basic ideology which ensures that, in an apparently random and accidental surface situation, the mediating relations form a "shifting pattern"—a pattern that is constantly reforming and renewing itself, and that cannot be attributed to an attitude of "subjective wit" any more than it can be linked with any symbolic or allegoric representation.

What we in fact do have, which incidentally again throws light on the subjective factor of the "shifting pattern," is indicated by Heine himself in one of his *Gedanken und Einfälle* (though not expressly referring to his own way of writing): "An association of ideas, in the same sense as association in industry, e.g., an alliance of philosophical ideas with economic, would lead to surprising new results" (VII, 433). This method—strongly reminiscent of Lichtenberg's need to "build canals" in the head—can in all respects be regarded as a correlative both of the desire to make out *Signaturen*, and of an esoteric exposition of human phenomena, events and objectivations. We need scarcely bring in examples from the text to show how in Heine's prose the association of ideas, alliance of differently related thoughts, functions in the sense described above—creating a link both of material and of perspective between, for instance, religious history and art theory, art theory and social psychology, social psychology and philosophy of history, philosophy of history and ethnology, etc., etc. In this combination of different angles is revealed above all the true significance of that much praised and often so naively and superficially appreciated phenomenon, Heine's wit[44]—a wit that

[44] It is painful to find people still hailing, as an epitome of this wit, the somewhat insipid jokes that in fact only begin to become less common in the texts written after 1831—jokes such as: "He [Rothschild, W. P.] treated me completely as his equal, quite famillionarily (III, 323)"—"Indeed she was often in the position where she gave the shirt off her back, if

consists not only of clever associations and combinations, but also of the art of estrangement as "supplying a sort of long-distance mirror for the over-familiar, so that people are concerned about it and also properly concerned in it."[45] But association of ideas is a part of this wit insomuch as differently centered, differently mounted areas and levels of thought interact, so that the reader must see things with new eyes, and so that the witty "order of imagination" loosens or shakes up stiff joints of thought, feeling, and evaluation.

In this context one might quote the association of ideas of theater criticism, popular psychology, sociology, and politics in *Über die französische Bühne*, which the author himself was probably alluding to when, in the third letter, apparently condemning himself, he spoke of the "confused thoughts in an even more confused style," and of a "written wilderness" (IV, 506). But even in the far from jocular piece *Die Nordsee*, one cannot mistake the principle of the horizontally as well as vertically associating wit. This early piece is also an excellent example of the importance of the ideological frame of reference for the association of ideas. Here one can discern a hidden principle of composition through the more or less hidden references to the problems of emancipation; it is only through these references that the individual views come together into something subjectively relevant and objectively significant. A list of contents of *Die Nordsee* would give one the impression of total randomness and disjointedness, and at most would lead one to ask wherein lay the rhetorical "art of transition" from the Catholic Middle Ages to seasonal work on Norderney, from Germany as the princely "stud" of Europe to Scott's novels. But when one reads it, one is made forcibly aware of the coherence of thematic scope and artistic structure.[46] For the

---

one asked for it" (IV, 101)—"A thickset person with white hair and blonde teeth," etc. Of course, such jokes reveal the emancipated lack of respect that is essential when conventions, clichés, taboos and emotional patterns are to be broken down. But a far more subtle, far more penetrating type of wit is that to be found, for instance, in the *Bäder von Lucca*, where—with reference to Plato—he wickedly associates the psychology of homosexuality with literary criticism; or in Chapters 4 and 14 of the *Stadt Lucca*, where reflections on mercantile-economic forms are drawn into the survey of the Protestant and Catholic clergy, the established Church, and pluralism of creed; or in Chap. 8 of *Schnabelewopski*, where culinary ideas give way to thoughts on national types of women. This form of wit, less obvious and less crude, but in the course of objectivation more enduring and productive, is often not even included when the "highlights" of Heine wit are being pointed out. The "top of the pops" position of the *Harzreise* must, alas, be taken partly as an indication of immature or underdeveloped taste.

[45] E. Bloch, "Entfremdung, Verfremdung," in *Gesamtausgabe*, IX (Frankfurt), p. 283.

[46] Cf. E. Feise, Heine's Essay "Die Nordsee," in *Xenion. Themes, Forms, and Ideas in German Literature* (Baltimore, 1950), pp. 90-104. This study shows convincingly that a

artistic side of the structure and way of writing is not something secondary or gratuitous; on it depends what we are to find represented in
place of the self-sufficient, transparent "world of the work," or "independent second world" of esthetic appearance—i.e., the dialectics of
political world orientation and concrete reference to reality, the connection between individual existence and supra-individual situations, processes, movements and conflicts. And these things are presented in such a
way that the individual existence and the reality that causes it so much
trouble are both shown as something factual, historical, and empirical;
neither pole is confined to a systematized continuity or to a "personal
world" of poetic fiction. In *Ludwig Börne* (v) Heine describes the effect
of the French Revolution on the "writer's world":

"The most solitary author, living in some isolated corner of Germany, took part in this movement; almost sympathetically, without
being properly informed about the political events, he felt its social importance and expressed it in his writings. This phenomenon reminds me
of the large sea-shells which we sometimes put on the mantelpiece for
decoration, and which, however far away from the sea they may be,
suddenly begin to make a noise the moment the tide starts to come in
and the waves break on the shore" (vii, 126).

But for Heine himself, it is more than a matter of this almost sympa-
thetic involvement. For him this historical, political, and social situation
is not just one distinct reality, but is in fact reality, as the setting in
which something affects and lays claim to him in its capacity as a real
thing.

At the same place, and in the same context, Heine also justifies the
other outstanding feature of his way of writing: "this constant affirmation of my personality [is] the aptest means of promoting self-judgment
in the reader" (vii, 132). For years this has been labelled extreme subjectivism. But that tells us far too little about the function and importance
of this feature. We can understand it properly only when we realize that
this constant affirmation, accentuation, and documentation of one's own

---

single theme is dealt with on changing levels and at the same time finds its expression in
the structure as such, which makes the essay into a "work of poetic self-expression." In
"disruption" as a state of consciousness and of society, Feise sees this actual theme, but his
profound interpretation of the meaning that Heine gives this catchword of the age, shows
the reciprocal relation of disruption and emancipation so clearly that his conception is
scarcely an obstacle to what is suggested here.—Incidentally, it is remarkable what little
difficulty Anglo-Saxons have, in comparison with German students of Heine, in regarding
Heine's prose—despite their insight into all that might gainsay it—as poetic and creative.
This is certainly because of the fact that they are not so much under the spell of Kant,
Schiller, and Hegel's "idea of art," and so when dealing with Heine are not so caught up in
the esthetic theory of "the period of art."

personality is something very closely connected with the ideological structure of experience—namely, the self-relativism of thought, feeling, will, and valuation.[47] The affirmation of one's own personality is essential if one is to show that one's own ideas and interests, and one's own mental and spiritual disposition, are an emanation of the *Zeitgeist* and expression of current spiritual and social forces, factors and progresses. Lukács rightly remarks that Heine presents the "contradictory interaction of reflections of reality in the poet's head." But this fact should not be interpreted as an emergency solution to the problem of presenting anachronistic German conditions which could not be presented in any other way (see note 20). What is thus presented is, rather, how the author sees his "own writings and aspirations" as a *Signatur*, so that he makes us aware of our own references to, and reflections of, reality as a field for mediating relations. Our attention is frequently and expressly drawn to this self-relativism, this functional definition of our own mentality, for example, everywhere that the author comes to the subject of the dichotomy of his own existence, as in *Ludwig Börne* (v): "Shall we one day rise from the dead? Strange! My daily thoughts answer this question in the negative, and out of a spirit of pure contradiction my nightly dreams answer it in the affirmative" (vii, 130) (cf. Heine's letter of Oct. 30, 1836, to Princess Belgiojoso). But the most striking of the many passages on this subject is that in Chap. 4 of the *Bäder von Lucca*:

"Dear reader, are you perhaps one of those pious birds that join in the song of Byronic disruption which, for ten years now, has been whistled and twittered to me in all forms, and as you have already heard has even found an echo in the skull of the Marchese? Oh, dear reader, if you want to lament that disruption, lament rather that the world itself is split in two down the middle. For as the heart of the poet is the center-point of the world, alas in this present age it must have been broken asunder. Anyone who boasts of his heart that it has remained whole, is merely confessing that he has a prosaic, isolated nook and cranny of a heart. But through mine there went the great world split, and for that reason I know that the great gods have blessed me more than many others, and have deemed me worthy of the poet's martyrdom.

"Once the world was whole, in Antiquity and in the Middle Ages, and despite the external struggles there was still a world unity, and there were whole poets. We will honor these poets and delight in them; but any imitation of their wholeness is a lie, a lie that any healthy eye can see through, and which cannot then escape derision" (iii, 304).

It is obvious that here, the poet's own historically fixed mentality, and with it his own writings and aspirations, is viewed as a *Signatur*, subor-

---

[47] As regards the difference between this self-relativism and epistemological relativism, see K. Mannheim, *Das Problem einer Soziologie des Wissens*, l.c., pp. 580 et seq.

dinate to a more comprehensive factor. It should be equally obvious that
the "great world split," that goes through the poet's heart, is not something metaphysical or ontological,[48] but the result of interdependent historical, social, and ideological processes. In his reflections on the *Signatur* nature of his own existence and his own work, the poet's historical
position-finding and self relativism are complementary forces; this is
even more clearly stated in *Die Nordsee*, after a few thoughts on the
significance of the Catholic church for the spiritual world of the Middle
Ages:

"But it is really laughable: while I am in the act of discoursing with
such great benevolence on the intentions of the Roman church, I am
suddenly seized by the customary Protestant zeal that always attributes
the worst to it; and this very division of opinion in myself once more
presents me with a picture of the disrupted mentality of our times (III,
93)."[49]

But the affirmation of the poet's own personality is not always made
so explicitly. Indeed, it occurs far more frequently in an indirect form;
the author presents himself, through the patterns of his experiences or
reflections, or through the intentions underlying his observations, or
through his esoteric reading, as an image or *Signatur* of the age. One
example of this may be found in Chap. 13 of the *Reise von München
nach Genua*, when for the first time the traveller has Italian soil beneath
his wheels. The attentive reader can scarcely fail to notice how, just at
this particular juncture, an ideological system of coordination is projected onto the description of this first encounter with Italian scenery.
This is especially striking in an image that might almost be called a pictorial formula for the contrast between Hellenism and Nazarenism: "On
one side stood a large wooden crucifix that served as a prop for a young
vine, so that it looked almost horribly gay, as life wound around death,
the juicy green shoots round the bloodstained body and the crucified
arms and legs of the Saviour" (III, 240). The description that follows inevitably evokes, in all its details, medieval icon-painting: "On the other
side of the little house stood a round dovecote, whose feathered folk flew
here and there, and an especially charming white dove sat on the pretty
little gable which, like the pious stone crown of a saint in a niche,
towered over the head of the beautiful spinner" (III, 240).

But then he dwells on the classical features of this spinner, so that

---

[48] Concerning the probable link between Heine's idea of disruption and Hegel's
Phänomenologie des Geistes, see Feise, pp. 103 et seq.

[49] The next paragraph is a shining example of everything that has been said about the
ideological frame of reference as guaranteeing mediating relations: "From a certain
standpoint, everything is equally great and equally small, and I am reminded of the great
European changes of epoch, as I contemplate the small state of our poor islanders" (III, 93).

finally the white dove sitting above her becomes ambiguous, no longer a clear evocation of the symbol of Christian painting, but reminding one now of another Holy Ghost, belonging to the "Third Testament." Until now the description can be regarded as a scene-setting, a pictorial formulation of the dualism into which the author's Italian impressions flow together, as into a vanishing point. But in the next paragraph come the internal aftereffects of what has been described, and now we see that basically this is all a picture of the thought-historical situation by which the author knows and feels himself to be influenced. A Greek sculptor, he reflects, seems to have shaped the sweet face of the spinner:

"Of course no Greek could have dreamt of the eyes, let alone have understood them. But I saw them and understood them, these romantic stars which so enchantingly illuminated the classical splendor. All day long I saw those eyes, and I dreamed of them throughout the night that followed. There she sat again and smiled, the doves fluttered here and there like angels of love, the white dove, too, moved its wings mystically over her head: behind her, ever mightier, rose up the helmeted guardians, ahead of her raced the brook, even wilder and stormier, the vines wound their way in fearful haste round the crucified wooden image—but she spun and smiled, and on the thread of her distaff, like a dancing spindle, hung my own heart" (III, 240 f.).

Here the subject is the enchantment of Antiquity, as transfigured by a romantic mentality, and in this the author, finding himself again in what he sees, appears himself as the *Signatur* of this complicated dialectic of the *Zeitgeist*: the playing off of Hellenic against Nazarene, the celebration and glorification of the Dionysiac as opposed to the religion of offenders, which has its roots, though, as a markedly romantic tendency, in the tradition against which it is played off. The author sees himself contained in the spectacle he describes, but he might just as easily allude to Keats as the author of the ode "On a Grecian Urn," for this indirect affirmation of the poet's own personality also gives expression to a universal situation of historical consciousness—and this is what forms the frame of reference for the succeeding chapters of the *Reisebild*.

In connection with self-relativism, there is one last aspect to be considered. We have seen that in the preface to the French edition of *Reisebilder*, Heine drew special attention to the types of progression and movement in his writing—"l'enchaînement, les transitions, les brusques saillies." We have seen that these possibilities of passing from one thing to another cannot ultimately be regarded as esthetically self-sufficient or as aiming merely at the attraction of particular movements and lineations.[50] The linking, the transitions, and the disjointedness

[50] In the way that for Wieland both the wavy line, since Hogarth and Baumgarten, raised to the level of the esthetic ideal, and the disconnectedness arising from the "Spirit

must be put together with the multifariousness and changeability of the subjective mind along with the linguistic modifications—in other words, with that which H. J. Weigand had in mind when he described *Ideen. Das Buch Le Grand* as a "mere rhapsodic hodge-podge of whims, moods and reflections" or "a weird sequence of lyrical and dramatic moods."[51] But this immediately obvious feature can be properly understood only when we realize that the perspectivism of attitude, form and language is intended—precisely like the affirmation of the poet's own divided opinions, the contradiction between thought and feeling, between daily thoughts and nightly dreams, between rational observation and irrational prejudice—as an index. Even the rich variety of wit, pathos, irony, mood, criticism, dreams, memory intoxication, polemics, reflections, sentimentality, detachment, ecstasy, etc. is meant as a *Signatur* and must be understood as such, for in this variety, too, with all its contrasts and contradictions, its twists and its turns, the *Zeitgeist* element of subjectivity, brought into view by the idea of disruption, is the real subject of discussion. The whole complex of personal subjectivity, of personal patterns of thought, feeling, and experience, is brought to light as the function and expression of a situation that transcends it.

And so "extreme subjectivism" and its structural correlatives are also subject to self-relativism; the many-sided affirmation of the poet's own personality is based on the recognition that poetry has a nonesthetic function. It is not only the "tribune," the "drummer," the political journalist Heine that renounces works in which the "integral unity of a world of art" might be found; the poet Heine, too, decides that his works and his aspirations are to be involved and interwoven with the "first real world" of history, politics, sociology and ideology. What arises out of this certainly does not conform to the idea of an independent *veritas aesthetica* (Baumgarten). Nevertheless, Heine's prose-writings are by nature complex and closely calculated linguistic textures, whose message comes out through the interaction of various levels of information and communication, and can be properly appreciated only by a literary approach that adapts itself to the many-layered references of an individual language of forms, which uses its artistic character to inform and communicate. Insofar as the search is for an "artistic whole," it may well be wrong to look for poetry here. Insofar as the search is for an artistic character, it appears to be right, for then one can still remain open to the factor of historical change in the idea of what is and is not poetry.

Capriccio," were important media for a "poetry of style" that was largely independent of the "poetry of things."

[51] Pp. 102, 131.

ODO MARQUARD

On the Importance of the Theory of the Unconscious for a Theory of No Longer Fine Art

1. THE following is an obituary to the living: Art, says Hegel in his lecture on esthetics, is "nach der Seite ihrer höchsten Bestimmung für uns ein Vergangenes" (on the side of its highest definition something past for us).[1] Perhaps Hegel was right; if so, then the time is ripe—indeed, overripe—for acceptance of the thesis that art and its theory, known since 1750 as "esthetics," from now on has no place in philosophy. "Nach der Seite ihrer höchsten Bestimmung," esthetics are a thing of the past. Undoubtedly—even from an unHegelian point of view—Hegel was right: for either the world is wholesome, in which case art in all seriousness is unnecessary, or the world is unwholesome, in which case art in all seriousness is too feeble—it is superfluous or impotent.

2. Nevertheless we shall now talk philosophically of art and its theory—and so, tentatively, of "esthetics." For, as the title of these reflections is meant to indicate, we shall be dealing with the question of what the "theory of the unconscious" actually signifies for a "theory of no longer fine art." Under "theory of no longer fine art" we understand the theory of an art for which beauty—mainly in the sense of material presence or imitation of a basically wholesome looking world—is no longer the main criterion. Such a criterion finally disappeared in the nineteenth and twentieth centuries at the latest. The question, then, might be put more directly: what, if anything, has the theory of the unconscious, which came to fruition during this same period, to do with the destruction of that criterion? What has it to do with the movement through which art has become indifferent to the obligation to be "fine," or beautiful?

3. So let the battle commence: in the one corner, the theory of the unconscious—a theory mainly represented today by Freud; in the other corner, the theory of no longer fine art—a theory concerning which Freud and his disciples unfortunately had very little to say. The outcome of the battle will *not* be discussed here. What will be discussed is:

(a) The theory of the unconscious and a particular theory of art, but

[1] Hegel, *Ästhetik*, ed. F. Bassenge (Frankfurt, no date), I, 22.

not the influence of the (psychoanalytical) theory of the unconscious on artistic productions. Certainly there is an influence—and a very strong one—especially of the Freudian theory on art; but a poor philosopher has neither the breadth of vision nor the competence to utter words of wisdom concerning this influence.

(b) The theory of the unconscious, but not the theory of the *subconscious*. Freud rejected the latter. He calls the "designation of a . . . 'subconsciousness' . . . incorrect and misleading."[2] The "subconscious" for Freud, then, is certainly not the source of anything esthetic but, at most, the source of great exasperation. So we shall be considering only the theory of the unconscious.

4. The theory of the unconscious is introduced here primarily as the Freudian theory, i.e., as a theory of psychoanalysis, or, in the Freudian sense, "Tiefenpsychologie" (depth psychology).[3] "The division of the psyche into conscious and unconscious is the basic condition for psychoanalysis."[4] All the same, the idea of the unconscious does not stem from Freud. It is not possible to go into a detailed account here of the history of the idea, but we can have a look at one of the threads of the tradition: this is the question of Freud's link with Nietzsche, which in spite of (or, perhaps, because of) two remarks by Freud,[5] in spite of one remark by Jones,[6] in spite of R. J. Brandt's analysis,[7] and in spite of Freud's ac-

---

[2] Freud, *Gesammelte Werke* (Collected Works), ed. M. Bonaparte, E. Bibring, W. Hoffer, E. Kris, O. Isakower (London, 1940 seq.), x, 269 (*Das Unbewusste*, 1913), see II-III, 620 (*Die Traumdeutung*, 1900); XIII, 242, note 1 (*Das Ich und das Es*, 1923).

[3] See Freud, ed. cit., XIII, 228 (*Psychoanalyse und Libidotheorie*, 1923): "When the analysis of dreams gave insight into the unconscious operations of the soul, and showed that the mechanisms which create pathological symptoms are also active in the normal life of the soul, psychoanalysis became depth psychology and, as such, capable of application to the arts." Cf. XIV, 88 (*Selbstdarstellung*, 1925).

[4] Freud, ed. cit., XIII, 239 (*Das Ich und das Es*, 1923).

[5] Freud, ed. cit., x, 53 (*Zur Geschichte der psychoanalytischen Bewegung*, 1914): "Then in later times I forwent the extreme pleasure of Nietzsche's works, with the conscious motivation of not wanting to be hindered by any kind of preconception in my processing of psychoanalytical impressions."

Cf. XIV, 86 (*Selbstdarstellung*, 1925): "Nietzsche . . . whose presentiments and insights often coincide in the most astounding manner with the laborious results of psychoanalysis, I have for this very reason long avoided; this was for me less a matter of preference than of preserving my impartiality."

[6] E. Jones, *Sigmund Freud. Life and Work* (New York, 1954 seq.), II, 385: "The Vienna Society held discussions on Nietzsche's writings on April 1 and October 28, 1908. On the first occasion Hitschmann read a selection of Nietzsche's *Genealogie der Moral* and raised several questions for discussion. Freud related . . . Nietzsche had in no way influenced his ideas. He had tried to read him, but found his thought so rich that he renounced the attempt."

[7] R. J. Brandt, "Freud and Nietzsche: a comparison," in *Revue de l'Université d'Ottawa*, XXV (1955), pp. 225-34.

quaintance with Adler (till 1911) and Lou Andreas-Salomé (after 1911), is still a matter for conjecture.[8] In 1893 there appeared Breuer and Freud's *Vorläufige Mitteilung* (Preliminary Information).[9] In 1883-1884 Josef Paneth, a colleague of Freud's, called several times on Nietzsche in Nice; they talked together, and Paneth wrote about it to Freud.[10] These accounts are not available, but there are letters—or extracts from letters

[8] As regards Freud's links with Nietzsche, one can say at present that "Freud's Nietzsche" is

(a) Nietzsche quoted (mainly incorrectly) from secondary literature: see, for example, Freud, ed. cit., II-III, 554; IV, 162, note 2, repeated VII, 407; X, 391.

(b) Nietzsche present through key-words at contemporary salon discussions: see, for example, *Übermensch*, XIII, 138; *Ewige Wiederkehr des Gleichen*, letter to Ferenczi of Dec. 16, 1917; also XIII, 21; *Es* (with reference to G. Groddeck), XIII, 251, note 2, and XV, 79; *Umwertung aller Werte*: Reflections of 1897, quoted by Jones, I, 390-91.

(c) Nietzsche as presented by friends common to Nietzsche and Freud: e.g., Lou Andreas-Salomé (1911, Weimar, after 1912, Vienna); see Jones, III, 227: "He (i.e., Freud in a previously unpublished letter to A. Zweig of Nov. 3, 1937) described her as the only real bond between Nietzsche and himself." A similar bond, though, was J. Paneth—see note 10.

(d) Nietzsche present in the conversation of those close to Freud. Apart from Hitschmann (see note 6), members of the early Freud circle were H. Sachs (who in Weimar in 1911, commented to E. Förster-Nietzsche "on the similarity between some of Freud's ideas and her famous brother's": Jones, II, 97), Th. Reik and O. Rank—i.e., at least three people who devoted enormous energy and zeal in searching the arts for spheres of application, parallel, and precursors of psychoanalysis; the search was often successful only with the aid of some very doubtful interpretations. Nevertheless, it would certainly have been difficult for Freud to avoid hearing their oral reports on Nietzsche. In addition there was—until 1911—A. Adler, who sought explicit links with Nietzsche: "Nietzsche's *Wille zur Mach* and *Wille zum Schem* embrace many of our own ideas" in: *Über den nervösen Charakter* (Munich and Wiesbaden, 1912, 1922), p. 5. Adler was also quite rightly regarded by C. G. Jung as an exponent of a Nietzsche wing of psychoanalysis: *Über die Psychologie des Unbewussten* (1916, ⁶1948), p. 54 seq. Adler's adherence to Nietzsche no doubt hindered Freud's response to the latter, and Freud's break with Adler (1911) must certainly have had some effect on Freud's willingness to take further interest in Nietzsche or to declare himself a convert to the latter. Later on, Nietzsche was also present in the persons of G. Groddeck and A. Zweig: see Freud's letters to Zweig, Jones, III, 488-90, and Freud, *Briefe 1873-1939*, ed. E. L. Freud (Frankfurt, 1962), p. 414. Of course, the question of which Nietzsche was present in the Freud circle can only be answered accurately by someone who has nosed out which Nietzsche works and books were read in this circle, and has studied all the Nietzsche quotations in all the works of this circle—a task which no-one has yet attempted.

[9] J. Breuer and S. Freud, *Über den psychischen Mechanismus hysterischer Phänomene*, included in their *Studien über Hysterie*, 1895.

[10] See Jones, III, 489: an otherwise unpublished letter—here translated into English—from Freud to A. Zweig, 11.5.1934: "A friend of mine, Dr. Paneth, had got to know him (Nietzsche) in the Engadine and he used to write me a lot about him." Information about the relationship between Josef Paneth (1857-1890) and Freud is to be found in Freud's letters to Martha Bernay and her family between Aug. 22, 1883, and Oct. 24, 1887—see Freud, *Briefe von 1873-1939*, ed. cit., esp. pp. 102 ff.

—available which Paneth (who was evidently a passionate recorder of conversations) wrote to his fiancée; we read, for instance: "we agreed that the unconscious life of every man . . . is infinitely richer and more important than the conscious," and: "There is much that lies embryonic in man . . . and works unconsciously."[11] From this one can see at least that Paneth, the letter-writing friend of Freud, spoke with Nietzsche about the unconscious; furthermore, that he spoke with him rather as an enthusiastic disciple with a revered master, discussing the commonplaces of the time. For of course the idea of the unconscious was then known to everyone, thanks to E. v. Hartmann's highly relevant *Philosophie des Unbewussten* (Philosophy of the Unconscious) (first published, 1869). Hartmann referred back to C. G. Carus: "The Dresden doctor Carus . . . with his 'Psyche' is rightly regarded as the precursor of the philosophy of the unconscious."[12] Carus in his turn, with his thesis: "The key to knowledge of the conscious life of the soul lies in the region of the unconscious,"[13] professed his loyalty to Schelling. For in Schelling, the theory of the unconscious—adapting the *term used by Fichte*[14] and the originally Kantian idea[15] of an imagination unconsciously producing reality—is clearly formulated:

"There is nothing to prevent one from assuming (the existence of) a

[11] E. Förster-Nietzsche, *Das Leben Friedrich Nietzsche's*, II, 2 (1902), pp. 481 and 484; see generally pp. 481-93.

[12] E. v. Hartmann, *Philosophie des Unbewussten* ([12]1923), p. ix.

[13] C. G. Carus, *Psyche. Zur Entwicklungsgeschichte der Seele*, 1846-1860, ed. L. Klages (Jena, 1926), pp. 1, 9, 39. It was, wrote Carus, a mistake to set up a "partition between the unconscious and the conscious, for this caused one to separate from the realm of the soul what . . . lay outside consciousness . . . so that one was unwilling to recognize anything as soul that could not be attributed to this faculty": p. 1; for: "All soul-life depends on the unconscious"; we must recognize "the unconscious soul-life as the basis of the conscious": *loc. cit.*, and we must "reconstruct our existence mentally, from conscious existence back into unconscious": p. 3.

[14] Schelling, *Sämtliche Werke* (Collected Works), ed. K. F. A. Schelling (Stuttgart and Augsburg, 1856-61), x, 93: we are "firmly convinced of the reality of things outside ourselves . . . because we do not become conscious of the faculty by which they are produced": *loc. cit. (Zur Geschichte der neueren Philosophie*, 1821 seq.); this is also—see A. Gehlen, "Über die Geburt der Freiheit aus der Entfremdung," in *Archiv für Rechts- und Sozialphilosophie*, XL (1952-1953), p. 340—the "Fichtian formula of the 'lost freedom,' of the alienation and apparent, deceptive independence and superiority of what we have produced. In psychological usage, this Fichtian formula became world-famous: in Freud. For what are the dreams, the whims, the irresistible urges, and indeed the whole neurotic arsenal, if they are not unconscious products of the independence of the ego—products which alienate themselves from it and confront it as a superior force, and which are now broken up by analysis that 'makes them conscious,' traces their genesis and the history of their origins, and so re-establishes the ego's freedom from and dominance of its own after-birth?"

[15] *Kritik der reinen Vernunft* B, p. 103.

region beyond the presently existing consciousness and an activity that
enters into the conscious mind, no longer as itself but only through its
result . . . a past of this ego that precedes and transcends consciousness
. . . a transcendental history of the ego. . . . The . . . ego finds in its
consciousness nothing but, as it were, the monuments, the memorials of
that way, and not the way itself. But for this very reason it is the task of
science, and that is of the primeval science—philosophy—to make this
ego of consciousness recover consciousness, i.e., come into consciousness. In other words, the task of science is . . . an anamnesis. . . .[16] . . .
What we call science, is . . . striving for a return to consciousness. . . .[17]
. . . The peculiarity of transcendental idealism, in the light of this doctrine, is this . . . that it shifts into a region that lies beyond common
consciousness. . . .[18] . . . The nature of the transcendental approach
must therefore consist in the fact that . . . what . . . escapes consciousness, is . . . brought back to consciousness. . . .[19] . . . Philosophy therefore . . . depends on the . . . ability . . . to reflect . . . the unconscious.
. . .''[20]

This genealogy of an idea could be continued and supplemented,
either as regards the idea of the unconscious itself, or with reference to
other ideas and theories which are still current today as individual elements of the theory of psychoanalysis.[21] From this, we should learn two
things:

(a) Psychoanalytical ideas belong to the history of philosophy, and
have philosophical relevance (i.e., relevance to the philosophy of history). They are philosophical ideas at least on account of the fact that
they *were* philosophical ideas before they became psychoanalytical, and
also, surprisingly, not because they demand philosophical validity but
quite the reverse, because they were able to give up their philosophical
validity. The psychoanalytical theory of, among other things, the unconscious, should not be viewed as an "antithesis," but rather as a definite "state" of philosophy.

(b) Anyone seeking some philosophical significance in the theory of
the unconscious—including significance for no longer fine art and its
theory—would do best not to start with Freud, but earlier, with the
Romantics and their philosophy.[22]

[16] Schelling, pp. 93-95.   [17] Schelling, ed. cit., VIII, 201 (*Die Weltalter*, 1813).
[18] Ed. cit., III, 391 (*System des transzendentalen Idealismus*, 1800).
[19] P. 345.   [20] P. 351.
[21] See M. Dorer, *Historische Grundlagen der Psychoanalyse*, 1932; see also O. Marquard, "Über einige Beziehungen zwischen Ästhetik und Therapeutik in der Philosophie
des 19. Jahrhunderts," in *Literatur und Gesellschaft* (Festschr. B.v. Wiese), 1963, pp.
22-55.
[22] See Th. Mann, *Die Stellung Freuds in der modernen Geistesgeschichte*, *Gesammelte
Werke* (Collected Works), X, 278: "There is an independent dependence; and of this de-

5. For in the Romantic era at the very latest, the theory of the unconscious becomes relevant to the philosophical theory of art.

In doing so, it takes its place in a process which—as Hegel said—was
put into operation by Christianity. This is the progress of the derestriction of art—i.e., what one might call the ending of the "numerus
clausus" as regards *what* can be dealt with artistically and *how* it can be
dealt with artistically.

Hegel analyzes this process in his esthetics of the *Romantic Art
Form*.[23] His analysis leads to a sociological-theological thesis: as far as
Christianity is concerned, religion becomes increasingly "inward-
looking"; at the same time the external world becomes increasingly
"irreligious"—Max Weber would say "disenchanted";[24] and the two
trends intensify each other:

(a) The more disenchanted the world gets, the more deeply religion
becomes intensified:

"Religion builds its temples and altars in the heart of the individual,
and sighs and prayers seek the God the sight of whom the heart denies
itself, because the danger of the intellect is there, which would recognize
what it sees as a thing, the wood as trees . . .[25] i.e., only the present
prosaic conditions . . .[26] of middle-class society[27] . . . and . . . in the
midst of this industrial formation and the reciprocal exploitation and
suppression of the rest . . . the harshest cruelty of poverty. . . ."[28]

(b) The more deeply intensified religion becomes, the more disenchanted grows the world:

"Now . . . the mind is indifferent to the way the immediate world is
shaped, for immediacy is unworthy of the spirituality of the soul. . . .
What appears outwardly . . . takes on . . . the function of merely showing that the external is the unsatisfying existence. . . .[29] . . . The . . .
Universe is said to be . . . god-forsaken, so that in accordance with this
atheism of the moral world, what is true may be situated outside [the
moral world]. . . ."[30]

The esthetics of the Romantic form of art belong to the theory of

---

scription are obviously the most remarkable links between Freud and German Romanticism, the features of which are almost stranger than those of his unconscious descent from
Nietzsche, but which have till now attracted little critical attention."

[23] Hegel, *Ästhetik*, ed. cit., I, 498-584.

[24] P. 505.

[25] Hegel, *Sämtliche Werke, Jubiläumsausgabe*, ed. H. Glockner (Stuttgart, 1927 seq.),
I, 281-82 (*Glauben und Wissen*, 1802).

[26] Hegel, *Ästhetik*, ed. cit., I, 192.   [27] P. 256.

[28] P. 255.   [29] P. 508.

[30] Hegel, *Grundlinien der Philosophie des Rechts*, 1821, ed. J. Hoffmeister (Hamburg,
⁴1955), p. 7.

this general history of spiritualization through disenchantment, and disenchantment through spiritualization. These esthetics assert that when
reality becomes both externalized and internalized to the extreme, and
the world of things and the world of sentiments become increasingly
divergent, reality can no longer present itself as beautiful or express
itself solely and truly in beautiful art. Reality requires other, more
appropriate, means of opening up its truth and of getting a clear understanding of itself. The prime means of doing this in our modern, self-
conscious world is no longer art, but science: *thought and reflection
have outstripped the fine arts*.[31] Conditioned by the 'split' between mind
and reality (between subjectivity and objectivity), art loses its absolute
status; but at the same time it gains new possibilities: for as a result of
this split, art thus becomes derestricted. While the "absolute content appears to be compressed into the point of subjective sentiment, so that
every process is transferred to the human mind, in this way the range of
content is again infinitely expanded. It opens itself up to unlimited
diversity. . . .[32] . . . through which art casts off every firm restriction to
a particular range of content and interpretation, and . . . excludes no
interest—for art no longer has to present only that which is at home on
one of its particular levels, but [can present] everything which man generally is able to feel familiar with. . . .[33] For this very reason . . . Romantic art lets the external world indulge itself freely, and in this respect
allows uninhibited presentation of each and every object, right down to
flowers, trees, and the commonest household utensils, in the natural
contingency of their existence. . . ."[34]

This, of course, is only an indication of the tendency towards dere-
stricting art—nothing more. For Hegel only outlined this tendency. But
in principle—on the basis of this trend and its theory—Art has a perfectly free hand from now on.

[31] Hegel, *Ästhetik*, ed. cit., I, 21; cf. p. 22: "Our present age in its general state is not
favorable for art. Even the practising artist is not only led astray and infected by the reflections given expression all around him, so that he brings more and more ideas into his
works themselves; but the whole intellectual climate is such that he himself stands inside
this contemplative world and its conditions, and would never be able to abstract himself
from it through will or resolve, or—through a particular upbringing or removal from these
living conditions—to devise and achieve a special isolation, replacing what has been lost.
. . . What is aroused in us now through works of art is, apart from direct enjoyment, our
judgment. . . . The science of art is therefore even more necessary in our time than it was
in the days when art as art gave a certain guarantee of satisfaction. Art invites us to contemplative consideration—not for the purpose of evoking art again, but in order to take
scientific note of what art is." And so for Hegel, art in the modern world is the opportunity
to reflect that world; this thesis paves the way—not visualized by Hegel—for a further
thesis: that art itself increasingly becomes the opportunity to reflect itself.

[32] P. 506.   [33] P. 581.   [34] P. 508.

6. Hegel's theory of the *Romantic art form* is neither current nor popular today. But to your author—as regards what is under discussion here—it appears plausible, and I see no reason to abandon it.

Undoubtedly real beauty remains, for Hegel, reserved in the *Classical art form*: "The Classical art form . . . has attained the highest peak that art . . . can reach, and if anything is deficient in it, then it is only the art itself and the confinement of the art sphere. . . .[35] . . . Classical art (became) . . . the perfection of the realm of beauty. Nothing can be or become more beautiful."[36]

But what follows from this? Merely that post-classical and, particularly, present-day art can no longer be optimally defined through beauty. And so Hegel's theory of the Romantic art form—which Hegel undoubtedly did not follow through to its conclusion—is in fact a theory of the progressive reduction of beauty as a principle of art. Hegel, then, was describing a history of degeneration. And yet he writes: "All the same one can hope that art will continually ascend and perfect itself."[37] So what he actually means is no more a history of world degeneration than one of degeneration in art.[38] However, he adds: "its form has ceased to be the highest need of the spirit."[39] Therefore what Hegel means is a history of the degeneration of the relevance of art. His esthetics of the Romantic art form is the philosophy of the history of the degeneration of the fundamental *importance* of art.

Of course, the philosophy of the history of this degeneration is also the philosophy of the history of a progression—progress in the technical and thematic spheres of art. Art becomes increasingly less confined in what it is allowed to do. Where it makes radical use of this freedom—which to a certain extent it pays for with the loss of its importance—it eventually takes on the form of "no longer fine art": i.e., art which is indifferent at least to the obligation to be beautiful. Hegel's expression for this art—the extreme consequence of which he did not consider—is "Art exceeding itself, but . . . in the form of art itself."[40] Bearing this in

[35] P. 85. [36] P. 498. [37] P. 110.

[38] See p. 21: only "if one enjoys (i.e., unlike Hegel) indulging in complaints and reproofs, one can regard this phenomenon (i.e., the loss of importance of art) as a calamity and attribute it to the preponderance of passions and selfish interests that banish both the seriousness and the light-heartedness of art; or one may lament the misery of the present, and the complicated state of middle-class and political life, which does not allow the mind caught up in petty interests to be liberated for the loftier purposes of art, while the intellect itself is subservient to this misery and its interests, in forms of science that are only useful for such purposes, and it allows itself to be seduced into exile in this aridity." As against this, Hegel wants to identify "what is real" as "rational," and even in the present to give art a "high status": *loc. cit.*

[39] P. 110. [40] P. 87.

mind, one comes inevitably to the thesis that a theory of no longer fine art must be the logical development—going far beyond Hegel—of the Hegelian theory of the Romantic art form.[41]

7. For this theory is the philosophy of the process of ending the "numerus clausus" as regards *what* can be dealt with artistically and *how* it can be dealt with artistically.

As we have already seen, this is where the theory of the unconscious takes its place in the process. It does so mainly in the period of what Hegel called the "disintegrating forms of Romantic art":[42] a period which—according to his analysis—is too extremely outward and too extremely inward to possess that "inner outwardness" and "outer inwardness" which, as the "beautiful," can be artistically imitated. But—and this is the Romantic question—how can this be expressed in fine art? Furthermore, how—in spite of the loss of importance analyzed and accepted by Hegel—can the absolute importance of art be sustained and strengthened? Romantic esthetics seeks the answer to this question in three theories: the theory of genius, the theory of the naturalness of genius, and the theory of the unconscious.

(a) *The theory of genius.* Its question is: how can a historical reality, no longer beautiful in itself, nevertheless express itself absolutely in fine art? Its answer is: there must be something which—when beauty cannot be found in the existing world—will actually *bring* beauty into

---

[41] A similar expansion of Hegel's esthetics is also the intention of D. Henrich, *Poetik und Hermeneutik II*, 11-32; see also pp. 524 seq. I was not able to read this essay until after writing my own. His thesis on the "Reflektiertheit" and "partialen Charakter" of modern art leads to a variety of far more complex and undoubtedly fruitful conclusions. In contrast to my own questioning of esthetic immanence, Henrich appears to construct a new esthetic immanence which he seeks to consolidate through a sort of alliance with immemorial facts. Thus his "reflections with regard to Hegel" are quite "regardless" of Hegel, since they become the philosophy of a "Vermittlung" (mediation), which "must be accomplished without one's being able to assure oneself of it" (p. 20)—the philosophy of an "immemorial mediation" (pp. 20, 21, 23, 26), of an "unavailable basis" (pp. 17, 20, 22, 23, 24, 25), of an "intangible basis" (p. 21) with the "character of menace" (pp. 21, 22) etc. Henrich's protest against "evasion by fixing the mind" (p. 22) and his philosophy of "unavailable autonomy" (p. 24) aim at correcting Hegel's "defects" (p. 17) and the "shortcomings of his theory" (p. 27): they are—he writes—"all impulses which belong to an immemorial communication and which have not become a subject of his thinking" (p. 20). This objection was first raised against Hegel by the older Schelling. And so I find it difficult to regard Henrich's thesis primarily as an extension of Hegel, whereas I find it easy to see it as an extension of themes reflected on by the older Schelling—though admittedly involving a turn-around of the latter's esthetics; the basic dispute with Henrich would obviously be along the lines of these themes and—it goes without saying—of the duty-bound awareness that a charge is often only a modified version of defection, and a large-scale attack the penultimate stage of total desertion [See present vol., pp. 107-33.]

[42] Hegel, p. 582.

reality: in other words, a medium not to imitate, but deliberately to surpass reality through art. This medium of surpassment (or transcendence) is *genius*. Schelling, whose place of authority in the Romantic movement is identified by Hegel's Schelling Critique,[43] writes that the genius performs *this transcending of reality through art*[44] with his *enthusiasm*.[45] Like the Romantics generally, Schelling releases art theory from the tradition of the theory of mimesis, and then logically falls back on the tradition of the theory of enthusiasm.[46] Naturally this gives rise to further problems, and so we come to

(b) *The theory of the naturalness of genius.* Its question is: from where does the genius draw his power of transcendence, if not from the present historical reality? Its answer is: if this power of transcendence cannot come from history, then it must come from non-history. It cannot come from history, for history is to be transcended. There follows from this obligation of transcendence, on the one hand, the compulsion to regard history as that which *has* to be transcended—so that history will theoretically degenerate into an ensemble of motives for abandoning history; on the other hand, the compulsion to find some remedial power as a starting point from which history *can* be surpassed; and if this cannot be history itself, then it must be non-history. For historical man, the radical non-history which he is acquainted with is that which, for the most part, he has left behind him: that is—for a world that has become partly artificial, partly private, and so altogether extremely unnatural—the non-history of Nature. The artistic genius lives and creates out of this prehistoric Nature.[47] And so there comes into play a new form of

[43] Hegel, *Phänomenologie des Geistes*, 1807, ed. J. Hoffmeister (Hamburg, ⁵1949), pp. 12 seq., 20, 42 seq., and esp. 55-57.

[44] Schelling, ed. cit., VII, 295 (*Über das Verhältnis der bildenden Künste zu der Natur*, 1807).

[45] Schelling, pp. 326 and 327.

[46] This comes out particularly clearly with Schelling's attempt to recruit Plato as an ancestor, not only in matters concerning the doctrine of anamnesis, but also in relation to the philosophy of art: he manages to do this only by minimizing poetic criticism: see Schelling, ed. cit., V, 345 seq. (*Vorlesungen über die Methode des akademischen Studiums*, 1803), esp. p. 346: "What else is Plato's disapproval of the art of poetry, particularly in comparison with the praise he gives in other works to enthusiastic poetry, but polemics against poetic realism . . . ?" For position-finding as regards Romantic esthetics of genius, see J. Ritter, *Philosophische Ästhetik* (*Münstersche Vorlesungen*, 1947 seq.).

[47] For pertinent definitions of genius, see, amongst others, Kant, *Kritik der Urteilskraft* (1790), 46: "Genius is the inborn state of mind (*ingenium*) through which Nature gives art the rule"; Schiller, *Sämtliche Werke. Säkular-Ausgabe*, XII, 181: it "is Nature . . . that is the single flame at which the poetic spirit feeds itself; out of it, (the spirit) creates its whole power (*Über naive und sentimentalische Dichtung*, 1795); Schelling, ed. cit., III, 612 seq. (*System der transzendentalen Idealismus*, 1800), esp. p. 617: Genius produces thanks to the "grace of its nature"; see also note 50, below.

imitatio naturae: imitation of Nature is, at one and the same time, romantically demolished and preserved. Nature can no longer be copied as something existing,[48] for what exists—as artifact plus feeling—is the historical world; how can "Nature" be imitated there? Obviously only through an *imitatio* which is no longer a copy but a successor: Genius presents not Nature, but *as* Nature[49] and *like* Nature.[50] In maintaining this, the Romantic esthetics of genius is, basically, a natural philosophy of art. This, of course, raises further problems, and so we have

(c) *The theory of the unconscious.* Its question is: how can Nature, if historical man has left her behind him, nevertheless be present? Its answer is: Nature is present unconsciously. The aporia that Nature in the historical world is, at the same time, past (disappeared) and present (still here), is resolved by the theory of the unconscious. Through this, one can at once see that Nature "is not" (not consciously), but at the same time "is" (unconsciously).[51] As far as art is concerned, the exemplary embodiment of this state of unconscious Nature is the genius: Schelling writes: "It has long been realized that in art not everything is oriented with the conscious mind, that an unconscious power must be linked with the conscious activity;[52] the philosophy of art in accordance

[48] See Kant § 47: "Genius is to be completely opposed to the spirit of imitation"; so too with Kant's Romantic pupils.

[49] *Ibid.*, § 46: "that it gives the rule as Nature. . . ."

[50] Schelling, ed. cit., v, 349: "that the true artists . . . are . . . like Nature" (*Vorlesungen über die Methode des akademischen Studiums*, 1803); see in the same volume, p. 460 (*Philosophie der Kunst*, 1802-1805): "this is also considered in the idea of genius, that on the one hand it is thought of as a natural principle just as on the other it is thought of as an ideal principle. . . . It is one and the same condition, through which the world itself is produced in the original act of perception, and through which the world of art is produced in the act of genius. . . ." See ed. cit., VII, 301 (*Über das Verhältnis der bildenden Künste zu der Natur*, 1807): the "artist . . . if he wanted . . . to subjugate himself completely to the real, and to reproduce the existing world with slavish fidelity, would probably bring forth masks, but not works of art. And so he must move away from the product or the creature, but only in order to raise himself to creative power and to comprehend this intellectually. . . . But the artist should emulate every natural spirit that operates in the interior of things and speaks through form and gestalt only as if through images; only when he grasps this spirit in live imitation has he created something truthful himself." Cf. Schelling's self-interpretation, p. 321, note 1: "This whole situation demonstrates the basis of art and also of beauty in the vitality of Nature." See also Jean Paul, *Vorschule der Ästhetik* (1812), § 3: "Aber ist es denn einerlei, die oder der Natur nachzuahmen, und ist Wiederholen Nachahmen? ("But does it not then matter how Nature is imitated, and is repetition imitation?" Quoted by W. Preisendanz.)

[51] Obviously this problem does not yet arise in those cultures that are "close to Nature," but only in the "artificial" culture of the developed, historical, i.e., advanced modern world. This explains why the solution to the problem, in the form of the theory of the unconscious, only gets underway during the period of the Romantics.

[52] Schelling, p. 300.

with basic principles of transcendental idealism"[53] must, in the "genuis,[54] reflect conscious activity as determined by the unconscious."[55] Jean Paul expresses the same view: "The mightiest [force] in the poet, which breathes the good and the evil spirit into his works, is precisely the unconscious [force]."[56] And Carus later formulates the same idea:[57] "Genius distinguishes itself . . . by the fact that it is everywhere urged on and controlled . . . by the unconscious." This first Romantic theory of the unconscious saves Nature for art and from history: in connection with art, it is necessary and representative when the absolute claim of fine art—despite Hegel and in obstruction to the factual fate of art—is once more to be maintained and strengthened, and when this occurs through turning away from history and falling back on the prehistoric, alleged remedial power of Nature.

8. This recourse, however, is actually a regression. The immediacy of Nature is, in the historical world, an anachronism. It does not heal, it imperils. Also anachronistic in the modern world—which has become conscious and artificial—is everything that still produces as and like Nature. Therefore, to be a genius and to produce as a genius is also an act of regression. The plight of the genius and all the genius stands for is thus a sort of foundering, for the fine art of the genius increasingly becomes nothing more than a productive self-deception, which itself can be only momentary. As long ago as 1819, Schopenhauer was already writing that the art of the genius "does not release [man] for ever, but only for moments . . . and is . . . only an interim consolation."[58] The transitoriness and subsequent breakdown of this consolation leaves man in direct confrontation with a Nature that is no longer esthetically "enchanted." He is then faced with its dangerousness. The Romantic attempt to call on Nature through the genius as a saviour has fallen flat. What was to bring rescue is now a menace. The philosophy of later Romanticism—that of the older Schelling or of Schopenhauer—already departs from that of the earlier Romantics in characterizing Nature not through organic attributes but through attributes of chaos.[59] Nature imperils and destroys.

---

[53] Schelling, III, 612-29.   [54] Pp. 616 seq.   [55] P. 613.

[56] Jean Paul, § 13.   [57] C. G. Carus, *Phyche*, ed. cit., p. 158; cf. p. 242.

[58] Schopenhauer, *Die Welt als Wille und Vorstellung*, I (1819), 52.

[59] See the discussion of Nature in the early philosophy-of-freedom stage of Schelling's late philosophy, ed. cit., VII, 357 seq. (*Philosophische Untersuchungen über das Wesen der menschlichen Freiheit und die damit zusammenhängenden Gegenstände*, 1809): Nature is the "dark principle" (p. 362 etc.), "irrational principle" (p. 374 etc.), "obscure principle" (p. 377 etc.), "chaos" (p. 374 etc.); it is "a mere hankering or desire—i.e., blind will" (p. 363) and "the possibility of evil" (p. 363) etc. See pp. 359-60:"At the base there is always disorder, as if it could once again break through, and nowhere does it seem as though order and form were the original, but only that an original disorder had been

And so this Nature and the natural genius can be still desired only by those who desire destruction: their own, or, as a substitute, that of others. Destructive Nature becomes dominant; but artistic genius—the highest potential of the man at play—is played out: obviously it was invented and brought to life only in order to cover up and put off the confrontation with that situation of horror which we have indicated. And so—once the genius episode is over—man must surrender to this situation. He cannot withstand it for any length of time. He needs at least new forms of escape. Since previous esthetic solutions are no use, this situation must inevitably become a *non-esthetic* problem. And now at least two new possibilities arise for escape. From the beginning of the nineteenth century at the latest, this problem has become

(a) A non-esthetic problem *within* the range of esthetics. This points up something which was implicit in Hegel, but was certainly not explicitly set out: the way to a *no longer fine art*. All those failures, which man must fear to live out in reality, he seeks to translate into artistic unreality. He concentrates artistically on the bad, precisely because he fears it. He tries to spare himself from the realization of the bad through making an artistic theme out of it and through the technique of this thematizing. And so at once the esthetics of the beautiful is joined by that of the unbeautiful—that of the sublime, the tragic, the comic, the ironic, the humorous, the eccentric, the uncanny, the ugly, etc. This esthetics of the unbeautiful develops out of the role of a secondary esthetics which ultimately becomes universal; and in so doing it discloses a wealth of new themes and forms.[60] The problems connected with this

---

straightened out. This feature of things is the ungraspable basis of reality, which cannot be unravelled in the intellect even with the greatest of efforts, but remains forever down at the bottom of things. . . . Without this preceding obscurity, there is no reality of the creature; darkness is its inevitable heritage." Cf. not only the Romantic *Nachtseiten* (night sides) discussion, but also Schopenhauer's response to this clouded doctrine of will, *Sämtliche Werke*, ed. P. Deussen, IV, 131: "that 'natura naturans,' or the thing in itself, is . . . the will" (*Parerga und Paralipomena, I*, 1851), but this "endless striving" to which belongs "the absence of all purpose" and "boundless suffering," because it "usually preys upon itself: so everywhere in Nature do we see conflict, fighting and change of conquest, . . . the split with oneself essential to the will"—*Die Welt als Wille und Vorstellung, I* (1819), §§ 27, 29, 56 ff. Integral to all this is the fact that the dominant outlet is no longer that of natural philosophy and aesthetics, but—so typical of the older Schelling—theology and—as in Schopenhauer—ascetic quietism.

[60] Here to an increasing extent—see Hegel, *Ästhetik*, ed. cit., p. 22—the principal esthetic standard of "direct enjoyment" is replaced by that of "judgment" and "contemplative observation": henceforth art no longer coincides with emotion but with reflection. And this very fact perhaps makes possible a phenomenon of transference: when art becomes "no longer fine," the theory of this art—according to its intentions—becomes "fine"; a "de-estheticizing" of art compels an "estheticizing" of its theory. We shall not go into the question of whether this is true or not.

possibility of escape bring to the surface another possibility: the esthetically unsolved problem becomes

(b) A non-esthetic problem *outside* the range of esthetics. This again
points up something which was perhaps implicit in Hegel but was certainly not explicitly set out: the way to a *no longer artistic art*. An obvious example is the art of healing. All those failures which man must fear
to live out in reality, he seeks to translate into forms of damage which
can be negotiated, contemplated, endured, cured, or attended to in some
way or another: he seeks to experience them as diseases, under the pro-
tection of the doctor. And so even within the Romantic movement, the
central philosophic interest in esthetics is supplemented by an interest in
medicine; poetry becomes increasingly attentive not only to itself, but
also to sickness and the doctor. Art begins to see itself more and more as
a therapy, or as a symptom, or—pharmaceutically and toxicolog-
ically—as a neutralizer of both, as a stimulant or sedative drug, and an
artificial paradise. Genius becomes the symptom of all symptoms, esthetics the speciality of diagnostic praxis. The problem that was previously
expressed in esthetic terms is now expressed—at least, when
necessary—medically.[61]

9. In the course of the nineteenth century—*at the same time and in
the same context*—both possibilities become acute and representative:
that of a no longer beautiful art, and that of the medical sphere of influence. What does this signify? The same challenge—the unconscious
naturalness of the historical world—can be met equally by artistic and
by non-artistic measures. And this gives rise to the *principle of the convertibility of art and non-art*. The interchangeability or identity of phenomena relevant to art and to medicine—perhaps an erroneous finding,
but certainly one from which an element of truth can be extracted[62]—is
only a special case, but with regard to this special case, certain general
categories of such convertibility can be worked out. The fact that it
achieved this is what gives relevance to the significance of Freud's
theory.

This significance is easily overlooked, partly because of the short-
circuiting of some of Freud's analyses of art and artists, and partly be-

[61] For this whole phenomenon, see O. Marquard, *Über einige Beziehungen zwischen
Ästhetik und Therapeutik in der Philosophie des 19. Jahrhunderts* (Festschr. B.v. Wiese),
1963, esp. pp. 42 seq.: and the relevant references there; in my opinion C. Heselhaus explains a part of this whole phenomenon in his essay.

[62] Medical esthetics from—at the latest—G. Lombroso, up to W. Lange-Eichbaum,
whose theses are certainly problematical, is not only of symptomatic value; its provocative
capacity is considerable; and what can scarcely be disputed is that amongst the most decisive accomplishments in the history of thought is the outcome of those errors which led to
that which later generations have come to regard as true findings.

cause of the apparent conventionality of his theses on art theory. When
Freud expresses his ideas on art, he seems principally only to repeat the
Romantic theory of genius: art is connected with imagination; it preserves pleasant indulgences within a hard reality; it presents Nature
within culture; it is a game, an elevated daydream:[63] all this had also
been said by the Romantic genius theorists. It is quite possible to come
away with the impression that the psychoanalytical or depth-
psychological theory of art is particularly conservative—the last effort,
so to speak, to maintain the Romantic theory of genius. But this is only
apparently so. In reality, Freud, by once again constructing the theory
of art on a theory of the unconscious, opened up new possibilities for
this theory of art. Art, when it is "unbeautiful," no longer remains suspect; one can see and understand that art is interchangeable with non-
art. Freud offers up these possibilities of understanding chiefly by means
of two theoretical operations.

[63] Freud, ed. cit., VII, 214 and 222 (*Der Dichter und das Phantasieren*, 1907): "The poet
does . . . the same as the child at play; he creates a world of fantasy . . . so . . . that poetry
is like day-dreaming—a continuation of and substitute for former child's play." See also
ed. cit., VIII, 234 and 236 (*Formulierungen über die zwei Prinzipien des psychischen
Geschehens*, 1911): "With the setting up of the reality principle, a sort of thought activity
was separated off, which kept clear of reality tests and remained subject to the pleasure
principle alone. . . . Art, in a peculiar way, brings about a reconciliation of the two principles. . . ."
   See, above all, fantasy theory, of considerable importance for art theory—ed. cit., IX,
386-91, esp. 387 (*Vorlesungen zur Einführung in die Psychoanalyse*, 1917): "In the activities of the imagination, man . . . continues to enjoy that freedom from outer constraints which in reality he had long since renounced. . . . The creation of the spiritual
realm of fantasy has its exact counterpart in the erection of 'indulgences,' 'nature reserves,' where the demands of agriculture, trade and industry have threatened swiftly to
change the original face of the earth till it is unrecognizable. The nature reserve maintains
this old condition which otherwise has everywhere been regretfully sacrificed to necessity.
Everything can grow and proliferate there, as it will, useless things, and even harmful
things. Just such an indulgence, withdrawn from the principle of reality, is the spiritual
realm of the imagination."
   Such statements about art are only to be found in the younger Freud; but he does have a
more detailed, overall theory of art; in his later period—with the single exception of ed.
cit., XIV, 439—there is no theory of art; and so the explicit supplementation of the thesis
"art is erotic sublimation" through the thesis "art is death-wish sublimation" never takes
place. Apart from those works already quoted, Freud's ideas on art and artists are to be
found especially in: *Der Wahn und die Träume in W. Jensens 'Gradiva,'* 1907; *Eine Kind-
heitserinnerung des Leonardo da Vinci* (1910); *Das Motiv der Kästchenwahl* (1913); *Der
Moses des Michaelangelo* (1914), including the appendix to this piece (1927); *Eine Kind-
heitserinnerung aus Dichtung und Wahrheit* (1917); and, recapitulating: *Selbstdarstellung* (1925), esp. ed. cit., XIV, 90 seq.; *Dostojewski und die Vatertötung* (1928). But still
more important and pertinent are the general "arts studies" on dreams, failures, wit,
mythology, humour and suchlike. Mention must also be made of O. Rank, *Der Künstler.
Ansätze zu einer Sexualpathologie* (1907), if only to take note of the coarsening of the
Freudian school and to append general reflections on discipleship and caricature.

First, Freud interpreted the unconscious as something repressed:[64] "We get our idea of the unconscious from the doctrine of repression."[65] This doctrine makes it more plausible than Romanticism could ever do, how something good is excluded from official reality; and at the same time this doctrine gives validity to the post-Romantic idea that what is officially allowed is not always what is good, and might even have to be pushed aside when it is regressive and destructive. Freud's definition of the unconscious through repression gave the unconscious two "departments," in the sense that two things were repressed: the wrongly rejected good—called *Eros*—and the rightly rejected bad—called *Todestrieb* (death-wish).[66] At the same time, this new definition relieved the idea of the unconscious of its traditional tediousness—only the doctrine of repression made it something really explosive.[67]

Second, on the basis of this doctrine of repression, Freud was able to throw light on an event which he called "the return of the repressed":[68]

[64] After 1893 (ed. cit., ɪ, 89: *Über den psychischen Menchanismus hysterischer Phänomene*, together with J. Breuer) and despite the corrections in 1923 (ed. cit., xɪɪɪ, 243-45: *Das Ich und das Es*).

[65] Freud, ed. cit., xɪɪɪ, 241 (*Das Ich und das Es*, 1923).

[66] This is the terminology of the later Freud, definitively laid down in: ed. cit., xvɪɪ, 70 seq. (*Abriss der Psychoanalyse*, 1938).

[67] This is to say that in Freud the idea of the unconscious is not the most vital idea. It is only that which gave most offence to Freud's contemporaries and which the organizing committee for this colloquy thought to be the most vital. The idea of repression is more important. And the English translation of the German term "*Verdrängung*" also has association with the ideas of oppression and suppression integral to revolutionary theories. Much more topical than Freud's link with the Romantics—through the idea of the subconscious, which is our prescribed theme—would be his link with Marx: see, for instance, H. J. Sandkühler, *Freud und der Marxismus. Die Entdeckung der Zukunft im Vergangenen*, in: *Bogawus*, ɪv (1965), pp. 7 seq.—and his link with Hegel: see J. Taubes, *Psychoanalyse und Philosophie. Noten zu einer philosophischen Interpretation der psychoanalytischen Methode*, Radio Script, 1963. See also Freud's merely conditional allegiance to the idea of the unconscious, ed. cit., xɪɪɪ, 244 seq. (*Das Ich und das Es*, 1923): "If we see ourselves faced with the necessity of . . . setting up an unrepressed unconscious, then we must confess that the nature of the unconscious loses its importance for us."

[68] First in 1896, ed. cit., ɪ, 387 (*Weitere Bemerkungen über die Abwehr-Neurophychosen*): "Return of repressed memories. . . . But the resuscitated memories never enter the conscious mind unchanged . . . they are compromise formations between the repressed and the repressing ideas. . . . Return of the repressed. . . ." Or 1907, ed. cit., vɪɪ, 60 (*Der Wahn und die Träume in W. Jensens 'Gradiva'*): "As a rule the repressed cannot assert itself directly as a memory, but it remains productive and effective, and one day under the influence of an external action it gives rise to psychic consequences, which can be interpreted as transformations and off-shoots of the forgotten memory, and which remain incomprehensible if they are not interpreted in this way . . . then . . . one can expect such a return of the repressed. . . ." Or 1911, ed. cit., vɪɪɪ, 304 seq. (*Über einen autobiographisch beschriebenen Fall von Paranoia*): "If we look more closely at what is called 'repression,' we find we can divide the process into three phases. . . . The third and most important phase for pathological phenomena is . . . that of the failure of repression, the break-

whatever good or whatever bad is thrust out of official reality inevitably creates a substitute presence. We experience—writes Freud—"that repression as a rule creates a substitute formation . . . as symptom of a return of the repressed."[69] For Freud, this return of the repressed is the key to sublimations, symptoms, and therapies. And, in any case, the return of the repressed is the keystone of the theory of art made possible by Freud: "art is perhaps the most visible return of the repressed."[70] With this idea, Freud was able to establish at least three things:

(a) Return of the repressed: whether the repressed is something good, or something bad, this can occur in two ways—and art, if we understand it as the return of the repressed, is also twofold: affirmation of the sup-

---

through, the return of the repressed. . . ." The most detailed discussion is in 1937, ed. cit., xvi, 236 (*Der Mann Moses und die monotheistische Religion*): "All phenomena of symptom forming can rightly be described as the 'return of the repressed.' " See pp. 240 seq.: Freud's theory of the return of the repressed was not developed for art theory, but for the theory of symptom forming. This, of course, is the microtheory of historical processes—see, amongst others, Freud's statement in ed. cit., xiii, 228 ("*Psychoanalyse*" und "*Libidotheory*," 1923): "The valuation of psychoanalysis would be incomplete if one omitted to point out that it is the only one of the medical disciplines to have the widest connections with the arts, and is in the process of assuming a similar significance for religious and cultural history, mythology and literature to that which it has for psychiatry. This could seem surprising, in view of the fact that originally it had no other aim than to comprehend and to influence neurotic symptoms. But it is easy to ascertain the point at which the bridge to the arts was set up. When the analysis of dreams . . . showed that the mechanisms that create the pathological symptoms are also active in the normal life of the soul, psychoanalysis . . . became capable of application to the arts. . . ." The phenomenon of the return of the repressed is part of Freud's catalogue of *Triebschicksale* (Instincts and their vicissitudes). Here—ed. cit., x, 219 (*Triebe und Triebschicksale*, 1915)—the same is said of instincts as is said today of institutions, problems, answers, etc.: "They are distinguished by the fact that, to a great extent, they can take one another's place and easily change their objects. As a result of this latter characteristic, they are capable of achievements that lie far distant from their original intentions." It would be fascinating to examine structural affinities between Freud's theory of *Triebschicksale* and H. Blumenberg's *Umbesetzungstheorie* (displacement theory), especially as the term *Besetzung* (transposition) plays an important part, not only in the field of staff politics, but also in Freud's writings (e.g., ed. cit., x, 279 ff.: *Das Unbewusste* (1913): *Besetzung, Entziehung der Besetzung, Neubesetzung, Gegenbesetzung*, etc.), and because in the analysis of minor individual events—e.g., rotation of conscience pangs and agoraphobia—basically one can work with the same vocabulary as in the analysis of major thought-historical events: e.g., the genesis of modern times. Freud and Blumenberg compete, with structurally related theories, in the attempt to fill in the gap caused by the "pensioning off" of the idea of a comprehensive philosophy. My object in mentioning this is to emphasize the fact that either both theories are currently irrelevant, or neither is; either both theories must "be heard" (Koselleck), or neither.

[69] Freud, ed. cit., x, 256 ff. (*Die Verdrängung*, 1915).

[70] H. Marcuse, *Eros and Civilization. A Philosophical Inquiry into Freud* (London, 1956), p. 144.

pressed "better," or mild presence of the "bad-regressive." It is the "bringing to light"[71] of the good, or the appeasement of the barbaric.[72] It anticipates happiness, or tames aggressions. The once beautiful now prepares the way, or spares. It is a tempered protest, or that "mild narcosis into which art transports us,"[73] so that we may bear the unbearable. Revelatory protest and sparing narcosis; at times they are indistinguishable. When does protest become sparing? When does the sparing turn into protest? Both questions are part of this theory of art; but whenever they are asked, they always presuppose one thing: *art is a function of something which itself is not art.*

(b) Return of the repressed: this is not only art. It is also pathological symptoms, dreams and delirium, failures, absurdities. It is also historical actions, institutions, ideologies. And, finally, it is also theoretical operations and the forms in which they are carried out—for instance, research groups concerned with border phenomena of esthetics. Art, therefore, is just one form among many of the return of the repressed: it is just one substitute formation among many; among all these parallel activities, it is just "one more." Art is interchangeable with non-esthetic phenomena; it can be replaced by non-art; the apparent qualitative distinction between art and non-art disappears: *art loses its distinctive status.*

(c) Return of the repressed: through this definition, which puts it on a level with all sorts of other substitute formations, art is cast by Freud in "a relatively humble role;"[74] and so, in Freud, the theory of art also loses its exceptional position. But of course this also has its consequences for the "sphere of content and interpretation"[75] of art: if art and non-art are interchangeable phenomena, then the border of art is irrelevant and there is no longer any restriction on what it is permitted to it. If art and non-art are interchangeable, then—regardless of whether Freud said so explicitly or not—there is nothing which is not subsumable under art.

---

[71] E. Bloch, *Das Prinzip Hoffnung*, I, 1954; see, in general, the analysis of the *Noch-nicht-Bewusstsein oder der Dämmerung nach Vorwärts* (not yet consciousness or the forward-looking down), pp. 128 ff., with the critique typical of Bloch—aiming at Freud to hit Jung.

[72] Th. W. Adorno, *Minima Moralia* (1951), p. 201: "Every work of art is a crime prevented."

[73] Freud, ed. cit., XIV, 439 (*Das Unbehagen in der Kultur*, 1930).

[74] D. Riesman, *Freud und die Psychoanalyse* (1935), p. 35; against this, H. Marcuse can scarcely be right when (pp. 172 seq.) he revalues *The Esthetic Dimension* within the psychoanalytically oriented position, and in passing declares that Freud was more or less the best Schiller that ever lived and thought. What is important is that a preferential status for art simply does not exist in Freud; and Marcuse's line of thought is only of interest because it allows one to ask why he needs it.

[75] Hegel, *Ästhetik*, ed. cit., I, 581.

The restriction of art to the beautiful is utterly meaningless: for Freud, even more radically than for Hegel, art "on the side of its highest definition" is something past.

10. What does the theory of the unconscious accomplish for a theory of no longer fine art? As we have seen, quite a lot. First, the theory of the unconscious collaborates with that of genius. But then—above all in its radical, post-Romantic, Freudian form—it takes on vital significance for a theory of no longer fine art.[76] Freud's definition of art as the return of the repressed makes art interchangeable with non-esthetic phenomena, and precisely for this reason it also makes art extremely insensitive to any obligation to be fine. I have tried to indicate the implications of this definition: for Freud, art—like many other activities—is either a form of revealing a repressed good reality (protest) or a form of sparing the subject from a suppressed bad reality (narcosis), or it is both— narcotic protest or protesting narcosis. To a certain extent it is inevitable that art should be all this, at the present stage of a general process already analyzed by Hegel: the increasing lifting of all restrictions as to what may be dealt with artistically and as to how it may be dealt with artistically. In this sense, the obituary with which we began, concerning the absolute significance of art, is strictly identical with an *epinikion* to its newly acquired capacity for handling any subject in any conceivable way.

[76] In this particular context it will be useful to recall Freud's own valuation of psychoanalysis for the theory of art; see Freud, ed. cit., VIII, 416 (*Das Interesse an der Psychoanalyse*, 1913): "As regards some of the problems relating to art and artists, psychoanalytical observation gives a satisfactory explanation; others elude it completely."

MAX IMDAHL

Overstepping Esthetic Limits in Visual Art:

Four Aspects of the Problem

THIS subject is open to many different approaches. One might, for instance, discuss such themes as hell and damnation, which produce something unmistakably and positively ugly that casts no esthetic doubts on itself or on its beautiful antithesis. However, we shall not be dealing with this positive ugliness. Nor shall we discuss H. Sedlmayr's[1] reflections on *Ars humilis* as a (specifically Christian) *"complexio oppositorum* of the poles *humilis—sublimis."*

We shall confine ourselves here to considering four aspects of the problem of overstepping esthetic limits:

1. The destruction of traditional esthetics and the consequent release of a new esthetic consciousness.

2. The misinterpretation of an inner-esthetic solution.

3. The misinterpretation of an extra-esthetic solution.

4. The destruction of traditional esthetics and the consequent release of a new extra-esthetic consciousness.

We shall try to illuminate these four aspects with reference to modern or ultramodern works of art. This is not, of course, to be taken as meaning that no other works would provide an adequate illustration.

I

A well-known work by Marcel Duchamp is the reproduction of the Mona Lisa, with the legend L.H.O.O.Q. and defaced with a beard and moustache (1919, in a print of 35 copies, numbered and signed).[2] If the letters L, H, O, O, Q are read aloud, they give the sentence *Elle* (- L) *a chaud* (- H O) *au* (- O) *cul* (- Q).[3] Whether this sentence is an allusion

---

[1] H. Sedlmayr, "Ars humilis," in *Hefte des Kunsthistorischen Seminars der Universität München* (Munich, 1962), pp. 7 et seq. Also important in the context of our discussion is H. Sedlmayr, *Das Problem der Wahrheit. Vier Texte zur Unterscheidung der Geister in der Kunst,* in *Kunst und Wahrheit,* 3rd ed. (Hamburg, 1961), *Rowohlts Deutsche Enzyklopädie,* pp. 128 et seq.

[2] *Dada-Katalog der Galerie Krugier & Cie (Suites 10),* (Geneva, 1966), No. 20.

[3] R. Hamilton, *Duchamp* (Arts Council Exhibition at the Tate Gallery), (London, 1966), No. 134, p. 60.

to Sigmund Freud's study of Leonardo, or not, "this usurping of the masterpiece's privileges by the pun is aimed at destroying its prestige more effectively than any thesis could do" (Buffet-Picabia, 1945).[4]

The same letters also occur in Picabia's own painting *Le Double Monde*.[5]

The exceeding of esthetic limits through the defacement of the Mona Lisa strikes one immediately as polemic—but precisely what is being controverted? First, the defacement could stand for the destruction of the precritical, uncritical, sentimental attitude towards this picture, emphasizing instead the pictorial or lineal qualities of the work, perhaps in accordance with the axiom of Matisse that the decisive expression arises not from a face, but from the disposition of the picture as a whole.[6] Second, however, the defacement could mean the destruction of all traditionally oriented esthetics. And so we can ask whether the defacement is in favor of, or at the expense of, esthetics. Third, of course, it can be taken, quite independently of all esthetics, as indicating the destruction of all idealistic naturalism and even—to go to the extreme—of all levels of meaning. Marcel Duchamp said on occasion that in Dada there was no solution because there was no problem,[7] and so perhaps one might also argue the other way around that in making the problems total, all solutions are excluded. In his recollections of Marcel Duchamp, H. P. Roché gave the following meaning to the defacement: "Ne vous hypnotisez pas sur les sourires de demain."[8] And according to Roché's note, Duchamp said, in a general context: "Je me force à me contredire pour éviter de suivre mon goût."[9] Our study comes up to date with Duchamp's issue in 1965 of a series of unaltered Mona Lisa prints, with the inscription *Rasée L.H.O.O.Q.*[10] With this procedure, one might say that through the restoration of her identity, the Mona Lisa has finally lost her identity. The triumph of aporia—jesting in earnest.

Viewed from the standpoint of Dada theory, Duchamp's 1919 Mona Lisa is obviously a paradigmatic anti-work-of-art, destroying art in general, and not just traditional esthetics. It is reproduced in Picabia's magazine *391* as *Tableau Dada par Marcel Duchamp*, directly above Picabia's *Manifeste Dada*, in which ironic complaints about the power of art-dealers are followed by: *Plus de chiures de mouches sur les murs.* And later, in an attack on Cubism:

---

[4] *The Dada Painters and Poets: An Anthology*, ed. R. Motherwell (New York, 1951), p. xxvii.

[5] R. Lebel, *Sur Marcel Duchamp* (Trianon Press, 1959), Cat. No. 141, p. 169.

[6] G. Diehl, *Henri Matisse* (Paris-Munich, 1958), p. 91.

[7] Lebel, p. 85: "Il n'y a pas de solution parce qu'il n'y a pas de problème."

[8] *Ibid.*, p. 86.   [9] *Ibid.*, p. 85.   [10] Hamilton, No. 185, p. 78.

"Le cubisme représente la disette des idées. Ils ont cubé les tableaux des primitifs, cubé les sculptures nègres, cubé les guitares, cubé les journaux illustrés, . . . maintenant il faut cuber de l'argent!!! Dada, lui, ne veut rien, rien, rien, il fait quelque chose pour que le public dise: 'nous ne comprenons rien, rien, rien.' "[11]

According to Hans Arp's definition, offered in the book *Die Kunstismen* published by himself and El Lissitzky, "Dadaism descended on the Fine Arts. It pronounced art to be a magic defecation, applying an enema to the Venus di Milo, and allowing Laocoon and Sons, after their thousand year struggle with the rattlesnake, to go to the bog at last. Dadaism brought affirmatives and negatives to the point where they became nonsense. In order to achieve indifference, it was destructive."[12] Or there is Tristan Tzara's definition: "Peut-être me comprendrez-vous mieux quand je vous dirai que dada est un microbe vierge qui s'introduit avec l'insistence de l'air dans tous les espaces que la raison n'a pu combler de mots ou de conventions."[13] Picabia, again, put on the picture of a chimpanzee the legend "Portrait de Cézanne, Portrait de Renoir, Portrait de Rembrandt."[14] Such attitudes, destructive, anti-esthetic, skeptical of art and of convention, themselves make possible, intentionally or unintentionally, a new esthetic consciousness, which disregards every norm and for this very reason sheds an esthetic light on whatever is under attack. This, of course, presupposes that the relevant subject will have attention paid to it—a condition radically fulfilled in Dadaism by the vehemence of its anti-art. In the words of Hans Arp: "Dada is as direct as Nature and seeks to give every object its essential place."[15]

One interesting work—if we are to single out just a few examples—is Arp's picture, made of pieces of paper, entitled "Nach dem Gesetz des Zufalls" (1920).[16] When the glass of Marcel Duchamp's "Large Glass Picture (1915-1923)" was broken during transport, and covered with a network of innumerable cracks, Duchamp acknowledged the working of chance by saying that these cracks were the last refinement of his picture.[17] And when, back in 1917, Duchamp wanted to exhibit his famous—or notorious—*Fontaine* in New York (but was refused permission), this meant: "Le beau est là où vous l'inventez."[18] Robert

---

[11] 391. *Revue publiée de 1917 à 1924 par Francis Picabia*, Réédition par M. Sanouillet (Paris, 1960), p. 79.

[12] *Die Kunstismen. Les Ismes de l'Art. The Isms of Art*, ed. by El Lissitzky and H. Arp (Etlenbach-Zürich, Munich and Leipzig, 1925), p. x.

[13] H. Richter, *Dada—Kunst und Antikunst* (Cologne, 1964), p. 197.

[14] Richter, Fig. 86, p. 176.

[15] H. Arp, R. Huelsenbeck, T. Tzara, *Die Geburt des Dada*, ed. P. Schifferli (Zurich, 1957), p. 106.

[16] Richter, Fig. 12, p. 48.   [17] Richter, p. 98.   [18] Lebel, p. 86.

Rauschenberg found Duchamp's bicycle (a front wheel with its fork mounted on a footstool) "one of the most beautiful sculptures" he had ever seen.[19] Henceforward it will be difficult to deny the "Ready-Mades" their esthetic content—once taken out of their context—for only then can the thesis hold good that "The separating is an operation."[20] In the studio of a well-known contemporary sculptor I have seen a bottle drier that is very similar to the famous one discovered by Duchamp.

As anti-art, which means, first, the possibility of esthetically evaluating non-artistic contingencies, and, second, the consequent possibility of innovating the self-evident, Dada is a negation both of normative idealism and of genius in art. And yet perhaps this historical movement can still be considered as part of the flow of recent art history: just as the artistic genius follows normative idealism and—by its standards—brings about an extension of esthetic consciousness in the direction of a relative, i.e., subjective contingency, so the art of the genius is followed by an extension of esthetic consciousness into the limitless, by virtue of the now possible esthetic evaluation of the absolute and unconditioned contingency. Disregarding whatever degree of profit and loss one might attribute to this movement, one might say that Dadaism is to be viewed as an ironic treatment of the work of art and of the esthetics connected with art; it can also be regarded as a process provoking an esthetic liberation of Nature, insofar as Nature ceases to be a mere object of art and is therefore freed from the restriction that it can only appear perfect by means of art, or that it is nothing but material for the work of art.

II

We shall now discuss the bold style of Hans von Marées' figure-painting, at times almost anticipatory of Archipenko, as revealed in his most important work, the picture of the Hesperides (Fig. 1). The picture was painted in the period 1884-1887, and is contemporary with Seurat's famous "Grande Jatte." The *Allgemeine Deutsche Biographie* of 1906 contains an article on Hans von Marées, written by Hyazinth Holland. In this we read: "In no orthopedic institution is there cure or recovery for his (Marées') figures."[21] A somewhat gruesome view of Arcadia! Holland's remark is a criticism of the striking elongations and distortions of Marées' figures as exceeding esthetic limits—a nude by Luca Signorelli, dealing with a similar subject, reveals no such distor-

---

[19] R. G. Dienst, *Pop Art. Eine kritische Information* (Wiesbaden, 1965), p. 19.

[20] Motherwell, p. xvii.

[21] J. Meier-Graefe, *Hans von Marées. Sein Leben und Werk* (Munich and Leipzig, 1909 and 1910), III, p. 337.

tions (1490, Fig. 2).[22] Undoubtedly Holland's negative judgment is unfair. To adopt terms used by Adolf von Hildebrand, Hans von Marées' pupil, Holland obviously confuses a merely mechanical, illusory rendering of the *Daseinsform* (existence-form) of the figure—of no relevance to the impact of the picture—with what in Marées is actually a thematic representation of the figure's expressive *Wirkungsform* (effect-form); just as "in algebra one disregards numerical values, and expresses values only as possible relations between a and b," so the *Wirkungsform* raises all "real geometrical quantities" to the level of such "relative values," "which only have validity for the eye."[23] As regards the painter's task of producing a "situation that suits the eye,"[24] prior to Hildebrand, Konrad Fiedler expressed the view that painting was a matter of producing the world in and for the conscious human mind, with exclusive regard to its visible appearance, or, to put it another way, the Gestalt that comes about "through and for the eye."[25] Fiedler's thesis also differentiates between *Daseinsform* and *Wirkungsform*—one might also say between actual and expressive realities. But if, as with Holland, actual and expressive realities are mixed up, then inevitably the observer concerned will see only distortions and thus phenomena that are no longer esthetic. To this extent, Holland's judgment is logically consistent. One can also say that it is characteristic of Marées' style that it opens up the alternatives of suitable and unsuitable manners of observation: misunderstanding accompanies the claim to artistic insight.

In depicting the human figure with maximum emphasis on the joints, Marées was concerned, first, with presenting an organic composition, and second—perhaps more importantly—with "special modifications of the forms in which that organic structure presents itself to the eye."[26] Seen from the standpoint of this particular artistic aim, the distortions of Marées' figures are, among other things, well suited to showing up the joints that were so important to him. For, the more emphatic and ex-

[22] The picture was burned in the war. Concerning Marées and the style of the Italian Renaissance, see among others L. Vauxcelles in *Gil Blas* (October 1, 1909): "Ce fut un très pur artiste que Hans von Marées, un isolé, un chercheur insatiable qui s'epuisa à vouloir renouer—o chimère—le lien entre le passé et le présent, entre les grandes traditions des maîtres italiens et le naturalisme de son temps"—though the reference here to "naturalism" is not to be taken too literally (see Meier-Graefe on this quotation, III, p. 384).

[23] A. V. Hildebrand, *Das Problem der bildenden Kunst* (Strassburg, 1893), p. 20 (*Daseins- und Wirkungsform*), p. 22 (Algebra).

[24] An expression used by H. Konnerth, *Die Kunsttheorie Konrad Fiedlers. Eine Darlegung der Gesetzlichkiet in der bildenden Kunst* (München-Leipzig, 1909), p. 131.

[25] K. Fiedler, *Schriften über Kunst*, ed. H. Marbach (Leipzig, 1896), pp. 55 and 248.

[26] K. V. Pidoll, *Aus der Werkstatt eines Künstlers. Erinnerungen an den Maler Hans von Marées aus den Jahren 1880-81 und 1884-85*, reprinted (Augsburg, 1930), p. 17.

pressive each angle becomes, because of the length of its sides, in Marées the figures and their limbs are elongated, so that the angles of the joints can be that much more expressive. What matters is not the objective reality, but the subjective conspicuousness of that reality, through its enhanced tectonic and optic impact. For Hyazinth Holland, the figure is non-esthetic insofar as it is interpreted as a *Daseinsform*. But for Marées the figure is esthetic, since it is interpreted as a *Wirkungsform*. Contrary to Holland's interpretation, the theme according to Marées' artistic aim is not the figure as such, but the appearance of the figure, or, to be more precise, the composition of the appearance of the figure, and not the composition of the figure. If one judges by the proportion of the figure as such, the distortions take on a negative esthetic value; this corresponds to Holland's view. But if one judges by the proportions of the appearance of the figure, these same distortions take on a positive esthetic value, as elements of a clarified vision; this is Marées' intention. It must be added that under the particular conditions that prevailed in the late nineteenth century, the Arcadian subject matter of Marées' famous triptych of the Hesperides could be presented credibly only if, first and foremost, the style idealized the vision without bringing about an idealistic naturalism, for—as can be seen from the pictures of Anselm Feuerbach—this in the nineteenth century could easily lead perilously near to the so-called "Lebendes Bild" (Living Picture).[27] To sum up, what Hyazinth Holland objects to as unesthetic is, in reality, what Marées intends as esthetic. And this shows that the *Wirkungsform* and *Daseinsform* aspects of esthetics can no longer be separately conveyed.

A comparison with Signorelli's picture (Fig. 2) suggests that in the possibility of misunderstanding Marées' style there lies a modern phenomenon. Though Signorelli's figure can certainly be observed and interpreted on different levels, none will be inappropriate or damaging to the meaning. Signorelli's figure exists, in accordance with the principles of *Disegno*, as an ideal form perfecting Nature, an idea which recognizes no difference between *Daseinsform* and *Wirkungsform* since in such a context they virtually amount to the same thing. "From baroque on-

[27] Concerning the rival movements in Germany, at Marées' time, of Realism and Idealism, Fiedler considered the works of both to be "artistically insignificant." While the realists laid the main emphasis on the physical appearance, and could not raise this to any higher status or extend it beyond what was reflected in "normal heads," the idealists had an equally feeble mentality which they sought to enrich by means of a non-artistic content—one might term it the ponderous content of idealism balancing the dull vision of realism. For Pidoll, however, the works of Marées are "pictorial processes of Gestaltung." See Fiedler, p. 62 et seq.; Pidoll, p. 10; M. Imdahl, *Marées, Fiedler, Hildebrand Riegl, Cézanne, Bilder und Zitate*, in *Literatur und Gesellschaft*. Festgabe für Benno von Wiese (Bonn, 1963), pp. 142 et seq.

 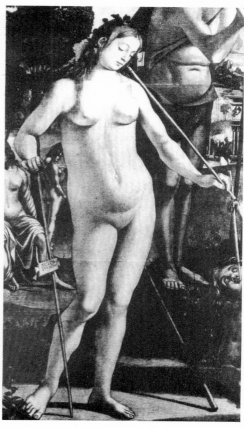

1. Hans von Marées, *Hesperides* (detail)   2. Signorelli, *The Education of Pan* (detail)

3. Picasso, *Mlle D. M.*

4. Picasso, *Child with Doll*

5. Rodin, *John the Baptist*

6. Victor Vasarely, *Tlinko*

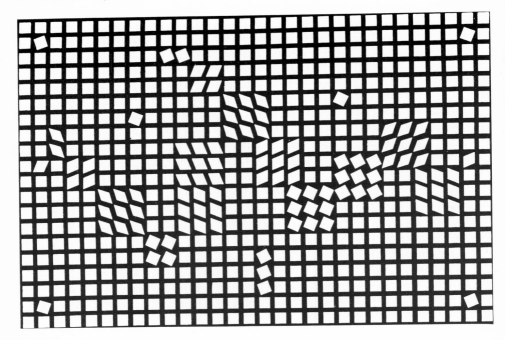

7. Jackson Pollock, *Number One*

wards," wrote the Poussin author Otto Grautoff, "there began a slow dissolution of forms in painting."[28] In this context one might refer to the thesis of the Reubenist Roger de Piles, concerning the relation between pictorial detail and the distance of the spectator from the picture: "que c'est une perte de tems, pour ne pas dire un manque d'intelligence, que de faire un travail inutile & qui se perd dans la distance convenable; & au contraire il y a beaucoup d'art & de science en faisant tout ce qu'il est nécessaire, de ne faire que ce qui est nécessaire." Undoubtedly there is a difference here between the form of the thing and the form of the vision, between objectivity and subjectivity—a differentiation full of consequence for later developments.[29]

III

The depiction of movement is one of the oldest, most immediate, and most constant problems in art. In the late nineteenth century, the physiologist Ernst Brücke applied the theories of Aristoxenos of Tarent to art; according to Aristoxenos, all movements of the body or of the voice are separated by ἠρεμίαι, that is, pauses. Brücke, who—as Eugen Petersen pointed out in his study of rhythm—was not aware of his conformity with Aristoxenos,[30] used the swing of a pendulum as a demonstration. He called the ἠρεμίαι "end-points" and considered them to be uniquely suited to depiction, since one could have the clearest possible view of the moving object during these temporary cessations of movement—albeit at the cost of the actual experience of movement. For Aristoxenos, however, movement can be best experienced during these pauses; this was pointed out with some emphasis by Petersen.[31] Erwin Panofsky also felt drawn to this aspect of Aristoxenos' theory. For the best possible depiction and momentary experience of a moving object, he favoured not the "partial phases of an actual movement that is in process," but the ἠρεμίαι or turning-points, as moments of a "latent movement" in the sense that "either a new movement seems to be on the point of beginning, or an old movement seems to have come to a halt." And: "Just as Aristoxenos declared that all movements can only

[28] O. Grautoff, Formzertrümmerung und Formaufbau in der bildenden Kunst (Berlin, 1919), p. 64.

[29] R. de Piles, "Conversation sur la Peinture," printed in Recueil de divers ouvrages sur la peinture et le coloris . . . , Paris, 1775, p. 159. See M. Imdahl, Die Rolle der Farbe in der Neueren französischen Malerei. Abstraktion und Konkretion, in Poetik und Hermeneutik II (Munich, 1966), pp. 195 et seq.

[30] E. Brücke, "Die Darstellung der Bewegung durch die bildenden Künste," in Deutsche Rundschau, xxvi (1881), pp. 39 et seq.; E. Petersen, "Rhythmus," in Abhandlungen der Königl. Gesellsch. d. Wissenschaften (Göttingen), N.F. xvi, 5 (1917), pp. 1 et seq.

[31] Petersen, pp. 13 et seq., 28 et seq.

be perceived at their stopping or, rather, turning-points, so do we feel we can maintain that—if their depiction is to convey an experience of energy, and in this way the preceding and the subsequent are to merge perceptibly into a now—they can be depicted only at their stopping or, rather, turning-points. Paradoxical though it may sound, the ἠρεμίαι—charged with potential movement because the actual movement rests in them—signify the really kinetic, the truly productive moments."[32] These words of Panofsky's contain a clear attack on Lessing's thesis of the productive moment,* and before Panofsky, Petersen too, for instance, had argued against Lessing, in his discussion of the discobolus as a paradigm of the ἠρεμίαι between two "opposed" but "to a certain degree homogeneous movements": "It is in truth, though some have tried to contest it, the most productive moment, and so the most suitable for depiction."[33] In recent times Hodler's well-known picture of the wood-cutter, for instance, is indebted to this most tried and trusted motif of the turning-point.

Apart from this method of "concentrating the course of movement in a single dynamically charged moment of suspense," in which the temporally preceding and subsequent become simultaneously perceptible in a "right-now," there is also the method of "splitting up the course of movement into several individual phases succeeding one another cinematographically"[34]: the successive parts of the action may be performed by a single figure recurring in different positions, or by different figures in different positions. This method, for which we may use Franz Wickhoff's general term of "continuing style,"[35] was not only dominant in early Christian and medieval narrative style, but is also to be found,

[32] E. Panofsky, "Albrecht Durers rhythmische Kunst," in *Jahrbuch für Kunstwissenschaft* (1926), pp. 141 et seq. Also E. H. Gombrich, "Moment and Movement in Art," in *Journal of the Warburg and Courtauld Institutes*, xxvii (1964), pp. 193 et seq.

*ED. NOTE. Cf. Laocoön, chap. 3, where Lessing argues that the moment either just before or after the action is most productive for imaginative effect.

[33] Petersen, p. 45. Th. Lipps, in *Ästhetik. Psychologie des Schönen in der Kunst*, ii (Hamburg-Leipzig, ²1906), pp. 104 et seq., also rejected Lessing's theory, mainly with arguments based on esthetic observation: "After all, the work of art always presents only that which it represents, and never that which it does not represent. And this means to say that in or for aesthetic observation, only what is directly represented—that is, the moment as such that is represented in the picture—actually exists, and that, on the other hand, neither the preceding nor the subsequent moment can ever exist for it, unless the preceding moment in reality is not preceding, and the subsequent in reality not subsequent—i.e., these moments are not separate in time but are included in the moment represented." But this is precisely what typifies the turning-point or the culmination of a movement.

[34] Panofsky, p. 143.

[35] F. Wickhoff, *Römische Kunst (Die Wiener Genesis)*, ed. M. Dvorak (Berlin, 1912), pp. 9 et seq., 168 et seq., 192, 199, 202.

for instance, in Mantegna's "Musentanz am Parnass,"[36] Breughel's "Blindensturz,"[37] Watteau's "L'Embarquement pour Cythère,"[38] and Géricault's "Pferderennen." Rodin had the following to say about this picture, in his attack on the possibility of producing any number of photographic snapshots:

"Or, je crois bien que c'est Géricault qui a raison contre la photographie: car ses cheveux paraissent courir: et cela vient, de ce que le spectateur, en les regardant d'arrière en avant, voit d'abord les jambes postérieures accomplir l'effort d'où résulte l'élan générale, puis le corps s'allonger, puis les jambes antérieures chercher au loin la terre. Cet ensemble est faux dans sa simultanéité; il est vrai quand les parties en sont observées successivement et c'est cette vérité seule qui nous importe, puisque c'est que nous voyons et qui nous frappe."[39]

Picasso's style of figure distortion is multifarious and certainly cannot be explained in terms of a single representative intention. But as far as his famous portrait "Mlle D.M." of 1937 (Fig. 3) is concerned, the depictions of movement that we have briefly described—demanding in the one case a simultaneous and in the other a successive kind of observation—appear essential to the understanding, even if for the time being they are non-artistic and also non-esthetic solutions to the problem. Picasso's picture can easily be misinterpreted as a distorted human portrait. And indeed it is open to misinterpretation, on grounds of exceeding esthetic limits or being non-esthetic, insofar as it depicts only one figure, but seeks to represent not movement concentrated in a single momentary pause, but a cinematographic succession of phases—in other words, through the one figure it attempts the perceptible simultaneity of a perceptible successiveness.

The head is multi-colored—almost piebald. Blending into a profile of quite classical ideality are elements of a turn into the frontal position,[40] which inevitably results in extensions or duplications of form, and so in distortions. The execution of the movement, the actual motion of the head, is represented as a process going on at this very moment. The left eye (directions from the observer's standpoint) is looking exactly *face à face*, its iris a flaming red: virtually dominating the picture, it signifies the anticipated completion of the movement of the head from the right.

[36] H. Kauffmann, *Albrecht Dürers rhythmische Kunst* (Leipzig, 1924), p. 82.

[37] R. Huyghe, *Die Antwort der Bilder* (Vienna-Munich, 1958), p. 149.

[38] A. Rodin, *L'Art. Entretiens réunis par P. Gsell* (Paris, 1911), p. 91 et seq.

[39] Rodin, p. 88.

[40] The catalogue of the Picasso exhibition held in 1955-1956 in Munich, Cologne, and Hamburg, describes this picture (No. 76) as the "joining together of front and side views of the same face."

The left eye in the opposite direction from the profile position of the head—with its less striking, pale green iris—has the effect of illuminating the tendency of the head to move from right to left. It would be quite wrong to see in this position of the eye, which in fact expresses the direction of a movement, or in any other of the distortions, the negative values of destructiveness; on the contrary, the distortions are a positive means of depicting movement, and so are a positive means of depicting life as well. And so the distortions do not function for the benefit of anything destructive or non-esthetic, but in order to bring the subject to life. And the extent to which movement is expressive of such life can be seen from what is undoubtedly Picasso's most provocative picture and the one most open to criticism: child with doll. The doll is certainly not distorted, but seems incapable of movement and so is lifeless, the child *is* distorted, but can move and so is alive (1938, Fig. 4).[41]

Not altogether dissimilar is the problem arising from Rodin's striding figure of John the Baptist (1878, Fig. 5). Here we have the highly unusual fact that the weight is placed equally on both feet; and so the question arises as to whether this is meant to typify an extreme form of antique striding position, the exaggerated tension of which can no longer be esthetically motivated, or, in accordance with the artist's declared intention, it represents two phases of one successive process, in which one placing of weight follows another.

"For instance, while my St. John is shown with his two feet on the ground, it is probable that a snapshot of a model executing the same movement would show the back leg already raised and moving towards the front. Or, the other way round, the front leg would not yet be touching the ground if the back leg in the photograph were in the same position as in my statue. Now it is precisely for this reason that the model in the photograph would present the strange appearance of a man suddenly struck with paralysis and petrified in his pose, as happens in Perrault's delightful fairy-tale to the servants of Sleeping Beauty, who are all suddenly immobilized in the position of their work. And this confirms what I have just shown you about movement in art. If in snapshots people, though caught in mid-action, actually seem to be suddenly frozen in the air, it is because every part of the body is reproduced at precisely the same twentieth or fortieth of a second, and so, unlike in art, there is no progressive development of the movement . . . it is the artist who is truthful, and it is the camera that lies."[42]

However, the question is whether of one's own accord one sees these

[41] One can regard as a kind of preparatory stage Cézanne's picture *Girl with Doll* (1900-1902), in which the doll has no face.

[42] Rodin, pp. 85 et seq.

moments of movement as Rodin sees them, or whether one can only recognize them when one is aware of the artist's theory. The alternatives are an impression of "going" as an organic execution of movement, or of an inorganic "standing still," with an otherwise organic modelling of the body. Undoubtedly Rodin's "Baptist," as a moving figure, has affinities to later futurism—it is more modern than people are generally willing to admit—but equally clear is the fact that it is as open as futurism to being misinterpreted. It is true that the equal weight on both feet can exclude the peculiarity of frozen movement to be seen on a snapshot, but it cannot defend itself against its own peculiarity being misinterpreted.

If one follows Rodin's instructions and sees the figure successively,[43] for instance looking first at the back foot and then at the front (the time needed to look from one to the other may correspond to the time in which the weight is shifted from one foot to the other), then one will miss seeing the figure as a unified, plastic form; but if, on the other hand, one looks at the figure as a plastic form, and sees it altogether or, say, from top to bottom, as a single unit, then one will miss the cinematographic movement. Picasso's moving figures—the full-length ones as well—[44]are perhaps able to lessen this conflict in two ways: first, by facilitating a kind of observation that is less concerned with the direction and succession of movement, thanks to the use of a pictorial syntax that lays more emphasis on independent values of direction, line, and color; and secondly because, as a result, from a concrete point of view, they seem all the uglier.

IV

It goes without saying that every appearance activates the eye and the faculty of seeing. The painter in his choice of colors can make demands on the eye: in the first place, well within the limits of its natural adaptability; in the second place, right up to those limits. In other words, in the first instance the eye can easily accustom itself to the colors, whereas in the second the colors make excessive demands, so that seeing becomes a conscious activity, and this conscious activity activates the thing that is actually to be seen. The first, and the most common, style of coloring is characteristic, for instance, of Courbet and Corot, whereas the second typifies painting before and after the turn of the cen-

---

[43] Rodin, pp. 88 et seq., in connection with Géricault's *Pferderennen*. According to Kauffmann, p. 5, it is not left to the spectator how he should see Rodin's figure. "Under no circumstances should he view it all at once, but starting with the organs embodying the earliest phase, he must read off all the others in the order in which they occur, and follow how the movement develops from limb to limb."

[44] E.g., *Guernica*.

tury, in particular the "Pointillism" of Seurat and the "Orphism" of Delaunay.* The demands on the eye that border on the excessive are dependent on the colors of the spectrum. In "Pointillism" these demands
arise principally from the unceasing "optical mixture"; in "Orphism,"
they come about because the eye is confronted with large, optically irreconcilable quantities of color which it always sees *simul et singulari-
ter*, so that it creates an agglomeration of various groups of harmonious
and dissonant forces. The effect of this—if we may cut short our
explanation—[45] is that in both "Pointillism" and "Orphism," the picture is experienced not as a once-and-for-all existence, but as one that is
permanently renewing itself. Robert Delaunay discerned the non-
esthetic knowledge produced by this effect in the striking presence of a
"forme en mouvement, statique—et dynamique,"[46] in the physical con-
ceivability of a "mouvement synchronique" as the "représentation de
l'universel Drame."[47] As far as the esthetic side is concerned, we have
the following basic principle: while what is to be seen, constantly renewing itself, remains identical it can still be reflected in the seeing. This is
what makes it possible for what is to be seen to unfold itself in a way that
is still esthetically traditional—provided that the esthetic is conditioned
by present relative values in painting. It was no coincidence that the
pointillist Seurat was more concerned than practically any other painter
of his time with the harmony of linear composition.

If one studies certain works of optical art, for instance, some colored
pictures by Victor Vasarely,[48] or even black-and-white pictures (1956,
Fig. 6), one will certainly find there a third category, in which the
boundary of optical adaptation is exceeded, the eye physically overwhelmed. The act of seeing which is demanded becomes painful, because
the eye can no longer experience the continual renewal of the same
thing, but undergoes a constant and abrupt change of vision. It is possible with Vasarely's picture to recognize an overstepping of the esthetic
borderline, and also the destruction of traditional esthetics: the first on
account of the painfulness of the stimulated vision; the second because
the composition of the picture—an esthetic experience that might be reflected in relative values present—has a constantly renewed potential existence which, however, is being constantly and newly destroyed every
moment, thanks to the overstepping of the borders of optical adaptabil-

---

*Illustr. in *Poetik und Hermeneutik, II* (Munich, 1966), after p. 208.

[45] Imdahl, pp. 219 et seq.

[46] R. Delaunay, *Du Cubisme à l'Art abstrait*. Documents inèdits publiés par P. Francas-
tel (Paris, 1957), p. 146.

[47] Delaunay, p. 180.

[48] See the illustrations to H. van Lier's article in: *Quadrum. Revue International d'Art
Moderne*, XVII (1964), pp. 55 et seq.

ity. In any case, the exceeding of esthetic bounds would be the esthetic consolidation continually and stormily denied by the exceeding of optical adaptability bounds. "Ne songeons pas à une alternance figure-fond, phénomène banal bien connu de la Gestaltthéorie. . . . C'est une ambiguité instantanée où les formes perdent leurs conditions d'existence."[49]

One is bound to ask whether the overstepping of the border of adaptability is not a general symptom of all modern arts, including music; whether, in fact, basically it does not imply an extension of esthetic sensitivity—an idea suggested to me by S. Kracauer; whether, indeed, Kandinsky's statement does not apply even on this not merely historical level—that "the dissonance of today will be the harmony of tomorrow."[50] For optical art, though, the main consideration seems to be not so much this as the non-esthetic question of how far visual experience can be extended through excessive demands on the eye, and how much otherwise invisible energy can be physically revealed to the overexerted eye. In Vasarely's consciousness is realized the consolidation of appearances that is otherwise denied; in other words, the ambiguity, that constantly leaves open the way to the hoped-for clarity, fulfills the theoretic demand that the painting—since science has revealed to us a "nature infiniment plus vaste" and our "vision egocéntrique" must develop towards a "conscience totale"—should take part in the "plastique multidimensionnelle," with Gestalt and Nichtgestalt, clarity and obscurity, "l'informal et le formal" individually alternating on the basis of a nonetheless strict imposition of form, and so reaching to the very "confins de l'inconcevable": "Que nous traversions les amas interstellaires. . . . Ou les membranes des êtres microscopiques . . . Que nous allions vers l'électron ou vers les soleils . . . Le paysage habituel desparaît! Nous ne sommes plus sur la surface, mais dans la chose." Vasarely's picture uses the eye to convey something of the communicability of man and the unfathomable world of its inherent multidimensionality, with the picture itself actually producing this communication: "De contemplateurs statiques nous sommes mués en participants dynamiques."[51]

The attempt we have made to divide painting into the three stages or

[49] Van Lier, p. 56.

[50] W. Kandinsky, *Essays über Kunst und Künstler*, ed. M. Bill (Stuttgart, 1955), p. 229 (in the article *Der Wert eines Werkes der konkreten Kunst*).

[51] Vasarely, *Formel-Informel*, reproduced in M. Joray, *Vasarely* (Neuchâtel, no date), p. 61. Vasarely's note dates from 1956. In *Poetik und Hermeneutik*, ii, p. 447, U. Schramm's comments on Vasarely's pictures, "the principle behind which is the abrupt interchange of positive and negative forms," so that "there prevails a total thematic darkness together with total brightness: the thing represented explains itself by its own means (without any external 'literary' precondition) in its intention to be this kind of interplay."

degrees of demand on the eye, is valid only if there are different, historical changes in the conception of reality that correspond to these stages.
In connection with Vasarely, Henri van Lier made the following observation: "Nos techniques, nos sciences, nos morales se familiarisent, en
tous ordres, avec l'idée d'une unité non donnée mais en devenir, d'un
champ plurispatial, de relations qui soient non pas les effets mais les
causes des êtres."[52] This conception of a non-definitive reality is the
basis of Vasarely's artistic aim—as can be seen from his own theories—
and it is this reality that is to be made visible through an optical equivalent. In view of this, we are bound to ask ultimately whether the whole
question of art and esthetics, or exceeding of esthetic limits, is of any
relevance.

The same radical question might arise in regard to a tachist work by
Jackson Pollock (1948, Fig. 7), if one regards it less as an esthetic view of
contingency (cf. 1), than as an "open form" (see Jaroslav Serpan)[53]
which "incorporates the whole scope of its completely unlimited, unforeseeable, and superabundant structural development."

[52] Van Lier, p. 56.

[53] J. Serpan, "Offene Form," in J. Claus, *Theorien zeitgenössicher Maler* (Hamburg,
1963) (*rowohlts deutsche enzyclopädie*), p. 96.

IV

Myth and Modern Literature. From
Poetik und Hermeneutik IV

MANFRED FUHRMANN

Myth as a Recurrent Theme in Greek Tragedy and Twentieth-Century Drama

I. Myths recurrent in Greek tragedy: (1) Lost works: recurring titles. (2) Surviving works: the technique of repetition. (3) Aristotle's *Poetics* on the recurrent myth as material for tragedy. II. Recurrent myths in twentieth-century drama: (1) Types of myth drama. (2) The technique of repetition. (3) The principle of thematized repetition and its methods. III. Repetition as essential feature of the dramatized myth.

I

1. THE seemingly pedantic title *Amphitryon 38* points to a phenomenon which is obviously characteristic of dramatizations of Greek myths, i.e., repetition, the assiduous rehandling of well-worn material. Twentieth-century plays are not the first to conform to this principle of repetition, nor are all those "modern" dramas which have adapted ancient legends. Even the authors of Attic tragedies staged the same stories over and over again.

The principle of following on from one's predecessors has obviously existed right from the beginning. We know of about a dozen titles of tragedies written by Aeschylus' competitors, Choerilus, Phrynichus, and Pratinas. They show that both Phrynichus and Pratinas worked on the Tantalus story.[1] They also show that Phrynichus had already used some of Aeschylus' themes. The titles *The Egyptians* and *The Danaides* anticipate Aeschylus' two plays of the same name which formed a trilogy with *The Hicetides*, a play that still survives. All the other material of Aeschylus' three predecessors recurs at least once in later years.[2]

[1] Phrynichus: A. Nauck, *Tragicorum Graecorum Fragmenta* (TGF) (Leipzig, ²1889), p. 722. The *Tantalus* which Aristias, Pratinas' son, produced in 467 was proved to be Pratinas' work by the Didascalia Ox. Pap. 2256, Frag. 2; see A. Lesky, *Die tragische Dichtung der Hellenen*, Göttingen, ²1964, p. 49.

[2] Choerilus wrote an *Alope* (TGF, p. 719); so, too, did Euripides (TGF, p. 389 seq.) and Carcinus (4th cent. TGF, p. 797). The Pratinas title *Perseus* (Ox. Pap. 2256, Frag. 2) seems to be unique, but it probably deals with the Andromeda story which Sophocles and Euripides (TGF, p. 157 seq., 392 seq.) and also Lycophron (3rd cent. Suidas, s.v.) dealt with. The Phrynichus title *Pleuroniae* (TGF, p. 721 seq.) conceals the Meleager-Althaea myth; cf. Sophocles (TGF, p. 219 seq.), Euripides (TGF, p. 525 seq.), Antiphon (4th cent.

The heroic stage of ancient Greece was dominated by heroic themes. Historic material was dramatized only sporadically, i.e., in the early period by Phrynichus and Aeschylus, then again in the fourth century and during the Hellenistic era.[3] One might think that it was because Greek tragedians limited themselves to the heroic saga, that they rapidly exhausted their repertoire and were compelled to fall back on myths they had already used. However, the repetitions of the early fifth century which I have already mentioned lead us to assume that the frequent rehandling of the same themes was not only due to a lack of material.

There seem to be no statistics on the total number of tragic themes or the number of plays based on them. The indices of Nauck's collection of fragments do, however, provide a firm basis for a good estimate.[4] Approximately 140 tragedians are mentioned and about 400 drama titles.[5] According to this list, the Oedipus story was the most popular among dramatists. It was worked on by eleven different authors,[6] six of whom were fifth-century dramatists—the three great tragedians plus Achaeus, Philocles, and Xenocles. The title *Thyestes* is mentioned eight times. The plays of Sophocles and Euripides, Agathon, and probably Chaeremon were written in the fifth century. The Medea story, which is the subject of seven plays, is in third place. It was obviously Euripides who made it so popular.[7] Whether the seven plays called *Achilles* all dealt

---

TGF, p. 792), Sosiphanes (4/3 cent. TGF, p. 819). Apart from Phrynichus (Suidas, s.v.) Iophon, Sophocles' son (Suidas s.v.), and Cleophon (4th cent. Suidas, s.v.) all worked on the Actaeon material. Phrynichus found a successor in Euripides with his *Alcestis* (TGF, p. 720). A classical authority (Serv. Dan. ad Verg. Aen. 4, 694) claims that there is some point of similarity. *Antaeus* (TGF, p. 720) was staged again by Aristias (TGF, p. 726). *Milet's Receipts*, one of Phrynichus' two political plays, brought its author a fine of 1,000 drachmas (Her. 6,21); it is understandable that this material was never used again. For details on *The Phoenicians*, Aeschylus' model for *The Persians*, see p. 139, upper half.

[3] Theodectes of Phaselis wrote a *Mausolus* (4th cent. TGF, p. 802); Moschion wrote plays with the titles *Themistocles* and *Pheraei* (4/3 cent. TGF, p. 812 seq.; the latter probably about the tyrant Alexander of Pherae). The *Cassandreis* by Lycophron (Suidas, s.v.) seemed to deal with an aspect of contemporary history.

[4] See footnote 1. The following has mainly been taken from W. Schmid's *Geschichte der griechischen Literatur* (*Handbuch der klassischen Altertumswissenschaft* 7, 1), Munich, [5]1908, 1, p. 374; on the frequent repetition of the same material, see too K. von Fritz, *Antike und moderne Tragödie* (Berlin, 1962), p. 113 seq.

[5] Including the titles of satyr-plays. As about one-fourth of these titles are mentioned twice or several times we have approx. 570 dramas. K. Ziegler, *Tragoedia*, in *Realencyclopädie der classischen Altertumswissenschaft* 6 A (1937), col. 1931, estimates the number of plays known to be 600.

[6] If the anonymous author in Suet. Ner. 46 is not identical with any of the eleven, the number of Oedipus versions goes up to 12. Cf. for this and the following TGF, p. 963 seq. (*Index Fabularum*).

[7] The authors of the other versions are Dicaeogenes (5th cent. TGF, p. 775), Euripides' nephew (Suidas s.v.), Carcinus (TGF, p. 798), Diogenes of Sinope (a doubtful reference;

with the same material is uncertain. The titles *Alcmeon*, *Telephus*, and *Philoctetes*, each occurring six times, probably do denote the same story. The titles *Alcmene*, *Ixion*, and *Orestes* were each used by five different authors.[8] Twelve names were used four times, sixteen three times, and fifty-six twice.[9]

These rough figures are still striking, even though one must beware of equating the same titles with the same material: similar titles could denote different themes, though of course different titles might deal with the same themes. The two possibilities probably cancel each other out as far as statistics are concerned. Another fact to be considered is that we have evidence of only a fraction of all the dramas actually written. In Athens more than a thousand tragedies were produced up to the year 400.[10] Estimates for the period after the fourth century are impossible, for plays then started to be produced over the entire Greek world. It is obvious that we would have even more evidence of the frequent reworking of material if, instead of less than a tenth, we had, say, a fifth or more of the titles.

2. We also know something about the manner in which dramatists used material which had already been presented on the stage. Early methods, it is true, can only be gleaned from a few facts arising out of the interrelation between two historical dramas, Phrynichus' *Phoenicians* and Aeschylus' *Persians*. The same rules must have applied to mythical themes as to historical, for the number of myths was relatively

---

see TGF, p. 807 seq.), Neophron (TGF, p. 729 seq. As regards the ancient claim that Euripides' *Medea* is a copy of Neophron's play of the same name, see Lesky, p. 163), and Biotus (TGF, p. 825).

[8] One can certainly include the two *Amphitryon* plays by Sophocles (TGF, p. 156) and Aeschylus of Alexandria (TGF, p. 824) amongst the Alcmene-dramas. It is questionable whether all the plays entitled *Bacchae* dealt with the Pentheus story as in the case of Euripides and Iophon (TGF, p. 761). If so, then this would mean 7 dramatizations of the same myth. For reference to the Meleager story see Note 2.

[9] E. Diehl uses the example of the tragedian Timesitheus (*Realencyclopädie der classischen Altertumswissenschaft* 6 A [1937], col. 1251, s.v.) to show the network of connections revealed by the information on each individual author: Of the traditional titles *The Danaides* is known through Phrynichus and Aeschylus, *Heracles* through Sophocles and Euripides, *Ixion* through the three great tragedians, and Theodectes and Callistratus; Timesitheus' *Memnon* recalls the Aeschylus Trilogy and Sophocles' *Ethiopians*. The latter also wrote *Helena's Counter-Demand* and *Antenorides*.

[10] After the end of the 6th cent., the programme of the Great Dionysia demanded 3 tetralogies (i.e., nine tragedies and three satyr-plays) annually. After 432 the programme of the Lenaea required three lots of two tragedies a year. The classical theatre only had "Premières." The first repetition of an old play was in 386. A rough calculation of the total repertoire could be obtained also by the number of plays each poet is supposed to have written (Aeschylus wrote about 80, Sophocles 130, Euripides 88 etc.). But the lexicographic data are so unreliable that this method is not recommended.

limited, whereas the dramatic possibilities history offered were absolutely unlimited. As Aeschylus tried to keep as close as possible to his
predecessor in *The Persians*, although there were plenty of similar subjects he could have chosen, we can assume that he and his contemporaries would have done the same when it came to working on myths.

The theme of *The Persians* is the Greek victory at Salamis, which is
depicted from the loser's point of view. The action is staged in Susa, the
capital of the Persian Empire. Researchers are probably correct in assuming that Aeschylus took over all this data from Phrynichus' *Phoenicians*.[11] The Hypothesis, the table of contents preceding the text, reports
that Aeschylus "altered" and "copied" Phrynichus' *Phoenicians* to write
his *Persians*. The Hypothesis quotes Glaucus of Rhegium (approx. 400)
who also referred to the beginning of *The Phoenicians* (Frag. 8; TGF, p.
722): τάδ᾽ἐστὶ Περσῶν τῶν πάλαι βεβηκότων.[12] Aeschylus' *Persians*
starts with the words τάδε μὲν Περσῶν τῶν οἰχομένων.[13] The quotation is clear and so is the author's intention: he wanted to be measured
against his predecessor. For this purpose he chose the same extract of
history, and the same frame of action, only altering certain details.
Phrynichus had a prologue figure, a eunuch, reporting the defeat. Aeschylus left out the eunuch, and the news of the defeat comes during the
action, after due preparation has been made for it by the misgivings, expressed by the Chorus and Queen Atossa. In addition to this alteration,
he replaces the Chorus of Phoenician women (presumably sailors' wives)
by Persian Councillors. Aeschylus obviously tried to concentrate the
progress of the action. His aim was to work some sort of climax if not
suspense out of the melodramatic subject. Finally, he also put a religious
slant on the events.

There is only one surviving instance of plays by the three great tragedians dealing with the same subject: the *Choephoroe* by Aeschylus and
the two *Electras* by Sophocles and Euripides. They have always been the
showpiece of comparative studies. The differences of the contents are
usually the focal point of attention. Here we shall deal with just a few
points relating to the different techniques in which the material is handled.[14] The theme of the three tragedies is part of the saga of the Tan-

[11] See Lesky, pp. 47 and 61 seq.; id., *Geschichte der griechischen Literatur* (Bern,
²1963), pp. 258 and 273.

[12] "This is of the Persians who went forth a long time ago. . . ."

[13] "This (is) of the Persians who went forth (to the country of the Greeks). . . ."

[14] Cf. for the following chiefly von Fritz, p. 120 seq. The relative chronology of the two
Electras can only be based on internal criteria. Here it is assumed, as in von Fritz, p. 129
seq. and K. Reinhardt, *Sophokles* (Frankfurt/Main, ³1947), p. 279 seq., that the Sophoclean tragedy preceded that of Euripides. For lit. on this disputable point, see Lesky,
Tragische Dichtung, p. 124².

talides, and tells of Orestes' matricide. The hero has grown up in a
foreign country; he returns to his homeland to avenge his father
Agamemnon. He makes a sacrifice at his father's grave. He meets
Electra. Brother and sister recognize each other and agree on a plan. The
victims are enticed into a trap. Orestes kills Aegisthus and Clytemnestra. All three plays present this same plot, and they all deal with almost the same section of the saga. They begin with Orestes' return and
finish with the double murder. The most important characters are
Orestes, Electra and Clytemnestra.

The similar framework of the three tragedies shows up their fundamental differences. Aeschylus wrote an Orestes drama. His two successors had good reason for calling their plays *Electra*. The Aeschylean
tragedy is part of a trilogy; the two *Electras* are self-contained. In Aeschylus' and Sophocles' works the action takes place in front of the King's
palace. Euripides moves the scene to a farm out of town. There are also
slight differences in the choice of events to be shown on stage. Aeschylus
and Sophocles begin with Orestes' entrance. Euripides starts with a prologue. Aeschylus and Euripides both show how the murder affects the
murderer's emotional state. In Sophocles' play the curtain falls immediately after the murder. Various subordinate figures are grouped around
the main characters, and the number of characters increases from play to
play. Aeschylus and Sophocles put Aegisthus on the stage; Euripides
only shows his corpse. Sophocles invents the pedagogue and
Chrysothemis; Euripides adds the poor country squire, Electra's husband, some minor figures, and the Dioscuri as *dei ex machina*. The recognition scene is different in all three plays; the same applies to the intrigue before the deed. In Aeschylus' and Euripides' plays the intrigue is
after the recognition; Sophocles interwove the two events. The motif
that leads to recognition—the lock of hair that Orestes sacrifices at his
father's grave—is varied very ingeniously in all three plays. In the two
older plays the intrigue is directed against Clytemnestra and Aegisthus;
in Euripides' tragedy it is only Electra who is the object of the intrigue.
In Sophocles' *Electra* Clytemnestra dies first and then Aegisthus; it is
different in the other two plays.

All these variations have a special function for the different basic concepts. Aeschylus' aim was to demonstrate the conflict between the necessity for and the wrongfulness of the murder. The necessity lies in Apollo's command and in what has happened before. The wrongfulness
causes Orestes' madness, which is to be healed only in the following play
of the trilogy, *The Eumenides*. This basic idea is the reason why the secondary character Aegisthus is killed before Clytemnestra. It is also the
reason why the end of the play shows the commencement of Orestes'

madness. All the other events in *The Choephoroe* are self-explanatory. It is not Aeschylus' simple construction, but the complicated alterations his successors made that are significant.

In Sophocles' play, Electra's suffering and obstinacy and her emotional climaxes are the focal point. Orestes is not particularly important. His problems are dealt with in Aeschylus' plays. This is why the two murders occur in a different order, and why Orestes' madness is not shown. In order to build up Electra's character, the dramatist introduces a foil, Chrysothemis, who is willing to compromise. For the purpose of creating emotional fluctuations, intrigue and recognition are interwoven, and both take up a relatively large proportion of the play. So, for a moment, Electra becomes a victim of the intrigue, too. This construction again necessitated the subordinate figure of the pedagogue and the alteration in the motif of the lock of hair.

Euripides' purpose is to prove that matricide is unwarrantable, and he alters the scene, the characters, and the motivation accordingly. Clytemnestra has saved Electra from Aegisthus (l. 25 seq.), Electra lives with her noble husband in poverty but in safety on a farm out of town. Hence the character of the countryman, and the prologue introducing the audience to the new state of affairs. Clytemnestra repents of her deed and begs her daughter to be understanding (l. 1011 seq., esp. 1105 seq.); Electra is hard-hearted and full of resentment. Orestes questions whether the divine commandments are binding or not and is driven into the deed by his sister (l. 962 seq.). In order to make this configuration work, the intrigue is only directed against Clytemnestra. Euripides makes her the victim of the low cunning of Electra, who takes advantage of Clytemnestra's motherly love in order to destroy her. For this reason the Aegisthus story remains off-stage; thus Euripides returns to the Aeschylean sequence of the murders and to Orestes' repentance at the end of the play. Only in Euripides' play, the motives and conditions are completely altered. The *dei ex machina* finally push the events along the route Aeschylus plotted for them, and the play ends with Orestes' absolution.

The relationship of Sophocles' drama to Aeschylus' trilogy is partly affirmative, and partly neutral: affirmative because his Orestes plot is preconditioned by the Aeschylean outcome, which acts its "insurance"; neutral because in his play the Electra problem has become the main issue whereas it had been at most only germinating in *The Choephoroe*. Euripides' play is meant to be set off against those of Aeschylus and Sophocles. Electra's external situation as well as the characters of mother and daughter are a reply to the Sophoclean drama. The contrast to Aeschylus is even more evident. Euripides' emancipated ethics reject the religious implications of the Aeschylean trilogy and, more indirectly, of

Sophocles' drama. At one point the polemic element is so strong that it almost shatters the dramatic illusion, and we feel it is the author, not the character, that is speaking. The lock of hair, the symbol which in Aeschylus leads to the anagnorisis, and in Sophocles only appears to be refuted through the deception of the intrigue—this symbol is used by Euripides as a means of unmasking and mocking his predecessor's scanty gifts of motivation (l. 524 seq.).

We may conclude from all this that the myth did not produce any "absolute" dramas. The plays which dealt with the same theme referred more or less directly to one another. The fact that the plot remains virtually the same in the plays all the more underlines their various differences (additions or corrections). If we can believe the few documents that still exist, then both the "early" Aeschylus and the "late" Euripides were inclined to accentuate their references to their predecessor. From time to time they even draw attention to their respective predecessors by using quotations or thinly disguised literary polemics. Sophocles, on the other hand, "the classicist par excellence," seems to have been more reserved: his plays were almost "absolute."

3. Some parts of Aristotle's *Poetics* confirm previous observations. The ninth chapter says that the comedy-writers invent their plots whereas the tragedians keep to traditional material, i.e., myths. Sometimes the poet only takes some of his characters from tradition, and adds others as he likes. It has even happened that the whole plot is fictitious, e.g., Agathon's *Antheus* (1451 b 11 seq.). Thus Aristotle does reckon with the possibility of the poet inventing his subjects. In all other passages, however, he assumes that the poet will write in the customary fashion. He takes it for granted that the myth predominates and is to be reused. And so it has been rightly claimed that he attaches too much importance to Agathon's experiment. Agathon's successors would have called dramas with fictitious plots comedies.[15] In the thirteenth chapter Aristotle refers to historical developments to prove his doctrine of the "average hero." He states that poets had started off by putting a large number of myths on the stage. Later, they limited themselves in the best tragedies to the sagas of just a few noble families. The favorites were the myths of Alcmeon, Oedipus, Orestes, Meleager, Thyestes, Telephus, and others (1453 a 17 seq.).[16] It is difficult to verify the devel-

---

[15] See Ziegler, col. 1963. Cf. ib., 2049 seq.: U. von Wilamowitz-Moellendorff, *Euripides: Herakles 1 = Einleitung in die griechische Tragödie* (Darmstadt, ⁴1959), p. 108 seq., criticizes the Aristotelian definition because it ignores the significance of the heroic saga as material for tragedy. This criticism, however, is unjustified, because Aristotle claims that myths are the customary material.

[16] Cf. Chap. 14 1454 a 9 seq., where this concentration is ascribed to τύχη, i.e. stage experience.

opment Aristotle speaks of, but his examples of particularly suitable myths confirm what we had already gathered from a quick glance at traditional titles: in both cases we come across the same favorite subjects of tragic drama. Aristotle's reasoning makes it even clearer that the frequent recurrence of certain subjects should not be considered as the obvious result of a limited repertoire. [17]

So much for the bare facts of dependence on myth and the repetition of selected stories. The Aristotelian theory of tragedy goes on to give information on how to handle myths, and it once more confirms the results obtained from a study of the extant material. The fourteenth chapter states that the traditional stories should not be "disintegrated" (λυειν) (1453 b 22 seq.): Clytemnestra must be killed by Orestes and Eriphyle by Alcmeon. The poet may make up events for himself, or must "make good use" (χρῆσϑαι καλῶς) of traditional material. Nothing more is said of fictitious plots. It is a kind of lacuna in the Aristotelian system, a mere possibility. All the more extensively he goes into "the good use" of traditional material. Under this heading he expresses his ideas on the link between knowledge and action, i.e., on the question of whether the hero knows from the beginning that there is a close relationship between himself and his adversary, or whether he only discovers this immediately before or after the deed. The argument makes it clear that the rule not to "disintegrate" traditional stories is directed at the framework of the dramatic action, at the skeleton of exterior facts. The term "good use" offers a wide scope of possible variations. This scope may be limited in actual practice by the plot in question, but in principle each dramatist is free to deal with the traditional story in the way he wants. The freedom of the dramatist lies in the subjective premises of the objective action. It is a matter of the motivation. Thus according to Aristotle, the tragedian is bound solely to the traditional skeleton of the story. He has a free hand as regards motivation.

Some other passages in the *Poetics* imply additional licenses as to the varying of myths. The sixteenth chapter (1459 b 19 seq.) classifies types of recognition, and gives some of them artistic priority. These ideas are obviously based on the assumption that the type of anagnorisis is a "variable" and not a "constant" in the dramatization of traditional stories. The criticism of Menelaus' "unnecessary wickedness," as Euripides presents him in his *Orestes* (1454 a 28 seq.), is based on the concession that the poet may alter the characters within limits imposed by the requirements of his play rather than by tradition. The same conclusion can be drawn from the general view that Sophocles portrays people as they should be, and Euripides as they actually are (1460 b 32 seq.). This

[17] Cf. p. 138, para. 3.

observation implies that each poet puts his own general view into his works.

Thus on the one hand Aristotle demands a constant plot, and on the other he concedes that some characters may be invented and that motives and characters may be altered. So, his *Poetics* gives us pretty well the same picture as our analysis of the three Orestes-Electra-dramas.

II

1. The title *Amphitryon 38* calls to mind the long series of Amphitryon dramas. It is not only the modern answer to the classical model, but also to the neoclassical plays of, for instance, Molière and Kleist.[18] Hauptmann's *Iphigenie in Delphi* also has a double reference. On the one hand, it harks back to the Greek basis, Euripides; on the other, it refers to Goethe's classic creation.[19] These two dramas, however, are exceptional. Generally speaking, the modern treatment of Greek myths links up directly with the ancient models. In the great variety peculiar to modern versions, this direct link is what we might call the common denominator. It lies not so much in the classical basis, which has vanished into the historical distance, or in the classical paradigms themselves; the link lies, rather, in a particular response to these paradigms, in their idealistic interpretation, and in the mentality of the middle-class, with its classical upbringing. Above all, these modern dramas presume the audience to be familiar with the classical model and its standard interpretation. In extreme cases, the modern versions demand a scene-for-scene comparison with the Greek original.

Certain phenomena tend to recur throughout these diverse modern myth-dramas. Any generalization is bound to involve distortion of some details, but it is quite useful to consider some of the principle features. First, it makes a good deal of difference whether the modern work follows on directly from a classical work of the same genre, a particular dramatization of the material, or whether ancient tradition as such stands god-father to the modern version, in the form of a narrative à la Ovid, a mythographic table of contents, or maybe a work of art.[20] The first mentioned type is the one found most frequently. Examples are Anouilh's *Antigone* and *Médée*, Giraudoux's *Amphitryon 38* and *Electre*, *Les Mouches* by Sartre, and O'Neill's trilogy *Mourning Becomes Electra*. Examples of the other type are Anouilh's *Eurydice*, Coc-

---

[18] See H. Jacobi, *Amphitryon in Frankreich und Deutschland*, Diss. Zürich, 1952, p. 74 seq., esp. 82 seq.

[19] See K. Hamburger, *Von Sophokles zu Sartre* (Stuttgart, 1962), p. 95 seq.

[20] The configuration Orphée-Eurydice-Heurtebise to be found in Cocteau's *Orphée* could have been inspired by the famous Neapolitan Relief.

teau's *Orphée*, Giraudoux's *La guerre de Troie n'aura pas lieu* and Hauptmann's *Iphigenie in Delphi* (as regards the material and not the "message"). There are also mixed forms, such as Cocteau's *Machine Infernale*. In this, the first act is a free invention, the second and third acts represent the traditional pre-history, hitherto undramatized, and only in the fourth act does the plot coincide with Sophocles' *Oedipus Rex*.[21]

This type of classification is not merely of an external nature; it shows to what degree the play is based on the classical tradition and is to be interpreted accordingly. Only the modern "replies" to classical plays are so closely linked to their originals that a comparison is essential for full comprehension. In the case of a myth taken from other sources, the modern dramatist allows himself far more freedom. He puts the individual characters and situations from the old myth into a plot of his own invention, and the myth tends to dissolve into a general symbol.[22]

This, it is true, also applies to O'Neill's trilogy, although it is based on a definite model, i.e., Aeschylus' *Orestea*. The reason for this is obvious. O'Neill transplanted the classical plot into a modern environment and replaced ancient points of reference with modern ones. Thus the Electra trilogy offers us a different classification: modern adaptations of ancient myths are presented partly in classical, partly in modern guise. However, it is the first category we have mentioned that is the most common. *Mourning Becomes Electra* and Anouilh's *Eurydice* belong to the second category, but the absurd setting of Cocteau's *Orphée* sets it apart from this classification.

Here, too, the difference is not of an external or accidental nature. Those modern dramas which put on "ancient apparel" also provoke a comparison with their classical predecessors. But the "transpositions" only show the original in outline, and here, too, the myth can become nothing but a symbol. Eliot's *The Family Reunion* represents an extreme form of refraction; the old Atride saga is barely noticeable.[23]

Apart from this, the "transpositions" and the "classical-type" plays usually tend towards different objectives. The dramatist presenting a classical structure in a modern context assumes that for all the difference in time, the basic core remains the same, thus confirming the continued validity of the content of the myth. The new context shows implicitly that there is a "constant," independent of all variants. The basic thought illustrated by the myth has the significance of an "archetype." This is

---

[21] Wilder's *The Alcestiad* is another play that does not fit into either of the categories mentioned.

[22] See P. J. Conradie, *The Treatment of Greek Myths in Modern French Drama*, in *Annale Universiteit van Stellenbosch* 29, Series B, No. 2 (1963), p. 25 seq.

[23] See Hamburger, p. 62 seq.

why plays which put mythical themes in modern guise seem to exist
more or less independent of their classical counterparts—they have no
desire to attack or argue against them.

The "classical-type" dramas are different. A number of them attempt
exactly to capture the classical atmosphere (e.g., Wilder's *The Alcestiad*
and Hauptmann's *Atridentetralogie*), but others destroy this illusion by
means of wild and whimsical anachronisms (e.g., the French
dramatists' plays). Their attacks on their classical counterparts tend to
be particularly vehement, and indeed this is an intrinsic part of them,
their *"raison d'être."* The attack, the correction or refutation can be directed against the classical model itself or, to be more precise, against the
idealistic aureole with which the bourgeois neohumanism of the
nineteenth century had encircled it. And so the polemic is ultimately directed at the ethic-social positions connected with the tradition of classical education. This is the basis of the myth-dramas of Anouilh and
Giraudoux. However, in some cases, it is not the ancient myth itself
which is the object of the criticism. It serves as a vehicle for a third element, the actual meaning. The figures and situations represent ideas
which were originally completely beyond the scope of the myth, and the
polemic is concerned precisely with this new "underlaid" meaning. The
prize example illustrating this complicated link is *Les Mouches*, in which
Sartre sets out to unmask Christian attitudes. The symbolism of Cocteau's drama *Orphée* also seems partly to concern things which are only
indirectly connected with the classical Orpheus figure, i.e., the importance which the romantic-symbolist age attached to poetic inspiration.[24]

Thus we can say that repetition is most evident in those plays which
(a) refer to a classical drama, and (b) present their material in classical
garb. It is obviously of no importance whether contrastive effects arise
directly from the ancient drama and its neohumanistic interpretation, or
from the meaning the modern author has put into the myth. In both
cases the repeated myth seems to achieve the same effect.

2. The following observations concern mainly those myth plays which
attempt to form a critical-dialectic relation to a classical drama. In these,
the manner of repetition reveals recurrent characteristics and a specific
technique. Other plays, e.g., Anouilh's *Eurydice* and Giraudoux's *La
guerre de Troie n'aura pas lieu*, follow these rules only at certain focal
points in their plots, and in a more indirect way. But even a quick glance

---

[24] See Conradie, p. 52 seq., esp. p. 58. The clearest example is the parody of the *"écriture automatique"* of Bréton's *Manifeste du surréalisme*; see E. Kushner, *Le mythe d'Orphée dans la littérature française contemporaine* (Paris, 1961), pp. 183 seq. and 212. On
the other hand, P. Dubourg, *Dramaturgie de Jean Cocteau* (Paris, 1954), p. 40 seq., does
not seem to reckon with the possibility of elements of critical parody.

at the "antidramas" we have in view, shows how similar the technique of repetition is to the rules observable in the ancient Orestes-Electra tragedies. Euripides especially seems to have anticipated the *modus procedendi* of modern dramatists.

Both Sophocles and Anouilh present the same plot in their Antigone dramas. The heroine ignores King Creon's orders and attempts to pay tribute to her dead brother Polynices, who has been branded a traitor. At her second attempt she is discovered. Creon carries out the threatened penalty and Antigone is imprisoned in a cave. Haemon, Creon's son and Antigone's betrothed, kills himself at her side and finally Eurydice, Creon's wife, also kills herself after hearing of her son's death. The setting is the same in both plays. Both versions show roughly the same part of the story on stage. Antigone and Creon are the main characters in both dramas, and Anouilh has hardly altered Sophocles' list of characters. The most obvious thing the modern version copies is the sequence of the scenes. In both plays the actual action commences with a dialogue between Antigone and her sister Ismene, and the same attitudes are revealed: Ismene's flexibility contrasts with Antigone's unbending resolution. The guardian of Polynices' corpse reports on Antigone's first attempt to bury her brother. It is the deed which has been discovered and not the offender. The guard enters again with Antigone, who has been arrested while trying a second time to bury her brother. Anouilh's drama continues to develop like the Sophoclean model. Antigone confesses her deed to Creon (Ismene tries to join her sister, but is brusquely dismissed).[25] Haemon tries in vain to save his bride. Antigone is seized with horror at the thought of approaching death. A messenger brings news of the catastrophe, and Eurydice dies.

The exact parallel between the two plays also throws their differences into relief. The parts of the story that Anouilh puts on the stage differ slightly from those of Sophocles. During the course of the play, we learn that Antigone had already made her first attempt to bury her brother before the play began. Anouilh also invents the maid and her expository dialogue with Antigone, but leaves out the seer Tiresias and his whole scene. He adds a dialogue between Haemon and his betrothed at the beginning of the play. As usual, the most radical alterations are in the characters and motivations, and it is not difficult to see that all the changes are made to serve a new overall concept of the myth.

Hegel maintained that Creon and Antigone opposed each other in the Sophoclean tragedy as representatives of equally justifiable principles:

---

[25] Here a word-for-word quotation accentuates the similarity: *"Tu as choisi la vie et moi la mort"* (p. 105, quoted from the separate edition of the *La Table Ronde* Press [Paris 1947]), = l. 555.

State and family; the conflict was inevitable and insoluble. This dialectic interpretation has long proved to be erroneous.[26] In the drama of Sophocles, justice and injustice, truth and semblance, confront one another. Truth and justice are on Antigone's side, and the dramatic development has the sole purpose of demonstrating the fundamental differences in the two main characters. Sophocles did, however, take care not to put just the empty personifications of two principles on the stage. Sóme of the maxims which Creon pronounces when he first comes on stage (l. 162 seq.) sound relevant and objective. It is only the later course of events that drives the hero to inexcusable vehemence and unmasks his principles as the gross offspring of egocentric tyranny. There are traits in Antigone's character, especially, which are not absolutely essential to her function of showing the limitations of State reasoning. She seems from the outset to be strangely willing to die, even before the actual situation demands her death (l. 69 seq.).[27] On the other hand, she laments her cruel fate before the end (l. 891 seq.). She is full of passion, but harsh. Her love for her brother knows no limits (l. 21 seq., 422 seq., 499 seq., etc.), and she reacts bitingly to Ismene's half-heartedness (l. 69 seq.). The way in which she rejects Ismene's willingness to die with her is almost repugnant (l. 538 seq.).[28]

It is these characteristics which turn the ancient drama into something more than a mere thesis, and it is these that Anouilh uses as a starting-point for his variations. His play can be divided into three relatively independent sections. The exposition (pp. 9-48) ends with the surprise that Antigone has already accomplished her deed. The main part (pp. 49-106) shows Creon's attempts to cover up the deed and to save Antigone. He fails as a result of the heroine's stubbornness. The conclusion (pp. 106-133) shows how the main characters react to the catastrophe. Antigone admits that she does not know why she is dying. Creon, however, with shocking callousness, sets about his everyday political business.

This concept differs greatly, though not totally, from the Sophoclean model. It is based on traits of the two main characters which are already inherent in Sophocles' tragedy: on the surplus of individuality which the ancient drama cannot accommodate. Sophocles' Antigone acts according to objective norms, the "unwritten, unchangeable law of the Gods" (l. 450 seq.). What subjectivity she shows is like a reflection of the power of these norms over her. Anouilh's Antigone is completely subjective. The purpose of the first scenes is to illustrate the heroine's strange nature,

[26] See e.g., Reinhardt, p. 73 seq.; Lesky, p. 113 seq.

[27] See also l. 96 seq., 460 seq., 497, 555, 559 seq., 777 seq. Cf. Hamburger, p. 193 seq.

[28] "Rude" (ὠμός) is the verdict which the Chorus pronounces on Antigone's acknowledgement of the eternal laws (1. 471 seq.).

her obstinacy, set against the background of ordinary life. These are the preconditions for the central action of the play, the great dialogue between Creon and Antigone. Creon claims the burial rites are a clerical swindle, reveals the baseness of both, Polynices and Eteocles, and convincingly explains the political necessity of the decree. He even admits that he does not know whose corpse is decaying in the sun. He says that only unrecognizable torsos had been found on the battlefield and merely the least mutilated body had been sorted out for the State burial. Creon's arguments reveal Antigone's *"je le devais"* (p. 70) to be a superimposed motivation for her fundamentally uncompromising nature. Her "all-or-nothingness," her relentless striving for the absolute, becomes nothing but a mere facade which she has to defend to the outside world at her hour of death by denying that she has confessed *"j'ai peur"* (p. 124).

Anouilh lets the characteristics of Sophocles' Antigone—her faith in the norms and her readiness to die—arise naturally out of her total subjectivity. For his Creon he also uses the starting-point of the older play—Creon's apparent sense of justice. The modern Creon personifies objectivity, common sense, awareness of real situations, of what is humanly possible. In Sophocles' play he is a narrow-minded tyrant defending his own personal power. In Anouilh's play he seems to be like this only for a moment.[29] What he only appeared to be at the beginning of the older play is, in the modern version, revealed as his true nature by the great dialogue between himself and his adversary. This new interpretation was the reason for the abrupt end to Anouilh's play. There was no room for a prophet's warning or for a delayed understanding and repentance on the part of the hero. This enabled Anouilh to dispense with the "diptych" structure of Sophocles' tragedy. In the modern version the heroine is the only focal point of the action.

Although it is clear that Anouilh has adopted elements of the naturalistic theatre, and has used a psychological approach to his characters, his methods of contrast—repetition—are basically the same as those of his classical predecessors. The basic facts of the external action are fixed; it is only the characters, the motives and the play's message that are free for modern adaptation.

Giraudoux's *Electre* takes over only the basic structure of its classical models: Orestes' return, the recognition between brother and sister, and the double murder. It also adopts the heroine's main feature, which is her unbounded hatred of Clytemnestra and Aegisthus, as Sophocles and Euripides portrayed it. The other references are more complicated. They reflect the fact that three original sources were combined to be played

[29] The reasoning *"L'opposition brisée qui sourd et mine déjà partout"* etc. (p. 54) corresponds to Soph., *Ant.* l. 280 seq.

off, each one against the other. The strange figures of the Eumenides refer to Aeschylus. Giraudoux has reversed the phases of their former double role. They accompany the action as "Gracious Ones" (2, 3; 2, 7),[30] and turn irrevocably into avengers at the end of the play, after the deed (2, 10). They are the foils proving that Electra's behavior is a negation of reality. They try to prevent the fatal end that the heroine strives for, and personify the basic concept of the play. Giraudoux's links with the two classical *Electra* dramas are more obvious. From Sophocles he inherited the heroine's uncompromising nature and the dreadful principle of "strike again if you can" (l. 1415), which in the modern version governs the relationship between brother and sister: the brother is a tool for Electra's revenge. The anti-Sophoclean concept originates from Euripides, as do some of the methods used to form it. There are none of the hardships[31] which motivate Electra's bitterness in Sophocles' work; also, the action presents in Clytemnestra (Euripides) and Aegisthus (Giraudoux) the opponents who rob the heroine's hatred of its legitimacy. Finally, the character of the gardener, and the plan to get Electra to marry him, correspond to Euripides' poor farmer.

Amidst this unusually subtle network of repetitions and references, there are also obvious differences. The modern version uses the Aristotelian theory of the variable relation between knowledge and action. Electra at first does not know what happened on Agamemnon's return, and the process dominating the play is the heroine's discovery, step by step, of the murder and of Aegisthus' role as Clytemnestra's lover. Giraudoux has reversed the relation between cause and effect which was common to all the classical plays. For his Electra, hatred is the primary feature. Her subjectivity proves to be the relentless urge to let "truth" win, a life-destroying, disastrous truth which at the same time is absolute justice (1,2; 1,13; 2,2; 2,8; 2,10). Electra can think and act as uncompromisingly as she does, because of her connection with the Gods, i.e., she has devoted herself to the unbreakable link between murder and expiation (1,3). It is this metaphysical background to her deeds which reveals the Euripidean, antimythic tendency of the modern play.

The heroine's environment illustrates a process running diametrically contrary to her destructive fanaticism for the truth, a process which catches up and overtakes whatever her shrewdness brings to light. External and internal enemies are endangering the State. Aegisthus experi-

[30] Consequently, Electra herself is the "Erinye," the bloodhound in the action; see 1,8: "*alors, je prends la piste*"; 1,9: "*j'ai pris la piste*"; 2,5: "*. . . la seule preuve qui m'échappe encore, dans cette chasse.*"

[31] They are milder in Euripides' play and are increased by the heroine herself for the purpose of provocation (l. 54 seq.).

ences his hour of vocation and achieves a truly sovereign sense of responsibility. He is even prepared to submit to Electra's judgment as soon
as he has saved the State, and he finally gives the brother and sister in
his power the opportunity to make a free decision. The "Sophoclean"
heroine of the modern drama thus stands in a world of completely altered conditions. She represents the "Absolute," the "Mythic"; and
when the mythic returns, despite all attempts to prevent its return, it is
shown to be senseless and absurd. The form of this repetition has
changed into a decree demanding emancipation from the fatality of the
myth. La guerre de Troie had already set a model for this basic
schema,[32] and it is evident that Anouilh's Antigone, with the uncompromising nature robbed of its explanatory motivation, follows the lines
laid down by Giraudoux's Electre.

3. The title Amphitryon 38 combines poetic statement with a consciousness created by literary scholarship. It announces that the action
will repeat something that has already been repeated. The paradoxical
title La guerre de Troie n'aura pas lieu also refers explicitly to the model
on which it has been based, to the traditional myth. As has already been
explained,[33] this tradition did not only offer repetition, variation, or a
counter-version; sometimes it also enabled the schema of the repetition
to be made clear by extra-scenic means, e.g., a quotation at a significant
point of the action, or criticism of the predecessor's motivation. These
means can be termed "extra-scenic" inasmuch as they were not required
by the scene or action itself. They were not so "extra-scenic" that they
would have disturbed or destroyed the scene, or the dramatic illusion.
The classical tragedians only left a thin wall between themselves and the
"absolute drama." They did not dare to break down this wall. To abolish
the illusion was the sole privilege of the comedians. This highlights a
fundamental difference between the modern myth-repeats and the conventions of the ancient and neoclassical theatre: the thematization of the
structure of the repetition, transcending the illusion. We have seen to
what extent the modern technique of reworking, with its network of
constants and variables, was similar to classical practices. We shall now
examine the methods that led beyond these practices.

Giraudoux's Electre repeats the mythic event as an unsuccessful attempt at prevention.[34] It constantly refers to the supposed "fatality."
There are numerous methods that link the modern version with the orig-

[32] Criticism of the fatality of the myth, demonstrated by the repetition of the myth, had
already begun before him with the Oedipus dramas of Gide and Cocteau.
[33] See p. 139, upper half.
[34] See H. Meyer, Das französische Drama des 20. Jahrhunderts als Drama der
Wiederholung, Diss. Heidelberg, 1952 (masch.), p. 195 seq.

inal. There are several mysterious symbolic figures in the play that serve this purpose without having very much to do with the actual dramatic action. They are the beggar and the Eumenides, personified by three girls who are little children at the beginning of the play and grow up with it to Electra's age.

The beggar—said to be a God—is on stage from the third scene on. He tells the parables of the hedgehog and the she-wolf. The second parable obviously anticipates the actual outcome of the drama, whereas the lesson he draws from it indicates a possible outcome that, in fact, does not take place (1,3). The beggar goes on to declare that Electra will "reveal herself" (1,3), and his reflections at the end of the first act are a commentary on the main figure: *"Elle est la vérité sans résidu, la lampe sans mazout, la lumière sans mèche"* (1,13). The end of the second act shows even more clearly that the beggar is outside the framework of the drama so as to "thematize" the mode of repetition. He describes Agamemnon's death, at a dramatically "unsuitable" point, and continues immediately afterwards with a report on the murder of Clytemnestra and Aegisthus (2,9). This report coincides with events off-stage, and is finally even seconds ahead of them. The abolition of dramatic dialogue is followed by the abolition of dramatic time. It seems as if the myth and its modern copy have merged into one. At the same time the paradoxical end indicates that the supposed fatality of events is foreseeable, but not inevitable.

The Eumenides are strange, symbolic beings. Like the beggar, they anticipate the actual outcome of the play, but also indicate solutions which would have been possible if the myth did not "have to" repeat itself. Examples are their speeches about Clytemnestra and Electra at the beginning of the play (1,1), and their parody of the Clytemnestra-Orestes recognition scene, in which reality and potentiality had already interpenetrated (1,11-12). In other respects, too, their position is usually outside the drama, and their function is to comment on the events, or to interpolate "stage directions": while, at one point they fight with Electra about the decision Orestes has to take, as though they were real characters (2,3), at another they dismiss a minor character (who had thwarted the first attempt to prevent the return of the myth)[35] as if they were the author's mouthpiece themselves. Soon afterwards they appear to slip into Aegisthus' role.[36]

---

[35] 2,7: *"Sei du endlich still. Du hast uns um die Heirat mit dem Gärtner gebracht"* (only in the version used for the German translation; see the German edition by H. Rothe, List Verlag, Munich, 1964, p. 110).

[36] 2,7: *"Pauvre fille! Tu es simple! Ainsi tu imaginais que nous allions laisser Oreste errer autour de nous, une épée à la main. . . . Nous l'avons enchaîné et bâillonné."*

This latter example shows that not all the "alienating" methods of illusion-breaking, and of violating the unity of character etc., thematize the resumption of the myth. On the other hand, not all the elements of the play which refer to the repetition and the classical paradigm, explicitly violate the dramatic construction. Destroying the illusion and making the audience conscious of the repetition are not identical. However, in Giraudoux's *Electre* they often coincide—the former as a means, the latter as an end. The plan dominating the beginning of the play is one of the elements which refer to the repetition without defying the rules of conventional drama: Electra is to marry the gardener so that her known powers of destruction will afflict another family. Another reference of this kind lies in some remarks leading to the quarrel between the two women (1,4). It is as if Sophocles' model for this scene (l. 516 seq.) were still ringing in our ears.[37]

On the other hand, the modern drama also contains an extra-dramatic element, which is not or at most indirectly intended to make one conscious of the repetition: the "Entreacte," the "Lamento" of the gardener. But some of his reflections do refer to the central theme of the play, and so they revert back to the basis on which the whole of the repetition mechanism is built. He says that in a tragedy with incest and patricide one will experience pure hatred, pure anger, real purity itself—in short, innocence. His spirits are heightened, when, for instance, Pharaoh's wife commits suicide, he feels secure, when a soldier commits treason, and tender, when a duke commits a murder. His conclusion is: tragedy is an enterprise of love. These paradoxes are only understandable, if we presuppose that the tragedy, or the dramatic myth, is something which should not happen in real life, something that must be prevented at all costs. The myth with its "purity" and absoluteness thus appears as a negatively regarded pseudo-fatality, and the repetition of the myth through its "realization" in a play—the vital message of which is that repetition must not occur in real life—ultimately cancels itself out. "Purity" indicates compromise and conciliation, "innocence" indicates the will to bear active responsibility etc. The gardener describes reactions which the audience is supposed to have; and the audience can experience them because the play proves that the heroine's "purity" and "absoluteness" are nothing but despotic egoism, rigid abstractions, and absolute subjectivity, and because in the antagonist, Aegisthus, it presents a per-

---

[37] 1,3 i.f. (Egisthe) "*Vous allez en* (sc. de femmes) *avoir deux, et qui parlent.*" (Le Mendiant) "*Et qui vont se disputer un peu, j'espère.*" 1,4 init.: (Le jardinier) "*Ce seraif la première fois qu'on verrait se fâcher Electre.*" These signs of repetition only apply to the fact that the two women had a quarrel in Sophocles' tragedy. They do not refer to the contents of the classical model.

son whose actions are governed by such complementary ideas as concili-ation, a sense of responsibility, etc.

This is how Anouilh seems to have understood his predecessor. His *Antigone* does not only reproduce the general outline of *Electre*, in which he creates his polemic reply to the classical model; it also takes over the reflections, partly dramatic and partly metadramatic, which indicate the structure of the repetition and its intention. The successor has portrayed these connections in a less complicated, less mysterious fashion, appealing more directly and less intensely to the intellect of his audience.

The function of Giraudoux's beggar, the Eumenides and the "Entre-acte," has its parallel in Anouilh's "Prologue," which is later called the "Chorus."[38] This anonymous figure takes no part in the dramatic dialogue. It usually delivers the comments and reflections of the author. Shortly before the catastrophe, it personifies Creon's inner voice. It raises objections and indicates possibilities which could have caused things to turn out differently.[39] In this connection, those characteristics that emphasize the repetitious nature of the play are of prime impor-tance. One of these is the solemn titles given to this speaker, i.e., "The Prologue," "The Chorus," which are obviously intended to draw atten-tion to the stylistic gap between the modern and the ancient drama. This contrast is continued through the way in which the Prologue plunges the characters into a common, middle-class environment. Moreover, it at-tempts to prepare the audience for the interpenetration of repetitions and deviations, just as the play itself will execute it—"*Voilà. Ces per-sonnages vont vous jouer l'histoire d'Antigone.*" A sentence of this type indicates that the audience is quite familiar with Sophocles' tragedy, which forms the basis of the modern drama. This is borne out by a refer-ence immediately afterwards to the heroine's role: "*Elle s'appelle Anti-gone et il va falloir qu'elle joue son rôle jusqu'au bout. . . .*" And about another character: "*Ce garçon pâle, là-bas, au fond, qui rêve adossé au mur, solitaire, c'est le Messager. C'est lui qui viendra annoncer la mort d'Hémon tout à l'heure. . . . Il sait déjà. . . .*" But, in addition to this, the Prologue also contains surprising new elements, which correspond to the differences between the modern author's characters and the concep-tion that his classical predecessor had of them. This is true especially of Creon, who is depicted already as the character who will hold his own in the great debate with Antigone: "*Cet homme robuste, aux cheveux*

---

[38] See H. R. Jauss, *Racines Andromaque und Anouilhs Antigone* in *Die neueren Sprachen*, N.F. 9 (1960), pp. 427-444; Meyer, p. 10 seq.

[39] See p. 106 seq., esp. 109: "*Est-ce qu'on peut imaginer quelque chose, dire qu'elle est folle, l'enfermer?*" etc.

blancs qui médite là, près de son page, c'est Créon. C'est le roi. Il a des rides, il est fatigué. Il joue au jeu difficile de conduire les hommes. . . . Oedipe et ses fils sont morts. Il a laissé ses livres, ses objets, il a retroussé ses manches et il a pris leur place."

One of the dramatic means of accentuating the repetitious element of Anouilh's play is the way in which the quarrel between the two sisters Antigone and Ismene begins: (Ismene) *"Tu sais, j'ai bien pensé, Antigone,"* and finishes: (Antigone) *"Je te laisserai me parler, oui. Je vous laisserai tous me parler"* (pp. 24 and 33). The debates of the Sophoclean tragedy have already taken place. They resound and they continue.[40] Another device which makes the drama turn upon itself without destroying it is the image of "playing a part" (it loses its metaphoric character in proportion to the degree in which not the "reality" of the illusion, but the illusion of the "part" is to be taken for reality). Creon says to Antigone: *"Ecoute-moi bien. J'ai le mauvais rôle, c'est entendu, et tu as le bon."* And soon afterwards: *"Ecoute-moi tout de même pour la dernière fois. Mon rôle n'est pas bon, mais c'est mon rôle et je vais te faire tuer."*[41] Thus the author reminds us of the original character and the original attitude of the audience, at the very moment when he is preparing to refute that attitude and to turn the "bad part" into a good one.

The longer part of the "Choeur" which follows the exposition (p. 56 seq.) corresponds to Giraudoux's "Entracte." It, too, refers back to the intentions of the myth-repeat. With ironic refractions it reduces the tragic *schema ad adsurdum.* The parallel between non-dramatic reflection and dramatic structure is complete. The Chorus is not content with Giraudoux's keyword *"tragédie,"* but adds the complementary term *"drame"* as well—categories which are obviously to be embodied in the conflict between the main characters Antigone and Creon. From the viewpoint of the Chorus, tragedy appears to be a mechanical process, working like clockwork *"bien huilé depuis toujours."* Death is part of the plan and there is neither freedom nor hope, but man remains innocent and can "realize himself" completely. *"La petite Antigone va pouvoir être elle-même pour la première fois"* are the words with which the Chorus introduces the next phase of the action. It states that there are good and bad characters in drama; one wants to survive, and there is a chance, *"on se débat parce qu'on espère en sortir."* The price that drama (and life, as a model of which this drama is conceived here) de-

---

[40] The fact that Ismene's words apply to the changed situation (Anouilh's play begins a little later than the Sophoclean original) is another question. At this moment, the audience knows nothing of the altered situation.

[41] Pp. 80 and 90; cf. p. 10 (Prologue) and p. 58 (the Chorus on the tragedy): *"C'est une question de distribution"* (i.e., of the parts).

mands for survival is a renunciation of absolute individuality, but this price is not mentioned by the Chorus. We find it where *"tragédie"* and *"drame"* are weighed against each other, in the great confrontation between Creon and Antigone.[42]

III

So much for the literary and historic details, which have been chiefly concerned with one phenomenon, i.e., the principle of varying repetition in Greek and modern drama. The possibility of repetition seems to be inherent in the dramatized myth. As classical tragedy dealt mainly with myths, we can also say that for the Greeks and Romans, the principle of varying repetition was characteristic of a whole dramatic genre, i.e., tragedy. We cannot extend this observation to modern drama. We can only say that the principle of varying repetition is particularly suitable for those plays which deal with myths. This also implies that modern dramatists have copied the principle from traditional, classical tragedies. Furthermore, classical tragedy and the modern myth-drama follow the same rules in applying this principle. One rule is that the skeleton of the plot should remain unaltered, whereas workings of the plot, the motivation, the characters, and the whole meaning of the play can, and should, be altered.

So far we have attempted to show how this interaction of "fixed" and "variable" elements functions in Greek and in modern drama. We have seen that the Greek tragedians aimed, to a greater or lesser extent, at making it obvious to the audience that their plays were repetitions of earlier ones. The Phrynichus quotation in Aeschylus' *Persians* and Euripides' criticism of Aeschylus in his *Electra* show a certain tendency to hammer home this fact. In short, they aimed at a "relative" type of drama which also made itself relative. However, Sophocles, who must be regarded as a classic author not only for this reason, but for others also, tries to disguise the repetitious nature of his tragedies. He makes tacit assumptions, he avoids obvious references, and, in short, he aims at an "absolute" drama. Perhaps this contrast in Greek tragedy anticipates the intensified antagonism of modern times between neoclassical and modern myth-plays. Anyway, whether this be true or not (this is not the time to debate the question), modern myth-dramas emphasize the repetitious trait with such sophisticated intensity that the few analogies in classical plays seem very tentative in comparison. They frequently use methods which dispense with the illusion of the conventional

---

[42] See p. 83 seq. e.g., p. 85: (Créon) *"Eh bien, oui, j'ai peur d'être obligé de te faire tuer si tu t'obstines. Et je ne le voudrais pas."* (Antigone) *"Moi, je ne suis pas obligée de faire ce que je ne voudrais pas,"* etc.

theatre, i.e., those methods which constitute the modernity of modern drama.[43]

It might be apposite to make a few general comments on what we have observed so far. It has no doubt become clear what is involved in the notion of repetition we have assumed in this essay. It is, of course, true that repetition—which is often varying repetition—is one of the elementary principles of form in all art, and it can affect the material or theme even outside the genres of tragedy and myth-dramas. One example from Greek literature is "The New Comedy," the plays of Menander. These have the typical ingredients of tragedy, particularly those used by Euripides, such as abandoned children, recognition scenes, and they even transferred entire plots and applied them over and over again to the world of the middle-classes. Obviously the genre of comedy repeats features and themes of tragedy, but it goes without saying that we are not concerned here with such a general interpretation of repetition. For our purpose repetition is taken to mean that the same events, which have happened to persons of the same name, are reproduced. The recurring events and the recurring names show that repetition has been thematized since the beginnings of Attic tragedy, and in this sense it is not merely a general principle of form, but a striking individual phenomenon of classical tragedy and the modern myth-drama.

---

[43] See Jauss, p. 439; some basic observations on the significance of the repeated myth in modern drama in E. Ternoo's *De mythe in de literatuur*, in *Handelingen van het 27. Nederlandse Filologencongres* (Groningen, 1962), p. 80 seq. P. Szondi, *Theorie des modernen Dramas* (Frankfurt/Main, 1956, [4]1967) does not include those French myth-dramas we have called modern here, and M. Kesting, *Das epische Theater* (Stuttgart, [3]1959), p. 150, states: "The attempts of Giraudoux and Anouilh, Sartre . . . to extend the Aristotelian drama were factored out from the standpoint of subject matter." This view is understandable. It is based on the assumption that the "epic" methods, which already annul the absolute drama of the neoclassical tradition by their forms, constitute the modernity of the modern theatre. But it does not seem to give sufficient consideration to the extent to which in French myth-dramas, the "material," i.e., the myth as a repetition and the continual reference to the classical model, already achieves what specifically epic methods accomplish in other plays. The myth is able to take over this function because, as a repetition, it is both material and form at the same time (see p. 149, para. 3). The same thing applies in music to the *Passacaglia*, the *Tema con variazioni*. Here, too, the *Tema* dictates the formal structure, the network of constants (harmonic, melodic, rhythmic) and variables. The French myth drama shows similar features to those of the "epic" theatre. The action is relative and the dialogue on stage stands for the dialogue between the author and the audience, for his appeal to the intellect of his audience. The structure of the repetition, with its open, paradoxical outcome, serves this purpose: the efforts of the dialogue on stage come to nothing since they are frustrated by the plot, which repeats itself and becomes a sort of "fate" in itself. The audience goes home asking itself whether fatality does not originate from subjective conditions, which would mean that the chance of surmounting is inherent in the obstacle that appears to be insurmountable.

This concrete repetitive quality, reminiscent of the laws of historiography, appears to be conditioned both by the myth and by the dramatic form.[44] Before tragedies were written, the Greeks presented their myths in two ways: through ritual dances, and through epic, and subsequently lyric narratives. It is obvious that these two forms of presentation were legitimized by basically different modes of "reality." The ritual dance represented the myth as a direct presence; epic and lyric poetry represented it as an account of the past. In the ritual dance, the myth "took place" in the present, and performers were identical with what they performed. In the epic or lyric account, the myth had happened in the past, and the narrator remained aloof from his narrative. In the ritual dance, the presentation was through people; in epic or lyric poetry it came through words. In the former, the event itself was re-enacted; in the latter there was only a copy of something that was presumed to be unique.

These two forms of presentation were in principle incompatible with each other. And so there arose a general feeling that the more modern, indirect technique of reporting was more credible than the older one of direct ritual dance. Just as in Athens inscriptions on statues were altered from "I am X" to "I am the statue, the monument of X," so people also realized that the dancers were not in actual fact what they seemed to be, but only represented certain persons. The literary category of mimesis was transferred to the act of religious worship. This first step was followed in Athens by a second that was by no means inevitable but in fact more paradoxical. The act of worship was not debased, but put into a literary form. It broke away from concrete ritual, from being limited to the Dionysos myth, and entered a new dimension, a hitherto unknown category of "reality." This is how tragedy came into being.

Tragedy broke away from concrete ritual. Its theme was the myth—not the individual myth of a particular cult, but the universal myth of literature. It entered a new dimension of "reality." It was not confined to the direct presentation of an event, as the act of worship had been, or to giving a report, as the recited epic had done. Externally it appeared to do both. It retained the form of the ritual dance, in that it was a direct presentation: it also retained the form of the literary work in that what it presented merely served as a medium for the actual meaning behind it. But the actual meaning, the message of the tragedy, was no longer the myth as a definite past event, as it was in the epic or lyric poem, but the myth as a model, conveying abstract ideas, constantly present in the background and never forming a tangible foreground: the power of the

[44] See B. Snell, *Mythos und Wirklichkeit in der griechischen Tragödie*, in *Die Entdeckung des Geistes* (Hamburg, [3]1955), pp. 138-160.

Gods and of fate, and human actions and their premises, such as justice, reason and passions. Tragedy thus documents the fact that existence can be understood on different levels; the events of the myth are merely an external, visual manifestation, and each interpretation of these events is the actual meaning, the essential "reality."

The paradoxical compromise, or rather the loftier unity of ritual and literary communication which the tragedy achieved, also explains the specific technique of repetition which this class of literature applied. The mythic material was what tragedy had inherited from its two fore-bears—the ritual dance and the epic-lyric report. It made use of its inheritance by taking over two contrasting principles from these forebears: from ritual dance it adopted the admission of repeatability; from the literary work the demand for variation. It was able to reconcile these two principles by making the plot, or story, "repeatable," and everything else—e.g., details of the action, motivation, characters—"variable." This solution, which reduced the unchangeable core of the myth to a bare skeleton of facts and names, avoided one drawback—the need for true historicity, for if all the details of the traditional myth had to be considered, the possibilities of variation would have been very limited; the need for nothing but pseudohistorical residue left the poet sufficient scope for his own ideas and intentions. On the other hand, this solution, i.e., keeping to a "reduced" myth, had a considerable advantage: the myth did not serve only as material but also as a form, or, to be more precise, it took over functions which were normally attributed to form. For it was a factor that kept recurring, an element which the author and his audience fully agreed upon from the start. Its generally accepted constancy formed a background against which the particular intention of the individual works could be seen that much more clearly.

Tragedy is based on the idea that there are distinct levels of existence, and the world can be divided into what is apparent and what is basically true. The special character of the myth in tragedy resulted from its ambivalent function as part content, part form. The interplay of all these factors enabled tragedy to "save" the myth in two ways. First, it mitigated criticisms levelled at the myth by showing their object to be a mere outside covering, and by exchanging this covering for a hard core of essential validity. This method aimed directly at "saving" the myth. Second, it aroused a critical attitude towards the myth by proving that what was supposed to be essentially valid was in fact conditional and unessential. This second method "rescued" the myth involuntarily, for it used it only as the indispensable basis for its polemics. If the poet's main aim was to protect the myth from criticism by giving it a new basic interpretation, then paradoxically he used it more as an "idea" or "form." If, however, he aimed at querying a recognized interpretation of the myth, then he used it more as a "theme," or as "material." It was not that he was concerned with the actuality of the mythical events, but his attack was directed against the myth as a bearer of meanings, e.g., fate as an insurmountable force limiting human actions. This dialectic process of dogmatism and emancipation had already taken place during the development of the Attic tragedy, from Aeschylus to Euripides, and it repeated itself when the modern myth-drama set itself the task of attacking the attitudes of classical humanism. If this attack did not differ in principle from its predecessors, it certainly did in the dramatic methods it employed.

WOLFGANG ISER

Patterns of Communication in Joyce's *Ulysses*

I

Myth and Reality

JOYCE called his novel *Ulysses* after Homer's hero, though the latter never appears in the book. Instead Joyce deals with eighteen different aspects of a single day in Dublin, mainly following the involvement of two characters—Leopold Bloom and Stephen Dedalus—in events that take place between early morning and late at night. What, then, is the connection between the *Odyssey* and June 16th, 1904? Most answers to this question try to join these two poles of the novel through the "tried and tested" ideas of the recurrence of archetypes, or the analogy between the ideal and the real.[1] In the first case, the explanation is provided by the permanent nature of basic human conduct—and so *Ulysses* has its roots in things we already know; the second, Platonizing interpretation claims that the basic idea of the *Odyssey* is a homecoming, while that of Bloom's wanderings is just a copy of a homecoming: for Ulysses this means release from his sufferings, but for Bloom it is merely a critical moment in the restless monotony of everyday life.

Although one is reluctant to dispute these lines of interpretation, they certainly suffer from the fact that not a single character from the *Odyssey* actually appears in *Ulysses*—in contrast to many modern texts, where the return of mythical figures is a fundamental theme—and Joyce's deliberate allusions to Homeric heroes and epic events show them in a different light from what we are familiar with through the *Odyssey*. The permanence idea gets into difficulties here, as it is never clear what is to be equated with what, and who with whom. There are similar objections to the analogy thesis, which postulates a sort of declivity from Homer to the present. One simply does not have the impression that everyday life in Dublin has been conceived as the woeful de-

---

[1] For a detailed discussion of these two interpretations, see W. Iser, *The Implied Reader. Patterns of Communication in Prose Fiction from Bunyan to Beckett* (Baltimore, ³1978), pp. 180 ff. For a critical assessment of the Homeric parallel, see also A. Esch, *James Joyce and Homer. Zur Frage der Odyssee Korrespondenzen im Ulysses*, in *Lebende Antike*—Symposium for Rudolf Sühnel, ed. H. Meller and H.-J. Zimmerman (Berlin, 1967), pp. 423 ff.

cline of an ideality that existed in the past. And again there is no clear parallel between past and present. Nevertheless, one can understand why the permanence and analogy theories have proved so attractive to those trying to combine past and present in a single vision: they do, after all, offer a means of organizing the seemingly opaque chaos of everyday life by referring it back to meanings drawn from Homer. The solution is convincing by virtue of its simplicity—but from an esthetic point of view it is quite inadequate. Joyce himself once said ironically of his novel: "I've put in so many enigmas and puzzles that it will keep the professors busy for centuries arguing over what I meant, and that's the only way of insuring one's immortality."[2] If for a moment one examines this statement with a little more seriousness than was perhaps intended, one is faced with the question of what actually gives rise to this preoccupation with the enigmas. Is it the enigmas themselves, or is it perhaps the critical armory which the professors are constantly dipping into as they try to solve the riddles? Whichever it may be, the parallelism indicated by the title of the novel compels one to see Dublin and Homer in conjunction, principally because one is anxious to extract some kind of meaning from the apparent senselessness of everyday life. But, like all compulsions, this makes one blind to certain not insignificant facts; one of these is the peculiar nature of the two poles that constitute the novel.

No Homeric figures actually appear in *Ulysses*, and yet the novel cannot be described as a realistic depiction of ordinary life in Dublin, despite the vast number of verifiable details that run right through it. We have since learned that a great deal of this material was drawn from Dublin address books, topographical descriptions, and the daily press of that time, so that an astonishing wealth of names, addresses, local events, and even newspaper cuttings can actually be identified,[3] though in the text they frequently form a montage that is stripped of its context. Sometimes these details vanish away into the impenetrable private sphere of Joyce himself, and sometimes they seem to lead the reader into a veritable labyrinth when he attempts to collate them. In searching for and visualizing connections, he often loses the organizing principle of those connections he thought he had discovered. And frequently it seems as though the many details are simply there for their own sake and, through sheer weight of numbers, more or less deliberately blur the outline of events in the narrative.

[2] Quoted by R. Ellmann, *James Joyce* (Oxford, 1966), p. 535.

[3] It is the great merit of R. M. Adams's *Surface and Symbol. The Consistency of James Joyce's Ulysses* (New York, 1962) that he extracted this material from the novel and was able to identify it.

The effect of all this is somewhat paradoxical, for it runs completely contrary to the expectations that the realistic novel had established in its readers. There, too, one was confronted with a wealth of details which the reader could see reflected in his own world of experience. Their appearance in the novel served mainly to authenticate the view of life offered.[4] But in *Ulysses* they are, to a great extent, deprived of this function. When details no longer serve to reinforce probability or to stabilize the illusion of reality, they must become a sort of end in themselves, such as one finds in the art-form of the collage. The unstructured material of *Ulysses* is taken directly *from* life itself, but since it no longer testifies to the author's preconception of reality, it cannot be taken *for* life itself. Thus the details illustrate nothing; they simply present themselves, and since they bear witness to nothing beyond themselves, they revoke the normal assumption that a novel represents a given reality. It is not surprising, then, that one is constantly returning to the title in order to try and create—through recourse to the *Odyssey*—some sort of frame of reference that will bring this chaos of detail under control and will endow everyday life with a pattern, with meaning, and with significance.

We now have a double frustration of our expectations: not only do the Homeric figures fail to appear in *Ulysses*, but also the many details are deprived of their usual function. As a result, our attention is drawn to the evocative nature of the novel. We realize that all these details constitute a surplus that projects far beyond any organizational schema that the novel may offer us. And so each reading gives us a new chance to integrate the details in a different way—with the result, however, that each form of integration brings about a sort of kaleidoscopic reshuffling of the material excluded.

By giving his novel this structure—whether consciously or unconsciously—Joyce was complying with a basic disposition of the reader, described by Northrop Frye as follows: "Whenever we read anything, we find our attention moving in two directions at once. One direction is outward or centrifugal, in which we keep going outside our reading, from the individual words to the things they mean, or, in practice, to our memory of the conventional association between them. The other direction is inward or centripetal, in which we try to develop from the words a sense of the larger verbal pattern they make."[5] These two tendencies seem to take the reader of *Ulysses* in completely different directions, which are divergent rather than convergent. As he reads, he

---

[4] See also H. R. Jauss, "Nachahmungsprinzip und Wirklichkeitsbegriff in der Theorie des Romans von Diderot bis Stendhal," in *Nachahmung und Illusion*, ed. H. R. Jauss (Munich, 1964), pp. 161 f. and 241 f.

[5] N. Frye, *Anatomy of Criticism. Four Essays* (New York, ⁵1967), p. 73.

finds that everyday life in Dublin is, so to speak, continually breaking its banks, and the resultant flood of detail induces the reader to try and build his own dams of meaning—though these in turn are inevitably broken down. Even the signal contained in the title seems to dispel rather than fulfill one's hopes of controlling the material, for the central frame of reference that one would so like to deduce from the *Odyssey* is never formulated anywhere in the text. According to whether one reads the novel from the Dublin viewpoint or from that of the *Odyssey*, one will get quite different "images." In the first case, the apparent lack of connection between the many details creates the impression of a thoroughly chaotic world; in the second, one wonders what the return of Ulysses in modern trappings is supposed to signify. Both approaches are, in themselves, relatively flabby, and the task of stiffening them up, and indeed bringing them together, is what the novel sets its reader.

Soon after the publication of *Ulysses*, Eliot and Pound both described the interaction of the two constituent poles of the novel, each using different metaphors. In his discussion of *Ulysses*, Eliot saw in the novel's references to tradition a demand that was to be made of all literature: "In using the myth, in manipulating a continuous parallel between contemporaneity and antiquity, Mr. Joyce is pursuing a method which others must pursue after him. They will not be imitators, any more than the scientist who uses the discoveries of an Einstein in pursuing his own, independent, further investigations. It is simply a way of controlling, of ordering, of giving a shape and a significance to the immense panorama of futility and anarchy which is contemporary history."[6] According to this, the mythic parallel is meant to give a constant outline to an order that is to be read into the events in Dublin. But this cannot mean—at least for Joyce—that the chaotic and enigmatic present is measured against the significance of Homeric archetypes. It would be closer to the truth to say that the mythic parallel offers patterns of perception, though what is perceived never conforms completely to these patterns. Indeed, the revelation of the irreducible differences is what constitutes the real function of the mythical patterns through which we are to look upon the modern world. The very fact that these cannot incorporate everything endows the non-integrated material with the necessary degree of live tension to make us immediately aware of it. It is not by chance that Eliot refers back to Einstein in order to indicate how the "discovery" of Joyce is to be evaluated and handled. The mythic parallel here is more in the nature of an explanatory hypothesis, and is scarcely to be interpreted as the return of the myth. It is simply a repertoire of patterns

---

[6] T. S. Eliot, "Ulysses, Order and Myth," in *James Joyce: Two Decades of Criticism*, ed. S. Givens (New York, 1948), p. 201. (The essay originally appeared in 1923.)

serving an overall strategy through which the present-day world is to be presented.

Ezra Pound, on the same subject, writes: "These correspondences are part of Joyce's mediaevalism and are chiefly his own affair, a scaffold, a means of construction, justified by the result, and justifiable by it only. The result is a triumph in form, in balance, a main schema, with continuous inweaving and arabesque."[7] Pound sees in the mythical correspondences nothing but preconditions for the construction of the novel—the scaffolding round the shell of the building to be erected. But the novel itself is more than the sum of its preconditions, and is in no way reducible to this sum. Ultimately, the network of mythical correspondences forms nothing but a framework of presentation, which is so clearly delineated in the novel in order to draw attention to the limitations of all such organizational patterns. This applies in equal measure to the recognizable archetypes, but the question then arises as to what such limitations actually are meant to achieve.

II

Experiments in Style

The Homeric allusions in *Ulysses* open up an horizon which is certainly not identical to that of the modern "World-Weekday,"[8] for between the present and the archetypes of the Homeric epic lies the whole of history, which could be passed over only if *Ulysses* were concerned with nothing but the return of archetypes. One should not forget, when considering the Homeric parallel, that Joyce permeated his novel with as many Shakespearean as Homeric allusions. And even if one tries to equate Shakespeare's presence in *Ulysses* with the return of the archetypes, nevertheless there is no denying the fact that Joyce was obviously more interested in the various manifestations of such archetypes than in merely establishing their return. This certainly indicates that for him the archetype was, at most, a vehicle, but not a subject. The history of its manifestations takes precedence over its mythical nature. But what is this history, and in what form is it reflected in the novel?

Our answer to this question can, perhaps, best proceed from the experiments in style. These in themselves are an innovation, insofar as the eighteen chapters of the novel present the narrative through eighteen differently structured perspectives. Normally, when reading a novel, we are asked only once to adopt the author's chosen standpoint in order to

---

[7] E. Pound, *Literary Essays*, ed. T. S. Eliot (London, 1960), p. 406. (The essay on Ulysses originally appeared in 1922.)

[8] "Welt-Alltag"—a term coined by H. Broch, *Dichten und Erkennen* (Zürich, 1955), p. 187, to designate June 16, 1904.

fulfill his intentions—but here the same demand is made of us no less than seventeen extra times, for each chapter is written in a different style. Style, according to John Middleton Murry, "is a quality of language which communicates precisely emotions or thoughts, or a system of emotions or thoughts, peculiar to the author."[9] We can talk of style when systematic viewpoints bring about a frame of reference that is to direct the reader's observations by selecting which facts are or are not to be presented.

This function of style is both its strength and its weakness, for inevitably it must restrict the field of observation. The meaning that it is to express can take its shape only through the process of selecting particular aspects of the phenomena to be presented, and so phenomena are reproduced mainly for the sake of what they will communicate to the reader. As style imposes a specific meaning and edits reality to coincide with this meaning, it reveals itself to be a "mythical analogue,"[10] which—as Clemens Lugowski has shown—not only implies a particular conception of reality, but is also the agent that actually forms it. Although this " 'mythical artifice' . . . is the result of a deeply unconscious and indirect act of interpretation,"[11] for this very reason, it will freeze the historical conditions under which such acts of interpretation came into being.

In *Ulysses* Joyce shows up these limitations by thematizing the capacity of style itself. By constantly changing the perspective throughout the eighteen chapters, he draws attention to the normative pressure caused by the modes of observation inherent in any one style, thus revealing the extreme one-sidedness of each individual "act of interpretation." While the change of styles shows up these limitations, the process is underlined in the individual chapters by the surplus of non-integrated, unstructured material. This, too, makes one aware of the limitations of the style in question, so that it often seems more real than the view of reality being presented at the time.

And so we have changes of style and non-integrated material to show up the limitations of each style, and in addition to these two factors, there is even a kind of authorial commentary,[12] which has these very limitations as its subject. This is the chapter "The Oxen of the Sun," which Joyce critics have always approached with a kind of embarrassment.[13] T. S. Eliot had the impression that this chapter showed the

[9] J. M. Murry, *The Problem of Style* (London, ⁹1960), p. 65.

[10] C. Lugowski, *Die Form der Individualität im Roman* (Berlin, 1932), p. 12.

[11] *Ibid.*, p. 206.

[12] See also S. L. Goldberg, *The Classical Temper. A Study of James Joyce's Ulysses* (London, 1961), p. 288.

[13] For details and bibliography see Iser, pp. 180 ff.

"futility of all the English styles,"[14] and this must certainly have been at least one of the effects that Joyce was aiming at.

In this display of individual and period styles, we are made aware of the various assumptions that condition the different presentations of the theme. By parodying the styles, Joyce makes sure that we do not over-look the "interpretative" nature of the forms of presentation. Leopold Bloom finds himself transformed into a variety of figures, in accordance with the particular style used: the medieval *traveller Leopold* changes into the Arthurian knight *Sir Leopold*, who in turn leaps into a new context as *childe Leopold*.[15] The reader cannot help being aware of the one-sidedness of all these characterizations, as he has already become familiar in the preceding chapters with the many-sidedness of Bloom's character. This same one-sidedness is equally evident in the central theme of the chapter. This does not deal with love, but only with the way in which Malory, Bunyan, Addison, and the other writers con-ceived of love. The basically comic effect arises out of the impression one has that the views, expressed in such a variety of styles, exclude rather than supplement one another. With each author the main theme takes on a different shape, but as each style automatically and unquestioningly assumes that it has captured the reality of the phenomenon, a latent naïveté comes to the surface. The question arises as to which of these individual views comes closest to the truth, but even then we realize that the individual authors, precisely through their selection of a particular means of presentation, have in fact edited the subject to form a single meaning and a single evaluation. The very fact that these meanings and evaluations seem to assume a normative validity makes us aware of the extent to which they depend on the historical situation from which they have sprung. If "The Oxen of the Sun" is taken, then, as the author's own "commentary" on his work, one can scarcely expect him to organ-ize his novel as yet another "act of interpretation." It is the *presentation* of everyday life that concerns him, and not the evaluation.

However, such a presentation also requires a form, and inevitably any form that Joyce chose would automatically foreshorten the phenomenon to be presented. And so one might assume that the chapters of the novel were organized, each as a sort of rebuttal of the others with their respec-tive *principium stilisationis*. The consequences of this principle of con-struction are very far-reaching. Joyce could parody the different styles in order to show the limitations of their capacity, but if he applied this technique to the whole novel, it would mean that in trying to present the

---

[14] Quoted by Ellmann, p. 490.
[15] Joyce, *Ulysses* (London: The Bodley Head, 1937), pp. 369 f.

events etc. of June 16th, 1904, he would have continually to parody himself. There are certainly traces of this in the text, but a constant self-parody would ultimately distract the reader from coming to grips with the events of June 16th, 1904. And would not this in turn—like all parodies—lead primarily to a negative evaluation, as limited in its own way as the evaluations of the authors parodied? Such a form would itself constitute an "act of interpretation."

Is it possible for anything to be presented, and yet at the same time for the "act of interpretation" to be suspended without the object of presentation becoming incomprehensible? *Ulysses* is the answer to this question. In order to moderate, if not actually to neutralize, the interpretative nature of style, Joyce called upon virtually every stylistic mode that the novel had evolved during its comparatively short history. These he enriched with a whole armory of allusions and with the recall of archetypes. The multiplicity of these schemata, together with the complexity of their interrelationship, results in the presentation of each incipient meaning simultaneously with its own diffusion. Thus the novel does not paint a picture of the "World-Weekday"—which means, ultimately, that it does not "present" anything in the conventional sense —but, through the great variety of its perspectives, it offers possibilities for conceiving or imagining the "World-Weekday." These possibilities must be fulfilled by the reader himself if he wants to make contact with the reality of the novel. One must therefore differentiate between "presentation" (i.e., by the author) and "imagination" (on the part of the reader). Of course, even if the "interpretative acts" of the novel are obvious, the reader still has to imagine things for himself. But he himself will conduct these "interpretative acts" only if the system of presentation leaves out the coordinating elements between observable phenomena and situations. In *Ulysses* this is brought about mainly through the over-precision of the system, which presents more conceivable material than the reader is capable of processing as he reads. And so it is not the style of the novel but the overtaxed reader himself that reduces the amount of observable material to manageable proportions. In doing so, he can scarcely avoid equating this reduced amount with the meaning. If one considers reactions to *Ulysses* over the last forty years—insofar as these can be gauged by the different interpretations offered—one can see how historically conditioned such meanings are. At the same time, it cannot be denied that the many possible permutations of meaning in *Ulysses* act as a constant inducement to the reader to formulate a meaning—and in doing so, he is forced to enter into the action of the novel.

The individual chapters of *Ulysses* act, to a greater or lesser degree, as signposts that point the way through the "World-Weekday," rather than guidebooks that impose on the reader a specific interpretation of the regions they represent. If we want to get a proper understanding of the function of the patterns of presentation, the allusions, and also the archetypes, it might be well first to examine one or two concrete examples.

The novel begins with the parody of a church ritual. Mulligan, the medical student, holds his shaving-bowl aloft at the top of the Martello tower, and intones: "Introibo ad altare Dei."[16] If this little curtain-raiser is a sign of what is to come, then we appear to be due for one long parody. At first this impression seems to be confirmed by the subsequent conversation between Mulligan and Stephen, for as he talks the former jumps abruptly from one stylistic level to another, everyday slang alternating with scholarly allusions to Greece, Irish mythology, and even Zarathustra.[17] Indeed, individual allusions are sometimes broken up and even corrupted. Are we now to have a series of parodied stylistic levels? If so, there would be a danger of the tension soon flagging, for a parody of stylistic levels here might seem trivial after the initial "exposing" of the mass. Moreover, it is scarcely possible to find a *tertium comparationis* for the various intersecting levels of Mulligan's speech.

It is also impossible to establish a purpose for such a parody, unless one wanted to conclude from the diffusion of stylistic levels that Joyce was advocating a purist use of language—an idea that is hardly worth considering. In fact, one gets the impression that what is stated is nothing but a stimulus to call forth its own reversal. Thus the profane distortions of the ritual of the mass take on another significance than that of mere parody. Like the subsequent conversation, they point up the limitations of all clearly formulated statements and induce the reader to supply his own connections between the segmented stylistic levels. As the text offers no point of convergence for the phenomena it sets before him, the reader tends to load each detail with meaning, and since the meaning cannot be fully realized, there arises a latent tension between the unconnected phenomena. This basic pattern, with a few variations, runs right through the first chapter, which Joyce called "Telemachus."[18] The most important type of variation is the abrupt switch of narrator. In the middle of a third-person narrative we are suddenly confronted with statements in the first person,[19] which strike the reader so forcibly that he

---

[16] *Ibid.*, p. 1.   [17] See *ibid.*, pp. 5, 9, 20.

[18] These chapter headings are to be found in Joyce's "note-sheets," and he used them in grouping together his material. See A. W. Litz, *The Art of James Joyce. Method and Design in Ulysses and Finnegans Wake* (New York, 1964); for an assessment of their importance, see esp. *ibid.*, p. 39.

[19] See Joyce, *Ulysses*, pp. 7 f.

soon becomes more conscious of narrative patterns than of things narrated. And so here, as elsewhere in the novel, one gets the impression that one must constantly differentiate between the linguistic possibilities of style and the possible nature of the phenomena concerned.

The predominant pattern of reversal in this first chapter reduces all that is clear and concrete to a mere position in life, but life itself goes far beyond such positions. The next chapter, originally called "Nestor," reveals the implications of this fact, and naturally another collection of stylistic patterns is necessary to uncover these hidden consequences. Stephen's interior monologue is the dominant pattern in this chapter, but it is broken up by authorial passages, direct speech, and also quotations from Milton's *Lycidas*,[20] all set against and arising out of the background of the morning lesson. They lead to reflections on history and man's possible place in history:

"For them too history was a tale like any other too often heard, their land a pawnshop. Had Pyrrhus not fallen by a beldam's hand in Argos or Julius Caesar not been knifed to death? They are not to be thought away. Time has branded them and fettered they are lodged in the room of the infinite possibilities they have ousted. But can those have been possible seeing that they never were? Or was that only possible which came to pass? Weave, weaver of the wind. . . . It must be a movement then, an actuality of the possible as possible."[21]

It is not insignificant that this reflection on the possible is inspired specifically by historical processes in which everything appears to be so irrevocably fixed. Is this determinacy ultimately to be seen only as one possibility amongst many? What about the existences of historical individuals? If, through their deeds and sufferings, they stepped outside the jurisdiction of infinite possibilities, why should they now fall back into it? It seems almost like a sophism when Stephen asks whether Pyrrhus and Caesar even considered the possibility, when they were alive, that one day they would not be there, or that they would end as they did. Although he himself considers such thoughts to be mere speculations, they do not stop him from concluding that real life can be understood only as an actuality of one possibility among many. But if what happened did not happen inevitably, then the real is nothing but a chance track left by the possible. And if reality is nothing but one chance track, then it pales to insignificance beside the vast number of unseen and unfulfilled possibilities; it shrinks to the dimensions of a mere curiosity. The tendency apparent in these reflections of Stephen's runs parallel to that at the beginning of the novel, where whatever was said pointed the

[20] *Ibid.*, pp. 22 f.   [21] *Ibid.*

way to its own reversal, and whatever possibilities were excluded by each utterance were brought out by another.

The children are bored by the history lesson, and want Stephen to tell them a story: "Tell us a story, sir.—Oh, do, sir, a ghost story."[22] Stephen himself has just had the impression that, when one thinks about it, history changes into a ghost story, albeit a different type from the one the children would like to hear. Bored by the factual, they are now asking for the fantastic, without realizing how much incomprehensibility lies in the factual. The text, of course, does not state this, but the manner in which the different perspectives are thrust against one another compels the reader to search for a link between them. The text offers him no guide as to how the different standpoints might be evaluated, and at best he can orient himself only through the next perspective which, like that of the children, is inserted into Stephen's monologue. There is no ghost story; instead, the children begin to read verses from Milton's "Lycidas"—those lines where the mourning shepherd is consoled with the assurance that the dead do not perish. Evidently only poetry eternalizes; but poetry is fiction.

In this comparatively short section of text, there are three different intersecting patterns: interior monologue, direct speech and literary quotation—all focused upon a relatively uniform theme, which, however, takes on three different forms as it is presented to the reader. For Stephen reality is so overshadowed by the possible that it is deprived of its unique significance. The children are bored by what has been, and want the titillation of the unreal. The literary quotation shows clearly that eternalization exists only in the medium of fiction. The text does not say how these three viewpoints are to be joined together, but simply offers three different possibilities of relating the real to the unreal. As the individual stylistic patterns intersect within the text, there is no hierarchic construction. The reflections of the inner monologue point inevitably to the private nature of the opinion expressed; the desires of the schoolchildren appear as something spontaneous and naïve, and the quotation as a kind of insurance without any reality. Although this need not be regarded as the only possible interpretation of the different patterns of the text, the conditions are certainly there for such an interpretation. Since these patterns are without a point of convergence, their meaning arises out of their interaction—a process which is set in motion by the reader himself, and which will therefore involve the reader personally in the text.

Apart from the patterns we have mentioned, this process is encour-

22 *Ibid.*, p. 22.

aged above all by the end of the chapter, which deals with a conversation between Stephen and the headmaster, Mr. Deasy. The headmaster gives Stephen a letter which he wants published in the *Evening Telegraph*, because it contains his (Deasy's) solution to an important problem: foot and mouth disease. "I have put the matter into a nutshell, Mr. Deasy said. It's about the foot and mouth disease. Just look through it. There can be no two opinions on the matter."[23]

For Mr. Deasy there can be no two opinions about this or about a number of other political problems in Ireland. But now the segmented text pattern of Stephen's history lesson becomes the background to Mr. Deasy's unequivocal utterances, through which he seeks once and for all to set right existing realities. Again the text says nothing about any relationship between these two passages, but the reader will soon find a relatively straightforward way to bridge this gap. Viewed against the background of infinite possibilities, Mr. Deasy's self-confidence appears absurdly narrow-minded, and so the reader will most likely come to two conclusions: first, that Mr. Deasy is a pompous ass; second, and far more important, that any claim to knowledge is an automatic reduction of the infinite and discounts above all the changeability of phenomena. However, let it be emphasized once again—this interpretation will be the reader's, for there is no such statement in the text itself.

As regards the original chapter-heading—"Nestor"—this offers yet another perspective, insofar as the reader will try to link the wisdom of Nestor with the pretensions of Mr. Deasy. He will most likely find that not only does Mr. Deasy suffer from the comparison, but so, too, does Nestor. For if, in Mr. Deasy's case, claims to knowledge presuppose unawareness of the changeability of phenomena, then the mythical wisdom of Nestor is open to re-evaluation by the reader.

The third chapter, originally called "Proteus," takes the experiment in yet another direction, at the same time bringing to a close the sections grouped under the heading "Telemachia," which deal with Stephen's inner situation before the appearance of Bloom. In comparison with the preceding chapters, one is struck by the relative uniformity of the stylistic pattern used here. Stephen's monologue forms the dominant *principium stilisationis*, though there are occasional traces of the authorial narrator. These latter, however, are of a special nature. Instead of relating the monologue to an overall situation, the author's voice here seems to be unable to keep up with Stephen's reflections, and is virtually swamped by them. It no longer acts as a mediator between the context

[23] *Ibid.*, p. 30.

and the narrated situation; instead, the monologue seems to abstract itself even from the authorial medium. With the authorial narrator thus deprived of his normal function, we are left with a gap between monologue and overall situation, and, as always when such gaps arise, the reader is stimulated into forming his own connections. But in this case, the reader's task is made doubly difficult by the fact that Stephen's monologue has no consistent pattern. At one moment it seems like a stream of consciousness, stirring up the past, the next it is a mere recording of observations on the beach at Sandymount, and then it is like a soliloquy or an introspective reflection which—unlike the conventional interior monologue—is not concerned with memory or observation, but with the conditions that initially give rise to memory and observation.

In the very first sentence of the monologue, we are made aware of the peculiar nature of Stephen's reflections: "Ineluctable modality of the visible: at least that if no more, thought through my eyes. Signatures of all things I am here to read, seaspawn and seawrack, the nearing tide, that rusty boot. Snotgreen, bluesilver, rust: coloured signs. Limits of the diaphane."[24]

Stephen tries to show the consequences that arise out of his inescapable restriction to his own perceptions. This is apparently only possible through concrete consideration of the actual mode of perception. If observation automatically involves so many preconceptions, then how is one to read the signatures of things? At best, seawrack and tide might be described as colors, but such a reduction not only impoverishes them—it also leads one swiftly to the borderline at which they resist perception and retreat into total opacity. It is perception itself that ultimately produces this opacity, which in turn appears to be a characteristic of the object which is to be perceived. Thus, for Stephen, the subject under discussion is the frame of reference of perception itself. Perhaps this frame is such that in approaching objects, it changes them in order to make them accessible to one's comprehension.

Stephen tries to test this idea; he closes his eyes in order to "see" if such a change really is produced by vision. He opens them again with the statement: "See now. There all the time without you: and ever shall be, world without end."[25] Obviously, things exist independently of one's comprehension and observation of them, and if this comprehension is, in turn, to be comprehended, it must be through the idea that the act of seeing is what produces the opacity of things. The monologue that follows is like an attempt to give form to this idea. Stephen's reflections on the limitations of observation culminate in a welter of fragmentary situations, images, characters, and contexts. The reader is

[24] *Ibid.*, p. 33.   [25] *Ibid.*, p. 34.

perplexed, not least because this is not what he expects from analytical reflection in a novel. Normally, the aim of this sort of reflection should be progress towards clarity and truth—it should enlighten and not obscure.[26]

The perplexing effect of the monologue derives mainly from the fact that the individual sentences or passages, which all deal with recognizable but unrelated themes, are simply set side by side without any apparent connection. Thus the vacant spaces in the text increase dramatically in number. These may irritate the reader—but as far as the intention of the monologue is concerned, they are perfectly consistent. They prevent the reader from joining up what he observes, with the result that the facets of the external world—as evoked by Stephen's perception—are constantly made to merge into one another. However, the perplexity that this process causes in the reader cannot be the sole purpose of the text, if one considers Stephen's preceding train of thought. Here as elsewhere, perplexity should rather be regarded as a stimulus and a provocation—though, of course, the reader is not obliged to take the bait and will, indeed, ignore it if he feels himself to be overtaxed. The point is that one *can* read something into this fragmentary text. Stephen's reflections on his acts of perception reveal a state of consciousness which has been described, in a different context, by Cassirer as follows: "The further consciousness progresses in its formation and division, and the more 'meaningful' its individual contents become—i.e., the more they take on the power to 'adumbrate' others—the greater is the freedom with which, through a change of 'viewpoint,' it can transform one gestalt into another."[27] It is this disposition of consciousness that is brought out through the ceaseless transformation of *gestalts* in the monologue. But it should be added that the transformation is effected primarily by the way in which Stephen varies the distance between the observed reality and himself as the conscious observer. This variation ensures that the world which is open to perception cannot be confined to any one conscious frame of reference. A vital element of it is the continual retraction of each adopted attitude to everything that occurs on the beach at Sandymount, and the whole process functions through the gaps, interrupting the images formed by acts of perception, thus focusing the reader's attention on the interaction between perception and reality.

The text also offers indications of this process: "I throw this ended

---

[26] Stephen is also conscious of this: "You find my words dark. Darkness is in our souls, do you not think? Flutier. Our souls, shame-wounded by our sins, cling to us yet more, a woman to her lover clinging, the more the more." *Ibid.*, p. 45.

[27] E. Cassirer, *Philosophie der symbolischen Formen III* (Darmstadt, ⁴1964), p. 185.

shadow from me, manshape ineluctable, call it back. Endless, would it be mine, to form my form? Who watches me here?"[28] This awareness of the necessity to separate modes of perception from the thing perceived, so that the observed world can take on its inherent multifariousness, is conveyed in the text through the gaps which prevent us from joining up the phenomena processed by observation. And so the monologue appears to release all the observed and recorded details from any overriding structure.

In the face of this impression, one might be tempted to regard this chapter as offering a focus for the whole manner of presentation of the "World-Weekday." Stephen's reflections on his own mode of observation, self-observation as a constant check on things observed, and the liberation of things perceived from the clutches of perception—these could easily be taken for the basic schema of the novel. But if this were so, Joyce would fall victim to his own trap. For then he would simply be replacing the styles he parodies with another of his own. For this very reason it is essential not to overlook the demarcation points through which he indicates the limitations of the mode of presentation in this chapter. First, we have nothing but the view of one character in the novel. The perspective is offered in the form of a monologue which sometimes seems to lose its way in the impenetrable individuality of the person delivering it. Second, even if one can follow these reflections, the very form of the monologue emphasizes the private nature of the ideas expressed, for the interior monologue is a private form of presentation, the ego addressing itself. And, finally, elsewhere in the novel Joyce gives certain indications as to how Stephen's cogitations are to be judged. Much later in the book—352 pages to be precise—in the chapter on the parody of styles (nota bene!), Stephen's introspective searchings are labelled "perverted transcendentalism."[29] Of course, the Joyce reader needs a very good memory (and usually does not have one good enough) to recall all such indications, but even an average, if overburdened, memory will record enough to show that the mode of presentation in the "Proteus" chapter is to be seen only as a facet of, and not as a paradigm for, the presentation of everyday life.

We might add one more reflection on this chapter, and that concerns the Homeric parallel. Joyce called the chapter "Proteus," and we know from the Odyssey that Proteus keeps escaping from Menelaus and transforming himself into different shapes, because he does not want to yield the secret of how Menelaus can best get home. But Menelaus has been warned in advance not to be put off by these changes of form, because it

---

[28] Joyce, Ulysses, p. 45.   [29] Ibid., p. 399.

is his courage that will compel Proteus to give away the vital secret. The transformations brought about by Stephen's thinking are somewhat different. Certainly it seems as though a secret is being kept from him, but in contrast to the Homeric story, he is producing this secret himself. He knows his inescapable restriction to observation, and he knows that things change the moment one observes them. Every approach changes them into something different. And so the "courage" of knowing just what it is that we can see and understand, actually blocks the way to the secret. The act of knowing itself produces the secret of things that change when they are observed. While the Homeric world order enabled Menelaus to learn the secret he coveted, the modern world uses its knowledge to reveal the fact that there *is* a secret—the indeterminate nature of all phenomena. As far as Menelaus is concerned, the knowledge wrested from Proteus leads directly to action; for Stephen, the knowledge that he is bound to his own forms of perception leads to an endless delving into the ultimate constitution of the world.

As it would be beyond the scope of this essay to deal with all the experiments of style in *Ulysses*, we shall confine ourselves to those that evince the most striking variations. One of these is undoubtedly the "Aeolus" chapter, which is especially relevant to our discussion as in many respects it forms a contrast to the "Proteus" chapter. Bloom's visit to the newspaper office provides the framework for a curiously patterned form of narration. Analysis reveals two separate levels of the text, which one might call, for the sake of convenience, the micro- and the macrostructure of the chapter. The microstructural level consists of a large number of allusions which basically can be divided into three different groups: (1) those dealing with the immediate situation, Bloom's effort to place an advertisement at the newspaper office and the events connected with it; (2) those referring to completely different episodes outside the chapter itself, sometimes relating to incidents already described, and sometimes anticipating things; (3) those passages which seem to slide into obscurity when one tries to work out exactly where they might be heading. However, as these allusions are not distinctly separated but are in fact woven into an intricate pattern, each one of them tends to entice the reader to follow it. Thus the allusions themselves turn into microperspectives which, because of their very density, simply cannot be followed through to the end. They form abbreviated extracts from reality which inevitably compel the reader to a process of selection.

This is also true of the other stylistic pattern to be discerned within the microstructural stratum. Just as with the allusions, there is throughout an abrupt alternation between dialogue, direct and indirect speech, authorial report, first-person narrative, and interior monologue. Although such techniques do impose a certain order on the abundance of allusions, they also invest them with differing importance. An allusion by the author himself certainly has a function for the context different from that which is made in direct speech by one of the characters. Thus extracts from reality and individual events are not contracted merely into allusions, but, through the different patterns of style, emerge in forms that endow them with a varied range of relevance. At the same time, the unconnected allusions and the abrupt alternation of stylistic devices disclose a large number of empty spaces.

All this gives rise to the stimulating quality of the text. On the one hand, the density of allusions and the continual segmentation of style involve an incessant changing of perspectives, which seem to go out of control whenever the reader tries to pin them down; on the other hand, the empty spaces resulting from cuts and abbreviations tempt the reader to fill them in. He will try to group things, because this is the only way in which he can recognize situations or understand characters in the novel.

The macrostructure of the chapter lends itself to this need for "grouping," though in a peculiar way. Heading and "newspaper column" form the schema that incorporates the allusions and stylistic changes. The heading is an instruction as to what to expect. But the text which follows the caption reveals the composition described above, and so in most cases does not fulfill the expectation raised by the heading. As the newspaper headlines refer to various incidents in the city, the situation of Ireland, and so forth, they would seem to be concerned with everyday events, the reality of which is beyond question. But the column that follows frustrates this expectation, not only by leading commonplace realities off in unforeseeable directions, thus destroying the grouping effect of the headline, but also by fragmenting facts and occurrences in such a way that to comprehend the commonplace becomes a real effort. While the heading appears to gratify our basic need for grouping, this need is predominantly subverted by the text that follows.

In the "Aeolus" chapter, the reader not only learns something about events in Dublin on June 16th, 1904, but he also experiences the difficulties inherent in the comprehension of the barest outline of events. It is precisely because the heading suggests a way of grouping from a particular viewpoint that the text itself seems so thoroughly to contradict our familiar notions of perception. The text appears to defy transcription of the circumstances indicated and instead offers the reader nothing but attitudes or possibilities of perception concerning these circumstances. In exploiting these possibilities, the reader is stimulated to a form of activity that B. Ritchie, in another context, has described as follows:

"The solution to this paradox is to find some ground for distinction between 'surprise' and 'frustration.' Roughly, the distinction can be made in terms of the effects which the two kinds of experiences have upon us. Frustration blocks or checks activity. It necessitates new orientation for our activity, if we are to escape the *cul de sac*. Consequently, we abandon the frustrating object and return to blind impulsive activity. On the other hand, surprise merely causes a temporary cessation of the exploratory phase of the experience, and a recourse to intense contemplation and scrutiny. In the latter phase the surprising elements are seen in their connection with what has gone before, with the whole drift of the experience, and the enjoyment of these values is then extremely intense . . . any esthetic experience tends to exhibit a continuous interplay between 'deductive' and 'inductive' operations."[30]

Now it does sometimes occur in this chapter that the expectations aroused by the headings are fulfilled. At such moments, the text seems banal,[31] for when the reader has adjusted himself to the non-fulfillment of his expectations, he will view things differently when they *are* fulfilled. The reason for this is easy to grasp. If the text of the column does not connect up with the heading, the reader must supply the missing links. His participation in the intention of the text is thus enhanced. If the text does fulfill the expectations aroused by the heading, no removing of gaps is required of the reader and he feels the "let-down" of banality. In this way, the textual pattern in this chapter arouses continual conflicts with the reader's own modes of perception, and as the author has completely withdrawn from this montage of possibilities, the reader is given no guidance as to how to resolve the conflicts. But it is through these very conflicts, and the confrontation with the array of different possibilities, that the reader of such a text is given the impression that something does happen to him.

It is perhaps not by chance that in this chapter the Homeric parallel has shrunk to the barest recollection, for the basic schema of composition is determined not by the scattering of news to all winds, but by the manner in which this scattered news is received. Joyce makes his theme out of that which did not concern Homer, and this also reveals something of the strategy of literary allusions that Joyce used in *Ulysses*.

A highlight of the experiments in style is the chapter Joyce originally called "Circe"—often designated as "Walpurgis Night." This presents scenes of "nighttown" Dublin in a series of dialogues in dramatic form. The very use of this form automatically precludes any long stretches of

---

[30] B. Ritchie, "The Formal Structure of the Aesthetic Object," in *The Problems of Aesthetics*, ed. E. Vivas and M. Krieger (New York, 1965), pp. 230 f.

[31] See Joyce, *Ulysses*, p. 118.

narrative. If one regards the grouping together of events as a basic element of narrative, it would seem as though here the novel is in fact trying to free itself from this basic condition. Even where there is some narration, it is in the form of stage directions, which deprive it of its real narrative character. However, despite its layout the chapter can scarcely be called a play at all. The monologues, dialogues, stage directions, exits and entrances it consists of, have almost completely lost their dramatic function. The conflicts between the characters end as abruptly as they began, and the cast grows bigger and bigger, for it is not only the characters in the novel that take part in the play—we are also suddenly confronted with Lord Tennyson[32] and Edward VII,[33] the gasjet whistles,[34] the retriever barks,[35] the voices of all the damned and those of all the blessed ring out,[36] and the end of the world—a two-headed octopus—speaks in a Scottish accent.[37]

The unremitting expansion of the cast list is combined with the most extraordinary dialogues. In dramatic dialogue characters generally aim at influencing one another, but here this basic function is carried to extremes. When, at the beginning, Bloom is surrounded by different partners and is confronted with events of the past and present, he assumes the form that is being alluded to.[38] Sometimes this tendency is taken to absurd lengths—as in the scene with Bella Cohen, the whoremistress, when he changes into a woman and creeps timidly under the sofa in order to play a subservient role opposite Bella, who meanwhile has swollen up into a masculine monster.[39] The effect of dramatic dialogue here is so exaggerated that Bloom simply falls into the role assigned to him by his partner. This speedy compliance is not without its problems for the partners either, for Bloom's change of form does not exactly increase their security as regards the process of acting and reacting.

Such scenes show clearly that the dramatic elements are no longer part of any dramatic structure, so that the "play" rapidly divorces itself from its own "genre." While the narrative residue is confined to mere setting of the scene, the dramatic text loses all dramatic teleology. The reader is simply confronted with what is said "on stage," and in view of the erosion both of narrative and dramatic forms here, he will feel that the effects of these dialogues get more and more out of control. Consequently he will be inclined to regard the whole thing as a ridiculous fantasy.

The question is, though, *what* constitutes the fantasy. While the

[32] Joyce, *Ulysses*, p. 555.   [33] *Ibid.*, pp. 557 and 560.   [34] *Ibid.*, pp. 485 and 550.
[35] *Ibid.*, p. 567.   [36] *Ibid.*, p. 565.   [37] *Ibid.*, p. 481.
[38] See, for instance, *ibid.*, pp. 423 f., 433 f.   [39] *Ibid.*, pp. 500 f.

ramifications of the "action" become ever more unpredictable, the figure
of Bloom becomes ever more dominant. And this figure is shown from a
variety of quite astonishing angles. At the very beginning there is a significant, if somewhat indirect, allusion to this process, for the stage direction describes Bloom walking through Dublin in the darkness, and
looking in convex and concave mirrors which continually change his appearance.[40] This is the theme that is developed throughout the chapter.
What Bloom is seems to depend on the perspective from which he is
viewed, and his mirror image depends on his environment at the time. It
is not surprising, then, that in the course of the night Bloom becomes
Lord Mayor of Dublin[41] and, indeed, the illustrious hero of the whole
nation.[42] The beautiful women of Dublin's upper crust go into ecstasies
over him[43] and, in the passion of their hero-worship, many commit
suicide.[44] However, these same women also take part in a court scene,
accusing Bloom of perverse conduct.[45] The question remains open as to
whether Bloom is projecting his own feelings onto the accusers, or is trying to rid himself of these feelings by ascribing them to others. In such
indeterminate situations, all statements are potential revelations of
character. There are innumerable examples of this kind, and if we
wanted to list them all, we should virtually have to retell the whole
chapter.

The basis of this expansion of Bloom appears to consist of two factors,
the one rather more obvious than the other. To deal with the more obvious factor first: in nighttown, everything becomes real for Bloom that is
omitted, concealed, or repressed in his daily life. If these aspects of himself are given the same degree of reality as the others, then his life up to
now will appear in a somewhat different light. Everyday life, it would
seem, has made him into a fragmented character, and only now, in
nighttown, can this character once more take on its full potentiality. An
obvious case, one might assume, for psychoanalysis. But to preclude any
premature analysis, Joyce has already parodied this type of interpretation through the medical student Buck Mulligan, in one of the earlier
scenes of the chapter.[46] It seems, then, that the emergence of Bloom's
hidden selves is not to be viewed as a symptom of repression, or as a way
round the censorship imposed by the superego, but rather as an attempt
to realize the potential of a character which, in everyday life, can never
be anything more than partially realized.

This potential becomes richer and richer with the great variety of
forms that the hitherto familiar character of Bloom adopts. And con-

[40] *Ibid.*, p. 414.   [41] *Ibid.*, pp. 455 f.   [42] *Ibid.*, pp. 460 f.
[43] *Ibid.*, pp. 458 f.   [44] *Ibid.*, pp. 467 f.   [45] *Ibid.*, pp. 443 f.
[46] *Ibid.*, pp. 468 f.

versely, if one wished to identify the Bloom of everyday life, one would be obliged more and more to pare down this rich virtual character. The everyday Bloom is merely a collection of individual moments in the course of his life—a collection which is infinitely smaller than that of the unlimited possibilities of the Bloom that might be. In the "Circe" chapter, it seems as though each Bloom character is simply a starting point for a new character, and he himself is present only as the dynamic force producing, linking, and invalidating manifestations of his own potential.

We must now consider how this indeterminate force is translated into all these determinate, if limited, forms; and the answer lies in the second, less obvious, factor characterizing the "Circe" chapter. Whatever Bloom reveals of himself is revealed because he is in a particular situation; the forms of his character arise out of changing contexts of life, and so each form is bound to a particular perspective—indeed, this is the only way in which the potential can be realized. With each situation, the character is displayed under specific circumstances, and the faster these change and the more impenetrable the sequence of these individual situations, the more abundant will be the array of possibilities through which the character can reveal itself.

We can now see clearly the function of the extraordinary mode of presentation in this chapter. The drastic reduction of narrative and the abandonment of dramatic coherence intensify the isolation of the individual situations. The disconnectedness virtually makes each one an end in itself, and the reality of the chapter consists in the change from one situation, and hence one manifestation of character, to another. This process is supported by the stage directions—the narrative residue—which relegate the reality of the town of Dublin to a mere theatrical setting. When the obtrusive reality of environment has been cancelled out, the character is inevitably abstracted from all outside restrictions and left free to develop its vast array of possibilities.[47] However, if the unreality of a changing character is to be presented as the reality of this chapter, then it is essential that the reader should constantly be prevented from joining up the patterns of the text. And precisely because there are so many patterns in this text, coupled with the particular expectations which each produces, the omission of connecting links gives rise to a greater degree of reader-provocation than is normal even in this highly provocative book. Here we have dramatic forms with no dramatic inten-

---

[47] F. Kermode, *The Sense of an Ending. Studies in the Theory of Fiction* (New York, 1967), p. 141, says with reference to a remark of Sartre's concerning characters in a novel: "The characters . . . ought surely to be 'centres of indeterminacy' and not the slaves of some fake omniscience." In the *Circe* chapter, Bloom's character is revealed most emphatically as a "centre of indeterminacy."

tion; we have narrative traces of an author, but he has concealed himself almost completely behind stage directions that serve no stage and head in no direction. The whole chapter seems to drift on unpredictable tides, and if it is to be brought to anchor, then the only weight heavy and steady enough is that of Bloom's potential character. This, however, seems like some sort of fantastic hallucination, for such a reversal of the possible and the factual simply does not correspond to our own experiences, but "if one were to speak only of experiences with which one coincided, one should no longer speak of anything at all."[48]

If one considers the multifarious potential of Bloom as a fantasy, one is already entering into a kind of trap. For such an impression—bordering on a judgment—implies that one knows all about the difference between reality and possibility. Here such differences are extremely blurred—though whether the ultimate effect of this blurring is to perplex or to illuminate must depend on the reactions of the individual reader. What can be said, though, is that an hallucination arising out of pure nonsense would certainly lack any sort of tension, whereas this chapter can scarcely be described as lacking in tension. The high degree of indeterminacy ensures a variety of tensions which, in their turn, will lead the reader to recall to mind—and possibly to see in a different light—all that he had previously learned about Bloom.

This collection of memories is almost certain to be conjured up as a background to the "Circe" chapter. In them the reader will seek the connecting principle denied him, but, whatever he may find there, every manifestation of Bloom's character prior to the "Circe" chapter is bound now to seem like the faintest shadow of the vast potential. Who, then, is the real Bloom? Is he what is manifested, or is he the possible? At one point Stephen remarks: ". . . the fundamental and the dominant are separated by the greatest possible interval."[49] If we take the fundamental as the potential, and the dominant as the manifestations, we have in a nutshell the "argument" of "Circe." Bloom, unlike the traditional character in a novel, has no identity but only a "constitutive instability"[50] which enables him to change character as often as he changes situation. The only enduring feature of Bloom is his changeability. Against this background, the conventional assumption that man can be defined in terms of actions, reactions, urges, fantasies, and embodiments of consciousness, appears as pure myth.

[48] M. Merleau-Ponty, *Phänomenologie der Wahrnehmung*, German transl. by R. Boehm (Berlin, 1966), p. 388.

[49] Joyce, *Ulysses*, p. 479.

[50] This is the translation of a term used by Ortega y Gasset to describe the given nature of man. See details in Kermode, pp. 140 f., footnote.

There remains the question of the Homeric allusion. Harry Levin's observation that the *Odyssey* and *Ulysses* are parallels "that never meet,"[51] applies to this chapter even more than to most others. While Ulysses' friends were turned into swine by Circe, he himself was able to resist the sorcery, thanks to the magic plant Moly given to him by Hermes. Ulysses remained himself because he was able to resist Circe's witchcraft. Bloom becomes himself by being transformed into the possibilities of his own character. Transformation means reduction in the *Odyssey*, and expansion in *Ulysses*.

Of a quite different sort is the stylistic experiment in the chapter originally called "Ithaca," which is of particular interest since it deals with the theme of homecoming. This archetypal situation is presented here as an uninterrupted sequence of questions and answers involving the main characters. To all appearances this interrogation is conducted by an anonymous narrator, who more or less asks himself what Bloom and Stephen think, do, feel, intend, communicate, mean, etc., and then proceeds, himself, to give answers that are as wide-ranging as they are detailed. But what exactly is the purpose of this inquiry, and why should the narrator be asking all the questions, since he appears to know all the answers anyway?

The effect of the mode of presentation in this chapter is that it seems constantly to place a barrier between the reader and the events of Bloom's nocturnal homecoming that are to be narrated; instead of describing these events, it appears to be continually interrupting them. In this way, the characters in the novel seem to fade into the distance— especially since each question is assigned an answer which is so loaded with precise detail that the reader's comprehension is in danger of being utterly swamped. This tends to divert the reader's attention away from the events and onto the curious nature of this question-and-answer process. For obviously the intention of the chapter must lie in this and not in the details of the nocturnal events. But if the mode of presentation sets aside rather than describes the events, and obtrudes on the reader instead of orienting him, then the only justification for this "going against the grain" must be that it exposes something which generally would be obscured by the mode of presentation.

Let us examine an example. When Bloom comes home, he puts some water on the stove because he wants to have a shave. The question and answer process now concerns the boiling of the water:

"What concomitant phenomenon took place in the vessel of liquid by the agency of fire?

[51] H. Levin, *James Joyce. A Critical Introduction* (New York, ²1960), p. 71.

"The phenomenon of ebullition. Fanned by a constant updraught of ventilation between the kitchen and the chimneyflue, ignition was communicated from the faggots of precombustible fuel to polyhedral masses of bituminous coal, containing in compressed mineral form the foliated fossilised decidua of primeval forests which had in turn derived their vegetative existence from the sun, primal source of heat (radiant), transmitted through omnipresent luminiferous diathermanous ether. Heat (convected), a mode of motion developed by such combustion, was constantly and increasingly conveyed from the source of calorification to the liquid contained in the vessel, being radiated through the uneven unpolished dark surface of the metal iron, in part reflected, in part absorbed, in part transmitted, gradually raising the temperature of the water from normal to boiling point, a rise in temperature expressible as the result of an expenditure of 72 thermal units needed to raise 1 pound of water from 50° to 212° Fahrenheit."[52]

The amount of scientific data—in this chapter a typical feature which becomes even more complicated elsewhere—shows how difficult it is to give the required reason for the phenomenon in question.

An impression akin to fantasy is evoked by the chain of cause and effect which, instead of going straight back to the primal cause, seems only to bring out more and more dependent factors. The more precise the description of these factors, the further into the distance recedes the primal cause and the more aware we become of the unexplainability of what is to be explained. As the narrator asks more and more questions, the answers demonstrate not his knowledge so much as the unobtainability of the right answer—and this is emphasized by the very preciseness of what *is* known. Thus the tendency underlying this question-and-answer process is one that aims at showing the degree of indeterminability inherent in all phenomena. It is scarcely surprising then that new questions are constantly thrown up which are meant to limit the amount of indeterminacy, but instead—thanks to their very precision—in fact increase it.

One's immediate reaction to the mass of scientific detail offered in answer to often quite banal questions is bewilderment. And this is so because a simple process is given a precise description. Obviously, then, our normal conception of such processes must be less precise and consequently seems to be straightforward. Why should it be made complicated? Perhaps in order to show the extent to which our knowledge and our decisions are based primarily on pragmatic considerations? However, it is only in this way that we can in fact form conceptions of every-

[52] Joyce, *Ulysses*, p. 634.

day phenomena. The question-and-answer process makes us aware that the degree of indeterminacy is irreducible, thus indicating that all the semi-consistent conceptions we have of everyday phenomena can only become conceptions because they ignore the unexplainability of reality. They are, in this sense, a fiction.

Now if indeterminacy is to be removed only by means of fiction, the reader finds the ground cut away from beneath his feet whenever he realizes this. The "Ithaca" chapter keeps maneuvering him into a position he can escape from only by taking up a definite attitude. He might decide that the chain of ironic answers forms a parody of scientific pedantry. But, as Northrop Frye states in another context, the ironic solution is: ". . . the negative pole of the allegorical one. Irony presents a human conflict which . . . is unsatisfactory and incomplete unless we see in it a significance beyond itself. . . . What that significance is, irony does not say: it leaves that question up to the reader or audience."[53] This is the sort of irony we find in the "Ithaca" chapter, which uses its ironic elements to give the reader responsibility for finding his own solution. This, of course, involves interpreting, and in order to ensure that interpretation be kept in its proper perspective, certain warning signals are built into the text. To the question: "What qualifying considerations allayed his (i.e., Bloom's) perturbations?" comes the answer: "The difficulties of interpretation since the significance of any event followed its occurrence as variably as the acoustic report followed the electrical discharge and of counterestimating against an actual loss by failure to interpret the total sum of possible losses proceeding originally from a successful interpretation."[54]

The main problem of interpretation, then, lies in the fact that the meaning of any one event is incalculably variable. The image of the electrical discharge, which disperses its sound waves in all directions, shows that every event, as soon as it happens, sets up a whole spectrum of meanings. If we try to extract one of these meanings and pass it off as *the* meaning of the event, then automatically we are shutting out all the other meanings.

Normally we understand by a successful interpretation one that conveys a specific meaning. But, according to the answer given here, an interpretation can be successful only if it takes into account the "possible losses" caused by interpretation—in other words, if it succeeds in returning to the phenomenon interpreted its whole spectrum of possible meanings. And this, as the answer makes clear, is difficult.

[53] N. Frye, "The Road of Excess," in *Myth and Symbol. Critical Approaches and Applications*, ed. B. Slote (Lincoln, ²1964), p. 14.

[54] Joyce, *Ulysses*, p. 637.

Meanings have a heuristic character which, particularly in these scientifically couched answers, bring out the many-sidedness of the phenomena described. In such a description, the phenomena will appear all the richer in meaning if no one meaning dominates. In the "Ithaca" chapter, aspects are not static but seem to be moving, offering an infinitely wider range of perspectives than could be offered if the author were merely to present the reader with his own classified interpretation of the phenomenon. And, however confused the reader may feel through this bewildering multiplicity, at least he now has the chance of experiencing for himself something of the essential character of the phenomena. The heightened indeterminacy enables him to view so many different aspects from so many different standpoints, and from the interaction of these aspects and perspectives he himself continually and dynamically formulates the meaning. In this way it is possible for the reader to experience the phenomenon more as itself than as the expression of something else.

Joyce called this chapter "Ithaca." But what sort of homecoming is this? For Ulysses it meant the end of his adventurous journey, with all its attendant dangers and sufferings, and also his reckoning with the suitors; but for Bloom the homecoming passes with innumerable trivial acts, and a fantastic, if impotent, condemnation of all Molly's lovers. No one is excepted from this universal anathema; it applies ultimately to marriage as an institution and even to Bloom himself. "What then remains after this holocaust? Only himself with his desires—not as husband or householder but as Leopold Bloom, an Einziger with no Eigentum."[55] Yet again, then, we have in the Homeric allusion a parallel which, if anything, runs in the opposite direction from the original, showing up the individuality of Bloom against the background of what the reader might expect from the archetypal homecoming.

The stylistic experiments of *Ulysses* end with Molly Bloom's much discussed interior monologue, which has the difficult task of bringing to an end an action which essentially cannot be ended. Here the old familiar problem of how a novel is to end appears in its most radical form. The end cannot be presented as a completion, for whose completion should it denote? The conventional rounding off is clearly impossible here, and so, too, is its companion piece, the slow fade-out: for after what the experiments have revealed, this would be nothing but a sign of resignation and, in the long run, a meaning grafted on. Joyce had resolved that he would finish the novel with the word "Yes,"[56] and whatever feelings one may have about this intention, the tenor of the whole is one of

---

[55] F. Budgen, *James Joyce and the Making of Ulysses* (Bloomington, 1960), p. 261.

[56] See S. Gilbert, *James Joyce's Ulysses* (New York, ⁷1960), p. 403, and also a statement of Joyce's quoted by Litz, p. 46.

affirmation. Thus the end had to incorporate the movement of the novel as a whole, enabling the reader to forget that it *was* the end.

Molly Bloom, as the Penelope of *Ulysses*, closes an action that began with Telemachus. It is not only in this external sense that we have a movement doubling back on itself; the interior monologue also shows how a return to memory becomes a new present. The total lack of punctuation suggests a continuum. The ego is united with itself, addressing to itself its own remembered past, and from this world of private reference, the reader is to a large extent excluded. To him, this ego appears less as a continuum than as a kaleidoscopic juggling of fragmentary facets. The framework of the monologue is given by a number of external details. Molly notes that Bloom has come home, has obviously brought someone with him, and finally goes to bed. The alarm clock tells her the time, and in the pale light of early morning she sees the flowers on the wallpaper, which remind her of stars.[57] The external impulses keep losing themselves in the memories they evoke, and these in turn broaden out into events that have *not* taken place. The present of this nocturnal hour is also overshadowed by a different present, and yet remembered past and existing present are not confronted one with the other; instead, what is remembered actually becomes the present simply because it has been freed from the conditions that originally called it into being. It takes on an existence of its own. But, in contrast to its original state, the past now is liberated from all restrictions of time and space, and so situations flow into one another elliptically, regaining the openness of outcome which they had been deprived of long ago in the past.

Here, then, we have the first characteristic of the monologue. Not only does it bring back past life, but it also frees this from its past determinacy. Individual situations which had formed links in the chain of the course of life now become open again, once more assuming their inherent richness of potential. The monologue eradicates the teleology of this course of life. It does not convey past and present in the style of an autobiography that is to deliver the meaning of the life concerned, but it shows that the life concerned is like a chain of coincidences if one bears in mind all the possibilities that were inherent in the situations before they became linked together. Once they are released from their specific life-order, situations can be seen through the perspectives of other situations which, through limitations of time and space in "real" life, had not even the remotest connection. Thus the past remembered suggests completely new combinations, and Molly's own life comes back to her with a surplus of possibilities which can at least give the illusion of a different life-order.

[57] See Joyce, *Ulysses*, p. 740.

Like the other stylistic patterns in *Ulysses*, the interior monologue
here breaks situations into fragments, and withholds from the reader
any principle that might bind them together. In view of this disconnectedness, all events of the past, all future wishes, all lost opportunities are
placed on the same level, so that Molly's life, as she recalls it, appears to
be in a constant state of transformation. But what is transformed into
what? Normally in a novel we are able to define the changes and to hold
onto the similarities as our connecting points, but here there seems only
to be perplexity. If the remembered past were brought back as a sort of
compensation for frustrated desires, then the reader could be oriented to
Molly's memories—through her particular situation at this particular
hour of the night. And if it were a matter of returning to that stage in
the past where it was still an unresolved present, then we should have a
constant unwinding of retrospective possibilities—like a film being run
backwards. But neither of these standpoints is clearly discernible in Molly's monologue. She does not seem to be looking back at the past from
the standpoint of the present, or to be returning to the past in order to
gaze at her situation at five o'clock this morning. As a person, in fact,
she seems to disappear behind the richness of her own life. The more
indeterminate her character threatens to become, the more dynamic is
the impression we have of her life: dynamic, because the reader is confronted with more and more viewpoints to which the individual facets
are to be related, or into which they can be transformed. As the
monologue does not accentuate any one organizing principle behind all
the transformations, these convey an impression of continual expansion—and indeed suggest the inexhaustibility of the past—precisely because there is no point of convergence. The reader finds himself constantly driven by the urge to group things together, to unravel the
tangle, but any attempt to do so will tend to reflect his own personal
preferences rather than any supposed "objective" meaning. But perhaps
the meaning is the reflection of these preferences.

There remains the question of the Homeric parallel. With the past returning into the present, and the present releasing the past from its determinacy, there arises the idea of the recurrent cycle. Molly would then
be even more than Penelope—she would be Mother Earth herself. But
her monologue by no means fulfills the conditions of the mythic cycle. It
lacks that essential element—the fact that when things have passed
through all the different stages and forms of their realization, they return once more to themselves. It is true that at the end Molly returns to
the point where she began—she recalls the first love scene with
Bloom—but even the recollected love scenes in this monologue are far
more like serial variations than a cyclic return. Molly cannot be reduced

to any of her aspects, or even to her love-memories. Nowhere does her *whole* being come to light, but it is this very emerging of aspects that brings out the driving force which constitutes the *inner* being. And it is only fitting that the interior monologue should end the novel in a form which sets a life free from all the restrictions of—precisely—its form.

III
The Function of the Experiments in Style

The implication of a novel written in several different styles is that the view expressed by each style is to be taken as only one possible facet of everyday reality. The accumulation of facets has the effect of making these seem like a mere suggestion to the reader as to how he might observe reality. The perspectives provided by the various chapters of the novel abruptly join up, overlap, are segmented, even clash, and through their very density they begin to overtax the reader's vision. The density of the presentational screen, the confusing montage and its interplay of perspectives, the invitation to the reader to look at identical incidents from many conflicting points of view—all this makes it extremely difficult for the reader to find his way. The novel refuses to divulge any way of connecting up this interplay of perspectives, and so the reader is forced to provide his own liaison. This has the inevitable consequence that reading becomes a process of selection, with the reader's own imagination providing the criteria for the selection. For the text of *Ulysses* only offers the conditions that make it possible to conceive of this everyday world—conditions which each reader will exploit in his own way.

What does the achievement of the various modes of presentation consist of? First, one can say that they bring to bear a form of observation which underlies the very structure of perception. For we "have the experience of a world, not understood as a system of relations which wholly determine each event, but as an open totality the synthesis of which is inexhaustible. . . . From the moment that experience—that is, the opening on to our *de facto* world—is recognized as the beginning of knowledge, there is no longer any way of distinguishing a level of *a priori* truths and one of factual ones, what the world must necessarily be and what it actually is."[58] Through their countless offshoots, the different styles of *Ulysses* preclude any meaning directed toward integration, but they also fall into a pattern of observation that contains within itself the possibility of a continual extension. It is the very abundance of perspectives that conveys the abundance of the world under observation.

[58] M. Merleau-Ponty, *Phenomenology of Perception*, trans. Colin Smith (New York, 1962), pp. 219 and 221.

The effect of this continual change is dynamic, unbounded as it is by any recognizable teleology. From one chapter to the next the "horizon" of everyday life is altered and constantly shifted from one area to another through the links which the reader tries to establish between the chapter styles. Each chapter prepares the "horizon" for the next, and it is the process of reading that provides the continual overlapping and interweaving of the views presented by each of the chapters. The reader is stimulated into filling the "empty spaces" between the chapters in order to group them into a coherent whole. This process, however, has the following results: The conceptions of everyday life which the reader forms undergo constant modifications in the reading process. Each chapter provides a certain amount of expectation concerning the next chapter. The gaps of indeterminacy, however, which open up between the chapters tend to diminish the importance of these expectations as a means of orienting the reader. As the process continues, a "feedback" effect is bound to develop, arising from the new chapter and reacting back upon the preceding one, which under this new and somewhat unexpected impression is subjected to modifications in the reader's mind. The more frequently the reader experiences this effect, the more cautious and the more differentiated will be his expectations, as they arise through his realization of the text. Thus what has just been read modifies what had been read before, so that the reader himself operates the "fusion of the horizons," with the result that he produces an experience of reality which is real precisely because it happens, without being subjected to any representational function. Reality, then, is a process of realization necessitating the reader's involvement, because only the reader can bring it about. This is why the chapters are not arranged in any sequence of situations that might be complementary to one another; in fact, the unforeseen difference of style rather seems to make each chapter into a turning point as opposed to a continuation. And as the whole novel consists of such turning points the process of reading unfolds itself as a continual modification of all previous conceptions, thus inverting the traditional teleological structure of the novel.

IV

The Archetypes

What part do the Homeric allusions play in the overall effect of the work? Do they, or do the archetypes recognizable in *Ulysses*, offer a means of comprehending the novel and ultimately giving it a representative meaning after all? It must be said that the intention underlying the stylistic experiments does not seem to point in that direction. The Homeric allusions vary in density and directness. It is worth noting that

they always take on an ironic note when they are clear and direct;
Bloom's cigar as Ulysses' spear is a typical example.[59] Such ironic traits
draw attention to differences, and however these may be interpreted
they are bound to prevent us from equating *Ulysses* with the Homeric
parallel. At the same time, the allusions—assuming we take note of
them in the first place—draw the archaic world into the everyday life of
the novel, though the outline of the ancient story cannot be regarded as
encompassing this life.

We might say that the main function of the allusions is to draw attention to the virtual features of the two worlds. At times the Homeric
myth is even inverted, with the episodes from the *Odyssey* to be understood as pointers to specific empirical or everyday aspects of life. Everyday appearances are not to be referred back to some underlying meaning; we proceed from the myth and its meaning, and see the variety of
appearances into which it can be broken up. Things which remain implicit or even totally concealed in the *Odyssey* are revealed in *Ulysses*,
and the change of perspective—from Homer to the present, and from
the present back to the archaic world—enables both past and present to
illuminate one another.

Through the allusions is projected a background that embraces the
whole of European literature from Homer to Shakespeare. The reader is
provoked into a process of recognition, for recognition, like grouping, is
part of his natural disposition and is an elementary activity in reading.
As he recognizes the implications of the allusions, he tries to equate
them with the events now being set before him, but he finds that they do
not actually coincide. There is just enough common ground to make him
aware of the differences, and the process of equating and differentiating
is one that will be both disturbing and stimulating.

If *Ulysses* does not hark back to the *Odyssey*, and Joyce does not—so
to speak—rise out of Homer, then the various transformations which
the reader feels constantly forced to experience will not cease with the
establishment of a common pattern. As we have already seen, the whole
structure and stylistic texture of the novel is geared to such transformations, and a common pattern of whatever type would run counter to its
basic intentions. The allusions offer a background which, in its own way,
remains as fluid as the foreground it sets off, and this very fluidity is the
fundamental prerequisite for the effect of the novel.

What of the archetypes themselves? To what extent can they be described as elements of a recurrent myth? The homecoming, the city and

---

[59] For such parallels, see R. Ellmann, "The Divine Nobody," in *Twelve Original Essays on Great English Novelists*, ed. Ch. Shapiro (Detroit, 1960), pp. 244 f., esp. 247.

the quest[60]—these are three archetypes which constitute an important structural pattern in the novel and which make *Ulysses* into a sort of glorified epic (the city being a considerably rarer archetypal ingredient of epic literature). In fact, the closest link between *Ulysses* and the *Odyssey* is the homecoming, although Bloom's homecoming does, of course, take place within the city. The quest already shows external differences, insofar as Telemachus searched for his father, while Bloom searches for his son. In the *Odyssey* there is no equivalent to the city as "new Bloomusalem."[61] If we consider the closest link—the homecoming—we will find, just as we did with the direct Homeric allusions, that the similarities serve in fact to point up the differences. For Ulysses the homecoming means the end of his sufferings, whereas for Bloom— the "conscious reactor against the void incertitude,"[62] as he is called in the "Ithaca" chapter—it brings nothing but a heightened sensitivity to the unforeseeable; even more significantly, there is no recognizable parallel anywhere in the novel between characters or archetypal situations. But since the title indicates a connection, we automatically become aware of the differences.

If one looks at Bloom against the background of Ulysses, one is immediately struck by two things: the difference in stature between the humble citizen of Dublin and the Homeric hero, and the many features of Bloom's conduct that either go beyond or fall short of what we know of Ulysses' character. Bearing in mind that Joyce considered Ulysses himself to be the most comprehensive specimen of human conduct,[63] one must also say that Bloom adds a few variants of his own to this "perfection"—though of course without ever becoming more "perfect" than Ulysses. Clearly, Bloom lacks most of Ulysses' characteristics, and vice versa, but however far Bloom may fall below the exalted standards of the Homeric hero, the very allusion of the title makes us think of Bloom as a Ulysses, and so offsets those elements of the character which prevailing conventions prevented Homer from dealing with. Human conduct in Homer appears rigidly stylized against that of the everyday Dubliner, while Bloom's conduct (and that of the other characters, too) is as fluid as the other is rigid. And so it would seem that the Homeric parallel is drawn, not to demonstrate the hopeless decline of the modern world compared with its former state, but to communicate the enormous variety of possibilities of human conduct. By evoking and simultaneously deforming archetypal patterns, Joyce succeeds in conveying and throwing into relief the uniqueness of Bloom as a citizen of the modern world.

[60] See N. Frye, *Anatomy of Criticism*, pp. 118 f. and 141.
[61] Joyce, *Ulysses*, p. 461.   [62] *Ibid.*, p. 694.
[63] See R. Ellmann, *Joyce*, p. 430.

The Homeric archetype provides a starting point for this individualization of Joyce's Ulysses (i.e., Bloom). Just as a cartoonist takes an existing face and then distorts its features in order to bring out its uniqueness, so, too, does Joyce (though obviously in a far less obtrusive manner) take an existing form and manipulate it this way and that in order to convey its singularity. Indeed, it is the very fact that Bloom *can* be pulled and pushed in this way that sets him apart from the ideality of Ulysses and makes him recognizable as an individual human being, with all the complications and uncertainties. The archetype is the general mould; the form Joyce extracts from that mould is the unique character of Bloom.

There is, then, a form of interaction between the Homeric archetype and its modern counterpart. As Joyce evolves constantly changing patterns from the former, so Ulysses' reactions assume a paradigmatic character, and the homecoming, for instance, is transformed into an "ideal" homecoming. However, one must bear in mind the fact that the "archetype"[64] does not exist in itself, but must be brought into existence by a realization. It is, so to speak, an empty frame that requires the concrete powers of style and language to provide the picture. The archetype, then, can take on as many forms as there are forms of presentation, so that we cannot really say even that the homecoming in the *Odyssey* is *the* archetype. It is only one rendering among many possible renderings, and in the light of all the variations apparent in the novel, it becomes retrospectively as restricted as they are. The archetype as such remains a structured blank that bears all potential realizations within itself, and provides the basis for all its own subsequent variations.

Clearly, if archetypal situations are potentially subject to so many different presentations, then no one presentation can claim representative significance. For this insight, again we are indebted to the Homeric parallel: by reducing the *Odyssey* homecoming to the level of one idealized realization, *Ulysses* shows all its limitations—and the same applies to the other archetypes of city and quest. Dublin is no heavenly Jerusalem, but as "Bloomusalem"[65] it is the place of exile of one of the unredeemed; the quest is characterized by the uncertainty of what is found, for although Bloom and Stephen finish under one roof, Molly's thoughts are already on relations with the young "intellectual,"[66]

---

[64] N. Frye has a very different conception of the archetype. The most succinct definition I could find in his writings is in the essay "The Archetypes of Literature," which is reprinted in his collection of essays: *Fables of Identity. Studies in Poetic Mythology* (New York, 1963). "The myth is the central informing power that gives archetypal significance to the ritual and archetypal narrative to the oracle. Hence the myth *is* the archetype, though it might be convenient to say myth only when referring to narrative, and archetype when speaking of significance" (p. 15).

[65] See Joyce, *Ulysses*, p. 461.   [66] See also Gilbert, pp. 386 and 394.

Bloom's son. In each case, the recurrent archetypal situation lacks the expected archetypal fulfillment—it is left open-ended.

The function of the archetype in relation to the presentational strategy of the novel is, then, to offer a kind of framework. Homecoming, city, and quest are the frames within which the picture of everyday life can be put together. This, of course, does not mean that the composition is determined by the frame. The mode of presentation ensures that the countless literary and historical allusions will not be marshalled into a single cut-and-dried meaning—not for the sake of making the allusions appear meaningless, but purely in order to preserve the infinite *potential* of their meaning.

V
The Reader's Quest and the Formation of Illusion

If the archetypes provide the action with a frame, the different styles and allusions to literature, both ancient and modern, give the reader more than enough scope to piece together his own picture. David Daiches has observed that: "If Joyce could coin one kaleidoscopic word with an infinite series of meanings, a word saying everything in one instant yet leaving its infinity of meanings, reverberating and mingling in the mind, he would have reached his ideal."[67] Certainly this is the direction in which Joyce was striving, and as the limitations of each separate meaning are uncovered, giving rise to new meanings, so the reader is made to feel the overall inaccessibility of the events and characters in question. Any presentation implies selection, and any selection implies omission. Here the omissions lead to new selections in the form of new styles, but as the styles and selections increase, so does the range of implication and omission. The more determinate the presentation, the more "reality" there is to catch up on, but in his very efforts to catch up, the reader produces in himself the awareness that the world he is trying to comprehend transcends the acts of comprehension of which he is capable.

The composition of *Ulysses* mirrors this impression. Edmund Wilson has summed up both the reader's impression and the structure of the novel as follows: "I doubt whether any human memory is capable, on a first reading, of meeting the demands of 'Ulysses.' And when we reread it, we start in at any point, as if it were indeed something solid like a city which actually existed in space and which could be entered from any direction."[68] The reader is virtually free to choose his own direction, but he will not be able to work his way through every possible perspective,

[67] D. Daiches, *The Novel and the Modern World* (Chicago, ⁴1965), p. 129.
[68] E. Wilson, *Axel's Castle. A Study in the Imaginative Literature of 1870-1930* (London: The Fontana Library, 1961), p. 169.

for the number of these is far beyond the capacity of any one man's naturally selective perception. If the novel sometimes gives the impression of unreality, this is not because it presents unreality, but simply because it swamps us with aspects of reality that overburden our limited powers of absorption. We are forced to make our own selections from the perspectives offered and consequently, in accordance with our own personal disposition, to formulate ideas that have their roots in *some* of the signs and situations confronting us.

This form of reading is predetermined by the novel itself, with its network of superimposed patterns that evoke constantly changing "pictures" of everyday life. Each reading is a starting-point for the composition of such "pictures," and indeed the whole process of reading *Ulysses* is a kind of composition. (The same, it is true, can be said of all reading, but in the case of this novel the demands made on the reader's creativity are far greater than normal.) No one picture is representative, and one cannot even say that any one pattern is in itself determinate or determinant, for the different sections of the text only go so far as to offer signs that can be grouped together to form a context. The patterns are, as it were, transitory units which are necessary if everyday life is to be experienced, but are in no way binding as to the nature of the experience.

Each "picture" composed out of each pattern represents one possible meaning of the text concerned, but the reader will not be content to accept each "picture" as an end in itself. He will search for a "complete picture" of everyday life, and this is precisely what the novel withholds from him. The patterns offer him nothing but the conditions for and variations of the presentability of everyday life. There is no overriding tendency, and the mass of details presents itself to the reader to organize in accordance with his own acts of comprehension. This, in turn, demands a heightened degree of participation on the reader's part. The novel thus places itself in the category of "cool media,"[69] as McLuhan called those texts and other media which, through their indeterminacy, allow and even demand a high degree of participation.

Herein lies the main difference between *Ulysses* and the tradition of the novel. Instead of providing an illusory coherence of the reality it presents, this novel offers only a potential presentation, the working out of which has to be done actively by the reader. He is not led into a ready-made world of meaning, but is made to search for this world. Thus reading itself has an archetypal structure which, just like the archetypes in the text, is unable to lead to any defined goal. It is a quest which brings to the surface the possibility of any number of findings.

[69] See M. McLuhan, *Understanding Media. The Extensions of Man* (New York, ³1966), pp. 22 f.

Thus it is possible to discover many different "pictures" of the everyday world, but they will never converge into a defined picture—and it is this very fact that compels the reader to continue his search. Even though he will never find the object of this search, on his way he will meet with a vast array of possible conceptions, through which the reality of everyday life will come alive in a corresponding number of ways. As these conceptions are not joined together, every picture remains representative of no more than one aspect of reality. The reading process unfolds as a "categorical aspection,"[70] in the sense that the aspects of reality that group together into a "picture" are continually merging and diverging, so that the reader can experience that reality as he goes along, but being thus entangled in it, he can never hope to encompass it all.

The reader, however, will still be continually tempted to try and establish some consistency in all the signs, patterns, fragments, etc. But whenever we establish consistency, "illusion takes over."[71] "Illusion is whatever is fixed or definable, and reality is at best understood as its negation: whatever reality is, it's not *that*."[72] The truth of this statement becomes apparent as one reads *Ulysses*. At first the inconsistency of the stylistic patterns and structures impels the reader to formulate illusions, because only by joining things together can he comprehend an unfamiliar experience. But even while he is in the process of linking things up, he is bringing into being all the other possibilities of the text that defy integration; and these in turn proceed to overshadow the consistency he had begun to establish, so that in the process of illusion-forming the reader also creates the latent destruction of those very illusions. He will begin to distrust the convenient patterns he has been building, and will eventually himself perceive that they are nothing but the instruments he uses to grasp and pare down the mass of detail. Now the very fact that it is *he* who produces and destroys the illusions makes it impossible for him to stand aside and view "reality" from a distance—the only reality for him to view is the one he is creating. He is involved in it, in precisely the same way that he gets involved in "real life" situations. Thus for many Joyce readers, "interpretation" is a form of refuge-seeking—an effort to reclaim the ground which has been cut from under their feet. Perhaps Bloom's attempts to instruct his wife contain the most succinct summary of Joyce's whole method:

"With what success had he attempted direct instruction? She followed not all, a part of the whole, gave attention with interest, comprehended

---

[70] For the use of this term in describing esthetic objects, see V. C. Aldrich, *Philosophy of Art* (Englewood Cliffs, 1963), pp. 21-24.

[71] E. H. Gombrich, *Art and Illusion* (London, ²1962), p. 278.

[72] Frye, *Anatomy of Criticism*, pp. 169 f.

with surprise, with care repeated, with greater difficulty remembered, forgot with ease, with misgiving remembered, rerepeated with error.

"What system had proved more effective?

"Indirect suggestion implicating self-interest."[73]

[73] Joyce, *Ulysses*, pp. 647 f.

JURIJ STRIEDTER

The "New Myth" of Revolution—A Study of Mayakovsky's Early Poetry

In wild destruction
Sweeping away the old
We will thunder out into the world
A new myth.
(MW. II, 125, l. 355 seq.)[1]

IN these lines from Vladimir Mayakovsky's revolutionary poem *150,000,000* (1919/20), revolutionary action is linked to the demand for a "new myth"; out of them arises the question of the extent to which revolution can be mythicized, the relation of the old myth to the new, and the function of poetry in the creation of new myths. A full discussion of these questions, either in general or in relation to Mayakovsky's poetry, would be far beyond the scope of this essay, but we shall attempt to provide a basis for such discussion by outlining certain facets of the subject, with concrete reference to some of Mayakovsky's early poems.

I

Mayakovsky's cry for a "new myth" harks back indirectly to the Romantics' discussion of myths, and directly to Nietzsche's demand for "new myths." The introduction of this term brought the myth discussion to life, and also complicated it.[2] It did, however, show that where "late horizons" of myth are under discussion, a difference has to be made between: (a) the adoption and reshaping of particular motifs, techniques, and structures of traditional myths in fulfillment of non-mythical intentions, dispensing with a "mythical view of life," and (b)

[1] Quotations from Vladimir Mayakosvky, *Polnoe sobranie sočinenij* (MW.), 13 vols. (Moscow, 1955 seq.)

[2] Cf. for a Marxist viewpoint with emphasis on the German tradition: R. Weimann, "Literaturwissenschaft und Mythologie. Vorfragen einer methodologischen Kritik," in *Sinn und Form*, 19th year, vol. 2 (Berlin, 1967), pp. 484 seq. The variety and contradictions of modern western myth-definitions, problems, and research methods can be seen from such introductory anthologies as: *Myth. A Symposium*, ed. T. Sebeok (Bloomington and London, 1958), esp. the contribution by Lévi-Strauss, and *Myth and Method*, ed. J. Miller Jr. (Lincoln, 1960), esp. the contributions by R. Chase and N. Frye. See also J. B. Vickery, *Myth and Literature. Contemporary Theory and Praxis* (Lincoln, 1966).

the intention of reviving this "mythical view of life" and creating "new myths," either through recourse to the tradition of myth, or with the aid of new themes and new techniques of mythicizing.

As it is far easier to limit and to analyze the first of these two fields of study, the literary historian is tempted to confine himself solely to it. But, for various reasons, such a self-imposed restriction can raise its own problems. First, in the literature of the nineteenth and twentieth centuries, the second trend has been at least as significant as the first. Second, outside the purely literary sphere, the second trend has been and still is extraordinarily productive. And, third, there is such a close interaction between the two that even a deliberately non-mythical, purely esthetic re-shaping of ancient myths can be properly judged only from the standpoint of production and—especially—response, in relation to the simultaneous effectiveness of "new myths." Allusion to traditional myths, which in a truly unmythical age and environment *can* be made and perceived as a purely esthetic effect, takes on completely different connotations in a situation shaped by "new myths"—either as poetry that fosters a general tendency towards mythicizing, or alternatively, as poetry which through its very fictitiousness unmasks the myth as a fiction, ironically debases it, or destroys it in some other way.

The actual choice of material, the preference for particular myths, myth traditions (e.g., classical, or biblical), the ways in which myths are passed on (e.g., as holy scripture, or as epic poetry)—these are all conditioned by whichever of the two trends predominates. If, from a purely esthetic standpoint and with a purely esthetic intention, a poet turns to a particular myth, the fact that this myth is no longer believed in will be to his advantage. For, as far as the material is concerned, the poet and his reader are freed from all non-esthetic considerations, and so their familiarity with the material can be used for purely esthetic purposes without offending against its "sanctity." In this way knowledge of the originally mythical nature of the material can be used for additional esthetic effect, perhaps through deviation from the old, known motivations behind the myths; the fact that the ancient myth can be viewed as a fiction, but as a creative fiction interpreting the world and once believed in as an interpretation, can be productively exploited for poetry in its guise as an interpretation of the world. This is one significant reason for the attraction and fecundity of the ancient myth in western poetry and fiction. One important factor is that the Greek myth itself—or at least its classical translation into epic and drama—maintained a greater esthetic distance and allowed a far wider scope for variation than did other more rigid ritual or religious myths. When the Christian religion excluded all non-Christian tenets while allowing the ancient myths to survive as fictions, classical mythology for the "Christian West" became an inexhaustible treasure-house for the estheticizing of the mythical and the mythicizing of the esthetic.

For the creators and defenders of "new myths," the situation is different. Since they are concerned with a revival of the mythical view of life, they are eager to make connections where myths are still believed or where there are mythical elements in the faith of the particular society. This link can be made by borrowing individual features or whole structures that enable the inherent religious possibilities to be taken over and set in a new context to fulfill new intentions. But it can also come about by the "new myth" directly challenging the "old," whose claim to credibility is disputed and conferred only on the "new myth." Particularly in this second case, but often in the first as well, one can reasonably talk of "usurpation," since this is not a matter of a "vacant space" being occupied, but of a directly or indirectly "occupied" space being taken over.

Nietzsche, regardless of his classical education and his embodiment of the Apollonian and Dionysian, as creator of "new myths" usurped the name Zarathustra, founder of a religion, and defied Christ, founder of a religion, thus playing to the full his role of provocator and usurper. And Mayakovsky, who in his very first poem calls himself "the scream-lipped Zarathustra of the present day" (MW. I, 184, l. 307), constantly usurps the figure of Christ, both for his new revolutionary myth and for himself, as the poetic harbinger of the revolution.

This allusion to the link between the German "new Zarathustra" of the nineteenth century and the Russian of the twentieth is worth making insofar as the striking preference for Christian motifs and ideas, together with the almost total lack of classical mythology in Mayakovsky's pre-revolutionary works, suggests certain specifically Russian premises. Through Russia's link with East Roman-Byzantine—as opposed to West Roman—tradition and through the correspondingly oriented, centuries-old dominance of the orthodox church in almost all spheres of culture, the heritage of classical antiquity played a far smaller part in Russia than it did in Roman Catholic regions, including those that were later to become Protestant. The Christian tradition was thus all the livelier, both as a religious and as a cultural factor. In view of this, reference to Christian ideas was bound to be infinitely more effective than evocations of classical mythology. This, of course, applies also to Mayakovsky. But with him, as with all Russian poets, it would be wrong to explain this preference for Christianity over antiquity as merely the result of tradition, without first taking into account the fact that this tradition only comes into play when a particular intention is involved. For classical mythology in the West, too, had long been nothing but an article of

education and not of faith, so that "piety" could again best be evoked
through recourse to Christianity (either by adopting it or by opposing
it); and also in Russia, too, there had of course been classically educated
and esthetically cultured circles before the twentieth century. And so if a
Russian poet's "mytho-poetic" experiments were conducted primarily
for esthetic effects, and if he was satisfied with a relatively small circle of
the initiated or aspired to some sort of esotericism, then just like his
western counterpart he would find a native audience that would know
how to evaluate his poetic reshaping of classical myths. As examples
contemporary with Mayakovsky, it is sufficient to quote the names of
the symbolist Vjačeslav Ivanov and the non-symbolist Osip Mandel'-
štam, who used such a vast amount of classical material that many of
their verses are practically incomprehensible unless one has a thorough
knowledge of classical mythology. But they were concerned just with a
relatively small circle of the esthetically initiated. Only when the poet
sought a wider sphere of influence did he find that the specific cultural
tradition of Russia made classical mythology unsuitable as a frame of
reference, whereas Christian myths and models offered ideal points of
contact, regardless of whether he himself was a practicing Christian, ag-
nostic, or atheist. The question might well be asked as to whether this in
fact was a specifically Russian phenomenon. For all the differences between Russia and Germany, it is worth considering whether in German
literature the clear preference of individual authors, and indeed whole
schools of writing, for the classical repertoire did not inevitably involve
confining that literature to those who had had a classical education; despite the considerably older and more widespread tradition of classicism
in Germany, this must certainly have restricted the real sphere of influence of literature and must have led to poetry's being accessible only to
the educated bourgeoisie. And so if the Russian literature of the late
nineteenth and twentieth centuries seems infinitely more oriented towards Christian ideas than towards classical mythology, this may, it is
true, be explained in terms of educational background, but only if at the
same time it is realized that the Russian poets themselves for the most
part were concerned with making allowances for this general background
and with reaching beyond the ears of just the educated circles to which
most of them belonged.

We have now observed two general advantages that the Christian tradition has over the classical, in respect of its application to "new myths."
First, we have the fact that all levels of society, and not just the classically educated, can be addressed along these lines. Second, at least parts
of the Christian system are still believed in or automatically connected
with religion by the majority of readers or listeners, a fact that can be
exploited in the creation of "new myths," either for the purpose of

provocation or in order to lend support to belief in the newly created myth. In contrast, the classical myth—even allowing for its anthropological significance and poetic, symbolic power—is historically and esthetically so distant that it can be felt only as the offspring of imagination, which will have a corresponding effect on one's response to the "new myth." Above all, wherever a phenomenon affecting the whole of a society is to be condensed into a mythology that will be meaningful for that society, the poet will find that, regardless of his own political and religious situation, he is well-advised to have recourse to Christian ideas. In the revolutionary poem "The Twelve" by the "bourgeois," "Christian" symbolist Blok, and in the early revolutionary poems of the socialist-revolutionary, atheistic futurist Mayakovsky, the October Revolution is linked with the figure of Christ and not with that of Dionysus or Prometheus.

II

As regards the question why and in what way Christian ideas influenced Mayakovsky's revolutionary myth and poems, a good deal can be learned simply from the selections he made out of the general fund of Christian tradition and, more especially, from his different evaluations of individual elements. He shows an obviously polemic attitude towards the God of the Old Testament, God the Father, who, as creator and ruler of the world, is made responsible for the imperfection and injustice of it: either he is made the object of pathetic protest, or he is ridiculed as a foolish old man.[3] There is a similar attitude towards the church and clergy, who, as administrators of this type of religious order and as followers of the ruler, are also ridiculed or attacked with bitter passion. The church sits with its front steps at the throat of the rebelling street, threatening to choke it, and when the street shakes it off, one awaits the approach of the *deprived* Father God to inflict punishment.[4]

While God the Creator and his church are held responsible for the defects of this world, the "other world" of Christianity is seen primarily as a polemic counter to demands for a better world on this earth. Some works show this in the form of a simple negation. The poet wants liberation from personal and social suffering, not later, in the other world, but in this, his own world; as perfect love he does not want that of heaven but that of earth; he wants the happiness of himself and everyone else to come, here and now.[5] But this other world can also be directly repre-

---

[3] Cf., among the early poems especially, "Cloud in Trousers," Parts 2 and 4, and "The Backbone Flute," Part 1.

[4] "Cloud in Trousers," Part 2 (MW. i, 182, l. 247 seq.).

[5] In connection with personal love, see especially "Cloud in Trousers," Part 4; for mankind as a whole, esp. "War and Universe," Part 5.

sented in the poem: the poet Mayakovsky, suffering on earth, is personally raised up into heaven; but there he finds a familiar, hated bourgeois
idyll, with Verdi's music, small-talk, etc. As a man with a *heart* and
with lusts of the flesh he has nothing in common with fleshless, sexless
angels and saints ("Where do the bodiless have their heart?"), and he
hastens longingly down again to the earth, even though he may not
have his longing fulfilled there either.[6] And what the proletarian poet
experiences is experienced by the proletarians themselves—the *impure
ones*, who do manage to reach the heavenly paradise, but are bored stiff
and leave it again at once, handing it back to its inhabitants Chrysostom,
Methuselah, Leo Tolstoy, and Jean-Jacques Rousseau.[7] Thus the Christian "other world" is used as a poetic foil, the renunciation of the
other-worldly ideal intensifying the grievance over the imperfections of
this world, while the satirical image and style of the other world provide
an effective contrast to the pathetic sufferings of this and so give fuel to
the revolt against both types of world.

The attitude towards Christ is quite different. No other figure in the
early poems and plays is referred to directly or indirectly with such frequency as Christ. These references are without any satirical overtones,
and indeed he is often set parallel to or on a level with the poet himself.
This striking integration is based on a view of Christ as a human god in
the broadest sense. Unlike the distant Father God, inhuman in his sever-
ity towards personally guiltless beings, Christ is the god that became a
man in order to suffer like a man and through his personally guiltless
sufferings to redeem suffering mankind. As god of the poor, the afflicted, the humiliated, he is closely akin to the poet of the hungry and
rejected, of the rogues and whores, as the young Mayakovsky sees himself. And so it is with this image of the guiltlessly martyred and crucified
Christ that the poet identifies himself.[8] What is vital in this conception

---

[6] *Man*, Parts: *Ascension of Mayakovsky, Mayakovsky in Heaven*, and *Return of
Mayakovsky*.

[7] *Mystery-Bouffe*, Act III, Scene 2: *Paradise*.

[8] Most directly in "Cloud in Trousers," Part 2, l. 329 seq. and Part 3, l. 500 seq. But
Mayakovsky also uses the words "crucifixion" and "crucified" at other, often vital, moments in the early poems, and with different kinds of association. Cf. for instance the closing lines of "The Backbone Flute":

> Color today's date red for a feast-day.
> Create thyself,
> magic as that of the crucifixion.
> You see—
> With the nails of words
> I am hammered to the paper.
> (MW. I, 208, l. 311 seq.)

of Christ and its poetic application to the revolution, is that he is no longer seen as the human, redeeming embodiment of that same god whose creative and law-giving aspects are personified in God the Father, but as the human *antitype* to this god. As a guiltless expiatory sacrifice he stands implicitly as a bitter accusation against the one who, as creator and ruler of a bad world-order, first arranged this sacrifice, as he arranged all sacrifices and sufferings of the innocent. Inherent in this new interpretation and application of the Christ figure is a strong element of protest, even though Christ himself, as the loving and innocently suffering one, is not portrayed as a protester. Apart from his purely charitable features, the figure is given clearly defined social-revolutionary traits, implying a general revolt against this whole world-order. And this is what makes it possible for the Christ figure to be integrated into the revolutionary myth.

Anyone who knows the history of Russian thought and literature in the nineteenth and twentieth centuries will see at once how deeply rooted Mayakovsky is in Russian tradition. One need only think of Dostoyevsky, who was led by experience of the limitless suffering of innocent children to return to God his "entrance ticket" to this world, and yet on the other hand saw in the meekly suffering Christ or his imitators the ideal, indeed the only, way to overcome the social injustice and other defects of this afflicted world. It is not possible to deal here with the whole history of this idea and its translation into literary form, but a word of warning should be given against offering too narrow a definition of it as "specifically Russian." Certainly this trend was particularly marked and particularly styled in Russia from the middle of the nineteenth century onwards. But there were sources and adherents all over Europe, not the least of them being Pierre Joseph Proudhon, whose influence on Russians such as Dostoyevsky and Mayakovsky is as clear as that on the most important West European theorist of the "new myth" at the turn of the century: Georges Sorel.[9] The idea of justice as the driving force and criterion of historical progress, experience of the injustice of the prevailing world-order, and the resultant endeavor to "recognize the reality and intensity of evil, to seek out its causes, and to discover the cure"—these were the determining factors behind Proudhon's *Idée générale de la révolution.* [10] This gave rise to the possibility of playing off one's own social-revolutionary ideas of justice against the church, and its close ties with the prevailing injustice (*De la*

[9] See H. Barth, *Masse und Mythos. Die ideologische Krise an der Wende zum 20. Jahrhundert und die Theorie der Gewalt: Georges Sorel* (Hamburg, 1959). Regarding Proudhon's influence, see esp. II, 2, p. 52 seq.

[10] Proudhon, *Idée générale de la révolution au XIXe siècle . . .* (Paris, 1851).

justice dans la révolution et dans l'église);[11] it also gave one the chance
to equate love of one's neighbor and expiatory sacrifice, as personified in
Christ, with one's own social-revolutionary actions and the socialist revolution. And this was the view taken by many West European as well as
Russian revolutionaries. This, then, is the tradition in which stands the
equation of Christ with social revolution in Mayakovsky's pre-
revolutionary writings.

For the purpose of this essay, however, it is not quite enough to refer
to the humanization and revolutionary interpretation of the Christ
figure. For this very view of the religious figure as a human and social
phenomenon involves a reduction of its specifically Christian, religious
nature and so a kind of "demythicizing." But for Mayakovsky, it is essential that the mythical or religious aspects should not be de-
mythicized: in being transferred to other contexts, these mythical or religious possibilities are to take on new effects to serve new purposes.

Such transfers of a myth from one system to another are at one and
the same time a reduction and a generalization of the traditional potential of meaning. The first stage in the reduction occurs through the separation of the mythical element from its old canon (Christ is no longer an inseparable part of the Holy Trinity, but is an individual figure). Then from
all the remaining possibilities of interpretation there is a further concentration on those which matter for the transfer into the new system
(Christ as the guiltless sufferer and as the redeeming sacrifice). Here one
can distinguish between those non-mythical elements that allow the
myth to be transferred to its new, social-historical context, and those
mythical aspects which enable the new theme to be presented as a "new
myth." As the humanized God Christ is reduced to a loving, suffering
man, he can be transposed from the sphere of religion and metaphysics
to that of worldly, social, political revolution; and as he is made into an
abstract myth, embodying the sacrifice for the sake of world redemption,
he can take on the vital function of worldwide redeemer and renovator in
the "new myth" of the revolution.

The linking of a traditional myth with a new one presupposes the
abstraction of both according to a common schema, a mythical "archetype."[12] The mythical archetype, or archetypal myth, that forms the
basis of all the revolution myths in Mayakovsky's pre-revolutionary

[11] Proudhon, *De la justice dans la révolution* . . . (Paris, 1858).

[12] "Archetype" is not used here in the Jungian sense, but indicates groups of motifs and
narrative schemata that can be derived as a common core from traditional myths and
legends. Today it is used in this sense both by myth scholars (see, for instance, M. Eliade,
Le mythe de l'éternel retour. Archétypes et répétition (Paris, 1949) and by literary critics,
e.g., N. Frye, "Archetypes of Literature,"in *Myth and Method* [see note 2], and *id.*,
Anatomy of Criticism (Princeton / London, 1957).

poetry, can be outlined as follows: the world of personal and general experience is a world of imperfection, injustice, and undeserved suffering, and hence a sick world. A cure is possible only through a radical upheaval and a new beginning. Everything existing, rigid, binding, must be released, must be returned through fire and flood back into its original state of chaos, so that the new year of a new chronology for new people in a new world can begin; and this new era will be a golden age or the paradise regained of a new Adam. An indispensable part of this mythical process is the sacrifice which, as a personal and general purification, is a pre-condition, a turning-point, and a ritual sign of the process of redemption.[13]

It is only against this background of the archetypal myth that one can understand the full significance of the Christ figure in Mayakovsky's revolution myth, and that one can follow the different variations in the relation between Christ, revolution, and revolutionary poet Mayakovsky. When Christ is seen as the Redeemer, the *whole* of the revolution (as redemption) can be compared or equated with him. When he is seen as the "new man," he is comparable to the *aim* of the revolution. When he is seen as the indispensable sacrifice, the scapegoat for the redemption, he can be compared to pre-conditions and elements of the revolutionary process, and those that suffer for and before the revolution can be compared to him. In the first instance—the equation of Christ and revolution as a single whole—the revolutionary poet, as herald of the revolution, becomes a "prophet" or "apostle"; in the last instance, when he sees himself as a martyr and a sacrifice for the revolution, he can be identified with Christ, he is a "new Christ."

This pervasive reference to the archetypal myth offers a kind of matrix, with the aid of which the reader himself can construct the basic possibilities of coordination, and so the writer can fulfill his poetic intentions by continually drawing parallels or simply making allusions, leaving out unwanted links in the chain of transposition, but also combining elements that might logically seem contradictory.

Thus the poem "Man," for instance, draws a consistent parallel between Christ and Mayakovsky. In direct line with the birth, passion, and ascension of Christ and with the liturgy that refers to these, the poem is divided into the following sections: *Birth of Mayakovsky, Life of Mayakovsky, Passion of Mayakovsky, Ascension of Mayakovsky, Mayakovsky in Heaven, Return of Mayakovsky, Mayakovsky to the*

---

[13] The link between revolution and the "scapegoat" motif as central themes in Mayakovsky's writings has already been pointed out by R. Jakobson in his article, "*Von einer Generation die ihre Dichter vergeudet hat*" (*Slavische Rundschau* 2 [1930], pp. 479 seq., esp. pp. 485 seq.). (English: "On a generation that squandered its poets.")

Centuries, and *The Last*.[14] As far as theme and style are concerned, the poem revolves round the contrast between the sacredness of the model and the satirical banality of the blasphemy. The technique used in the poem "Cloud in Trousers" is more complex and more refined, as it is continually moving from one type of coordination to another. This poem originally bore a title that relates very closely to our theme but was censured as being offensive to religion: "The Thirteenth Apostle."[15] The poet's designation of himself as the "thirteenth apostle" is also to be found in the text.[16] But in the same canto, during the dialogue between the poet and the mother of God, we read:

> I,
> am perhaps,
> the most beautiful
> of all thy sons.
> (MW. I, 190, l. 509 seq.)

and:

> Seest thou—again
> Barrabas is preferred
> to the bespat Golgothan?
> (MW. I, 190, l. 503 seq.)

These lines refer back to lines in the second part, where Mayakovsky draws a direct parallel between his personal sufferings during a lecture tour of Russia, and the martyrdom of Christ:

> That led to the Golgothas of the auditoria
> of Petrograd, Moscow, Odessa, Kiev,
> and there was not one
> who
> would not have cried:
> "Crucify,
> crucify him!"
> But to me—
> you people,
> even those that offended—
> you are dearer and closer to me than anything.
> (MW. I, 184, l. 329 seq.)

[14] Cf. MW. I, p. 243 seq.
[15] Cf. Mayakovsky's preface to the 1918 edition, quoted in MW. I, p. 441.
[16] At the end of Part 3 (MW. I, 190, l. 527).

While here, and a few lines later,[17] Mayakovsky the poet is himself the crucified one, he is also, and at the same time, *prophet* of the revolution with its Christ attributes:

> I see the one who is coming through the mountains of time,
> whom no-one sees.
> Where the short-tailed vision of the people breaks off,
> at the head of the hungering hordes,
> in the crown of thorns of revolutions
> strides the year 16.
> But I amongst you am his prophet!
> (MW. I, 185, l. 346 seq.)

Students of Mayakovsky's work have drawn attention—partly in censure, partly in praise—to the fact that the poet as prophet of the revolution was (only) one year out in his calculations. But, since these lines were written in 1915, one must bear in mind the significance of the fact that 1916 was the coming new year. The setting of the date can be taken as a concrete prophecy as to when the revolution would take place—just as the coming of the Messiah and the end of the world have been expected "next" or "this" year. But it also represents (as do the Christian examples) the mythical approach of the expected upheaval to be brought about by the great "New Year," which as one of the most familiar mythical archetypes stands for the immediate future and for the sum of the past (*crown of thorns of revolutions*) and eternal present. Thus the arrival of this mythical year of revolution cannot mark the end of the poet's mythical function as a scapegoat for the revolution; he is, rather, elevated within the symbol of permanent revolution, and himself becomes that symbol:

> And when
> in tumult heralding
> his arrival,
> you go forth to the Redeemer—
> for you I will
> tear out my soul,
> trample on it
> to make it grow greater!—
> and give it you, blood-stained, like a flag.[18]
> (MW. I, 185, l. 360 seq.)

---

[17] L. 354 seq.: At every drop of the river of tears
    I have stretched myself on the cross.
[18] The Russian text of lines 364/365 (*vam ja dušu vytaščju*), if translated literally, could

These closing words of the second part of "Cloud in Trousers" show very clearly how the connection between Christian ideas, and the Communist revolution, and the revolutionary poet Mayakovsky, comes about—and indeed can only come about—as a kind of projection back onto a mythical archetype and as a renewed realization of that archetype. This very dependence on the archetype preserves the evocative mythical power of the "new myth," even when the Christian element of the archetype has been deprived of its religious authority. For the person who regards Christianity as a binding religion of tradition, the equation of Christ with the revolution (and with the revolutionary poet) will act as a provocative usurpation of Christian revelation; for the non-Christian reader, the poetic and the religious elements interact as different realizations of the same mythical archetype, with the poetic "new myth" bringing to life what for him is the real point of reference—namely, the "old myth." In neither instance is it the final purpose of literary analysis merely to reduce all elements to the archetype; our concern must be to realize the reductions, reproductions, and associations made possible by the archetype, and to bring out the way in which such poetic techniques function, together with the "mythical" possibilities of the archetype or its religious elements, as exploited poetically by these techniques.

III

In order for Christian ideas to be integrated into the new poetic "myth" of the revolution, not only Christian tradition, but also the two other main factors, have to be transformed: the revolution, as the social and historical subject of the myth, and the poet and his work, as the medium through which the myth is conveyed. In both cases the question arises as to whether the phenomenon concerned, in its autonomy, does not contradict certain basic premises of myth.

As has already been mentioned, both the old and the new myth—if they are to be seen as myths and not as mere allusions to material that was once mythical—presuppose a belief in the reality of what is expressed. However, an essential feature of poetry as art is the very fact that both the writer and the reader are perfectly aware that it is a fiction. As far as modern Russian poetry is concerned, this is especially so of futurism, which opposed Russian symbolism with its conception of the word as symbolizing a higher reality that can be sensed behind the poetic utterance, and instead demanded that the word be understood expressly

---

either mean "I will tear out *my* soul (for you)," or "I will tear out *your* soul"; but the context favors the first of these, and the whole thing is most likely meant as the poet's self-sacrifice.

as word as such.[19] Mayakovsky, as poetic representative and theorist of Russian futurism, was bound to find, in his obligation as a poet to realize "new myths," that he was up against this inherent contradiction between the claim to credibility of the myth, and the conscious art of the poem.

Another factor in the question of the different obligations imposed by myth and poetry is that of objectivity. The modern poet is all too aware that his poetic utterances are those of a poetic subject, are received as such, and therefore are possessed of no objective authority, such as is claimed not only by the old but also by the new myth—including all those "myths" of the modern world which Roland Barthes calls "everyday myths."[20] The very fact that a group of Russian futurists actually called themselves "Ego-Futurists,"[21] shows how conscious the movement was of this problem. It is true that Mayakovsky was not a member of this group, but his poetry, including his early revolutionary poems, is permeated more than virtually any other revolutionary poetry by the ego of the poet (even going into personal details of the life of Vladimir Mayakovsky). And so the conflict between the subjectivity of the poetic utterance and the claim to authority of the "new myth" also had to be perceived and overcome. And just like the conflict between poetic "art" and mythical "reality," it had to be resolved in the poetic work itself, so that the reader or listener, who expected the poem to offer him a subjective fiction, could experience for himself its "revaluation" to the level of a real and authoritative myth.

In this context, the literary polemics included by Mayakovsky in his revolutionary poems take on a particular function. Most critics tend to interpret them as evidence of the violent and, on the part of the futurists, particularly intense dispute between the individual schools of poetry, and also as "self-advertisement"[22] by the young poet Mayakovsky and the equally young movement of futurism. And indeed these arguments which, like other futuristic proclamations, were directed against conventional poetry, with its lack of topicality, its insist-

---

[19] Cf. the titles of the two futurist Programmes: "The Word as Such" (*Slovo kak takovoe*), Moscow, 1913, by A. E. Kručenykh and V. Khlebnikov, and "Declaration of the Word as Such" (*Deklaracija slova kak takovogo*), Petersburg, 1913, by Kručenykh. The same trend is to be observed in nearly all futuristic programs; see V. Markov, ed., *Manifesty i programmy russkikh futuristov* (Munich, 1967).

[20] This corresponds to the German title of R. Barthes' *Mythologie* (Paris, 1957): R. Barthes, *Mythen des Alltags* (*edition Suhrkamp*), (Frankfurt/M., 1964).

[21] Cf. V. Markov, *Russian Futurism: A History* (Berkeley and Los Angeles, 1968), esp. Chap. 3: "Ego-Futurism and the Mezzanine of Poetry," p. 61 seq.

[22] "Self-advertisement" (*Samoreklama*) was one of the slogans with which the futurists were reproached by their critics, and which they themselves used on their own behalf.

ence on a conventional ideal of beauty, its restriction to a few supposedly "poetic" subjects, etc., can and should be evaluated in this way. But this is not the whole story. As the poet attacks the conventionality and "artificiality" of such poetry, and emphatically sets his own poetry apart from it, he reduces his reader's awareness of the conventional, artificial character of *all* poetry—including his own. This effect is enhanced when he himself then advances "real life" as a contrast to his own poetry. The interaction of the two phases can be demonstrated through one of the many polemic attacks in "Cloud in Trousers":

> What is Faust to me,
> fairytale firework,
> gliding with Mephisto over the celestial parquet!
> I know—
> the nail in my boot
> is more agonizing than the imagination of Goethe!
>
> (MW. i, 183, l. 290 seq.)

This could be interpreted as a typical futurist "slap at public taste,"[23] through abuse of venerated authorities and through "self-advertisement." But one can also see in these lines that at least as important as the Mayakovsky-Goethe confrontation is that between poetic invention as merely subjective fantasy, and real physical pain. (It is also worth noting that for Mayakovsky, experience of reality and experience of pain are here one and the same thing.) The lines that follow continue the self-aggrandisement, as Mayakovsky declares himself to be the new "scream-lipped Zarathustra" who, more "golden-lipped" than Golden Mouth Chrysostom, can "regenerate the soul" and "baptize the body" with every word he utters. But then the climax overrides and indeed almost obliterates this ego, through the message of the new Chrysostom:

> I say unto you:
> the tiniest grain of dust of the living
> is worth more than everything I can do and have done!
>
> (MW. i, 184, l. 301, seq.)

The "living" take on a mythical greatness, before which all the poet's verses and his own person pale into insignificance. The "new myth" entails the glorification of the *vital*—a feature that was emphasized by its originator, Nietzsche, and was then given a new force and a new color by

[23] "A slap at public taste" (*Poščečina obščestvennomu vkusu*) was probably the most famous and provocative proclamation of early Russian futurism (Moscow, 1912). Text in Markov, ed. cit.)

Bergson's philosophy of the "élan vital," which in its turn influenced, among others, Georges Sorel, in his theory of the "new myth."

The animation and personification of phenomena played an essential part in ancient myths. But the technique of personification is also one of the most common forms of poetic imagery. And the poetry of Mayakovsky—especially his early works—is notable for its wealth of metaphors, particularly "expanded" or "realized" metaphors. Even when he uses the technique of personification, there is basically no reason for speaking of "mythicizing," so long as the images are clearly recognizable as poetic metaphor. But the poetic, clearly metaphoric personification can also be used to conceal, and almost distract from, an underlying personification and vitalization of the social phenomenon it represents.

We shall now look at an example of Mayakovsky's poetry that is not peculiar to him or to Russian poetry, or indeed to poetry in general, and has played a not insignificant role in, for instance, German tradition, including that of the not so distant past. When, in his poem "Good and Beautiful," Mayakovsky not only compares Communist Russia to a *youth*, but actually equates them as *youth-land* or *the land—the youth*,[24] every reader knows that this is a poetic personification. But the more the poet develops this personification, the greater is one's impression that only the "coloring" is a poetic process, whereas the premise, the idea, of the "young land" stems from the subject itself. And so a whole series of associations seems to arise out of the subject and not to be mere metaphoric suggestion. The idea of "youth," transferred from the sphere of vitality to that of politics evokes a feeling, in contrast to all that is old, of unfettered strength, the prospect of and right to full development, the certainty of future and fruition; "age" belongs to the past, must stand aside, etc. History, both past and present, might present us with any number of clear proofs that this application of organic ideas to the sphere of political history is unacceptable, for nations and states with a long historic tradition and experience often show themselves to be much more "vital" than "young" nations, etc. But where vital ideas are generally on the move, these "new myths" of "young" peoples to whom the future belongs, and who are on the verge of a new thousand year "millennium," will find fertile soil to breed on. As we have pointed out, this kind of myth is not specifically poetic, and indeed one might almost call it pre-poetic. But the poet can make use of it for his own ends and, conversely, poetry can be useful for this kind of mythicizing: the reader's attention is focused on the poetic imagery, and he loses sight of the analogies that already underlie this level of imagery and have been

[24] MW. VIII, 320, l. 2879: *podrostok-strana*; p. 327, l. 3142 seq.: *strana-podrostok*.

accomplished, before the poetizing, by conventions of language and thought. Through this process, within the poetic fiction and the imagery perceived as poetry, there comes into effect a kind of mythicizing of the phenomena concerned.

In his "Everyday Myths" Roland Barthes writes: "Does every primary language fall victim to the myth? Is there no meaning that could resist this captivity threatened by form? In fact nothing is proof against the myth. . . . Perhaps the best weapon against the myth is, in reality, to mythicize it itself, i.e., to create an artificial myth. It is sufficient to make the myth itself the starting-point for a third semiotic chain, taking its meaning as the first step of a second myth. The power of the second myth consists in the fact that it sets up the first as an observed naïveté."[25] Barthes is fully aware of the danger and of one means of warding it off. In his later period Mayakovsky, too, created "artificial myths" of precisely this type and with precisely this same intention.[26] However, Barthes appears to overlook the fact that the raising of the myth as such to a higher power, so to speak, is not enough to expose the first myth as "observed naïveté" or as naive observation. This can only take place when the second myth applies its insight into its own artificiality, directly or indirectly, to the prerequisite first myth, revealing the homogeneity of the two myths. Otherwise the very emphasis on the artificiality of the second "layer" can, through direct contrast or indirect distraction, actually conceal the artificiality of the first and the invalidity of the way in which it mythicizes the phenomenon.

The example we have quoted of Russia as a youth is significantly taken from a post-revolutionary poem of Mayakovsky's. His prerevolutionary poems are typified by the mythicizing personification not of nationality so much as of social phenomena. Very typical and very revealing is the personification of the street in the second part of "Cloud in Trousers." The "tongueless street," whose breast is "trodden flat," "stoops" as if "vertiginous," and seeks to "swallow" or "spit out" her agony, but the "taxis" stand in her way. And when at last she succeeds in spewing out the choking phlegm and in pushing off the step of the church that is throttling her, she crouches down in expectation of the vengeful God and cries: "Let's go and feed" (MW. I, 181 seq., l. 230 seq.).

Anyone who reads these lines will realize at once that the street is figuratively personified and that the metaphor is then elaborated. But in the course of this process we lose sight of the fact that "the street" itself

---

[25] German edition, pp. 115 and 121 seq.

[26] Cf., at the end of this esssay, the short description of the late phase and its tendency critically to destroy certain "mythicizings" of the established revolution.

is already something artificial, a "synthetic" phenomenon, whose real nature can only be revealed by its context. The street is, for example, obviously not a "way" (in the sense of the Russian *put'* of folk-poetry and of Romantic, symbolist, or "acmeistic" poetry), but a proper city street. However, it is not simply to be identified with the city, a motif that is just as popular in the "new myth" of the symbolists and of other modern schools of poetry. In the context of this particular poem, the town symbolizes more the static, hermetic force. It is the "leprosorium" of those "interned" in it (MW. I, 182, l. 244 seq.); it also "blocks" the way of the street (MW. I, 182, l. 244 seq.). In contrast, the street is a dynamic force, striving to break through. But also, more than anything else, it is a world in contrast to the settled, civilized milieu of the "fat," smug bourgeoisie—which is an equally essential feature of the city; it is the world of the socially exploited masses, of the social misfits, or of the "antisocials":

> street-thousands:
> students,
> prostitutes,
> laborers.
>
> (MW. I, 183, l. 270 seq.)

The conventionally "poetic," figurative personification of the street as a being with breasts, throat, lips, etc., that stoops, spits, screams, etc., presupposes an idea of the "street" that subsumes a variety of individual features under this word, and thus creates the pre-condition for the phenomenon to be mythicized. The example also shows, incidentally, that it would be risky simply to call this process "pre-poetic" just because it precedes the poetic expansion of personifying metaphors. For it, too, can be fulfilled only in the context of the work itself and its literary tradition (the latter, for instance, through a direct link with previous and contemporary poetry and with the poetic "mythicizing" of the city). If, in this respect, one must talk of the myth's being dependent on its context, nevertheless it does not exclude the possibility of that myth's being abstracted from the concrete text and transferred to non-poetic spheres. It is precisely this type of myth that can very easily and successfully turn into "everyday myths," either by moving out of the poem and into other spheres, or by developing independently in various spheres through the common medium of language. We can stay with the same example and apply it to the present-day social political situation: the dynamic revolt that finds itself confined by the civilized, middle-class "establishment," is going literally and metaphorically out into the streets, and indeed once again, as in Mayakovsky's poem, it is the "students" that are to represent the "street-thousands." Once again the street—viewed positively by some and negatively by others—"demands its right"; politicians and professors "bow" or "do not bow to the street," etc., etc.

But let us return to the poems of Mayakovsky. Here as we have said, the "myth of the street," despite all its non-poetical associations, remains part of the poetic context. But as one essential factor of the text it must therefore come in contact with the other essential factors, and may have an effect upon these. This applies particularly, for instance, to the poet's own self-estimation, which we have already discussed, and to his polemic against conventional "poets." They, the others, are merely poetic talkers or entertainers of the "smug," who "cook up" "some brew out of love and nightingales" (MW. ɪ, 121, l. 229), try to concoct verses out of the "corpses of dead words," and yet reject the only still "living" words of the street-masses, such as "riff-raff" and *"Boršč,"* as unpoetic, and indeed "run snivelling away from the street" (MW. ɪ, 182 seq., l. 257 seq.). I, Vladimir Mayakovsky, however, am the spokesman of this very street, her "scream-lipped Zarathustra" (MW. ɪ, 184, l. 307), her preacher, apostle, and prophet. And for this reason I share in the "reality" of the phenomenon I have celebrated, extolled, and represented, whereas the conventional "poets" and their poetry are condemned to unreality and so to foolishness.

The contrast between the fictitious character of poetry and its claim to "reality" is expressly brought out in order for it then to be played down again in relation to the poet's own statements. This is done through the interplay of mounting negations and identifications. Just as the lyric "I" builds itself up by negating "artificial" verse-making, so by negating itself in relation to what is real and alive, it makes room for the linguistic invocation of individual phenomena such as "the street" or "the revolution" as "mythical realities," and with these it can then identify itself and so have a share in the "higher" reality. The "poet of the street," who alone can enable the "tongueless street" to speak, in return takes from it the certainty of mythical reality which he had previously "conferred" upon it.

Unlike those poets who simply repeat ancient myths, the poet who seeks to found a "new myth" must himself produce it through the creative use of language, and furthermore he can do this only if he incorporates in the act of creation his own relation to the subject. The poetic consistency and suggestive power of Mayakovsky's poetic revolution myths are derived not least from the fact that he himself draws attention to this element of his work instead of trying to conceal it, and indeed this interdependence of myth and myth-maker is a basic structural principle of his poetry. Hence, the qualitative and quantitative significance that the "lyric I" takes on in his works, as the very personal presence of the poet Vladimir Mayakovsky.

How very basic all this is to the whole of Mayakovsky's pre-revolutionary writing comes out clearly when one considers his one dramatic work of this early period. The large poem genre was traditionally a kind of mixture of "epic" and "lyrical," with varying degrees of emphasis on one or the other. Mayakovsky's early poems are characterized by a very pronounced emphasis on the "lyrical." But in drama, the withdrawal of the poetic "I," and the disappearance of its immediate presence, appears to be an integral element of the genre. However, Mayakovsky's *Tragedy* of 1913 is not only a lyrical drama; it is also, very directly, the lyrical drama of the poet Mayakovsky. The poet also gives it a quite unmistakable title: *Vladimir Mayakovsky. Tragedy*. V. Mayakovsky is the speaker of the entire prologue and epilogue, and is the main character in both acts of the play. And when the play was performed, Mayakovsky took the part himself.[27] Not only the content—the poet Mayakovsky collects the limitless suffering of mankind in the tears that are borne to him, so that he can accusingly reproach "the dark god of fear" with it (MW. I, 171, l. 510)—but also the form of this pre-revolutionary tragedy corresponds to that of the pre-revolutionary poems, and indeed Mayakovsky reversed the genres by calling his next work—the poem "Cloud in Trousers"— his *second tragedy*.[28] It might be mentioned in passing that he was not alone in this equation of tragic poem and lyric tragedy, but shared the trend with the Russian symbolists—however, we are not so much concerned with historical links here as with the question of the relation between the literary work, the writer, and the mythicized revolt.

Most of what we have said about the pre-revolutionary works can also be applied to the rest of Mayakovsky's writings. Roman Jakobson, in his article on Mayakovsky that was written just after the latter's death, called him an eminent lyric poet.[29] And he interpreted all Mayakovsky's writings from the standpoint of a tension between a very personal "lyricism" and the desire to be a poet of the revolution.[30] In contrast, Soviet

[27] Text in MW. I, p. 151 seq.; notes on the performance, *ibid.*, p. 439. Cf. also L. Stahlberger, *The Symbolic System of Mayakovsky* (The Hague, 1964), Chap. 1 is devoted specially to *Tragedy*.

[28] When Mayakovsky quoted a few lines before the poem was published (Miscellany *Strelec*. Feb., 1915), and when he discussed the poem himself in his article "About the Various Mayakovskys" (*Žurnal žurnalov*, August, 1915), he himself called it his second tragedy (see MW. I, p. 347).

[29] *Loc. cit.* (see note 13), p. 31 seq.

[30] In his 1930 article, Jakobson views this tension, despite the fatal conflicts that arose

Russian literature on Mayakovsky tried for a long time to minimize this
aspect of his work, if not actually to taboo it. However, recent theses are
now also willing to interpret his work at the two extremes of "I" and
"Revolution"; but unlike Jakobson and the western interpretations inspired by him, they regard this polarity as a poetically productive,
dialectic relationship advocated by Mayakovsky himself, and not as a
corrosive rivalry between the two trends.[31]

But while the argument goes on as to whether this conflict is to be
viewed as negative or positive, and what effect it had on the personal fate
of Mayakovsky, there remains the vital question how such a very
"egocentric" and "purely lyrical" poet could have become the most convincing creator of a poetic "new myth" of revolution. Perhaps this was
not *in spite of* his "lyricism," or *in spite of* the passionate and painful
entanglement of the poetic "I" and the revolution, but directly *because*
of them. For despite the inevitably subjective fictitiousness of poetic utterances, it was only these factors that made it possible for a "new
myth" to be constituted and expressed in this medium. In this respect,
his poetic revolution myth is not only eminently "lyrical," but also
eminently "modern." For: "The modern poet, who does not proceed
from or live by any common religion or myth, can never be simply an
organizer to the degree that earlier poets were; he must first be the
creator of his myth and of his inner attitude towards the world (. . .) and
every lyric verse of our age is charged with the self-created totality of
relationships to the world."[32]

IV

So far we have talked mainly of two methods by which
Mayakovsky creates his poetic myth of revolution; we might put them
under the headings of "Christ" and "Street." From the point of view of

---

out of it, rather as a poetically effective tension integral to Mayakovsky's writing. Later,
particularly in his article "*Novye stroki Majakovskogo*," in *Russkij literaturnyj arkhiv*
(New York, 1956), p. 173 seq., he interprets both poles more unequivocally and one-sided-
ly as irreconcilable, and M.'s political "engagement" as intolerable for his poetry. This is
the interpretation favored, often with direct reference to Jakobson, by most Western
critics; but in my opinion Jakobson's earlier view is better suited to the particular character
of the works in general.

[31] See, for instance, the book by Z. Papernyj, *Poetičeskij obraz u Majakovskogo* (The
Poetic Image in Mayakovsky), (Moscow, 1961), which takes as its structural starting-point
the poles of "I" and "Revolution," and sets out to reconcile the two.

[32] M. Susman, "*Das Wesen der modernen deutschen Lyrik*," in *Kunst und Kultur*, vol.
9 (Stuttgart, 1910), p. 12 seq. I have deliberately chosen a description that is more or less
contemporary, but stands in a completely different cultural context and proceeds from different conceptions of poetry, in order to reveal the common ground that even then is still
present.

"age," the first is a reference to "ancient myths," and the second a mythic neologism achieved through personification. The "new myth" here, as usual, is neither exclusively derived from new subject-matter, nor exclusively transferred from old subject-matter to new objects, but it is a combination of the two. In this case, the two contrasting techniques also serve two different functions. The "usurpation" of Christian ideas and their transference to the revolution, despite the total rejection of "the other world," turns the revolution in an "upward" direction; the reference to organic ideas, and the emphasis on the activities of the socially "lower" regions, directs the revolution "downwards." Obviously this "upwards" and "downwards" orientation of Mayakovsky's should not be mistaken for any kind of world judgment. But as the revolution is, so to speak, stretched out between these two poles, it appears to be a kind of intersecting point between high and low, between heaven and hell etc.

This setting of earthly events between the upper regions of the divine and the lower regions of the demonic, and the idea of the earth's being the intersecting point or sphere of activity of both forces, corresponds directly to the scenic form of the myth in Mystery plays, and indeed to the view and presentation of myths in general. And so whenever revolution is mythicized, there is often a tendency not only to idealize it "upwards," but also to demonize or vitalize it "downwards," and to minimize the area in between—that of the concrete, social-historical events and activities. Both in Blok's revolutionary poem "The Twelve" and in Mayakovsky's pre-revolutionary poems, the revolution is embodied partly in Christ, and partly in villains, whores, and cads—and not in the class-conscious, Marxist-oriented proletariat or in the leaders of the Communist Party. The very fact that the active revolutionary Mayakovsky takes this same attitude should make one hesitate to call Blok's attitude a one-sided judgment of the Communist revolution through aversion or through ignorance. One can hardly accuse Mayakovsky of ignorance of, or aversion to, a revolution which he proudly called "my revolution."[33] It is in fact the desire poetically to proclaim the revolution as a "new myth" that led both poets (and many others) to this "upwards" and "downwards" orientation, and to the sanctifying and demonizing of the revolution at the expense of its history—which, of course, does not exclude a prior "mythicizing" of the events in the poet's personal experience, but does not necessarily make that an indispensable precondition.

[33] In Mayakovsky's poetic autobiography *I Myself*, under the heading *October* (1917): "To accept or not to accept? Such a question has never existed for me (or for the other Moscow futurists)." *My Revolution*. (MW. I, p. 25).

Despite these structural similarities, however, there remains a difference that was fundamental, not only to the basic premises of the two poets in their attitudes towards the revolution, but also to their poetic rendering of this phenomenon. In contrast to the non-Communist, non-revolutionary Blok, the Communist revolutionary Mayakovsky, as a poet, was bound to be disturbed by the question whether the Communist Revolution and the Marxist-Leninist ideas behind it could permit this kind of mythicizing and abstraction from history. For, regardless of whether the revolution is oriented "upwards" into the metaphysical or "downwards" into the elemental, in both cases it is robbed of its social and historical character as the product of human activity.

It is the old conflict between myth and history, which permeates the whole discussion of myths ancient and modern. It is beyond the scope of this essay to deal with this complex theme. It is enough to observe that nearly all studies of myth and history are in agreement that when the myth is placed in an historical setting it loses its specific function as a myth, and when historical events or personages are mythicized, they lose their specifically historical character. This contrast remains unaffected by the different interpretations of individual critics and theorists. The mythical may be regarded as the source of the historical, and so viewed positively as the more original or negatively as the superseded; or both may be seen as equally basic possibilities of elucidation; or, finally, the attempt might be made to merge them into a "myth of history." But in all cases, the contrast between the two remains as a conflict that has to be resolved.

In the context of our discussion, there are two aspects of this conflict that are directly relevant. (1) The timelessness or permanence of the myth, its "eternally recurrent"[34] nature, stands in contrast to the uniqueness and unrepeatability of the historic event, the historic personage, the historic situation. (2) History appears as that which can be made by man, while myth essentially avoids this man-made appearance.

There might be some objections to this second contrast, and indeed the part it plays varies considerably in the different systems and theories of historical philosophy and myth. But it does occur—for instance, in Vico—wherever history is conceived as something created by God to be implemented by man. And it is also present when history as an autonomous force dispenses with the deeds of the individual but nevertheless is viewed as the history of *mankind.* At the other end of the scale, there

[34] Cf. the title of M. Eliade's book, *Le mythe de l'éternel retour* (see note 12). It is true that this refers in particular to the myth of the "eternal recurrence," but the interpretation of earthly and cosmic events as an "eternal recurrence" is also a basic feature of the mythical world-view.

are many myth theories that set the myth apart from religious dogma, because of its changeability and adaptability, and place it closer to or even on a par with fiction—as in the mythopoetic view of the German Romantics, in the more recent Anglo-Saxon conception of *Myth as Literature*[35] (and "Literature as Myth"), and in many anthropological and sociological interpretations of the function of the "myth-maker." But even in these cases, no one disputes the fact that the world of the "made" myth appears to be peopled by superhuman powers, and not by ordinary human beings engaged in the historical struggle for power.

Marx brings forward these two differences between myth and history as arguments against the mythicizing of revolution. Marx and Engels did not, of course, reject the idea of the myth out of hand, but in fact fully appreciated its function as a pre-historic, pre-rational means of interpreting and coping with the world. However, Marx radically rejected myth-making in the revolution that he strove for, because he saw it as an historical phenomenon to be achieved in history. In the very first chapter of his *Eighteenth Brumaire*, he writes:

"Men make their own history, but they do not make it spontaneously or out of circumstances of their own choosing; they make it out of immediate, given, and traditional circumstances. The tradition of all the dead generations haunts the brains of the living like a nightmare. And when they seem to be in the very act of transforming themselves and everything else, of creating something not yet in existence—at those very times of revolutionary crisis, they fearfully call up the spirits of the past to aid them, borrow from them names, battle-cries, costumes, in order to construct the new scene of world-history in this venerable dress with this borrowed language."[36]

Here or elsewhere in this work, Marx takes as his main examples the retrogressive orientation of the 1848 revolution towards the 1789 revolution, the 1789 revolution towards Rome, and Cromwell's revolution towards the Old Testament. While with the two older revolutions this sort of "raising of the dead" was at least a necessary "self-deception" to spur the revolutionaries on to something that was new and their own, he says that the revolution of 1848, in attempting to imitate and directly repeat an historically unique event, was a "farce" and a "parody" of a past "tragedy": "The earlier revolutions needed the world-historical memory, in order to intoxicate themselves over their own content. The revolution of the nineteenth century must let the dead bury their dead, in order to arrive at its own content."[37] Hence the basic precept: "The

[35] See R. Chase, "Myth as Literature," in *Myth and Method* (see note 2).
[36] Karl Marx, Friedrich Engels, *Werke* (Berlin, 1958 seq.), vol. 8, p. 115.
[37] P. 117.

social revolution of the nineteenth century cannot create its poetry out of the past, but only out of the future."[38]

Here Marx is primarily concerned with the question whether *any* retrogressive orientation does not hinder the revolutionary force; and so at this point it is more a problem of the "historicizing" than of the direct "mythicizing" of revolution. But even here it is clear that such recourse to historic events and the attempt to imitate them strips the events themselves of their historic uniqueness (regardless of whether the "model" is the "sacred" history of the Old Testament or the stylized history of Rome), and also that "self-deception" and "intoxication" are seen in the attempt to imitate mythicized models and symbols, which in itself is a form of self-mythicizing.

How something historically developed and socially made can be falsified into something given by God or Nature, proof against all revolutionary change, immune to all human making and unmaking, so that it can be perpetuated as a condition of social relations, was demonstrated with particular vividness by Marx in the famous 24th chapter of *Das Kapital*, with the example of *so-called original accumulation.*[39]

The economic and social inequality and injustice of human society, which has been "made" historic by the interested parties through accumulation of capital, is mythicized by being attributed to "original accumulation." Along the lines of the "legend of the theological fall of man" there is invented a "history of the economic fall of man." The prevailing mode of production becomes a kind of "self-evident law of nature," which eventually even the working class itself believes in because of its "upbringing, tradition, and customs." And so "the worker can remain resigned to the 'natural laws of production,' i.e., to his dependence on capital, which arises out of the actual conditions of production, and is guaranteed and perpetuated by them."[40] "Arises" instead of being made; "perpetuity" instead of historic temporality, and in both an inviolable "guarantee"—these are characteristics of the myth. Carried over to historic processes and situations, they conceal what has been historically developed and socially made, and so hinder its improvement. This is why in Marx's eyes the task of social revolution is to unmask such myths, to show that present economic, social, and political conditions are an "artificial product of modern history" and not "eternal laws of nature," and to prepare and carry out social revolution through this form of scientific enlightenment and not through new myths.

It is a known fact that Marx's ban on myths has been opposed even by

[38] *Ibid*.
[39] Ed. cit., vol. 23, pp. 741-91: *Die sogenannte ursprüngliche Akkumulation*.
[40] P. 765.

some passionate champions of social revolution, most trenchantly perhaps by Georges Sorel, whose theory of the social myth has penetrated even as far as Russia. In the context of our discussion it is neither possible nor necessary to go into details of Sorel's criticisms of Marx, of Sorel's theory of the social myth and its significance for the revolution, or of later Marxist-Leninist criticisms of Sorel's thesis. What matters here is the attempt to show that Marx himself mythicized revolution, and the attempt to rationalize the necessity of myth for both nineteenth- and twentieth-century social revolution. As we have seen, Marx resolutely refused to elevate the historical development of economic, social, and political conditions to the level of a kind of "natural law" and so to mythicize it. But at the end of this same twenty-fourth chapter, he writes: "With the inevitability of a natural process, capitalist production generates its own negation."[41] Is not this, asks Sorel, his own mythicizing of the revolutionary process? And at this point, where Marx passes from an analysis of the past to a prophecy for the future, does not his own language generally change into that of prophecy and myth? What Marx is depicting here, argues Sorel, is precisely what he, Sorel, understands by "social myth." And this is not a lapse on Marx's part, but is in fact the very strength of his teaching, even if he himself would deny it out of orthodox dogmatism. Social revolution, says Sorel, is a revolution of the poor; but the poor cannot be inspired to revolt just by rational, scientific analyses. They must be emotionally stimulated, and this can be done only with the aid of social and revolutionary myths.[42]

Such a conception of the social myth might be regarded as purely tactical, and has often been interpreted in this way. Indeed, Sorel's myth theory itself is open to tactical interpretation, which is perhaps why it could be taken up and abused by pure tacticians of violence. But it would certainly be wrong to pin Sorel's conception of the myth to this purely tactical standpoint. Behind it stands the idea, already born in his early writings, that the rational, causal, all-illuminating world-view would in turn lead to an impoverishment, and that in a "mythless age," as Nietzsche said, there is need for "new myths" in order for life to take on a meaning and for the dynamic forces of the individual and of the social structure to be mobilized.

It need scarcely be pointed out that such ideas were very much in line

[41] P. 791.
[42] The most direct and polemic treatment of this theme in Sorel's writings is *La décomposition du marxisme* (Paris, 1908). Concerning Sorel's theory, apart from H. Barth's book (see note 9), see J. L. Horowitz, *Radicalism and Revolt against Reason; the Social Theories of Georges Sorel* (London, 1961), and K. Götzle-Claren, *Mythos und Moral. Rationalismus und Irrationalismus in der politischen Philosophie Georges Sorels*, Diss. Berlin, 1963.

with certain views and demands of the social-revolutionary movement in Russia, too; and they found echoes in the pre-revolutionary writings of Mayakovsky. But in order to avoid the mistake of simply lining up the young Mayakovsky's conception of revolution with these currents of thought, and in order not to lapse into a debate of Sorel versus Marx, revolutionary Marxism-Leninism versus social-revolutionary utopianism, irrationalism, and anarchism, we must take note of the fact that in Marx, too, the possibilities of revolution being mythicized are at least implicit.

As evidence, we need only turn once more to the *Eighteenth Brumaire*. We have seen how Marx said that every revolution "created" from somewhere its "poetry," but social revolution must create it not, as before, from the past but from the future. The term "poetry"[43] is certainly used here in a highly indeterminate manner, but what Marx means is made clear by the preceding sections on the revolutions of the seventeenth and eighteenth centuries: "In this way . . . Cromwell and the English people had borrowed language, passions, and illusions from the Old Testament for their middle-class revolution."[44] And: "The raising of the dead in those revolutions served therefore to glorify new struggles, not to parody the old; to exaggerate the given task in the imagination, and not to run away from its fulfilment in reality; to revive the spirit of revolution, and not to make its ghost walk again."[45]

"Poetry" appears as the product of imagination and as exaggeration, but also as the possibility of rousing "passions" for the revolutionary "fulfilment in reality," and of giving "language" to one's own revolutionary activities or will. Shortly before, Marx compares the borrowing of historic and mythical names and symbols in "epochs of revolutionary crisis" with the learning of a language. "The beginner who has learnt a new language always translates it back into his mother tongue, but he has only adopted the spirit of the new language and he can only produce freely in it, when he moves around in it without searching his memory, and forgets his hereditary language in it."[46] This comparison is striking in that he regards learning a "new language" as a process of recourse to a familiar "mother tongue," and sees this "memory-searching" as an aid and a pre-condition for learning just as much as an inhibiting dependence endangering free production. The comparison is not quite true in that he proceeds from the premise of two ready-made languages, for even the "new" language is in fact new only for the "beginner" coming

---

[43] For Marx and Engels' general conception of poetry and literature, see P. Demetz, *Marx, Engels und die Dichter* (Stuttgart, 1959); English edition revised and extended, *Marx, Engels and the Poets* (Chicago / London, 1967).

[44] P. 116.   [45] *Ibid*.   [46] P. 115.

from another language. The new language of revolution, which has to be learned in "epochs of revolutionary crisis," is one that is new for everyone and is to express a new reality. As far as this "new language" is concerned, everyone is a "beginner"; and so everyone needs to refer back to a "mother tongue" as a starting-point for learning the new language. This "mother tongue," if it is to be of use to people as an "aid to learning," must also be familiar to everyone. Its symbols must be vivid enough to enable old ideas to reveal new phenomena; but they must also be general enough not to be rigidly confined to familiar objects and so distort instead of facilitate one's view of these new phenomena. Such a general, original "mother tongue," which can be referred back to when one has to formulate and learn the "new language" of a "new reality," is the language of the myth. If the possibility and the task of reactivating the myth in "epochs of revolutionary crisis" is viewed from this standpoint, then there can be no objection to poetry as a linguistic fiction. On the contrary, it shows quite clearly how vital the myth is, as a kind of "mother tongue," to the learning of the "new language," without its being degraded to the level of a mere didactic tool.

And so from the early writings of Marx we can, if not deduce, then at least explain, two basic possibilities for the mythicizing of revolution, and these were of vital importance to all Mayakovsky's revolutionary writings and the revolution myths contained in them. In the early, pre-revolutionary works, it is the first aspect that dominates—the clear orientation towards the future, and the attempt to "create" the "poetry" necessary for the revolution still to come, to "exaggerate" his "own tasks" of the present, in order to free himself with "illusions" or "self-deceptions" from the agony of the past and present in preparation for this revolutionary, poetic future. But in the works written immediately after the revolution, e.g., especially the poem *150,000,000* and the play *Mystery-Bouffe*, it is the second aspect that dominates. Precisely because it is now no longer a matter of the myth's being "believed in," but of the mythical structure as a structure, in *these* works of Mayakovsky's the thing believed in (Christ) as a mythical point of crystallization can retreat into the background or disappear altogether, while at the same time myths or similar material can be chosen as historically or esthetically much more distant models. From the biblical tradition, for instance, there is the great flood, and the passage through hell and heaven.[47] From classical poetry—which in these new circumstances can now be made use of by the Russian revolutionary poets too—there is the Trojan War, especially the Trojan Horse.[48] From traditional Russian

[47] Cf. *Mystery-Bouffe* (MW. II, p. 167 seq.).
[48] Cf. *150,000,000* (MW. II, p. 113 seq.).

folk-tales there are the wanderings and the triumph of the rascally Ivan.[49] These different subjects, myths, and schemata constantly interweave, sometimes supplementing one another, sometimes cancelling one another out, and in this way they show that the aim is not to reactivate one single myth, but to bring out a common "mythical mother tongue" which can serve as the basis for the new, and constantly to be renewed, poetic "myth" of the revolution in process. With the pre-revolutionary works one could speak of a "usurpation" of the still current Redeemer myth being combined with new "mythicized" phenomena such as the "street," but in the works written during the revolution, the "mythicizing" is deliberately more artificial. It comes about through a transparent, constantly alternating materialization and destruction of "mythical archetypes," which give expression to the as yet non-existent "new language" of the revolutionary process, but also "unmask" themselves in order to prevent too close a dependence of the revolutionary present on the myths of the past, and in order to demonstrate the free play of the poetry.

In an even later phase, this second principle of construction gives way to a third, which might be described as the polemic, poetic destruction of the continual self-mythicizing of a now firmly established revolution. One can distinguish several variants. The destruction can be accomplished by countering the false "monumentalizing" of the "red October" and of Lenin with the very subjective view of the "Witness," and his emphasis on "Facts" (e.g., in the poems "Vladimir Il'ič Lenin" and "Good and Beautiful").[50] But it can also be brought about by contrasting the supposedly revolutionary present, in its Philistine or bureaucratic smugness and hollowness, with the poet's mythicizing of himself as a "scapegoat" and "expiatory sacrifice" for a revolution conceived as permanent—as for instance in the unfinished poem "At the Top of My Voice." And, lastly, it can be poetically accomplished by the "myth" of a negative future Utopia, in which certain tendencies of post-revolutionary Soviet society are satirically unmasked—as in, particularly, the two comedies The Bedbug and The Bathhouse.

To deduce from all this that Mayakovsky "renounced" the revolution, would be as inadmissible a simplification and distortion of this complex process as would be any attempt to proclaim just one of these three principles as the "true Mayakovsky," or to dismiss his personal "lyricism" and "self-mythicizing" as a "futuristic aberration" (as do most Soviet

[49] In 150,000,000.

[50] See in the 1st Canto of Good and Beautiful: "Throw thyself down and drink from the river with the name 'Fact' " (MW. VIII, 235, ll. 13-16), and: "That out of the book, through the joy of eyes, from happy tongues, may flow the power . . ." (ibid., l. 40 seq.).

critics), or, conversely, to condemn his involvement in the October Revolution and the new Soviet Union as a "betrayal of his real poetic self" (as do most Western critics). Within the scope of this essay, it has been possible only to deal in detail with the first of these three principles, and a closer analysis of the other two must be left for another occasion; however, perhaps it will already be clear how very much Mayakovsky's writings, from the earliest right through to the last poems and plays, were characterized by a personal "lyricism" and revolutionary subject matter, and how, for this very reason, the structure of these writings and the function of their "mythical" element could and had to change, according to whether they were conceived and poetically realized before, during, or after the October Revolution.

V

History and Literary History. From
Poetik und Hermeneutik V

KARL-HEINZ STIERLE

Story as Exemplum—Exemplum as Story:
On the Pragmatics and Poetics of Narrative Texts

> I fancy that something like an Ariadne thread has been found, that leads one out of all sorts of half-understood intricacies, once one resolutely defines speech as action.—K. Bühler, *Sprachtheorie*, p. 52

I

To BEGIN with, a few remarks concerning the methods we shall use in approaching this subject.

If one understands texts as a permanent rendering of continuous speech actions, then the most common frame of reference as regards the constitution of texts must be a theory of action.[1] At the beginning of his *Philosophische Untersuchungen*, Wittgenstein makes the far-reaching

[1] The claim is that the study of literature, as the systematic study of texts, has its place in the framework of the active sciences. Under this premise, the adaptation of theoretical concepts integral to the active sciences may provide substantial stimuli for the study of literature. The following essay, however, makes only a very limited allowance for this. It is first and foremost an attempt to apply the concept of the speech action, which is attracting increasing attention in modern philology, philosophy of language, and sociology, to texts and not merely to minimal speech utterances. For the concept of speech action, see especially J. L. Austin, *How to Do Things with Words* (Harvard University Press, 1962); K. Bühler, *Sprachtheorie* (1934), (2nd ed., Stuttgart, 1965); J. Frese, "Sprechen als Metapher für Handeln," in *Das Problem der Sprache. 8. Deutscher Kongress für Philosophie* (Munich, 1967); A. Gehlen, *der Mensch* (1940), (8th ed., Frankfurt, 1966), esp. chapter on "Handlung und Sprache"; J. Habermas, "Vorbereitende Bemerkungen zu einer Theorie der kommunikativen Kompetenz," in Habermas-Luhmann, *Theorie der Gesellschaft oder Sozialtechnologie* (Frankfurt, 1971); W. Kamlah, P. Lorenzen, *Logische Propädeutik* (Mannheim, 1967), esp. II, 2: "Sprache und Rede"; K. Lorenz, *Elemente der Sprachkritik* (Frankfurt, 1970); N. Luhmann, "Sinn als Grundbegriff der Soziologie," in Habermas-Luhmann, *Theorie der Gesellschaft oder Sozialtechnologie* (Frankfurt, 1971); B. Malinowski, "The Problem of Meaning in Primitive Languages," in Ogden and Richards, *The Meaning of Meaning* (1923); G. H. Mead, *Mind, Self and Society* (Chicago, 1934); K. L. Pike, *Language in Relation to a Unified Theory of the Structure of Human Behavior*, 2nd ed. (The Hague, 1967); S. J. Schmidt, "Sprachliches und soziales Handeln. Überlegungen zu einer Handlungstheorie der Sprache," in Linguistische Berichte 2 (1969); J. R. Searle, *Speech Acts. An Essay in the Philosophy of Language* (London, 1969); L. Wittgenstein, *Philosophische Untersuchungen* (Frankfurt, 1967); D. Wunderlich, "Die Rolle der Pragmatik in der Linguistik," in *Der Deutschunterricht* (1970), *Heft* 4.

observation that speech occurs in actions.[2] This is only a short step away from the idea that speech occurs as an action. It is characteristic of actions that the impulses of which they consist are orientated towards a particular meaning, which in principle is easy enough to understand. The object of this understanding, however, is not simply the relation between action and meaning, but the schema of action through which it is conveyed, and which transcends the individual action and indeed is the prime influence on it. For Max Weber, such "types of courses of action" are the actual subject of sociology. "Within social activities one can perceive real regularities, i.e., courses of action, in a typically, homogeneously *intended sense*, that are repeated by the same doer and/or are spread amongst many doers. Sociology is concerned with these *types* of courses of action, in contrast to history as the causal accounting of important, i.e., fateful, individual contingencies."[3] Actions, insofar as they are based on such a schema, are conventional—they stand within a cultural and social frame of reference which endows them with a "meaning" that extends beyond mere rational expediency. This conventional aspect of actions is their "sign." F. de Saussure, for whom linguistics counted as part of a science which he called *sémiologie*, and which he regarded as "science qui étudie la vie des signes au sein de la vie sociale,"[4] saw the meaning structure of conventional actions in the context of these "signs": "considérant les rites, les coutumes etc. . . . comme des signes" (p. 35).

If Saussure's concept of semiology might be called "action as speech," when we come to consider texts the term might be reversed to "speech as action." Texts can be understood in two ways—as speech and as action. W. Kamlah and P. Lorenzen, in their *Logische Propädeutik*, use the terms "Handlungsverstehen" (action understanding) and "Redeverstehen" (speech understanding) in order to differentiate between the two approaches.[5] Understanding a text as action is based on understanding a text as speech. The correlatives of this form of understanding have been aptly described by J. L. Austin[6] as "the act of saying" and its reification, the "act by saying" (or perlocutionary act).[7] Both levels follow their

[2] L. Wittgenstein, p. 24: "The word *'Sprachspiel'* (language game) is meant to bring out the fact that speaking a language is part of an activity or a form of life."

[3] Max Weber, *Wirtschaft und Gesellschaft*, 2 vols., ed. J. Winckelmann (Cologne, 1964), I, 20.

[4] F. de Saussure, *Cours de linguistique générale* (Paris, 1968), p. 33.

[5] Kamlah, Lorenzen, p. 57.

[6] J. L. Austin, *How to Do Things with Words* (Oxford, 1965), pp. 101 ff.

[7] For our purposes it is unnecessary to consider Austin's second category of speech actions, the "illocutionary acts" (acts in saying), which relate to the special case of definite, explicit, linguistically normalized acts.

own rules in the composition of the text, and it is only their interaction that brings about the complexity of the concrete text structure itself. The "act of saying" might be called the object of the text, and coincides with those aspects of the text that remain identical when it is translated into other languages. It is what has long been known, somewhat unsubtly, as *content*. The "act of saying" culminates in the object's becoming a text, captured by an "act of saying" which divides it up in accordance with the possibilities of a given vocabulary, and sticks it together again on a new level, in accordance with the rules of a given syntax. As regards the concrete text, there is an interaction between the structures that go to make up these two acts.

Austin's distinction between the "act of saying" and the "act by saying" presupposes two different theoretical frames of reference. That of the "act of saying"—in its extra-syntactical consistency—might be called *text-semeiotic*, and that of the "act by saying," *text-pragmatic*.[8] The latter might be joined to a third frame of reference—*text-poetic*. As regards the schemata of pragmatic speech actions, Ch. Morris[9] distinguishes between their "primary use" and their "secondary use"; an essential object of the text-poetic is the "secondary use" of schemata of pragmatic speech actions and their liberation from the pragmatic context—whether this be for the purpose of reflecting them (a simple example, a kind of linguistic "minimal art," would be P. Handke's[10] arrangement of a football team as a "poem"), or in order to make possible an illusory identification with an implied reader. A borderline case of our text-poetic would be speech actions without pragmatic correlatives, as in concrete writing in which speech action is enclosed in itself, and the criteria of its composition have first to be deciphered.[11]

As far as text-pragmatic is concerned, A. Jolles' studies of the "simple

---

[8] Ch. Morris, *Signification and Significance* (Cambridge, 1964), p. 44: "Pragmatics is the aspect of semeiotics concerned with the origins, uses and effects of signs." For Morris, semantics, syntactics, and pragmatics stand on one level; together they form the sphere of semeiotics. Our suggestion is that only syntactics and semantics be subsumed under semeiotics, and pragmatics be set up as an opposing field on its own. In *Linguistische Berichte*, there is a report by H. Schnelle on a discussion of Morris' schema that took place during the 1970 colloquy in Jerusalem on Pragmatics in Natural Languages.

[9] Ch. Morris, *Signs, Language and Behavior* (New York: Braziller, no date), p. 94. Cf. also the fundamental observations on "Endzweck und Selbstzweck des Handelns," in A. Gehlen, *Urmensch und Spätkultur* (Bonn, 1956), pp. 33 ff.

[10] P. Handke, *Die Aufstellung des I. FC Nürnberg vom Jan. 27, 1968*, "Die Innenwelt der Aussenwelt der Innenwelt," ed. Suhrkamp (Frankfurt, 1969).

[11] Only this type of text, which is constituted purely on the text surface, is dealt with in M. Bense's text theory, which purchases its conciseness at the price of an arbitrary narrowing down of its subject matter. See M. Bense, *Einführung in die informationstheoretische Ästhetik*, in *Rowohlts Deutsche Enzyklopädie* (Hamburg, 1969).

forms''[12] of literature are of immediate significance. By "simple forms,'' Jolles means those forms "which, so to speak without the aid of the writer, occur in the language itself and arise out of the language'' (p. 10). They are determined by their "Bündigkeit'' (p. 22)—the arrangement of a distinct coherence of linguistic "gestures.'' According to Jolles, the simple form itself is not something one actually comes across in the text. The concrete form is what he calls "vergegenwärtigt'' (p. 264)—"realized.'' Out of the interaction of constant and variable elements of these "realizations'' there emerges the inherent schema of the simple form. However, Jolles does not stop at tracing the realized back to the simple form. He also asks—and herein lies the pragmatic side of his approach—about the "Geistesbeschäftigung'' (spiritual occupation) which manifests itself through the simple form and in the realized form. The term "Geistesbeschäftigung'' is certainly linked with ideological presuppositions which must be put on one side if anything is to be gained from Jolles' account. This "Geistesbeschäftigung'' he calls "Arbeit der Sprache'' (work of language) (p. 16), but for him work is typologically confined to that of the farmer, the mechanic, and the priest. What these people do is performed once more in speech, and is preserved in speech as a simple form. Jolles' sentimental conception of a thus-constituted "division of labor,'' with little or no regard for economic or social history, has as little attraction as his restriction to a system of simple forms which, in the guise of primal forms of linguistic behavior, are supposed to correspond to primal forms of human activity. The question of the pragmatic, extra-syntactic forms cannot be narrowed down a priori. Historic change, which implies a change in society and its modes of communication, results in the emergence of new schemata of linguistic action, together with new possibilities for their poetic development and variation; in the context of text-pragmatic and text-poetic, these possibilities cannot be discussed in isolation, but must be related to their historical position.

The simple forms that Jolles describes are almost exclusively *narrative*. Narrative forms have an exceptional degree of self-containment, which at the same time allows a good deal of variation. Jolles' work shows the particular relevance of the pragmatic aspect of texts to the constitution of the story as a text. The essential distinction between the forms lies in the way the narrative is put together, and the way in which differently expressed interests correspond to the object presented— interests from which the speech action emerges as the force that captures the narrative cohesion. Here Jolles is demonstrating something that has

[12] A. Jolles, *Einfache Formen*[2] (Darmstadt, 1958).

frequently been overlooked in subsequent narrative theory. Weinrich,[13] for instance, with his distinction between "discussed and narrated world," proceeds from a typical "speech situation of narrative" (p. 48). The great number of possible narrative approaches are traced back to a single one, from which all others are supposed to be deducible. The narrator is defined as one particular prototype: "The prototype of the *narrator*, with which literature continually confronts us in its stories within stories, is the storyteller. We have a quite definite conception of him: he is old rather than young; in fairytales he is the kind uncle or—if it is a woman—the kind aunt or grandmother. He does not stand up, but is seated—in an armchair, on a sofa, or by the fireplace. His hour is evening, after work. He likes to interrupt his story in order to have a puff on his pipe or cigar (rarely a cigarette!). His movements are slow; he takes his time, looking at his audience one after the other, or he gazes thoughtfully up at the ceiling. His gestures are sparing, his expression reflective rather than animated. He is *quite relaxed*" (p. 49). Weinrich regards storytelling as a kind of primal phenomenon. But the story of the accused describing the details of a crime, the story the parson inserts in his sermon, the story the newspaper puts on its front page, the story the historian reports on, the eyewitness account the policeman notes down—these are all speech actions that cannot be deduced from Weinrich's picture of a narrator. The fact that something is to be narrated does not tell us all we need to know about the speech situation. It is this situation which in fact determines the narration. The composition of narrative texts is independent of the use that is made of them, and so it is independent of their position in any particular linguistic or non-linguistic context. It would be possible to examine the word story, together with all its connotations, as Wittgenstein has examined the word *game*. Instead of asking what basic, common idea underlies all games, he investigates the use of the word—i.e., the contexts in which the word occurs, and the activities revealed in these contexts. At one point in his *Philosophische Untersuchungen*, Wittgenstein, anticipating Chomsky, differentiates between "Oberflächengrammatik" (surface grammar) and "Tiefengrammatik" (depth grammar).[14] What on the surface seems to suggest agreement proves in its deeper structure to stretch further and further apart. "The indescribable diversity of all our daily language games does not enter into our consciousness, because the clothes of our language make everything the same" (p. 261).

Despite this diversity, the category of narrative texts is unmistakably

---

[13] H. Weinrich, *Tempus. Besprochene und erzählte Welt* (Stuttgart, 1964).
[14] P. 203.

separated from that of systematic texts by the narrative schema that underlies them all. A. C. Danto, in his "Analytical Philosophy of History"[15] defines this as follows:

(1) x is F at t-1
(2) H happens to x at t-2
(3) x is G at t-3. (p. 236)

This formula describes the basic structure of narrative. The subject of the story takes on the predicate F at the time of t-1, and the predicate G at t-3. F and G denote a change. Between the two conditions the story tells us H during the period of t-2. (1) and (3) represent the thing to be explained, and (2) is the explanation. In this sense, Caesar's "veni, vidi, vici" could be taken as an example of a minimal, irreducible story. Between the times of t-1 (*veni*) and t-3 (*vici*) lies the period t-2 with its *vidi*, which is so effective precisely because of the witty, impressive way in which it reduces the long period to a mere nothing.

For Danto history is certainly an illustration of a process which upsets the balance of a situation and, after a series of changes, creates a new situation which forms a contrast to the first. However, Danto makes it quite clear that it is not the subject which determines its form of organization, but the form of organization which primarily gives rise to the subject. What constitutes this form is *contrasts* and the way in which they are conveyed. At this point we must differentiate between *system* and *process*—a difference inherent in language itself. According to L. Hjelmslev, language as a system is determined by the correlatives either-or, and as a process by both-and.[16] The basic difference between language as a process and language as a system, between the syntagmatic and the paradigmatic perspectives, occurs again on the level of texts as the difference between systematic and narrative texts.

The mode of narration follows the both-and construction, the sequent poles of which determine the scope of the story. The narrative schema makes possible a syntagmatic unfolding of paradigmatic poles, which can "act out" their parts as they are embodied in the text. There is one class of poles that has an especially important part: such contrasts as life-death, young-old, inexperienced-experienced, which have a fixed,

[15] A. C. Danto, *Analytical Philosophy of History*[2] (Cambridge, 1968).

[16] L. Hjelmslev, *Prolegomena to a Theory of Language*, revised English edition (Madison, 1963), p. 36: "This is what is behind the distinction between process and system: in the process, in the text, is present a both-and, a conjunction or co-existence between the functives entering therein, in the system is present an either-or, a disjunction or alternation between the functives entering therein." For remarks on this statement, see A. Greimas, *Du Sens* (Paris, 1970), esp. the chapter "Éléments d'une grammaire narrative."

sequent relation (what Hjelmslev calls "determinations"). On these narrative contrasts depend all other contrasts.

A story does not take shape solely through its narrative schema, but also through the implementation of the schema on the different levels of the text. The task of describing this implementation as a speech action and of tracing it back to its context is fulfilled by the text-pragmatic and the text-poetic respectively. If one wishes to extract a story out of the narrative schema formulated by Danto there would have to be a whole series of transformations which we do not have time to go through in detail here. One might call the dimension arising out of the narrative schema, the *disposition* of the story. In this, the narrative schema is subject to a thematic situation. What lies between story disposition and story is the actual composition of the story. This might be regarded as analogous to the different "situations" of a printing-block.

The pragmatic connection between story disposition and story can be illustrated by a simple example. There is a whole collection of pragmatically determined story dispositions—namely, the paragraphs of the penal code. From every premise one can deduce stories, or at least incomplete halves of stories. Alternatively, there are stories that can be reduced to the premises of paragraphs in the penal code,[17] though they, too, are incomplete and in need of a conclusion. This is provided by the conclusion of the paragraph, in accordance with the given pragmatic context. The story can end only with the conclusion of the paragraph—a story the poles of which are offense and punishment. T-1 and t-3, offense and punishment, are named by the paragraph; t-2, in between, is implicitly presumed in the paragraph—namely, the judgment. Obviously under these conditions there must be two separate modes of narration in court (*diegesis* and *narratio* in classical rhetoric). In his narration the accused will take care not to allow a story to unfold. The accuser, on the other hand, will set out to arrange the "facts" as a story. It will be one of those stories which, as it comes under the premise of a paragraph, will be only "half a story," i.e., the first half. This is the kind of story we mean when we use such phrases as "a likely story," "telling stories" etc. It is no accident that Wilhelm Schapp's book is called *In Geschichten verstrickt*[18] (Entangled in Stories), and it is no accident that the last horizon in these stories is the *"Weltgeschichte im christlichen Sinne"* (p. 202)—a world history coordinated with a world court.

---

[17] From another standpoint A. Jolles has also referred to this connection: "We see how a rule, a legal paragraph, merges into an event; an event comes into existence, and as it is captured by language, it takes on a gestalt." Instead of "event," we should prefer the term "story" here.

[18] W. Schapp, *In Geschichten verstrickt* (Hamburg, 1963).

II

The transition from paragraphs of the penal code to the story that is implicit in them, is a transition from the systematic to the narrative text. It is conceivable that the story could be narrated in such a way that it contained nothing but the characteristic features of that category of stories to be associated with the particular paragraph. In the sphere of juridical narration, this would mean that the more serious the case, the less would be told. In other spheres there is normally a narrative surplus, which, however, has another pragmatic function: namely, to enhance probability by means of realistic detail.

It would seem that the borderland between systematic and narrative texts contains much that will help us to understand the way in which "stories" are constituted as texts. This territory was closely explored by Lessing in his *Abhandlungen über die Fabel.*[19] The fable and the exemplum are minimal narrative forms arising from minimal systematic texts such as maxims, proverbs, and moral precepts. Lessing shows step by step how a narrative text can be extracted from the systematic text that is its subject:

"The weaker is generally a prey to the stronger. This is a generalization that brings to my mind a series of things, one of which is always stronger than the next, and which can therefore destroy one another in the descending order of their various strengths. A series of *things*! Who will enjoy spending his time thinking about the dreary idea of a *thing* without alighting upon this or that *definite thing* whose qualities will conjure up a clear picture for him? And so here, too, instead of a series of *indefinite* things I will assume a series of *definite, real* things. I could seek out a series of states or kings in history; but how many people are so conversant with history that, the moment I named my states or kings, they could recall the size and power these states and kings had in relation to one another? I should have made my sentence only a little more conceivable, and I should like to make all of it as conceivable as possible! I hit on the idea of animals; and why shouldn't I be allowed to choose a series of animals—especially if they are well-known animals? A cock, a marten, a fox, a wolf: we know these animals; we only have to hear their names to know which is the weaker and which the stronger. So now my sentence reads: the marten eats the cock, the fox the marten, the wolf the fox. It *eats*? But perhaps it isn't eating. This is not yet definite enough for me. And so I say: it *ate*. And now, you see, my sentence has become a fable!"* (P. 16.)

What brings about the transformation of the general into the particu-

[19] G. E. Lessing's *Collected Works*, ed. P. Rilla (Berlin, 1955), vol. IV.

lar is the effect. Through this, a moral statement is to be made vivid and "conceivable." Thus the sum total of a moral statement is translated into the sum total of an *action*: "An action is what I call a series of changes which together make up a whole. This unit of the whole rests on the conformity of all the parts to a single purpose. The purpose of the fable—that for which the fable has been devised—is the moral precept" (pp. 24 f.). The "purpose," i.e., the pragmatic connection, determines the constitution of the narrative text—the manner in which the narrative schema is put together.

Lessing's idea of the "unit of the whole" has implications for the tense of his narrative. The chronologically arranged whole of the "action" can be a whole only if one has a complete view of it. And this means that the story has to be in the past. The preterite here, as in all narrative texts, is the tense denoting completeness of action, i.e., its state of being past. Käte Hamburger, who cannot see the connection between completeness and "pastness," has, in her book *Die Logik der Dichtung*,[20] developed a series of imaginary problems out of the difference between the role of the preterite in texts of fiction and non-fiction. For her the narrative as fiction has, to a certain degree, no narrator. What is presented here is "a fictional reality with an existence of its own, which *as fiction is just as independent of a narrator as is a 'real' reality*" (p. 112). As the fictional narrative, according to Hamburger, is not narrated, it is also not in the past but in a fictional present. In fiction, "the grammatical form of the imperfect (loses) its function of informing us about the past state of the facts conveyed" (p. 64). But in fact she is overlooking the particular function of the preterite: that right up to the penultimate sentence of the narrative text it denotes an already completed situation which, precisely because it is a "whole," is the determining factor in the style of text construction. The preterite always denotes this all-embracing completeness. In this it differs from the present tense and has a special (cataphoric) quality in that it makes possible a "whole" that may extend over a period of time.

Exemplum and fable coincide insofar as they constitute a narrative completeness relating to a systematic completeness. The style and method, of course, are different, with the fable approaching closer to the borders of the systematic text. At one point in his thesis, Lessing deals with the difference between fable and exemplum. In the "inner probability" (p. 45) that is uninfluenced by the factual nature of the real case, Lessing—in contrast to Aristotle—sees an advantage that fables have over historical examples, with regard to the power of conviction (p. 45).

---

[20] Käte Hamburger, *Die Logik der Dichtung*[2] (Stuttgart, 1968).

Lessing's idea of the "inner probability" distinguishing the fable from the exemplum is not altogether apposite. It conceals the programmatic improbability of the fable and hence what really separates fable and exemplum from each other.[21] Every improbability in a fable has a particular function: it is a sign of the allegoric intention underlying the "genre." In the fable, the general appears *as* the particular; in the exemplum, it appears *in* the particular. In the first case, the general is represented, in the second it is implied. If one draws a difference between "blind" and thematic implications, the exemplum makes a theme of those implications that give rise to the whole of the underlying moral precept. What the exemplum implies is this moral precept, and the medium through which it makes itself explicit is the story, or the history. The exemplum is a form of expansion and reduction all in one— expansion as regards its underlying maxim, reduction as regards a story from which is extracted and isolated that which the speech action of the exemplum needs in order to take on a concrete form. As far as the direction of the text composition is concerned, there is no doubt. The basic rule underlying the unity of the whole is the "purpose" of the exemplum—the moral precept.

In his book *Die Rechtsmetaphysik der Göttlichen Komödie*,[22] Hugo Friedrich interprets the exemplum as the embodiment of a moral type: "The story refers to something lying beyond the events it depicts—a moral type freed from time" (pp. 28 f.). He is concerned particularly with Dante, in whose work the exemplum contracts to a great and memorable exemplary figure, thus changing its status. It is in these exemplary figures as transformations of the exemplum that the architectural structure of Dante's symbolic world is to be seen. But the exemplum, in this basic structure, does not denote moral types so much as moral relations. It is the relations between good and evil, cleverness and naïveté, power and impotence, or illusion and disillusionment, that emerge from the narrative range of the exemplum. This is composed of the three elements of situation, decision, outcome. The resultant tripartition is shaped by the pragmatic context in which the exemplum is to be placed. In accordance with what in fact is its rhetorical aim, the exemplum is set in a pragmatic situation that is inconclusive and demands a decision. The pragmatic situation and the ultimate situation of the exemplum are isomorphic. Insofar as the given situation and the exemplum are isomorphic, the outcome for the exemplum can be interpreted as an anticipation of the outcome for one's own situation. The

---

[21] On the function of the improbable in fables, see the author's "Poesie des Unpoetischen. Über La Fontaines Umgang mit der Fabel," in: *Poetica*, 1 (1967).

[22] H. Friedrich, *Die Rechtsmetaphysik der Göttlichen Komödie* (Frankfurt, 1942).

exemplum, in fact, shows what it will lead to if one makes a particular decision in a particular situation. It is this form of parallelism that gives the exemplum its power of persuasion in the matter of action or non-action. The fact that the exemplum can be understood as anticipating the outcome of an isomorphic but still incomplete situation, is based on certain deep-lying premises concerning the story-comprehension out of which the exemplum arises. The ideas which Aristotle expressed in his *Rhetorica* on the difference between fable and exemplum, are valuable evidence of this:

"Fables are suitable for addresses to popular assemblies; and they have one advantage—they are comparatively easy to invent, whereas it is hard to find parallels among actual past events. You will in fact frame them just as you frame illustrative parallels: all you require is the power of thinking out your analogy, a power developed by intellectual training. But while it is easier to supply parallels by inventing fables, it is more valuable for the political speaker to supply them by quoting what has actually happened, since in most respects the future will be like what the past has been."[23]

What happens in history is by nature not unique but recurrent. One could therefore say that history in the Aristotelian sense is not unique but recurrent. And so the exemplum indicates a unit of situation and outcome which, because it is recurrent, is of general significance. This is why the Aristotelian exemplum really does have an anticipatory character, for it enables one to assess a still inconclusive situation in the light of earlier experience, and so to take a reasoned decision that is not merely the result of a rhetorical sophism. Quintilian[24] also advised his rhetor to have as many exempla as possible at the ready. Quintilian had in mind the juridical case in particular, and the testimonial value that a skilfully chosen example might have. The exemplum has—or appears to have—the higher authority of detachment and impartiality. Here the authority is no longer that of the recurrent but of the completed past, which lends it greater exemplary validity. In both cases—Aristotle and Quintilian—history is shown in a particular perspective, which Cicero described in a slogan that has lasted right up to the present: "historia magistra vitae."[25] This maxim draws attention to the connection, ex-

[23] *The Works of Aristotle*, vol. xi, *Rhetorica*, transl. by W. R. Roberts (Oxford, 1946), ii, 20.

[24] Quintilian, *Institutio oratoria*, X.1.34, ed. H. E. Butler, The Loeb Classical Library, in 4 vols., iv, p. 22: "(. . .) ex cognitione rerum exemplorumque, quibus imprimis instructus esse debet orator, ne omnis testimonia expectet a litigatore, sed pleraque ex vetustate diligenter sibi cognita sumat, hoc potentiora, quod ea sola criminibus odii et gratiae vacant."

[25] Cicero, *De oratore II*, c. 9,36.

tending beyond the scope of any single lesson, between history and moral philosophy—a connection that establishes the frame within which the exemplum as a "simple form" has its own position. The maxim offers us, to a certain degree, the perspective through which history first becomes visible. History itself is shaped from a moral-philosophical standpoint and appears separated from the historical continuum, bearing its own meaning within itself. History is a macroexemplum. The criteria by which events may be translated into history are those of moral philosophy, which find their expression in the context of a "story." What occurs during the translation of events into history is repeated during the translation of history into exempla, except that here the moral-philosophical substrata undergo a new compression. The "Umwegstruktur"[26] (digressive structure) that is peculiar to history as a "macroexemplum," is lost in this second translation. The exemplum as a minimal narrative unit relates to the minimal systematic unit of the moral-philosophical precept in such a way that they virtually form a compound. "Solum quod facit ad rem est narrandum"[27] runs one of the exemplary rules of Humbert de Romance. The "res" here is the moral precept.

The historical process, as Antiquity understood it and as it underlies the "simple form" of the exemplum, might be described by a term of modern linguistics as "paradigmatic." Wherever history takes on a concrete form, it does so in a manner related to its subsumption under categories of the moral system. Only if a history has its place in the moral system and stands surety for one of that system's precepts, can it assume an exemplary character; only then can it claim the right to be extracted from the continuum of mere events or from the digressiveness of history as a "macroexemplum," and placed in its new paradigmatic context. As a result of this process, the exemplum dispenses with the difference between "mythology, legend, poetry on the one hand, and real history on the other" (Friedrich, p. 28). "What is given in a continual and many-sided tradition is regarded as an event" (p. 28). The drive to gain systematic control of the ever-expanding surfeit of noteworthy material, and the insatiable gathering and sorting of traditional material into a paradigmatic moral system, increased in the Middle Ages and the Renaissance until it became a kind of obsession which is difficult for us to understand today. "It is as if history, pulped and shredded, returned again to the primal force of its boundless material—as is manifested in the encyclopedias of the twelfth and thirteenth cen-

[26] I have taken the term from H. Blumenberg, "Wirklichkeitsbegriff und Wirklichkeitspotential des Mythos," in *Poetik und Hermeneutik*, IV.

[27] Quoted by Friedrich, p. 28.

turies, as elsewhere, in which norms and types are no longer capable of mastering the material of experience and history" (Friedrich, p. 32).

With the reactions of the Christian Middle Ages, however, the exemplum changes its character. Now it is seen as a *figura* and enters into a figure typology[28] that determines the frame of reference for all figures, and in this respect it can be read on two levels—the paradigmatic and the syntagmatic. As history is at one and the same time "magistra vitae" and the story of Christ, so, too, does the exemplum relate both to its paradigmatic classification in the context of the moral-philosophical system and, as a figure, to the proclamation and fulfillment of the story of Christ.

R. Koselleck[29] connects the disappearance of the exemplum since the late eighteenth century with a changed conception of history, the underlying experience of which could no longer be that of the "magistra vitae." The adherence to the continuum of events, which is integral to this new conception of history, can be termed "syntagmatic." As history frees itself from the clutches of the moral-philosophic system, it goes out of the paradigmatic and into the syntagmatic sphere of endless interconnections which continually overlap but can never be conclusively defined. Only now does history as such appear as the quintessence of all "stories" that touch on the factual. With Voltaire, the two possibilities of historical orientation still co-exist. History is narrated (a) in the syntagmatic framework of world history, and (b) in the paradigmatic framework of a collection of exempla for the never-changing condition of human baseness.[30]

So long as the story as an exemplum is related to a moral-philosophical system, the narrative schema will continue to appear fixed, as it were, by outside influences. But this foreignness is not confined to narrative texts. The relation between "case" and penal code, between exemplum and moral precept, is not exceptional. It merely illustrates with particular clarity a more or less prominent determinant of every story. It is characteristic of all stories that there is a specific imbalance of narrative expansion, due to the particular pragmatic context to which the story belongs. As with the exemplum, the paradigmatic conception of history comes closest to the sphere of systematic texts, so history seeks

---

[28] See the fundamental essay by E. Auerbach, "Figura," in *Archivum Romanicum*, XXII (1938), pp. 436-89.

[29] R. Koselleck, "Historia Magistra Vitae. Über die Auflösung des Topos im Horizont neuzeitlich bewegter Geschichte," in *Natur und Geschichte, Karl Löwith zum 70. Geburtstag* (Stuttgart, 1967), pp. 196-218.

[30] See the author's Einleitung zu Voltaire, *Aus dem Philosophischen Wörterbuch*, Sammlung Insel (Frankfurt, 1967).

in its syntagmatic context to minimize the "foreignness." Its aim is to represent things "as they actually were." But, ultimately, instead of removing the foreignness, it can only achieve the illusion of having removed it. This is precisely what Roland Barthes, in an essay on *Le discours de l'histoire*,[31] describes as history-writing's pretension to reality, with which an implicit ideology covers itself. The writing of any story presupposes an interest that needs to be theorized.

III

The idea of poetic autonomy has, with some exceptions, so far prevented literary critics from seeking out the pragmatic forms underlying poetic forms, and from working out the connection between the latter and their pragmatic correlatives. Once one is aware of this connection, one realizes that a critical treatment of pragmatic speech actions is the great source for the origin of poetic forms. An analytic attitude towards the pragmatic form entails a change of focus, to which there corresponds a speech action that is in direct opposition to a speech action as manifested by the pragmatic form. A pragmatic speech action does not become concrete in its context, but as regards its final purpose it arranges itself, so to speak, spontaneously. An act of attentiveness is necessary, an "intentio obliqua," to give a concrete form to the "intentio recta" of the pragmatic speech action as such. If the pragmatic form turns out to be the shortest way to the fulfillment of an intention, the release of the pragmatic form entails the possibility of provoking this intention through the manner of its presentation, and calling into question its pragmatic stylistic principle. Flaubert acts rather in this manner when, in *Bouvard et Pécuchet*, he makes the speech action "popular scientific representation" the subject of a quotation which inexorably brings to light its ideological implications and ridicules it simply by the manner of its repetition. This example illustrates the possibilities of the "secondary use" of pragmatic speech actions, which enables a problem to be made implicitly conceivable without going beyond the confines of the thing that is criticized—in contrast to explicit criticism, which takes place on the level of a metalanguage and is therefore bound to enter into an abstract relationship with the object of the criticism.

Following the transformation of the exemplum into its problematical

---

[31] R. Barthes, "Le Discours de l'Histoire," in *Information sur les Sciences Sociales* (1967), p. 73: "Comme on le voit, par sa structure même et sans qu'il soit besoin de faire appel à la substance de contenu, le discours historique est essentiellement idéologique, ou pour être plus précis, imaginaire, s'il est vrai que l'imaginaire est le langage par lequel l'énonçant d'un discours (entité purement linguistique) 'remplit' le sujet d'énonciation (entité psychologique ou idéologique)."

situation means tracing the reversal of "story as exemplum" to "exemplum as story." But before the end of the eighteenth century, when for historical and philosophical reasons the exemplum as a simple form faded out, there were two instances of a paradigmatic accomplishment of this reversal: first in the stories of Boccaccio, and then in Montaigne's essays.

Of the medieval narrative forms that Boccacio subsumes under the new "genre" of the short story, the exemplum—as H.-J. Neuschäfer has shown in his comprehensive study *Boccaccio und der Beginn der Novelle*[32]—is pre-eminent. A simple instance of Boccaccio's method of handling the speech action of the exemplum is the way he deals with the exemplum of the good friend—in the collection *Disciplina clericalis*.[33] Neuschäfer has made a perspicacious comparison between the exemplum and the story that proceeds from it. He shows that the example of the generous man, who unhesitatingly gives his bride to his friend who falls in love with her, becomes problematical in the story because "the characters are no longer there merely as the vehicle for an idea, but have a consciousness of their own" (p. 45). And so the clarity of the exemplum is obscured in particular through the fact that in Boccaccio's story the bride is not simply an object but is conscious, is horrified by the demand made on her, and so sets off a whole chain of ever-widening complications, which quite undermine the exemplarity of the exemplum. As the ideal conception of generosity is now confronted with problems and resistance, opposed as it is by existing factors of reality, Neuschäfer goes so far as to state "that the story throws direct doubts on the meaning of the exemplum" (p. 47). This is certainly an "overexposure" of the story's intention, for the exemplary element is not completely lost, but simply complicated and made into an object for reflection. "Santissima cosa adunque è l'amistà" is still the last word even here.[34] Neuschäfer himself refers to Boccaccio's "peculiar method" of "so to speak applying the brake and catching up the uncertainties of his story at a particular point" (p. 48). Boccaccio's "critique" involves explaining "blind implications" on the level of the text itself. As he makes a particularity out of the exemplum which is to illustrate a generality, he lays bare the purely formal side of this claim to particularity. And so he passes beyond the

---

[32] H.-J. Neuschäfer, *Boccaccio und der Beginn der Novelle* (Munich, 1969). On the relation between exemplum and story, see also W. Pabst, *Novellentheorie und Novellendichtung*, 2nd ed. (Heidelberg, 1967), and S. Battaglia, *Giovanni Boccaccio e la riforma della narrativa* (Naples, 1969).

[33] Boccaccio, *Il Decameron*, ed. Ch. S. Singleton, 2 vols. (Bari, 1955), *Giornata de cima, novella ottava*, I, 275-91.

[34] I, 290.

exemplum in the direction of a story whose surplus of determinants makes it impossible for it to be reduced to a simple moral precept or, in this case, a moral idea.

There is a fundamental difference between the case that is offered for judgment and the example that is meant directly or indirectly to inspire imitation. As speech actions they appeal to two quite different modes of thought. The "one-sided emphasis on *one* standpoint," which Neuschäfer sees as the "characteristic of the mediaeval exemplum" (p. 54), can easily be explained in terms of the intention immanent in the exemplum—an appeal for *imitatio*.

The explanation of "blind implications"—i.e., such implications as are not taken up thematically—will result in one's calling into question the priority of the generality that gave rise to the exemplum. What this secondary level of narrative allows is primarily a change of attitude, from "imitation" to "judgment." Through this change of attitude, which the secondary narrative represents, the exemplum becomes a case, or a story demonstrating the case. The link between case and story has been convincingly drawn by A. Jolles. His definition of the case coincides exactly with what we have termed the attitude of "judging." "In the case, the form results from the criterion used as a measure during the evaluation of actions, but in the realization the question concerns the value of the norms. The existence, validity, and range of different norms are considered, but this consideration contains the question: where lies the weight, and according to which norm is one to evaluate?" (p. 190). The case is the form of the uncertainty itself: "The strange thing about the case form is the fact that although it asks the question, it cannot give the answer; it imposes on us the duty of deciding, but it doesn't contain the decision itself—what is realized in it is the weighing, but not the result of the weighing" (p. 191). Jolles' account of the original connection between case and story is directly confirmed by the fact that Boccaccio himself had a predilection for using the term in referring to his stories. Thus at the end of the fourth day, Dioneo looks back on the "infortunati casi d'amore"[35] which the company had learned about that day. Or at the beginning of the eighth story on the second day, when the narrator intervenes, reference is made, not without a smile, to the coming story and the "vari casi della bella donna."[36]

The problematic exemplum does not, of course, coincide simply with that speech action which, as a "case," has its firm position in the context of law. The *casus* as a problematic case has a particularly complex relation to the norm of the law; the communication of case and legal norm

---

[35] I, 326.   [36] I, 143.

presupposes a high degree of discernment on the part of the presiding judge. If we want to find out the particular link between the short story and the case and exemplum, we had best go back to an examination of the structure of discernment, as provided by Kant's *Kritik der Urteilskraft*. For Kant, *discernment* is "the ability to realize the particular as contained in the general."[37] Discernment "with regard to a conception through which an object is conveyed, needs and indeed demands the concurrence of two powers of conception: the imagination (for the perception and combination of the manifold) and intellect (for the definition that will cover this combination)" (p. 137). In this regard there is one category of judgment that is particularly relevant—that in which there is no definition that corresponds to the conception. Kant calls this category *judgments of taste*. "As there is no definition of the object as a basis for the judgment, it can only exist in the subsumption of the imagination itself (with a conception through which an object is given), on condition that the intellect proceeds from perception to definitions" (p. 137). The object of the judgment of taste, produced by the imagination itself, is "esthetic ideas" (p. 167). "But by esthetic idea I mean that conception by the imagination which stimulates much thought, without any definite idea—i.e., definition—being adequate to express it, and which consequently no language can fully encompass or make intelligible" (p. 168). The relation between the esthetic idea and the definition is determined by the fact that "a host of feelings and secondary conceptions is stirred up for which there is no expression" (p. 170). "In a word, the esthetic idea is a conception of the imagination associated with a given definition—a conception which is linked to such a multiplicity of partial conceptions in its free application that no expression denoting a particular definition can be found for it; a conception, then, that makes one think much that is indefinable in addition to what one thinks about a definition, and it is the feeling for the indefinable that animates the faculty of cognition and provides a spiritual link with language, as mere letters" (p. 171). It is precisely this confirmation of discernment, which transcends the limits of legally fixed norms and is no longer definable but, as a reflection, i.e., a search for definitions, remains inconclusive, that forms the intentional correlative which distinguishes the poetic speech action "short story" from the pragmatic speech actions "case and exemplum." What is demanded of the reader is not a real but a "specimen" judgment. The pragmatic structure becomes a tentative pragmatic

[37] I. Kant, *Kritik der Urteilskraft*, ed. K. Vorländer (Hamburg, 1959), introduction, p. 15. On Kant's theory of the example, see G. Buck, *Lernen und Erfahrung* (Stuttgart, 1967).

structure; the reader no longer merely accepts a part that is assigned to him—he *plays* a part.

When the exemplum is exposed to a "multiplicity of partial conceptions," it loses its generality and tends towards the individual case. "The place of the legal typicality is taken by a unique case, which can be problematical precisely because of its uniqueness; for only the particular and the unique, not the general and what is always so, raises problems" (Neuschäfer, p. 43). However, this uniqueness is not absolute. It is true that the complexity of the moral situation can no longer be resolved by an underlying moral precept, and thus retains its uniqueness; but the Boccaccio short story, as a story, still retains its exemplary structure, insofar as it illustrates a narrative arrangement that forms the basis of a large number of stories. What always happens in the *Decameron* is that on each evening the narrative arrangement is explained that is to be the meeting point of the stories to be told the following day. And so in spite of their "uniqueness," the stories generally stand within a common paradigmatic frame which must be taken into account when we are confronted with each individual story. If the exemplum used to be nothing more than the narrative transposition of a moral precept, in Boccaccio the story is told in three different "situations," which in their interrelation move ever farther away from the paradigmatic center-point. This gradated narrative expansion is what is special about Boccaccio's stories. The reader first learns about the narrative arrangement. This is outlined in the "argument" that precedes each story and "summarizes" the story—i.e., fixes on an element of the constitutional process of the narrative text, from the standpoint of which the narrative expansion can be analyzed.

In Boccaccio's *Decameron*, the (fictional) narrators are identical with the (fictional) audience. Narrator and audience as constituent implications in the story itself become explicit in the overall framework, and so are directly conceivable. If one proceeds from the fact that the intended use of a text prescribes the rules that direct its composition, then from the narrator-audience society pictured in the framing story, one can derive the poetics of the story arising out of the pragmatic element of the exemplum. The new mode of presentation of the story is made into a theme, as denoting the self-evidence of the society made explicit in the framing story. Perhaps the idea of maturity can give the clearest description of this self-awareness. What Neuschäfer says of Boccaccio's characters also—indeed, especially—applies to the little society of the framing story, i.e., that "they are not mere objects" of some superhuman power, or one-sided representatives of a superordinate idea, but are independent "subjects" who are capable of discussing and judging the given data for themselves (p. 61). This maturity has a Utopian character. The little company that flees from the fear of the plague in Florence, to live together for a few days in complete and undisturbed harmony, anticipates the reconciliation between nature and reason that was a continual subject of discussion right up to Schiller's letters on the esthetic upbringing of man. Reasonable nature and natural reason are the factors that govern the conduct of this ideal society. The two together form the basis for that liberality of judgment that each individual in this society must maintain, both in narrating and in listening, if he is to have a feeling for the multiplicity of human appearances and for the inexhaustible residue of cases that lie outside the established norms.

In this framing story, Neuschäfer sees, above all, the "intention to confront us with human nature in its very inconsistency" (p. 134). He feels that this inconsistency can be ironed out only from case to case through a "compromise" (p. 64). "One can say that in the stories of the Decameron human nature is revealed for the first time with all its own uncertainties, and that this is the first attempt to present it in its inconsistency, and that the framework of the stories, with Miseria and Dignitas, circumscribes those two poles which for Boccaccio denoted the absolute extremes of its possibilities" (p. 134 ff.). For Neuschäfer, the polarity of Miseria and Dignitas represents Boccaccio's final word. But this reveals only the medieval Boccaccio. It leaves out what lies between the lines—the liberating laugh, the superior smile, the reconciliation of nature and reason in anticipation of the ideal, emancipated society. It is this very force of anticipation—which makes possible the cheerful composure of the members of this society—that stands out in such stark contrast to the terror of the plague in Florence.

The reader of the *Decameron* is not identical to the audience evoked in the framing story. But he does not stand in a direct relation to the narratives either. However, his perspective is mapped out. It lies in the process of *identification* with that ideal society in which—if only exceptionally and for a short time—nature and reason are reconciled. And so he becomes a partner in this foretaste of a mature society, from the standpoint of which the new "genre" of the short story first takes on its real meaning.

IV

In R. Koselleck's essay *Historia magistra vitae*, which is a "dissolution of the topic against the background of the violent history of modern times," Montaigne's attitude plays only a minor role. This appears to be a borderline example of that skeptical view of history which amounts to the doctrine that there is nothing to learn from history.

"Even the fact that one could learn nothing from history was, after all, a definite experience, an historical lesson, which could make the knower more discerning, cleverer, or—to use Burckhardt's terms—wiser" (p. 200). The process of "dissolving the topic"—this is Koselleck's thesis—starts off with the eighteenth century and with certain specific premises. "Up until the eighteenth century, the use of this expression remained an infallible indication of the constancy—taken for granted—of human nature, whose activities lend themselves to the provision of repeatable proofs of moral, theological, or political doctrines" (p. 197). However misguided it might be to regard Montaigne as the precursor of dissolution of the paradigmatic dimension of history set off in the eighteenth century as a result of a new experience of history, this certainly does not mean to say that his skeptical attitude towards the exemplum has no place in history. The position occupied by Montaigne's skepticism can be described, in terms used by Roland Barthes, as *degré zéro*[38] of history. Where Montaigne makes his attitude most clear, history finds itself an equal distance away from both the syntagmatic and the paradigmatic level. Thus past faith in the consistency of history is abandoned, along with Christian faith in the salvationary orientation of history. But under this premise it is just as impossible to reach a decision concerning the statement that something can be learned from history as it is to reach one on the opposite, and yet implicitly confirmatory, statement that nothing is to be learned from history. Montaigne's concern is with the suspense that has become a principle of representation itself. In Montaigne, the vast number of historically viewed stories neither fulfill their traditional paradigmatic function, nor take on any syntagmatic relationship, nor bear their own value within themselves. But this very inconclusiveness gives room for reflection, though this will no longer arrive at a goal that can be reified as a "doctrine." It is true that the "historiens" give a picture of "homme en général de qui je cherche la connaissance," but if here this picture is to be found "plus vif et plus entier qu'en nul autre lieu," then this is only as "la diversité et vérité de ces conditions internes en gros et en détail, la variété des moyens de son assemblage et des accidents qui le menacent."[39] But Montaigne is not concerned solely with the endless diversity of events, which continually reveals the end-

---

[38] R. Barthes, *Le degré zéro de l'écriture*[2] (Paris, 1969), p. 67. Barthes has transferred the linguistic term ("on sait que certains linguistes établissent entre les deux termes d'une polarité . . . l'existence d'un troisième terme, terme neutre ou terme zéro") to the new field of "écriture."

[39] Montaigne, *Essais*, ii, 10, *Des Livres*, ed. A. Thibaudet, Bibliothèque de la Pléiade (Paris, 1950), p. 458.

less diversity of "homme en général" and thus makes the whole concept increasingly problematical, but his interest lies even more with the higher level of the relation between events and history, i.e., the manner in which the diverse approaches of the historians first compose the history. Two things may be regarded as exemplary: one, a form of representation that makes a theme of the multiplicity of communications between events and history, "qui nous représente la diversité même des bruits qui courent et le différent rapport qu'on lui faisoit" (II, 10, p. 459); two, a manner of representation, the excellence of which is attributable not so much to the "histoire" itself as to the discernment of the historian. In the one case, the events withdraw behind the "diversité" of the evidence guaranteeing them; in the other, they withdraw behind the perfection of a well-grounded but therefore only "probable conception." As such problematic stories are continually set in a state of suspense, they are drawn into the sphere of reflection, which is continually made concrete as a speech action of suspense. To the extent that the "final purpose" becomes problematic, the speech action can take as its subject only its own movement. This priority of speech action over its purpose is shown clearly by Montaigne himself when he chooses as the title of his work the mode of treatment that he intends to use: *Les Essais*. The essay is at one and the same time a pragmatic and a poetic speech action. As pragmatic, it is a reflection on the possibility of knowing "homme en général"; as poetic, it takes as its subject this very reflection, in the unforeseeability and inconclusiveness of its movement. When, in the essay "De l'exercitation" (II, 6), Montaigne says of himself "Je peins principalement mes cogitations, subjecte informe, qui ne peut tomber en production ouvragère" (p. 416), with "peindre" and "cogitations" he is denoting this very bipartition.

Montaigne's view of history is a view of stories, and his view of stories is a view of exempla. It is only because stories are presented to him as exempla that he can in turn reduce them to stories that are no longer exemplary representatives of something general but, as they represent only themselves, become components of an immeasurable "diversité" of what is actually possible. However, the process of this reduction does not simply lead back to the "original" state of the story before it was given the status of an exemplum. The stories from which exempla were traditionally extracted were already designed for this purpose. They were macro-exempla which could also be read as a series of micro-exempla. If a story is taken out of its context and raised to the level of an exemplum and then in a second reproduction is withdrawn from its exemplarity, it will express an ambiguity which was not built into the original context of the story. The "meaning" of the story will no longer be fixed, and can be only tentatively grasped by a reflective process:

"Et combien y ay-je espandu d'histoires qui ne disent mot, lesquelles qui voudra esplucher un peu ingenieusement, en produira infinis Essais. Ny elles, ny mes allegations ne servent pas tousjours simplement d'exemple, d'authorité ou d'ornement. Je ne les regarde pas seulement par l'usage que j'en tire. Elles portent souvent, hors de mon propos, la semence d'une matiere plus riche et plus hardie, et sonnent à gauche un ton plus delicat, et pour moy qui n'en veux exprimer d'avantage, et pour ceux qui rencontreront mon air" (Considération sur Cicéron, i, 40, p. 289).

The course that Boccaccio took from the exemplum, through the problematic exemplum, to the short story was determined by the fact that in the narrative process itself he unfolded the "blind implications" of the exemplum, thus challenging its clarity. Montaigne, however, through his process of reduction, liberates the "blind implications" by making them the subject of a study that is fully aware of the inexhaustibility of its subject.

Exemplum and maxim are complementary. The exemplum is an exemplum with reference to a maxim; the maxim can take on a concrete form only through the perspective of an exemplum. The parallel in Montaigne is the complement of the *problematic* exemplum and the *problematic* maxim, i.e., reflection. It is only in the light of this complementary structure that the construction of Montaigne's essays can be understood. This fact has long been obscured by a misconception that the actual relevance of the essays must be found in the "artistic" self-presentation of the later essays. Even Hugo Friedrich makes this a point of his book on Montaigne, therein following Villey[40] and especially Burckhardt's conception of the Renaissance as an era of discovery of individuality;[41] he sets out to "give expression basically only to the dominant ideas of the middle and later periods, i.e., those which frequent

---

[40] P. Villey, Les sources et l'évolution des essais de Montaigne, 2 t. (Paris, 1908), t.2, l'évolution des Essais, p. 43: "Il n'est personne qui n'ait été surpris de tous ces petits chapitres, si grêles, qui ouvrent le premier livre. On s'étonne qu'ils puissent être de la même main qui a écrit l'essai 'De la vanité' ou celui 'De l'expérience.' Ces chapitres-là coûtent peu à Montaigne, il n'y met rien du sien. N'importe qui les multiplierait à l'infini, car ils n'ont aucune personnalité."

[41] J. Burckhardt, Die Kultur der Renaissance in Italien, Ges. Werke, III (Darmstadt, 1962). See especially the second part "Entwicklung des Individuums" and the notes on the "Vollendung der Persönlichkeit."

repetition guarantees to be an integral part of his spiritual organism."[42] The reference of the ego to itself seems in this context to guarantee the unity: "His writing, which judged from the standpoint of systematization appears to be a ramble without a destination, proves to be the organic radiation of an ego that can remain completely occupied by itself." But if one replaces this very isolated theme of self-presentation back in the general framework of the essays, it becomes clear that the theme is only the logical development of problems that were already the subject of the earliest essays.

For the link between problematic exemplum and problematic maxim, from which Montaigne's essays proceed, the introductory essay "Par divers moyens on arrive à pareille fin" offers a model which is continually developed in the essays that follow.[43] The title of the essay is itself a maxim, but of so general a nature that one cannot gauge any idea of the mode of treatment from it. Here to a certain extent the maxim only denotes a form of its own absence, for it sets up as a theme something that directly contradicts the traditional clarity and finality of maxim and exemplum—namely, *diversité*. The essay itself also begins with a maxim or at least a pseudomaxim: "La plus commune façon d'amollir les coeurs de ceux qu'on a offensez, lors qu'ayant la vengeance en main, ils nous tiennent à leur mercy, c'est de les esmouvoir par submission à commiseration et à pitié" (ɪ, 1, p. 27). This introductory maxim is an illustration of the titular maxim, insofar as it is a qualification of the original maxim and makes it something to be reflected upon. Parallel to the "la plus commune façon" with which it is introduced, there is in the very next sentence a qualifying "toutesfois," which brings into play the contrasting possibility: "Toutesfois la braverie, et la constance, moyens tous contraires, ont quelquesfois servi à ce mesme effect." To illustrate this latter possibility, he then offers three examples: Edward Prince of Wales captures a town that he intends to punish, and after all pleas for mercy have done nothing but increase his wrath, he is so impressed by the sight of three of his enemies heroically defending themselves that his wrath disappears and he pardons them and all the other inhabitants of the town. Scanderbeg forgives a soldier because he defiantly faces him with his sword drawn at the ready. Emperor Conrad pardons the women of Weinsberg, who with cunning and with courage try to rescue their menfolk. To these three examples of anger suddenly appeased by cour-

---

[42] H. Friedrich, *Montaigne* (Bern, 1949), p. 8. But the perspective of this important representation extends far beyond its program.

[43] On this essay, see also the interpretation by Friedrich, pp. 181-86. As I have subsequently discovered, the following account largely coincides with that of Friedrich.

age, Montaigne adds a personal reflection of his own:[44] with him, pity and courage would be equally successful, but pity would be more natural for him. The confession is at once qualified, as it is contrasted with the Stoic standpoint, according to which pity is nothing but a "passion vitieuse." Montaigne returns to his examples and tries to systematize them: weak natures lapse into pity, "femmes, enfants, le vulgaire" (amongst whom Montaigne counts himself with ironic self-debasement); admiration of fearless virtue is the sign of "une âme forte et inployable." But this is again followed by a qualifying "toutesfois." Also with "âmes moins généreuses," "étonnement" and "admiration" may be equally effective. On the one hand, Pelopidas is pardoned by the people of Thebes because he confesses his crime and begs for mercy; but, on the other, Epaminondas, who arrogantly challenges everyone, is also released by the people. Finally, Dionysius, who wishes to make a "tragique exemple" of his enemy, finds that the imperturbability of the latter threatens to have an influence on the attitude of his army, and so has to have him killed in secret. Following on directly from this new collection of examples comes a reflection that does away with all tendencies to systematize and defines the Montaigne view of mankind: "Certes, c'est un subject merveilleusement vain, divers, et ondoyant, que l'homme. Il est malaisé d'y fonder jugement constant et uniforme" (p. 29). Following this reflection come the contradictory exempla of Pompey, who pardoned a town because of the greatness and virtue of a single citizen, and the guest of Sylla who sacrificed himself for nothing—and these put the titular maxim in reverse. In the light of these new examples it ought to read: "Par pareils moyens on arrive à diverses fins." What is here only the implicit enigma and incalculability of human conduct becomes explicit in the last exemplum, which Montaigne sets "directement contre mes premieres exemples" (p. 30) and which is of especial significance if only because it is by far the most expansive example in the essay.[45] Alexander, who after a long period of siege has captured the town of Gaza, takes prisoner the commander, whose heroism is evinced by the most astonishing deeds of valor. The imperturbability of the commander, whom he confronts with the prospect of an agonizing death, so enrages Alexander that he has him tortured to death on the spot. In ever wilder rage, he has the whole town razed to the ground. What is vital in this anti-exemplum, which again calls into question the

[44] This reflection is added in the second edition (1588).

[45] The exemplum of Alexander's anger is added in the 1588 edition. The conjectures on the reasons for Alexander's conduct, which conclude the text, are extended by two new possibilities in the posthumous edition of 1595. Here the conclusion is the depiction of the destruction of Thebes.

titular maxim, is the inherent incalculability of human conduct. What happens between the time t-1, when the commander is taken prisoner, and t-3, when he is put to death—i.e., the period t-2—can no longer be comprehended. And so the story falls into two sections, and what lies between them does not occur on the level of the story but on the level of the narrator's conjectures. At this vital point, there is mention only of possibilities, which take the place of any definite answer. Thus the "explanation" is offered only in the form of a threefold question: "Seroit-ce que la hardiesse luy fut si commune que, pour ne l'admirer point, il la respectast moins? Ou qu'il l'estimast si proprement sienne qu'en cette hauteur il ne peust souffrir de la veoir en un autre sans le despit d'une passion envieuse, ou que l'impetuosité naturelle de sa cholere fust incapable d'opposition?"

It is the vital middle section, which binds together the situation and the outcome and thus constitutes the "meaning" of the exemplum, that in Montaigne becomes problematic. Whereas in the classic exemplum the link between situation and solution was indisputable and had only to be taken note of, now the link itself has become a puzzle, and is therefore an interesting subject of psychological and moral cogitation. With this change of orientation, the frame of reference is removed, which is essential if an exemplum is actually to be an example. The change of status of the exemplum in Montaigne's essay involves its no longer setting an example for actions, but an example for *re*actions. The spontaneity and unforeseeability of the reactions captures the essence of human mystery and unfathomableness. The human enigma becomes the theme. As reactions, the "exemplary" actions in this essay are no longer the responsibility of the subject. If traditional forms of exemplum presupposed the possibility of a decision—as is implied by the moral category of responsibility—the reactions in Montaigne's exempla are conditioned by the irreducible complexity of the character and the dramatic moment. This means that the exemplum loses its representative function and is directed back to a story the meaning of which is no longer obvious, but is a starting point for purely subjective and constantly renewed conjecture.

While the early essays are generally problematic chains of self-cancelling exempla with occasional reflections, in the later essays the "simple form" of the historic exemplum fades further and further into the background. The authenticity of the exemplum, which was the traditional foundation of its authority, itself becomes questionable in the same proportion as the supposed exemplarity of the example is open to question. The best exempla are now those that are most obvious, taken from one's own experience and authenticated by it. "La vie de César n'a point plus d'exemples que la notre pour nous" (III, 13, p. 1205). This turning away from "exemples étrangers et scholastiques" (III, 13, p. 1214) arises out of the discovery of the self as an inexhaustible source of exempla, backed by the authority of experience. Thus the ego replaces history as the quintessence of authenticated stories. But just as in Montaigne "historia" cannot be "magistra vitae," so neither can the ego itself become "magistra vitae." As it (the ego) presents itself with all its endless contradictions and inconsistencies, it induces not learning—for this presupposes something dependable—but endless reflection. The examples in Montaigne—even the examples from his own life—have the paradoxical function of being examples for the particular and not for the general. This new meaning of "exemple" in Montaigne is illustrated in the essay "De l'expérience" (III, 13). The problematic relation between the general and the particular is considered here with reference to the incongruity of laws and human conduct. Even the subtlest refinement of the laws is still bound to be inadequate in view of the immeasurable diversity of human actions. At this point Montaigne continues: "La multiplication de nos inventions n'arrivera pas à la variation des exemples" (p. 1196). The exemplum here is the individual case, which cannot be subsumed and to which even the widest diversification of the laws cannot do justice, because finally it conforms only to itself.

Ultimately for Montaigne the impossibility of exempla implies the impossibility of stories and hence even of one's own life-story. Montaigne begins his essay "Du repentir" (III, 2) with a basic idea that sets up the program for a life-story and at the same time demonstrates its impossibility. The first sentence leads one to expect a biography: "Les autres forment l'homme: je le récite" (p. 899). But in the reflections that follow immediately afterwards, the conditions that would make such a story possible are done away with. The world is nothing but an incessant fluctuation, and the things in it fluctuate in two ways—by themselves and through the movement of the whole. Consistency is only a border-line case of this fluctuation: "La constance mesme n'est autre chose qu'un branle plus languissant." And so even the representation cannot be certain of the object it is representing: "Je ne puis asseurer mon object; il va trouble et chancelant, d'une yvresse naturelle." The fluctuation of the object also corresponds to the impermanence of the perspective in which it appears—a perspective that changes from one moment to the next: "Je le prens en ce point, comme il est, en l'instant que je m'amuse à luy." Out of this arises the program of a representation that is the program of an "anti-story," insofar as from the story are extracted the integrant elements that first enable it to be meaningfully split up. "Je ne peints pas l'estre. Je peints le passage: non un passage d'aage en autre, ou, comme dict le peuple, de sept en sept ans, mais de jour en jour, de minute en minute." But not only does the story break up into ever smaller segments determined by an ever decreasing unit of time; the story itself continually has to be adjusted, since it changes from hour to hour as it comes under ever new perspectives. "Il faut accommoder mon historie à l'heure. Je pourray tantost changer, non de fortune seulement, mais aussi d'intention." Thus the representation of one's own life is "un contrerolle de divers et muables accidens et d'imaginations irresolues et, quand il y eschet, contraires: soit que je sois autre moymesme, soit que je saisisse les subjects par autres circonstances et considerations. Tant y a que je me contredits bien à l'adventure, mais la vérité, comme disoit Demades, je ne la contredy point" (p. 900). However, this "vérité" is no longer that of a "récit," but that of an essay: "Si mon ame pouvoit prendre pied, je ne m'essaierois pas, je me resoudrois; elle est tousjours en apprentissage et en espreuve." What makes the "histoire" impossible makes the essay possible. What was revealed by the Alexander exemplum in Essay i, 1—the disintegration of the story—has itself become the object of reflection. The radicality with which this occurs is of theoretic significance, and does not simply reflect the difficulties of writing a biography. In his reflections, just as when he is actually speaking about himself, Montaigne is not solely concerned with himself; references to the authenticity of one's own existence also have a philosophic significance, and this is strikingly revealed by the fact that the essay which follows these programmatic introductory reflections—"Du repentir"—makes astonishingly little reference to the problems of self-representation—a fact which until now has constantly been overlooked. The *"programme* of self-representation" has generally been separated both from the closely related reflections on the impossibility of the life-story and from the actual subject of the essay itself, repentance. Thus E. Auerbach, for instance, in the Montaigne chapter of his *Mimesis*,[46] does not even consider the link between the "programme" and the essay. But it is only through this link that the actual philosophic intention of the introduction becomes apparent. To understand this, it is necessary to return once more to Montaigne's contrast between *être* and *passage* (je ne peints pas l'estre. Je peints le passage). Set against the timeless substance, *l'être*, is the *passage*—a time structure that is not to be understood as a directed process or as a transition, but as a skipping from one moment of time to another in accordance with a basic principle of unforeseeability. The temporality of man appears as something discontinuous. Just as there is no constituent connec-

[46] E. Auerbach, *Mimesis*, 2nd ed. (Bern, 1959), pp. 271 ff.

tion between moments of time, and each moment is basically only itself and separated from all others, so one's own existence breaks up into a succession of discontinuous moments of existence, which make up the ego in its immeasurable diversity throughout an extent of time. The unity of the person can be captured only in the unity of the moment. But the ever decreasing reduction of the moment of time must still remain illusory because this unity is not to be found in even the smallest moment, for the simple reason that the ego is already contradictory in itself. This contrariness is manifested in the synchronism of the individual moment just as much as in the diachronism of the sequent moments. From now on we can see that "peindre le passage," apparently intended only as an illumination of the subjective individual, is in fact related to a quite different intention—namely, the refutation of the Christian demand for repentance. Repentance, "le repentir," has a time structure of its own. It involves a qualitative differentiation in the sequence of moments of existence, in such a manner that the present moment is privileged and stands out from the rest of the sequence so far, in that it enables us not only to view the past as it was, but also as it should have been. Present repentance and the combining of past moments of existence into the story of a lapse are mutually constituent factors. Thus the confessions of Augustine, for instance, are a story that can be composed only from the privileged standpoint of the present moment with its superior insight. For Montaigne, however, this elevation of the present self, which is indispensable for the possibility of repentance, is naive and blind to perspectives, and cannot take responsibility for the relativity of the most immediate, i.e., the present moment. Once this relativity is recognized, the task must be not to judge the moments of past existence from the standpoint of the present, but to leave them alone in their wholeness and so enhance one's awareness of the diversity of one's own self. Seen in this perspective, the possibility of composing a story and the possibility of repentance appear equally illusory.

As Montaigne lights the way from exemplum to story and thence to the dissolution of the story, he shows that the problem is one of the premises under which stories become possible in the first place. The problem of the constitution of stories is an example of the wider problem of the relation between the general and the particular, which in Montaigne's eyes represents the overall problem of cognition. If Descartes' *Discours de la méthode* is in principle a reply to Montaigne's principled problematic view of cognition, the philosophy of history in the eighteenth century is a reply, however tortuous, to Montaigne's problematic view of the story—a reply which sought to counter his atomization of the moments of a story with a philosophic legitimization of historic construction. But despite Montaigne's skeptical argument against the possibility of historic construction, the philosophy of history remains as far from conclusion as the theory and practice of "stories." The modern novel has taken up Montaigne's ideas in earnest, and has set itself the task of bringing about the poetic speech action of the "impossible story."

RENÉ WELLEK

The Fall of Literary History

SOME thirty years ago I wrote a book entitled *The Rise of English Literary History*.[1] Today one could write a book on its decline and fall. George Watson, in *The Study of Literature*, speaks of "the sharp descent of literary history from the status of a great intellectual discipline to that of a convenient act of popularization."[2] Christopher Ricks, in a review of Watson's book, even doubts that "literary history is a worthwhile activity" and that it ever was "a great intellectual discipline."[3] Ricks cannot think of any literary historians who would represent the "tradition of confident historiography of literature," except perhaps Saintsbury and Oliver Elton. It never occurs to him that literary history might have been written elsewhere than in England. There *is* a great tradition of narrative literary history, in Germany beginning with the Schlegels, in France with Villemain and Ampère, in Italy with De Sanctis, in Denmark with Brandes, in Spain with Menéndez y Pelayo, in Russia with Veselovsky. Among nineteenth-century Americans George Ticknor and Moses Coit Tyler wrote important narrative literary histories, whatever their shortcomings. Ricks also ignores the fact that literary history need not necessarily cover the whole of a literature or a very long span of time, as Elton's six volumes do. It might be a history of a genre, such as comedy, epic, or ode; it might be the history of a technical device, such as prose-rhythm, or the sonnet; it might be the history of a theme or themes, such as classical mythology in English poetry; or it might be the history of a mode, such as allegory, humor, or the grotesque. I cannot see why the history of ideas in literature should be excluded from literary history. Examples could be found in plenty.

Still, whatever we may advance against Mr. Ricks's dismissal of literary history or however much we may deplore that Louis Kampf, as president-elect of the Modern Language Association of America, could issue a premature death certificate of all "academic literary study,"[4] we can hardly help agreeing that something has happened to literary his-

---

[1] Chapel Hill, 1941. New edition, with new Preface (New York, 1966).

[2] London, 1969, p. 66.

[3] In *The Cambridge Quarterly*, Vol. iv (Autumn-Winter, 1969-1970), pp. 400-402.

[4] "The Scandal of Literary Scholarship," in *The Dissenting Academy*, ed. Theodore Roszak (New York, 1966), p. 43.

toriography which can be described as decline and even as fall. Particularly in the interval between the two World Wars, widespread dissatisfaction with literary history was voiced in almost every country. It was directed against several related features of established literary historiography which should nevertheless be kept separate. One was the general dissatisfaction with what could be called the atomistic factualism of much literary scholarship and the resultant inconsequential antiquarianism, still with us; the second target was the uncritical scientism which pretends to establish causal relationships and provide causal explanation by a listing of parallels between works of literature or by correlations between events in the life of a poet with the themes or figures of his works. Thirdly, it was widely felt that literary history suffered from a lack of focus, that it surrendered its central concern to general history, a trend which, in the United States, was endorsed in Edwin Greenlaw's *Province of Literary History*.[5] I like to quote Roman Jakobson, who, in 1921, compared literary historians to "police who are supposed to arrest a certain person, arrest everybody and carry off everything they find in the house and all the people who pass by chance in the street. Thus the historians of literature appropriate everything—the social setting, psychology, politics, philosophy. Instead of literary scholarship we got a conglomeration of derivative disciplines."[6] Literary history was (and often still is) the *Allerleiwissenschaft* taught by Professor Diogenes Teufelsdröckh. The national limitations and nationalistic commitments of much literary history, particularly in Germany and France, excited some dissatisfaction which found expression in the newly constituted discipline of "comparative literature." One particular strand of nineteenth-century literary history—the attempt to emulate the evolutionism of Herbert Spencer and Darwin—fell, however, almost silently into oblivion.

I shall not try to rehearse this debate. One of my earliest articles in Czech was a demolition of the evolutionary theory behind Legouis and Cazamian's *Histoire de la littérature anglaise*.[7] In severe reviews of Herbert Grierson's *Critical History of English Poetry*[8] and of the collective histories of English and American literatures edited by Albert C. Baugh[9] and Robert E. Spiller[10] I criticized the mixture of biography, bibliography, anthology, information on themes and metrical forms,

[5] Baltimore, 1931.
[6] *Noveyshaya russkaya poeziya* (Prague, 1929), p. 11. My translation.
[7] In *Casopis pro moderní filologii*, XII (1926), pp. 78-81.
[8] In *Western Review*, XII (1947), p. 5204.
[9] Baugh's "Literary History of England," in *Modern Philology*, XLVII (1949), pp. 39-45.
[10] Robert E. Spiller, W. Thorp, T. H. Johnson, eds., "Literary History of the United States," in *Kenyon Review*, XI (1949), pp. 500-506.

sources, attempts at characterization and evaluation, sandwiched into background chapters on political, social, and intellectual history which is called "literary history." Many others, independently, have voiced similar misgivings. Harry Levin, for instance, has well exposed the failure of *The Oxford History of English Literature*.[11]

The dissatisfaction and the reasons for dissatisfaction are thus obvious enough. We must rather ask what can be done to reform literary history and what proposals have been made to do so. I suggest that they can be discussed under three headings. Some advocate the abolition of literary history; some propound its absorption or subordination to some related discipline, mainly general history or sociology; and, finally, some try to define a specific method of writing literary history.

The main argument for the abandonment of literary history comes from those who deny the pastness of literature. As early as 1883 W. P. Ker, later an eminent literary historian, stated that a work of literature is not a link in a chain and is above the world of movement.[12] In a later lecture[13] he elaborated the contrast between literary history dealing with an ever-present matter which it can point to, as a guide in a gallery points to the pictures, and political history, which has to reconstruct a vanished past. In a fragment, published as late as 1955, Ker asserts that "literary history is like a museum; and a museum may be of use even if ill arranged: the separate specimens may be studied by themselves."[14] Ricks echoes Ker when he points to the radical difference between literary study and military, social and political history, "not least in this that you cannot have an edition of the battle of Waterloo or of George III's madness."[15] Most insistently Benedetto Croce, in a paper written in 1917[16] and since in many contexts, argued that works of art are unique, individual, immediately present, and that there is no essential continuity between them. There is none, for instance, except an external technical sequence between Dante, Boccaccio, and Petrarch. In a letter in which he summarized a conversation I had with him in the year of his death (1952), Croce says expressly that "one can write only little monographs and critical essays if one asks that these essays be put into some order, the answer is that everyone can put them into any order he

[11] "Reflections on the Final Volume of *The Oxford History of English Literature*," in *Refractions: Essays in Comparative Literature* (New York, 1966), pp. 151-70.

[12] "Philosophy of Art," in *Essays in Philosophical Criticism* (1883). Reprinted in *Collected Essays*, Vol. II (London, 1925), pp. 231-68.

[13] On Thomas Warton (1910), also in *Collected Essays*, Vol. I, p. 100.

[14] On *Modern Literature*, eds. T. Spencer and J. Sutherland (Oxford, 1955), p. 265.

[15] As in note 3, p. 401.

[16] "La Riforma della storia artistica e letteraria," in *Nuovi Saggi di estetica*, 2nd ed. (Bari, 1926), pp. 157-80.

pleases."[17] Croce's assumption sounds almost Neo-Platonic: "A work of art is always *internal*; and what is called *external* is no longer a work of art."[18]

Without Croce's idealistic presuppositions, the American New Criticism has said substantially the same. Allen Tate, for instance, told us that "the historical method will not permit us to develop a critical instrument for dealing with works of literature as existent objects" and "that the literature of the past can be kept alive only by seeing it as the literature of the present. Or perhaps we ought to say that the literature of the past lives in the literature of the present and nowhere else; that it is also present literature."[19] In England F. R. Leavis said it with his customary violence: "Literary history . . . is a worthless acquisition; worthless for the student who cannot as a critic—that is, as an intelligent and discerning reader—make a personal approach to the essential data of the literary historian, the works of literature."[20] In German scholarship the same reaction against literary history brought about the dominance of "interpretation," most strikingly expounded and exemplified by Emil Staiger. The introduction to *Die Zeit als Einbildungskraft des Dichters* (1939) formulates the rejection of literary history most clearly. One cannot explain a work of art. One can only exhibit its traits. A "phenomenology" of literature is the only fruitful method of literary study.[21] I need only allude to the more recent vogue of "phenomenology" in France. The possibly oversharp distinction between extrinsic and intrinsic methods which organizes the order of the chapters in my and Austin Warren's *Theory of Literature* may have contributed to the singling out of the work of art as an isolated object outside history, even though the last chapter of our book is expressly devoted to a program of literary history.

Even more widespread and successful have been the attempts to absorb literary history into general history, particularly the attempts to reduce it to a mirror of social change. I need only allude to the oldest systematic scheme of this kind: Hippolyte Taine's triad of *milieu-race-moment* which is, however, misunderstood if interpreted as a version of positivistic determinism. I have tried to show that Taine was rather something of

---

[17] Dated June 5, 1952. "Si dirà che la critica così diventa una serie di monografiette o di saggi critici, che bisogna pure mettere in qualche ordine. E per far ciò non occorre il permesso di nessuno. Ciascuno può metterle in quell' ordine che più gli piace."

[18] *Estetica*, 8th ed. (Bari, 1945), p. 57. "L'opera d'arte . . . è sempre *interna*; e quella che si chiama *esterna* no è più opera d'arte."

[19] "Miss Emily and the Bibliographer," in *Reason in Madness: Critical Essays* (New York, 1941), pp. 107, 116.

[20] *Education and the University* (London, 1943), p. 68.

[21] Zurich, 1939, pp. 13, 18.

a Hegelian.[22] Harry Levin, particularly in his *Gates of Horn*, fruitfully developed the idea of literature as an institution.[23] Renato Poggioli has proposed an application of Pareto's sociology to literary historiography, using terms such as "residue" and "derivation" for a new periodization of literature.[24] Poggioli's *Theory of the Avant-garde* analyzes a mastercurrent sociologically. He believes in the imperative of the period. The artist dwindles to the dimension of a victim of social forces.[25]

Obviously, Marxism has been by far the most influential in interpreting literary history as a reflection of social and economic forces. Literature becomes "ideology," overt or implied statement about class situation and consciousness. To give an example with which I am intimately acquainted: the *History of Czech Literature*, published by the Czechoslovak Academy of Sciences, reduces Czech literature to a commentary on the social and national struggles of the Czechs, minimizing religion and neglecting the art of poetry almost completely.[26]

Outside bureaucratic Marxist history-writing more sophisticated versions were produced. Georg Lukács knows of the "specificity" of literature, of the oblique and often distant relation between literature and the "substructure," but he also reduced literature to a species of knowledge, to a "reflection of reality," a term repeated with obsessive frequency in the first volume of the *Aesthetik*. It occurs there no less than 1,032 times. Literary history is seen as a "moment" of general history, as an illustration of the struggle between progress and reaction.[27] The lyric and poetry in general are slighted as they do not yield the characters, types and plots Lukács examines in novels and dramas. It would be easy to demonstrate the insensitive distortions to which he subjects Hölderlin, Eichendorff, Dostoevsky, Nietzsche, Rilke, and others in the interest of his ideology. "Content" in the brute sense of involvement in the progress toward communism is the main criterion, even though Lucács, as a theorist, has insight into form and its function.

Lucien Goldmann is a follower of the early Lukács: he told me once that Lukács complained to him that Goldmann wanted him to have

[22] See my *History of Modern Criticism*, Vol. IV (New Haven, 1965), pp. 27-57.

[23] New York, 1963, esp. pp. 16-23.

[24] "For a Literary Historiography Based on Pareto's Sociology," in *The Spirit of the Letter* (Cambridge, Mass., 1965), pp. 291-322. First published in Italian in 1949.

[25] *Teoria dell'art d'avanguardia* (Bologna, 1962). English translation by Gerald Fitzgerald (Cambridge, Mass., 1968). See comments by Roger Shattuck in *The New York Review of Books*, March 12, 1970, p. 43.

[26] See my review in "Recent Czech Literary History and Criticism" (1962), in *Essays on Czech Literature* (The Hague, 1963), pp. 194-205.

[27] See, e.g., *Skizze einer Geschichte der neueren deutschen Literatur* (Neuwied, 1965), pp. 12, 13. Written in 1952.

dropped dead at the age of thirty. Goldmann, in *Le Dieu caché* (1956), construes analogues between the economic conditions of the *noblesse de robe*, the theology of Jansenism, and the tragic world view of Pascal and Racine, making Pascal sound like Kant and vice versa. Goldmann tells us at least bluntly that literary history is a "really non-existent subject," though in an earlier paper he admits that "sociological analysis hardly touches a work of art."[28]

All these attempts—and many more could be cited—to absorb literary history into social history raise such problems as the integration of human history and the interrelationship between the activities of man, the role of the individual in history, and the nature of explanation of one activity by another. One has the impression that at least in the West the grand "philosophies of history" in the style of Hegel, Marx, Spengler, and Toynbee are discredited in sober scholarly thinking. I do not share Karl Popper's extreme view of *The Poverty of Historicism* but rather sympathize with Jakob Burkhardt's tolerant reference to "the centaur on the forest edge" of historical studies.[29] Also the more cautious schemes of social evolution with their pervasive metaphors of growth and decay have been subjected to much trenchant criticism: most recently in Robert A. Nisbet's *Social Change and History* (1969). Others have shown that the different activities of man do not cohere as closely as general historians assume and that one may doubt the unbroken continuity of linear developments. Siegfried Kracauer, in his posthumous *History: The Last Things before the Last* (1969), has argued in favor of special histories and their comparative independence from general history. Hans Blumenberg, in *Die Legitimität der Neuzeit* (1966), has tried to show that many assumptions about continuity in intellectual history are mistaken, that we can rather speak of breaks in the tradition and even of a spontaneous generation of ideas. The whole concept of the *Zeitgeist* which was basic to German *Geistesgeschichte* has been called in doubt. Certainly the very close parallelism of the arts presents great difficulties: the difference between the arts as to their relation to antiquity should make us pause. Much of the parallelism among the arts is only metaphorical analogizing. In Mario Praz's recent *Mnemosyne: The Parallel between Literature and the Visual Arts* (1970), for instance, the

---

[28] *The Hidden God*, English translation by Philip Tody (New York, 1964), p. 96. "Matérialisme dialectique et histoire de la littérature," in *Recherches dialectiques* (Paris, 1959), p. 62 "Mais *l'analyse sociologique* n'épuise pas l'oeuvre d'art et parfois n'arrive même pas à la toucher."

[29] *Weltgeschichtliche Betrachtungen*, ed. Rudolf Marx (Leipzig, n.d.), p. 6. "Immerhin ist man dem Kentauren den höchsten Dank schuldig und begrüsst ihn gerne hier und da an einem Waldesrand der geschichtlichen Studien."

Divine Comedy is contrasted with the *Canterbury Tales*, with the *Tales* testifying to the decay of the Middle Ages merely because they are unfinished.[30] One can take refuge in the idea of different time-schemes, as Henri Focillon and his pupil George Kubler have done. In *The Shape of Time: Remarks on the History of Things* Kubler conceives of historical time as intermittent and variable, in difference from the continuous time of a human being or animal.[31]

It would be foolish to deny the implication of literary history in general history: any reflective person even centuries ago must have noted the changes in literature which came with the fall of the Roman Empire, the advent of Christianity, or the Renaissance of the fifteenth and sixteenth centuries. Literary historians long before Marx or Taine noticed the differences, in medieval literature, between works written for a courtly audience, by clerics for the clergy or the laity, or by burghers for their fellow-artisans. But what the attempts at social explanation fail to achieve is the causal explanation of a specific work of literature, its individuality, its pattern and value.

I have read in the amazingly large literature stimulated primarily by Carl G. Hempel's paper "The Function of General Laws in History" (1942).[32] Hempel, a neo-positivist close to the Vienna Circle, argues that historical statements appeal implicitly to general laws he calls "covering laws." Historians are at least by implication considered defective scientists, as they cannot verify these laws, cannot predict the future, are sometimes unaware of the laws, and are often content with what Hempel calls mere "explanation sketches." A whole series of analytical philosophers—Arthur C. Danto, William Dray, W. B. Gallie, Patrick Gardiner, W. H. Walsh, and Morton White, to mention only a few[33]—have either elaborated on Hempel's thesis or modified it or rejected it in favor of a concept of historical explanation which actually ceases to be causal. Some historians—often labeled "idealists"—reject all causal explanation and defend narration as the only proper historical

---

[30] Princeton, 1970, pp. 69-70.

[31] New Haven, 1962. Kubler is much concerned with artifacts from pre-Columbian America. He must rely on purely archeological and stylistic evidence unrelated or hardly related to any definable historical events.

[32] First in *Journal of Philosophy*, xxxix (1942); reprinted in *Readings in Philosophical Analysis*, eds. Herbert Feigl and Wilfred Sellars (New York, 1949), pp. 459-71.

[33] Arthur C. Danto, *Analytical Philosophy of History* (Cambridge, 1968); William Dray, *Laws and Explanation in History* (Oxford, 1957); William B. Gallie, *Philosophy and Historical Understanding*, 2nd ed. (New York, 1968); Patrick Gardiner, *The Nature of Historical Explanation* (Oxford, 1952); W. H. Walsh, *Philosophy of History: An Introduction* (New York, 1960); Morton White, *Foundations of Historical Knowledge* (New York, 1965).

method. R. G. Collingwood can say, "When the historian knows what happened, he already knows why it happened."[34] Michael Oakeshott speaks of "the continuous series model of explanation,"[35] suggesting that a historical event is explained if we narrate it with no lacuna, as we might account for a collision between two cars by describing the exact course of their movements. Most of this enormous, often hair-splitting and logic-chopping, discussion is concerned with questions of responsibility, ethical culpability, normal and abnormal behavior, accidents such as sudden deaths in history, and is completely oblivious of the very different problems of literary or art history. Questions such as "why did Brutus stab Caesar?" or "why did Louis XIV die unpopular?" are characteristic problem cases. Only Morton White discusses intellectual history.

Some of the distinctions between types of causal explanations made in this debate, however, are applicable to literary history. We can, for instance, speak of accidents such as the deaths of Shelley and Byron or we might think of the (possibly apocryphal) "person on business from Porlock" who interrupted Coleridge while he was writing down *Kubla Khan*.[36] We might try to distinguish between "standing conditions" and outside influences such as the effect of the French Revolution or the sudden influx of German ideas and themes toward the end of the eighteenth century. We might speak of "proximate causes" for this influx in singling out Coleridge's trip to Germany in 1798 made possible only by the Wedgwood annuity. But all this concerns biography or large-scale historical trends which might be described as "conditions," but we never succeed in naming the cause or even a cause of a single work of art. Morton White gives examples of causal explanations for certain views of John Dewey[37] but does not produce more than psychological motivation: Dewey, for instance, wanted to defend ethical naturalism because he was a political liberal. It is difficult, however, to see in what sense his liberalism "caused" his naturalism: there were plenty of liberals not given to ethical naturalism. We can only guess at the workings of Dewey's mind, his reasons and arguments; we do not establish causes. Louis Kampf, in criticizing my paper "German and English Romanticism: A Confrontation,"[38] complains of my neglect of "causal explana-

---

[34] *The Idea of History* (Oxford, 1946), p. 214. Written in 1936.

[35] *Experience and Its Modes* (Cambridge, 1933), esp. p. 131.

[36] Coleridge's account, first printed in 1816, differs from an earlier shorter version first printed by Alice Snyder in the *Times Literary Supplement*, August 2, 1934, p. 541, which does not mention the interruption nor the "person from Porlock."

[37] Morton White, *Foundations of Historical Knowledge*, *loc. cit.*, pp. 200-201.

[38] In *History and Theory* (Middletown, Conn.), vi (1967), 77.

tion" and comes up with the old idea (also discussed in my paper) of the "German artist's almost total separation from his society"; but Kampf cannot suggest how this situation explains more than, at most, the preference for the lyric or the grotesque and fantastic, art-forms well represented in other presumably less alienated societies. Alienation cannot account for a single work of art: not even for *Heinrich von Ofterdingen* or *Kater Murr* nor for their differences. Actually, some of the most fantastic and subjective German writers were, in their private lives, successful landowners or government officials such as Achim von Arnim or Joseph von Eichendorff. Cause, in the sense as defined by Morris R. Cohen—"some reason or ground why, whenever the antecedent event occurs, the consequent must follow"[39]—is, we must conclude, inapplicable to literary history. A work of art need not to have caused another one. One can only argue that any work of art would be different if another work of art had not preceded it. Obviously if there had not been an *Iliad* or an *Odyssey* or an *Aeneid* or a *Divine Comedy*, subsequent literature would be different. We can speculate rather futilely on these eventualities but can never argue even that works of art as closely related as the pre-Shakespearean *King Leir* and Shakespeare's *King Lear* or *Hamlet* and the German *Bestrafter Brudermord* are connected causally: we can only say that Shakespeare knew the earlier play and can describe the use he made of it, and we can show that the German play is ultimately derived from *Hamlet*. One work is the necessary condition of another one but one cannot say it has caused it.

The so-called laws of literary history boil down to some vague psychological generalities: action and reaction, convention and revolt, the "form-fatigue" formulated by a German architect Adolf Göller in the 1880's.[40]

Cause may, it should be granted, be used loosely and widely. R. S. Crane, in a paper "Principles of Literary History," which was published in the year of his death (1967), and has, I believe, received no attention, uses cause in the fourfold meaning derived from Aristotle. He constantly speaks of causes in Aristotle's fourth sense of "purpose" or "aim." He considers the "causes in the work which condition its effect on readers" when we would more clearly speak of traits, characters, or qualities of a work, or he speaks of "causes in the author which condition his acts of composition" which seem nothing other than his motives or intentions.[41] We must concede the final inexplicability of a great work of

---

[39] *The Meaning of Human History* (La Salle, Illinois, 1947), p. 102.

[40] Adolf Göller, *Zur Aesthetik der Architektur* (Stuttgart, 1887). "Formermüdung."

[41] "Critical and Historical Principles of Literary History," in *The Idea of the Humanities and Other Essays Critical and Historical* (Chicago, 1967), Vol. II, pp. 45-156. Quotations from p. 151.

art, the exception of genius. Long ago Emile Faguet objected to Taine's method that may account for a burgher from Rouen in the 1630's, and even for Thomas Corneille, but not for the genius of Pierre Corneille.[42] The art historians who more commonly deal with collective styles and anonymous works than literary historians have often come to the same conclusion. Thus Henri Focillon, who studied *The Life of Forms in Art*, reflects, in the context of the rise of the Gothic style in architecture, that "the most attentive study of the most homogenous *milieu*, of the most closely woven concantenation of circumstances, will not serve to give us the design of the towers of the cathedral of Laon." "It emerges with a highly efficient abruptness."[43] Like Focillon we might argue that even if we knew the life of Shakespeare in the greatest detail, knew the social and theatrical history of the time much better than we know it now, studied all the sources, we still could not predict the peculiar shape and physiognomy of a play like *Hamlet* or *King Lear* if we did not know the text or imagine it would have been lost. Causal explanation as deterministic scientific explanation by deduction from a general law or demonstration of a necessary efficient cause fails if applied to literature.

The absorption of literary history into general history, the determinism of social explanation has been opposed not only by the proponents of criticism but by theorists who proposed the idea of an internal evolutionary history of literature. Its earlier version, heavily dependent on Darwinian evolutionism, has been generally abandoned. The Russian formalists, however, worked out a restatement which avoids the analogies with biology and adopts rather Hegelian (and Marxist) dialectics as the model. The parallel to similar attempts in art history, particularly Wölfflin's "history without names," must have been also in their mind. But they developed it in a literary context as they could appeal to the example of Alexander Veselovsky, who tried to write collective developmental literary history, largely drawing on folk material and as they, with their sympathies for Russian futurism, could think in terms of poetic revolutions and completely new starts. They interpreted literary history largely as a wearing out or "automatization" of conventions followed by an "actualization" of new conventions using radically new devices. Novelty is the only criterion of change. "A work of art will appear as positive value when it regroups the structure of the preceding period. It will appear as a negative value if it takes over the structure without changing it,"[44] says Jan Mukařovský, the main theorist of the

---

[42] In *Politiques et moralistes du dix-neuvième siècle*, 3ème série (1900), pp. 237-314.
[43] New York, 1948, pp. 60, 63.
[44] In *Polákova Vznešenost přírody* (Prague, 1934), p. 9; reprinted in *Kapitoly z české poetiky*, Vol. II (Prague, 1948), pp. 100-101. My translation.

Prague Linguistic Circle who adopted the concepts of the Russians. In a paper criticizing Mukařovský's history of Czech versification based on this idea of internal evolution, dating back to 1934 and substantially repeated in "The Theory of Literary History" (1936),[45] I made an attempt to reconcile this concept of evolution with a theory of criticism. Mukařovský (and the Russians), I argued, are unable to answer the basic question about the direction of change; it is not true that evolution proceeds always in opposite direction. The single criterion of novelty would make us value initiators more highly than the great masters, to prefer Marlowe to Shakespeare, Klopstock to Goethe. We are expected to forget that novelty need not be valuable, that there may be, after all, original rubbish. The very material of literary history, I argued, must be chosen in relation to values, and structures involve values. History cannot be divorced from criticism. Criticism means constant reference to a scheme of values which is necessarily that of the historian. The mere selection of texts out of hundreds and thousands surviving is an act of judgment, and the selection of the particular traits, details, or qualities which I choose to discuss is another act of judgment which is inevitably performed with the conceptual tools the historian is able to apply. This is not advocacy of anarchical subjectivism. We still must require submission to the texts, respect for their integrity, "objectivity" in the sense of a desire to overcome personal prejudices and to criticize one's own standpoint. Nor can the recognition of the inevitability of a personal or temporal point of view—what Lovejoy has called the "presenticentric predicament"—mean simply surrender to skepticism, sheer relativism, as we would then have to doubt the possibility of all knowledge. I cannot adequately discuss this problem here: it has worried me and many historians.

Still, whatever its difficulties, I cannot see why one reviewer of my *History of Modern Criticism*, Bernard Weinberg,[46] denied me even the title of a historian because I believe that the history of criticism should "illuminate and interpret our present situation" and because I single out theories by Lessing and Friedrich Schlegel with approval. The unargued assumption seems to be, in the words of his mentor, Ronald S. Crane, that a "history without prior commitments as to what criticism is or ought to be," a "history without a thesis,"[47] is the only legitimate way

[45] "Dějiny českého verše a metody literární historie," in *Listy pro umění a kritiku*, II (1934), pp. 437-45; "The Theory of Literary History," in *Travaux du Cercle Linguistique de Prague*, VI (1936), 173-91.

[46] *Journal of the History of Ideas*, XXX (1969), pp. 127-33, and my answer, *ibid*. (1969), pp. 281-82.

[47] *The Idea of the Humanities*, loc. cit., Vol. II, p. 174.

of writing history. I am surprised to hear that my attention to anticipa-
tions of modern theories or my references to contemporary poetic
theory "invalidates my *History* as history." Judged by such a criterion,
Bosanquet's *History of Aesthetic*, Croce's history of aesthetics in *Estetica*, Saintsbury's *History of Criticism* and, on analogous grounds,
almost all literary, philosophical, and political historiography would be
"invalidated." I prefer to side with Croce, Meinecke, Troeltsch,
Huizinga, Collingwood, Carr, and many others who have argued that
"historical thinking is always teleological,"[48] that "History properly so
called can be written only by those who find and accept a sense of direction in history itself."[49]

I am not alone with the emphasis on criticism as value judgment: long
ago Norman Foerster cogently formulated the view that "the literary
historian must be a critic in order to be a historian."[50] Though sketchily,
English literary history has been rewritten with new value judgments in
the essays of T. S. Eliot, in F. R. Leavis' *Revaluation*, and in Cleanth
Brooks's "Notes for a Revised History of English Poetry."[51]

Still, the idea of an internal evolution of literature has fallen on deaf
ears. I myself, in a paper "The Concept of Evolution in Literary History" (1956),[52] modified (and as I see now implicitly rejected) my earlier
view. I argued that an artist, as any man, may reach, at any moment,
into his remote past or into the remotest past of humanity. It is not true
that an artist develops toward a single future goal. What is needed is a
modern concept of time, modeled on an interpenetration of the causal
order in experience and memory. A work of art is not simply a member
of a series, a link in a chain. It may stand in relation to anything in the
past. It is not only a structure which may be analyzed descriptively. It is
a totality of values which do not adhere to the structure but constitute its
very nature. The values can be grasped only in an act of contemplation.
These values are created in a free act of the imagination irreducible to
limiting conditions in sources, traditions, biographical and social circumstances.

I have read two numbers of the new periodical *New Literary History*,
which contain valuable articles, but no new ideas of literary history beyond the traditional study of periods, genres, influences, etc., are sug-

---

[48] Jan Huizinga, "The Idea of History," in *The Varieties of History*, ed. Fritz Stern
(New York, 1956), p. 293.

[49] E. H. Carr in *What is History?* (Harmondsworth, Middlesex, 1964), pp. 123-24.

[50] *The American Scholar* (Chapel Hill, 1929), p. 36.

[51] Brooks's sketch in *Modern Poetry and the Tradition* (Chapel Hill, 1939), pp. 219-44.

[52] In *For Roman Jakobson* (The Hague, 1956), pp. 653-61; reprinted in *Concepts of
Criticism* (New Haven, 1963), pp. 37-53.

gested. D. W. Robertson, for instance, restates historicism which asks us to reconstruct the situation of the writer in the past; Hallett Smith defends his approach to Elizabethan poetry through genre tradition; Robert Weimann rehearses Marxism; W. K. Wimsatt discusses imitation in English eighteenth-century poetry. Geoffrey Hartman's piece, called expressly "Toward Literary History,"[53] comments on the idea of the progress of poetry from antiquity to England with the apparent aim of emphasizing again the national tradition of poetry. Wimsatt's and Hartman's papers corroborate W. J. Bate's *Burden of the Past* (1970), which speaks eloquently of the English poet's sense of the crushing weight of tradition and the way of overcoming it not merely by escaping or denying it (as much modern art does) but by reaching into the past: Wordsworth going back to Milton, Keats to Spenser, Milton, and, above all, Shakespeare.[54] A history of Renascences is suggested: a sense of the presence of the whole past, as it was suggested in T. S. Eliot's "Tradition and the Individual Talent." All these three items buttress my rejection of linear development, the conception of a free reaching into the past.

One more proposal for immanent literary history has come recently from Germany: the "Rezeptionsgeschichte" advocated by H. R. Jauss.[55] This is not merely a demand for a history of readers' reactions, of criticisms, translations, etc.—first voiced, I believe, in the now forgotten book, *Critique scientifique* by Emile Hennequin in 1888—but assumes, with Gadamer and Heidegger, a "fusion of horizons": a necessary interplay of text and recipient in which the text is assumed to be transformed by the reader. Jauss argues that the attitude of an author to his public can be reconstructed not only from addresses to the reader or external evidence but implicitly: through the assumption, for instance, in *Don Quijote* of a knowledge and concern for chivalric romances. Lowry Nelson, in a paper "The Fictive Reader and Literary Self-Reflexiveness,"[56] has made, independently, concrete suggestions on different types of this relation. One must welcome emphasis on hitherto unexplored aspects of literary history, but in practice "Rezeptionsgeschichte" cannot be anything else than the history of critical interpretations by authors and readers, a history of taste which has always been included in a history of criticism.

The new literary history promises only a return to the old one: the history of tradition, genres, reputations, etc., less atomistically con-

---

[53] In *Daedalus*, Spring 1970, pp. 355-83.

[54] *The Burden of the Past and the English Poet* (Cambridge, Mass., 1970), p. 130.

[55] Cf. "Was heisst und zu welchem Ende studiert man Literaturgeschichte?"

[56] In *The Disciplines of Criticism*, eds. P. Demetz, T. M. Greene, Lowry Nelson, Jr. (New Haven, 1968), pp. 173-92.

ceived as in older times, with greater awareness of the difficulties of such concepts as influence and periods but still the old one.

Possibly, this is a good and right thing. The attempts at an evolutionary history have failed. I myself have failed in *The History of Modern Criticism* to construe a convincing scheme of development. I discovered, by experience, that there is no evolution in the history of critical argument, that the history of criticism is rather a series of debates on recurrent concepts, on "essentially contested concepts,"[57] on permanent problems in the sense that they are with us even today. Possibly, a similar conclusion is required for the history of poetry itself. "Art," said Schopenhauer, "has always reached its goal."[58] Croce and Ker are right. There is no progress, no development, no history of art except a history of writers and institutions or techniques. This is, at least for me, the end of an illusion, the fall of literary history.

[57] Cf. W. B. Gallie, *Philosophy and Historical Understanding*, 2nd ed. (New York, 1968), pp. 153 ff.

[58] *Die Welt als Wille und Vorstellung*, 3rd Book, Paragraph 36, in *Sämtliche Werke*, ed. Arthur Hübscher (Leipzig, 1938), Vol. II, p. 218. "So ist dagegen die Kunst überall am Ziel."

HANS ROBERT JAUSS

History of Art and Pragmatic History

I

AT first sight, history in the realm of the arts presents two contradictory views. With the first, it would appear that the history of architecture, music, or poetry is more consistent and more coherent than
that of society. The chronological sequence of works of art is more
closely connected than a chain of political events, and the more gradual
transformations of style are easier to follow than the transformations of
social history. Valéry once said that the difference between art history
and social history was that in the former the products were "filles vis-
ibles les unes des autres," whereas in the latter "chaque enfant semble
avoir mille pères et réciproquement."[1] One might conclude from this
that the claim "man makes his history himself" is most strongly borne
out in the realm of the arts.

With the second view, the paradigms of art historiography, in their
pre-scientific and then again in their positivistic phase,[2] show that this
greater consistency of detail is purchased at the price of an overall inconsistency as regards the links between art *genres* as well as their relation
to the general historical and social process. Before it turned to tracing the
history of style, art history had always taken the form of artists' biographies, which were linked only through chronological order. The literary historiography of the humanists also began with "stories," i.e.,
biographies of writers, in the order of their dates of death, sometimes
divided up into categories of authors.[3] The model was Plutarch's *Lives*,
which also established the pattern of "parallels." This form of integration, which until the end of the eighteenth century underlay the response to classical art and the dispute over its exemplariness, belonged
specifically to the first stage of the "histories of art appreciation."[4] For

---

[1] "Letter to André Lebey," Sept., 1906, *Œuvres II* (Paris, 1960), p. 1543; also
S. Kracauer, in *Die nicht mehr schönen Künste*, ed. H. R. Jauss (Munich, 1968), *Poetik
und Hermeneutik*, III, p. 123.

[2] Concerning the change of paradigm in the history of science, see Th. S. Kuhn, *Die
Struktur wissenschaftlicher Revolutionen* (Frankfurt, 1967), and H. R. Jauss, "Paradig-
mawechsel in der Literaturwissenschaft," in *Linguistische Berichte*, I (1969), pp. 44-56.

[3] P. Brockmeier, *Darstellungen der französischen Literaturgeschichte von Claude
Fauchet bis Laharpe* (Berlin, 1963).

[4] See H. R. Jauss, *Literaturgeschichte als Provokation* (Frankfurt, 1970), pp. 35 ff.

the literary form of "parallels" presupposes the idea of perfection as a criterion that transcends time, even when authors or works extend it to "genres" of art or to national "golden ages." The historical appearance of art splits up into a variety of different elemental courses, each of which is directed towards its own "point of perfection" and, through esthetic norms, can be compared with earlier histories or "forerunners." The appearance of all histories in the arts can then be joined together again in the composite historical picture of a periodic recurrence of the golden age—a picture that is typical of humanistic historiography, and also of Voltaire's social history.[5]

A second stage of the "histories" came about through Historism (overestimation of historical singularity) in its positivistic phase. The principle of explaining a work of art by the sum of its historical conditions meant that, with every work, study had to start right from scratch, so that the "beginnings" could be ascertained from its sources, and the determinant factors of time and environment could be extracted from the author's life. The question of sources, which inevitably leads to the question of sources of sources, loses its way in "histories" just as completely as that of the link between life and work. Thus the sequent link between one work and the next is lost in a historical vacuum, which would be obvious simply from the chronological order if it were not concealed by the vague generalization of "currents" or "schools," or bridged by an external nexus, borrowed from pragmatic history—first and foremost, that of nationhood. As against that, the question may justifiably be asked whether art history can in fact do anything else but borrow its overall coherence from pragmatic history.

Between the first and second stages of the "histories" lies the historism of the Enlightenment, in which art history played a not insignificant part. The epochal turning point at which singular history, together with the newly founded *philosophie de l'histoire*, won the battle against plural histories,[6] began at the start of the eighteenth century through perceptions made in the study of art. The dispute that flared up again at the height of French classicism concerning the exemplariness of classical art, brought both sides—the *Anciens* and the *Modernes*—ultimately to the same conclusion, which was that ancient and modern art in the long run could not be measured against the same standard of perfection (*Beau absolu*), because each epoch had its own customs, its own tastes, and therefore its own ideas of beauty (*Beau relatif*). The discovery of the historical element of beauty, and the historical perception

[5] See H. R. Jauss, *Ästhetische Normen und geschichtliche Reflexion in der Querelle des Anciens et des Modernes* (Munich, 1964), pp. 23-33.

[6] R. Koselleck, "Historia magistra vitae," in: *Natur und Geschichte, Karl Löwith zum 70. Geburtstag* (Stuttgart, 1968), pp. 196-219.

of art that it initiated, led up to the historism of the Enlightenment.[7] In the eighteenth century, this process resulted in an increasing emphasis on the time element of both art history and philosophical history, which since Fénelon's *Projet d'un traité sur l'histoire* (1714) had deliberately utilized the unifying means and classical norms of the epic in order to legitimize its superiority over the merely factual ruler-and-state type of history.[8]

Winckelmann's *Geschichte der Kunst des Altertums* (1764) is the first landmark of the new historiography of art, which was made possible through the historicizing of Antiquity, and was set on its way by the abandoning of comparative description in the form of "parallels." In turning away from the traditional "history of artists," Winckelmann sets the new "history of art" the task of "teaching the origin, the growth, the change and the decline of the same, together with the different styles of nations, times, and artists."[9] Art history, as Winckelmann inaugurated it, does not need to borrow its overall coherence from pragmatic history, as it can claim a greater consistency of its own: "The arts . . . , like all inventions, began with necessity; afterwards one sought for beauty, and finally there followed the superfluous: these are the three outstanding stages of art."[10] As against the course of events in pragmatic history, the sequence of works in the art of Antiquity is distinguished by a complete and therefore normative course: in the realm of the arts, the historical element can complete itself naturally. Friedrich Schlegel, who carried this principle over to poetry, looked for and found in Greek poetry "a complete natural history of art and of taste," in the course of which "even the incompleteness of the earlier stages and the degeneration of the later" could take on exemplary significance.[11] Herder's critique of Winckelmann can, in this context, be interpreted as an attempt logically to extend the time element of art history to "the whole sequence of times,"[12] and to assert the historical universality of beauty, as against the singularized art of the Greeks which had nevertheless been raised to the level of a norm.[13] Poetry "as a tool or as an artistic product

[7] See thesis quoted in note 5.

[8] See *Nachahmung und Illusion*, ed. H. R. Jauss (Munich, 1964), *Poetik und Hermeneutik*, I, p. 191.

[9] *Geschichte der Kunst des Altertums* (1764), ed. W. Senff (Weimar, 1964), p. 7.

[10] *Ibid.*, p. 21.

[11] *Über das Studium der griechischen Poesie*, ed. P. Hankamer (Godesberg, 1947), p. 153.

[12] *Briefe zur Beförderung der Humanität*, 7th and 8th collections, ed. Suphan (Berlin, 1883), XVIII, p. 57.

[13] See H.-D. Weber, *Fr. Schlegels "Transzendentalpoesie" und das Verhältnis von Kritik und Dichtung im 18. Jahrhundert* (Munich, 1973), pp. 88-101.

and flower of civilization and humanity" reveals through its history something that "could only be brought about progressively in the great course of times and nations."[14] And here the point is reached at which art history and social history enter into a relationship that raises a new question: whether the history of art, which is usually regarded as a dependent "poor relation" of general history, might not once have been the head of the family, and might not once more become a paradigm of historical knowledge.

II

The decay of the traditional form of literary history, shaped in the nineteenth century and now drained of all scholarly exemplariness, makes it almost impossible for us to realize the high rank that was enjoyed by art history at its birth, with the formation of historical perception in the thought of the Enlightenment, in the philosophy of history of the German Idealists, and at the beginning of historism. With the turning away from traditional histories, chronicles, and accounts of rulers, states and wars, the history of the arts seemed like a paradigm of the new form of history, which—above all—could claim a philosophical interest: "Tous les peuples ont produit des héros et des politiques: tous les peuples ont éprouvé des révolutions: toutes les histoires sont presque égales pour qui ne veut mettre que des faits dans sa mémoire. Mais quiconque pense, et, ce qui est encore plus rare, quiconque a du goût, ne compte que quatre siècles dans l'histoire de monde."[15] Pragmatic histories are of monotonous uniformity; only through the perfection of the arts can the human spirit rise to its own particular greatness and leave behind works that engage not only the memory, but also thought and taste. Thus Voltaire justifies the new undertaking of his *Siècle de Louis XIV* (1751). Voltaire's change-over to the "philosophy of history" was followed by Winckelmann and Herder's founding of the history of art and literature. They made the same claims, and made their criticisms of traditional political and war history no less clearly.

Before his famous works, Winckelmann wrote down *Gedanken vom mündlichen Vortrag der neuern allgemeinen Geschichte* (1754), in order to distinguish "what is truly useful in history" from the "nice and beautiful." He sets himself apart from "our pragmatic scribes" and from the "diverse general histories," demands "great examples" and "decisive studies," sets up a canon: "Of scholars and artists, general history im-

[14] This is the basic principle behind the history of modern poetry, with which Herder, in letters 81-107, along with Schiller and F. Schlegel (1796-1797), again takes up the questions of the *Querelle des Anciens et des Modernes*; see work quoted in note 4, pp. 72-74.

[15] Voltaire, *Le siècle de Louis XIV*, Intr.

mortalizes only inventors, not copyists; only originals, not collectors: a Galileo, Huygens and Newton, not a Viviani, not a Hopital . . . ," and thus follows the basic principle: "Everything subordinate belongs to specialist history."[16] The new demands of Winckelmann's *Geschichte der Kunst des Altertums* (1764) denigrate not only the previous "History of Artists," but also the chronological presentation of previous history. The history of art is to be "no mere narration of chronology and changes within it," but history and system all in one; it is to bring out the complete "essence of art" and the idea of beauty throughout its historical development.[17]

For Herder, too, the advantages of a history of the poetry of times and nations were clear. This can be seen from the panoramic presentation of current poetry with which, in his "Humanitäts-Briefen" of 1796, he refers to the historical-philosophical problem of the *Querelle*: "In this gallery of different ways of thinking, aspirations and desires, we certainly get to know periods and nations more deeply than on the deceptive, dreary route of their political and war history. In the latter we seldom see more of a people than how it let itself be governed and killed; in the former we learn how it thought, what it hoped and wished for, how it enjoyed itself, and how it was led by its teachers or its inclinations."[18] The history of the arts becomes a medium through which the historical individuation of the human spirit is presented throughout the course of times and nations. Thus the ideality of the Greeks, which Winckelmann had still maintained, is pushed back into its historical setting, the normative element of perfection carried over to the diversity of individual beauty, and the world-historical study of poetry related to a conception of history that has no further need of any immanent teleology[19] and yet again promises the *esthete* a coherent whole. Those aspects of a natural history of art that are still to be found in Herder—the imagery of growth and old age, the cyclic completion of every culture, and the "classical" as the "highest of its (respective) kind"—bring into view the coherence of

---

[16] The fragment, dating from 1754, is quoted from *J. Winckelmanns sämtliche Werke*, ed. J. Eiselein (Donaueschingen), XII, pp. iii-xv; see also Fontius, *Winckelmann und die französische Aufklärung* (Berlin, 1968), *Sitz.-Ber. d. dt. Akad. d. Wsch. zu Berlin*, Cat. for language, literature and art, 1968, I, to whom I am obliged for the reference.

[17] P. 7.   [18] Ed. Suphan, XVIII, p. 137.

[19] In his presentation of modern poetry, 1796, Herder still holds fast to a "telos" of history, insofar as he asks, at the outset: "What is the law of this change? Does it change for the better or for the worse?" (p. 6), and at the end, concludes from a comparison of periods: "*tendimus in Arcadiam, tendimus!* To the land of simplicity, truth and morals goes our path" (p. 140). As regards the esthete (XXXII, p. 63) or *poetic philologist* (XXXII, p. 83) that one must be, in order to risk oneself on the ocean of historical observations, see Weber (note 13), p. 110.

art history in the traditional way as conditioned by the outcome of the *Querelle*. The path-finding approach with which Herder outstripped this immanent teleology and also the progress theory of the arts, arose out of his return to the tradition of biblical hermeneutics. Herder—as Weber showed—developed a theory of beauty which once more asserted its historical universality against the relativism of national and epochal individualities: the beautiful, which is no longer something metaphysically definable or essentially imitable, can be reassembled through the hermeneutic critical process as the "supra-historical" quintessence of historical manifestations, taking on an eidetic form for the expert or the critic.[20] Thus history exposes itself to "esthetic study as a spiritual continuity in a sense different from that of the literalness of facts."[21]

We shall be looking later at the question of whether the historian of fully developed historism owes something to Herder's *Ästhetiker* and whether in fact the hermeneutic science of history of the nineteenth century had a latent paradigm in the *poetic heuristics*[22] of art history. The course which literary and art history followed in the nineteenth century can be characterized through the progressive reduction of all claims to advance a unique insight of their own. Under historicism, which entailed the historical study of ancient and modern art as a new paradigm of historical experience, art history handed over lock, stock, and barrel its legitimation as a medium for esthetic, philosophical or hermeneutic reflection. The new history of national literatures, however, became an ideal counterpart to political history, and claimed to develop, through the context of all literary appearances, the idea of how national individuality could attain its identity, from quasi-mythical beginnings to the fulfillment of national classicism.

Positivism did gradually reduce this ideological orientation through a greater emphasis on science, but this merely left research into literary history without *any* particular framework. What Herder said of the old annalistic literary history can again be applied to the positivistic, which is a mere imitation of the external linking of events in pragmatic history: it "steps through nations and times with the quiet tread of a miller's mule."[23] The modern theory of literary science, dating from the First World War, lays emphasis on stylistic, formalistic, and structuralistic methods, and in turning away from positivism has also turned away from literary history. Now the literary historian tends to keep quiet when the discussion is on problems of the science of history and historical hermeneutics. But even today the history of literature can still awaken that same interest it took on in the ideas of the Enlightenment and the

[20] Note 13, p. 123.
[21] *Ibid.*, p. 119.
[22] Ed. Suphan, I, pp. 441-44.
[23] Ed. Suphan, II, p. 112.

period of Idealism, if only the appearance and function of literature in history are liberated from the rigid conventions and false causalities of literary history, and the historicity of literary works is put in its right perspective against the positivistic idea of knowledge and the traditionalist idea of art.

III

The scientifically sanctioned form of literary history is conceivably the worst medium through which to display the historicity of literature. It covers up the paradox of all art history, which Droysen touched on when he explained why the past reality of historic facts and their posterior interpretation are different, as for instance with pictures in an art-gallery: "Art history establishes a connection between them which, in themselves, they do not have, for which they are not painted, and from which there arises a sequence, a continuity, under the influence of which the painters of these pictures stood without being aware of it."[24]

Representing the "objective facts" of literary history are data of works, authors, trends, and periods. But even when their chronology can be fully confirmed, their interconnection, as seen in retrospect by the literary historian, is quite different from that "which once in its present [time] had a thousand other connections than those which concern us historically."[25] The retrospectively established, "actual" connection of literary "facts" captures neither the continuity in which a past work arose, nor that in which the contemporary reader or historian recognizes its meaning and importance. What has been the "event" of a literary work cannot be directly gauged from the facts listed by literary history. The question, left open by Droysen, as to how one is to extract from the sequence of works that continuity in which works are first created and received, can be answered only when one realizes that the analogy between "literary facts" and "historical facts" is an epiphenomenon.[26] This analogy, positivistic in origin, debases the historicity of the work of art and at the same time the interconnection of literary works. As a literary fact, or intersecting point of definable factors, the literary work forfeits its historically concrete appearance. This latter has its basis in the form and meaning created by the author, realized by his readers, and to be realized by them over and over again. When literary history adopted the paradigm of positivistic history, reducing the experi-

---

[24] *Historik: Vorlesung über Enzyklopädie und Methodologie der Geschichte*, ed. R. Hübner (Munich, ⁵1967), p. 35.

[25] *Ibid.*, p. 34.

[26] Droysen himself was caught up in the idea that in the history of art or literature "the sought-for, objective facts lie directly in front of us" (*ibid.*, p. 96).

ence of literature to causal links between work and work or author and author, the historical communication between author, work, and reader disappeared behind an hypostatized succession of monographs, which only retained the name of history.[27]

Behind the appearances of literary history, however, there is basically no objective link between work and work that is not brought about by the creating and receiving subjects of literature.[28] It is this intersubjective communication that separates the historicity of literature from the factual objectivity of pragmatic history. But this difference narrows if one follows Droysen's critique of the dogma of "objective facts," and accepts that diffuse events are only "understood and combined through the interpretation (of them) as a coherent process, as a complex of cause and effect, of aim and fulfillment, in short as A Fact," and that these same events can also be interpreted differently from "the point of view of the new fact" or from the later standpoint of the observer.[29] In this way Droysen gave back to the historical fact its basic character as an event, which like the work of art is an open field as far as interpretation is concerned. For it is not only the "right of historical study" but also an equally primary right of esthetic interpretation, to view works or "facts in the light of the significance they have gained through their effects."[30] And so the analogy that constitutes the link between art history and pragmatic history lies in the character both of the work of art and of the historical fact as an event—a character which in both cases was levelled out by positivism's objectivist idea of knowledge.

The problem of the connections and structural interactions of art history and pragmatic history is one that needs to be looked at again. On the one hand, one must infer, from Droysen's critique of the objectivism of the Historical School, that there may have been unacknowledged fictional narrative forms and esthetic categories of the history of style which made possible this classical form of historiography. And, on the other hand, one must ask whether Droysen's idea of "the event," which includes the consequences of things as well as the standpoint of the retrospective observer, does not itself presuppose the paradigm of the past work of art and its undefined meaning.

IV

"The science of history is not an encyclopaedia of historical sciences, or a philosophy (or theology) of history, or a physics of the his-

---

[27] See the critique of literary history by R. Barthes, *Literatur oder Geschichte* (Frankfurt, 1969), p. 12.

[28] See *op.cit.* in note 4, pp. 171-73 (Thesis VI).

[29] *Historik*, pp. 133, 167.   [30] *Ibid.*, p. 91.

torical world, or—least of all—a poetics for historiography. It must set itself the task of being an organon of historical thought and research."[31] Droysen's science of history is, in its approach, hermeneutic. This makes it hard for it to give the lie to the expectation that it will merely be a "poetics for historiography," like Gervinus' *Grundzüge der Historik* (1837). The fact that it also implies a philosophy (the continuity of progressive historical *work*) and a theology of history (the highest aim of a *theodicy*) is less harmful to its claims to independence than the suspicion that history is an art, and therefore cannot be raised to the rank of a science. For the method of investigating sources—the "physics of the historical world"—could not suffice to assure history of this rank. Despite its triumphs—as Droysen ironically points out—people hailed "as the greatest historian of our time the man who, in his presentation (of history), was closest to the novels of Walter Scott" (p. 322). Droysen's polemic against Ranke and the objectivity ideal of historism is aimed principally at exposing the illusions that accompany the apparently objective narration of traditional facts.

The first is the illusion of the completed process. Although every historian knows that our knowledge of history must always remain incomplete, the prevailing form of the narrative creates "the illusion, and wants to create it, that we are faced with a complete process of historical things, a finished chain of events, motives and purposes" (p. 144). The historical narrative uses the law of fiction, that even disparate elements of a story come closer and closer together for the reader, and ultimately combine in a picture of the whole; if this esthetic effect is to be avoided and the imagination prevented from closing the gaps, then special preventive measures are required which, paradoxically, are more common to modern artistic prose than to historiography.

The second is the illusion of the first beginning and the definitive end. Here, with a sagacity rare for his time, Droysen uncovered and denounced the "false doctrine of the so-called organic development in history" (p. 152): "It is completely beyond the scope of historical research to get to a point that would be . . . the beginning, the sudden origin" (p. 150). It is untrue of history "that all conditions for the later are present in the earlier" (p. 141), and it is equally untrue that things in history have as definite a conclusion as Ranke makes out in his history of the period of the Reformation—for "what has become bears in itself all elements of new unrest" (p. 298). When the historical narrative proceeds genetically and tries to explain things from the standpoint of their origin, it once more falls back upon a law of fiction—namely, the Aristote-

[31] Droysen, *Historik*, § 16 (henceforth quoted only with page number or §).

lian definition of the poetic fiction, which must have a beginning, a middle, and an end: a beginning that does not originate out of something else, and an end that can be followed by nothing.

The third illusion is that of an objective picture of the past. Whoever believes with Ranke that the historian need only disregard his partialist self and cause his present to be forgotten (p. 306), in order to capture an undistorted past, is as little able to guarantee the truth of the resultant "pictures from the past or illustrations of what is long since lost" as are "poets and novelists" (p. 27). Even if a past could be "established in the full breadth of its former present" (p. 27), in the past things themselves there would still not be that "criterion for the important and characteristic" which can only be gained by reflecting on the standpoint from which the whole variety of phenomena can be viewed as a (relative) whole. "Only the thoughtless is objective,"[32] for: "Here the 'facts' only seem to be speaking, alone, exclusive, 'objective.' They would be dumb without the narrator, who makes them speak" (§91).

The epic fictions of the completed process, of the first beginning and the definitive end, and of the self-presenting past, are the consequences of what Droysen showed to be the illusion of Romantic historism, according to which the historian need only repeat the pure facts as extracted from his sources, "and the resultant illusion of handed-down facts then passed off as history" (§360). The flourishing historiography of the nineteenth century, which sought to disavow the artistic character of history writing in order to gain recognition as a science, devolved on a fictionalization of its subject matter to the extent that it followed the principle that the historian must efface himself for history to be able to tell its own story. The poetics involved in this is no different from that of the contemporary peak of literature—the historical novel. However, it is not enough to characterize this new poetics of historical narrative just by the material revelation and poetic, anecdotal animation of the past with which Sir Walter Scott's novels satisfied the historically curious. The fact that Scott was able to bully scientific historiography into an individualized presentation of the past such as history had never been capable of before, was also due to a principle of form.

What so impressed A. Thierry, Barante, and other historians of the Twenties, in Scott's novels, was not only the suggestive power of historical color and detail, the individual physiognomy of a past epoch, and the perspective enabling historical events to be followed through persons instead of the usual impersonal actions. It was also, above all, the new form of the "drama"—one of Scott's major claims to fame—by which

[32] Variant in manuscript print of 1858.

his contemporaries meant not so much the dramatic plot-weaving as the still unfamiliar dramatic form of the narrative: as the narrator of the historical novel remains completely in the background, the story can unfold itself like a play, giving the reader the illusion that he himself is present at the drama of the persons involved. This also means that the reader is put in the position of being able to make his own judgments and draw his own moral conclusions—which had previously always been denied him by argumentative historians like Hume or Robertson.[33] These analogies between the poetics of the historical novel and the ideal of objectivity sought by contemporary historiography speak for themselves.[34] In both cases we have a narrator who is explicitly withdrawn, but implicitly present, all the time communicating and passing judgment—this situation arising out of the illusion of an unmediated presentation of the past. Even more than the novelist Scott, who could delegate his narrative functions to his characters—or hide them through perspectives—the historian Ranke continually reveals himself through *a posteriori* viewpoints and esthetic classifications which could have played no part in the lives of those who actually experienced the historical event. The fact that he defiantly cuts the thread joining the period "as it actually was" with that "which resulted from it" becomes painfully obvious whenever a judgment, selection, motivation, or linking of events presupposes the hindsight of the historian, and whenever the impression has to be conveyed that a view made possible only by this hindsight and by the aftereffects of the event in question was a pattern inherent in that original event. In Ranke's historiography, these inconsistencies are concealed by the illusion of a completed process—and this in a manner no longer reminiscent of Scott's handling of historical plots, but of the stylistic approach to the sequential continuity of events evinced by the form of art history.

V

We shall now illustrate the thesis that Ranke's historiography is determined by esthetic categories that fall in with the latent paradigm of

[33] A. Thierry: *Sur les trois grandes méthodes historiques en usage depuis le seizième siècle* (1820); De Barante, *Préface de l'Histoire des Ducs de Bourgogne* (1824), and the anonymous article: "De la nouvelle école historique" (1828); quoted from K. Massmann, *Die Rezeption des historischen Romans von Sir Walter Scott in Frankreich von 1816 bis 1832*, Diss. Konstanz, 1969, esp. p. 118.

[34] The fact that there was here a "parallelism of intention . . . which justifies the assertion that the historical novel of the Scott type . . .was capable of fulfilling the programme of the eighteenth-century Scottish school of history more completely than it could itself" is also shown by E. Wolff, "Zwei Versionen des historischen Romans: Scotts 'Waverley' und Thackerays 'Henry Esmond,' " in *Lebende Antike, Symposium für R. Sühnel*, ed. H. Meller and H.-J. Zimmermann (Berlin, 1967), pp. 348-369 (esp. 357).

the history of style, by analyzing the period of the English War as presented in Ranke's *Französische Geschichte* (Chap. i, 3; 1852-1861).[35] History of style, in the form created by Winckelmann, has the following characteristics: turning point through the introduction of something new (change of style);[36] division into phases (e.g., the four phases of Greek art: older style, high, beautiful, and the style of imitators); the completeness of periods (styles have clear beginnings and a definite end, sealed off by the success of the new).

In Ranke's presentation, the period of the English War starts off in several respects with a radical change to something new. Louis IX, the "original of all religious kings," is succeeded by a king from the same Capetian stock, but "a character of a different kind"—Philip the Fair, a believer in the specifically modern doctrine of power politics (p. 78). He was the first that "with ruthless ambition" dared to "violate" the frontiers to the German Empire maintained by his predecessors—a fact concerning which Ranke has this comment to make: "he knew, or felt, that he was in league with the nature of things" (pp. 78-79). This sentence is a perfect example of a narrative statement (henceforth to be abbreviated n.s.), possible only in retrospect, which the narrator Ranke obviously passes off ("or felt") as coming from the person of Philip. The change to the new is then thematized in the dispute with Pope Boniface VIII, the breaking off of crusade politics, and the destruction of the Order of the Temple. In the latter case, Ranke does not even attempt to test the truth of the accusations against the Templars, his reason being that "it is enough for us to take note of the change in ideas" (p. 79). And so the border between the old and the new can be defined in its full, epoch-making significance: "The age that had been enlivened by the ideas of general Christendom, was over (n.s.); the goods from which the profits were to be used in the reconquering of Jerusalem, were collected up and used in the service of the kingdom. . . . Through his (Philip's) whole being there blew already the sharp breeze of modern history (n.s., p. 80)." Historical processes of such a general kind as Ranke had in mind do not, in reality, take over one from the other at a single frontier between old ("was over") and new ("blew already"), but they merge into one another at a variety of levels and crossing-points, sometimes delayed, sometimes premature. Ranke's presentation, which is highly effective

[35] Ed. O. Vossler (Stuttgart, 1954), pp. 78-95 (henceforth quoted only with page numbers).

[36] The beginnings of a new style are, according to K. Badt (see note 87) "often not tentative or imperfect, but—like Athene out of the head of Zeus—the new style stands complete before us, perhaps a little coarse, but nevertheless fully and characteristically developed" (p. 139).

from the points of view of narrative and perspective, brushes aside the heterogeneity and gives this new impulse a function that one can only call esthetic, for here the "change in ideas," like the creation of a new style, proceeds as a sort of event from a definite beginning, and at a stroke changes the whole outlook of the world.

Ranke has stylized the political starting point of this epoch in a manner that betrays him: "But scarcely had this standpoint been adopted of a ruthless, isolated policy oriented only towards a furtherance of the State of France, when there occurred an event through which the country was plunged into a general confusion and thrown back completely upon itself" (n.s., pp. 80, 81). With this temporal vagueness ("but scarcely had . . . when there occurred") Ranke surreptitiously introduces a teleology which continues to show itself in the linking and phasing of events right up to the formulation of an end result: "The world was astonished to see not only French flags flying in Normandy, but also the English retreating from the hundred-year possession of Aquitania. They kept nothing except Calais. Perhaps as great a piece of good fortune for the conquered as for the conquerors, for the nations had to separate, if each of them (was to) develop in accordance with its own instincts" (n.s., p. 95). Just like the unfolding of a new style, then, the history of the new epoch also has its purpose, in the light of which all individual contingencies become meaningful and their connection clear—"Clear" as the sequence of works representing a particular style, sharing in every change in that style, and revealing only the sort of changes that can be included in a description of that style.

With Ranke's narrative style, the heterogeneous is often absorbed into the general course of things by means of temporal phasing and harmonizing. Heterogeneous elements of an event are brought in as it were in stages ("for centuries" . . . "long since" . . . "finally" . . . p. 79), then to be plunged into their main development with the "now" of a vital moment ("And this great faction now made contact with the struggle over the succession" [p. 83]). Or the main action might bring to the fore a long hidden, heterogeneous event through a highly significant "completely," so that it may thus be incorporated into the general process. Thus, for instance, the new power of the cities is first "prepared in secret," then "supported by all those elements working in the depths," and finally released "completely" by the English War (p. 82). The temporal sequence implied in "completely," in the typical "now" (which not infrequently has the meaning of "at this very moment"), or in the combination "already . . . but" (p. 86), leaves matters of chronology very vague where often it would be difficult to be precise or precision would destroy the harmonious flow, and it creates out of the contingency of events a continuity of significant moments.

This very idealized time sequence, like the history of a style, describes a steady upward and downward movement, except that here the curve runs in the opposite direction, as Ranke follows the line of the decline and subsequent rise of royal power. Corresponding to the culminating-point of a style history is the moment at which all the heterogeneous trends are homogenized: "Meanwhile, however, the English War had broken out again, and there came a moment at which all these questions, however little they originally had in common, merged into one another" (p. 88). The ideality of this moment is again betrayed by the fact that it is obviously not identical with any of the events of this phase (Agincourt, Treaty of Troyes, Henry V's entry into Paris), but rather symbolized the lowest ebb of the French crown. The upward movement begins with a reference to a higher need: "But his (the Dauphin's) sword . . . alone would scarcely have saved him; first he had to separate himself from the (. . .) union of the Armagnacs (. . .) if he really wanted to be King of France" (p. 89). Once again the "great and saving moment," which the narrator Ranke dwells on for some time (p. 90), does not coincide with any concrete event. The description of the upward movement homogenizes the events and changes that strengthen the monarchy, and leaves the defeated opposition nothing but its dying moments of decline. And so the idea concealed in the event, but brought out by the narrator as the decisive impulse behind the transition, can be fulfilled by the historical outcome already described—the idea of a new monarchical order, together with which is inaugurated a new idea of the nation "developed in accordance with its own instincts" (p. 95). But the historian, who describes the cut-and-dried historical individuality of this epoch with such apparent objectivity, still owes us the reasons for his interpretation and narrative perspective, which betray themselves in his *parti pris* for the consolidation of the "fixed order" of the monarchy (p. 94) and against the repressed ideas of the towns and estates movement.

VI

While the principle behind Ranke's presentation of history refers back to the latent paradigm of the history of style, Droysen's critique of the narrative presentation and the resultant artistic nature of "objective" historiography presupposes a hermeneutics that arose from the historical approach to art. Droysen tries to shatter the "conventional view (. . .) that the only type of historical presentation is the narrative" (p. 254) through the distinction of non-narrative forms of presentation (the "examining," the "didactic," the "discursive") and also through the attempt to draw a borderline between "artistic" and "historical" narrative. His statement that the artistic creation is "a totality, something complete in itself" (p. 285) is aimed at the historical novel ("a picture, a photograph of that which once was," p. 285), and applies equally to the history of the past and to the historical representation of respective epochs by historicism. Underlying this is Droysen's main argument: "That which was, does not interest us because it was, but because in a certain sense it still is, in that it is still effective because it stands in the total context of things which we call the historical, i.e., moral world, the moral cosmos" (p. 275). The narrative form of historical presentation, according to Droysen, can escape the suspicion of being artistic fiction only if, as a mimesis of development, it includes and reflects "our interpretation of important events from this standpoint" (p. 285). But this presentation of history—according to Droysen the only "historically" legitimate one—has its precedent in the hermeneutic process of experiencing and readapting the art of the past. The meaning of a work of art, too, is extracted only during the progressive process of its reception; it is not a mystic whole that can reveal itself totally on its first showing.[37] The art of the past, just like history, does not interest merely because it was, but because "in a certain sense it still is" and invites one to new adaptations.

Droysen's argument against the narrative technique leaves unanswered the question of how the classical narrative form of history can be cut out, and how the contrasting didactic form of presentation can be brought in—"in order to use the whole wealth of the past for the enlightenment of our present and for our deeper understanding of it" (p. 275). Droysen seems to have overlooked the fact that the new task "of showing the development of this present and of its thought content" (p. 275), like any "mimesis of development," cannot be performed linguistically without a narrative link—in other words, without the form of a "story." This also applies to the individual event if, as Droysen maintains, a historical fact as an event—just like a work of art—is constituted by the range of its possible meanings and can therefore be made concrete only through the interpretation of later observers or performers. Droysen's new definition of the historical fact—"What happens is understood and put together only by interpretation as a coherent event . . . in short, as A Fact" (pp. 133-34)—necessarily implies narration if the diffuse event of the past is to be grasped as a totality in the light of its present meaning. In this context, narrative is to be understood primarily as a basic category of historical perception, and only secondarily as a form of historical presentation. The different modes of narrative presen-

[37] See Droysen, p. 285, and also A. C. Danto, *Analytical Philosophy of History* (Cambridge, 1965), who overlooks the fact that the difference between the "whole" of a work of art, and the never completed "whole of history" only exists so long as one does not consider the work of art in the historical dimension of its reception.

tation have, throughout history, been subject to a process consisting of various phases and degrees of literariness and "anti-literariness." Droysen's polemic against the "artistically" closed narrative form of historism again implies an "anti-literary" form of presentation—with a limited perspective, aware of its own location, and a horizon that is left open; and, paradoxically, the poetics of modern literature offers paradigms for such a presentation.

This interweaving of poetics and history reappears in A. C. Danto's analytical philosophy of history. Danto's premise is: "our knowledge of the past is significantly limited by our ignorance of the future" (p. 16); he bases narrative logic on the posteriority of its statements: "[they] give descriptions of events under which those events could not have been witnessed" (p. 61); historical explanation presupposes "conceptual evidence" (p. 119)[38] and narrative ("A narrative describes and explains at once" [p. 141]); it should not try to reproduce the past, but with the aid of the past "organize present experience" (p. 79). All this is directly in line with Droysen's approach to history, though Danto makes no reference to it. Poetics comes onto the scene when Danto deals with the role of narrative in historical explanation and seeks an equivalent to the unprovable "historical laws" (Chaps. x-xi). He claims to find it in "temporal wholes," which first of all he explains by referring to the historical variability of literary forms (p. 226), and then traces back to definitions (pp. 233 ff.) that are basically just a rehash of the classical, Aristotelian norms of epic fiction. But if the narrative as a form of historical explanation is to keep open the possibility of further narrative statements about the same event (p. 167), the closed horizon of the classical narrative form must be surmounted and the contingency of history made to prevail against the epic tendency of the "story."

"A story is an account, I shall say an explanation, of how the change from beginning to end took place" (p. 234): this corresponds to the Aristotelian definition of the story (*Poetics*, 1450 b)—all the more so as Danto had already substituted "change," in the sense of the tragic dénouement (1450 a; 1452 a) for the mere event as the actual subject of historical explanation (p. 233). In this way Danto falls into the illusion, already uncovered by Droysen, of the first beginning and the definitive end; it immediately gets him into trouble when he observes—but

---

[38] This preconception, which Danto seeks to explain as a "social inheritance" (pp. 224, 242), like his general attempt to establish a relative legitimacy for the historical, would be easier to grasp through Droysen's idea of analogies of historical experience. See *Historik*, p. 159: "Whatever is given in the nature of the thing, we have learnt from our experience and knowledge elsewhere of analogous situations—as the sculptor, restoring an old torso, has this basic analogy in the constant form of the human body."

swiftly dismisses as a mere problem of causality—that the "change of things" might be the middle of a history that stretches as far back as it does forwards (p. 240). His thesis "that we are in fact referring to a change when we demand an explanation of some event" (p. 246) also narrows the idea of an event to a homogeneous change, and ignores the fact that in an event not only the change from before to after, but also the aftereffects and the retrospective importance for the observer or for the acting person need to be explained. Danto believes he can achieve homogeneity through what seems to him to be the obvious condition that the historical narrative requires a never-changing subject, and should include only details or episodes that will serve the cause of explanation (p. 250). But this is precisely how Aristotle defined the epic unity of the story (1451 a), at the same time drawing attention to the superiority of fiction—which is concerned with the possible or the general—over history, which can deal only with the factual and the particular (1451 b). If narrative logic, which here is still completely confined to the closed circle of classical poetics, is to fit in with the contingency of history, it could follow the paradigm of the modern novel: since Flaubert, this has systematically dismantled the teleology of the epic story, and developed new narrative techniques in order to incorporate the open horizon of the future into the story of the past, to replace the omniscient narrator by localized perspectives, and to destroy the illusion of completeness through unexpected and unexplained details.

Narrative as a basic form of historical perception and explanation can be viewed throughout in accordance with Danto's analogy to the basic form of literary genres and their historical appearance. Only one must then refute the substantialist misconception that in a history of genres the multiplicity of historical variants is countered by an invariable form which, as "historic law" subsumes every possible historical form of a genre.[39] The history of artistic genres in fact reveals the existence of forms that are possessed of no greater generality than that which shows itself in the change of their historical appearance.[40] What Droysen said of the individuality of nations also applies to the literary form or artistic genre as an historical unit: "they change to the extent that they have history, and they have history to the extent that they change" (p. 198). This sentence refers back to the basic view of history in Droysen's *Historik*, the "continuity of progressive historical work" (p. 29), or—in Droysen's interpretation—the ἐπίδοσις εἰς αὑτό, through which according to Aristotle (*De an.*, ΙΙ, 4.2) the species of man differs from that

[39] The metric scheme alone is not enough to determine the generic form of a sonnet, as Danto, p. 256, obviously assumes.

[40] See H. R. Jauss, "Littérature médiévale et théorie des genres," in *Poétique, revue de théorie et d'analyse littéraires* (1970), pp. 79-101 (esp. p. 92).

of animals, which can only reproduce *as* species. It is obvious that the history of art, as regards the historical appearance of its forms, fulfills in a very distinct manner Droysen's idea of a continuity "in which everything earlier extends and supplements itself through the later" (p. 12). If it is inherent in the idea of "historical work" that "with every new and individual appearance it creates a newness and an addition" (p. 9), then artistic productions correspond to this idea more than other manifestations of historical life which, in the framework of continuing institutions, change more slowly and not always in such a way that every change "creates a newness and an addition" as the work of art in fact can with every new and individual appearance. The analogy between the historical event and the past work of art, which Droysen's *Historik* presupposes, therefore extends even further. The history of art, through its manner of progression in time, and the study of art, through its continuous mediation of past and present art, can become a paradigm for a history that is to show the "development of this present" (p. 275). But art history can take on this function only if it itself overcomes the organon-type principle of style history, and thus liberates itself from traditionalism and its metaphysics of supratemporal beauty. Droysen was already pointing the way when he tried to bring the histories of individual arts back into the "progression" of historical work, and when he spurred on the art history of his day, which was "still only in its beginning," with the words: "The idea of beauty will progress in the same measure as the acknowledged beauty of ideas" (p. 230).

VII

The conception of a history of art that is to be based on the historical functions of production, communication, and reception, and is to take part in the process of continuous mediation of past and present art, requires the critical abandonment of two contrasting positions. First, it defies historical objectivism, which remains a convenient paradigm ensuring the normal progress of philological research, but in the realm of literature can achieve only an apparent precision, which in the exemplary disciplines of natural and social science scarcely earns it any respect. It also challenges the philological metaphysics of tradition and with this the classicism of a view of fiction that disregards the historicity of art, in order to confer on "great fiction" its own relation to truth— "timeless present" or "self-sufficient presence"[41]—and a more substan-

41 M. Heidegger, "Der Ursprung des Kunstwerks," in *Holzwege*, Frankfurt, 1950, p. 18; also the corresponding definition of *classical* in H. G. Gadamer, *Wahrheit und Methode* (Tübingen, 1960), p. 272: ". . . a consciousness of permanence, of the unlosable meaning independent of all temporal circumstances . . . a kind of timeless present, which means contemporaneousness for every present"; or E. R. Curtius, *Europäische Literatur*

tial, organic history—"tradition" or "the authority of the traditional."[42]

Traditionalism, which holds fast to the "eternal store" and guaranteed
classicality of "masterpieces" and so creates for itself the spectacle of a
Sonntagsstrasse der Literaturgeschichte (Sunday street of literary history),[43] can appeal to a secular experience of the fine arts. For, as
Droysen remarks in his *Historik* (1857): "No-one before Aristotle
thought that dramatic poetry might have a history; until about the middle of our century it did not occur to anybody to talk of a history of
music."[44] The fact that the timelessly beautiful is also subject to historical experience because of historical influences, elements of which will
remain in the work of art, and because of the open horizon of its meaning, which becomes apparent in the never-ending process of interpretation, and the fact that the fine arts also have a history, to the extent that
they do change in this way—these facts are a comparatively recent discovery, which the triumph of historism could not make self-evident.
What Droysen's contemporary Baudelaire provocatively formulated in
1859 as a "théorie rationnelle et historique du beau," illustrated with
the outrageous example of clothing fashions, and contrasted with the
low-brow bourgeois taste for the "immortal,"[45] has continually been
regarded ever since the *Querelle des Anciens et des Modernes* as a new
challenge to the classical interpretation of art by the enlightened or historical consciousness.

The conception of tradition which this idea of art goes back to is—
according to Theodor W. Adorno—carried over from natural, spontaneous situations (the link between generations, traditions of crafts and
trades) to the realm of the mind.[46] This carrying over endows what is
past with an authoritative orientation, and sets the creations of the mind
into a substantial continuity which supports and harmonizes history, at
the cost of suppressing the contrary, the revolutionary, the unsuccessful.[47] In accordance with the transmission image (*tradere*), the process
of historical action here turns into a self-activating movement of im-

---

und lateinisches Mittelalter (Bern, 1948), p. 23: "The 'timeless present' which is an essential element of literature, means that the literature of the past can always remain effective
in any present."

[42] H. G. Gadamer, pp. 261 seq.: *Die Rehabilitierung von Autorität und Tradition.*

[43] W. Krauss, *Literaturgeschichte als geschichtlicher Auftrag*, in: *Sinn und Form* 2
(1950), p. 113.

[44] P. 138.   [45] In: *Le Peintre de la vie moderne* (Paris, 1951), pp. 873-76.

[46] "Thesen über Tradition," in *Insel Almanach auf das Jahr 1966*, pp. 21-33.

[47] See Adorno, p. 29: "(Here) one meets with the true theme of the recollection of tradition, which brings together all that has remained by the wayside, the neglected, the defeated, under the name of the out-of-date. There the living element of tradition seeks ref-

perishable substances or into the sequent effect of original norms. To put it as briefly as possible: "In truth history does not belong to us, but we belong to it."[48]

In the sphere of art, the changing of the historical praxis of human creativity into self-sufficient recurrence of shaping historical entities reveals itself in the hypostatized metaphor of the *after-life of Antiquity*. This stands for an historiographic model which, in the humanist's credo, has its counterpart as "imitation of the ancient" and, in the course of history, witnesses nothing but the continual alternation of decline and return to classical models and lasting values. But tradition cannot transmit itself by itself. It presupposes a response whenever an "effect" of something past is recognizable in the present. Even classical models are present only where they are responded to: if tradition is to be understood as the historical process of artistic praxis, this latter must be understood as a movement that begins with the recipient, takes up and brings along what is past, and translates or "transmits" it into the present, thus setting it in the new light of present meaning.

Along with the illusion of self-activating tradition, esthetic dogmatism also falls into discredit—the belief in an "objective" meaning, which is revealed once and for all in the original work, and which an interpreter can restore at any time, provided he sets aside his own historical position and places himself, without any prejudices, back into the original intention of the work. But the form and meaning of a tradition-building work are not the unchangeable dimensions or appearances of an esthetic object, independent of perception in time and history: its potential of meaning only becomes progressively visible and definable in the subsequent changes of esthetic experience, and dialogically so in the interaction between the literary work and the literary public. The tradition-forming potential of a classic work can only be seen by its contemporaries within the horizon of its first "materialization."[49] Only as the horizon changes and expands with each subsequent historical materialization, do responses to the work legitimize particular possibilities of understanding, imitation, transformation, and continuation—in short, structures of exemplariness that condition the process of literary tradition-forming.

---

uge, and not in the store of works that are to defy time"; and see especially S. Kracauer, whose philosophy of history in *History: The Last Things Before the Last* (New York, 1969) vindicates in many respects the demand "to undo the injurious work of tradition" (p. 7).

[48] Gadamer, p. 261.

[49] Concerning the term *"Konkretisation"* (materialization), which I have taken over from F. Vodička, see below.

If one wishes to give the name "tradition" to this discontinuous process of an active, normative, and changing reproduction of what is past in the sphere of art, then one must do away with the Platonic idea of art and with the substantialist conception of history as an "event of tradition." The receiving consciousness certainly stands among traditions that precondition its way of understanding, but, just as certainly, the traditional cannot be fitted out with predicates and a life of its own, for without the active participation of the receiving mind, these are simply not conceivable. It is therefore a substantialist relapse in the historical hermeneutics of H. G. Gadamer when—obviously indulging a predilection for the classics—he expects of the traditional text per se (regardless of whether it is a work of art or a historical document) "that it asks a question of the interpreter. Interpretation . . . always contains a basic reference to the question that has been asked of one. To understand a text means to understand a question."[50] But a past text cannot, of its own accord, across the ages, ask us or later generations a question that the interpreter would not first have to uncover or reformulate for us, proceeding from the answer which the text hands down or appears to contain. Literary tradition is a dialectic of question and answer which is always kept going—though this is often not admitted—from the present interest. A past text does not survive in historical tradition, thanks to old questions that would have been preserved by tradition and could be asked in an identical way for all times including our own. For the question whether an old or allegedly timeless question still—or once more—concerns us, while innumerable other questions leave us indifferent, is decided first and foremost by an interest that arises out of the present situation, critically opposes it, or maintains it.

W. Benjamin, in his critique of historism, reaches an analogous conception of historical tradition: "To put into operation experience with history—which for every present is an original experience—is the task of historical materialism. It turns to a consciousness of the present, which shatters the continuum of history."[51] Why this task should fall to the historical materialist alone is not made clear by this essay. For, after all, a historical materialist must presumably believe in a "real historical continuity" if, with Benjamin, he declares his allegiance to the ideas expressed in Engels' letter to Mehring (14 July 1893). Anyone who, with Engels, wishes to proclaim the apparent triumph of thought as "intellectual reflections of changed economic fact," cannot also impute to the conscious mind the achievement of "shattering the continuum of

[50] *Wahrheit und Methode, loc.cit.* pp. 351-55.

[51] "Edward Fuchs, der Sammler und Historiker," in *Angelus Novus* (Frankfurt, 1966), p. 304.

HANS ROBERT JAUSS 453

history." According to materialist dogma, he cannot apply any consciousness to the present that is not previously conditioned by changed economic facts in the midst of the real, historical continuity which, paradoxically, that consciousness is meant to shatter. The famous "tiger leap into the past" (*Geschichtsphilosophische Thesen*, XIV) completely brushes aside historical materialism: Benjamin's anti-traditionalist theory of reception superseded it in the Fuchs essay before he himself realized it.

VIII

The classical idea of art as the history of creative spirits and timeless masterpieces, together with its positivistic distortion in the form of innumerable histories of "Man and Work," has since the Fifties been the subject of critical examination conducted in the name of the "structural method." In Anglo-American criticism this proceeded from Northrop Frye's theory of archetypal literature, and in French from Claude Lévi-Strauss; it aimed at a predominantly elitist idea of culture and art, contrasted this with a new interest in primitive art, folklore, and sub-literature, and demanded a methodical approach starting with the individual work and finishing with literature as a system.[52] For Frye, literature is an "order of words," not a "piled aggregate of works": "Total literary history gives us a glimpse of the possibility of seeing literature as a complication of a relatively restricted and simple group of formulas that can be studied in primitive culture."[53] Archetypes or "communicable symbols" mediate between the structure of primitive myths and the forms or figures of later art and literature. The historical dimension of literature withdraws behind the omnipresence or transferability of these symbols, which obviously change gradually, with literary means of expression from myth to mimesis; it reemerges only when, at the last moment, Frye attributes to the myth an emancipatory function regarding ritual, so that—like Matthew Arnold—he can set art the task of removing class barriers, enabling it to participate "in the vision of the goal of social effort, the idea of complete and classless society."[54]

The gulf between structure and event, between synchronous system and history, becomes absolute in Lévi-Strauss, who searches behind the myths for nothing but the structure in depth of the closed synchronous

[52] See the detailed critique by G. Hartman, "Toward Literary History," in *Daedalus* (Spring, 1970), pp. 355-83; also C. Segre, *I segni e la critica* (Turin, 1969), who also subjects the claims of semasiological literary theory to well-argued criticism.

[53] Northrop Frye, *Anatomy of Criticism* (New York, 1967), pp. 16 seq.

[54] P. 348.

system of a functional logic. The latent Rousseauism of this theory is apparent in the chapter "Du mythe au roman" from *L'Origine des manières de table*.[55] When the structural analysis of the Indian myths, which in one breath are awarded and refused "liberté d'invention" ("nous pouvons au moins démontrer la nécessité de cette liberté," 104), throws up a historical process such as the development from myth to novel, this process appears as an incontrovertible degradation in the general *"débâcle"* of history (pp. 105-106). In this downward movement of the real through the symbolic to the imaginary, the structures of contrast decline into those of repetition. Lévi-Strauss is reminded here of the "serial," which also draws its life from the denatured repetition of original works and, like the "mythe à tiroir," is subject to a short periodicity and the same "contraintes formelles." But this new version of the old theory of the "decayed matter of culture" (or here, "matter of Nature") is contradicted by the fact that in the nineteenth century the serial novel was not the "état dernier de la dégradation du genre romanesque" but, on the contrary, the starting point for the great, "original" novel of the Balzac and Dostoyevsky type—not to mention the fact that the *Mystères de Paris* kind of novel developed a new mythology of city life that cannot be fitted in with the idea of a decline in the "exténuation du mythe." Ultimately Lévi-Strauss's theory of a decline itself surreptitiously takes on the nature of a new myth, when in the moral outcome of the serial novel he claims to find an equivalent to the closed structure of the myth, "par lequel une société qui se livre à l'histoire croit pouvoir remplacer l'ordre logico-naturel qu'elle a abandonné, à moins qu'elle-même n'ait été abandonée par lui" (p. 106). History as the deviation of society from Nature, personified in the "ordre logico-naturel," if one were not to assume that Nature herself (comparable to Heidegger's "Kehre") has turned away from Man: with this, Heidegger's myth of "Seinsvergessenheit" (oblivion of existence) is given a worthy, panstructuralistic companion-piece!

For Lévi-Strauss every work of art is completely explicable through its function within the secondary system of reference of society; every act of speech is reduced to a combinatory element in a primary system of signs; all meaning and individuation merges into an anonymous, subjectless system, establishing the priority of a spontaneous natural order over any historical process. And so we may assume, with Paul Ricoeur, that the paradigm of anthropological structuralism will only be productive for the methodology of the study of art and literature if, along with the results of structural analysis, the latter takes up and regains what the

[55] Paris, 1968 (*Mythologiques*, III), pp. 69-106.

former seeks dogmatically to exclude: "une production dialectique, qui fasse advenir le système comme acte et la structure comme événement."[56]

An approach to bridging the gap between structure and event is already to be distinguished in the literary theory of Roland Barthes, who in France paved the way for criticism of the "Lansonist system" of university literary history, and was the first to show what structural analysis of a literary work could really achieve. His Racine interpretation penetrates behind the historical explanation and naive psychology of literary creation, and establishes a kind of structural anthropology of classical tragedy. The archaic system of characters is transplanted into a surprisingly rich context of functions, a context which extends from the three dimensions of topography right up to metaphysics and the inverted redemption theology of the Racinian hero, and which stimulates and expands one's historical understanding.[57] The question left open in *L'homme racinien* as to what literature meant to Racine and his contemporaries is, for Barthes, one of those problems that literary history can solve only through a radical conversion "analogous to that which made possible the transition from the chronicles of kings to genuine history." For literary history can only "deal on the level of literary functions (production, communication, consumption), and not on that of the individuals who have exercised these functions."[58] From a scientific point of view, literary history would accordingly be sociologically possible only as a history of the literary institution, while the other side of literature—the individual connection between author and work, between work and meaning—would be left to the subjectivity of criticism, of which Barthes can, quite rightly, make the demand that it confess to its preconceptions if it wants to prove its historical legitimacy.[59] But this raises the question whether the thus legitimized subjectivity or series of interpretations of a work is not itself again "institutionalized" through history, forming a system in its historical sequence. The question also arises as to how one is to conceive the structure of a work which, in opposition to the structuralistic axiom of completeness, remains open to an interpretation that in principle is incapable of completeness and, indeed,

[56] "La structure, le mot, l'événement," in: *Esprit*, 35 (1967) pp. 801-21, esp. 808; special attention should be paid to this fundamental critique, which develops hermeneutic approaches to the problem of overcoming structural dogmatism.

[57] *Sur Racine* (Paris, ²1963), see esp. p. 17: "Les trois espaces extérieurs: mort, fuite, événement" and p. 54: "La faute (La théologie racinienne est une rédemption inversée: c'est l'homme qui rachète Dieu)", p. 55.

[58] *Ibid.*, p. 156.

[59] *Literatur oder Geschichte*, pp. 34-35.

takes on its specific character as art through this very openness and dependence on individual response.

Barthes has not asked the first of these questions, but his answer to the second is equally exasperating for the dogmatists of Positivism and of Structuralism:[60] "Ecrire, c'est ébranler le sens du monde, y disposer une interrogation indirecte, à laquelle l'écrivain, par un dernier suspens, s'abstient de répondre. La réponse, c'est chacun de nous qui la donne, y apportant son histoire, son langage, sa liberté; mais comme histoire, langage et liberté changent infiniment, la réponse du monde à l'écrivain est infinie: on ne cesse jamais de répondre à ce qui a été écrit hors de toute réponse: affirmés, puis mis en rivalité, puis remplacés, les sens passent, la question demeure."[61] Here the open structure of the literary work is observed in the open relation between meaning, question, and answer, but the cost of this is a yawning gap of subjective arbitrariness between the past work and its progressive interpretation—a gap that can be bridged only by the historical mediation of question and answer. For the implicit question, which in fact is what first awakens our present interest in the past work, can be obtained only through the answer that the esthetic object, in its present materialization, holds or seems to hold ready for us. Literary works differ from purely historical documents precisely because they do more than simply document a particular time, and remain "speaking" to the extent that they attempt to solve problems of form or content, and so extend far beyond the silent relics of the past.[62]

If the literary text is taken primarily as an answer, or if the later reader is primarily seeking an answer in it, this by no means implies that the author himself has formulated an explicit answer in his work. The answering nature of the text, which provides the historical link between the past work and its later interpretation, is a modality of its structure—seen already from the viewpoint of its reception; it is not an invariable value within the work itself. The answer or meaning expected by the later reader can have been ambivalent or have remained altogether indeterminate in the original work. The degree of indetermi-

---

[60] See statements of R. Picard and C. Lévi-Strauss, quoted by G. Schiwy, Der französische Strukturalismus (Hamburg, 1969), p. 67 and p. 71 respectively.

[61] Sur Racine (Paris, ²1963), p. 11; cf. Literatur oder Geschichte: "In literature, which is an order of connotation, there is no pure question; a question is always nothing but its own scattered answer, which is split up in fragments, between which the meaning springs up and at the same time escapes." This new accentuation of the problem in itself implies what Barthes did not see—the answer nature of the text, which is the prime connecting-point for its reception.

[62] Hence the greater resistance of art to time—that "paradoxical nature" of the work, unexplained by R. Barthes: "it is a sign for history, and at the same time resistance against it" (p. 13).

nacy can—as W. Iser has shown—actually determine the degree of esthetic effectiveness and hence the artistic character of a work.[63] But even the extreme case of an open-structured fictional text, with its quantity of indeterminacy calculated to stimulate the imagination of the active reader, reveals how every fresh response links up with an expected or supposed meaning, the fulfillment or non-fulfillment of which calls forth the implicit question and so sets in motion the new process of understanding. This process emerges most clearly in the history of the interpretation of great works, when the new interpreter is no longer satisfied with the conventionally accepted answer or interpretation, and looks for a new answer to the implied or "posthumous" question. The open, indeterminate structure makes a new interpretation possible, whereas on the other hand the historical communication of question and answer limits the mere arbitrariness of interpretation.

It makes no difference whether the conventionally accepted answer of a text has been given explicitly, ambivalently, or indeterminately by the author himself; or whether it is an interpretation of the work that first arose at its reception—the question implied in the answer presented by the work of art—a question which, according to Barthes, each present must answer in its own way—is now set within a changed horizon of esthetic experience, and so is no longer asked as it was originally by the past text, but is the result of interaction between present and past.[64] The question, which enables the past work of art to affect us still or anew, has to be implicit because it presupposes the active mind's testing the conventional answer, finding it convincing or otherwise, discarding it or putting it in a new light so that the question implied first and now for us may be revealed. In the historical tradition of art, a past work survives not through eternal questions, or through permanent answers, but through the more or less dynamic interrelationship between question and answer, between problem and solution, which can stimulate a new understanding and can allow the resumption of the dialogue between present and past.

Analysis of the tradition-forming dialectic of question and answer in the history of literature and art is a task which literary criticism has scarcely even begun. It goes beyond the semiotic conception of a new

[63] *Die Appellstruktur der Texte: Unbestimmtheit als Wirkungsbedingung literarischer Prosa* (Konstanz, 1970) *Konstanzer Universitätsreden*, ed. G. Hess, vol. xxviii.

[64] This interaction has been described by H. G. Gadamer as a "fusion of horizons: (*Horizontverschmelzung*), pp. 289 seq., 356. In my opinion, this description, with which I concur, does not necessarily give rise to the reversal of the relationship between question and answer which Gadamer (pp. 351-56) brings about in order to ensure the precedence of the "event of tradition" over understanding as "a productive procedure" (p. 280).

science of literature, which Barthes sees in an all too narrow framework: "It cannot be a science of contents (which can only be suckled by historical science proper), but a science of the conditions of contents, i.e., of forms: what will concern it is the variations of meaning applied and to a certain extent applicable to the works."[65] However, the constantly renewed interpretation is more than an answer left to the discretion of the interpreter, for literary tradition is more than just a variable series of subjective projections or "fulfilled meanings" over a mere matrix or "empty meaning" of works, "which bears all of those."[66] It is not only the formal constitution and variability of the meanings applicable to works that can be described in accordance with the linguistic rules of the symbol. The content, the sequence of interpretations as they have appeared historically—this, too, has a logic: that of question and answer, through which the accepted interpretations can be described as a tradition-forming coherence; it also has a counterpart to the language or "literature competence"[67] that is a prerequisite for all transformations: the initial meaning or problem structure of the work, which is its "a priori" content, conditioning all subsequent interpretations, and providing the first instance against which all these must prove themselves. And so there is no reason why the science of literature should not also be a science of contents. And indeed it will have to be, because the science of history cannot relieve it of the task of closing the gap which Barthes, through his formal rigorism, has widened between author and reader, reader and critic, critic and historian, and furthermore between the functions of literature (production, communication, reception).[68] A new science of literature will cease to be a mere auxiliary to history at the moment when it uses the privilege of its still "speaking" sources, and their communication of response and tradition, to attempt the move away from the old "history of development" and towards a new "history of structure"—a move which the science of history is also concerned with making.

IX

How can the history of art and literature contribute towards closing the gap between structural method and historical hermeneutics?

---

[65] *Kritik und Wahrheit* (Frankfurt, 1967), p. 68.

[66] *Ibid.*, p. 68.   [67] *Ibid.*, p. 70.

[68] *Ibid.*, pp. 88-91. In *Literatur oder Geschichte*, the programmatic "literary history without individuals" is understood as a history of the literary institution; the mediation between production, communication, and reception remains quite open, and in the end R. Barthes has to confess that the result of this reduction is "simply history," and so no longer specific to the historicity of art (pp. 22-23).

This problem is common nowadays to various approaches to a theory of literature which—like my own attempt[69]—regard as necessary the destruction of literary history in its old monographic or "epic" tradition, in order to arouse a new interest in the history and historicity of literature. This is especially true of the French *Nouvelle Critique* and Prague Structuralism,[70] whose standpoint we must examine here, at least as it is represented in a few pioneer works.

One representative advocate of the *Nouvelle Critique* is G. Genette. In his programmatic essay *Structuralisme et critique littéraire* (1966),[71] he shows different ways in which literary criticism could use structural description, and theory of style could integrate already current analyses of immanent structures in a structural synthesis. The contrast between intersubjective or hermeneutic analysis and structural analysis would not require literature to be divided into two separate spheres of mythographic or sub-literature, on the one hand, and artistic literature, in the exegetic tradition, on the other—as Ricoeur suggested, in his critique of Lévi-Strauss.[72] For the two methods could expose complementary meanings of the same text: "à propos d'une même oeuvre, la critique herméneutique parlerait le langage de la reprise du sens et de la récréation intérieure, et la critique structurale celui de la parole distante et de la reconstruction intelligible."[73] Thematic criticism, which until now has been concerned almost exclusively with the individual works of authors, would have to relate these to a collective topic of literature, dependent on the attitude, taste and wishes—in short, the "expectation of the public."[74] Literary production and consumption would act in the same way as *parole* and *langue*; and so it must also be possible to formulate the

---

[69] *Literaturgeschichte als Provokation der Literaturwissenschaft* (Konstanz, 1967).

[70] For my account of this, I am indebted to Jurij Striedter and the Research Group for the Structural Study of Language and Literature at the University of Constance, who have prepared a detailed presentation and a German edition of the most important texts of Prague Structuralism for the series *Theorie und Geschichte der Literatur und der Schönen Künste*, published by W. P. Fink, Munich, and have allowed me to quote from their translation of F. Vodička's book *Struktura vývoje* (published in the meantime: *Die Structure der literarischen Einbildung*, intro. by J. Striedter, Munich, 1976). The semiotic structuralism of Soviet literary study does not yet appear to be concerned with the problem of a structural history of literature so much as with structural analysis of literary genres. See K. Eimermacher, "Entwicklung, Charakter und Probleme des sowjetischen Strukturalismus in der Literaturwissenschaft," in *Sprache im technischen Zeitalter*, 30 (1969), pp. 126-57. Of prime importance are the writings of Jurij Lotman: *Lekcii po struktural' noj poetike* (Tartu, 1964), repr. Providence, Rhode Island, 1968.

[71] In the collection of essays *Figures* (Paris, 1966), pp. 145-70.

[72] "Structure et herméneutique," in: *Esprit* 31 (1963), pp. 596-627; continued with: "La structure, le mot, l'événement." in: *Esprit* 35 (1967), pp. 801-21.

[73] P. 161.   [74] *Ibid.*, pp. 162-64.

literary history of a system in a series of synchronous sections, and to translate the mere sequence of autonomous, mutually "influencing" works into a structural history of literature and its functions.[75]

J. Starobinski, on the other hand, with his new definition of literary criticism (*La relation critique*, 1968), proceeds from the belief that structuralism in its strict form is applicable only to literatures that represent a "regulated play in a regulated society."[76] The moment literature questions the given order of institutions and traditions, oversteps the closed limits of the surrounding society with its sanctioned literature, and thus opens up the dimension of history in a culture, the result is that the synchronous structure of a society and the appearance of its literature as an event no longer belong to the homogeneous texture of the same logos: "la plupart des grandes oeuvres modernes ne déclarent leur relation au monde que sur le mode du refus, de l'opposition, de la contestation."[77] The task of a new criticism will be to bring this "relation différentielle" back into the structural context of literature. This does not only require that thematic criticism opens the closed hermeneutic circle between work and interpreter (trajet textuel) onto the work's path to the world of its readers (trajet intentionnel); it also requires that critical understanding should not frustrate the differential or "transgressive" function of the work: if history continually cancels out the protest element and the exceptionality of literature, absorbing it as a paradigm of the next order, the critic must fight against this levelling out of works in the line of tradition, and must hold fast to the differences,[78] thus emphasizing the discontinuity of literature in the history of society.

Furthest from the dogma of the irreconcilability of structural and historical analysis is probably Prague structuralism. Here approaches of formalistic literary theory have been developed into a structural esthetics, which seeks to comprehend the literary work with categories of esthetic perception and then to describe the perceived gestalt of the esthetic object diachronically, in its "concretizations" conditioned by response. The pioneer work of J. Mukařovský has been continued, par-

---

[75] *Ibid.*, p. 167: "L'idée structuraliste, ici, c'est de suivre la littérature dans son évolution globale en pratiquant des coupes synchroniques à diverses étapes, et en comparant les tableaux entre eux . . . . C'est dans le changement continuel de fonction que se manifeste la vraie vie des éléments de l'oeuvre littéraire."

[76] In *Quatre conférences sur la "Nouvelle Critique"* (Turin, Società editrice internazionale, 1968), p. 38.

[77] *Ibid.*, p. 39.

[78] *Ibid.*, p. 39: "Les grandes oeuvres rebelles sont ainsi trahies, elles sont—par le commentaire et la glose—exorcisées, rendues acceptables et versées au patrimoine commun. . . . Mais la compréhension critique ne vise pas à l'assimilation du dissemblable. Elle ne serait pas compréhension si elle ne comprenait pas la différence en tant que différence."

ticularly by F. Vodička, to form a theory of literary history that is based on the esthetics of response.[79] In his book *Struktura vývoje* (1969) he sees the main task of literary history in the context of the polarity between the literary work and reality, which is to be materialized and historically described according to the manner of its perception, i.e., the dynamic connections between the work and the literary public.[80] This requires, on the one hand, the reconstruction of the "literary norm," i.e., the "totality of literary postulates" and the hierarchy of literary values of a given period, and, on the other, the ascertainment of the literary structure through the "concretization" of literary works, i.e., through the concrete gestalt that they have assumed in the perception of the public of the time. Prague structuralism therefore sees the structure of a work as a component part of the broader structure of literary history, and sees the latter as a process arising out of the dynamic tension between work and norm, between the historic sequence of literary works and the sequence of changing norms or attitudes of the public: "Between them there is always a certain parallelism, for both creations—the creation of norms and the creation of a new literary reality—proceed from a common base: from the literary tradition that they overcome."[81] This presupposes that esthetic values, like the "essence" of works of art, only reveal their different forms through a process and are not permanent factors in themselves. The literary work—according to Mukařovský's bold new version of the social character of art—is offered not as a structure that is independent of its reception, but simply as an "esthetic object," which can therefore be described only in accordance with the succession of its concretizations.

By *concretization*, Vodička means the picture of the work in the consciousness of those "for whom the work is an esthetic object."[82] With this idea, Prague structuralism has taken up and historicized an approach of R. Ingarden's phenomenological esthetics. According to the latter, the work, in the polyphonic harmony of its qualities, still had the character of a structure independent of temporal changes in the literary norm; but Vodička disputes the idea that the esthetic values of a work could be given complete expression through an optimal concretization: "As soon as the work is divided up on its absorption into new contexts

[79] The most important writings of J. Mukařovský are to be found in "Chapters from Czech Poetry," *Kapitoly z české poetiky* (Prague, 1948), 3 vols., and *Studie z estetiky* (Studies from Aesthetics) (Prague, 1966).

[80] The book *Struktura vývoje* (Structure of Development), published in Prague in 1969, takes up two older works: *Konkretizace literárního díla* (Materialization of the Literary Work, 1941), and *Literární historie, její problemy a úkoly* (Literary History, Its Problems and Tasks, 1942); see note 70.

[81] *Struktura vývoje*, p. 35.   [82] P. 199.

(changed state of the language, different literary postulates, changed social structure, new system of spiritual and practical values etc.), one can
feel the esthetic effect of precisely those qualities of a work which earlier
. . . were not felt as esthetically effective."[83] Only the reception, i.e.,
the historical life of the work in literature, reveals its structure, in an
open series of aspects, through the active interrelationship between the
literary work and the literary public. With this theory, Prague structuralism has gained a position for the esthetics of reception which re-
lieves it of the twin problems of esthetic dogmatism and extreme subjectivism: "Dogmatism found eternal, unchangeable values in the work, or
interpreted the history of responses as a way to the ultimate, correct perception. Extreme subjectivism, on the other hand, saw in all responses
proof of individual perception and ideas, and sought only in exceptional
cases to overcome this subjectivism through a temporal determination."[84] Vodička's theory of reception links up with the methodological
principle that the materialization legitimated by a literary public—which
itself can become a norm for other works—is to be distinguished from
merely subjective forms of materialization which do not enter any current tradition as a value judgment: "The object of cognition cannot be
all materializations possible with regard to the individual attitude of the
reader, but only those which show a confrontation between the structure
of the work and the structure of the norms currently valid."[85] Thus the
critic who records and publishes a new materialization joins the author
and the reader as someone with his own particular function within the
"literary community," whose constitution as "literary public" is only
one of several perspectives that can offer this theory of a structural literary history as a shot in the arm to the methodologically stagnating
sociology of literature.

X

A theory that sets out to destroy the substantialist idea of tradition, and to replace it with a functional idea of history, is bound to be
open to the charge of one-sidedness precisely in this sphere of art and
literature. Whoever abandons the latent Platonism of the philological
method, dismisses as illusory the eternal essence of the work of art and
the timeless standpoint of its observer, and begins to regard the history
of art as a process of production and reception, in which not identical
functions but dialogic structures of question and answer mediate between past and present—such a person must run the risk of missing a
specific experience of art that is obviously in opposition to its historicity.

---

[83] P. 41.   [84] P. 196.   [85] P. 206.

Art historiography that follows the principle of the open structure and the never completable interpretation of works, in accordance with the process of productive understanding and critical reinterpretation, is concerned primarily with the intellectual and emancipatory function of art.[86] Is it not, then, bound to ignore the social and, in the narrower sense, esthetic character of art—its critical, communicative, and socially influential function and those achievements which the active and the suffering man experiences as impulses of ecstasy, pleasure, and play, and withal as impulses that remove him from his historical existence and his social situation?

It cannot be disputed that the emancipatory and socially formative function of art represents only one side of its historical role in the process of human history. The other side is revealed in the fact that works of art are "directed against the course of time, against disappearance and transience," because they seek to immortalize, i.e., "to confer on the objects of life the dignity of immortalization."[87] And so, according to Kurt Badt, art history also has the task of showing "what art has been able to present of human perfection, for instance even in suffering (Grünewald's *Christus*)."[88] However, recognizing the supratemporal character of this glorifying and immortalizing function does not mean contrasting the historicity of art with the timeless essence of an absolute beauty that has manifested itself only in the immortality of the work. The glorified immortality of the work of art is something that has been created *against* transience and within history itself.[89] The history of art incorporates the historical appearance of works and their immortality as the result of esthetic activities of mankind. If, with Karel Kosík, we understand the dialectics of history as a process in which history "contains both the historicity that is transient, sinks into the past and *does not return*, and historical character, the formation of the immortal—i.e. the self-forming and self-creating"[90]—then the history of art is distinguished from other spheres of historical reality by the fact that in it the formation of the immortal is not only visibly carried out through the production of works, but also through reception, by its constant re-

---

[86] This objection is raised by M. Wehrli in his address: *Literatur und Geschichte, Jahresbericht der Universität Zürich* (1969-1970), p. 6.

[87] K. Badt, *Wissenschaftslehre der Kunstgeschichte* (p. 160). This is a yet unpublished work, which the author has kindly allowed me to quote from; it also proceeds from a consideration of Droysen's *Historik*, in order to establish a new methodological basis for the history of the fine arts (published in the meantime, Cologne, 1971).

[88] *Ibid.*, p. 190.

[89] Here I am following K. Kosík, *Die Dialektik des Konkreten* (Frankfurt, 1967), esp. the chapter: "Historismus und Historizismus," pp. 133-49.

[90] *Ibid.*, p. 143.

enactment of the enduring features of works which long since have been committed to the past.

The history of art maintains this special status even if one concurs with the Marxist literary theory that art and literature cannot claim any history of their own, but only become historical insofar as they participate in the general process of historical praxis. The history of art keeps its special position within pragmatic history to the extent that, through the medium of perception and by means of interpretation, it can consciously bring out the historical capacity of "totalization, in which human praxis incorporates impulses from the past and animates them through this very integration."[91] Totalization, in the sense of "a process of production and reproduction, animation and rejuvenation,"[92] is presented in exemplary form by the history of art. For here—as T. S. Eliot pointed out—it is not only the authentically new work that revises our view of all past works. Here the past work, too, which has the appearance of immortal beauty and—according to Malraux—embodies art as a counter to fate, needs the productive work of understanding in order to be taken out of the imaginary museum and appropriated by the interpretative eye of the present. And here, too, ultimately, art historiography can win back its disputed legitimation insofar as it seeks out and describes the canons and contexts of works, rejuvenating the great wealth of human experience preserved in past art, and making it accessible to the perception of the present age.

[91] *Ibid.*, p. 148.   [92] *Ibid.*

Notes on Contributors*

ABRAMS, M. H. Professor of English at Cornell University, where he
 has held endowed chairs since 1960. Member of the American
 Philosophical Society and the American Academy of Arts and
 Sciences as well as an honorary permanent member of the
 Royal University of Malta. He gave the Alexander Lectures at
 the University of Toronto in 1964. He has held Guggenheim,
 Rockefeller, and numerous other fellowships. During 1977 he
 was Visiting Fellow at All Souls College, Oxford. His books and
 numerous essays on romantic poetry and literary criticism are
 widely known: *The Mirror and the Lamp* won the Christian
 Gauss Prize for 1954 and *Natural Supernaturalism* won the
 James Russell Lowell Prize for 1972. One of his earliest works,
 The Milk of Paradise, was reprinted in 1970. He is an editor of
 the *Norton Anthology of English Literature*. Most recently he
 collaborated with Jonathan Wordsworth and Stephen Gill in
 editing *Wordsworth's "Prelude"* (W. W. Norton, 1978).

BLUMENBERG, HANS. Professor of Philosophy at the University of
 Münster (since 1970). Previous professorships at Hamburg,
 Giessen, and Bochum. Guest professor at the Berlin Technical
 University, 1967-1968. Member of the Mainz Academy of Science and Literature (since 1963). Member of the Senate of the
 German Research Society (1962-1968). Fields of special interest
 include phenomenology (especially in relation to anthropology
 and history of philosophy), history of science and humanistic
 history of applied science, and conceptual theory (particularly
 metaphorology). Publications: *Paradigmen zu einer Meta-*
 phorologie (Bonn, 1960); *Die kopernikanische Wende* (Frankfurt, 1965); *Die Legitimität der Neuzeit* (Frankfurt, 1966); *Der*
 Prozess der theoretischen Neugierde (Frankfurt, 1973); *Die*
 Genesis der kopernikanischen Welt; articles on Copernicus,
 rationalism, pseudo-Platonism and phenomenology, some
 translated into Italian.

* The order of authors is alphabetical. Limitation of space has made it possible to enter
only a few of the publications by each author. Publications which have appeared in English
are so indicated.

DIECKMANN, HERBERT. Professor Emeritus of French and Comparative Literature at Cornell University. Formerly Professor of French at Harvard University. Recent publications include: Introduction to the Preface of *La Religieuse* in the new edition of Diderot's works, vol. XI, and the Introduction and annotation of *La Promenade du sceptique*, vol. II, by Diderot (Paris, 1976). He is also editing the correspondence of Ernst Robert Curtius with Valery Larbaud, André Gide, and Charles Du Bos. Professor Dieckmann's collected writings are currently being prepared for publication in book form by the Cornell University Press.

FUHRMANN, MANFRED. Professor of Latin Philology at the University of Kiel (1962-1966) and at the University of Konstanz (since 1967). Fields of special interest include the late classical period, Roman law, and rhetoric and poetics. Publications: *Das systematische Lehrbuch: Ein Beitrag zur Geschichte der Wissenschaften in der Antike* (Göttingen, 1960); *Die Antike und Ihre Vermittler* (Konstanz, 1969); *Einführung in die antike Dichtungstheorie* (Darmstadt, 1973); *Alte Sprachen in der Krise?* (Stuttgart, 1976). Editor of a multi-volume translation of Cicero's speeches into German; and of *Poetik und Hermeneutik*, IV—*Terror und Spiel: Probleme der Mythenrezeption* (Munich, 1971).

HENRICH, DIETER. Joint Professor of Philosophy at Heidelberg and Harvard universities. Held earlier chairs at the Free University of Berlin, Heidelberg, and Columbia. Fields of special interest— history of modern philosophy, philosophy of the mind, ethics, and esthetics. Numerous publications in German since 1952 include studies of such figures as Kant, Fichte, Hegel, Husserl, and Max Weber. Writings in English include, besides further work on Kant and Hegel, such essays as "Self-Consciousness, A Critical Introduction to a Theory," in *Man and World*, IV (1971) and "Hegel and Hölderlin" in *Idealistic Studies*, II (1972). Recent work in German: *Identität und Objektivität, eine Untersuchung über Kants transzendentale Deduktion* (Heidelberg, 1976); "Identität: Begriffe, Probleme, Grenzen," in *Poetik und Hermeneutik*, VIII (Munich, 1978). President of the International Hegel Association.

IMDAHL, MAX. Professor of Art History at the University of Bochum, with special interest in theory and history of painting. Member of the Council on Documents in Kassel (1968). Member of the Advisory Council of the University of Bielefeld. Co-editor of *Theorie und Geschichte der Literatur und der Schönen Künste* (Munich, 1963ff). Books include a recent study of an American artist, *Frank Stella* (Stuttgart, 1970) and *Barnett Newman: Who's Afraid of Red, Yellow and Blue* (Stuttgart, 1971). Articles on Cézanne, optical art, concretist painting, and graphic syntax and semantics, e.g.: "Cézanne, Braque, Picasso" in *Wallraf-Richartz Jahrbuch* XXXVI (Cologne, 1974) and "Überlegungen zur Identität des Bildes" in *Poetik und Hermeneutik*, VIII (Munich, 1978).

ISER, WOLFGANG. Professor of English and Literary Criticism at the University of Konstanz. Special interest—esthetics and literary theory. Chairs at Universities of Würzburg (1960-1963), Cologne (1963-1967), and Konstanz (since 1967). Visiting professorships at Colgate University (1968); University of California at Irvine (1976 and 1978); Princeton University (1978). Fellow of Center for Humanities, Wesleyan University (1970-1971). Netherlands Institute for Advanced Study in the Humanities and Social Studies (1973-1974). Fellow of the Heidelberg Academy of Arts and Sciences. Publications: *Die Weltanschauung Henry Fieldings* (Tübingen, 1952); *Walter Pater, die Autonomie des Ästhetischen* (Tübingen, 1960); *Spensers Arkadien: Fiktion und Geschichte in der englischen Renaissance* (Krefeld, 1970); *Die Appellstruktur der Texte: Unbestimmtheit als Wirkungsbedingung literarischer Prosa* (Konstanz, 1970). In English translation: *The Implied Reader: Patterns of Communication in Prose Fiction from Bunyan to Beckett* (Baltimore, 1974); *The Act of Reading: A Theory of Aesthetic Response* (Baltimore, 1978); "Indeterminacy and the Reader's Response" in *Aspects of Narrative*, ed. J. Hillis Miller (New York, 1971); recent articles in *New Literary History*.

JAUSS, HANS ROBERT. Professor of Literary Criticism and Romance Philology, University of Konstanz. Special interests—reception esthetics, theory of literary genres, historical writings and literary history. Previous chairs at University of Münster (1959-1961) and Giessen (1961-1966). Visiting professor at Columbia (1973), Yale (1976) and the Sorbonne (1978). Publications: *Kleine Apologie der äesthetichen Erfahrung*, with notes on art history by Max Imdahl (Konstanz, 1972); *Zeit und Erinnerung* in Marcel Prousts "A la recherche du temps perdu": Ein Beitrag zur Theorie des Romans (Heidelberg, 1955; 2nd ed., 1970); Untersuchungen zur mittelalterlichen Tierdichtung (Tübingen, 1959); Genèse de la poésie allégorique française au moyen âge (Heidelberg, 1962); Ästhetische Normen und geschichtliche Reflexion in der "Querelle des Anciens et des Modernes" (Munich, 1964); Literaturgeschichte als Provokation (Frankfurt, 1970); Alterität und Modernität der mittelalterlichen Literatur (Munich, 1977); Ästhetische Erfahrung und literarische Hermeneutik (Munich, 1977). Editor of Grundriss der romanischen Literatur des Mittelalters, VI (Heidelberg, 1968). Articles in English in the periodical New Literary History.

KOSELLECK, REINHART. Professor of History at the University of Bielefeld. Formerly Professor of Political Science at the University of Bochum and Modern History at Heidelberg University. Special interests—social history, theory of history, and political semantology. Director of the Center for Interdisciplinary Research at the University of Bielefeld. Reuchlin Prize (1974). Member of the North Rhine-Westphalian Academy of Sciences. Publications: Kritik und Krise: Ein Beitrag zur Pathogenese der bürgerlichen Welt (Freiburg, 2nd ed., 1976), English translation forthcoming; Preussen zwischen Reform und Revolution: Allgemeines Landrecht, Verwaltung und soziale Bewegung von 1791 bis 1848 (Stuttgart, 2nd ed., 1975). Co-editor of six-volume lexicon, Geschichtliche Grundbegriffe (Stuttgart, 1972ff); and (with Wolf-Dieter Stempel) of Poetik und Hermeneutik, V—Geschichte: Ereignis und Erzählung (Munich, 1974). Editor of Studien zum Beginn der modernen Welt (Stuttgart, 1977).

MARQUARD, ODO. Professor of Philosophy at University of Giessen since 1965. Special interests—German idealism, philosophy of psychoanalysis, esthetics, philosophy of history, philosophical anthropology and its history. Publications: Skeptische Methode im Blick auf Kant (Freiburg, 1958); "Über einige Beziehungen zwischen Ästhetik und Therapeutik in der Philosophie des 19. Jahrhunderts" in Literatur und Gesellschaft (1963); "Zur Geschichte des philosophischen Begriffs 'Anthropologie' seit dem Ende des 18. Jahrhunderts" in Collegium Philosophicum (Basel/Stuttgart, 1965); Schwierigkeiten mit der Geschichts-

philosophie (Frankfurt, 1973). Co-editor of *Historisches Wörterbuch der Philosophie* (Basel/Stuttgart, 1971ff) and of *Poetik und Hermeneutik*, VIII—*Identität* (Munich, 1978).

PREISENDANZ, WOLFGANG. Professor of Modern German Literature at the University of Konstanz since 1966. Guest professor at the University of Pittsburgh (1965); University of California at Davis (1966-1967); University of Virginia (1979). Special interests: semiotics, narrative structures in relation to historical periods, theory of the droll. Publications: *Die Spruchform in der Lyrik des alten Goethe und ihre Vorgeschichte seit Opitz* (Heidelberg, 1952); *Humor als dichterische Einbildungskraft: Studien zur Erzählkunst des poetischen Realismus* (Munich, 1963; 2nd ed., 1975); *Über den Witz* (Konstanz, 1970); *Heinrich Heine: Werkstrukturen und Epochenbezüge* (Munich, 1973); *Wege des Realismus: Zur Poetik und Erzählkunst im 19. Jahrhundert* (Munich, 1977). Essays on Goethe, Heine, E.T.A. Hoffmann and Gottfried Keller in *Beiträge zur Geschichte der deutschen Sprache und · Literatur* (periodical issued at Tübingen). Co-editor of *Theorie und Geschichte der Literatur* (Munich, 1963ff).

STEMPEL, WOLF-DIETER. Professor of Romance Languages at the University of Hamburg since 1973. Earlier professorships at Bonn (1963-1967) and Konstanz (1967-1973). Special interests: Romance linguistics and textual theory. Publications: *Untersuchungen zur Satzverknüpfung im Altfranzösischen* (Braunschweig, 1964); "Mittelalterliche Obszönitat als literästhetisches Problem" in *Poetik und Hermeneutik*, III (Munich, 1968; "Pour une description des genres littéraires," *Actes du XIIe Congrès de Linguistique et Philologie Romanes*, II (Bucharest, 1971); "Perspektivische Rede in der französischen Literatur des Mittelalters" in *Interpretation und Vergleich: Festschrift für W. Pabst* (Berlin, 1972); "Gibt es Textsorten?" in *Textsorten*, ed. E. Gülich and W. Raible (Frankfurt, 1972). Edited and contributed an essay to the following German editions of Slavic writings: "Zur formalistischen Theorie der poetischen Sprache" in *Texte der russischen Formalisten II* (Munich, 1972); "Zur literarischen Semiotik Miroslav Červenkas" in the German edition (co-edited by F. Boldt) of *Miroslav Červenka, Der Bedeutungsaufbau des literarischen Werks* (Munich, 1977).

STIERLE, KARL-HEINZ. Professor of Romance Philology at the University of Bochum. Recent publications: *Text als Handlung: Perspectiven einer systematischen Literaturwissenschaft* (Munich, 1975); articles on several topics of discourse theory and theory of literature and on French literature (Pascal, Baudelaire, Mallarmé, Valéry). Co-editor with Odo Marquard of *Identität— Poetik und Hermeneutik*, VIII (Munich, 1978).

STRIEDTER, JURIJ. Professor of Slavic Languages and Literatures at Harvard University. Has held chairs in Slavic and comparative literature at the Free University of Berlin (1961-1966), and the University of Konstanz (1967-1977) as well as earlier visiting professorships at Harvard, Yale, Columbia, and the University of Zürich. Among his books are: *Der Schelmenroman in Russland* (Berlin, 1961); *Texte der Russischen Formalisten* I (Munich, 1969, 1971); and (forthcoming in English) *From Formalism to Structuralism* (Harvard University Press). His latest articles in English include: "Poetic Genre and the Sense of History in Pushkin," *New Literary History*, VIII, 1976-1977; "The Russian Formalist Theory of Prose," *PTL*, II, no. 3, 1977; and "The Russian Formalist Theory of Literary Evolution," *PTL*, III, no. 1, 1978.

WELLEK, RENÉ. Sterling Professor Emeritus of Comparative Literature at Yale University. A central figure in 20th-century international literary scholarship, he has held professorships at the universities of Prague, London, Iowa, and Princeton. Publications (among many): *Theory of Literature* with Austin Warren, 3rd ed. (London, 1966); *A History of Modern Criticism*, 5 vols. (New Haven, 1955-65; vol. 5 forthcoming); *Confrontations: Studies in the Intellectual and Literary Relations between Germany, England and the United States during the 19th Century* (Princeton, 1965); *Discriminations: Further Concepts of Criticism* (New Haven, 1970).

Index of Names

IN addition to names of writers and other persons mentioned in the text and footnotes, some subject headings such as Freudianism and Phenomenology have been indexed (in capitals) for the convenience of the reader. Names of editors have not been indexed. For an indication of topics covered in each essay, consult the table of contents, pp. v-vii.

Library of Congress Cataloging in Publication Data

Main entry under title:

New perspectives in German literary criticism.

  Includes index.
  1. Literature—Addresses, essays, lectures.
I. Amacher, Richard E., 1917- II. Lange, Victor, 1908-
PN45.N39   809   78-12472
ISBN 0-691-06380-X